JAMES W. VANDER ZANDEN, Ph.D., University of North Carolina, is Associate Professor of Sociology at The Ohio State University. He previously taught at Paine College and at Duke University. Professor Vander Zanden has contributed numerous articles to leading sociological and professional journals, and is the author of two other books, including *Sociology: A Systematic Approach*, published by The Ronald Press Company.

AMERICAN MINORITY RELATIONS

The Sociology of Race and Ethnic Groups

James W. Vander Zanden

THE OHIO STATE UNIVERSITY

SECOND EDITION

THE RONALD PRESS COMPANY • NEW YORK

Library of Congress Catalog Card Number: 66–16853
PRINTED IN THE UNITED STATES OF AMERICA

To
Deak

Preface

There is no dearth of literature dealing with American religious, ethnic, and race relations. Within recent years, a good many materials have appeared contributing to both data and theory. This work has encompassed and cut across many disciplines. Although courses in the field have traditionally been placed under the rubric of sociology, there has been an increasing need to give recognition to the contributions of other disciplines, most notably anthropology and psychology.

In approaching the vast amount of data and theory that has appeared, it is necessary to find some meaningful and systematic framework for handling and organizing the materials for textbook purposes. The approach I have employed focuses on the sociological foundations of race and minority relations, striking what I believe is a judicious balance between the purely descriptive and the purely theoretical. This avoids the disadvantages of a mere descriptive rundown of each of the minority groups, on the one hand, and a too ambitious theoretical and conceptual approach, on the other. The former, it seems to me, fails to provide a firm grounding in theory or to give the reader an understanding of the considerable dimensions and processes involved in intergroup relations, while the latter strikes me as presumptuous and unsatisfactory in terms of our understanding of human behavior in general and of religious, ethnic, and race relations in particular.

The first part of the book sets the stage for the consideration of American minority relations. It treats a number of key concepts, examines various processes of social and cultural contact between peoples, considers the sources of American minorities, and analyzes some of the facts and myths revolving about race.

Part II examines various theories dealing with the sources of prejudice and discrimination. The discussion of economic, power, status, and personality factors incorporates new research findings—especially in regard to the scapegoat theory.

Part III considers four processes of intergroup relations—conflict, segregation, stratification, and assimilation— particularly in terms of recent developments in these areas.

In Part IV there is an examination of the reactions of minorities to their disadvantaged status, which are discussed primarily in terms of acceptance or aggression and avoidance or assimilation. This approach permits a study of assimilationist-oriented minorities, and an extensive analytical consideration of the Negro "protest" movement. There is also an examination of still other minority responses, including obsessive sensitivity, efforts at ego enhancement, group self-hatred, and attempts to flee from reality.

Finally, Part V focuses upon the fact that dominant-minority relations are anything but static, and that social change is an inescapable fact of social existence. The concluding chapter examines that body of sociological literature dealing with means by which democratic goals may be advanced and prejudice and discrimination combated.

Once again I should like to acknowledge the help my wife, Deak, has given me in preparing this new edition. She has meticulously edited the manuscript and suggested many sound revisions.

JAMES W. VANDER ZANDEN

Columbus, Ohio
March, 1966

Contents

vii

Part III: INTERGROUP RELATIONS WITHIN AMERICA

Part IV: MINORITY REACTIONS TO DOMINANCE

I

INTRODUCTION

1

INTRODUCTION

1

The Nature of Minority Relations

Our domestic well-being and the dictates of our world position have compelled us as a nation to focus increasing attention upon our racial and ethnic relations. Lewis Killian and Charles Grigg, two prominent sociologists, in an appraisal of America's current racial crisis, observe: "Americans, particularly white Americans, must soon awake to the fact that the crisis in race relations is second in gravity only to the threat of nuclear war." [1] And former Harvard University president James B. Conant, on the basis of a far-reaching study of public education, concludes:

. . . without being an alarmist, I must say that when one considers the total situation that has been developing in the Negro city slums since World War II, one has reason to worry about the future. The building up of a mass of unemployed and frustrated Negro youth in congested areas of the city is a social phenomenon that may be compared to the piling up of inflammable material in an empty building in a city block. Potentialities for trouble—indeed possibilities of disaster—are surely there. [2]

On the world scene American racial and ethnic patterns, both North and South, have assumed considerable importance. Joseph Modupe Johnson, a Nigerian leader, notes:

If the government only knew how much damage was being done they would not continue this costly indulgence. For every penny of aid poured

[1] Lewis Killian and Charles Grigg, *Racial Crisis in America* (Englewood Cliffs, N.J.: Prentice-Hall, Inc., 1964), 130.
[2] James B. Conant, *Slums and Suburbs* (New York: McGraw-Hill Book Co., Inc., 1961), 18.

into Africa, America continues to lose tons of goodwill because of the racial discrimination in this country. Something drastic must be done, fast, before it is too late.[3]

And the United Press International reports:

Secretary of State Dean Rusk Monday called on Americans to solve racial problems which he said are causing "deep injury" to U.S. foreign policy abroad.

Rusk said that because of remaining U.S. racial barriers, U.S. diplomats must conduct American foreign policy like someone running in a foot race "with one of our legs in a cast."

Rusk said the United States "is now confronted with one of the gravest issues that we have had since 1865 . . . and this issue deeply affects the conduct of our foreign relations." [4]

Indeed, within this context the scientific study of minority relations assumes the greatest gravity.

The problem of minority relations within the United States is primarily a sociological problem, since it involves relations between people not merely as individuals but as members of groups. Such groups may be differentiated on the basis of physical or cultural characteristics, or a combination of both. To these differences are assigned various meanings which influence and pattern interaction in wide areas of human life. Sociologists are interested not only in the relations between peoples with differing physical or cultural backgrounds; they are also interested in the social structures which develop out of contacts between peoples and in the dynamic processes that contribute to these structures.

A SCIENTIFIC APPROACH TO THE STUDY OF MINORITY RELATIONS

Sociology undertakes to examine minority relations with a scientific orientation characterized by objectivity in analysis and observation. Science is not to be defined as some single method or routine, for example, the application of the experimental method, but by an attitude, a point of view. Sociology is entitled to be classified as a science to the extent to which its theories are refined and tested by observation, and its ideals are characterized by universality and exactness. To possess scientific validity and reliability, conclusions and observations must be independent of the values and beliefs of the scientist. Two

[3] Arnold H. Lubasch, "Racial Strife Pictured as Losing Friends for U.S. in Africa," *New York Times*, May 20, 1964.
[4] *Atlanta Constitution*, May 28, 1963.

plus two equals four whether it is calculated by an American, a Russian, or an Indonesian, or by a Communist, a Methodist, or a Hindu spiritualist. Such objectivity is often difficult to achieve when men begin thinking about, and analyzing, themselves and their society.

To the extent to which an integrationist and a segregationist are similarly biased, although in different directions, they are probably equally capable of undertaking studies of interracial behavior that are scientific in character. Scientific objectivity dictates, however, that they not introduce their respective biases into their studies. This is not to suggest that science requires the integrationist or the segregationist to give up his moral convictions and beliefs. It only requires that he be prepared to control his own convictions and beliefs in order to examine evidence in a dispassionate manner. In fact, Shibutani and Kwan observe:

> Ironically, one of the major barriers to a better comprehension of these phenomena is the indignation of the investigators. Social scientists are human beings, and their emotional reactions to the injustices they see make difficult the cultivation of a detached standpoint. Men who are angry often look for a responsible agent to blame, and this search for culprits often vitiates research. . . . When difficulties are perceived in moral terms, there is a tendency to explain events by imputing vicious motives to those who are held responsible. Furthermore, moral indignation often blinds the student to many facts that would otherwise be obvious.[5]

We have noted that scientific knowledge is ethically neutral. By itself it is neither good nor bad, and it can be used in a great many ways. In contrast, decisions involving the *use* to which scientific knowledge is put entail value judgments, e.g., pragmatic and moral considerations. Nuclear physics can provide data on atomic fusion, but it cannot provide the answers as to whether or not an atomic bomb should be built, and, if built, when and if it should be used. Similarly, sociologists may secure considerable scientific data concerning the mechanics of race rioting, but the use to which this information will be put rests outside the province of sociology as a pure science. The sociological

[5] Tamotsu Shibutani and Kian M. Kwan, *Ethnic Stratification* (New York: The Macmillan Company, 1965), 15. A somewhat different and extremely controversial approach is set forth by Dan W. Dodson: ". . . we [sociologists] are of necessity reformers. If we are not reformers, we have no place in relations and other areas where groups have unequal opportunities. Ours is the task of restructuring intergroup relations to the end that basic human rights are translated into civil rights, i.e., undergirded by law, and that the total society is brought to respect equality of relationships between us." Dan W. Dodson, "The Creative Role of Conflict Reexamined," *The Journal of Intergroup Relations*, 1 (Winter, 1959–1960), 5.

findings may be ignored, used to reduce race rioting, or employed to foment "bigger and better" riots.

Sociology as a *pure* science—a science of man and society—does not take a position on social issues. Whether prejudice and discrimination or integration and segregation are good or bad—desirable or undesirable, right or wrong—are not matters that legitimately belong within the province of sociology. Sociologists usually have opinions on such matters as do other members of society, but sociology as a science does not. When sociologists take positions on public issues, they do so not within their scientific capacity but within the context of other roles, e.g., that of a citizen. To the extent to which sociology contains valid, reliable propositions concerning human behavior, it can find application within social life in that such knowledge can be used to realize goals commonly defined as worthwhile. It is then *applied* science. But, since men frequently differ in their goals, there is no reason why antagonistic groups may not utilize sociological knowledge for their own ends or in combating each other.

PREJUDICE AND DISCRIMINATION

Prejudice

In approaching human behavior, tools of analysis are crucial—concepts with which the vast array of social phenomena may be examined. The term *prejudice* is one such concept. In recent years prejudice has taken on a good many unfavorable connotations, so that today people are generally quick to disassociate themselves from it. "I'm not prejudiced," is a frequently heard comment. "In fact, one of my best friends is a Jew. But, you know, I just can't stand most of 'em! They're so loud, sneaky, and stingy. They're just full of gall!" It is difficult to examine dispassionately and objectively something that is so widely condemned yet simultaneously so prevalent.

The term *prejudice* is used with somewhat differing meanings by various individuals. Prejudice is commonly taken to mean a "pre-judgment" about a person or group without bothering to verify the opinion or to examine the merits of the judgment. Implicit in this definition is the assumption that prejudice involves a hasty or premature appraisal of individuals or groups. If this is the case, knowledge and experience should be all that is necessary to dispel prejudice. In truth, however, considerable evidence is available which suggests that knowledge and experience frequently have little impact upon prejudice. Furthermore, some of the prevalent beliefs about particular groups, although containing many half-truths and distortions, may in some instances have a "kernel of truth" to them. Thus this definition of prejudice as a "pre-judgment" is not adequate or satisfactory.

Probably one of the most common failures in examining prejudice is the tendency to view it as a unitary phenomenon. Actually prejudice is not one thing but, rather, many things. Kramer makes a useful distinction between three major levels of orientation toward any minority group: (1) the cognitive, (2) the emotional, and (3) the action levels.[6] Research testifies to the fact that these three levels constitute analytically distinct aspects of prejudice and that the levels are not necessarily interrelated.[7] Let us examine each of these levels in turn.

The *cognitive* level of orientation refers to the individual's picture of the minority group. It deals with how an individual perceives a minority, what he believes about it, and what common traits he attributes to its members. An individual's "picture" of Negroes may be that they fight and brawl, have criminal instincts, live like animals, and are mentally inferior, lazy, slow, unimaginative, and sloppy. Jews may be pictured as possessing unbounded power and control in money matters, as sticking together, as conniving to outwit gentiles, and as pursuing unscrupulous, ruthless, and unpatriotic activities.

The *emotional* level of orientation refers to the emotions—the feelings —that the actual or symbolic stimulus of the minority evokes within the individual. Fear, sympathy, pity, hate, anger, love, contempt, and envy are among the emotional responses that may be experienced by individuals within the context of racial interaction or when confronted with the prospect of such interaction. The idea of patronizing a washroom, of eating at the same restaurant, or of shaking hands with a Jew or Negro may excite horror or disgust within some individuals. Negro movement into a previously all-white neighborhood may produce fear and anxiety among many whites. The social standing of a prominent Jewish businessman or doctor may elicit envy among some gentiles. Identification with the persecuted may lead some whites to experience sympathy for Negroes, and to desire that a Negro win in a prize fight with a white. It should be noted that although the emotional level is distinct from that of the cognitive, the two may appear together—one may overlay the other.

The action level of orientation refers to the tendency or disposition to act in certain ways toward a minority group. Here the emphasis is

[6] Bernard M. Kramer, "Dimensions of Prejudice," *The Journal of Psychology*, 27 (1949), 389–451.

[7] See, for example, John H. Mann, "The Relationship between Cognitive, Affective, and Behavioral Aspects of Racial Prejudice," *Journal of Social Psychology*, 49 (1959), 223–228.

upon tendencies to act, not upon the actions themselves. Whites may desire to keep Negroes out of their circle of friends and may be disposed to reject any direct personal relations with them. Similarly, whites may favor barring Negroes from their social clubs, athletic organizations, and business and professional associations. They may prefer segregated schools, parks, buses, washrooms, lunch counters, and waiting rooms. Accordingly, they may be viewed as disposed toward discriminatory behavior.

Prejudice may be viewed as a system of negative conceptions, feelings, and action-orientations regarding the members of a particular group. This definition reflects the three major levels of an attitude system: the cognitive, the emotional, and the predisposition to act in a given fashion.

Discrimination

It has been seen that prejudice is a state of mind. It involves attitudes and feelings. But attitudes and feelings are not to be equated with overt action. The former constitute merely a predisposition to act, a predilection for certain kinds of behavior, but not the actual response itself. Overt action, on the other hand, involves the actual response or series of responses that an individual makes. Feelings and attitudes are not necessarily correlated with actual behavior. A student may feel considerable antipathy for his professor, yet he may take great pains to hide his feelings and to act instead in a very personable, friendly, and ingratiating manner. His failure to act out his genuine feelings in hostile, aggressive, and antagonistic actions may be the product of fear lest his professor retaliate and lower his grade. By the same token, a student may bear warm, friendly, and sympathetic attitudes and feelings toward a professor, yet engage in cool, ritualistic, and formalized responses. His failure to act out his friendly feelings may be the product of concern lest his fellow students consider him an "oddball" or an "apple polisher."

Similarly with prejudice. A white businessman may bear considerable prejudice toward Negroes yet nevertheless display friendly responses toward Negro customers in order to gain their goodwill. Thus his negative sentiments are not translated into overt action. On the other hand, a businessman who lacks prejudice may refuse to accept Negro customers, because he believes their presence would injure his business. In this instance, he fails to translate his non-prejudiced outlook into overt action. Accordingly, it is necessary to distinguish between *prejudice,* which is a state of mind, and *discrimination,* which entails overt action in which members of a group are accorded unfavorable treatment on the basis of their religious, ethnic, or racial membership.

We have seen, then, that discrimination is not simply the result—the acting-out—of prejudice. Discrimination occurs without prejudice and prejudice without discrimination. Overall, however, a correlation exists between prejudice and discrimination such that the more prejudiced are also more likely to practice discrimination. Yet there are numerous occasions in real life when there is far from a one-to-one relation between them. In the 1930's, for instance, a sociologist, Richard T. LaPiere traveled throughout the United States with a Chinese couple. In the course of the trip, LaPiere and the Chinese couple asked for service in hundreds of hotels, auto camps, tourist homes, and restaurants. They were refused service only once. Six months later, LaPiere wrote each of the establishments and asked if Chinese guests were welcome. Over 90 per cent replied that they would *not* accommodate Chinese, clearly in contradiction to their earlier actions. Here is a clear case of verbal prejudice combined with no actual face-to-face discrimination.[8]

Similarly, in a more recent experiment, two white women and a Negro woman entered 11 restaurants in a fashionable Northeastern suburban community. They encountered no problems, and received nothing less than exemplary service. Two weeks later a letter was sent to the same restaurants requesting reservations for a similar group. There were no answer to the letters and great resistance to the follow-up phone calls.[9]

DESEGREGATION AND INTEGRATION

Prior to the Supreme Court's 1954 decision in the school-segregation cases, the terms *desegregation* and *integration* were generally used interchangeably. As used by the press, public officials, and the legal profession, they still tend to be regarded as more or less synonymous. However, there has been a growing insistence among social

---

[8] Richard T. LaPiere, "Attitudes vs. Actions," *Social Forces,* 13 (1934), 230–237.

[9] Bernard Kutner, Carol Wilkins, and Penny R. Yarrow, "Verbal Attitudes and Overt Behavior Involving Racial Prejudice," *Journal of Abnormal and Social Psychology,* 47 (1952), 649–652. For other related experiments, see: Melvin L. DeFleur and Frank R. Westie, "Verbal Attitudes and Overt Acts," *American Sociological Review,* 23 (1958), 667–673; Robert O. Blood, Jr., "Discrimination without Prejudice," *Social Problems,* 3 (1955), 114–117; Lawrence S. Linn, "Verbal Attitudes and Overt Behavior: A Study of Racial Discrimination," *Social Forces,* 43 (1965), 353–364; and Robin M. Williams, Jr., *Strangers Next Door* (Englewood Cliffs, N.J.: Prentice-Hall, Inc., 1964), 50 and 314.

scientists that the words, if used precisely, have different meanings. *Desegregation* refers to the removal of formal barriers within a society, both legal and social, that are premised upon racial or ethnic membership. Desegregation thus involves the elimination of segregation in the operation of public or quasi-public facilities, services, and institutions. It entails the achievement in full of what is often referred to as "civil rights." *Integration,* however, embraces the idea of the elimination of prejudice as well as discrimination, and hence refers to much more:

> Integration, as a subjective and individual process, involves attitudinal changes and the removal of fears, hatreds, suspicions, stereotypes, and superstitions. Integration involves problems of personal choice, personal readiness, and personal stability. Its achievement necessarily requires a longer period of time. It cannot come about "overnight." It requires education and deals poignantly with the problems of changing men's hearts and minds.[10]

Although school desegregation has advanced rather far in some southern states, integration has not necessarily been accomplished. Negro students, for example, have often been admitted to previously all-white schools, yet their acceptance within informal, personal, intimate, and voluntary relationships of whites has in large measure not been realized. The belief had been quite prevalent, prior to the Supreme Court's ruling, that desegregation would more or less automatically result in integration. This view now appears somewhat naïve. It assumes that, if formal discrimination ends, prejudice in due course will also end. But such an interpretation ignores the complexity of prejudice and the multiplicity of factors contributing to its existence.

MINORITIES

The Concept

What is a minority? Probably the most satisfactory answer to this question is that suggested by Wagley and Harris, who identify five definitive features of a minority.[11] Let us examine each of these five features in turn.

1. *A minority is a social group whose members experience at the hands of another social group various disabilities in the form of preju-*

---

[10] Kenneth B. Clark, "Desegregation: The Role of the Social Sciences," *Teachers College Record,* 62 (1960), 16–17.

[11] Charles Wagley and Marvin Harris, *Minorities in the New World* (New York: Columbia University Press, 1964), 4–11.

dice, discrimination, segregation, or persecution (or any combination of these). The group that administers these disabilities is generally referred to as the *dominant group.* Note that the term *minority* does not necessarily have any numerical connotation. Despite its literal meaning, a minority is *not* a statistical category. Although minority groups are generally of smaller size than the dominant group, this is not always the case. Within the Union of South Africa and some areas of our southern states, Negroes constitute a majority of the population. Moreover, at least until recently, a limited number of Europeans dominated "minority" peoples in Indonesia, in the Congo, and other former colonial areas. Yet despite the fact that they are a numerical majority in such settings, the minority occupies a disadvantaged position and experiences various disabilities.

2. *The disabilities experienced by minorities are related to special characteristics that its members share, either physical or cultural or both, which the dominant group holds in low esteem.* The disapproval ranges from ridicule or mere suspicion to hate. Most frequently the special traits distinguishing the minority from the dominant group are differences in physical appearance (for example, Negroes within the United States) or in language, religion, or some other cultural traits (for example, Jews). Groups identified on cultural grounds are commonly referred to as *ethnic* minorities; those identified on physical grounds, as *racial* minorities.

3. *Minorities are self-conscious social units; they are characterized by a consciousness of kind.* The individuals making up a minority recognize the fact of their membership and this recognition affects their behavior. Minority members are aware of something that they share in common with others like themselves—that is, "I am one of them." The common traits that they share often form the basis of an *esprit de corps,* an in-group feeling, a sense of belonging to a group distinct from the dominant group. Wagley and Harris note:

In addition to whatever special traits they share, their sense of isolation, of common suffering, and of a common burden makes most minorities self-conscious groups apart from all others in their society. It is often this self-consciousness, this awareness of common problems, that keeps a minority intact. A person who no longer practices the traditional Jewish religion and who is completely acculturated to the dominant culture patterns and language of his society, often continues to identify himself as a Jew. Individuals whose physical features are mainly Caucasoid identify themselves as Negroes in the United States because of their feelings for their group.[12]

[12] *Ibid.,* 6–7.

4. *Generally a person does not become a member of a minority voluntarily; he or she is born into it.* Members of a minority usually (but not always) conceive of themselves as being alike by virtue of their common ancestry. At any rate, and this is critical, by virtue of their real or presumed ancestry, members of the dominant group ascribe minority group status to them. At times but one parent (father or mother) is sufficient to insure the membership of a child in a minority, and in certain cases, a single grandparent or great-grandparent suffices. Within the United States an individual who is physically indistinguishable from the dominant white group but who has a known Negro grandparent is defined as a Negro. In Nazi Germany it was of no avail that a "Jew" looked like German non-Jews, had been converted to Christianity, and had taken a Christian spouse—he was still, according to the Nazis, a "Jew."

5. *Members of a minority group, by choice or necessity, tend to marry within their own group (endogamy).* In-group marriage is sometimes enforced by the dominant group, sometimes by the minority, and frequently by both. Within some areas of the United States, for example, Negro-white marriage is barred by the white group, but informally is also discouraged by the Negro group. The rule of endogamy functions to perpetuate the physical and cultural differences between the dominant and minority groups as well as inequalities in status.

Robin M. Williams, Jr., captures the core of the above five features in this summary definition: *"Minorities . . . are any culturally or physically distinctive and self-conscious social aggregates, with hereditary membership and a high degree of endogamy, which are subject to political, or economic, or social discrimination by a dominant segment of an environing political society."* [13] Table 1 presents a breakdown for the United States of all racial groups enumerated in the 1960 Census, while Table 2 indicates the religious composition of the United States estimated on the basis of a sample survey conducted by the Census Bureau in 1957.

Minorities on the World Scene

Clearly minority groups are by no means unique to the United States. Europe especially has been noted for a long history of social movements and conflicts revolving about demands for political self-determination among various nationality groups. Although often distinguished in language, cultural heritage, and even religions, they have

[13] Williams, *op. cit.*, 304.

TABLE 1

Racial Groups in the United States, 1960

Race	Number	Per Cent of Total
White	158,831,732	88.6
Negro	18,871,831	10.5
Other Races		0.9
Indian	523,591	
Japanese	464,332	
Chinese	237,292	
Filipino	176,310	
All Other	218,087	
	179,323,175	100.0

SOURCE: U.S. Bureau of the Census, *1960 Census of Population, Supplementary Reports, PC (S1)-10,* September 7, 1961, 3.

TABLE 2

Religion Reported by the Civilian Population 14 Years Old and Over, in the United States, March, 1957

	Number (000's)		Per Cent of Total
Protestant	78,952		66.2
Baptist		23,525	19.7
Lutheran		8,417	7.1
Methodist		16,676	14.0
Presbyterian		6,656	5.6
Other Protestant		23,678	19.8
Roman Catholic	30,669		25.7
Jewish	3,868		3.2
Other religion	1,545		1.3
No religion	3,195		2.7
Religion not reported	1,104		0.9
Total	119,333		100.0

SOURCE: *Statistical Abstract of the U.S., 1958* (Washington, D.C.: Government Printing Office, 1958), table 52, 50.

not enjoyed nationhood. In fact, as Arnold Rose points out, the territories covered by political nations have never been, and could not possibly be, exactly the same as the territories inhabited by the nationality groups.[14] Very frequently nationality groups occupy only small pieces of territory or are dispersed by residence and place of occupation throughout the territory of the dominant group. Thus political self-determination for one nationality may be quite incom-

[14] Arnold Rose, ed., *Race Prejudice and Discrimination* (New York: Alfred A. Knopf, Inc., 1951), 3.

patible with political self-determination for another. There are a large number of contemporary nation-states that contain multiple nationality groups, including Great Britain (Scotch, Welsh, and English), Belgium (Flemish and Walloons), Czechoslovakia (Czechs and Slovaks), Switzerland (Germans, French, and Italians), Canada (French and English Canadians), and the Soviet Union (fourteen major and many smaller nationality groups, e.g., Great Russians, Georgians, Ukrainians, Tartars, Kirghiz, Turks, etc.).

Since modern nations have classically pursued the interests of a particular nationality, other nationality groups within their physical boundaries have often occupied the status of minorities. Not only have minorities frequently suffered through persecution, but at times they have posed a serious source of friction between nations. The presence of Greeks in Bulgaria and Turkey, Turks in Bulgaria and Greece, and Bulgarians in Greece and Turkey has served to keep relations between these three nations strained and even periodically turbulent during the twentieth century.

The Relativity of Minority Membership

A given racial, nationality, or religious group may be dominant in one area and a minority in another. Jews constitute the dominant group in Israel, while Arabs represent a minority group. In the Arab nations the situation is reversed. Roman Catholics are a dominant group within Spain and Italy but a minority within Norway. Chinese exercise dominance over Tibetans and the various nationality groups within contemporary China but constitute a minority throughout most other areas of the world. In various historical periods the dominant-minority relationship may also be altered or, in fact in some instances, reversed. During the Nazi occupation of Czechoslovakia, the Sudeten Germans secured a position of dominance over the Czechs among whom they previously had been a minority.

Furthermore, dominant and minority group memberships are not necessarily mutually exclusive. As Barron points out, it is possible for an individual to have dominant and minority roles simultaneously.[15] This possibility derives from the fact that the minority-dominant group classification has a threefold basis: race, religion, and nationality. Roman Catholics within the United States are members of a prominent religious minority, yet many of their members may simultaneously be whites and thus racially grouped with the dominant group. Negroes, on the other hand, are racially grouped with a minority, yet in terms

[15] Milton L. Barron, *American Minorities* (New York: Alfred A. Knopf, Inc., 1957), 4–5.

of religion may be members of the dominant Protestant group. Norwegians in some areas of the Midwest, by virtue of their national descent, are accorded minority status, although they are members of the dominant white race and the dominant Protestant religion.

Visibility

In order for a dominant-minority situation to exist, it is essential that there be some visible and conspicuous feature or features present by which the members of the two groups can be differentiated. The individuals within the society must be able to identify one another in terms of ethnic or racial membership. The distinguishing traits may be of a physical, cultural, or combined physical-cultural character. In the absence of such traits, the boundaries between the in-group and the out-group could not be maintained.

While some of the differences between people are personal and unique, a good many of the differences can be typed, such as sex and age differences. Japanese, Chinese, Mexicans, Indians, and Negroes are distinguished from the dominant whites within the United States by certain hereditary physical traits that they share in common with the other members of their respective groups. Cultural traits likewise provide identifying clues. Names, language, accents, mannerisms, dress, gestures, typical facial expressions, food habits, religious practices, and various types of folk behavior supply "marks," or "signs," of ethnic membership. The evidence of ethnic membership may be quite manifest in terms of dress as among many Amish and Puerto Ricans. Then again, the identifying traits may be less readily apparent. In most respects, Catholics are undifferentiated from the great mass of Protestant Americans. Yet clues to Catholic membership are frequently discernible. The individual who wears a Saint Christopher medal, who attaches a statue of the Virgin Mary to his car's dashboard, who indicates he goes to mass, or who has attended and whose children attend a Catholic school is customarily identified as a Catholic.

The identifying "marks," or "signs," of group membership are sometimes perceptible by senses other than sight. Language and accent involve audibility. Odors, the product of differing hygienic or dietary practices, may provide evidence of ethnic membership. Yet olfactory hallucinations are not uncommon. Individuals may associate garlic with Italians and cheap perfume with immigrants, and accordingly, even in the objective absence of the particular odor, "smell" garlic when they meet Italians, and cheap perfume when they are in contact with immigrants. Association may also provide clues of group membership—individuals who are frequently found in the company of known Jews are often identified as Jews; similarly, with individuals in frequent association with Negroes.

Individuals who decide to escape from their membership in particular racial or ethnic groups may undertake to diminish or to eliminate their "visibility." Negroes may employ hair straighteners and bleach; Jews may change their names from "Cohen," "Blumberg," and "Finkelstein" to Anglicized names and display crosses as jewelry. Where visibility is so minute as to make it impossible to detect by simple observation who is a member of the minority group and who is a member of the dominant group, the minority may be compelled to display some identifying symbol. In Nazi Germany Jews were required to wear the Star of David or a yellow armband. Pope Innocent III, unable to distinguish Christians from heretics, decreed that the latter dress in a distinctive manner.

Types of Minorities

As Louis Wirth suggests, minorities can be classified in any number of ways.[16] Among these are (1) the number and size of the minorities within the society, (2) the degree to which minority status involves friction and discrimination, (3) the nature of the social arrangement governing the interaction between the minority and dominant groups, and (4) the goals toward which the minority and dominant groups are striving. In view of the contemporary world setting, Wirth feels that the last criterion is the most meaningful and satisfactory. Accordingly, he distinguishes between four types of minorities: (1) pluralistic, (2) assimilationist, (3) secessionist, and (4) militant.

A *pluralistic minority* desires to live peacefully side-by-side with the dominant group. It seeks tolerance for its differences. But while craving tolerance for various of its cultural idiosyncrasies, a pluralistic minority also seeks to maintain its cultural identity against dominant-group absorption. Switzerland provides an example of a culturally pluralistic nation. A majority of the Swiss speak a variety of German known as *Schwyzertütsch;* about 20 per cent speak French; another 6 per cent, Italian; and slightly more than 1 per cent speak an ancient language known as Romansh. Within the various cantons, there are notable differences in costume, dialect, and patterns of life. Although a majority of the people are Protestant, there is a sizable Catholic population. Within this setting, Switzerland officially recognizes all

---

[16] Louis Wirth, "The Problem of Minority Groups," in Ralph Linton, ed., *The Science of Man in the World Crisis* (New York: Columbia University Press, 1945), 347–372.

four languages, although only German, French, and Italian have been declared "official languages" into which all federal documents are translated. Although religious and ethnic prejudice is by no means non-existent, the Swiss have learned to live harmoniously with their differences.

Whereas a pluralistic minority seeks to maintain its group integrity, an *assimilationist minority* expects to be absorbed within an emergent common culture that is the product of the blending of divergent racial and ethnic strains. Assimilation is viewed as a two-way process in which, through a fusion of the differing racial stocks and cultural traditions, a new people and culture emerge. This has been the prevailing orientation among the various European immigrant groups within the United States as well as the aim of American Negroes generally.

The *secessionist minority* repudiates both assimilation and cultural pluralism. Although desiring to maintain their own cultural identity, they are not satisfied, as are the cultural pluralists, with mere toleration or cultural autonomy. The aim of the secessionists is statehood—full political self-determination. Frequently the secessionist minority enjoyed national sovereignty at an earlier period and cultivates among its members the romantic sentiments associated with it. No matter how archaic the cultural patterns, strong emphasis is placed upon the revival of the language, lore, literature, and ceremonial institutions associated with the group's prior independence. The Irish, Czech, Polish, Lithuanian, Estonian, Latvian, and Finnish nationalistic movements that culminated in the establishment of independent nations at the end of World War I are illustrative of secessionist movements. The Jewish Zionist movement and the Garveyite movement among Negroes in the 1920's are other examples.

A *militant minority* goes far beyond the demand for equality, or even cultural and political autonomy, and insists upon reversing the statuses. Domination over others is set as its goal. Such a group is frequently convinced of its own superiority. The Sudeten Germans, aided and abetted by the Nazis, made claims upon the Czechoslovakian republic which in effect would have reduced the Czechs to minority status.[17]

Wirth's types have not gone without criticism. The fourth type, "militant," is not the same kind of concept as the others, dealing as it does with tactics. Similarly, there is no reason why some of the other types may not also be "militant" in their tactics. Still another effort to classify minorities has been undertaken by Oliver C. Cox, who dis-

[17] *Ibid.*, 354–363.

tinguishes between the differing kinds of situations which characterize dominant-minority relations:

1. Situations in which the colored person is a stranger in a white society, such as a Hindu in the United States or a Negro in many parts of Canada and in Argentina—we shall call this the stranger situation.
2. Situations of original white contact where the culture of the colored group is very simple, such as the conquistadors and Indians in the West Indies, and the Dutch and Hottentots in South Africa—the original-contact situation.
3. Situations of colored enslavement in which a small aristocracy of whites exploits large quantities of natural resources, mainly agricultural, with forced colored labor, raised or purchased like capital in a slave market, such as that in the pre-Civil War South and in Jamaica before 1834—the slavery situation.
4. Situations in which a small minority of whites in a colored society is bent upon maintaining a ruling-class status, such as the British in the West Indies or the Dutch in the East Indies—the ruling-class situation.
5. Situations in which there are large proportions of both colored and white persons seeking to live in the same area, with whites insisting that the society is a "white man's country," as in the United States and South Africa—the bipartite situation.
6. Situations in which colored-and-white amalgamation is far advanced and in which a white ruling class is not established, as in Brazil—the amalgamative situation.
7. Situations in which a minority of whites has been subdued by a dominantly colored population, as that which occurred in Haiti during the turn of the eighteenth century, or the expulsion of the whites from Japan in 1638—the nationalistic situation.[18]

It is not always clear, however, as to which variable Cox is using in his classificatory approach: the nature of the original contact, the degree of cultural contrast, the proportionate size of the minority, or some other.

CONTACT BETWEEN PEOPLES

Migration as a Source of Contact

If people were content to live among their own kind in communities that were more or less isolated from one another, racial and ethnic

[18] Oliver Cromwell Cox, *Caste, Class, and Race* (New York: Doubleday & Co., 1948), 353–354.

prejudice would be virtually unknown. Religious sects conceivably may spring up within a society, but racial and nationality groups have traditionally arisen among people more or less isolated from others. When for one reason or another people have engaged in territorial movement, they have often come into contact with other groups. Frequently the groups within the contact situation have differed from one another in race, religion, or national origin. In turn, one or more of these elements may furnish the foundation for the emergence of a dominant-minority relationship.

In examining migration, it is useful to distinguish between a number of different types of movement. Petersen [19] provides us with a convenient system by which to classify migrations:

1. *Primitive migration.* The movement of primitive peoples appears related to their inability to cope with the forces of nature. By virtue of their limited technological level, primitive people exercise little control over their subsistence. The resources available within one locality are generally inadequate to support a food-gathering or hunting people. Instead they must range over a wider area, frequently moving haphazardly or back and forth over their traditional territory. Although a herding people generally have greater control over their food supply than do gathering and hunting peoples, they too need to migrate for new grazing lands. Similarly an agrarian people may migrate when there is a sharp disparity between the produce from the land and the number of people subsisting upon it. The disparity may come about suddenly, as by drought or an attack of locusts, or by the steady Malthusian pressure of an increasing population on land that is limited in extent or fertility. Within their new settings, the migrants typically seek to resume their previous way of life. In the modern period, however, the more usual destination for migrants has been the city, where new ways of thinking and acting are demanded of them.[20]

2. *Forced and impelled migrations.* In forced migrations it is the state or a functionally similar institution that has served as the activating agent for the migration. Petersen distinguishes between impelled migration, where the migrants retain some power to decide whether or not to leave, and forced migration, where they lack this power. The early Nazi policy of encouraging Jewish emigration by various anti-

[19] William Petersen, "A General Typology of Migration," *American Sociological Review*, 23 (1958), 256–266.
[20] *Ibid.*, 259–260.

Semitic measures is illustrative of impelled migration, whereas their later policy of herding Jews into cattle trains and transporting them to camps is an example of forced migration.

Impelled migration frequently takes the form of flight. As a new people moves into a territory, it may drive before it the weaker former occupants. This apparently was the case during the early centuries of the Christian era, when invaders from the East made their way into Europe. In the modern period, flight has constituted a major form of migration as well as a source of intense friction between the Free and Communist worlds. The mass flight of East Germans to West Germany had so undermined the East German Communist regime that in the summer of 1961 the Soviet Union precipitated a Berlin crisis and unilaterally closed the border between East and West Berlin. Coolie trade is likewise a form of impelled migration, e.g., the movement of Asians to plantations and the migration of white indentured servants to the British colonies in the eighteenth century.

Forced migration has assumed considerable importance since the turn of the twentieth century, with millions of people forcibly uprooted and transferred from their homelands. Following World War II, some 7 million Germans were expelled from the former German territory east of the Oder-Neisse River line by the Polish government. Included were Germans in the states of Pomerania, East Prussia, and Silesia. The separation of Pakistan from India was accompanied by the migration of more than 12 million Moslems and Hindus, in part induced by terrorism and in part arranged under government auspices. During World War II, the Soviet Union, on the claim that they were "disloyal nationalities," resorted to the forced deportation from their homelands of the Volga Germans, the Chechen-Ingush, the Crimean Tartars, and the Kalmuks, each of whom had constituted an autonomous Soviet republic. More than 2 million people were involved. The overseas shipment of Africans during the mercantile age similarly constituted a forcible movement of people.

3. *Free migration.* In primitive migration the activating force is primarily the lack of means to satisfy basic physiological needs, and in forced migration the migrants are largely passive. In free migration, on the other hand, the decisive element is the will of the migrants. The overseas migration of Europeans to the New World during the nineteenth century affords an important illustration of this type of migration. The numbers involved in the free migration were not large —they were pioneers who helped to break the ice and clear the way for later mass migrations. The pioneers were often adventurers or intellectuals who were motivated by their ideals. Their letters home and

their accounts in European newspapers encouraged others to follow them to the New World.[21]

4. *Mass migration.* The pioneers blazed the trails that others followed. Migration soon became the style. Once it began, it stimulated still further migration. Emigration became a *social* pattern, and it can be largely understood in terms of the mechanisms of collective behavior. In various parts of Europe there developed what became known as "America fever": Emigration became an important aspect in the atmosphere of the times. In Sweden, children were "educated to emigrate"; they followed a tradition that made emigration the "natural" thing to do. In fact, the failure to emigrate may actually have posed difficulties for the individual, in terms of the expectations that had been set for him.[22]

Modes of Interaction Between Peoples

When peoples with differing racial and/or cultural backgrounds come into contact, various patterns tend to emerge governing their interaction. Since the interaction between such groups usually involves a continuous process, specific configurations appear that serve to direct and channel their relations. Although never static and unchanging, these modes of interaction may be relatively enduring. Some of the more common forms of interaction may be summarized as follows [23]:

1. *Conflict.* Conflict involves a struggle over values and claims to wealth, power, and prestige in which the opponents aim to neutralize, injure, or eliminate their rivals. It may find expression in riots, lynchings, rebellions, warfare, and other types of violence, and in its most extreme expression may result in the extermination of a group. In Nazi Germany the annihilation of the Jews was pursued as a deliberate policy. Conflict may also be expressed in non-violent forms such as boycotts, sit-ins, legal litigation, humor, and related mechanisms. It should not be concluded, however, that conflict is an inevitable consequence of contact between groups. In western Manchuria, for example, the Tungus, a Mongoloid people, and the Cossacks, a Caucasoid people, have managed to live together for generations in peace and harmony despite their vast cultural differences.[24]

2. *Subjugation.* Subjugation involves the establishment of dominance by one group over another, in which the members of the one

---

[21] *Ibid.*, 263.

[22] *Ibid.*, 263–264.

[23] In this connection, see: Brewton Berry, *Race and Ethnic Relations* (3d ed., Boston: Houghton Mifflin Co., 1965).

[24] *Ibid.*, 115–118.

group are made the subjects of the other group. Subjugation may find expression in colonialism in which the dominant group maintains its authority over the minority group at a territorial distance. In still another arrangement, the dominant group may bring the minority group within its own territorial boundaries, e.g., slavery.

3. *Segregation.* Segregation involves the process or state whereby people are separated or set apart. Segregation may be territorial; groups may undertake to disengage from interaction through the realization of spatially distinct areas of habitation. Spatial separation may be undertaken voluntarily by a group that seeks to insulate itself from others (e.g., the Amish of Pennsylvania [25] and the Basques of Idaho [26]) or involuntarily where a dominant group imposes separation upon a minority (e.g., the Indian-reservation policy within the United States). Segregation may also find expression in discrimination where individuals, by virtue of their group membership, are unequally and differentially treated.

4. *Stratification.* Stratification involves the ranking of people in a vertical arrangement—a hierarchy—that differentiates them as superior or inferior, higher or lower. Vertically people may be differentiated along racial, ethnic, and religious lines, and in turn each of these vertical cleavages may be differentiated horizontally by a series of social classes. Negroes, by virtue of their racial membership, and Poles, Greeks, and Italians, by virtue of their ethnic membership, are frequently found disproportionately concentrated in the lower rungs of the class hierarchy.

5. *Pluralism.* Pluralism involves the peaceable, harmonious living together of peoples with differing cultural backgrounds in which differences are permitted within a range consonant with national welfare. Switzerland probably represents the outstanding example in which pluralism has been pursued as a thoroughgoing national policy. The United States has tended to follow a pluralistic approach in its handling of religious differences, in its policy since 1933 toward the American Indians, and in its toleration of the associations and foreign-language newspapers of immigrant groups.

6. *Assimilation.* Assimilation involves the fusing together of peoples with diverse beliefs and behavior patterns within a common unity or culture. The fusion may be largely realized through a unilateral approximation of one group to the culture of the other, e.g., the relin-

[25] See Chapter 10 for a discussion of the Amish.
[26] See: John B. Edlefsen, "Enclavement among Southwest Idaho Basques," *Social Forces,* 29 (1950), 155–158.

quishing by European immigrant groups of their native cultures and the assuming of Anglicized cultural patterns. Assimilation may also be acomplished by a bilateral, reciprocal fusion in which a genuine third culture appears through the merging of two or more cultures, e.g., the Mestizo culture of Latin America.

7. *Amalgamation.* Whereas assimilation refers to a social process, amalgamation involves a biological process—a biological fusion of distinct racial and sub-racial groups. Biological mixing between differing racial groups has been an extremely common phenomenon in human history, going on since prehistoric times.

Consequences of the Type of Contact

Lieberson suggests that the type of contact which occurs between groups assumes critical importance in determining whether conflict or assimilation will ensue.[27] Most situations of intergroup contact involve at least one indigenous group (a group native to and already established in an area) and at least one group migrating to the area. Usually the groups in contact differ in their capacity to impose changes on one another. One group, then, tends to be "superordinate" and the other "subordinate." Hence, Lieberson distinguishes between *migrant superordination* and *indigenous superordination.*

Migrant superordination generally occurs when the population migrating to a new contact situation is superior in technology (especially weapons) and is more tightly organized than the indigenous group. These conditions enable the migrant group to impose its political and economic institutions upon the indigenous population. Through its political and economic dominance, the migrant group can effectively cultivate its own cultural practices and maintain its distinct social institutions (educational, family, religious, and so on). In this setting warfare often accompanies the early contacts between the two groups. Even where the initial contact is friendly, conflict is generated as the migrants begin to interfere with the natives' established order. Price notes the following consequences of white invasion and subordination of the indigenous populations of Australia, Canada, New Zealand, and the United States:

During an opening period of pioneer invasion on moving frontiers the whites decimated the natives with their diseases; occupied their lands by

---

[27] Stanley Lieberson, "A Societal Theory of Race and Ethnic Relations," *American Sociological Review,* 26 (1961), 902–910. For still another effort to develop a general theory of race relations see R. A. Schermerhorn, "Toward a General Theory of Minority Groups," *Phylon,* 25 (1964), 238–246.

seizure or pseudo-purchase; slaughtered those who resisted; intensified tribal warfare by supplying white weapons; ridiculed and disrupted native religions, society and culture, and generally reduced the unhappy peoples to a state of despondency under which they neither desired to live, nor to have children to undergo similar conditions.[28]

With the passage of time the subordinated indigenous people begins to participate in the economy introduced by the migrant group, a fact that often accentuates the disruption of their native institutions. This, in turn, has frequently fostered both nationalism and a greater sense of racial unity. In many African states, where Negroes were subdivided in tribal groups prior to white contact, racial consciousness and unity among Africans were actually created by white European colonialism. Contact characterized by migrant superordination is especially likely to breed a high incidence of racial and ethnic turmoil.

In contrast with migrant superordination, indigenous superordination entails the political and economic domination of the migrants by the indigenous population. When a population migrates to a subordinate position, Lieberson argues, considerably less conflict results. The movements of many European and Oriental populations to the United States, for example, did not give rise to warfare, nationalism, or long-term conflict. The occasional labor and racial strife marking the history of immigration to the United States is not on the same level as efforts to eliminate or revolutionize a particular social order.

In appraising differences in the effects of migrant and indigenous subordination, it is necessary to consider the options available to the migrants:

Irish migrants to the United States in the 1840's, for example, although clearly subordinate to native whites of other origins, fared better economically than if they had remained in their mother country. Further, the option of returning to the homeland often exists for populations migrating to subordinate situations. . . . Finally, when contacts between racial and ethnic groups are under the control of the indigenous population, threats of demographic and institutional imbalance are reduced since the superordinate populations can limit the numbers and groups entering. For example, when Oriental migration to the United States threatened whites, sharp cuts were executed in the quotas.[29]

In indigenous superordination, then, conflict is likely to be limited and sporadic, while considerable emphasis is placed upon the assimilation of migrants. The history of migration to the United States provides

[28] A. Grenfell Price, *White Settlers and Native Peoples* (Melbourne: Georgian House, 1950), 1.
[29] Lieberson, *op. cit.*, 905–906.

a classic example. Hence, the consequences ensuing from indigenous superordination are in marked contrast to those of migrant superordination.

SOURCES OF AMERICAN MINORITIES

American Indians

In 1492 there were about 700,000 to 1,000,000 Indians in that area which now comprises the United States. In the regions of earliest contact with Europeans, the area along the Atlantic seaboard and the Gulf of Mexico, the tribal territories of the Indians were appropriated and the aborigines were either annihilated or driven inland. Some made their way into the swamps, coves, and wooded mountains of these regions. Following the American Revolution, the new government followed a policy of negotiating treaties of land cession with the Indians. Where the Indians failed to agree, they were confronted with military force. Local groups of whites often moved on their own against the Indians. When the Indians resisted white encroachments upon their lands, warfare ensued, the Seminole War in Florida and the Black Hawk War in the Illinois Territory being among the better known of the wars fought east of the Mississippi. Eventually, with the exception of portions of the Iroquois nations, the tribes signed treaties of cession and moved westward. Some went resignedly, others at bayonet point.

West of the Mississippi, similar patterns prevailed. Against the Plains Indians, a policy of systematic annihilation was pursued. The slaughter of buffaloes was deliberately encouraged as a war measure to force the Indians into capitulation. In 1871, Congress made the Indians wards of the United States, and a reservation policy was followed. It was a program directed at destroying Indian cultures and forcing the assimilation of the Indians as individuals within the American way of life. The policy had devastating consequences for the Indians, a fact recognized in 1933 with the reorientation of Indian policy toward a program of pluralism. In 1924, Indians were finally granted American citizenship, a right denied them for nearly 150 years.

Negroes

In 1619 twenty Negroes were purchased from a Dutch man-of-war by the settlers at Jamestown. Since there was no precedent in English law regarding slaves, it appears that Negroes initially assumed the status of indentured servants, much in the fashion of whites. However, the Negroes' distinctive physical characteristics doubtless furthered their differential treatment from the beginning, and in time facilitated their enslavement. The growth of Negro slavery was closely tied with the development of the plantation system of agriculture that evolved within the South. Prior to the invention in 1793 of the cotton gin, slaves were primarily used in commercial agriculture based upon tobacco, rice, indigo, and naval stores. To supply the considerable demand for slaves, an elaborate trade system emerged. The voyage of the slaves from Africa to America, often referred to as the "Middle Passage," was a veritable nightmare. Overcrowding and epidemics were common.

At the time of the first federal census, taken in 1790, there were 757,208 Negroes in the country, of which more than 90 per cent were concentrated in the South. However, it was not until Eli Whitney solved the problem of separating the cotton seed from the close-adhering lint that cotton became the major crop of the South. By 1815

TABLE 3

Growth of the Negro Population Since 1790

Census Year	Number of Negroes	Percentage of Total Population	Percentage Increase of Negroes During Decade	Percentage Increase of Whites During Decade
1960	18,871,831	10.5	25.4	17.5
1950	15,044,937	9.9	17.0	14.4
1940	12,865,518	9.8	8.2	7.2
1930	11,891,143	9.7	13.6	15.7
1920	10,463,131	9.9	6.5	15.7
1910	9,827,763	10.7	11.2	21.8
1900	8,333,940	11.6	18.0	21.2
1890	7,488,676	11.9	13.8	27.0
1880	6,580,793	13.1	34.9	29.2
1870	4,880,009	12.7	9.9	24.8
1860	4,441,830	14.1	22.1	37.7
1850	3,638,808	15.7	26.6	37.7
1840	2,873,648	16.8	23.4	34.7
1830	2,328,642	18.1	31.4	33.9
1820	1,771,656	18.4	28.6	34.2
1810	1,377,808	19.0	37.5	36.1
1800	1,002,037	18.9	32.3	35.8
1790	757,208	19.3		

SOURCE: U.S. Bureau of the Census, *Negroes in the United States, 1920–1932,* 1–2; *Sixteenth Census of United States, Population,* II, 19.

the production of cotton had increased at a phenomenal rate. This expansion of the cotton economy was accompanied by the growth of the slave population. Although by 1808 England and the United States had outlawed the traffic in slaves, the slave trade persisted, merely having been driven underground. Nevertheless, by far the chief source of growth in the slave population was natural increase. The growth in the Negro population of the United States since 1790 can be seen in Table 3.

Immigration to the United States

The total number of immigrants admitted to the United States throughout our history is not known. In 1820 the government began maintaining a record of immigration, but until 1907 the enumerations suffered from serious limitations. According, only a rough approximation of total immigration to this country can be gained from federal sources. These data are presented in Figure 1 (page 28). Until the depression years of the 1890's, the volume of immigration generally increased each decade. Immigration remained high until the passage of restrictive legislation in the 1920's, which set ceilings upon the number of migrants to be admitted from each nation. Many immigrants to the United States eventually returned home. Between 1907 and 1930 the ratios of outflow to inflow for total alien migration ranged from 23.7 to 32.0 per cent, with the exception of the World War I period when it rose to 55 per cent. During the depression years of the 1930's emigration exceeded immigration, but, since World War II, there has been a sharp decline in outflow relative to inflow.[30]

The data on the number of immigrants to the United States from particular countries suffer from an even greater number of limitations than the data on immigration generally. Owing to the changes in the list of countries separately reported and to changes in boundaries, data for a number of nations are not comparable throughout. Furthermore, prior to 1906, the enumeration was made with reference to the country from which the alien came rather than the country of the alien's last permanent residence. Table 4 (page 29) gives a rough approximation of the total immigration to the United States from various nations since 1820.

The Period from 1783 to 1830. In 1790 the white population of the United States was predominantly of English stock. There were com-

---

[30] Simon Kuznets and Ernest Rubin, *Immigration and the Foreign Born* (New York: National Bureau of Economic Research, Inc., 1954), 46.

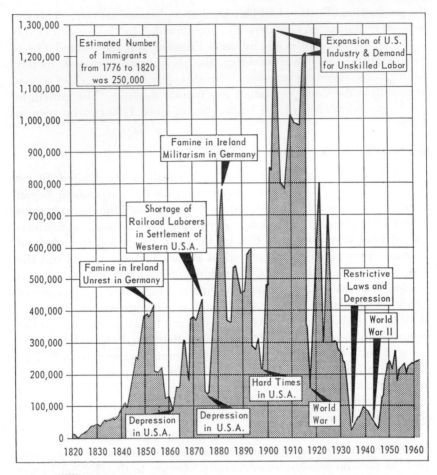

Figure 1. One hundred and forty-one years of immigration into the United States. (Source: *Philadelphia Inquirer*, William Streckfuss, Staff Artist. By permission.)

paratively few Germans, Irish, and Dutch, and even fewer French, Canadians, Belgians, Swiss, Mexicans, and Swedes. Between 1783 and 1830 about 10,000 immigrants came to the United States each year.[31]

31 The material that follows has been summarized primarily from: Donald R. Taft and Richard Robbins, *International Migrations: The Immigrant in the Modern World* (New York: The Ronald Press Co., 1955); Conrad Taeuber and Irene B. Taeuber, *The Changing Population of the United States* (New York: John Wiley & Sons, Inc., 1958), chapter 3; and Donald J. Bogue, *The Population of the United States* (New York: The Free Press of Glencoe, 1959), chapter 14.

TABLE 4

Immigrants, by Country of Origin: 1820–1963

Country	Total, 144 Years 1820–1963	Country	Total, 144 Years 1820–1963
All countries	42,702,328	Portugal	293,420
		Spain	188,974
Europe	34,896,219	Sweden	1,255,296
Austria ⎱ Hungary ⎰	4,280,863	U.S.S.R.	3,344,998
		Yugoslavia	69,834
Belgium	191,981		
Czechoslovakia	129,704	Asia	1,160,758
Denmark	354,331	China	411,585
Finland	28,358	Japan	338,087
France	698,188	America	6,218,631
Germany	6,798,313	Canada and	
Great Britain	3,844,058	Newfoundland	3,697,649
Greece	499,465	Mexico	1,291,922
		West Indies	684,175
Ireland	4,693,009		
Italy	5,017,625	Africa	53,186
Netherlands	338,722	Australia and New	
Norway	843,867	Zealand	84,468
Poland	451,010	Pacific islands	22,332

SOURCE: U.S. Bureau of the Census, *Statistical Abstract of the United States,* 1964, 94.

The Period from 1830 to 1882. The next period, from 1830 until 1882, was marked by a great increase in immigration. The great land areas beyond the Mississippi served to induce many foreigners to come to America. Rapid industrialization created major demands for unskilled labor to build canals, railroads, and roads, to work in factories, and to carry on many non-mechanized tasks. During these fifty-two years, English, Irish, Germans, and Scandinavians predominated among the migrants. The Irish came in especially large numbers after 1840 when the failure of their one crop, the potato, caused famine and resultant widespread suffering throughout Ireland. More than 1,350,000 Irish were recorded as having arrived in the United States during the eight years from 1847 to 1854. For the most part the Irish settled in the tenements of American cities, under slum conditions similar to those found among the southern and eastern Europeans of later date. In contrast with the Irish, the Germans and Scandinavians clung less tenaciously to the cities, many of them settling on farms in the Midwest. The German immigration reached its peak between 1880 and 1892 when more than 1,770,000 Germans were admitted; the Scandinavian immigration, between 1881 and 1890 when more than 656,000 were admitted.

The period from 1830 to 1882 was characterized by varied attitudes toward immigrants. Since organized labor was still struggling to secure recognition as an integral ingredient within the American system of labor-management relations, opposition from the trade unions on economic grounds had as yet not reached its full strength. Manufacturers generally eagerly sought the cheap labor provided by successive waves of immigrant groups and were not anxious to see this flow impaired. However, considerable objection was raised to the admission of paupers, criminals, and other "undesirables" among the aliens, as well as to the increase of the Catholic element within the population. In particular, considerable opposition was directed against the Irish. Prior to the Civil War, the Know-Nothing movement gained widespread support, as nativistic sentiment was spurred on by economic competition and apprehension over the increasing number of culturally different Irish and German immigrants. The party blossomed from a splinter group into a political force that elected nine governors and displayed a striking measure of strength in state legislatures and Congress.

1882—A Turning Point. The year 1882 represents a turning point in the history of American immigration. It marked the climax of the movement of migrants from northern and western Europe to the United States and the beginning of the large-scale movement of migrants from southern and eastern Europe. It was also the time of the passage of the Chinese Exclusion Act, and it inaugurated the beginning of federal control of immigration in general. Included in the so-called new migration (as opposed to the "old" migration from England, Germany, Scandinavia, France, Holland, etc.) were the Italians, Poles, Jews, Greeks, Portuguese, Russians, and a varied assortment of other Slavs. Within the span of some twenty years there was a complete reversal in the proportions of immigrants from northern and western, and southern and eastern Europe. Whereas, in 1882, 87 per cent came from the former area and only 13 per cent from the latter, by 1907 the corresponding figures were 13 per cent and 81 per cent, respectively. In the decade from 1901 to 1910 Italy's 2 million immigrants alone exceeded the 1.9 million from all the countries of northern and western Europe combined. By virtue of significant cultural differences between the "new" immigrants and the native American population, as well as a variety of other factors, the "new" immigrants were considered less desirable than the "old." Whereas the "old" migration had been predominately Protestant except for Irish Catholics and some Catholic Germans, an overwhelming percentage of the new immigrants were Catholic, Jewish, or Greek Orthodox in religion.

With the turn of the twentieth century, public sentiment in favor of restricting immigration became intense and widespread. The farmlands of the Midwest had all been homesteaded, and the settlement of the West and Southwest was well underway. The great railroads had been built, and great industries were flourishing. The "new" migration flowed into the large cities where ethnic islands emerged. New York, Chicago, and other large cities each came to have its "Little Italy," "Little Poland," etc. Within these separate neighborhoods and communities, the native languages and customs were kept alive.

With the influx of the large-scale immigration from eastern and southern Europe and a marked increase in ethnic antipathies, Congress in 1907 authorized an immigration commission to make "full inquiry, examination, and investigation of immigration." Clearly, the United States was moving in the direction of a policy aimed at regulating and restricting immigration. As early as 1882, Congress had enacted a law prohibiting Chinese from entry, save for a small group of scholars, ministers, and merchants. In the same year, legislation was also passed excluding paupers, criminals, "lunatics," and other undesirables, and imposing a head tax. In 1884, contract labor was outlawed; in 1903, insane persons, beggars, and anarchists were added to the exclusion lists; between 1907 and 1910, new types of mental "defectives" and persons involved in crimes of "moral turpitude" were included; and in 1917, a literacy test was added. The inflow of Japanese had been curtailed in 1907 by an agreement between Japan and the United States.

Numerical Restriction of Immigration. Following World War I there occurred an upsurge in American isolationist sentiment, a wave of antipathy for immigrants and foreigners, and a mass fear of aliens as "Reds" and "radicals." Within this context Congress was finally persuaded to take direct action toward the numerical restriction of immigration, the result being the act of 1921. The purpose of the act was to curtail the total volume of immigration and to favor migrants from western and northern Europe. It provided for a quota system under which each nation was allocated an annual immigration allowance equal to 3 per cent of the number of its foreign-born in the United States as reported by the 1910 Census. As the quotas of 1921 still gave to the nations of the "new" migration a large share of the persons to be admitted each year, the law was revised in 1924. The act of 1924 established a new formula for computing a country's quota, based on 2 per cent of the number of people born in that country who were residing in the United States in 1890. In 1890 the flow of "new" immigrants had not been large enough to build up a large foreign-born population of southern- and eastern-European origin. The 1924 act also provided that beginning July 1, 1929, the quota of any country would have the same ratio to 150,000 as the number of persons of that national origin living in the United States had to the total population living in the United States, as determined by the 1920 Census. Table 5 lists the quotas under these acts and clearly suggests how they discriminated against immigrants from southern and eastern Europe. Under the quota system, an estimated 84 per cent of the quotas went to northern and western Europe and only 14 per cent to southern and eastern Europe. The act of 1924 also barred Orientals from migrating to the United States. However, these restrictions were largely removed during World War II, and under the act of 1952 Orientals were assigned a token quota.

Post World War II Legislation. A more recent step in legislation was the passage of the Immigration and Nationality Act of 1952. The act simplified the national-origins formula of the 1924 act by basing the annual quota on a flat $\frac{1}{6}$ per cent of the population according to the 1920 Census. By presidential action, new quotas were established in 1953 for each quota area, totaling 154,657. These quotas have been periodically revised. Congress has also passed a number of acts relating to the admission of displaced persons and refugees. The Displaced Persons Act of 1948 authorized the entry of certain displaced persons and refugees, without regard to the availability of quotas, but subject to charges against future quotas. The act expired in 1952, but in 1953 Congress authorized the issuance of 214,000 special non-quota visas until the end of 1956 to refugees from Communist-dominated nations. Similarly, special legislation was enacted in 1958 which permitted Hungarian refugees from the abortive 1956 revolution to enter the United States. It is important to note that the quota system actually provides only one-third of the yearly immigration into the United States. These supplementary laws have authorized the entry of hundreds of thousands of displaced persons, political refugees, and others without regard to the quota system. In addition, Congress yearly approves thousands of individual "private" laws to permit the entry and naturalization of named individuals.

1965 Legislation. Critics charged that America's immigration laws judged persons by race and place of birth rather than personal worth to society. In response to this criticism Congress enacted new legisla-

TABLE 5

Annual Immigration Quotas, by Country, Under Successive
Immigration Laws and Amendments: 1921–1963

Country	1921 Act (3%, 1910)	1924 Act Effective 1924 (2%, 1890)	1924 Act Effective 1929 (national-origin ratio)	1952 Immigration and Nationality Act (as amended)
Total	356,995	164,667	153,714	156,987
Asia	1,043	1,300	1,323	3,290
Africa and Oceania	481	1,420	1,400	3,900
Europe	355,406	161,546	150,591	149,597
Northern and Western Europe				
Belgium	1,563	512	1,304	1,297
Denmark	5,694	2,789	1,181	1,175
France	5,729	3,954	3,086	3,069
Germany	68,059	51,227	25,957	25,814
Great Britain	77,342	34,007	65,721	65,361
Ireland	—	28,567	17,853	17,756
Netherlands	3,607	1,648	3,153	3,136
Norway	12,202	6,453	2,377	2,364
Sweden	20,042	9,561	3,314	3,295
Switzerland	3,752	2,081	1,707	1,698
Total, Northern and Western Europe	197,990	140,799	125,653	124,965
Southern and Eastern Europe				
Austria	7,451	785	1,413	1,405
Bulgaria	302	100	100	100
Czechoslovakia	14,282	3,073	2,874	2,859
Finland	3,921	471	569	566
Greece	3,294	100	307	308
Hungary	5,638	473	869	865
Italy	42,057	3,845	5,802	5,666
Poland	25,827	5,982	6,524	6,488
Portugal	2,520	503	440	438
Romania	7,419	603	295	289
Spain	912	131	252	250
Turkey	656	100	226	225
U.S.S.R.	34,284	2,248	2,784	2,697
Yugoslavia	6,426	671	845	942
Total, Southern and Eastern Europe	154,989	19,085	23,300	23,089

SOURCE: U.S. Bureau of the Census, *Statistical Abstract of the United States,* 1964, 91.

tion in 1965 which provided for the abolishment of the old national-origins quota system after June 30, 1968. After this date an annual ceiling of 179,000 immigrants will apply on a basis of strict equality to all nations of the world outside the Western Hemisphere. There will be no country-by-country quotas, and the national of an Asian or African country will receive the same consideration as a citizen of Great Britain or France. No country, however, will be allowed more than 20,000 immigrant visas in a single year.

After June 30, 1968, an overall ceiling of 120,000 annually will apply to the Western Hemisphere, but without the 20,000 country-by-country limitation. This will be the first time that such a restriction has been placed on immigration from Canada and the independent nations of Latin America and the Caribbean. The new legislation gives preference to applicants chiefly on the basis of (1) family ties to Americans and (2) occupational skills in short supply in the United States. Whereas the Statue of Liberty bears the inscription "Give me your tired, your poor, your huddled masses yearning to breathe," the immigration pattern that will ensue under the new legislation will be "Give me chiefly your skilled workers and trained professionals."

Internal Migration

In both urban and rural areas of the United States the proportions of foreign-born are steadily declining. Foreign-born persons who die are simply not being replaced by other foreigners. The immigrants' place in the social and economic life of American cities is being taken by migrants from rural areas within the United States. The major rural groups migrating to American cities are Negroes, Puerto Ricans, Mexican-Americans, and white southern "hillbillies." These groups differ from the immigrants in that they are American citizens and, except for some Puerto Ricans and Mexican-Americans, their native language is English. The migrants have taken over many of the unskilled, low-paying, low-status jobs vacated by the immigrants who are declining in numbers and ascending the status ladder. As did the bulk of the immigrants before them, these migrants from rural America face the dual burdens of poverty and urban inexperience.[32]

The so-called "hillbillies" present a good example of the norms, values, beliefs, and general habits that lower-class rural groups bring to the urban environment. Although Protestant, native white descendants of early Anglo-Saxon Americans, these migrants from the Southern Appalachian and Ozark regions constitute a minority group within a

[32] Noel P. Gist and Sylvia Fleis Fava, *Urban Society*, 5th ed. (New York: Thomas Y. Crowell Company, 1964), 464–466.

number of our large cities. Their way of life often conflicts with that of other urban dwellers:

Settling in deteriorating neighborhoods where they can stick with their own kind, they live as much as they can the way they lived back home. Often removing window screens, they sit half-dressed where it is cooler, and dispose of garbage the quickest way. . . .

Their children play freely anywhere, without supervision. Fences and hedges break down; lawns go back to dirt. On the crowded city streets, children are unsafe, and their parents seem oblivious. Even more, when it comes to sex training, their habits—with respect to such matters as incest and statutory rape—are clearly at variance with urban legal requirements, and parents fail to appreciate the interest authorities take in their sex life.[33]

The rural background of the "hillbillies" has ill-prepared them for the highly formal, circumscribed behavior required by American industrial life. The "hillbillies," used to individual work on farms or in hunting and fishing, carry over into the factory the habit of working at their own pace, a practice incompatible with highly coordinated industrial operations. As yet not fully committed to the city, workers often quit their jobs and fall back upon their rural kin for support or take weekends to go "home" for family occasions. Some even limit their city sojourn to the winter months when they are not needed on the farm. Absenteeism and unreliability lead to low seniority and little advancement. Within the city, the migrants, many of whom are young adults, are freed from traditional moral codes; sexual transgressions and general demoralization are a frequent result. The difficulties experienced by the "hillbillies" are all the more distinctive because the group has no "strikes" against it in terms of race, religion, or national origin.[34]

SUMMARY

In this chapter we have presented an overview of minority-dominant group relations. We noted that sociology approaches this study with scientific objectivity. In examining human behavior, tools of analysis are crucial—concepts with which the vast array of social phenomena may be approached. Hence, we looked at a number of key concepts: prejudice, discrimination, desegregation, integration, and minority. We then proceeded to examine what occurs when groups with differing racial and/or cultural backgrounds come into contact. And finally, we discussed the sources of American minority groups.

[33] Albert N. Votaw, "The Hillbillies Invade Chicago," *Harper's Magazine*, February, 1958), 65.
[34] Gist and Fava, *op. cit.*, 466–468.

2

Race: Fact and Myth

No treatment of minority relations would be complete without a consideration of "race." By virtue of the ignorance, superstition, and prejudice that have surrounded the matter for generations, we have postponed this consideration until we could thoroughly examine it. Various questions need to be dealt with: What is race? Are there "pure" races? Are Jews a "race"? Are there intellectually superior races? Are there "racial" personalities and temperaments? Is there a "racial" morality? Is racial interbreeding harmful? How are races formed? Although myths of one sort or another have clouded these basic human questions, scientific evidence can help to dispel some of the mystery and confusion.

WHAT IS RACE?

Definition

Throughout the world, people differ in the color of their skin, eyes, and hair, in stature, in bodily proportions, in head form, in nasal shape, and in many other characteristics. Each of these characteristics is apparently determined by more than one, often by many, genes. From the strictly biological viewpoint, homo sapiens is made up of a number of populations, each one of which differs from others in the frequency of one or more genes. These genes are responsible for the hereditary differences between men. Theodosius Dobzhansky, a noted geneticist, defines races as "populations differing in the incidence of certain genes, but actually exchanging or potentially able to exchange genes across whatever boundaries (usually geographic) separate them." [1] In his definition, Dobzhansky points to the fact that, by virtue of their common biological descent, the members of each race share certain types of genes. These genes in turn are responsible for the physical similarities that occur among the members of particular racial groups. Dobzhansky also notes that races are capable of interbreeding with one another and of producing fertile offspring. In this respect they are to be distinguished from species, for example, although the horse and donkey, each a distinct species, are hybridized on a large scale to produce mules, mules are wholly, or almost wholly, sterile, so that no gene interchange results. As can be seen from our discussion, scientists define "race" exclusively in *biological* terms. Human differences that are socially acquired and transmitted are not used as criteria of race.

It is important to distinguish between the scientific use of the term *race* and the *social* definition commonly given it in popular usage. Thus an individual with no apparent Negroid physical features but with known Negro ancestry is commonly classed by Americans as a Negro. Despite the fact that an individual may have one-sixteenth Negro ancestry—where a great-great-grandparent was a Negro—and fifteen-sixteenths white ancestry, he is still usually classified by Americans as a Negro. Indeed, as Warner notes, some Americans socially defined as Negroes:

. . . could not produce a racial Negro no matter how often and hard they might try. This is true for the very good reason, that by all physical tests an anthropologist might apply, some social Negroes are biologically white and, when mated with their own kind, can produce only white children.[2]

This contrast between social and genetic definitions of "Negro" often produces bizarre results. A beard, a turban, and an accent can do wonders for an American Negro traveling within the United States; mistaken for a "foreigner," such an individual often has access to otherwise segregated facilities. Similarly, Africans attached to the United Nations in New York City can frequently obtain housing denied American Negroes by virtue of "race." A New York real-estate woman reports:

The other day an African called me for a six-room apartment. I called a building I knew had a vacancy and the landlord asked, "How dark is he?" I said he was black as the ace of spades but that his wife wore her national

---

[1] Theodosius Dobzhansky, "On Species and Races of Living and Fossil Man," *The American Journal of Physical Anthropology*, N.S., 2 (1944), 251–265.
[2] W. Lloyd Warner, "Introduction," in Allison Davis, Burleigh B. Gardner, and Mary R. Gardner, *Deep South* (Chicago: University of Chicago Press, 1941).

dress. That always helps because then the other tenants won't mistake them for American Negroes. He got the apartment.[3]

Classification of Races

Having defined "race," we then face the task of differentiating between the races of the world. Estimates of racial types range from three—Caucasoid, Mongoloid, and Negroid—to thirty or more.[4] The simplest and most widely used classification involves the threefold division. The late E. A. Hooton, a noted physical anthropologist, employs the threefold approach and describes the more important hereditary traits distinguishing the Caucasian, Mongoloid, and Negroid stocks. These may be summarized in abbreviated form as follows:

> Caucasoid: skin color, light brown to pale white; hair color, shades lighter than black; eye color, never black; hair form, wavy or straight; nose form, usually high and narrow; facial protrusion (prognathism), usually lacking; membranous lip thickness, medium to thin, little eversion; and pelvis, broad in both sexes.

> Mongoloid: skin color, yellow or yellow brown; hair color, black; eye color, medium to dark brown; hair form, straight, coarse texture; nose form, infantile, root very low, no nasal depression; eye form, opening slit-like, slanting; and teeth, shovel incisors usually present.

> Negroid: skin color, dark brown to black; hair color, black; eye color, dark brown to black; hair form, woolly or frizzly; nose form, bridge and root usually low and broad; lip form, membranous lips usually puffy and everted; and facial protrusion, often marked in subnasal region.[5]

Seemingly such a division is simple and clear-cut. But is it? In which of these categories can one place the people of Polynesia? Polynesia represents a group of islands scattered over the mid-Pacific within an equilateral triangle of which the Hawaiian Islands form the apex, Easter Island the eastern angle of the base, and New Zealand the western basal point. The skin color of the Polynesians ranges from almost white to dark brown; some are roundheads, others are longheads; their noses may be slender and high, or broad, short, and concave; their hair is prevailingly wavy but sometimes straight and even frizzly. Upon examination some Polynesians show Mongoloid features, others Negroid traits, and yet others European features. In the majority of the

---

[3] Jane Krieger Rosen, "Africans in Darkest New York," *New York Times Magazine,* February 28, 1965, 31.

[4] See Stanley M. Garn and Carleton S. Coon, "On the Number of Races of Mankind," *American Anthropologist,* 57 (1955), 996–1001.

[5] E. A. Hooton, *Up from the Ape* (New York: The Macmillan Co., 1949), 572 ff.

Polynesians these racial characteristics are blended into a harmonious and pleasing whole. As a group they are distinct from any of the three main racial types.[6] How does one classify them? Authorities are in disagreement on the matter. Similarly, such peoples as the Australian aborigines, the Melanesians of New Guinea and neighboring islands, the Ainus of northern Japan, and many others cannot be fitted into the threefold classification.

Indeed, some leading anthropologists, including Sherwood L. Washburn, argue that there simply are not three primary races. Take the Bushman, a people inhabiting the Kalahari Desert in southern Africa. They are a pygmy people who, however, are not at all like the Congo Pygmies or the other Negritoes of the world. They are not so short, and they are typically yellowish in skin color, not black. The Bushmen possess the most extraordinary specialization to be found in the races of man. This is steatopygia, or the ability to lay up fat on the upper thighs and backside, until it is quite conspicuous, and to use this fat to sustain life when on a starvation diet (much in the fashion of a hibernating animal). Here, then, is a race that cannot be aligned with any other. The ancestors of these Bushmen lived 15,000 years ago in an area at least twice that available to Europeans of that time. While the Bushmen were living in a land of optimum game, the Europeans were living close to an ice sheet. It is estimated that 15,000 years ago there were from three to five times as many Bushmen ancestors as there were European ancestors. Washburn observes:

> If one were to name a major race, or a primary race, the Bushmen have a far better claim in terms of the archeological record than the Europeans. During the time of glacial advance more than half of the Old World available to man for life was in Africa. The numbers and distributions that we think of as normal and the races whose last results we see today are relics of an earlier and far different time in human history.[7]

Dobzhansky, a leading geneticist, likewise insists that a close look at the theory of ancient pure races discloses fatal weaknesses. These presumed ancestral races have been selected by choosing among living people a few clans, tribes, or even individuals with a convenient combination of traits, and declaring them the original "types" and the sources of the blends observed in people elsewhere:

> . . . One may, for example, select some very tall, blond, straight-haired, round-headed, straight-nosed, and thin-lipped persons and some short, black, frizzle-haired, long-headed, broad-nosed, and thick-lipped ones to be the pure races. Everybody else, then, may be represented on paper as de-

<hr>

[6] *Ibid.*, 616–618.

[7] Sherwood L. Washburn, "The Study of Race," in Melvin M. Tumin, *Race and Intelligence* (New York: Anti-Defamation League of B'nai B'rith, 1963), 49.

rived from the recombination of traits that resulted from mixtures between the chosen prototypes. Alas, there is no reason to think that mankind ever consisted of uniform races with requisite combinations of traits (or any other pure races), or that the people now living came from such a mixture.[8]

Hence critics have dealt rather harshly with traditional racial typologies and the premises underlying them.

Additional Problems Associated with Racial Classification

Most people recognize that Scandinavians such as the Swedes manifest a series of physical characteristics that differentiate them from Mediterranean peoples such as the Italians. Swedes are often classified within the Caucasian sub-race of Nordics; Italians within the Caucasian sub-race of Mediterraneans. Between the Nordics and the Mediterraneans in the central zone of Europe are the Alpine sub-race. Yet among what people or where geographically in Europe can one say with definitive authority, "Here Nordics end and Alpines start"? Or, "Here Alpines end and Mediterraneans begin"? Or, for that matter, why distinguish between merely Nordics, Alpines, and Mediterraneans? Why not five or nine or some other number of sub-races? Might not one classificatory system have as much merit as another? Moreover, if one studies, district by district, the inhabitants of Germany, France, or northern and central Italy, one finds Nordic, Alpine, and Mediterranean types and every conceivable intermediate type.

On a larger scale one might ask, "Where and among what people in Africa can one with justice to the evidence indicate that here and among these people Caucasians cease and there and among those people Negroids start?" The problem is readily seen. It stems from the fact that most racial differences are *continuous* rather than *discrete*. With regard to skin color, hair form, stature, head shape, and the like, populations often show no sharp distinctions. Variations on the contrary are gradual and continuous. Blood types, however, are discrete. An individual's blood is either A, B, AB, or O, never a mixture or a shading of all four. Yet, as we shall see later in this chapter, blood types cut across "race" lines and hence are of little help in racial classification. In summary, races are not characterized by fixed clear-cut differences but by fluid, continuous differences.

There is still another problem associated with attempts to classify peoples on the basis of racial types. People differ in a great many ways, in skin color, hair texture, nose form, head shape, stature, nasal shape, and the like. If the variations in all these traits paralleled each other,

---

[8] Theodosius Dobzhansky, *Mankind Evolving* (New Haven: Yale University Press, 1962), 255.

racial classification would be facilitated. But often they do not. Some people in southern India, for example, have very dark skin but straight or wavy hair, while the Bushmen in South Africa have peppercorn hair (it curls tightly to form little individual spirals) but yellowish skin. A racial classification made on the basis of skin color would be quite different from that based on hair shape. Present classifications often arbitrarily ignore many of these differences and hence do not do justice to the evidence.

In conclusion, human races do not lend themselves easily to cut-and-dried classifications and neat labels. Where two or more peoples come into contact, populations are usually found that are intermediate or combine the traits of the different stocks. The longer the time over which such contacts occur, the more widely spread are the intermediate populations and the more blurred the racial divisions. In time there unfolds a situation such as in contemporary Europe where one or a multiple number of sub-races can be identified according to one's own predilections. Most of us readily recognize that nobody is simply a Caucasian, a Negroid, or a Mongoloid, since these peoples may in turn be divided further into Nordics, Pygmies, American Indians, and so on. Thus the racial panorama is complex and varied, and no two people would probably classify races in the same way. Here we will not attempt the task at all. Present-day scientists are far from agreement in making a division of the human races. Indeed, the number of races one identifies depends upon the purpose of the classification, and hence is a matter of convenience and judgment. By necessity any classification of races is almost entirely arbitrary, and depends upon the particular characteristics on which one chooses to base it. Any number of racial classifications of the same populations but based on different gene frequencies may be equally valid and useful. The concept "race" merely enables us to place a "handle" upon a phenomenon, to look at, to describe, and to analyze it. Classification and systematization are tools employed to make diversity intelligible and manageable. But this need not bar us from recognizing the shortcomings or relative nature of our tools.

Are There Pure Races?

Prominent in the philosophy of Nazi Germany was the notion of the "Aryan race." It was alleged that the German people constituted a "pure race," whose destiny it was to rule the world by virtue of its inborn "superiority." To the "Aryan race" were ascribed such traits as tallness, blue eyes, fair hair, and long heads, along with such psychic qualities as virility, innate nobility, natural aggressiveness, precise intelligence, the spirit of independence, sternness to themselves and others, a well-developed sense of responsibility, great foresight, tenacity of will, and qualities of world leadership—in a word, the qualities most admired by the German racist writers. Professedly it was a "pure" race in no way "contaminated" by other biological stocks.

No scientific evidence is available that substantiates this thinking. Authorities are agreed that "pure" races do not exist in the contemporary world. Ample evidence testifies that all peoples are the products of racial intermixing through the ages, from which the German people are no exception. Migrations and invasions from the earliest time passed across the face of central Europe, including the Danubians, the Bell Beaker peoples, the Goths, the Vandals, the Huns, and many others.[9] Thus in Berlin one may meet a lot of tall, blond, and blue-eyed people, but one will also find many with brown eyes and dark hair. There is no reason to believe that the latter are any less German than the blue-eyed blonds. Hence, it seems slightly ludicrous that the main exponents of the theory of racial superiority and pure races should be inhabitants of one of the most thoroughly hybridized areas in the world.

Closely associated with the notion of the "Aryan" race and frequently overlapping with it are notions relating to a "pure" Nordic race. Here again there is no evidence to substantiate the doctrine. Most people would probably agree that the Swedes are among the most Nordic people of Europe. Yet in 1897–1898, when some 45,000 Swedish army conscripts of twenty-one years of age were measured for army service, only 11 per cent were of the "pure" Nordic type, with tall stature, blond hair, blue eyes, and long skulls. The maximum of "pure" Nordics in any province was 18.3 per cent in Dalsland. Thirty years later similar measurements were made of 47,000 conscripts. Of these, 87 per cent were found to have light eyes, 8 per cent eyes of mixed shade, and 5 per cent brown eyes. Only 7 per cent had flaxen hair, while 63 per cent had light brown hair, 25 per cent had medium brown hair, 2 per cent brownish-black hair, and 3 per cent red hair. Obviously the Swedes do not constitute a "pure" race. Their genetic heritage is one of racial intermixture.

Are Jews a Race?

There are a good many people who assert that Jews constitute a "race." They go on to claim that they can identify a Jew from other people simply on the basis of appearance. The distinguishing physical

[9] Carleton Stevens Coon, *The Races of Europe* (New York: The Macmillan Co., 1939).

traits are allegedly short to medium stature, black hair, a long hooked nose, greasy skin, a dark complexion, and a tendency for the women to be somewhat hefty. We are then faced with the question, "Do Jews possess a complex of physical characteristics which makes them a distinct racial group?" Science answers the question with an unequivocal "No." In fact even the Nazis implicitly answered the question negatively, as they required Jews to display on their clothing the Star of David or yellow armbands so that "Aryans" might identify them. Apparently, in the absence of such insignia, the "Aryans" were having difficulty distinguishing the Jews.

Jews have a wide distribution throughout the world. During the Babylonian captivity in the sixth century B.C., they intermingled and intermixed with the Mesopotamian peoples. During the Hellenistic period they followed Alexander the Great into Egypt, Syria, Asia Minor, and other regions. At the time of the Maccabees, in the second century B.C., the Jews moved to the farthest corners of the Roman Empire, including Spain, Italy, France, and the Rhineland of Germany. With the coming of the First Crusade in the eleventh century and the persecution of the Jews by Christian knights, Rhineland Jews migrated to present-day Poland, Russia, and the Ukraine.[10] Likewise, there are Chinese Jews who are identical in Mongoloid traits with other Chinese; there are Abyssinian and American Negroids who are Jews; and in Italy there is a Jewish community of ex-Catholics. Jewish settlements are found in Transcaucasia, Syria, Turkistan, Persia, Afghanistan, Morocco, and Algeria.

Obviously it is not possible here to present the detailed statistics demonstrating the considerable variability in physical characteristics among the misnamed "Jewish race." The type usually regarded as typically "Jewish" is actually prevalent among the peoples of the eastern Mediterranean area, most of whom are not Jews and never have been. Thus Turks, Greeks, Syrians, and others are often mistaken for Jews by those who claim to be able to identify Jews by their appearance. Actually the Jews involved in the widespread migrations just described tended through time to interbreed with the inhabitants of the new lands. Accordingly, they frequently became indistinguishable from the aboriginal groups. By way of illustration, it is calculated that in Germany, between 1921 and 1925, for every 100 Jewish marriages, there were 58 all-Jewish and 42 mixed marriages. In 1926, in Berlin, there were 861 all-Jewish and 554 mixed marriages.[11] In the light of

---

[10] Ashley Montagu, *Man's Most Dangerous Myth: The Fallacy of Race* (New York: Columbia University Press, 1942), 221–222.

[11] Juan Comas, *Racial Myths* (Paris: UNESCO, 1951), 30.

such evidence it is not surprising to note that a census of schoolchildren taken in Germany during the nineteenth century reveaied that among 75,000 Jewish children, 32 per cent had light hair and 46 per cent light eyes.

Other evidence likewise points to the fact that different populations of Jews at one time or another have intermixed with the various populations among whom they were living. Among Jews in Yemen (Arabia) 100 per cent had dark eyes and dark hair. But among Jews in Baden (part of Germany), the dark-eyed Jews were in the minority (48.8 per cent), although nearly 85 per cent had dark hair, while 2.3 per cent had red hair. Some 51.2 per cent had light eyes and 12.8 per cent had fair or blond hair. A significant number of Baden Jews, accordingly, had the so-called "Aryan" traits. Similarly, in Lithuania 34.8 per cent of the Jews had light eyes and 29.0 per cent had fair or blond hair. When head shape is considered, Jews in different regions of the world show considerable differences from one another. Jews residing in the Daghestan Caucasus are predominantly round-headed; those in North Africa and especially those in Yemen Arabia are predominantly long-headed; and those in Europe tend to be of all varieties with the intermediate types predominating.

Quite clearly Jews are not of a uniform physical type. Even the hooked nose, ostensibly so characteristic of Jews, was shown by one study to be prevalent among only 44 per cent of the Jews of one group, while straight noses were found in 40 per cent, the "Roman" nose in 9 per cent, and the tip-tilted nose in 7 per cent. A trip to the new nation of Israel testifies to the absence of a Jewish "race." Jews have migrated to Israel in recent times from the far corners of the globe, a fact reflected in the multitude of physical differences among its people.

In summary, the existence among Jews of Caucasian, Mongoloid, and Negroid types, the presence of blonds and brunets, of hooked and Roman noses, of round, long, and intermediate heads, etc., is demonstrable evidence of the non-existence of a Jewish "race." Those emotional and temperamental reactions which may characterize some Jews, such as distinctive facial expressions, bodily posturings and mannerisms, styles of speaking and intonation can be traced to Jewish cultural traditions and to the treatment Jews received at the hands of the non-Jews. Who then is a Jew? We need to resort to a *social* definition. A Jew is an individual who is defined as a Jew by the community-at-large or by Jews or both.

ARE THERE SUPERIOR RACES?

Notions of Racial Intellectual Superiority

In the field of minority relations probably few other aspects have attracted as much attention as the question of whether certain racial or ethnic groups enjoy an inherent intellectual superiority over others. The notion of racial and ethnic superiority and inferiority has had wide currency in the modern age. It formed a cornerstone of official government policy in Nazi Germany. Traditionally it has provided a firm ideological foundation in defense of the southern segregated race pattern. A book by Tom P. Brady, a Yale-educated Mississippi circuit judge, is a case in point. The book, *Black Monday* (signifying the day of the Supreme Court's school-desegregation ruling), has been given wide distribution by the pro-segregation southern Citizens Councils in their war against desegregation.[12] Brady declares that the Negro, "like the modern lizard," has failed to evolve beyond "primitive status." He argues:

. . . he [the Negro] did not evolve simply because of his inherent limitations. Water does not rise above its source, and the negro could not by his inherent qualities rise above his environment as had the other races. His inheritance was wanting. The potential did not exist. This is neither right nor wrong; it is simply a stubborn biological fact.[13]

With the development in 1905 of the first tests to quantitatively measure intelligence, developed by Alfred Binet, a noted French psychologist, seemingly a scientific instrument was at hand to substantiate the doctrine of white intellectual superiority. Early authorities alleged that the Binet scale was a true test of inborn intelligence, relatively free of the disturbing influences of environment. Investigations based upon the Binet and related tests indicated that racial and ethnic groups differed markedly from one another in innate intelligence. In the various studies of Negro children by means of the Binet test, the intelligence quotient (I.Q.) ranged from 83 to 99, with an average around 90. A score of about 100 was considered normal for the population at large, thus Negroes performed at a lower-than-average level. With American Indians, I.Q. scores were also low, the majority ranging between 70 and 90. Mexicans did only slightly better. Chinese and Japanese, however, showed relatively little inferiority to whites, the scores rang-

12 Tom P. Brady, *Black Monday* (Winona, Miss.: Association of Citizens' Councils, 1954).
13 *Ibid.*, 2.

ing from 85 to 114, with an average only slightly below 100. Among European immigrant groups, Italians ranged from 76 to 100, with an average about 87, and the Poles did equally poorly. On the other hand, immigrants from Great Britain, Holland, Germany, and the Scandinavian countries were superior to others in test performance.

Contemporary intelligence testing, employing a variety of tests, tends to corroborate the findings that American Negroes, on the average, score lower than whites. During World War II, the Army administered intelligence tests to 9 million inductees. The average score was a few points above 100. The results for men processed from June, 1941, to February, 1942, were as follows: [14]

	Above 129	110–129	90–109	70–89	Below 69	No. Tested
White	8.5%	30.1%	32.1%	20.9%	8.3%	493,651
Negro	0.5	4.9	16.7	31.4	46.3	56,027

How Valid Are Intelligence Tests?

During the first two decades of the twentieth century, authorities tended to conclude that Negroes were the intellectual inferiors of whites. Robert M. Yerkes, chairman of a committee of psychologists that designed intelligence and aptitude tests for the U.S. Army during World War I, concluded that intelligence tests "brought into clear relief . . . the intellectual inferiority of the negro. Quite apart from educational status, which is utterly unsatisfactory, the negro soldier is of relatively low grade intelligence." This discovery was "in the nature of a lesson, for it suggests that education alone will not place the negro race on a par with its Caucasian competitors." [15]

By the 1930's, however, authorities were beginning to question intelligence tests in terms of their ability to measure innate, native intelligence. Social and cultural factors were shown to influence test results. Social scientists came to recognize that membership in a particular culture influences what the individual is likely to learn or fails to learn. This is reflected in the following illustration: In one portion of the National Intelligence Test, a psychological test in wide use in the United States, the individual is presented with a series of incomplete sentences in which he is asked to supply the missing word. One such sentence reads, "_____ should prevail in churches and libraries"; the correct answer is "silence." But in the southern Negro church,

[14] Robert D. North, "The Intelligence of Negroes," *Research Reports of the Anti-Defamation League,* Vol. 3 (November, 1956), 3.

[15] Robert M. Yerkes, "Psychological Examining in the United States Army," National Academy of Sciences, *Memoir,* 15 (1921), 870.

silence is neither the rule nor the ideal. The worshipers are expected to respond, to participate actively and audibly; in fact, a church service characterized by silence might well be considered a failure. Accordingly, many southern Negro children might be expected to answer this question "incorrectly." [16]

The effect of environmental changes on intelligence-test performance also led educators to take a second look at the tests. During World War I, over a million recruits including Negroes were given psychological tests. Beta tests were administered to illiterates and semi-literates, and Alpha tests were administered to literates. The results showed that Negroes from the South, where economic and educational handicaps were greater, did more poorly than northern Negroes. But most striking perhaps of all was that *Negroes* from some *northern* states turned out scores averaging higher than *whites* from some *southern* states. It has been suggested that the superior performance of northern Negroes was due to selective migration, i.e., Negroes with superior intelligence, energy, and initiative would leave the South, leaving behind Negroes with lesser intelligence. But the evidence in this connection for a theory of selective migration is slim. Klineberg, on the basis of a careful search through the school records in several southern cities and a detailed statistical comparison of the school marks obtained by the migrants and non-migrants, found no differences between the two groups. Apparently the environmental opportunities of northern Negroes were the crucial factor.[17]

This conclusion regarding the operation of environmental factors is strengthened by other studies. Klineberg made tests in New York City which demonstrated that I.Q. scores of Negroes in that city increased with length of residence. This would hardly be the case if such tests exclusively measured innate intelligence. Everett S. Lee confirmed the Klineberg findings in an analysis of intelligence tests given by the Philadelphia school system. There was a steady upward trend in the average I.Q. scores of the Negro migrants, so that, by the time all were in the ninth grade, those who came in at the first grade were less than a point below those born in the city.[18]

As was already noted, the test scores of American Indians are among the lowest of the groups examined in the United States. But Rohrer found that the performance of the Osage Indians was comparable to

[16] Otto Klineberg, *Race and Psychology* (Paris: UNESCO, 1951), 11.

[17] Otto Klineberg, *Negro Intelligence and Selective Migration* (New York: Columbia University Press, 1935).

[18] Everett S. Lee, "Negro Intelligence and Selective Migration: A Philadelphia Test of the Klineberg Hypothesis," *American Sociological Review*, 16 (1951), 227–233.

that of whites. The noteworthy point here, however, is that these Indians are exceptional in that they live under conditions which are similar to those of the whites with whom they were compared. Oil had been discovered on their reservation, enabling them to acquire an economic position and a social and environmental condition far superior to those of most American-Indian communities. On two different tests—one a non-language test, the second depending on language—they obtained average I.Q. scores of 104 and 100, respectively.[19]

The net result of all the research relating to intelligence testing indicates that as yet a "non-cultural" and "non-environmental" test has not been devised. In fact, it is unlikely in the light of our present understanding of the problem that such a test will be devised. It is known that environmental factors account for large differences in measured intelligence performance, and that minority groups are usually disadvantaged in terms of favoring environmental conditions. Thus studies have repeatedly shown that Negro children taken as a group, especially those who come from segregated schools, do not enjoy educational and related opportunities commensurate with those of whites.

Still other questions have been raised regarding racist interpretations of differences in Negro and white I.Q. scores. Any research that seriously attempts to make comparisons between or among "races" must sooner or later grapple with the questions, "What constitutes a race?" and "How do we go about classifying an individual or a group of people in terms of race?" Yet as we have already observed, these remain unsettled matters. Most racial comparisons rest upon social definitions of race. They do not allow for the considerable penetration of Caucasian genes among Negro Americans, a penetration that renders any discussion of pure races invalid and any suspicion of massive genetic distinctions between Negro and white Americans unlikely.[20]

In conclusion, any claims regarding innate differences between Negroes and whites with regard to intelligence cannot be substantiated unless three conditions are met:

1. Adequate tests of native intelligence, uncontaminated by environmental influences, and with proved reliability and validity will have to be developed.
2. The environment—the social and cultural backgrounds—of the Negroes and whites being tested must be fully equal.

[19] John H. Rohrer, "The Test Intelligence of Osage Indians," *Journal of Social Psychology*, 16 (1942), 99–105.

[20] See R. M. Dreger and K. S. Miller, "Comparative Psychological Studies of Negroes and Whites in the United States," *Psychological Bulletin*, 57 (1960), 361–401.

3. The distinctive *genetic* homogeneity of the Negro group being tested, as well as that of the white group, must be *demonstrated*, not assumed.[21]

To date, none of these conditions has been met. Hence, it cannot be definitively asserted that innate, native differences in intelligence exist between racial and ethnic groups. Nor, on the other hand, can it be definitively stated that *no* differences exist between racial and ethnic groups in innate, native intelligence. On the basis of what evidence is currently available, however, most contemporary authorities are of the opinion that notions of appreciable inborn differences in intelligence between various racial and ethnic groups simply cannot be supported.[22] Moreover, should such differences be found in the future, they are unlikely to be of major consequence or to have any great importance for social participation.

ARE THERE "RACIAL" PERSONALITIES AND TEMPERAMENTS?

The Subjective Nature of Many Appraisals

The same exaggeration of the role of biological forces may also be noted in popular notions regarding differences in personality and temperament. Jews are alleged to be shrewd, sly, and mercenary; Negroes, happy-go-lucky, lazy, and superstitious; Italians, impulsive, passionate, and quick-tempered; American Indians, unshrinking, stalwart, and brave; etc. Such traits are supposedly the products of inborn, genetic properties. Here we have much the same situation and much the same scientific support that we found regarding innate intellectual differences. Often, the alleged traits are fictitious and change with the times. In 1935 most Americans thought of Japanese as "progressive," "intelligent," and "industrious"; by 1942 they were "cunning" and "treacherous"; and by 1950 the image had changed again. When there was a need for Chinese laborers in California, they were portrayed as "fru-

---

[21] In this regard, see Tumin, *op. cit.,* 9.

[22] A few psychologists, however, challenge this point of view. See: Henry E. Garrett, "The Equalitarian Dogma," *Mankind Quarterly,* 1 (1961), 253–257; Audrey Shuey, *The Testing of Negro Intelligence* (Lynchburg, Va.: J. P. Bell Co., 1958); Frank McGurk, "Psychological Tests: A Scientist's Report on Race Differences," *U.S. News and World Report,* September 21, 1956, 92–96; and Ernest Van Den Haag, "Intelligence or Prejudice?," *National Review,* December 1, 1964. However, these psychologists have won little support. Their conclusions have come under attack by the Society for the Psychological Study of Social Issues, a division of the American Psychological Association; the Society for the Study of Social Problems; the American Anthropological Association; as well as a number of other professional associations.

gal," "sober," and "law-abiding"; when labor was plentiful and they competed with white workers, they became "dirty," "repulsive," "unassimilable," and "dangerous." Much the same situation existed in India, where American troops found the natives "dirty" and "uncivilized," whereas Hindu intellectuals found Americans "boorish," "materialistic," "unintellectual," and "uncivilized." Accordingly, such appraisals often rest on subjective evaluation. This is not to deny that peoples may differ, but such differences are inconsistent and appear related to social and environmental factors, not to biology.

Rorschach-Test Results

One useful technique for determining personality characteristics is the Rorschach Test. The subject is shown an inkblot and is asked what he "sees" in the configuration. The individual gives his responses to each of ten inkblots. It is assumed that he portrays a "total action" picture of his state of adjustment without realizing that he is revealing his frustrations, hostilities, or emotional status. No matter what his interpretations—whether he sees a volcano, a bear, individuals bowing to each other, a genital organ, or a woman's face in the shadows—the subject is believed to be projecting his general personality pattern. Abel and Hsu administered the Rorschach Test to a group of Chinese born in China and a group of Chinese who had lived their entire life in the United States. Had the general personality pattern of the Chinese been biological, one would expect their responses to be similar. Yet the study revealed some striking differences in the personality patterns of the two groups. The authors of the study concluded that the reason for the divergences was the merging of the Chinese Americans within the American way of life.[23] In a word, environmental forces were responsible.

Such findings are supported by other evidence. As Montagu notes, the alleged "expansive and rhythm-loving Negro" reared in England becomes as composed, phlegmatic, and awkward rhythmically as the average Englishman.[24] And, despite the fact that between the sixteenth and nineteenth centuries there were no new invasions of England nor any major genetic infusions from the outside, the boisterous joy of life of the Elizabethan period gave way to the prudish Victorian age, while the rationalism of the eighteenth century gave way to the romanticism of the nineteenth century. Similarly, Australians, New Zealanders, Canadians, and South Africans show different typical per-

[23] Klineberg, *Race and Psychology*, 35–36.
[24] Ashley Montagu, *Statement on Race* (New York: Abelard-Schuman, Ltd., 1951), 102.

sonality structures from one another and from their English ancestors. Clearly such phenomena as these would seem incapable of interpretation in strictly biological terms. Yet any final, definitive conclusion would be premature, as science as yet lacks adequate tests for the measurement of personality characteristics.[25]

IS THERE A "RACIAL" MORALITY?

The Image of the Italian as a Gangster

Closely related to other racial myths is the notion that there is an association between races and ethical standards. Not infrequently, a nationality group is erroneously equated with a racial group. Thus blanket assertions are sometimes heard that some immigrant groups, most notably the Italians, are "racially" predisposed toward crime, racketeering, and acts of violence. Questioned, the proponent of this viewpoint is likely to respond with considerable indignation and recite a list of Italian names including Capone, Luciano, Costello, Fischetti, and those of many other notorious gangsters. It is always interesting to note that such infamous "bad men" of the 1930's as Dillinger, Van Meter, Floyd, Nelson, Barker, and Kelly—all with traditional old American names—are conveniently forgotten. Actually the rate of criminal convictions among foreign-born Italians was approximately the same as that for other foreign-language groups and less than that for native-born whites. Although crimes against the person were higher, other crimes had a much lower incidence, including those of drunkenness, forgery, and disorderly conduct.

The prevalence of crimes against the person within the total criminal behavior of Italian immigrants is sometimes attributed to their "hair-trigger" disposition. Some insist that Italians are easily offended at trifles and respond with violence. Yet closer analysis reveals some important flaws in this theory. Root and Giardini demonstrate that American-born sons of Italians, though involved in predatory crimes, are not usually violent in their offenses. In short, this supposed inborn Italian predisposition passes in a single generation. This phenomenon is inconsistent with our present knowledge of genetics. Rather, a social explanation appears more in order. Traditionally the lack of a strong government in southern Italy promoted the practice of self-defense. A "true" man would not go to court; he would draw his stiletto at the slightest imagined affront. But his American-born son has become "Americanized" in his crimes. He loses much of his father's alleged

25 See Dreger and Miller, *op. cit.*, 374–381.

hair-trigger temperament and seeks financial gain from crime, not personal honor.[26]

Criminality Among Negroes

Crime reports in America consistently show that the percentage of Negroes caught within the meshes of the machinery of crime repression is out of proportion to their percentage in the total population. Negroes tend to rank disproportionately high as compared with whites in arrests for gambling, aggravated assault, murder, carrying weapons, narcotics, robbery, and prostitution; they rank disproportionately low in arrests for forgery, driving while intoxicated, auto theft, embezzlement, manslaughter by negligence, and drunkenness. The high incidence of homicides and assaults is apparently a product of the special behavioral and cultural patterns that characterize Negro life in America. On the one hand, Negroes would quite understandably be found ranking low in "white-collar crime" such as forgery and embezzlement, owing to their less advantaged position and limited access to white-collar positions. Furthermore, in evaluating statistics of Negro crime, it should be realized that Negroes are more liable to be suspected of crime than whites. They are also more liable to be arrested. After arrest, they are less likely to secure bail, and accordingly are more liable to be counted in jail statistics. They are more liable to be indicted and less likely to have their cases dismissed. If tried, Negroes are more likely than whites to be convicted. If convicted, they are less likely to be given probation. Such factors would increase their proportion among prisoners.[27]

But, as Taft points out, "Even the staunchest friend of the Negro can hardly argue that if full allowance could be made in statistics for the effect of prejudice on the discriminatory treatment of the Negro, the two races would have identical crime rates. Such an argument would indeed 'prove too much.' "[28] He suggests that discrimination works in two ways: It causes frustration and may result somewhat directly in aggression and crime; secondly, it may account for the disproportionate exposure of a member of this minority to conditions and associates that would indirectly dispose him to criminal behavior.[29]

There is no foundation for a biological interpretation of the higher incidence of some types of crimes among Negroes. If there were such

[26] See: Donald R. Taft, *Criminology*, 3d ed. (New York: The Macmillan Co., 1956), 101–102.
[27] *Ibid.*, 134.
[28] *Ibid.*, 136.
[29] *Ibid.*, 136–137.

a biological predisposition, we would expect to find among *all* groups of Negroes, regardless of social or economic circumstances, a similar incidence in criminal behavior. But this is not the case. Shaw and McKay, in a study of juvenile delinquency in Chicago, found that the rate of delinquency among Negroes as among whites varied in relation to the organization or disorganization of the residential area. The rate of Negro delinquency declined from 42.8 per 100 boys, ten to seventeen years, in the First Zone to 1.4 per 100 in the Seventh Zone. The First Zone was a deteriorated area in the center of Chicago; the Seventh Zone was in an area in which there was a marked increase in the proportion of Negroes in professional and business occupations.[30] Similarly, there is relatively little crime among Negroes in rural areas where Negroes are the dominant population group. Mound Bayou, Mississippi, is a case in point. Mound Bayou is an all-Negro community of some 8,000 Negroes where for years no jail existed and no major crime was reported.

There is no scientific evidence available that demonstrates that such a phenomenon as a "racial" morality exists. As we will see in the next chapter, morality and ethical standards are cultural in nature and origin. Peoples throughout the world show a vast range in their evaluations of any particular type of behavior as "good" or "bad," "right" or "wrong." No demonstrable, consistent correlation occurs between racial groups and culture, nor between racial groups and "moral" patterns. If biology were at work, such correlations would exist. Similarly, from one generation to the next a people may demonstrate a considerable shift in ethical judgments and values. This is seen among groups converted to Christianity or communism, or groups assimilating a new culture, such as is true of immigrant Americans. Nor need the reader be reminded of the gulf that often exists between himself and his parents or grandparents in judgments of "appropriate" or "inappropriate" behavior. Clearly a biological interpretation would be erroneous.

INTERRACIAL MIXTURE

Is Racial Interbreeding Harmful?

Closely related to the doctrine of inborn racial superiority and inferiority is the notion that interbreeding, or crossing, between races results in the mental and physical deterioration of the groups involved. According to a popular superstition, the offspring of interracial unions

[30] Clifford R. Shaw and Henry D. McKay, *Juvenile Delinquency and Urban Areas* (Chicago: University of Chicago Press, 1942).

inherit most of the bad and few of the good qualities of the parental stocks. In turn these bad qualities are allegedly passed on to future generations, while the good qualities are further sifted out through continued interracial unions. Human degeneration is supposed to be the net result. A pamphlet of the pro-segregationist southern Citizens Councils asserts, "the intermingling of breeding stock results invariably in the production of 'scrubs' or mongrel types, and the downgrading of the whole herd. The same principle applies with equal force to the process of human development." [31]

For the proponents of this position, the consequences of race mixture are not merely academic, but of vast consequence to the fate of civilization. Hitler, writing on the issue in *Mein Kampf,* declares, "It is outstandingly evident from history that when the Aryan has mixed his blood with that of the inferior peoples, the result of the miscegenation has invariably been the ruin of the civilizing races." Similarly, U.S. Senator Herman E. Talmadge of Georgia writes, "history shows that nations composed of a mongrel race lose their strength and become weak, lazy and indifferent. They become easy preys to outside nations." [32] And Mississippi Circuit Judge Tom P. Brady declares:

> Whenever and wherever the white man has drunk the cup of black hemlock, whenever and wherever his blood has been infused with the blood of the negro, the white man, his intellect and his culture have died. It is as true as two plus two equals four. The proof is that Egypt, India, the Mayan civilization, Babylon, Persia, Spain and all the others, have never and can never rise again. [33]

Scientists reject all these notions regarding the harmful consequences of racial interbreeding. Available evidence suggests that race mixing has been going on from the earliest of times, having been a common occurrence when peoples of differing genetic heritage have come into continuous contact. We have already pointed out the fallacious character of the doctrine concerning "pure" races. Most social scientists agree, Hitler, Senator Talmadge, and Judge Brady not withstanding, that it was precisely the fact that divergent peoples met—in the process often biologically and culturally fusing—which contributed the impetus for the emergence of the Egyptian, Mesopotamian, Greek, Mayan, and Inca civilizations. Apparently it was not the mixing of genes per se that produced the result, but ensuing cultural cross-fertilization result-

[31] *A Christian View on Segregation,* pamphlet of the Mississippi Association of Citizens Councils (Greenwood, Miss., n.d.), 5.
[32] H. E. Talmadge, *You and Segregation* (Birmingham: The Vulcan Press, Inc., 1955), 44–45.
[33] Brady, *op. cit.,* 7.

ing from the contact of divergent ways of life. A look at a world map will demonstrate that the advance of civilization was most marked, not on the peripheries of continents, but precisely where continents joined. It was the Indians in Central America and its margins that attained the highest advances in civilization, not those to the far south or north. Likewise, it was near the juncture of three continents, Asia, Europe, and Africa, that the Egyptian, Greek, and Mesopotamian civilizations arose.

From time to time opponents of racial interbreeding have argued that such mixture produces morphological "disharmonies." According to such notions, a hybridized people are a "badly put-together people"— they inherit conflicting traits from the two parental stocks. It has been suggested that crossings between people with a large frame and large viscera and people with a small frame and small viscera may endanger the offspring, e.g., a danger exists of the combination of large viscera in a small frame, resulting in crowding, or of a small viscera in a large frame, contributing to inadequate support. Similarly it has been argued that interbreeding between two groups, one with large teeth in large jaws and the other with small teeth in small jaws, could result in disproportionate teeth and jaws in the offspring.[34]

W. E. Castle was one of the first to challenge this thinking.[35] Castle demonstrated that the theory of morphological disharmony is premised upon the fallacy of a unit-character inheritance of specific organs. Using an experiment with two divergent breeds of rabbits, one of which was four times the average weight of the other, Castle showed that no disharmony could be observed in the offspring. The hybrids were of intermediate weight, and all parts of the skeleton were intermediate and suited to each other. The 1950 UNESCO Statement on Race, issued by a group of eminent social scientists, concurs with the Castle position: "Statements that human hybrids frequently show undesirable traits, both physically and mentally, physical disharmonies and mental degeneracies, are not supported by the facts."

There are a number of traits, however, such as Rh-negative blood types, sickle-cell anemia, and thalassemia, that apparently can be transmitted through race crossings. While some groups possess the traits, others do not. Accordingly, where crossing takes place, the genes for

[34] See: C. B. Davenport, "The Effects of Race Intermingling," *Proceedings of the American Philosophical Society*, 56 (1929), 364–368; and, with M. Streggerda, *Race Crossing in Jamaica* (Washington, D.C.: Carnegie Institute of Washington, 1929).

[35] See: W. E. Castle, "Race Mixture and Physical Disharmonies," *Science*, 71 (1930), 603–606; and "Biological and Social Consequences of Race Crossing," *American Journal of Physical Anthropology*, 9 (1926), 145–156.

these conditions will be distributed among populations who either do not possess them or possess them in low frequencies. In the case of blood types, an Rh-negative mother mating with an Rh-positive male may have a number of babies who, by virtue of the consequent action of antibodies, may die either before or after birth (if untreated). Eight per cent of American Negroes carry the gene, as do about 16 per cent of the whites, while Mongoloids are free of the condition. Sickle-cell anemia is usually a fatal condition in which the red cells of the body take on an irregular curved shape which is likened to a sickle. It is found exclusively in Negroids or individuals with Negroid ancestry. Thalassemia is also a disease affecting the blood, and is found primarily among Mediterranean peoples and their descendants within the United States.

Racial Interbreeding and "Hybrid Vigor"

Some writers have argued that, not only are hybridized people not "inferior," "mongrels," or "scrubs," but they actually constitute a "superior" group by virtue of "hybrid vigor." Within the plant and animal worlds geneticists have been capable of producing hybrids that are superior to the parental stocks in size, fecundity, resistance, or other adaptive qualities. The same is true for humans, or so argues this school of thought. Kluckhohn, a prominent anthropologist, writes:

. . . where mixed bloods have had a fair chance, they seem by universal judgment to be superior in most particulars to either of the parent groups. Even under conditions of discrimination but where malnourishment has not been characteristic, the hybrids have been better specimens physically: taller, longer-lived, more fecund, healthier.[36]

The descendants of the mutineers of the *Bounty* are often cited as cases in point. In 1790, nine English sailors and about twelve Tahitian women and eight Tahitian men landed on Pitcairn Island in the mid-Pacific. The descendants of the English mutineers and the Tahitian women are living to this day on this and Norfolk Island. Shapiro, who studied both groups, concluded that the hybrids of white-Tahitian unions are more vigorous, robust, and healthy than the average Tahitian or Englishman. "This study of race mixture on the whole rather definitely shows that the crossing of two fairly divergent groups leads to a physical vigor and exuberance which equals if not surpasses either parent stock." [37]

[36] Clyde Kluckhohn, *Mirror for Man* (Greenwich, Conn.: Fawcett Publications, Inc., 1960), 101.

[37] H. L. Shapiro, *Descendants of the Mutineers of the Bounty* (Honolulu: Memoirs of the Bernice P. Bishop Museum, 1929), 69.

Whether or not "hybrid vigor" occurs among humans is by no means a settled question among scientists. Most authorities would probably agree that in terms of the present state of our knowledge there is nothing to prove that cross-breeding results in either degeneracy or improvement in the quality of the descendants. Montagu, who seemingly favored the "hybrid vigor" position in an earlier book,[38] later took a more cautious approach to the matter. In his more recent work he writes, "there appears to be very little evidence of *hybrid vigor* as a consequence of admixture between ethnic groups—the gene differences do not seem to be large enough. . . . This is not to say that hybrid vigor does not occur among human beings, but that if it does occur, it is not as evident as it is among plants and lower animals." [39]

Mistaken Pre-Mendelian Notions of Inheritance

An important source of mistaken notions concerning the consequences of racial intermixture are outmoded pre-Mendelian concepts relating to the nature of biological transmission through generations. This misunderstanding has been prevalent among those viewing racial mixture as harmful. The reader will note that, in the quotation from Hitler cited earlier in the chapter, Hitler refers to "blood" as mixing in Aryan and non-Aryan crossings. Likewise, Judge Brady refers to the "blood" of whites being "infused with the blood of the negro." This thinking represents a carry-over from the period before Mendel's work on the transmission of heredity.

Prior to Mendel, it was believed that "blood" was the agency of biological inheritance. Supposedly, parental "bloods" mixed, giving rise to the "blood" of the child, a compromise between those of the parents. In other words, the hereditary "bloods" of the parents mixed and fused in their offspring. In the process of crossing, hereditary substances were thought to mix much in the manner in which grapejuice may be mixed with water. A simple dilution takes place. Similarly, if a Negro is crossed with a white and simple dilution occurs, the result would be a mulatto. A mulatto was accordingly called a "half-blood." This myth of "blood" is reflected in such concepts as "blueblood," "good blood," "pure blood," "full blood," "English blood," "Jewish blood," "the voice of blood," etc.

Today we know that "blood" has nothing to do with hereditary transmission. Thus, if mulattoes are crossed, the result is not necessarily an

[38] Ashley Montagu, *Man's Most Dangerous Myth: The Fallacy of Race* (New York: Columbia University Press, 1945), 100–133.

[39] Ashley Montagu, *Human Heredity* (Cleveland: The World Publishing Co., 1960), 192.

individual half-way between the two parental mulatto types—a result that had been assumed by the old doctrine. The offspring may range from more or less white to more or less black. Furthermore, the blood of the mother and that of the child do not mix, the child having from the beginning its own blood. Accordingly, a mother may be of a different blood group than her child. Similarly, successful blood transfusions between individuals of different races are possible, given congruity of serological types, which presents new proof of the fallacy of the "blood myth." As the experiments of Mendel and later scientists have demonstrated, heredity is transmitted by more or less discrete packages called genes. Some of these genes may be dominant, others recessive. Genes segregate; they do not mix. If Mendelian segregation did not occur, and if the "blood" theory were correct, all the children of similar parents should be identical. Obviously this does not occur; and when it does occur, in cases of identical twins, it is due to factors other than "blood."

The Offspring of Interracial Unions

As Dunn and Dobzhansky indicate, the number of genes distinguishing the races involved in the cross is important. The number determines how often individuals resembling the parent races will appear in the second and later generations. Assuming for the moment that Negroes and whites differ in only two genes for skin color (the number of such genes involved is not precisely known), in the offspring of mulatto marriages (the grandchildren of the Negro and white involved in the interracial union) only 1 child in 16 will have a black skin, and 1 in 16 will have a white skin. If three genes are involved which show no dominance, the chance of a white-skinned child would drop to 1 in 64; if four, to 1 in 256. The reader should not jump to the conclusion that a white-skinned child of mulatto parents could "pass" as a white. He would probably have some other traits that would resemble the Negroid group, e.g., perhaps thick lips, woolly hair, etc. Thus, if only a dozen genes constituted the total difference in all characteristics between Negroes and whites (an extremely conservative figure), the chance of individuals indistinguishable from whites appearing among the offspring of first-generation mulattoes would be 1 in 16,777,216 children.[40]

In this connection, still another aspect of Negro-white mixture should be considered. A notion commonly found within the United States is that a white marrying another individual who is white in appearance, but who really is part Negro, can give birth to a coal-black child. This

[40] L. C. Dunn and Theodore Dobzhansky, *Heredity, Race and Society* (New York: The New American Library of World Literature, Inc., 1959), 59–60.

is entirely false. Genetically such parents *cannot* have a child darker than the darker of the parents. Only if *both* parents have Negroid ancestry can a child be darker than his parents. Thus in the children of mulatto parents, the children usually differ in color from each other, some darker or lighter than their parents.

If *completely* random mating with no regard to racial differences were to take place within the United States, in time the darker skin shades of Negroes would be virtually eliminated, but there would be little noticeable effect on the skin color of Caucasians. In brief, the Negro one-tenth of the nation would be "inundated by a white sea" in respect to skin color. One geneticist asserts:

> When complete fusion has occurred, there will probably be no more than a few thousand black people in each generation in the entire country, and these are likely to have straight hair, narrow noses and thin lips. I suppose that if some person now living could return at that distant time, he would ask in wonder: "What became of the Negro?" [41]

HOW ARE RACES FORMED?

Most of us readily recognize not alone that whites, Negroids, and Mongoloids differ in physical appearance, but that this racial division can be further subdivided. Thus we recognize within the white race numerous groups including Nordics and Alpines; within the Negroid race Pygmies and others; and within the Mongoloid race American Indians and "Classic" Mongoloids—all of whom differ in appearance. Close anatomical study demonstrates that these differences are "skin deep." Apparently no fundamental constitutional differences are involved. They merely comprise superficial characteristics. Thus the "peppercorn hair" (narrow and intertwining clusters of loops of hair appearing as a springlike coil) of the African Bushmen differs markedly from the straight hair of whites. Yet the resemblance between the two is greater than between the straight-haired ape and the straight-haired white man.[42] It is on the basis of such differences in appearance as hair and skin color that men divide their fellows into "races." The question then posed is this, "How did the various races get the way they are?"—in short, "How are races formed?"

The statement on race issued under UNESCO auspices answers the question in these terms:

> Scientists have reached general agreement in recognizing that mankind is one: that all men belong to the same species, *Homo sapiens*. It is further

[41] Curt Stern, "The Biology of the Negro," *Scientific American*, 191 (1954), 85.
[42] Montagu, *Statement on Race*, 58.

generally agreed among scientists that all men are probably derived from
the same common stock; and that such differences as exist between different
groups of mankind are due to the operation of evolutionary factors of differentiation such as isolation, the drift and random fixation of the material
particles which control heredity (the genes), changes in the structure of
these particles, hybridization, and natural selection. In these ways groups
have arisen of varying stability and degree of differentiation which have
been classified in different ways for different purposes.

Mutations

If men are of a common stock, we must look at the mechanism by
which they become differentiated. In short, how do new genes appear? The process is referred to as *mutation*. Mutation involves
physical change in the chemical structure or position of the gene in
relation to other genes. The exact cause of mutation is not known.
It is thought, however, that natural radiation such as cosmic rays may
play a large part in the process. Thus various hair forms seemingly
have been the product of mutation. It is known, for example, that
among swine, mice, rats, and rabbits curly hair has appeared spontaneously through mutation. Similarly, although kinky or woolly hair
is a normal characteristic of Negroids, such hair has occurred as a mutation among whites of exclusively white ancestry. On record are three
Norwegian families in which such a mutation appeared.

Mutations constitute the raw materials of evolutionary change and
racial differentiation. Some authorities assert that at least one mutation occurs in every human sometime between conception and death.
Most mutations, perhaps as many as 99 per cent, are harmful. Hemo-
philia, or "bleeder's disease," characterized by a defect in the clotting
power of blood, is a case in point. Estimates suggest that 1 in every
100,000 individuals in the English-speaking world today has the hemo-
philia gene, which came into being in each case quite spontaneously.
England's Queen Victoria apparently arose from such a cell; at any
rate, she transmitted the gene through her daughters and granddaugh-
ters to the royalty of Russia and Spain.[43]

Natural Selection

Occasionally a mutation appears that has a selective survival value.
Among rabbits, for example, in a territory where the ground is covered
with snow half the year, mutations in favor of a seasonal shift of coat
color to white would be of adaptive value in lessening their chance of
being killed by natural enemies. They would tend to possess an advantage over brown rabbits whose coats remained unchanged. Through

43 Dunn and Dobzhansky, *op. cit.*, 78.

the action of environment, the mutant rabbits would tend to be preserved so that they would tend to leave more offspring behind than the unchanging brown rabbits. And, through time, as would be expected, the mutant rabbits would flourish in comparison with the brown rabbits. This phenomenon is the Darwinian process of *natural selection.*

Coon, Garn, and Birdsell have suggested that natural selection probably operated in producing some of the racial differences among men. Body form is a case in point. Desert people, including the Tuareg of the Sahara and the Somalis of the Horn of Africa, are tall, lean, skinny people, with long arms and legs, shallow bodies, and narrow hands and feet. According to Coon, Garn, and Birdsell such a build is adaptive to dry desert heat. The skin surface area among such people is great in proportion to their volume and weight. The crucial factor seems to be that such a build presents the maximum skin surface area (in proportion to mass and weight) to the external environment, thus permitting a maximum of cooling surface for evaporation. Since roughly 50 per cent of the body's blood is inside of the legs at any one time, a long, pipelike leg is an excellent radiator. It exposes much more cooling surface than a short, barrel-like one.[44]

On the other hand, among people in the Arctic Circle, the opposite condition tends to prevail. In contrast to the inhabitants of desert areas, Arctic people present the least possible skin surface area to the environment in proportion to volume and weight. The Eskimo and Chukchi peoples are built to radiate as little heat as possible. Their bodies are thickset and chunky, their chests thick and wide, their legs short and thick, their fingers and toes short, and their wrists and ankles small and fat-covered. Likewise, Arctic-dwelling peoples often are at the door of starvation. Selection would favor those who could store and utilize fat, as "obesity" would have survival value where food is scarce.[45]

Coon, Garn, and Birdsell view the Mongoloid face as a piece of thermal "engineering." They argue that the presence of the world's most Mongoloid people in the coldest inhabited parts of the world, in Siberia and the Yukon, suggests that Mongoloids are adapted to cold. A man with thin, bony features, especially a narrow, prominent nose, would be in danger of freezing his face. On the other hand, a man with a flat face, padded with fat, and with a sparse beard would be well

[44] Carleton S. Coon, Stanley M. Garn, and Joseph B. Birdsell, *Races: A Study of the Problems of Race Formation in Man* (Springfield, Ill.: Charles C Thomas, 1950), 36–40.
[45] *Ibid.,* 41–45.

adapted. This is the Mongoloid face in its extreme form. Likewise, epicanthic folds (giving the appearance of slanting eyes) protect the eyeball with fatty layers of padding, bringing the lids close to one another. Whiskers are also a disadvantage, as moisture from the individual's breath freezes on the hair, and soon the face underneath freezes too.[46]

Such theories, however, are quite speculative. We lack experimental evidence for testing their validity. Indeed, the critics have dealt rather harshly with Coon, Garn, and Birdsell. Washburn, for instance, observes that large numbers of Mongoloids currently live in the hot, moist tropics, and many of them have lived for thousands of years under conditions that have been anything but cold. Moreover, Washburn fails to find the types of correlations that would support the Coon, Garn, and Birdsell position:

> If one follows the form of the nose, in Europe, as one moves north, narrow noses are correlated with cold climate; in Eastern Asia low noses are correlated with cold climate. In neither case is there the slightest evidence that the difference in the form of the nose has anything whatsoever to do with warming the air that comes into the face.[47]

Washburn insists that the Mongoloid face has nothing to do with adaptation to the cold. He argues that it constitutes a complex structural pattern related to the teeth, and hence is primarily the result of large masseter (chewing) muscles and the bones from which these muscles arise. Superficially a very similar pattern may be seen among the African Bushmen whose facial form can hardly be attributed to thermal engineering. Caution, then, is called for in attempting to ascertain the role played by natural selection in race formation.

Isolation

Mutations having adaptive value would have tended to become established among early man, as populations were characteristically small. The land mass of Asia, Africa, and Europe is considerable, and early man was frequently isolated from other groups of humans over considerable periods of history. Accordingly, breeding took place largely or entirely within isolated groups. Such natural factors as mountain ranges, rivers, forests, deserts, seas, and distance served to reinforce isolation. Thus, in time, no matter how much alike all peoples had initially been, groups isolated from one another would soon become different by virtue of the differing mutations among them. Isolation,

[46] *Ibid.*, 65–75.
[47] Washburn, *op. cit.*, 51.

then, is another factor contributing to racial differentiation. Four other processes played their role in racial differentiation as well: genetic drift, hybridization, sexual selection, and social selection.

Genetic Drift

Genetic drift involves the emergence of mutations which have no particular adaptive value in terms of survival but which spread throughout a particular population by virtue of its isolation. This chance assortment of genes over generations may lead to the loss or fixation of a particular trait. The blood groups A, AB, B, and O apparently represent neutral mutations, the product of genetic drift.

Hybridization

The role of hybridization has been seen in the earlier discussion of racial crossing. Hybridization involves crossings between individuals and populations differing in genetic characteristics. Such intercrossings increase the range of the recombinations of the genes. Allowing for the action of selection, isolation, genetic drift, etc., one can see that an entirely new physical type can be formed. New races are emerging in Latin America (alloys of Indian, Mediterranean white, and Negro), in Hawaii (Polynesians, whites, and Mongoloids), in parts of the United States (Negroes and whites), and elsewhere, the product of hybridization.

Sexual Selection

Sexual selection refers to the selection by the best equipped males of the most preferred females. Those males who are best endowed tend to crowd out the less well-endowed males in reproduction. "Best endowed" may involve in one population the possession of the greatest muscular power, in another the greatest social prestige, in yet another the "smoothest line." The traits selected by the best-endowed males are likely to be selective so that those women defined as least desirable would have the least number of children. Eventually a modification in the entire population would occur. In America the preference of darker Negro males for lighter Negro females tends to lighten in the long run Negro skin color.

Social Selection

Social selection involves the regulation of breeding by artificially instituted distinctions and barriers between socially differentiated individuals or groups. Marriage may be strictly regulated on the basis of class, caste, or other socially instituted devices. The effect is much the same as in sexual selection. In summary, the seven factors contributing to racial differentiation have been mutation, natural selection, isolation, genetic drift, hybridization, sexual selection, and social selection.[48]

BLOOD TYPES

What Is the Relationship Between Blood Types and Race?

Of all the inheritable characteristics of man, only the blood groups have been studied in all parts of the world with considerable detail. The blood groups are O, A, B, and AB. Prior to 1900 it was known that blood transfusions from one person to another sometimes produced severe shock and even death in the recipient, while in other cases transfusion was successful. At the turn of the twentieth century Karl Landsteiner discovered that, when some types of blood were mixed, the red corpuscles clumped together or "agglutinated." This was the source of trouble in transfusions. It was found that blood from individuals of group O can safely be given to persons of any group, but A blood can not be given safely to O or B persons; B blood caused trouble to O or A persons; and AB blood should not be given to O, A, or B persons. Because of the importance of blood transfusions in saving lives, peoples throughout the world have been "typed."

As can be seen from Table 6, type-O blood is found among every race. This also tends to be the case with A, although the latter apparently is not found among at least two Indian tribes of South America. In terms of the Old World land mass of Europe, Asia, and Africa, O tends to be relatively more prevalent at the continental margins. A and B, on the other hand, tend to be concentrated in the middle of continental areas or in centers of dense population and complex civilization. Proceeding from west to east in northern Europe, from Iceland to Russia, the proportion of individuals having group-O blood steadily falls, while that of A tends to rise. Group-B bloods picks up with a sharp rise in incidence from Finland to Siberia but is absent among the American Indians and the Australian aborigines.

The Value of Blood Types

Of what value are the blood-group types O, A, B, and AB, as well as the M-N blood types and Rh factor, in aiding our understanding of race? Since blood types are genetically *discrete* traits, they are useful in helping scientists unravel the past of man's origins and intermixture.

---

[48] For a consideration of these factors see: Montagu, *Statement on Race*, 23 ff.; and *Man: His First Million Years* (New York: The New American Library of World Literature, Inc., 1958), 73–79.

TABLE 6

Percentage of Individuals of the Four Blood Groups Among
Certain Populations

People	O	A	B	AB	People	O	A	B	AB
Europe					North America				
Icelanders	56	32	10	2	Eskimos	41	54	4	1
Scotch	54	32	12	3	Navahos	75	25	–	–
South English	43	45	8	4	Blackfeet	24	76	–	–
Spanish	42	47	9	2					
Norwegians	40	49	8	3	South America				
Swedes	38	46	9	7	Toba (Argentina)	97	3	–	–
Finns	34	42	17	7					
Sicilians	46	34	17	3	Africa				
Russians (Moscow)	32	34	25	9	Egyptians (Cairo)	27	39	25	9
Asia					Ethiopians	38	33	21	8
					Congo Pygmies	31	30	29	10
Tartars	28	30	29	13	Nigerians	57	19	19	5
Kirghiz	32	27	32	9					
Buriats	32	20	39	8	Australia				
Chinese (Peking)	31	25	34	10	Aborigines	48	52	–	–
Japanese (Tokyo)	30	38	22	10					

SOURCE: L. C. Dunn and Theodosius Dobzhansky, *Heredity, Race and Society,*
rev. ed. (New York: The New American Library of World Literature, Inc., 1952),
120. By permission.

A number of illustrations will serve to clarify the point. A colony of
Hungarian gypsies were found to have blood-group frequencies more
like those of the Hindus of India than those of the Hungarians. A
check of the history of the group, on the basis of their language structure, revealed that the ancestors of this colony of gypsies had migrated
from India some 500 years earlier.

In Wales it has been found that a significant number of individuals
bearing Welsh names make up a population distinctly different in their
blood-group gene frequencies from those bearing English names. They
tend to resemble the Scots and the Irish, which suggests a different
source of ancestry from that of the English. Blood groups proved useful in another case. In a study of thirty Aleutian mummies, Candela
discovered that eight showed the B and AB blood groups. This fact
suggested that the Aleuts were of Asiatic origin rather than, as was
previously expected, of Eskimo-Indian origin. Later studies of skeletal
remains by Hrdlička and of cultural remains by De Laguna confirmed
the finding first made possible by the analysis of blood types.[49]

[49] Ashley Montagu, *An Introduction to Physical Anthropology* (Springfield, Ill.:
Charles C Thomas, 1945), 131.

SUMMARY

Races are "populations differing in the incidence of certain genes, but actually exchanging or potentially able to exchange genes across whatever boundaries (usually geographic) separate them." Human races do not lend themselves easily to cut-and-dried classifications and neat labels. Racial and ethnic groups often display differences in certain physical features, in performance on intelligence, aptitude, and personality tests, in the incidence of certain types of crime and diseases, and in a good many other characteristics as well. Race bigots contend that these group differences reflect differences in genetic capacities. And from this they argue that certain peoples are inherently inferior to still others, usually themselves. Those who find such notions abhorrent have at times gone too far to the other side in their protest: They have insisted that all people are as similar in their abilities and potentialities as identical twins. In all candor we must confess that scientists cannot at this point definitively assert either that there are or that there are not native differences between various racial or ethnic groups in certain capacities or potentialities. None of the essential conditions for making such a scientific statement has as yet been met. However, on the basis of contemporary evidence most authorities are of the opinion that if in the future such differences should be established, they are unlikely to be of major consequence or to have any great importance for social participation.

II

SOURCES OF PREJUDICE AND DISCRIMINATION

3

The Sociocultural Factor

Peoples throughout the world exhibit markedly different patterns of behavior. The reason for this is their *culture*. Culture may be thought of as a "set of ready-made definitions of the situation which each participant only slightly retailors in his own idiomatic way." [1] It is a "set of blueprint for action." [2] Thus culture provides us with guideposts or a kind of map for all of life's activities. It tells us how to think and act. It gives us our moral values indicating what is "good" and "bad," "right" and "wrong." Americans "know" that suicide is "evil," "immoral," and "cowardly." But, for the Japanese, death by suicide can be "good," "moral," and "courageous." Such considerations are not simply matters of behavior, of overt action; they elicit strong emotional feelings—in this case, contrasting feelings. Knowing a person's culture tells us countless things about him.

THE ROLE OF CULTURE

Culture and Intergroup Relations

Culture can also be thought of as providing the guideposts for intergroup relations. The interaction between members of dominant and minority groups is mapped out, patterned, by the culture. The guideposts of the culture are *social norms*. Norms constitute generally accepted, sanctioned prescriptions for, or prohibitions against, various

[1] Clyde Kluckhohn and William H. Kelly, "The Concept of Culture," in Ralph Linton, ed., *The Science of Man in the World Crisis* (New York: Columbia University Press, 1945), 91.
[2] *Ibid.*, 97.

types of behavior. They tell us what we *should, ought,* and *must* do, as well as what we *should not, ought not,* and *must not* do. They are expectations shared by the members of the society-at-large or by the members of particular groups within the society. A large part of our behavior can be understood in terms of the operation of the norms of our society or of groups of which we are a member. This does not mean, however, that we are necessarily conscious of our cultural norms. Ralph Linton, an anthropologist, notes:

> It has been said that the last thing which a dweller in the deep sea would be likely to discover would be water. He would become conscious of its existence only if some accident brought him to the surface and introduced him to air. Man, throughout most of his history, has been only vaguely conscious of the existence of culture and has owed even this consciousness to contrasts between the customs of his own society and those of some other with which he happened to be brought into contact.[3]

Hence, we tend to take our culture for granted; it is more or less second nature to us.

Norms tell the dominant-group member how he is expected to think, act, and feel toward a minority-group member; similarly, they tell the minority-group how he is expected to think, act, and feel toward a dominant-group member. They may spell out, for example, the "proper" racial etiquette. The Negro in many rural areas of the South is "supposed" to go to the back door of the white's home, to knock on the door, to retreat down the steps to the ground level, and, with the appearance of the white, to remove his hat. He is "expected" to speak with deference, attempting to please the white, and to intersperse his speech with frequent expressions of "sir," "yes, boss," and "sho 'nuff." The white is "expected" to call the Negro by his first name, to avoid the use of "Mr." in reference to the Negro, and to tell, not ask, the Negro what to do.

A society may be made up of a number of subcultures, units smaller than the society which possess distinctive normative systems. The units may differ from the society of which they are a part in such ways as language, values, religion, diet, and style of life. The South can be thought of as constituting a subculture within the United States. There is some truth in the southerner's assertion that the region possesses a distinct "southern way of life." The northerner in the South is also well aware of it. As has been shown by the studies of the late Dr. Howard W. Odum, of the University of North Carolina, and the writings of W. J. Cash, the South is characterized by traits and a herit-

[3] Ralph Linton, *The Cultural Background of Personality* (New York: Appleton-Century-Crofts, Inc., 1945), 125.

age that set it apart from the nation at large.[4] These are found in the region's strongly fundamentalist religion, its exaggerated individualism, its famous southern manner, its strong allegiance to the family, its impatience with organization and formal law, and its fierce sense of honor and dignity. But above all, inescapably fashioning and molding the complexion of southern life, has always been the Negro and the accompanying white-supremacist pattern. This is not to suggest that there is an absence of discrimination and prejudice in the North. But in the North there is involved a substitution of private, informal, and indirect techniques for the more public, formal, and direct manifestations within the South.

Some authorities explain prejudice and discrimination on the basis of the operation of social norms. Black and Atkins argue:

"May it not be," we asked ourselves, "that what is often taken for prejudice in the Southerner may be just a 'learned-by-rote' set of definitions and rules regarding his relationship to a certain object (the Negro), much as we all learn by rote a certain set of definitions and rules regarding our relationship to the flag of our country?" By what metaphysical twist of logic is the one to be regarded as being prejudiced while the other is not? [5]

Black and Atkins go on to suggest that not eating with a Negro may be as "natural" to the southerner as is saluting the flag to most Americans.

According to this approach, the southerner may not be using the Negro as a scapegoat for projecting personal frustration. He may not be misinformed or uninformed about the characteristics of the Negro. He may not be suffering from some personality or situational insecurity. He may not be an "authoritarian personality." These are one group of factors advanced to explain prejudice. By the same token, the southerner may not be acting in response to widespread, external conditions of social or economic disorganization. Nor may he have a vested interest—political, economic, or status—in the prevailing intergroup structure.[6]

Rather, the individual can be viewed as functioning within a subculture in which racial prejudice and discrimination are prescribed by the prevailing norms. "The function which anti-Negro reactions serve for most citizens in the South is that of keeping them in harmony with

---

[4] See: Howard W. Odum, *The Way of the South* (New York: The Macmillan Co., 1947); and W. J. Cash, *The Mind of the South* (New York: Doubleday & Co., Inc., 1954).

[5] Percy Black and Ruth Davidson Atkins, "Conformity Versus Prejudice as Exemplified in White-Negro Relations in the South: Some Methodological Considerations," *The Journal of Psychology*, 30 (July, 1950), 111.

[6] *Ibid.*, 111–112.

their society—of gaining for them, social approval or at least averting for them social disapproval." [7] Only when the southerner is viewed by "outside" standards is he a "deviant." But if he were to act in conformity with the "outside" standards, or if he were to internalize these norms, he would be "out of step" within his home society. Within the southern social framework the white supremacist is not a deviant; rather, the deviant is the white who no longer fully practices and follows the southern patterns. The white supremacist would be a deviant, however, if his attitudes or actions, as judged by the community in which he resides, were less favorable to Negroes than those normally accepted. He would be deviating in over-conformity, in excessive conformity, such as is seen in the super-white, super-American behavior of Ku Klux Klansmen.

Social norms may not be limited to a particular subculture. They may pervade the entire culture. But in either case they serve to channel and regulate the patterns of interracial relations. In addition, culture tells us it is "right" and "proper" to think, act, and feel in this manner. A system of rationalizations, ideas, and myths emerges to justify the structure. By conforming to his society's expectations, the individual can find comfort, security, and a sense of well-being. His behavior becomes more or less habitual, a product of the institutionalized system of dominant-minority relations in existence. The behavior may not only become conditioned; it may be assigned strong emotional qualities.

Social Distance

One index of the role of culture in patterning prejudice is the degree of *similarity* that exists in the responses of a society's members to various racial and ethnic groups. If members rank the various groups within a society in a similar fashion, one concludes that this is the product of the operation of social norms. A familiar technique, devised by Emory S. Bogardus, seeks to measure the *social distance* at which members of one group hold another group and its members. Bogardus formulated a list of statements representing varying degrees of social intimacy or distance. He asked his subjects to mark those classifications to which they would willingly admit members of a given group. The scale of statements is

To close kinship by marriage (1 point)
To my club as personal chums (2 points)

7 *Ibid.*, 112.

To my street as neighbors (3 points)
To employment in my occupation (4 points)
To citizenship in my country (5 points)
As visitors only to my country (6 points)
Would exclude from my country (7 points)

In 1926, Bogardus secured the responses of 1,725 Americans to forty racial and ethnic groups. The individuals ware aged from eighteen to thirty-five, of which approximately half were college students and half were college graduates who were employed but were taking one or more post-graduate courses. The study was conducted among respondents from thirty-two well-distributed areas in the United States and included Negroes who constituted 10 per cent of the participants. Bogardus obtained a racial distance quotient (RDQ) for each racial and ethnic group. The racial distance quotient was obtained for each group by adding together the number of points associated with the statement nearest the top of the above list in the various completed questionnaires and then dividing this figure by the total number of completed questionnaires. The lowest possible RDQ would be 1.00 and the highest, 7.00. The results of the 1926 study and identical studies in 1946 (with 1,950 subjects) and 1956 (with 2,053 subjects) are indicated in Table 7. Near the top of the preference-ranking scale are English, native white Americans, and other northern Europeans; then Spaniards, Italians, and generally southern and eastern Europeans; near the bottom, Orientals and Negroes. In looking at the greatest distance score given any group in each of the three years (1926, 1946, and 1956), it is of interest to note that through the years a decline occurred in distance reactions (respectively 3.91, 3.61, and 2.83).[8]

Social scientists within the United States have been checking the social-distance positions of various groups by this means for some forty years. The most striking of their findings is that the pattern of preference is found across the nation, varying little with income, region, education, occupation, or even with ethnic group. With a few minor shifts, the relative positions of the groups remain substantially constant. Thus a similar social-distance ranking has been found from such diverse parts of the nation as Florida, New York, Illinois, Kansas, Nebraska, and Washington.[9] Meltzer, studying attitudes of schoolchildren of

[8] Emory S. Bogardus, *Social Distance* (Yellow Springs, Ohio: Antioch Press, 1959), chapter 6. For a more recent and modified version of the Bogardus Social Distance Scale see: Harry S. Triandis and Leigh Minturn Triandis, "Race, Social Class, Religion, and Nationality as Determinants of Social Distance," *Journal of Abnormal and Social Psychology*, 61 (1960), 110–118.

[9] J. P. Guilford, "Racial Preference of a Thousand American University Students," *Journal of Social Psychology*, 2 (1931), 179–204.

TABLE 7

Racial and Ethnic Distance in the United States in 1926, 1946, and 1956

Group	RDQ 1926	Rank 1926	Group	RDQ 1946	Rank 1946	Group	RDQ 1956	Rank 1956
English	1.06	1	Amer. (nat. white)	1.04	1	Amer. (nat. white)	1.08	1
Amer. (nat. white)	1.10	2	Canadians	1.11	2	Canadians	1.16	2
Canadians	1.13	3	English	1.13	3	English	1.23	3
Scotch	1.13	4	Irish	1.24	4	French	1.47	4
Irish	1.30	5	Scotch	1.26	5	Irish	1.56	5
French	1.32	6	French	1.31	6	Swedes	1.57	6
Germans	1.46	7	Norwegians	1.35	7	Scotch	1.60	7
Swedes	1.54	8	Hollanders	1.37	8	Germans	1.61	8
Hollanders	1.56	9	Swedes	1.40	9	Hollanders	1.63	9
Norwegians	1.59	10	Germans	1.59	10	Norwegians	1.76	10
Spanish	1.72	11	Finns	1.63	11	Finns	1.80	11
Finns	1.83	12	Czechs	1.76	12	Italians	1.89	12
Russians	1.88	13	Russians	1.83	13	Poles	2.07	13
Italians	1.94	14	Poles	1.84	14	Spanish	2.08	14
Poles	2.01	15	Spanish	1.94	15	Greeks	2.09	15
Armenians	2.06	16	Italians	2.28	16	Jews	2.15	16
Czechs	2.08	17	Armenians	2.29	17	Czechs	2.22	17
Indians (Amer.)	2.38	18	Greeks	2.29	18	Armenians	2.33	18
Jews	2.39	19	Jews	2.32	19	Japanese Amer.	2.34	19
Greeks	2.47	20	Indians (Amer.)	2.45	20	Indians (Amer.)	2.35	20
Mexican Amer.	—	21	Chinese	2.50	21	Filipinos	2.46	21
Mexicans	2.69	22	Mexican Amer.	2.52	22	Mexican Amer.	2.51	22
Japanese Amer.	—	23	Filipinos	2.76	23	Turks	2.52	23
Japanese	2.80	24	Mexicans	2.89	24	Russians	2.56	24
Filipinos	3.00	25	Turks	2.89	25	Chinese	2.68	25
Negroes	3.28	26	Japanese Amer.	2.90	26	Japanese	2.70	26
Turks	3.30	27	Koreans	3.05	27	Negroes	2.74	27
Chinese	3.36	28	Indians (East)	3.43	28	Mexicans	2.79	28
Koreans	3.60	29	Negroes	3.60	29	Indians (East)	2.80	29
Indians (East)	3.91	30	Japanese	3.61	30	Koreans	2.83	30

SOURCE: Emory S. Bogardus, *Social Distance* (Yellow Springs, Ohio: Antioch Press, 1959), 33. By permission.

varying socioeconomic classes in St. Louis, found preferences very similar to those of college students.[10] Hartley found that girls in Bennington College, Vermont, had for the most part the same attitudes toward various minority groups as did the Negro students of Howard University, in Washington, D.C. Hartley concluded, "Let us accept, then, the conclusion that there is a standardized pattern of preferences or prejudices prevalent in the United States." [11]

To a considerable extent the social-distance rankings of minority-group members are quite similar to those of dominant-group members. There is, however, one important difference. While the minority-group members tend to retain the standardized pattern, they move their own group up from its lower position to one near the top of the scale. Thus Bogardus found that Negroes placed Negroes at the top of their racial preferences, while Jews similarly put their own group on top.[12] Zeligs and Hendrickson found a high correlation (.87) between the rankings of Jewish and non-Jewish children.[13] One study, however, ran counter to these findings. Prothro and Jensen, in a study of Negro and white college students within the Deep South, found that the attitudes of the Negro students were no more favorable toward whites than the attitudes of white students toward the Negroes.[14] Moreover, Bogardus found that the distance scores for the groups in the top third of the preference rating are about the same for 1926 and 1946, but are higher for the same groups in the 1956 study (see Table 7). Bogardus explains this fact in these terms: ". . . in recent years the darker races seem to be developing an increasing degree of racial awareness and are reacting more than in earlier years against the 'superior' attitudes of some members of the white race." [15]

In summary, the evidence generally points to the fact that the distance at which various ethnic and racial groups are held is relatively consistent within the United States. This consistency suggests that culture, more particularly social norms, is a crucial factor in understanding prejudice and discrimination.

[10] H. Meltzer, "Group Differences in Nationality and Race Preference of Children," *Sociometry*, 2 (1939), 86–105.

[11] Eugene Hartley, *Problems in Prejudice* (New York: King's Crown Press, 1946), 23.

[12] Bogardus, *op. cit.*, 26–29.

[13] R. Zeligs and G. Hendrickson, "Racial Attitudes of 200 Sixth-Grade Children," *Sociology and Social Research*, 18 (September-October, 1933), 26–36.

[14] Terry E. Prothro and John A. Jensen, "Comparison of Some Ethnic and Religious Attitudes of Negro and White College Students in the Deep South," *Social Forces*, 30 (1952), 426–428.

[15] Bogardus, *op. cit.*, 34.

Perception and Culture

We never really "see" the physical world about us. Rather the world we "see" is the product of the interaction between our anatomy, the physical aspects of the universe, and what we have learned from our past experience. Thus our perception is never a photographic image of the physical world. Men differ considerably in the world they "see." Many variables enter into our perception of the world about us, one of which is culture. Hallowell gives an interesting example of the relation of culture to perception. He was discussing with a group of students the differing names that various peoples have given to the constellation Ursa Major (dipper, bear, otter, plow, etc.) and the influence that the assignment of such names has had upon the perception of these stars. When he finished, feeling he had made the point, one student spoke up, asserting, "But it *does* look like a dipper." As Hallowell's remarks indicate, it probably *does* look like a plow to those who use that label rather than a dipper.[16]

Bagby formulated an interesting experiment that demonstrates the part culture plays in our perception of the world about us.[17] Mexicans and Americans constituted the subjects in the study. Bagby set up ten pairs of slides to be viewed through a stereoscope. On one side he mounted pictures of objects familiar to most Mexicans, for example, a matador, a dark-haired girl, and a peon. On the other side he mounted a similar picture of objects familiar to most Americans, for example, a baseball player, a blonde girl, and a farmer. The corresponding photographs resembled one another in contour, texture, and the distribution of light and shadows. Most Americans saw only those objects that were already familiar to them (e.g., the baseball player rather than the matador), and most Mexicans likewise saw only those objects placed within the context of their culture (e.g., the matador rather than the baseball player). To a surprising extent, then, our selection and interpretation of the sensory cues reaching us from our environment rests upon cultural definitions and standards. The world we see is a world heavily colored and impregnated with cultural connotations.

Perception is always selective. For instance, at this moment you are chiefly aware of the page in front of you and, most of all, of this particular sentence. Yet the objects actually reflected in your vision extend

---

[16] A. Irving Hallowell, "Cultural Factors in the Structuralization of Perception," in J. H. Rohrer and M. Sherif, eds., *Social Psychology at the Crossroads* (New York: Harper & Row, 1951), 171–172.

[17] James W. Bagby, "A Cross-Cultural Study of Perceptual Predominance in Binocular Rivalry," *Journal of Abnormal and Social Psychology*, 54 (1957), 331–334.

above, below, and well to the sides of this page. As this sentence calls them to your attention, objects on the sides, top, and bottom may enter awareness. Similarly, you may have been unaware of various noises, smells, and pressures on the skin that have been present while you were reading.

It is not surprising that cultural definitions should play a major part in our perception of racial and ethnic groups. Here, too, selective perception operates. Within the United States, for instance, whites are capable of distinguishing between light brown and dark brown, yet mulattoes are defined as Negroes. Within Brazil, in contrast, mulattoes are not classified with black-skinned peoples; Brazilians make a distinction between the two groups.

Perception is not merely selective; it may also be distorted by cultural definitions. Eugene and Ruth Horowitz demonstrated this fact in an experiment involving southern children. They briefly showed the children a picture of a large apartment building fronted by a well-kept lawn, taken in brilliant sunlight. After the picture was removed, they asked the children: "Who was at the window?," "What was she or he doing?," "Who was cleaning up the grounds?." Actually, no figures of people had been in the picture. Nevertheless, most of the children readily described some individual in answer to each of the questions calling for such a response. When the children responded that they had seen a Negro woman at the window, they almost invariably attributed to her a menial activity, for instance, cleaning the window. The answer to the question "Who was cleaning up the grounds?" was usually "A colored man." [18]

Another interesting study indicating how cultural definitions can affect perceptions was made by Gregory Razran. One hundred college students and fifty non-college men were shown pictures of thirty young women, all strangers to them. They were asked to rank each photograph on a five-point scale that would indicate their general liking for the girl, her beauty, her character, her intelligence, her ambition, and her "entertainingness." Two months later the same group was again shown the identical photographs but with surnames added. For some of the photographs Jewish names were given, such as Finkelstein and Cohen; to others, Irish surnames such as O'Shaughnessy and McGillicuddy; to others, Italian surnames such as Valenti and Scadano; and to others, old American surnames such as Davis and Clark. The labeling of the photographs with the surnames had a definite effect upon the manner in which they were perceived. The addition of Jewish and

[18] Eugene L. Horowitz and Ruth E. Horowitz, "Development of Social Attitudes in Children," *Sociometry*, 1 (1938), 301–338.

Italian names resulted in a substantial drop in general liking and a smaller drop in the judgment of beauty and character. The falling of likability of the "Jewish girls" was twice as great as for "Italians" and five times as great as for "Irish." On the other hand, it also resulted in a general rise in the ratings in ambition and intelligence for the girls with Jewish surnames. Clearly, cultural definitions had a marked effect upon the perception of the photographs and upon the judgment of the characteristics assigned to the girls.[19]

The role of cultural definitions in influencing perception can be seen in other contexts. If we meet an Irishman at a social event and do not know his ethnic membership, we look at him with a more or less open mind. When someone tells us he is an Irishman, our perception is altered. We may expect him to be witty, quick-tempered, and quick to use his fists. If his anger flares, we say, "Aha! How like an Irishman!" But, if a non-Irishman shows the same traits, we say "Things have gone hard with him recently," "He has had one too many drinks," or "His health has been bothering him lately." We remember those Irish who are witty and quick-tempered; we tend to overlook and forget those who are not. Similarly with Jews. If we are in the supermarket and someone nearby is quite loud, we may turn and see it is a Jewish acquaintance. "Aha," we say to ourselves, "a typical Jew." But, if the individual were non-Jewish, we would say, "Boy, has that person got a loud mouth! How irritating!" The attribute is merely associated with the individual as an individual, and no larger ethnic category is involved. Subdued and quiet Jews we tend to overlook. They just do not "register." But let a Jew speak loudly and act aggressively, and we conclude, "You might know, a Jew!" He registers!

John Dollard, in his study of caste and class in a southern town, points to the role of culture in perception. He feels the master defense against "accurate social perception" within the South is tradition: "What is done is *de facto* right and is justified by the consideration that it has not been invented by current culture bearers but comes to them through sacred tradition. . . ."[20] Nor is the world merely seen; it is seen in terms of a "tremendous conviction of rightness." "So compelling is the traditional order that each and every sharer in it acts *as if* he had a mass of impartially seen experience to support his view." Dollard concludes, "Realistic social perception is specifically *not* cultivated; rather every precaution seems taken that it will not occur, and

---

[19] Gregory Razran, "Ethnic Dislike and Stereotypes: A Laboratory Study," *Journal of Abnormal and Social Psychology*, 45 (1950), 7–27.

[20] John Dollard, *Caste and Class in a Southern Town*, 3d edition (New York: Doubleday & Co., Inc., 1957), 368.

that the folkways and mores will persist." [21] For Dollard such a state of affairs in the race issue is distressing. Yet it is interesting to note that Dollard tends to equate his own northern normative system of racial equality with a "realistic social perception." The northerner Dollard and the southerner both "see" a "different" reality, and each views it as "realistic," and with a "tremendous conviction of rightness."

CATEGORIES AND STEREOTYPES

The Role of Categories

Without the aid of categories, i.e., generalizations, we could not think. Each day, we experience a great number of events. Without categories, each event would be a totally new experience, unrelated to old experiences. Each event, each object, would be particular, no generalization or abstraction being possible. Each dog would be viewed as a totally new and unique phenomenon. There would be no category to which to relate the dog. For practical purposes he would be undistinguished from a mountain, as there would be an absence of animate and inanimate categories, not to mention other meaningful and differentiating categories. Each new experience would be completely unique, incapable of being related from an overview to other previous experiences. To do so would be to generalize, to formulate categories. The world about us would be a glob—a seemingly undifferentiated mass, yet with finite, unique distinctions overwhelming us everywhere.

Categories enable us to put "handles" on phenomena, to say meaningfully, "This is a dog"; "This is a tree"; "This is a car." Words are the labels we place on such categories. Words enable us to generalize, to abstract from concrete reality some one feature. On the basis of this one feature we can assemble different concrete realities, but only with respect to this one feature. Thus the very act of classifying necessitates that we overlook all other features.[22] Katz points out that language is a poor substitute for the realities that it seeks to represent. "The real world is more complex, more colorful, more fluid, more multidimensional than the pale words or oversimplified signs used to convey meaning." [23] There is no easy solution to the problem. A language too close to perceptual reality would be useless for generalization. Language enables us to transcend the specificity of the single event.

21 *Ibid.*, 368.

22 Gordon W. Allport, *The Nature of Prejudice* (Boston: Beacon Press, Inc., 1954), 178.

23 D. Katz, "Psychological Barriers to Communication," *Annals American Academy of Political and Social Science,* 250 (1947), 17.

Thus it makes possible analysis and the comparison of experiences. But in the process something is lost. Lee notes this situaion in this illustration:

I knew a man who had lost the use of both eyes. He was called a "blind man." He could also be called an expert typist, a conscientious worker, a good student, a careful listener, a man who wanted a job. But he couldn't get a job in the department store order room where employees sat and typed orders which came over the telephone. The personnel man was impatient to get the interview over. "But you're a blind man," he kept saying, and one could almost feel his silent assumption that somehow the incapacity in one aspect made the man incapable in every other. So blinded by the label was the interviewer that he could not be persuaded to look beyond it.[24]

Some words such as "blind man" are words of considerable power. As Allport indicates, they tend to prevent alternative classification, or even cross-classification. Ethnic labels are frequently of this type, especially when they refer to some highly visible features, e.g., Negro, Oriental, etc. They point merely to one group of features, and often may blind us to all finer discriminations. This is a basic law of language, namely, that every label applied to a person refers properly only to one aspect of his nature. A man may be a *social worker,* an *athlete,* a *Negro,* and a *community leader.* But if these terms were given to someone, the chances are that *Negro* would stand out in his mind as the symbol of primary potency.[25] This brings us to a consideration of *stereotypes.*

The Nature of Stereotypes

Stereotypes are a special class of categories. Membership in the category, in terms of our interest in the religious, racial, or ethnic group, is sufficient to evoke the judgment that a given individual possesses all the attributes commonly assigned to that group. Thus, if one is Jewish, automatically such traits as shrewd, mercenary, industrious, grasping, intelligent, and ambitious tend to be attributed to the individual; if Irish, such traits as pugnacious, quick-tempered, witty, and very religious; and so it goes. An individual is recognized, then in terms of one feature, his membership in a particular religious, ethnic, or racial group. On the basis of this one feature, other attributes are assigned to him. In this manner each individual is "pigeonholed," that is, he is held to be a certain "type" of person, for example, a Negro, Jew, Catholic, or Italian. A stereotype is *a category that singles out an in-*

[24] Irving J. Lee, "How Do You Talk About People?" *Freedom Pamphlet* (New York: Anti-Defamation League of B'nai B'rith, 1950), 15.
[25] Allport, *op. cit.,* 179.

dividual as sharing certain assumed characteristics on the basis of his group membership.

Stereotypes are convenient timesaving devices. The world about us is complex, involving a good many events and people. Bogardus points out that it is "almost impossible for most people in a busy world of activities to weigh every reaction of every person, minute-by-minute, in terms of its individual meanings and merits. . . . Thus persons and also groups are typed in snap-judgment style." [26] Without stereotypes we would find it necessary to interpret each new situation as if we had never met anything of the kind before. They are convenient and have the virtue of efficiency although not always of accuracy.

We have noted that stereotypes represent a categorical response to religious, ethnic, and racial groups. This interpretation is supported by a study conducted by Paul Secord. Under differing conditions, a series of ten photographs of Negroes were shown in order to a number of subjects. The photographs were scaled to range widely from ones of individuals containing markedly Negroid to markedly Caucasian physical traits. The subjects were asked to rate the photographs on the basis of fifteen attributes constituting the Negro stereotype. Secord found no difference in the degree of personality stereotyping (lazy, stupid, dishonest, superstitious, etc.) of the ten Negro photographs. The identification of a photograph as that of a Negro was sufficient to evoke the judgment that the individual possessed all the attributes commonly assigned to Negroes. There was no decrease in stereotyping moving from the most Negroid to the most Caucasian Negroes. The generally accepted definition of a stereotype as a categorical response to a member of a minority group is thus confirmed.[27]

Some Characteristics of Stereotypes

A useful study shedding additional light on stereotyping was conducted by Vinacke among students at the University of Hawaii.[28] As a preliminary step in the experiment, a class of 90 students was asked to characterize eight national-racial groups. The groups were Japanese, Chinese, Haole (name used in Hawaii for Caucasians), Korean,

[26] Emory S. Bogardus, "Stereotypes Versus Sociotypes," *Sociology and Social Research,* 34 (1950), 286.

[27] Paul F. Secord, "Stereotyping and Favorableness in the Perception of Negro Faces," *Journal of Abnormal and Social Psychology,* 59 (1959), 309–314; and Paul F. Second, William Bevan, and Brenda Katz, "The Negro Stereotype and Perceptual Accentuation," *Journal of Abnormal and Social Psychology,* 53 (1956), 78–83.

[28] W. Edgar Vinacke, "Stereotyping Among National-Racial Groups in Hawaii: A Study in Ethnocentrism," *Journal of Social Psychology,* 30 (1949), 265–291.

Filipino, Hawaiian, Negro, and Samoan. Of special interest was the fact that the 90 students were not limited to any one group but included Japanese, Chinese, Caucasians, Koreans, Filipinos, and part Hawaiians. This contributed to an increase in the range of traits cited. From this data a list of 117 terms was prepared. The list was then given to a different set of subjects, some 375 students. The students were told to characterize the eight groups by selecting terms from the list or by adding other terms not on the list. In addition, the students were instructed to go down the list of 117 terms appraising each trait as to whether they considered it "favorable," "neutral," or "unfavorable." Finally each subject was asked to indicate his sex and ancestry.

The general stereotypes that emerged were as follows:

Japanese: Agreement was marked in characterizing Japanese as polite, close-knit family, industrious, clean, and neat in traits evaluated as good; as imitative and quiet in neutral traits; and as traditional and clannish in more unfavorable traits.

Chinese: One of the strongest and most definitive stereotypes was that of the Chinese, who were characterized as good businessmen, industrious, solid and careful (traditional, conservative, cautious), and expert financiers (money-conscious, shrewd, thrifty, stingy). In addition, they were commonly depicted as intelligent, scholarly, cultured, close-knit in family, and clannish. They described themselves as superstitious, but other groups did not ascribe the trait to them.

Haole: A fairly definite and uniform stereotype emerged of luxury-loving, sociable, expressive, confident, outspoken, and progressive. Some subjects regarded the Haoles (Caucasians) as feeling or acting superior (self-important, boastful, snobbish, show-off, conceited) and prejudiced.

Korean: Much less agreement was found on Korean characteristics, although they were frequently described as hot-tempered, stubborn, independent, talkative, and outspoken.

Filipino: The Filipino stereotype was definite and strong. Filipinos were characterized as flashy and hot-tempered, as well as good followers, musical, temperamental, ignorant, emotional (passionate), spendthrifts, sexy, unpredictable, sensitive, lower class, and show-offs. These traits were usually defined as largely unfavorable. The Filipinos agreed with many of the traits but assigned themselves such favorable traits as religious, sociable, friendly, industrious, and ambitious.

Hawaiian: Nearly all the traits assigned the Hawaiians were favorable: musical, easygoing, happy-go-lucky, jovial, sociable, and happy. The unfavorable traits that occasionally appeared were lazy, superstitious, lacking ambition, drink too much, slovenly, and noisy.

Samoan: Generally the Samoan was characterized as a sort of simplified Hawaiian.

Negro: There was much less agreement on the Negro stereotype than had generally been been found in studies on the American mainland. Traits assigned the Negro with some frequency were musical, athletic, flashy, smelly, lazy, sensitive, lower class, ignorant (uneducated), emotional (passionate), religious, and superstitious.

From the Vinacke study a number of useful insights on stereotyping emerge. First, stereotyping is not a one-way street with only the dominant group engaging in the practice. A group not only stereotypes other groups but is itself stereotyped by other groups. Thus the study found that a group may characterize another favorably and be favorably characterized in return, e.g., Haoles and Korean males; characterize a group favorably and be unfavorably characterized, e.g., Haoles and Chinese; or characterize a group unfavorably and be unfavorably characterized, e.g., Chinese females and Korean females. Furthermore, each group tends to stereotype not only other groups but also itself. The two images may not always coincide. Filipinos and Koreans saw themselves in a number of essentials different from those in which they were seen by others. Similarly, the various groups did not always see eye to eye in their evaluation of a trait. Thus "clannish" was characterized as "unfavorable" by Chinese males, Korean females, and Chinese-Hawaiian males but neutrally by others.

A second insight that can be gained from Vinacke's study is that stereotypes may reflect genuine cultural or national patterns. One of oldest and most widely held opinions concerning stereotypes is that they inevitably contain distortion and perpetuate inferior, shoddy, and "wrong" ideas about human groups. However, this and a number of other studies suggest that not all stereotypes reveal misinformation; some may have a "kernel of truth." Vinacke concludes:

1. Stereotyped concepts are bound to be wrong, either in details or in total, when they are applied to any given individual of the group.
2. Stereotypes tend to relate primarily to superficial traits, hence any assumptions that one gains about a group from a stereotype is bound to be somewhat naive.
3. Stereotypes frequently contain many half-truths and distortions.

4. Nevertheless, some stereotypes consist of actual characteristics of the group described. A common error often emerges, however, when people attribute these characteristics to biological rather than social sources. Thus some of the traits ascribed to Filipinos are associated with the fact that they are relatively recent arrivals to the Islands and have scarcely left the plantations in any great numbers. Their education is limited, and accordingly they appear as "ignorant" to other Islanders. The "good businessmen" trait that was attributed to the Chinese appears to be a product of their success in mercantile undertakings on the Islands.

A third insight provided by the Vinacke study is that not all groups are equally stereotyped. The stereotype of the Korean was found to be comparatively weak and slight, whereas those of the Chinese and Japanese were definite and strong. The fact that the Korean stereotype was relatively weak and slight may be a product of the comparatively limited opportunity the subjects had to form such a stereotype. On the other hand, the Negro, with whom the subjects apparently had had little direct contact, received a relatively definite stereotype. Vinacke concludes that stereotypes are at times the product of contact with a group; at other times a product of heresay and cultural tradition.

Do Stereotypes "Cause" Antipathy?

A study by Gerhard Saenger and Samuel Flowerman supplies still another insight on stereotypes.[29] Saenger and Flowerman sought to test the hypothesis that stereotypes are a causative factor in the determination of hostile or negative attitudes toward a group. Their study of 292 college students did not bear out the hypothesis. If the hypothesis were to be substantiated, it would be expected that the students would hold different stereotypes for those groups they generally liked, such as Americans, and groups often disliked, such as Jews. But on the contrary, the study revealed an almost complete overlap in the proportion of stereotypes most frequently ascribed to either group. Table 8 summarizes the results of the study. Both Americans and Jews are described most frequently as aggressive, ambitious, industrious, materialistic, efficient, practical, and intelligent. Furthermore, there was one group to whom the students ascribed an even greater proportion of "typically" Jewish characteristics: businessmen.

The content of the stereotype assigned to Jews, therefore, fails to explain the hostility directed toward them. The hypothesis that Jews

[29] Gerhart Saenger and Samuel Flowerman, "Stereotypes and Prejudicial Attitudes," *Human Relations,* 7 (1954), 217–238.

TABLE 8

Stereotypes Considered Most Typical of Jews, Americans, and Businessmen *

	Jews		Americans		Businessmen	
Stereotype	Per Cent	Rank	Per Cent	Rank	Per Cent	Rank
Ambitious	71	1	67	1	82	1
Industrious	57	2	62	2	68	4
Intelligent	57	3	44	8	67	6
Aggressive	53	4	44	7	65	7
Shrewd	53	5	18	15	59	8
Materialistic	39	6	56	3	67	5
Efficient	37	7	49	5	69	3
Practical	36	8	48	6	77	2
Liberal	36	9	31	9	7	15
Mercenary	31	10	24	12	38	9

* The table is based on 292 cases and arranged in declining rank order of the stereotypes ascribed to Jews. The rank order relates to 26 stereotypes given to the subjects in a checklist.

SOURCE: Gerhart Saenger and Samuel Flowerman, "Stereotypes and Prejudicial Attitudes," *Human Relations*, 7 (1954), 220. By permission.

are disliked because of such alleged traits as ambitiousness, aggressiveness, and materialism rests on the assumption that these traits are viewed as undesirable, regardless of the group to which they are applied. But this was not borne out by the study. Only 28 per cent of the students viewed materialistic behavior as undesirable; 25 per cent disapproved of aggressiveness; 17 per cent, of emotionality; and 3 per cent, of ambitiousness, the trait most frequently ascribed to Jews. If Jews are disliked because of such traits, Americans and businessmen should also be disliked. The study suggests that stereotyping is not *causative* of hostility, although unfavorable stereotyping may be *symptomatic* of it.[30]

Robert K. Merton similarly notes that the very same behavior may undergo a complete change of evaluation in its transition from the in-group to the out-group:

Did Lincoln work far into the night? This testifies that he was industrious, resolute, perseverant, and eager to realize his capacities to the full. Do the out-group Jews or Japanese keep these same hours? This only bears witness to their sweatshop mentality, their ruthless undercutting of American standards, their unfair competitive practices. Is the in-group hero

[30] In this regard also see Muzafer Sherif, "Superordinate Goals in the Reduction of Intergroup Conflict," *American Journal of Sociology*, 68 (1958), 351.

frugal, thrifty, and sparing? Then the out-group villain is stingy, miserly and penny-pinching. All honor is due the in-group Abe for his having been smart, shrewd, and intelligent and, by the same token, all contempt is owing the out-group Abes for their being sharp, cunning, crafty, and too clever by far. Did the indomitable Lincoln refuse to remain content with a life of work with the hands? Did he prefer to make use of his brain? Then, all praise for his plucky climb up the shaky ladder of opportunity. But, of course, the eschewing of manual work for brain work among the merchants and lawyers of the out-group deserves nothing but censure for a parasitic way of life. Was Abe Lincoln eager to learn the accumulated wisdom of the ages by unending study? The trouble with the Jew is that he's a greasy grind, with his head always in a book, while decent people are going to a show or a ball game. Was the resolute Lincoln unwilling to limit his stand-ards to those of his provincial community? That is what we should expect of a man of vision. And if the out-groupers criticize the vulnerable areas in our society, then send 'em back where they came from. Did Lincoln, rising high above his origins, never forget the rights of the common man and applaud the right of workers to strike? This testifies only that, this greatest of Americans, was deathlessly devoted to the cause of freedom. But, as you examine the statistics on strikes, remember that these un-American practices are the result of out-groupers pursuing their evil agitation among otherwise contented workers.[31]

Changes in Stereotypes

It is occasionally suggested that stereotypes are rigid, firm, and un-changing. Evidence, however, indicates that, while some stereotypes are relatively stable, others do change through time. An interesting study focusing upon the question of stereotype rigidity was undertaken by G. M. Gilbert.[32] After a lapse of about twenty years, Gilbert did a repeat study at Princeton of a pioneer investigation of stereotypes by Katz and Braly.[33] In 1932 Katz and Braly had asked Princeton under-graduates to select out of a list of eighty-four attributes five that they thought were most characteristic of each of the following: Ameri-cans, English, Germans, Jews, Negroes, Japanese, Italians, Chinese, Irish, and Turks. Gilbert's subjects were born about the time that the initial study was conducted.

Evidence for the *persistence* of ethnic and racial stereotypes is con-tained in the fact that the characteristics checked most frequently by the post-World War II students were, for the most part, the ones most

[31] Robert K. Merton, *Social Theory and Social Structure, revised edition* (New York: The Free Press of Glencoe, 1957), 428–429. By permission of the pub-lishers.

[32] G. M. Gilbert, "Stereotype Persistence and Change Among College Students," *Journal of Abnormal and Social Psychology*, 46 (1951), 245–254.

[33] D. Katz and K. W. Braly, "Racial Stereotypes of 100 College Students," *Journal of Abnormal and Social Psychology*, 28 (1933), 280–290.

frequently checked in 1932. But perhaps of greatest interest in the later study was a phenomenon Gilbert referred to as the "fading effect." The stereotypes for the ten groups were considerably weaker in the post-World War II period than in 1932. In no case were any traits assigned to a group by as high a proportion of the students as 60 to 80 per cent, as was the case in 1932. On the contrary, almost all the traits were checked by a significantly smaller percentage of students and many of the attributes were ignored. Thus while the characteristics most frequently checked for Negroes and Jews in the post-World War II period were about the same as those most frequently checked in 1932, they were checked by a far smaller proportion of the students.

Similarly, Americans were much less adulated. The favorable stereotypes of industrious, intelligent, ambitious, and efficient had diminished considerably. The greatest change in frequency was noted in the trait "progressive," reduced from 27 per cent to 5 per cent. The only two traits to show some slight increase were "materialistic" and "pleasure-loving." These latter traits correspond to foreign scholars' concept of the American national culture and may have some foundation in cultural reality. The trait "individualistic," hardly mentioned in 1932, emerged as one of the five most frequently cited attributes. Simultaneously "aggressive" faded out of the picture. Gilbert suggests that Americans now think of themselves as more "individualistic" and less "aggressive" than they did, having been made aware of the regimentation and aggression of foreign dictators. Overall these American college youths were less inclined to make flattering generalizations about themselves than had been their predecessors of a generation before.

Of considerable interest was the reluctance of the post-World War II students to engage in stereotyping at all. Many expressed sentiments indicating they felt it was unreasonable to force them to make generalizations about people. Some were especially concerned with the fact that they were asked to characterize people with whom they had never been in contact. One wrote:

I refuse to be a part of a childish game like this. It seems to me that the Psych. Dept. at Princeton, at least, ought to recognize the intelligence of students who choose courses in this department. As far as I have come into contact with these so-called ethnic groups I can think of no distinguishing characteristics which will apply to any group as a whole.

Gilbert concludes that post-World War II Princeton students were more reluctant than previous generations to make stereotyped generalizations about ethnic and racial groups. He indicates this may be the product of the gradual disappearance of stereotyping in American entertainment and communications media. By the same token there has been an increase in the study of the social sciences among students since 1932, fields in which stereotypes are held up to critical examination. Stereotyping runs counter to the image of the American "thinking man" who is not "supposed" to fall into such stylized modes of thought. If a person labels, there is a tendency to think of him as prejudiced, as thinking irrationally and contrary to an American idealized way of making choices.[34] Apparently the image of the "thinking man" took its toll of students who were prepared to stereotype, or at least to *admit* to stereotyping. Hence, caution is in order. It is quite conceivable that the giving up of stereotyping did not go very deep and that stereotypes survived in confidential conversations and in discriminatory behavior.

REFERENCE GROUPS AND PREJUDICE

Reference Groups and Attitudes

Our American society is organized about an almost infinite variety of functioning social groups. Each individual may be simultaneously a member of a surprisingly large number of such groups. In appraising an individual's attitudes or behavior, it is necessary to know which of the many groups is the actual referent for the individual within the given situation. The group providing the standards and anchorage regulating his behavior within the given context is called the "reference group." He may be a member of the group, relating himself psychologically to it, or he may be a non-member who aspires to membership, achieving the relation through psychological identification.[35] In any event, the individual uses the group as a model for his behavior. In the broadest sense, a reference group can even be an individual. Here we are concerned with the relationship between reference groups and attitudes.

Considerable research has been conducted on the relationship between the attitudes an individual holds and the reference groups of which he is a member. The research has ranged from attitude studies of the American soldier to studies of attitude shifts occurring with changing reference groups among Roman Catholic and Bennington College students. These studies demonstrate the close relationship be-

[34] Forrest La Violette and K. H. Silvert, "A Theory of Stereotypes," *Social Forces,* 29 (1951), 257–262.

[35] Muzafer Sherif and Carolyn W. Sherif, *Groups in Harmony and Tension* (New York: Harper & Row, 1953), 167.

tween an individual's attitudes and his reference group. This general finding has been confirmed in studies dealing with attitudes toward racial and ethnic minorities.

Schlesinger, for instance, devised an experimental situation where college students were exposed to information that they believed to represent the opinions of their fellow students regarding Jews (but information that in fact had been designed by Schlesinger). After exposure to the "peer" information, the students were asked individually to answer a variety of questions regarding their attitudes toward Jews. The answers to these questions were compared with the results of an anti-Semitism attitude test that the students had completed two weeks before the experiment. Schlesinger found that as a result of exposure to "peer" information, the students' expression of agreement or disagreement with favorable or unfavorable assertions about Jews changed in the direction of conformity with perceived peer opinion. Schlesinger concluded that most of the students were highly suggestible, tending to conform to supposed peer opinion, whether this was pro- or anti-Semitic, and almost regardless of their prior levels of prejudice.[36]

Leonard Pearlin conducted still another study investigating the role of reference groups among students at a southern woman's college. The majority of the students experienced at the college a climate of opinion with respect to Negroes that was more favorable than that to which they had been exposed prior to their coming to college. Thus many of the students came into contact with norms and attitudes that were inconsistent or in conflict with those they had previously experienced.[37]

The data from the Pearlin study indicate that the least prejudiced students were those who had experienced a weakening of ties to pre-college membership groups, while the more prejudiced were those who had retained firm affiliations with such groups. Likewise, the least prejudiced students were those who most strongly referred themselves to college groups, while the more prejudiced were those who referred themselves less strongly to campus groups. Thus the shift toward favorable attitudes toward Negroes was in part the product of a double-edged process. On the one hand, there occurred a weakening of ties to pre-college groups. This weakening of ties was accompanied by a decrease in the effectiveness of the pre-college groups in regulating

[36] Lawrence E. Schlesinger, "The Influence of Exposure to Peer Group Opinions on the Expressions of Attitudes toward a Minority Group" (unpublished doctoral dissertation, Boston University, Boston, 1955).

[37] Leonard I. Pearlin, "Shifting Group Attachments and Attitudes Toward Negroes," *Social Forces,* 33 (1954), 47–50.

the individual's attitudes in an unfavorable direction toward Negroes. On the other hand, it was not sufficient that one simply "drift away" from previously established social relationships. Of equal importance in the modification of attitudes was the establishment of strong identification with those groups possessing attitudes favorable toward Negroes. By virtue of identifying with new reference groups, one shifts his attitudes in accordance with those harbored by the new groups.

The process of acquiring more favorable attitudes toward Negroes, then, involves both *disattachment* and *attachment:* disattachment from previous reference groups unfavorable to Negroes and attachment to new reference groups favorable to Negroes. Attitude changes cannot be reckoned solely in terms of exposure to new attitudes. Not all the students underwent a modification of their attitudes toward Negroes although they had been exposed to the new ideas. Whether or not an individual undergoes a modification of his attitudes depends to a considerable extent upon the nature of his relationship to groups holding the opposing sentiments. Generally, where a shift in attitudes occurs, there will be found a detachment from those groups from which one initially derived and found support for one's attitudes. Correspondingly, the shift in attitude will be in the direction of the sentiments of those groups with which one develops the firmest attachments and identifications.

In summary, stereotypes and attitudes are group-anchored. Individuals view themselves as being members in good standing within certain groups or as wishing to become members in good standing. Within these groups various favorable and unfavorable attitudes toward minorities are found. The individual tends to accept the prevalent attitudes as part of his acceptance of the group and identifies himself with these attitudes so as to be accepted by the group. The group's views tend to become his views.

Reference Groups and Overt Behavior

Attitudes and overt behavior are not to be equated. Attitudes involve a *predisposition* to act, think, perceive, or feel; they constitute merely a predilection and not the actual response or series of responses that an individual makes. This is, of course, the distinction between prejudice and discrimination, a distinction that is important in our consideration of the role of reference groups. We have already noted the close relationship between reference groups and attitudes. We have also noted that an individual is a "member" of multiple groups. These multiple groups may make conflicting demands upon an individual in terms of the behavior expected of him. Accordingly, an individual's behavior may appear to be inconsistent. These inconsistencies in re-action frequently can be understood as the product of membership in diverse reference groups. When operating within the framework of one reference group he may behave one way; he may behave in quite a contradictory manner when operating within the framework of an-other reference group.

This analysis can be applied to the contradictory behavior of white union members during the Detroit race riots in 1943. These workers were members of unions with staunch anti-segregation policies. Ne-groes were members of the unions. The norms set by the unions were those fostering non-prejudiced behavior. Had these union men been *nothing but* good union members, they would not have engaged in the race riots. But they were also members of other reference groups in-cluding neighborhood and ethnic groups that directly and indirectly reminded the union men of "race." When they interacted within the context of these latter groups, their feelings were aroused as staunch members of their "racial" group. They followed the dictates of being "regular guys" in this situation no matter how contradictory such dic-tates were to the union role.

The inconsistency in the union members' reactions can be explained in part on the basis of the operation of differing reference groups within differing contexts. Thus as good union members these men partici-pated in campaigns for equal job rights for Negroes. But they were many things at the same time. They had conflicting loyalties. When acting as participants in a race riot they were acting in conformity with their loyalties as members of a particular neighborhood and "ra-cial" group. Still, on the job they could act on the basis of union loyalties in a non-discriminatory fashion toward Negroes.[38]

Considerable research has shown that new reference groups may serve to bring about conformity to new norms despite contrary and well-established practices and attitudes. Southern white migrants to Chicago reveal considerable antipathy to Negroes. They express strong attitudes and feelings of preference for southern race patterns, and they deplore the fact that Negroes are "taking over Chicago." But in most of their behavior they make a peaceful, if reluctant, accommodation to the Chicago patterns. This is not to imply that there is an absence of dis-crimination in Chicago, but the pattern of interracial interaction is of a type different from that customarily found in the South. Although the South continued to be, for the most part, the reference group for their attitudes, Chicago functioned as the reference group for their be-

[38] Muzafer Sherif, "The Problem of Inconsistency in Intergroup Relations," *Journal of Social Issues,* 5 (1949), 32–37.

havior. Similarly, as patrons of a "hillbilly" tavern these white migrants would be more likely to beat up a Negro than to permit him to be served. But within the context of a different reference group, the non-segregated restaurant next door, of which they were regular patrons, they ate lunch on a non-segregated basis.[39] And many of them not only worked in plants with Negroes, but shared the same rest rooms and dressing rooms.[40] Conformity to the interracial normative order in Chicago was realized despite contrary and well-established attitudes.

Similarly, in Panama there are places where one side of a street falls in the American Canal Zone, and the other side of the street falls in Panamanian territory. Biesanz and Smith found that Negro Panamanians tend to conform to discriminatory practices when they go to the Zone side of the street; white Americans tend to adjust to non-discriminatory practices when they go to the Panamanian side.[41]

Hence, a good deal of accumulating research points to the fact that an individual's attitudes and feelings toward various racial and ethnic groups are not simple and straight-forward, but rather diverse, complex, and often *contradictory*.[42] It appears that the *situation* in which the individual finds himself does much to determine which of his *heterogeneous* attitudes and feelings about a minority will be brought into open play. Individuals, then, come into situations of contact with minority groups prepared to respond to them in a number of different ways, some favorable, others unfavorable. *Which responses an individual in fact brings forth depends to a considerable extent upon which of his many reference groups is functioning within the situation to provide him with behavioral standards.*

Some sociologists, such as Lohman and Reitzes, go so far as to suggest that "individual behavior is, for all practical purposes, made a fiction." [43] They believe that the individual's personal attitude toward minorities is of little consequence in explaining his actual behavior. "The reality is the social fact: the key to the situation and the indi-

[39] Lewis M. Killian, "The Adjustment of Southern White Migrants to Northern Urban Norms," *Social Forces*, 33 (October, 1953), 66–69.

[40] Lewis M. Killian, "The Effects of Southern White Workers on Race Relations in Northern Plants," *American Sociological Review*, 17 (1952), 327–331.

[41] John Biesanz and Luke M. Smith, "Race Relations in Panama and the Canal Zone," *American Journal of Sociology*, 57 (1951), 7–14.

[42] In this regard see: Melvin M. Tumin, *An Inventory and Appraisal of Research on American Anti-Semitism* (New York: Freedom Books, 1961), Chapter 3; Richard Christie, "Authoritarianism Re-Examined," in Richard Christie and Marie Jahoda, eds., *Studies in the Scope and Method of the Authoritarian Personality* (New York: The Free Press of Glencoe, Inc., 1954), 152; and Robin M. Williams, Jr., *Strangers Next Door* (Englewood Cliffs, N.J.: Prentice-Hall, Inc., 1964), 66–68.

[43] Joseph D. Lohman and Dietrich C. Reitzes, "Note on Race Relations in a Mass Society," *American Journal of Sociology*, 58 (1952), 242.

vidual's action is the collectivity, and in our time the collectivity is increasingly of the nature of a deliberately organized interest group." [44] Most authorities would probably not concur in such an extreme statement of group determinism. Nevertheless, the role of reference groups in patterning behavior toward minorities is undoubtedly considerable and accepted by most authorities.

Conformity to the norms of the group is the product of both external and internal forces. The group itself exerts pressure for conformity to its norms by positive and negative means. Conformity is rewarded, encouraged, and approved. Non-conformity is responded to by corrective and coercive means including ridicule, scorn, warnings, ostracism, rejection, and even physical punishment. Conformity may also be the product of internal forces operating within the individual. In accepting the group definition of the situation, the individual develops self conceptions that in effect regulate conduct in accordance with the norms of the group. The individual may not see conformity as an act of coercion coming from the outside. Rather, through conformity the individual achieves pride, self-identity, a sense of security —products of belonging to a group. It is *his* group, *his* norm. He conforms because he has internalized his roles which are in accordance with the norms of the group.[45]

ACQUIRING PREJUDICE

Racial Awareness

A popular legend has it that a white baby will cry if it sees a colored face, thus demonstrating instinctive aversion. Actually babies pass through a period in their development when they will cry when they see any strange face including grandma's or even dad's if the latter has been absent long. In fact, in the South, colored nurses are frequently the ones to whom the child gives his first attachment. There is no evidence to suggest that prejudice and prejudiced behavior represent an instinctive response to minority groups. Nevertheless, many southerners believe that an instinctive repugnance for Negroes exists among whites. The gradual increase in prejudice among children tends to discredit this notion. If it were the product of "instinct," we would expect to find prejudice existing at birth or expressing itself suddenly during a specific stage in maturation. This is not the case.

A significant number of studies have been conducted in an effort to determine the ages at which children become aware of race. These

44 *Ibid.*, 242.
45 Sherif and Sherif, *Groups in Harmony and Tension*, 184–190.

studies show that children as young as three and four are capable of making distinctions between the physical characteristics of Negroes and whites. With advancing age, the frequency of such distinctions increases.[46] Morland's study of 454 nursery-school children in Lynchburg, Virginia, is representative of these studies. The measuring instrument consisted of a set of eight pictures about which the children were asked to make racial identifications. The ability to recognize racial differences was scored in terms of "high," "medium," or "low," depending on how many times the pictures of Negroes and whites were identified correctly. Each child had sixteen chances to do this, two

TABLE 9

Ability of 454 Children, by Age, To Identify Pictures
of Negroes and Whites

	3 years old		4 years old		5 years old		6 years old	
Ability	No.	%	No.	%	No.	%	No.	%
High	15	14.7	97	61.0	120	78.4	37	92.5
Medium	21	20.6	25	15.7	21	13.7	2	5.0
Low	66	64.7	37	23.3	12	7.8	1	2.5
Total	102	100.0	159	100.0	153	99.9	40	100.2

Chi Square $= 119.1856$; P less than .001.

SOURCE: J. Kenneth Morland, "Racial Recognition by Nursery School Children in Lynchburg, Virginia," *Social Forces*, 37 (1958), 134. By permission.

for each picture. He was scored "high" if he missed none or one out of the sixteen; "medium" if he missed two or three; and "low" if he missed more than three. Table 9 indicates the results of the study by the age of the children. Among the three-year-olds tested, fewer than two out of ten scored "high," while among the six-year-olds, more than nine out of ten scored "high." A regular progression in recognition ability by age occurs, with the most rapid spurt appearing during the fourth year.

Yet racial awareness is one thing. Prejudice is quite another. Although children may be conscious of racial differences, this does not

[46] R. B. Ammons, "Reactions in a Projective Doll-Play Interview of White Males Two to Six Years of Age to Differences in Skin Color and Facial Features," *The Journal of Genetic Psychology*, 76 (1950), 323–341; Harold W. Stevenson and Edward C. Steward, "A Developmental Study of Racial Awareness in Young Children," *Child Development*, 29 (1958), 399–409; M. E. Goodman, *Race Awareness in Young Children* (Reading, Mass.: Addison-Wesley Publishing Co., Inc., 1952); and J. Kenneth Morland, "Racial Recognition by Nursery School Children in Lynchburg, Virginia," *Social Forces*, 37 (1958), 132–137.

necessarily mean that they are prejudiced—that is, that they possess a system of negative conceptions, feelings, and action-orientations regarding the members of a particular group. We are confronted, then, with this question: At what age do children manifest prejudice? Our evidence is inconclusive and even somewhat contradictory. Horowitz, using three picture tests, sought to determine the racial preferences of white grammar school children in New York City schools and in segregated schools in Georgia and Tennessee. He found an overall preference for whites over Negroes in all grammar school grades in both northern and southern schools.[47]

Radke, Sutherland, and Rosenberg, in a study of lower socioeconomic class children in Pittsburgh, grades 2 through 6, found that on the wish level *both* Negro and white children tended to prefer whites. But, interesting enough, when confronted with situation-bound sociometric and projective contexts, the results were somewhat different. In questions phrasing the context as the classroom, interracial choices were common. On the other hand, in questions phrasing the context as the neighborhood (the larger community), interracial choices were less common. Further, when asked in situation-bound contexts (i.e., with reference to the classroom and neighborhood situations), the Negro children did not show greater preference for whites.[48] Yet this and the Horowitz study do not necessarily demonstrate that prejudice is channeling the children's racial choices. Indeed, in both studies the children were quite aware of what was expected of them in each situation (norms were operative) and they may well have responded accordingly.

Westie, in a study of Indianapolis grade school children, found that children in the early grades, for the most part, are unprejudiced and, in general, incapable of coherent, consistent stereotyping. He concludes:

The vast majority of the 232 grade school children . . . were as incoherent about their out-group preferences and images as children are about almost any other social phenomenon. It is one thing to demonstrate that prejudice and stereotyping *can,* in some cases, develop in young children; it is quite another to say that they are characteristic of children.[49]

Further, Westie is of the opinion that stereotyping develops considerably later in children than prejudice.

[47] Eugene L. Horowitz, "Development of Attitudes toward Negroes," *Archives of Psychology,* 28 (1936).

[48] Marian J. Radke, Jean Sutherland, and Pearl Rosenberg, "Racial Attitudes of Children," *Sociometry,* 13 (1950), 151–171.

[49] Frank R. Westie, "Race and Ethnic Relations," in R. E. L. Faris, ed., *Handbook of Modern Sociology* (Chicago: Rand McNally and Company, 1964), 591.

In conclusion, it appears that children develop racial awareness at an early age. Prejudice, however, seems to be a later development, but at just what age children commonly develop prejudice is not clear. More research is clearly needed on this matter.

The Transmission of Racial Attitudes

Learning that one is a "white" or a "Negro" is part of the process of acquiring one's self-identity. The child learns his racial role in much the manner in which he learns other roles. He acquires the symbols and expectations appropriate to his racial role, and in the process is achieving the answer to the question "Who am I?" Society provides him with the answer; it is defined for him in terms of a variety of situations. In answering the question "Who am I?" the child needs to answer its corollary "And who are all those?" The answers to these questions are already contained in the culture of the society and are transmitted to him through the intermediaries of parents and peers.

Olive Westbrooke Quinn's study of the transmission of racial attitudes among southern whites sheds additional light on the process. She interviewed high-school and college youths in Tennessee, Arkansas, and Mississippi.[50] Direct instruction played a relatively unimportant role in the transmission to them of racial attitudes. Even the most perceptive and self-analytical of the young people interviewed had difficulty producing any memories of the direct teaching of such attitudes. For the most part, verbal instruction had been avoided. There was, however, one exception. Repeatedly these youths told of explicit parental instructions in the use of the word "lady": "I remember when I learned that lesson. I told Mother the wash lady was here. She said to say 'woman,' and I asked why. Mother explained that you never say 'Negro lady.' She said 'lady' was a term of respect applied to few white ladies and to no Negroes at all."[51]

Racial attitudes were largely acquired indirectly. When verbal instructions were given, they were generally preceded by some incident where the child violated the racial norms: "One time when I was leaving to go to kindergarten, I kissed my nurse. Father waited until I was in the car with him, and then he told me not to. I asked why, but Father was very domineering, and he told me I was too young to understand and that I'd just have to do as he said."

While direct verbal instruction was seldom used, indirect verbal instruction was not avoided. Indirect verbal instruction, given by the

[50] Olive Westbrooke Quinn, "The Transmission of Racial Attitudes among White Southerners," *Social Forces*, 33 (1954), 41–47.
[51] *Ibid.*, 42.

simple expedient of letting the child "overhear" adult conversation, constituted a major means of transmitting racial attitudes.   As Quinn suggests, it is probably not accidental, except in a few cases, when parents permit their children to overhear adult conversation.   Ordinarily, parents exercise care that their children will not hear things about which they are considered "too young" to know.   However, when adults freely discuss sexual looseness and immorality among Negroes in the presence of children but maintain a strict silence on the subject of white sexual irregularities, it is difficult to escape the conclusion that they are not averse to their children hearing such talk:

I knew Alma [a Negro] lived with men.   It's funny, I never heard much talk about the morals of white people; it came to me as a decided shock that white people are often sexually immoral, but I have always known—or nearly always—that colored people are not hampered by morals.   I never heard any tales of sexual immorality involving white people until I was considered grown.[52]

The shortcomings and deficiencies of Negro servants are freely paraded before children, and stereotyped images of Negro behavior are related.   The following excerpt from a diary kept by Quinn is revealing on this point:

Tonight I went to Bea's for the evening.   She and her mother were very much elated that at last they had found a Negro woman who had agreed to come to the house and do the laundry.   All of us were sitting on the front porch, Bea, her mother, Sue and I.   Mrs. White was laying plans for the morrow.   "Bea," she said, "remind me to lock up the silver tomorrow.   We don't know a thing about this nigger."   Then she turned to me, "You know, you can't trust any of them.   I always lock up my good silver." [53]

These remarks of Mrs. White were not addressed to her granddaughter, Sue, but they did not escape her.   By listening to the casual conversation of adults, she had again had the lesson driven home that Negroes were untrustworthy.   In the process of growing up, children identify with their parents.   A common expression of this identification is found in imitative behavior; the child "tries on" the behavior of the adult.   In this manner, he assimilates and internalizes the norms of the world about him.   They become a part of his very existence, an integral part of his being.   The child, witnessing white adults' behavior toward Negroes, is likely to carry this pattern over into his own interaction with Negroes.

Another indirect means by which racial attitudes are communicated to children is through instructing them not to make disparaging remarks

52 *Ibid.*, 43.
53 *Ibid.*, 44.

about Negroes; rather, they are told that they must not let the Negro know their genuine feelings. But implicit within such instruction rests the assumption of Negro inferiority, the underlying premise of which appears as an unquestioned fact within this context. The child may be instructed to respect Negro feelings and rights, yet the overtone is unmistakably present that the Negro is helpless, servile, and inferior.[54] Furthermore, such instruction may have an additional impact as reflected in this observation by one youth: "You know, I think from the fact that I was told so often that I must treat colored people with consideration, I got the idea that I could mistreat them if I wanted to." [55] In short, this youth had come to view his parent's admonitions as an invitation to engage in the contrary behavior. When a parent seems excessive in his warnings, the fact may not escape the child. The child interprets the parent's words as in effect saying, "I don't really believe this myself. That is why I keep repeating it. I keep saying it over and over to convince *both* you and myself that I genuinely mean it. But I really have considerable inner doubt. That is why I can't be satisfied with just saying it once or twice. I need to constantly assert it. So don't take me seriously."

A Negro servant, having accepted his role, may also actively train the child to engage in the expected white behavior. Furthermore, the child who is treated with deference by members of a racial or ethnic minority subtly picks up the fact that he "must" be "superior" to members of the minority group. If in acquiring his roles he can evoke deference by imitating the behavior of his parents, the conception is reinforced.

Indeed, the entire social setting in which the white child finds himself is often saturated with evidences of Negro social inferiority. He does not have to be told that Negroes are "inferior." The fact is only too apparent. He is part of the white community and as such he behaves within the context of its patterns:

It is not just that his parents use a different rest room than do the Negroes. *He* uses a different rest room than the Negroes. *He* sits in the white section of the bus. *He* behaves towards them as social inferiors, and naturally comes to accept them as social inferiors. . . . By the time a child is told for the first time that "Negroes are inferior," he is already convinced of it. On the other hand, by the time he is told for the first time that "Negroes are *not* inferior" it is already often too late.[56]

54 *Ibid.*, 44.
55 *Ibid.*, 44.
56 Earl Raab and Seymour Martin Lipset, "The Prejudiced Society," in Earl Raab, ed., *American Race Relations Today* (New York: Doubleday & Company, Inc., 1962), 49–52.

A child takes on his society's "people habits" in much the same fashion he takes on its food habits. Just as all foods are not regarded as equally palatable, all peoples are not regarded as equally acceptable. The child soon learns which foods are "good" and which foods are "not so good"; he learns which people are "good" and which people are "not so good." [57]

In conclusion, there are numerous indirect means by which attitudes toward minorities are communicated to children. Cues are constantly given the children as to appropriate and inappropriate behavior. A general atmosphere may prevail of racial or ethnic antagonism, an atmosphere of which the child is not unaware. From parental actions and inactions—big and small—their gestures, facial expressions, tone of voice, rapidity of speech, muscular movement, speed and rhythm of breathing, and other cues, sentiments are communicated. Parents are usually under the impression that they are not the ones responsible for teaching their children prejudice. Often they are not doing so consciously, but unconsciously cues are being emitted by them. Parents may actually seek to avoid the topic, "We don't discuss race in front of him." But the very failure to openly discuss race suggests to the child that perhaps the parents feel "uncomfortable" on the subject, itself a significant cue.

CONCLUSIONS

The full story of prejudice and discrimination cannot be told in this or any other single chapter. Each chapter, of necessity, is one-sided when taken by itself. This is an inevitable consequence of any analytical treatment in the area of human relations. The problem of racial and ethnic relations is many-sided. In examining one aspect, it is necessary to simultaneously hold in mind many other aspects. In this chapter the ideological, power, economic, prestige, and personality factors have been held in abeyance.

Clearly the sociocultural factor in prejudice and discrimination is of considerable importance. We have seen how, via social norms, it serves to channel and regulate human feelings, thoughts, and actions. Prejudice and discrimination may be responses to a system of shared, interlocking, socially axiomatic expectations and values. They become institutionalized in the manner of other social institutions. Their existence is quite independent of the particular life histories of the individuals within any given society. Prejudice is shared by relatively

[57] Westie, op. cit., 583.

adjusted and maladjusted personalities, and by those with and without any vested interest in the existing intergroup structure. Thus, to the extent to which an individual has been exposed to prejudicial traditions by his reference groups, he is likely to be prejudiced. This factor helps to explain the continuation of prejudice and discrimination when the original causes have disappeared. Since prejudice and discrimination may become embedded within the social norms, they continue to operate when the initial factors in antagonism have been undermined or cease to operate.

But, as was noted, one factor cannot explain the entire matter. It leaves a number of aspects unexplained:

1. In and of themselves, social norms are not capable of explaining the origins or sources of the particular traditions.

2. The factor does not account for individual differences observed either in the intensity of prejudice or in discriminatory actions. It sheds light on merely those elements that are shared by a people, but it does not tell us why members of identical groups may vary in the degree or intensity with which they hold prejudicial attitudes or engage in discriminatory acts. Similarly, not all people are conformists; deviants are found within any society.

3. The factor does not account for the sharp alterations in the pattern of prejudice and discrimination such as those observed in the pre-Nazi, Nazi, and post-Nazi periods in Germany or for the changes in American attitudes toward the Japanese.

4. The social-norm factor does not explain why some groups are singled out as groups against whom prejudice and discrimination may be directed and why others are not. Nor does it explain why some groups, about whom there is no tradition when they enter a country, are singled out while other groups may largely escape prejudice and discrimination.

4

Economic, Power, and Status Factors

Within any social system people act in relation to certain values that can be shared by everyone. These values are not scarce in the sense that one individual's sharing in them reduces or interferes with others' enjoyment. Religious salvation and national prestige are conspicuous illustrations of this. The adherents of a religious faith can all participate in a great many of its values, for example, salvation, without detracting from the participation of others. By the same token, all Americans tend to share in any increase or decrease in national prestige. National prestige as such is "participated in" rather than "divided up." [1]

On the other hand, there are some values within any society that are scarce and divisible, such values as *wealth, power,* and *status.* In each instance, the more there is for the one, the less there is for others. [2] Some theories attempt to explain prejudice and discrimination in terms that stress this fact. Common to such theories are two themes found either singly or in some combination: (1) *groups in competition with one another for wealth, power, and/or status tend to develop prejudice toward one another* and (2) *a racial or ethnic group that commands a disproportionate advantage over another group in access to wealth, power, and/or status evolves and employs prejudice and discrimination*

[1] Robin M. Williams, Jr., *The Reduction of Intergroup Tensions* (New York: Social Science Research Council, 1947), 55.
[2] *Ibid.,* 55.

as instruments for defending its position of privilege and advantage.
Let us briefly consider each of these themes in turn.

Competition for Scarce Values

The literature in race relations abounds with statements that prejudice and discrimination are a product of competition between individuals and groups for scarce values. Several studies indeed lend
support to this hypothesis. Experiments by Sherif, for instance, have
shown that in the absence of institutionalized control, boys' groups
normally develop very hostile, discriminatory relationships after a relatively short period of competition in sports and games.[3] Similarly,
Blake and Manton, on the basis of their experiments dealing with competition, suggest that a loss in competition leads to hostility both toward
impartial judges and toward the winning group. Even though the
members of the competing groups reported that they understood the
competitor's views as well as they understood those of their own group,
they in fact, did not. In all groups, the members knew their own
group's position best and were inclined toward distortion in their comprehension of the other group's position.[4]

Hamblin, using quota samples of white adults in St. Louis, also found
some support for a competition approach.[5] His study found (1) a
correlation of .41 between frustration experienced by whites in *past*
competition with Negroes and the tendency of whites to discriminate
against Negroes and (2) a correlation of .62 between a *fear* of equal
status competition with Negroes (the prospect of *future* competition)
and the tendency of whites to discriminate against Negroes. Further,
Hamblin investigated the relationship between a number of other
variables (including family pressures and friends' pressures) and tendencies to discriminate against Negroes. Multiple regression-correlation
analyses showed that fear of equal status competition independently
explained 17 per cent of the variance, family pressures 32 per cent,
and friends' pressures 16 per cent, the three variables together explaining 65 per cent of the variance.

The Hamblin study demonstrates that one major determinant of the
tendency to discriminate is the actual or feared frustration arising out

[3] Muzafer Sherif, "Experiments in Group Conflict," *Scientific American*, 195
(1956), 54–58. See Chapter 7 of this book for a lengthy review of this study.

[4] Robert R. Blake and Jane S. Manton, "Comprehension of Own and of Out-
group Positions under Intergroup Competition," *Journal of Conflict Resolution*,
5 (1961), 309.

[5] Robert J. Hamblin, "The Dynamics of Racial Discrimination," *Social Problems*,
10 (1962), 103–120.

of competition with minority group members. But the results also show that frustration, actual or anticipated, is not the most important antecedent to the tendency to discriminate. Together family and friends' pressures appear to account for about 50 per cent of the variance, pointing to the critical role played by reference groups in influencing discriminatory tendencies.

Vested Interests

One of the clearest formulations of a vested interest approach is suggested by Herbert Blumer, who views prejudice and discrimination as arising from a sense of "group position." [6] The dominant group, Blumer asserts, comes to view itself as being entitled to certain rights and privileges. These rights and privileges may include the ownership of choice property, the right to certain jobs, occupations, and professions, the claim to certain positions of power, the right to exclusive membership in particular institutions including schools, churches, and recreation facilities, the claim to certain positions of social prestige and to the display of the symbols associated with these positions, and the claim to certain areas of intimacy and privacy.

In Blumer's view, race prejudice arises from a fear that the minority threatens or will threaten the advantaged position of the dominant group:

> The source of race prejudice lies in a felt challenge to this sense of group position. The challenge, one must recognize, may come in many different ways. It may be in the form of an affront to feelings of group superiority; it may be in the form of attempts at familiarity or transgressing the boundary line of group exclusiveness; it may be in the form of encroachment at countless points of proprietary claim; it may be a challenge to power and privilege; it may take the form of economic competition. Race prejudice is a defensive reaction to such challenging of the sense of group position. It consists of the disturbed feelings, usually of marked hostility, that are thereby aroused. As such, race prejudice is a protective device. It functions, however shortsightedly, to preserve the integrity and the position of the dominant group. [7]

Prejudice arises, Blumer asserts, through a collective process. It operates chiefly through the media of mass communication in which spokesmen for a racial or ethnic group—public figures of prominence, leaders of powerful organizations, and intellectual and social elites—

[6] Herbert Blumer, "Race Prejudice as a Sense of Group Position," in Jitsuichi Masuoka and Preston Valien, eds., *Race Relations* (Chapel Hill: The University of North Carolina Press, 1961), 215–227.

[7] *Ibid.*, 222.

publicly characterize another group. Such spokesmen foster feelings of racial superiority, racial distance, and a claim to certain rights and privileges. Other members of the dominant group, although often having different views and feelings, fall into line lest they be subjected to in-group ostracism. In this fashion a sense of group position—with its encompassing matrix of prejudice—becomes a general kind of orientation. It is a theory, then, that views the dominant group as having a vested interest in another group's subordination; the dominant group has a stake in preserving an order characterized by privilege and advantage. Prejudice becomes an instrument for defending this privilege and advantage.

Emphasis upon Particular Values

Thus far in our consideration we have not differentiated between wealth, power, or status factors. It has probably occurred to some readers that a favorable position with regard to either wealth, power, or status tends to be associated with a favorable position with regard to the other two. Although often true, it is not always the case. By way of illustration, the sheriff of many rural counties may possess considerable political power but be ranked low in economic wealth or status. Similarly, a member of one of the aristocratic "old" families of the South may enjoy considerable status but have little in the way of power or wealth. And the "new rich" may have wealth but lack comparable power or status, as in the case of some Texas oil barons. Since some writers tend to stress the role of one variable over the others, let us focus our attention upon each variable in turn.

THE ECONOMIC FACTOR

Economic Competition

We have noted that there appears to be some foundation to the notion that groups in competition for scarce values often develop prejudice toward one another. Some writers argue that economic competition plays a particularly critical role. Donald Young notes that within American history there is a direct correlation between peaks of agitation against minorities and the valleys of economic depression. The major "anti-foreign" movements—the Native American Party in the 1830's, the Know-Nothing Party of the 1850's, the American Protective Association of the late nineteenth century, and the post-World War I Ku Klux Klan—won their largest following in hard times. Various regional movements—against Chinese, Japanese, and Filipinos on the West Coast, Italians in Louisiana, and French Canadians in New England—have similarly coincided with economic difficulties in these areas.[8] At least two forces appear to operate in such settings. First, hard times have been associated with widespread unemployment that has intensified intergroup competition for jobs. Second, the frustrations associated with unemployment may breed hostile and aggressive impulses that are vented upon minority groups.

Race riots and violence have often been associated with intense intergroup competition. The 1919 Chicago race riot centered in two areas: the area about the stockyards, where Negroes had entered the meat packing industry in thousands and were accused of taking white men's jobs while the whites were away in the army; and in the Hyde Park area, where the chief grievance was the financial loss to white owners in Negro residence areas, allegedly through depreciation of property values. In the Atlanta riot of 1906 one of the chief incitements to violence was the circulation of cards showing Negro carpenters and bricklayers building houses, thus menacing the economic security of white craftsmen.[9] And in the 1943 Detroit riot, Negroes were in sharp competition with whites for housing accommodations in the areas surrounding the Negro ghetto of Paradise Valley, while competition for other goods and services, already scarce in the wartime economy, intensified antagonisms.[10] Further, in a comparative study of racial violence in the United States, Grimshaw found that, except during the peak of rioting, the incidence of violence was greatest in contested urban areas where Negros and whites were directly competing for housing and other accommodations.[11]

Cornell University sociologists, in studies in Elmira, New York, and Savannah, Georgia, found that middle and upper class gentiles are more likely to be prejudiced against Jews than their fellows in the less affluent and less educated strata. In contrast, whites in the lower socioeconomic strata are more likely to be prejudiced against Negroes than those in the upper socioeconomic strata. It should be noted, however, that none of the differences in prejudice between the various socioeconomic strata were strikingly large. Still, the Cornell studies lend support to the assumption that prejudice is most likely at the point

[8] Donald Young, *Research Memorandum on Minority Peoples in the Depression* (New York: Social Science Research Council, 1937), 133–141.

[9] Charles S. Johnson, "Race Relations and Social Change," in Edgar T. Thompson, ed., *Race Relations and the Race Problem* (Durham, N.C.: Duke University Press, 1939), 271–303.

[10] Alfred McClung Lee and Norman D. Humphrey, *Race Riot* (New York: Holt, Rinehart, and Winston, Inc., 1943). See Chapter 7 of this text for a discussion of this study.

[11] Allen D. Grimshaw, "Urban Racial Violence in the United States," *American Journal of Sociology*, 64 (1960), 114–115.

of greatest sensed threat from social and economic competition. In this case, Jews are more likely to be in competition with upper strata gentiles while Negroes are most likely to be in competition with lower strata whites.[12]

Negro Subordination and White Gains

Having examined the role of economic competition in fostering prejudice, let us turn to various vested interest approaches. Indeed, some evidence suggests that whites, both North and South, derive occupational and income gains from the prevailing race structure.[13] Glenn, who examined 1950 Census data for 151 Standard Metropolitan Areas, concludes:

> The data presented here leave little doubt that in 1950 whites in American metropolitan areas which had large Negro populations were benefiting occupationally from the presence and low status of Negroes. These data suggest that American whites in general were and still are benefiting from anti-Negro discrimination.
>
> The findings of this study lend credence to the view that discrimination and its supporting prejudice persist mainly because majority [dominant group] people gain from them. One should not go so far as to attribute the perpetuation of discrimination entirely to its functions to the majority, nor should the many known and possible dysfunctions of discrimination to the majority be overlooked. However, one should also avoid viewing discrimination as merely a self-perpetuating carry-over from a past era. . . .[14]

Property Values and Race

A widespread fear prevails among many white home owners that Negro movement into white neighborhoods forces property values down. Since whites may have an appreciable financial investment in their homes, this fear fosters white resistance to neighborhood desegregation and the perpetuation of discriminatory patterns. Laurenti has made a careful study that provides data enabling us to assess the relationship between property values and the movement of non-whites

---

[12] Robin M. Williams, Jr., *Strangers Next Door* (Englewood Cliffs, N.J.: Prentice-Hall, Inc., 1964), 53–54. Also see Irving R. Stuart, "Minorities vs. Minorities; Cognitive, Affective, and Conative Components of Puerto Rican and Negro Acceptance and Rejection," *Journal of Social Psychology*, 59 (1963), 93–99.

[13] For papers dealing with this matter and statistical procedures for measuring white gains, see: Norval D. Glenn, "Occupational Benefits to Whites from the Subordination of Negroes," *American Sociological Review*, 28 (1963), 443–448; "Reply to Cutright on Negro Subordination," *American Sociological Review*, 30 (1965), 416; and Phillips Cutright, "Negro Subordination and White Gains," *American Sociological Review*, 30 (1965), 110–112.

[14] Glenn, "Occupational Benefits to Whites from the Subordination of Negroes," 447.

into white neighborhoods.[15] He gathered data on sale prices for homes sold between 1943 and 1955 in 20 neighborhoods in San Francisco, Oakland, and Philadelphia that had been entered by non-whites. Home sale prices in each neighborhood were compared with a "control" area—a similar neighborhood in the same city except that it had remained all-white.

Laurenti found:

1. In 14 of the 34 comparisons (41 per cent), test prices (prices in the neighborhoods experiencing Negro influx) stayed within 5 per cent, plus or minus, of control prices during the observation period. He considered this to mean that no significant change had occurred in these property values.
2. In 15 comparisons (44 per cent), test prices ended relatively higher than control prices, by margins of more than 5 to 26 per cent.
3. In the remaining 4 comparisons (15 per cent), test prices ended relatively lower than control prices, by margins of 5 to 9 per cent.
4. From the date of the first non-white entry to the end of the observation period, 20 of 34 comparisons showed larger per cent increases each quarter for test prices than control prices.
5. These conclusions apply regardless of the extent of non-white influx.

Laurenti also examines previous studies and shows that they reach quite similar conclusions.[16] There is little factual support for the belief that non-white entry into a neighborhood produces a fall in property values; there is in fact a diversity of price outcomes according to circumstances, but the entry of non-whites into previously all-white neighborhoods is more often associated with price improvement or stability than decline. It should be added, however, that "panic" selling, if it occurs, may indeed lower home sale prices temporarily.

Economic Exploitation and the Rise of Racism

Notions that a particular group, usually one's own, is superior to other groups are not new to mankind. It is not uncommon for men anywhere in the world to believe that they, and they alone, belong to the "best people." As Ruth Benedict points out, "The formula 'I belong

---

[15] Luigi Laurenti, *Property Values and Race* (Berkeley: University of California Press, 1960). For a discussion of white fears see Arnold M. Rose, "Inconsistencies in Attitudes toward Negro Housing," *Social Problems*, 8 (1961), 286–292.

[16] For a recent study, see Erdman Palmore and John Howe, "Residential Integration and Property Values," *Social Problems*, 10 (1962), 52–55.

to the Elect' has a far longer history than has modern racism." [17]
Among even the most primitive peoples this formula is an integral part
of their whole life experience. Prior to mass contact with outside
groups, they were prone to look upon themselves grandiosely as *"the
human beings,"* as "Men." The designation applied exclusively to their
own group. Zuñi, Déné, Kiowa, and the rest were tribal names by
which primitive people knew themselves, and these terms were equated
with "mankind." Outside of their own closed group, human beings in
the true sense did not exist. Other peoples were seen within this
highly provincial outlook:

> They were not people with whom my own tribe had common cause.
> God did not create them of the same clay, or they did not spring out of the
> same water jar, or they did not come up through the same hole in the
> ground. But my own little group was under the special providence of God;
> he gave it the middle place in the "world" and he foretold that if ever it
> was wiped out, the world would perish. To my tribe alone he gave the
> ceremonies which preserve the world.[18]

Racism, on the other hand, focuses upon the differences in physical
features among various groups of mankind and makes this the basis
for the imputation of inferiority or superiority. The tendency to seize
upon physical differences as the badge of inborn mental and temperamental differences is not limited to modern times. As long as five
thousand years ago, we find some evidence of race prejudice in India.
Similarly we discover occasional ideas in early Chinese and Egyptian
thought that are explicitly racist. And Aristotle and other ancient
Greek writers speculated on the sources of both physical and temperamental differences among different peoples. Yet prior to the late
seventeenth and early eighteenth centuries, racist beliefs were of considerably less importance than might be supposed.[19]

Why, then, did an elaborate racist dogma emerge in the eighteenth
century? Some writers emphasize the economic factor in the appearance of racism.[20] The emergence and elaboration of racist ideas are
closely associated in time with the advent and development of Negro

[17] Ruth Benedict, *Race: Science and Politics* (New York: Modern Age Books,
1940), 155.

[18] *Ibid.,* 156.

[19] Thomas F. Gossett, *Race: The History of an Idea in America* (Dallas:
Southern Methodist University Press, 1963), Chapter 1.

[20] See: Gunnar Myrdal, *An American Dilemma* (New York: Harper & Row,
1944), 84–88; Oliver Cromwell Cox, *Caste, Class, and Race* (New York: Doubleday & Co., Inc., 1948), 321–352; and George Eaton Simpson and J. Milton Yinger,
Racial and Cultural Minorities, 3rd ed. (New York: Harper & Row, 1965), 84–89.

slavery. An integral aspect of Negro slavery was the economic gain realized by white slaveowners. Accordingly, it has been concluded by some and implicitly implied by others that the racist dogma was evolved primarily as a means to excuse and sanction the institution of slavery in general and the economic exploitation of slaves in particular.

Initially, Negro slavery in America was explained primarily on religious grounds—the Negro was a heathen and a barbarian, a descendant of Noah's son Ham, cursed by God and doomed to be a servant forever as the price of an ancient sin.[21] With the passing of time and the conversion of Negroes to Christianity, the heathen or infidel buttress no longer constituted a satisfactory defense of slavery. Gradually, then, the biological argument came into prominence. The Negro's physical appearance was increasingly made the foundation for the assignment to him of a fundamental physical, mental, and moral inferiority.

Thus slavery, of which the economic aspect constituted an integral ingredient, was surrounded with a belief or ideological system that sanctioned its existence. Yet Marxists would go even further and conclude that racism was *deliberately* and *rationally* evolved by the slaveowners as a means of justifying an institution in which they had a vested interest. But, while recognizing the role of the economic factor, as in the above account, there is no need to conclude with the Marxists that the race dogma was deliberately created by a class seeking to defend its privileges. In the first place, the emphasis upon biology constituted merely a new twist to the notion that one's own people represent "the Elect." Secondly, as Montagu indicates, whites had no need to search out reasons by which to justify their conduct. The disadvantaged state of the slave—his illiteracy, poverty, and spiritual benightedness—supplied plenty of material for elaboration on the theme of his essential inferiority. The Negro's differing physical appearance provided a convenient peg upon which to hang the argument of deeper inferiority. Obvious differences in *social* status were equated with *physical* differences and, in turn, with *biological* differences.[22] Thirdly, people more or less spontaneously tend to evolve a rationale for their behavior. This is true of any behavior, economic or otherwise. Accordingly, to focus exclusively upon economic institutions in this regard can be exceedingly misleading.

[21] William Sumner Jenkins, *Pro-Slavery Thought in the Old South* (Chapel Hill: The University of North Carolina Press, 1935), 18–19.
[22] Ashley Montagu, *Man's Most Dangerous Myth: The Fallacy of Race*, 2d ed. (New York: Columbia University Press, 1945), 19–20.

Economic Exploitation and the Ante-Bellum Period

In the years following the American Revolutionary War, the slave-holding states experienced a severe economic depression. Rice and indigo brought little profit to the planters, and tobacco production was plagued by the twin evils of soil exhaustion and a glutted market. The price of slaves declined and manumission increased. The opinion was frequently voiced in the nation that slavery was doomed. With the invention of the cotton gin in 1793, a means was found to increase the efficiency of unskilled labor and to infinitely lower the cost of cotton. The cotton crop, which had been 8,000 bales in 1790, increased phenomenally to 650,000 bales in 1820, to 2,500,000 bales in 1850, and to 4,000,000 bales in 1860. The need for Negro labor surged ahead with the increased crop. Slavery received a new lease on life. In 1790 there had been less than 700,000 slaves; by 1830 there were more than 2,000,000. Simultaneously, southern spokesmen and writers intensified their output of literature designed to defend the region's "peculiar institution."

Within these developments the economic factor clearly played an important role. In 1854, George Fitzhugh, writing in his *Sociology for the South,* reflected upon this fact:

Our Southern patriots, at the time of the Revolution, finding negroes expensive and useless, became warm anti-slavery men. We, their wiser sons, having learned to make cotton and sugar, find slavery very useful and profitable, and think it a most excellent institution. We of the South advocate slavery, no doubt, from just as selfish motives as induce the Yankees and English to deprecate it.

He proceeded to rationalize: "We have, however, almost all human and divine authority on our side of the argument. The Bible nowhere condemns, and throughout recognizes slavery." [23]

Yet, to focus exclusively upon the economic factor in developments leading to the Civil War would result in an oversimplified conclusion. The situation was much more complex. By the turn of the nineteenth century, racist notions were already widespread. The slaveholding South was under heavy fire from the Abolitionist movement, a movement which in the first two decades of the nineteenth century was as strong in the South as in the North, if not stronger.[24] An entire social order was at stake—a distinct "southern way of life." Under attack

[23] Quoted by Myrdal, *op. cit.,* 1188.
[24] *Ibid.,* 86.

from another "way of life" and from organized groups elaborating the anti-slavery theory, the white South responded with an intensification and elaboration of its pro-slavery beliefs. To see the struggle primarily or exclusively in economic terms is to cloud the picture. Ideas begot counter-ideas and counter-ideas begot new ideas. In essence two societies, the North and the South, although sharing many cultural elements in common, were locked in a struggle that eventually culminated in war. The South existed for nearly five years as a separate and distinct nation: a reflection of the two sections' different social and cultural systems. More was involved than a mere economic structure: An elaborate and far-reaching cultural and social system was at stake.

Racism and "The Class Struggle"

During and immediately after World War II the notion gained prominence that prejudice and discrimination were primarily products of exploitation in Western capitalist society. Handlin notes that the prestige of the Marxist view of the class struggle and the delusion that all race conflicts had been eliminated in the Soviet Union seemed to confirm the analysis that exploitation was at the root of prejudice.[25] Benedict, writing during this period, suggested that racism served a twofold function: It justified persecution in the interests of some class or nation, and it enabled exploiting classes to rechannel the anger of the masses away from themselves and onto a scapegoat.[26] Perhaps one of the clearest formulations of this position was set forth by Oliver Cromwell Cox.[27] Cox's bias within the traditional Marxist framework can be seen in such statements as these: "From the standpoint of degrees of development of democracy in the three great nations of the world—the United States, England, and Russia—the United States is probably most backward and Russia farthest advanced"[28] and "Indeed, we should expect that under some other form of economic organization, socialism, the relationship between whites and peoples of color would be significantly modified."[29]

Cox takes the position that "racial exploitation and race prejudice developed among Europeans with the rise of capitalism and nationalism, and . . . because of the worldwide ramifications of capitalism, all racial antagonisms can be traced to the policies and attitudes of the

[25] Oscar Handlin, *Race and Nationality in American Life* (New York: Doubleday & Co., Inc., 1957), 40.

[26] Benedict, *op. cit.*, 232 and 238. In this regard also see Isacque Graeber, "An Examination of Theories of Race Prejudice," *Social Research*, 20 (1953), 267–281.

[27] Cox, *Caste, Class, and Race*.

[28] *Ibid.*, 223.

[29] *Ibid.*, 345–346.

leading capitalist people, the white people of Europe and North America." [30] Essentially racism is seen as serving the economic interests of the capitalist class in three ways: First, by viewing another people as inferior—as mental, moral, and physical inferiors—capitalists find it easier to exploit, oppress, and ill-treat these people in good conscience, and by the same token they can make colonialism and Jim Crow appear palatable or acceptable to the white masses.[31] Second, racism is financially advantageous, since the white capitalists can then pay Negroes less in wages, realizing greater profits.[32] Third, racism serves to divide the working class, to pit white workers against Negro workers; in this manner capitalists can drive down wages and drain discontent away from themselves. It is a tactic of "divide and conquer." [33]

Critique of the Marxist Interpretation

The Marxist position suffers from a number of serious shortcomings, some of which it shares with other economic, power, and prestige theories which will be examined at the conclusion of the chapter. A number of these shortcomings, however, are peculiar to the Marxist orientation and can be indicated here.

First, the Marxist theory fails to account, as Handlin notes, for the "differences in tastes of the capitalists of other countries. Why should the Brazilians and Frenchmen not have picked on the Negroes?" [34] Second, many American minority groups have found their most prejudiced persecutors not among the capitalists, but among the lower white socioeconomic groups. Myrdal suggests this has been the case within the South.[35] Similarly, the anti-Oriental movement on the Pacific coast was initiated by workingmen, in fact by trade unions. And Lipset presents convincing evidence that the working class is the least tolerant stratum in modern societies.[36]

Third, if the Marxist interpretation were correct, one would expect to find racism most rampant in large urban and industrial centers where capitalism finds its most manifest expression. Yet the available evidence indicates that white southerners are typically more intolerant of the Negro than are white northerners, the latter of which reside in a

---

[30] *Ibid.*, 322.
[31] *Ibid.*, 334–336 and 393.
[32] *Ibid.*, 333.
[33] *Ibid.*, 534.
[34] Handlin, *op. cit.*, 52.
[35] Myrdal, *op. cit.*, 69, 583, 597–598.
[36] Seymour M. Lipset, *Political Man* (New York: Doubleday & Co., Inc., 1960), 101. Also see: William J. MacKinnon and Richard Centers, "Authoritarianism and Urban Stratification," *American Journal of Sociology*, 61 (1956), 610–620.

more highly urbanized and industrialized society.[37] Similarly, within the South, the urban centers have been generally more disposed to the initiation of desegregation policies than rural communities or small towns.

A fourth difficulty with the Marxist approach is that from it one would assume that capitalists would welcome communities with racial strife as desirable locations for new industry. Such communities would be especially ripe for a "divide and conquer" policy. Yet the contemporary South has repeatedly demonstrated, contrary to the Marxist expectation, that capitalists are quite averse to locating plants in such localities. With the explosive unfolding of the race issue in Little Rock in 1957, the city suffered severely in its ability to attract new industry, a factor contributing to the anguish of its city fathers.[38] Similarly, industrialists have been reluctant to locate in those states in which militant segregationism has been most prevalent. Clearly, factors associated with racial strife and segregationism make such states and cities undesirable as locations for new industry.

A fifth problem with the Marxist approach to racism is that it assumes that white upper-class members consciously use and facilitate the development of race prejudice for purposes of class economic advantage. It is true, of course, that some incidents of this sort have occurred. But the process is more complex and less rational than the Marxists would suggest. Capitalists are no less human—no more immune to social or psychological factors—than non-capitalists. They are socialized within the same overall normative system—they assimilate the same scale of social distance. If they gain from prejudice it is more often coincidental than a conscious, deliberate, intentional plan.

Sixth, the Marxist position fails to recognize that cheap labor is not necessarily profitable labor. Cheap labor is often inefficient labor characterized by low morale and pseudo-ignorant malingering.

An Economic Interpretation of the Rise of Anti-Semitism

A major effort to interpret the rise of American anti-Semitism in economic terms is found in Carey McWilliams' A Mask for Privilege.[39] McWilliams' position is of particular interest, as he played a prominent

[37] H. H. Hyman and P. B. Sheatsley, "Attitudes Toward Desegration," Scientific American, CXCV (1956), 35–39; and E. T. Prothro, "Ethnocentrism and Anti-Negro Attitudes in the Deep South," Journal of Abnormal and Social Psychology, XLVII (1952), 105–108.

[38] M. Richard Cramer, "School Desegregation and New Industry: The Southern Community Leaders' Viewpoint," Social Forces, 41 (1963), 384.

[39] Carey McWilliams, A Mask for Privilege: Anti-Semitism in America (Boston: Little, Brown & Co., 1948).

role in making popular the cause of America's minorities. As the title of his book conveys, anti-Semitism is seen as a "mask for privilege." McWilliams finds little evidence of anti-Semitism in the United States prior to the Civil War. He places the responsibility for the rise of anti-Semitism at the doorstep of the industrial and financial tycoons who emerged during and following the war: the Goulds, Vanderbilts, Huntingtons, Hills, Harrimans, Rockefellers, Carnegies, Cookes, Morgans, and Armours. Outside the East, in the rapidly growing communities of the Middle West, the Far West, and the South, many Jewish immigrants had made the transition from peddler to prosperous merchant with extraordinary swiftness. They were, says McWilliams, among the "first families"—possessing wealth and distinction. Counted among their number were such names as Straus, Rosenwald, Seligman, Warburg, Schiff, Morgenthau, Sloss, Sutro, and Lubin.

The non-Jewish tycoons, says McWilliams, evolved anti-Semitism as a weapon by which to block the rapid rise of Jews in the new social and economic hierarchy.[40] The exclusion first occurred in the "prestige" institutions—in the exclusive resorts, clubs, and schools.[41] Social discrimination led to economic and political discrimination, since the Jews were shut out from important social contacts that were vital to business success.[42]

Jewish business was then driven into marginal pursuits—scrap iron, waste products, clothing, liquor distilling, etc. This concentration in relatively undesirable trades left the Jews in an exposed position. As the spotlight was focused upon the Jews, it became easy to direct abuse against them: "anti-Semitism is a favorite weapon of proven efficiency in the socioeconomic conflicts of a class-driven society." [43] It is an instrument of the ruling classes: "a weapon of reaction . . . used for many interrelated purposes: to confuse the people; to obscure the basic causes of unrest; to divert attention from these causes; to cloak the real purposes and objectives of reaction; to arrest social progress; to fight democracy." [44]

As Handlin indicates, McWilliams labors under the burden of an untenable thesis and is frequently careless in matters of detail. McWilliams asks his readers to believe that somehow the non-Jewish tycoons conspired—plotted—to drive Jewish businessmen as "Jews" from positions of prominence. No evidence is submitted by him to document

40 *Ibid.*, 18–21.
41 *Ibid.*, 114 ff.
42 *Ibid.*, 120.
43 *Ibid.*, 87.
44 *Ibid.*, 88.

this thesis. He also leaves unanswered the question "Why were the Jews singled out; why not some other group?" Since McWilliams argues that a single line of development generated anti-Semitism in the United States, he assumes throughout that anti-Semitic forces grew up indigenously within this country. He neglects the influences of European anti-Semitism and the impact on America of the works of Gobineau, Lapouge, and Chamberlain. Thus McWilliams cannot answer the question, "Why were the Jews singled out?" by a resort to the European tradition.[45] Furthermore, the rise of American anti-Semitism may well be analogous in some respects to the emergence of prejudice against other religious groups. The Quakers and Mormons were at one time severely persecuted within the United States, but this was hardly rooted in economic reasons. Nor have Catholics enjoyed immunity from religious attack.

Does this evaluation indicate that the economic factor was of *no* consequence in the history of anti-Semitism? Certainly such a position would be as shortsighted as that outlined by McWilliams. But the McWilliams' analysis is illustrative of the danger of seeking to impose a rigid theoretical position, in this case a one-factor economic interpretation, upon the facts. By selecting "facts" carefully it probably would not be too difficult to "substantiate" any theory, no matter how preposterous. The economic factor can best be understood as one among many interrelated factors that contributed to the emergence and perpetuation of anti-Semitism.

The Emergence of Anti-Semitism in Europe

A study of the rise of anti-Semitism in Europe is useful in demonstrating the complexity of the problem of tracing the origins of prejudice and in suggesting the multiplicity of factors usually involved in such a phenomenon. In tracing the emergence of anti-Semitism, it is important to note the religious and cultural aspects of Jewish life that served to set the Jews apart from the inhabitants of the non-Jewish communities in which they lived. Judaism is more than a religious system regulating man's spiritual relation with God. It represents an interwoven complex of cultural, ethical, and spiritual ingredients. The dietary laws governing the permissible kinds and classes of food are only among the better known of many similar regulations for other types of behavior. With their dispersion to the far corners of the Occidental world, the Jews found themselves culturally differentiated from the native populations.

[45] Handlin, *op. cit.*, 41–42.

The dispersion of the Jews from Palestine was a protracted movement. As is true of any extensive migration, friction occasionally occurred between the Jews and the native inhabitants. But the friction was scarcely anti-Semitism. It was a friction similar to those between Gauls and Romans, between Greeks and Persians, and between other groups, hardly resting upon religious grounds as such, but upon a complex of interwoven factors including religious, cultural, national, and economic ingredients. Actually, the Jews found the pagan Roman Empire quite tolerant of religious and cultural differences so long as these did not interfere with political control. By A.D. 313 Christianity had become the official religion of Rome. Subsequent decades witnessed harsh and repressive actions directed against non-Christian faiths. Full citizenship rights became dependent upon religion; Jews were forbidden to convert Christians, and intermarriage was prohibited. Hostility was then engendered on religious grounds.[46]

Christianity became a dominant ingredient in medieval life, heavily permeating and coloring the thought and behavior of the period. Attention became focused upon the Jews as "non-believers." The Crusades further fanned the flames of fanatical religious intolerance, as Christianity became the keynote in the wars against the Moslems. Jews became the "Christ killers." It was easy for a superstitious age to believe that Jews had tails; that they had a special odor; that they sacrificed Christian children, using their blood in Passover rites; and that they got hold of the sacred Eucharistic wafers and tortured them until they bled. Such myths as these were the precipitating causes of thousands of deaths. In 1243, scores of Jews at Beelitz, near Berlin, were burned at the stake for allegedly torturing the sacred bread, and in 1420 the whole Jewish community of Vienna was exterminated on the same allegation.[47]

Scapegoating also played a role. When things are going badly for a people, it becomes convenient to search for targets of blame. People are not prone to accept their own failures or failures within their cherished institutions. It is much less painful to place the blame on out-groups—to search, as in Puritan New England, for witches. As a group against whom antagonism already existed on religious grounds, it was not difficult to make the Jews the scapegoats when misfortune struck. There is no need to assume, as do the Marxists, that anti-Semitism is the invention of ruling classes to divert attention and hostility from themselves. It can be quite a spontaneous occurrence,

[46] See Louis Golding, *The Jewish Problem* (West Drayton, Middlesex, England: Penguin Books Limited, 1938).
[47] Simpson and Yinger, *op. cit.*, 200.

given the previous history of Jewish and Christian interaction. The reaction to the Black Death is a case in point. During the middle of the fourteenth century, a quarter to a third of the population of Europe was wiped out by the plague. The suffering and fear were enormous. In need of an "explanation" to allay fears, community after community turned upon the Jews. By virtue of religiously prescribed diet and cleanliness, Jews were less frequently struck down by the Black Death. Myths circulated that the Jews were in league with the devil—that they poisoned wells. Some towns did not wait for the disease to strike but attacked the Jews as potential well-poisoners. Within a period of two years, nearly 350 Jewish communities were wiped out.[48]

Within this context the economic factor played a role. By virtue of the disabilities imposed upon them, a relatively higher proportion of Jews turned to trade and commerce, which initially enjoyed a relatively marginal position in a predominantly agrarian society. As is inevitably the case, some prospered more than others, and some were exceedingly successful. With the growth of cities in Italy in the tenth century and in Germany in the eleventh century, a strong increase in the practice of, and demand for, a money economy emerged. The Catholic church prohibited the lending of money at interest as a cardinal sin, although allowing the Jews to lend to non-Jews. The temptation to lend money at interest is considerable to men of wealth; money can beget money. And Jewish merchants were no exception. But the money lender is not a popular man; debtors harbor considerable antagonism for their creditors.

In the medieval period those who engaged in the lending of money for interest (usury) were considered little better than robbers—to make money from money was sinful and non-productive; the only legitimate source of money was labor. Although only a minority of Jews were usurers, the entire Jewish group came to be identified as usurers and hated for this injustice. Since the Jews lived isolated in their own communities, ghettos, the Jew known by the populace tended to be the Jewish usurer, and this became the image of the Jew—the Shylock of Shakespeare's *Merchant of Venice*. At times, by virtue of lending money to princes and nobles, the Jews became identified with the ruling classes at a period when the aristocracy was coming under growing fire. This served to fan the flames of hostility toward the Jews. Similarly, as in Spain in the thirteenth, fourteenth, and fifteenth centuries, and in Austria and other German states in the seventeenth and nineteenth centuries, the most prominent Jews were appointed councilors of the crown and served as tax gatherers and commercial monopolists.

[48] *Ibid.*, 202.

Tax collectors are hardly popular men, and the Jews reaped new antagonism.[49]

Other factors, including psychological factors, likewise contributed to the rise of anti-Semitism. Many of the forces that were operative in Europe were similarly present in America and served to foster the growth of anti-Semitism here. But America was also heir to the European heritage. In light of the exaggerated claims made for economic interpretations of prejudice and discrimination, it is necessary to set the economic factor within its proper perspective. While it probably plays a role, each case needs to be appraised and analyzed separately. Care is necessary lest one become the servant of a dogma, as has often been true of the Marxists.

THE POWER FACTOR

Power may be broadly defined as the ability to control or influence the behavior of others. As such it implies uneven interaction. While the interaction between individuals and groups may continue to be reciprocal, involving a two-way interchange, the reciprocity is unequal and uneven. Action on one side of the interaction equation is effective and decisive to a degree greater than that found on the other side.[50] Power is one ingredient of a minority-dominant relationship, a relationship in which the dominant group tends to enjoy the advantage. By virtue of the disproportionate power residing in the dominant group, that group possesses on the whole a greater access to the opportunities and rewards of the society. By the same token, the minority group has less access to these opportunities and rewards. These differences in power tend to become institutionalized.

Power and the Differentiation of Minority Groups

A power interpretation of minority-dominant relations has received growing attention among American sociologists.[51] But, for the most

---

[49] Werner J. Cahnman, "Socio-Economic Causes of Antisemitism," *Social Problems,* 5 (1957), 21–29. For two very suggestive and original papers dealing with middlemen traders and prejudice see Irwin D. Rinder, "Strangers in the Land: Social Relations in the Status Gap," *Social Problems,* 6 (1958–1959), 253–260, and Sheldon Stryker, "Social Structure and Prejudice," *Social Problems,* 6 (1959), 340–354.

[50] R. A. Schermerhorn, "Power as a Primary Concept in the Study of Minorities," *Social Forces,* 35 (1956), 53–54.

[51] *Ibid.,* 53–56; H. M. Blalock, Jr., "A Power Analysis of Racial Discrimination," *Social Forces,* 39 (1960), 53–59; Morton B. King, Jr., "The Minority Course," *American Sociological Review,* 21 (1956), 80–83; and R. A. Schermerhorn, "Toward a General Theory of Minority Groups," *Phylon,* 25 (1964), 238–246.

part, the work has been primarily of an exploratory nature. Schermerhorn suggests that power relations furnish the chief means through
which minorities become differentiated. When groups with differing
cultural lifelines come into regular contact, their interaction crystallizes
into a social structure reflecting their differing power. The instability
of the power situation sets in motion a trend toward equilibrium or
resolution of the power clash.

Efforts to resolve the clash tend to take one of three forms. The first
form involves *extrusion*, where the group with the greater power elimi-
nates the other group by annihilation or by driving the other group
from a specified territory. It was this approach which characterized
the predominant mode of early Indian-white interaction. Virginia
offered scalp bounties as an incentive for soldiers and farmers to kill
Indians siding with the French during the French and Indian War.
The practice of exterminating Indians was widespread in California,
beginning in 1849. One of the early settlers wrote, concerning events in
which he participated on August 15, 1865, "I had often argued with Good
regarding the disposition of the Indians. He believed in killing every
man or well-grown boy, but in leaving the women unmolested in their
mountain retreats. It was plain to me that we must also get rid of
the women." [52]

A second form for the resolution of the power clash involves *non-con-
tiguous control*. Here the superordinate group maintains dominance of
the other party at a territorial distance. This type of interaction is
characteristic of colonialism. It similarly constituted the basis for our
Indian-reservations policy prior to 1933. A third form is *incorporative
control*, where the superordinate group brings the subordinate group
within its own geographical boundaries. Here a day-to-day adjustment
is essential, and a more elaborate mode of accommodation is required,
at least on the part of the superordinate group. In general, the incorporative mode appears to be the dominant one in the United States,
where such techniques as slavery, Jim Crow, discrimination, and the
selective admission of immigrants have prevailed.

Power is of many types which constitute a continuum with traditional
values or norms at one end of the scale and coercion at the other. The
power of tradition is cultural, while that of coercion tends in a sense
to be extracultural in that it involves the threat to biological necessities.
Since equality of power between two groups in any situation is rare,
forms of superordination typically appear. Furthermore, the power
will tend toward the coercive end of the scale in encounters between

[52] Quoted by B. Schrieke, *Alien Americans* (New York: The Viking Press, Inc.,
1936), 7.

groups with widely different cultural traditions, simply because value and normative controls ordinarily do not extend to the out-group.[53]

Power as a Dominant-Group Gain

American culture places a premium upon power as an integral aspect of its success motif. Striving for success is encouraged to such an extent that it approaches the status of a culturally obligatory pattern. To occupy a powerful position—to be a "boss," "the guy on top"—is the challenge held out to Americans. The desired norm is "to be over others," not "to be under others"; "to give orders," not "to take orders." Honor is accorded the individual who possesses power. The question asked is "How many men do you have under you?" The "captain" of the athletic team, the "president," the "supervisor," the "superintend-ent," the "bishop," the "mother superior," the "general," these are es-teemed and desired positions. Similarly, "to be bossed" is disesteemed and undesirable, at times even humiliating. It is tantamount to be-coming a "flunky." Strength is equated with power; weakness, with compliance with the power of another.

But power is not only a cultural *goal;* it is a *means* to other goals. A society in which competition is exalted and in which it becomes the means through which the culturally defined "good things of life" are achieved must place a premium upon power. To the extent to which the society allocates rewards on a competitive basis—to which the society is an arena where, in the Darwinian sense, only the fittest sur-vive and the strong outdo the weak—survival, or at any rate "success," becomes dependent upon power. The pursuit of self-interest calls for the control of others. The means by which control may be realized are infinite. It may be direct or through indirect manipulation such as by means of oversolicitousness or putting people under obligation.

Accordingly, to enjoy a superordinate position in relation to others becomes both a cultural goal and a means to other cultural goals. Yet to be superordinate implies that others are subordinate. By the nature of the structure, not everyone can have power. Power is a scarce, divisible value; the more there is for one individual, the less there is for others. If there are to be leaders, there must be followers. If there are to be the powerful, there must be the powerless. Some segments of the population cannot realize the authoritative roles and positions which are held out to them as goals and means to other goals by the culture. They are effectively blocked by the dictates of the social structure. Within such a context, a dominant-minority pattern may

[53] Schermerhorn, "Power as a Primary Concept in the Study of Minorities," 55–56.

hold out to the dominant group certain benefits. It offers to its members one alternative means by which they can experience power. Power is forthcoming by virtue of membership in the dominant group. Through identification with, and sharing membership in, the dominant group the individual can feel powerful.

Power and Personality Needs

Power may also serve deep personality needs. Striving for power can be quite normal; but it also can involve compensatory striving. In the normal person, feelings of power may be born of the realization of his own superior strength, whether it be physical strength, mental capacities, maturity, or wisdom. The compensatory striving for power, however, is the product of anxiety, hatred, and feelings of inferiority. In a word, normal striving for power is born of strength; the compensatory, of weakness. Many Americans may choose the route of power-striving precisely because within our social structure power can give a feeling of greater security.[54] The striving for power can serve a number of functions for the individual. In the first place, it functions as a protection against helplessness, which is one of the basic elements in anxiety. In the second place, it functions as a protection against the danger of feeling, or being regarded as, insignificant.[55] Power-striving, then, may not only be derived from cultural, but also from personality sources.

Evidence points to the fact that high levels of prejudice may be associated with power-seeking personalities.[56] Power may be sought as an end in itself. Since power is commonly equated with the dominant racial or ethnic group, weakness—the absence of power—can be overcome through gaining a sense of participation in the dominant group. The power which one lacks but strives for can be realized, or so it seems, from identification with a powerful group, e.g., "the white race." The minority group is seen as weak and ineffective. Its weakness invites attack from the would-be powerful. It becomes a means to assert, "I am powerful." But, being weak—helpless and insignificant—the individual realizes by this means a power that is not genuine in that it is not rooted in the personality itself. Accordingly the power has to be repeatedly asserted and demonstrated in hopes of proving to oneself and the world that one actually is powerful. But the constant and excessive reassertion of prejudicial attitudes via statements, jokes and

---

54 Karen Horney, *The Neurotic Personality of Our Time* (New York: W. W. Norton & Co., Inc., 1937), 162–163.

55 *Ibid.*, 166–167.

56 T. W. Adorno *et al., The Authoritarian Personality* (New York: Harper & Row, 1950).

jibes, and prejudicial behavior betrays the precarious status of the individual's sense of adequacy and strength. On the other hand, the weakness of the minority serves to outrage the would-be powerful by reminding the individual of his own weakness. Thus, the minority must be attacked, even destroyed.

But the minority group is seen not only as inefficient and weak; simultaneously, it may be viewed as selfish, materialistic, aggressive, and power-seeking, e.g., the Jew and the Negro. For the insecure person, the world is a threatening world; a world of anxiety, hatred, and aggressiveness; a world in which the individual is helpless and insignificant. Thus it is easy to see minorities as threatening. Minority groups being weak, it is not difficult to picture them as dangerous to oneself as the weak strive insatiably for power—witness oneself. And minorities are dangerous in still another sense. Retaliation lurks in the wings. Injustice sown in life reaps retribution, or so it appears. One must pay for one's aggression; the minority will exact payment.

It has been noted how an individual may attempt to gratify his need for power by means of the minority-dominant relationship. But simultaneous with the striving for power is the need to submit to it. The two traits often go hand-in-hand.[57] An individual may both crave for power over men and long to submit to an overwhelming outside power. Through submitting to power, he hopes he can participate in it. By losing self-identity within a large collective, the race (e.g., "the white race"), he sacrifices his individuality but gains through his absorption by the whole. He submits to power; he is subservient to the large, powerful racial group, becoming little more than an atom. But he seems to overcome his weakness through gaining a sense of participation in the power of the whole.

Scapegoating for Political Ends

The role of scapegoating in the emergence of anti-Semitism has already been noted. By attributing evils and difficulties to an out-group, members of the in-group can escape feelings of blame for their own failures or for failures in cherished institutions. It is painful to admit and to recognize such failure. How much more convenient and comforting it is to place the responsibility upon another! Political leaders throughout history have found it expedient to divert the hostility and aggressiveness of the in-group to out-groups. Hitler and Goebbels were masters at the art. The German people—frustrated by defeat in war, plagued by economic chaos, disgruntled by the problems of life in

[57] See: *Ibid.*, 237–238, 804, and 856 ff.; and Erich Fromm, *Escape from Freedom* (New York: Holt, Rinehart & Winston, Inc., 1 941), 220–239.

general—were given the Jews, Reds, and international bankers as targets upon which to vent their rage. Russians and Chinese—restless under the failure of dreams for a "new world" and a "new life" to materialize and by the inevitable frustrations of life—are presented with "Yankees," "foreign imperialists," and "Wall Street capitalists" as permissible targets for hate and aggression. In pagan Rome, it was the Christian minority that was used as the target to divert attention from the problems, failures, and corruption within the Roman state. Tertullian observed, "If the Tiber rose to the walls of the city, if the inundation of the Nile failed to give the fields enough water, if the heavens did not send rain, if an earthquake occurred, if famine threatened, if pestilence raged, the cry resounded: 'Throw the Christians to the lions.'"

Political leaders need not create racial or ethnic prejudices; there is no evidence to suggest that they do. They may, however, capitalize upon incipient or marked tendencies toward prejudice among the in-group and exploit and intensify these tendencies. It is often assumed that only evil men with ignoble causes employ scapegoating as part of their devious ways. Yet the search for targets of blame is a common political technique. In election campaigns many Democrats are not averse to assigning Republicans the responsibility for the Great Depression of the thirties, nor are many Republicans reluctant to attribute World War II and the Korean War to the Democrats. The long-term "farm problem" in America of agricultural surplus is customarily attributed to the "failures" of the party in power by the party out of power, Democrat or Republican. Obviously, in all these situations a great many forces were operative. To assign the responsibility to one group is in essence to search for a target of blame.

Nor do frustrations and tendencies toward aggression in and of themselves necessarily account for prejudice. Blocked in realizing desires or goals, people tend to become angry—hostile. Aggressiveness may ensue. But there is nothing inherent in either frustration or aggression that necessarily leads to its expression in racial or ethnic prejudice. The object to which aggressiveness may attach itself is frequently determined by culture. It is the culture that defines the availability of an object as a source for expressing hostile impulses. The culture renders the object a permissible or impermissible target. Given a cultural heritage that stresses differences in religion, culture, and physical traits, and that draws highly value-laden conclusions about these differences, racial and ethnic groups are rendered appropriate avenues for the releasing of aggressiveness. Economic conditions, political strife, international strains, these or other tensions do not in and of themselves cause prejudice. They may, however, feed and fan the flames of prejudice when the culture defines particular groups as targets for wrath. Contributing to frustration and thus to aggressiveness, they intensify the need to vent hostile feelings. Political leaders may manipulate and encourage these feelings and their expression for partisan purposes. Here we will examine two such efforts: racism in southern politics and anti-Orientalism on the Pacific coast.

Race and Southern Politics

The use of "race" to advance one's own political fortunes has commonly been associated with southern political life. The names of Georgia's Tom Watson and "Old Gene" Talmadge, of South Carolina's "Pitchfork Ben" Tillman and "Cotton Ed" Smith, of Mississippi's James K. Vardaman and Theodore Bilbo, among others, have served to identify a racist appeal, with southern campaigning. Montagu writes:

In the South "race" hatred has long been kept alive and fanned to white heat at the instigation of unscrupulous industrialists and politicians, ever ready to capitalize on baseless popular superstitions, prejudices, and beliefs, because there is no issue more useful than "race" as a political platform for securing votes. Tell the poor whites that their condition is due to the competition of the Negroes and their very existence is threatened by the latter, and they will vote for anything to which such an issue is tied in apparent favor of themselves.[58]

The 1950 North Carolina Senatorial Race.   Illustrative of the use of the race issue in electioneering is the 1950 senatorial race in North Carolina, in which Senator Frank P. Graham suffered defeat. The election is of special interest on a number of counts. In the first place, it constituted, in the words of political analyst Samuel Lubell, one of "the most crushing setbacks Southern liberalism . . . suffered since the coming of Franklin Roosevelt." [59] Secondly, North Carolina had for decades been noted for its progressivism and for its exception to the southern pattern of race baiting. For nearly fifty years the issue of white supremacy had not been raised as a major issue in Tarheel State elections. Thirdly, the election occurred in 1950, four years *prior to* the Supreme Court's school-desegregation ruling which stimulated the emergence of the race issue as a major theme in elections throughout the South.

Prior to entering politics, Senator Graham had been president of the University of North Carolina. He enjoyed a distinguished record and

[58] Montagu, *Man's Most Dangerous Myth,* 81–82.
[59] Samuel Lubell, *The Future of American Politics,* 2d ed. (New York: Doubleday & Co., Inc.), 107.

considerable respect as an outstanding educator, humanitarian, and spokesman for southern liberalism. His reputation stood him in good stead in the May 27, 1950, primary, in which he ran 53,000 votes ahead of his closest opponent and came within 1 per cent of the needed majority. But a short step from victory in May, on June 24, the runoff election, Graham was defeated by 18,000 votes. Until the last few days of the campaign Graham seemed assured of winning over his opponent, Willis Smith.

In the last five days of the campaign, a torrent of racist literature flooded North Carolina. Handbills circulated in the state reading: "WHITE PEOPLE WAKE UP." Graham was portrayed as favoring the "mingling of the races," Negro use of "your toilet facilities," Negro occupation "of the same hospital rooms with you and your wife and daughter," etc. Advertisements appeared in the press proclaiming, "The South Under Attack" or "End of Racial Segregation Proposed." Radio stations carried spot announcements with "Do you know that 28 percent of North Carolina's population is colored?" or "The southern working man must not be sacrificed by FEPC!" Photographs of Negro G.I.'s dancing with white girls in night clubs in England were left at filling stations where farmers like to gather and chat; other leaflets listed prominent Negroes such as Richard Wright and Walter White as having white wives. At the "whispering campaign" level the main issue stressed was the threat of an end to segregation in public schools.

The mood of North Carolina changed. Graham stickers came off automobiles; people found it uncomfortable to admit support for Graham. In Durham, an election official favoring Graham was awakened during the night by a telephone call. When his wife answered, she was asked, "How would you like a little stewed nigger for breakfast?" The day before the voting, Graham stopped at a filling station near High Point. Five men were sitting around. Graham introduced himself and offered to shake hands. Muttered one, "We're all Willis Smith [Graham's opponent] men here. We'll have nothing to do with nigger lovers here." [60]

The Role of the "Black Belt." The late V. O. Key, Jr., an authority on southern politics, stressed the view that whites of the "Black Belt" counties constitute the core and backbone of the political South. [61] The Black Belt makes up only a small part of the area of the South—counties in which Negroes constitute 50 per cent or more of the total popula-

[60] This account has been summarized from *Ibid.*, 107–115.
[61] V. O. Key, Jr., *Southern Politics* (New York: Alfred A. Knopf, Inc., 1950).

tion. In 1960 there were some 144 such counties, a marked drop from the 286 Black Belt counties of 1900. In these counties large-scale-plantation or multiple-unit agriculture prevails. Here are located most of the large agricultural operators who oversee the work of many tenants, sharecroppers, and laborers, most of whom are Negro. Numerically, whites constitute a minority of the population, but in economic, power, and status terms they have considerable investment in the maintenance of the existing social order.

Although the Black Belt whites are few in number, Key argued that their unity and political skill enabled them "to run a shoestring into decisive power at critical junctures in southern political history." [62] It was this group of whites who were the prime movers in the fight to protect slave property and in the establishment of the Confederate States. Later, with conservative allies in the cities, they put down the radical Populist movement. And through the propagation of the racist position, they impressed on the entire South a philosophy agreeable to their needs and succeeded for decades in maintaining a regional unity in national politics to defend these necessities.[63] Their major vehicle has been the Democratic party. "The black-belt counties can be regarded as a skeleton holding together the South. They have, in a sense, managed to subordinate the entire South to the service of their peculiar local needs." [64] In essence Key's position was that the "race" issue has been consistently manipulated by Black Belt whites to maintain their vested interests. In short, he argued that economic, power, and status gains are derived from the existing order and that these gains potentially could be jeopardized if Negroes voted in number or if the white vote became divided. A white man in Hale County, Alabama, where Negroes constitute 70 per cent of the population observes,

"Look at the figures and tell me what we could do if Negroes had full voting rights. Why, the blacks would be in the judges' seats and running the schools. They'd stick together at the polls and elect their candidates to every office in the country." [65]

Anti-Orientalism on the Pacific Coast

Anti-Orientalism in California emerged against the backdrop of hostility toward Mexicans, Spaniards, and Indians and a tendency to lump together all persons of non-northern-European ancestry. It was during the gold rush in the early 1850's that the first Chinese arrived in Cali-

[62] *Ibid.*, 6.
[63] *Ibid.*, 5–11.
[64] *Ibid.*, 666.
[65] William A. Emerson, Jr., "A Political State of Mind," *Newsweek*, XLVII (May 21, 1956), 38.

fornia. Initially (1851–1859) there was a labor vacuum. The fortune seekers had no intention of performing menial, petty, and laborious tasks. Under these conditions the Chinese got their chances.[66]

Anti-Chinese sentiment surged with the completion of the Central Pacific Railroad (1864–1869), which filled San Francisco with unskilled labor at the same time white labor was migrating to the West Coast from the East. Business stagnated following the Civil War and the economy was hit by successive depressions. Unemployment was considerable. Discontent and frustration mounted among whites. Within this setting, anti-Chinese feelings intensified. At times the agitation against the Chinese took on violent aspects. The primary leadership in the anti-Chinese campaigns came from workingmen's groups, particularly the Workingmen's party, which exploited anti-Oriental sentiment in securing the election of its candidates to public office. However, with the passage of the Chinese exclusion acts beginning in 1882, and the decline in the Chinese population through 1920, anti-Chinese agitation and sentiment diminished.[67]

But the Japanese reaped a new harvest of anti-Oriental sentiment following 1900. The foundations had been laid in the earlier period. By 1890 there were 2,039 Japanese in the United States; by 1900 the number had increased to 24,236; and by 1910, to 72,157. Most of these settled in California. While a complex array of factors, including the rise of Japan as a great power with territorial ambitions, contributed to the appearance of intense, mass anti-Japanese feelings, here attention will be focused upon the political exploitation of the issue.

In 1901 the Workingmen's party, a leader in the earlier anti-Chinese movement, was revived as the Union Labor party. In that year it succeeded in electing Eugene E. Schmitz mayor of San Francisco. Schmitz, a former bassoon player in a San Francisco orchestra, was the henchman of Abe Ruef, an exceedingly able and notoriously corrupt politician. Although re-elected, Schmitz was facing indictment in 1906 for his many crimes. Attempting to save themselves, Schmitz and Ruef saw an opportunity to whip up and fan deep-seated anti-Oriental sentiment as a diversionary issue. On May 6, 1905, the San Francisco school board had gone on record as favoring the segregation of Oriental students in local schools, but, for lack of funds, the resolution had been tabled. However, on October 11, 1906, on the eve of the indictment of Schmitz and Ruef, the school board suddenly decided to carry the resolution into effect. Not only were the graft investigations pending, but a state election was less than a month off. There were only 93

[66] Schrieke, *op. cit.*, 9.
[67] *Ibid.*, 8–17.

Japanese students out of a total school population of 25,000. But the issue sparked a surge in anti-Japanese feelings in the state.[68]

THE STATUS FACTOR

Within the United States there are many standardized criteria by which people are evaluated and ranked in the status hierarchy. Among these criteria are occupation, source and size of income, style of life, length and type of education, possession of property, residential neighborhood, type and size of home, rank of associates, leisure-time activities, skill, family, and many more. One of the principal criteria of status, yet one among others, is religious, racial, and ethnic membership. The various religious, racial, and ethnic groups, as was noted in the previous chapter, can be ranked in a hierarchy on the basis of the social-distance scale.

Same Features of Status

In general, high status can be recognized by one or more of the five features suggested by E. Benoit-Smullyan.[69] These, in turn, can be applied to dominant-minority relations. First, the individual or group tends to be an object of admiration. This admiration may or may not be based upon objective characteristics or achievements. Within the United States, it is not unusual for the dominant white, Anglo-Saxon, Protestant group to be stereotyped as an "achieving," "creative" group. Frequently equated with this group are such highly valued aspects of American life as democracy, Christianity, and scientific advancement. Similarly, the accomplishments of minority groups are often felt to be minimal and insignificant. In fact, minority groups at home and abroad are not infrequently characterized as the "white man's burden," and it is often held that the dominant whites need—in fact, have the duty— to bring others the essentials of "the American way of life."

Second, high status tends to be associated with deference. Deference involves the symbolic expression of the individual's or group's priority. Within dominant-minority group interaction, membership within the dominant group gives the individual the presumptive right to take the initiative in many relations with the minority. Similarly, when present at minority-group functions, the dominant-group member may be

[68] Carey McWilliams, *Prejudice* (Boston: Little, Brown & Co., 1944), 16 ff.
[69] E. Benoit-Smullyan, "Status, Status Types, and Status Interrelations," *American Sociological Review*, 9 (1944), 151–161.

accorded a special "place of honor" or given special recognition. It is not unusual for a white in attendance at a Negro religious service to be shown to an honored or premium seat, to be extended various courtesies, to be freely flattered, and to be asked to address the group. By the same token dominant-group membership gives the individual the presumptive right of being addressed in certain distinctive ways by minority-group members. This is most clearly seen in rural sections of the South where the Negro is expected to address the white in terms of "sir," "boss," "cap'n," "Mr."; to express a continual flow of agreement such as "Yes, boss," "Sho 'nuff," and "Well, I declare"; to remove his hat; and the like.

Third, the behavior of the individual or group becomes a model and is deliberately or unconsciously reproduced by others. Deliberate imitation may be intended to create a favorable impression upon the one imitated, in so far as it is not designed or interpreted as an attempt to displace the advantaged individual or group. In fact, it may be quite flattering to those in dominant positions that members of a minority attempt to emulate certain of their qualities, yet fail in the endeavor. It contributes to a feeling of superiority. Thus, a Negro domestic worker may repeatedly reiterate her intention to bank the financial gift given her by her employer. But then, after spending it on trivialities, she returns to tell the employer, "It does not pay to give us Negroes much money because we just don't know how to take care of it." But imitation need not be only an effort to create a good impression; the minority may accept the superiority of the dominant group and the inferiority of their own and attempt to edge over toward the dominant-group model. Thus, there is a tendency for Negro men to "marry white" within the Negro group, i.e., marry Negro women lighter than themselves. Closely associated with this feature of status is the fourth, where high status tends to be a source for suggestion. Ideas expressed by the dominant-group member may be more readily accepted than the same ideas expressed by minority-group members.

Fifth, high status functions as a center of attraction. This results from the fact that status is contagious. Those who associate with people of high status participate in that status. The contact may be fleeting, yet may confer status, e.g., "Shake hands with the man who shook hands with the President." To enjoy the friendship of, to work for or with, to belong to the same group with, or to be in a family with a prestigious individual is to gain status. It is not uncommon to find Negroes being ranked by other Negroes on the basis of the status enjoyed by their white employers within the white community.

Status Gains

Most of us enjoy the feeling that we are not just average but perhaps, at least to some degree, special and important. We like to identify with a winning football team, the "best" school, fraternity, or community, and so it goes. Indeed, our American culture places considerable emphasis upon status. Yet not all Americans are able to realize the status that they desire.[70] For members of the dominant group, however, status is acquired simply through the fact that they are a white or a gentile. By virtue of one's dominant group membership, an individual can acquire a sense of status that his own achievements might not command. Dollard asserts in his study of a southern town:

In the North a man may have a prestige position because he has money, or is learned, or is old; the novelty in the South is that one has prestige solely because one is white. The gain here is very simple. It consists in the fact that a member of the white caste has an automatic right to demand forms of behavior from Negroes which serve to increase his own self-esteem. To put it another way, it consists of an illumination of the image of the self, an expansive feeling of being something special and valuable. It might be compared to the illusion of greatness that comes with early stages of alcoholization, except that prestige is not an illusion but a steadily repeated fact.[71]

Hence, membership in the dominant group can take on enormous emotional significance for status-starved individuals.

The feeling of status deprivation or depreciation, however, need not be limited to individuals in the lower socioeconomic classes. Upper class people can feel poorly about their status because they experience a sense of *relative* deprivation when they compare themselves with others whom they envy or desire to be like. Evidence suggests that feelings of relative deprivation can be as widespread and intense in upper status groups as on lower status levels. This may account, in part, for the anti-Semitism displayed by many upper status individuals. For instance, a wealthy, well-educated professional may feel more intense deprivation and end up more anti-Semitic than a relatively uneducated manual laborer, who, comparing himself only to his status equals, ends up feeling rather good about himself and his situation.[72]

[70] Robert K. Merton, *Social Theory and Social Structure*, rev. ed. (New York: The Free Press of Glencoe, Inc., 1957), 121–194.

[71] John Dollard, *Caste and Class in a Southern Town*, 3d ed. (New York: Doubleday & Co., Inc., 1957), 174. Some authorities feel that this characterization by Dollard represents a gross overstatement of the situation.

[72] Melvin M. Tumin, *An Inventory and Appraisal of Research on American Anti-Semitism* (New York: Freedom Books, 1961), 50.

The Klansman

The status gains derived by dominant group members are often complex. A consideration of the Ku Klux Klan is most revealing. From 1955 through 1958 the Ku Klux Klan experienced a revival in the South. An outbreak of bombings, fiery crosses, torchlight rallies, whippings, and beatings followed in the wake of the revival. Illustrative of Klan activity was the beating of Claud Cruell on the night of July 21, 1957, near Travelers Rest, South Carolina. Cruell, a fifty-eight-year-old Negro, and his wife were baby-sitting for a white neighbor. During the evening a group of white men, some of whom were identified as Klansmen, burst into the home. Accusing him of being "overly friendly with whites," the intruders bound and severely beat the elderly Negro. Previous to the incident, whites in Travelers Rest had harbored resentment against Cruell for his relative prosperity and ownership of a sizable farm. Judge Aaron, a mentally retarded Negro handy man, was another Klan victim. Klansmen abducted and castrated Aaron on Labor Day, 1957. Testimony at the subsequent trial revealed that they had selected Aaron merely by chance—the Klansmen had been out to find *any* Negro as their victim.

But the 1955–1958 Klan revival represented little more than a pallid ghost of earlier organizations. The Reconstruction Klan had arisen as a response to the assault upon white supremacy that had followed the Civil War. With the passing of Reconstruction, the Klan faded away. Called back to life in 1915 by William J. Simmons, kluxing reached its peak in the 1920's, gaining some 5 million members and political power within Oregon, Texas, Oklahoma, and Indiana. The 1955–1958 version of the Klan, however, garnered less than 10,000 members. Its strength was concentrated, not, as perhaps would be expected, in rural Black Belt counties, but in the urban centers of the southeastern Piedmont. By late 1958, the fortunes of the Klan again waned, only to experience a new revival in the 1960's. With this background in mind, let us turn to an examination of some of the status gains accruing to Klan members.

The author was able to locate the names and occupational positions of 153 Klansmen in the 1955–1958 revival.[73] They could be classified in four occupational groupings: (1) skilled workers (e.g., garage mechanics, machinists, carpenters, and stonemasons), (2) marginal small businessmen (e.g., small building-trade contractors and proprietors of food markets, grills, and gasoline stations), (3) marginal white-collar

[73] James W. Vander Zanden, "The Klan Revival," *American Journal of Sociology*, LXV (1960), 456–462.

workers (e.g., grocery-store clerks, service-station attendants, police-men, and salesmen), and (4) transportation workers (primarily truck drivers) and unskilled and semi-skilled workers in the textile, construc-tion, automotive, aircraft, coal, and steel industries. The sample was of unknown representativeness, and it was undoubtedly biased, yet it probably reflected the occupational breadth of the Klan's membership.

Two-thirds of the Klansmen were found in the first three categories. These positions—skilled workers, marginal businessmen, and marginal white-collar workers—are commonly ranked within the status hierarchy in the upper rungs of the working class and the lower rungs of the middle class. They occupy an intermediate position in the social struc-ture between clear-cut "blue-collar" manual jobs and "white-collar" jobs—between the "working class" and the "middle class"—positions that are somewhat hazy and vague in their placement in one or the other of the socioeconomic class divisions. American society, with its em-phasis upon success, its belief in an open class system, and its high valuation of middle-class status, places such individuals in a difficult position. Their status ranking tends to be nebulous and ambiguous. At best they have a toe hold within the middle class; at worst, middle-class status seems almost—but not quite—within their grasp. As a consequence their status tends to be insecure and they are anxious con-cerning their placement in the status hierarchy. Torn between the status America says they *ought* to have and what they in fact *actually* have, they feel disgruntled, discontented, and frustrated.

They tend to be "status-starved." The Rev. James W. ("Catfish") Cole told newsmen, after his group was routed by Lumbee Indians in an episode gaining national headlines in 1958, "I don't care what you write. Just be sure you write it. The name is easy to remember. The initials are J. C. as in Jesus Christ." Society gives such individuals a way out. They are still white, and they are still Americans, in a region where such things are most important. They seize upon those status elements which are available to them, but elevate and magnify them out of proportion to their place in the social order. They *over-conform* to the institutionalized caste pattern of the South and to patri-otic identification with America. Judged by white group standards, their adherence to the dominant white racial values and Americanism is excessive. This leads to conflict with other values, most particularly the sanctity of the individual and of private property.

This exaggerated magnification of values commonly esteemed in America is reflected in this statement appearing in the handbook of the U.S. Klans, Knights of the Ku Klux Klan:

We invite all men who can qualify to become citizens of the Invisible Empire, to approach the portal of our beneficent domain, join us in our noble work of extending its boundaries, and in disseminating the gospel of Klankraft, thereby encouraging, conserving, protecting and making vital the fraternal relationship in the practice of an honorable clannishness; to share with us the sacred duty of protecting womanhood; to maintain forever the God-given supremacy of the White Race; to commemorate the holy and chivalric achievement of our fathers; to safeguard the sacred rights, privileges and institutions of our civil government; to bless mankind and to keep eternally ablaze the sacred fire of a fervent devotion to a pure Americanism.

Secrecy plays a role similar to exaggerated conformity. The strongly emphasized exclusion of all outsiders makes for a feeling of possession. That which is secret and mysterious has a quality of importance and essentiality. By the possession of such secrets, the Klansman secures prestige. Similarly, Klan secrets give the Klansman a highly tangible and explicit group identification, since they set him apart from the amorphous mass of humanity. Without secure anchorage in the class structure, he compensates via the anchorage afforded by Klan membership.

Lacking prestive-giving symbols in the world-at-large, Klansmen establish their own world, an "Invisible Empire." It is a world with its own esteemed symbols—its grotesque, differentially valued purple, red, green and white gowns, its elaborate honorific insignia, and its exaggerated status-exalting nomenclature of Imperial Wizard, Grand Dragon, Grand Titan, Grand Giant, and Exalted Cyclops. Likewise, questions of power and status had been a major source of Klan factionalism and splintering. Although the U.S. Klans, Knights of the Ku Klux Klan, had been the largest of the Klans, at least fifteen splinter Klans had formed.

Social Mobility and Prejudice

So far as their status is concerned, many Americans are on the move. Some rise in the status hierarchy, other remain stationary, while still others fall. Various studies suggest that there is a relationship between social mobility and prejudice. Bettelheim and Janowitz, in a survey of seven studies, find general confirmation for the hypothesis that downward mobility is associated with racial and ethnic prejudice.[74] A common explanation for this association is that downward mobility is frustrating, giving rise to hostile and aggressive impulses that in turn are vented upon minorities. The evidence with regard to upward

[74] Bruno Bettelheim and Morris Janowitz, *Social Change and Prejudice* (New York: The Free Press of Glencoe, 1964), 29–34.

mobility is less clear. However, after surveying the evidence from six studies, Bettelheim and Janowitz conclude: "the evidence . . . goes a long way to support the minimum observation that moderate upward mobility does not increase ethnic prejudice and often brings some decline in hostility." [75]

Silberstein and Seeman refine matters further on the basis of interviews involving a sample of 665 persons in the metropolitan area of Morgantown, West Virginia.[76] They suggest that mobility by itself may not be enough of an explanation. Rather, we need to know, they argue, the extent to which an individual cares about his status and mobility. They distinguish between mobility-oriented and achievement-oriented individuals. The distinction "lies in the fact that the latter tend to give status and prestige a lower value—i.e., they choose to emphasize the relative importance of, for example, friendship, political freedom, community life, or intrinsic interest in the job as compared with the value of social rank." [77] Silberstein and Seeman discover that the mobility-oriented (the status-seekers) tend to be more prejudiced, whether they are downward or upward mobile or even stationary in their status history. In contrast, the downwardly mobile, achievement-oriented individuals showed much less prejudice. Hence, the critical variable may not be mobility itself so much as how individuals perceive and define status and mobility.

CONCLUSIONS

The chapter has examined the role that such scarce and divisible values as wealth, power, and status play in dominant-minority relations. Yet, while recognizing the importance of these factors, it was repeatedly necessary to exercise caution and qualification with regard to them. Dominant-minority relations are complex, and no single factor tells the entire story. In the discussion of each factor, not alone did other variables repeatedly intervene, but it was essential to consider them lest a distorted picture emerge.

Some of the more important limitations of an economic, power, or status analysis of prejudice and discrimination can be summarized as follows:

1. These factors may play an important role in the rise of a particular dominant-minority pattern, but they do not necessarily

[75] *Ibid.*, 36.

[76] Fred B. Silberstein and Melvin Seeman, "Social Mobility and Prejudice," *American Journal of Sociology*, LXV (1959), 258–264.

[77] *Ibid.*, 259.

account for the continuation of the pattern after such forces have subsided or ceased to operate.

2. Anti-Negro and anti-Semitic feelings run high in many American communities in which Negroes and Jews are either absent or represented by only a few members. Here economic, power, or status gains are absent or minimal.

3. The factors do not adequately explain the great diversity in the patterns of racial and ethnic prejudice and discrimination throughout the world.

4. The factors neglect the personality functions of prejudice in terms of frustration-aggression, projection, and personality structure. They fail to account for the differences observed either in the intensity of prejudice or in discriminatory actions among individuals with a vested interest in the prevailing social order.

5

Ideological Factors

Societies everywhere in the world have evolved sets of ideas by which life is made understandable for their members. These ideas tell people about the nature of their society and about its place in the world. Without such ideas on the important matters of existence, social life would be without meaning. People would lack means by which to fit together the multitude of specific events that touch them and others. These sets of ideas give people a framework for relating themselves to others and to life in general. Such ideas tell people about the history of the society, its friends and enemies, its gods and devils, its heroes and villains. They tell people about the structure and processes of the society, about such things as internal differentiation, for example, of social classes, how they came into being, how they differ, how people "get ahead" or fall behind. A society's ideas tell people about disaster, illness, birth, marriage, and death. They tell people about the approved goals and values of the society. Such sets of ideas are referred to as *ideology*.

Ideology provides the essential ideas that form the spiritual and intellectual foundation of group solidarity. Such a body of ideas functions as a kind of societal glue knitting people together in a fellowship of belief. Ideology has a cohesive, integrative function for the society. Obviously, ideas have a considerable influence on men's behavior. The role of religious, economic, political, and other ideologies in the contemporary world is only too clear. Such ideologies as Christianity, Islam, capitalism, communism, socialism, fascism, and democracy are major forces in directing human behavior. In this chapter we will be

concerned with major sets of ideas influencing racial and ethnic interaction.

AMERICA'S EUROPEAN LEGACY OF RACISM

Early European Roots of Racism

Racism is essentially the doctrine that one racial or ethnic group is
condemned by nature to inferiority and another group is destined to
superiority. Racism, like other *isms*, is often held to with considerable
conviction, much in the fashion of a religion. As has been true of a
good many other *isms*, be it Catholicism, Protestantism, fascism, communism, or the like, men have cut each other's throats in its name. In
Nazi Germany it probably reached its most virulent expression. An
estimated 5 million Jews perished in the Nazi endeavor to exterminate
all Jews. In Chapter 2 the various tenets of the racist doctrine were
considered in terms of contemporary scientific evidence. Here we are
interested in examining some of the diverse and manifold sources contributing to the emergence of European racism. To one degree or
another, America was heir to this heritage.

As was already noted in earlier sections, it is not uncommon for
men anywhere in the world to believe that they, and they alone, belong
to the "best people." Among even the most primitive the formula "I
belong to the Elect" constitutes an integral part of their whole life experience. Primitive peoples are prone to look upon themselves grandiosely as "*the* human beings," as "Men." Their outlook is highly provincial. They tend to equate themselves with "mankind." But this
notion is to be distinguished from racism by the latter's focus upon biology and biological features. The idea of inborn inferiority or superiority
of groups was not necessarily an ingredient in the formula "I belong
to the Elect." Early men merely saw their own group as occupying
the center of the stage of life and the universe, a universe that was
objectively quite geographically limited.[1] Such a perception of the
world probably fed into a later racial current.

Barzun has pointed out the apparent paradox that modern Aryan
racist ideology had roots in the writings of Latins such as Tacitus,
De Boulainvilliers, and De Gobineau.[2] Yet in many respects these
writers used the Aryans as Samuel Johnson used the Chinese and
Thomas More used the Utopians—for invidious comparisons in a cri-

[1] Ruth Benedict, *Race: Science and Politics* (New York: Modern Age Books,
1940), chapter 7.

[2] Jacques Barzun, *The French Race: Theories of Its Origins and Their Social and
Political Implications* (New York: Columbia University Press, 1932); and *Race: A
Study in Modern Superstition* (New York: Harcourt, Brace & World, Inc., 1937).

tique of their own society. Significantly these doctrines did not become an important aspect of the ideology and politics of the Latin countries.[3] Tacitus was a disaffected Roman moralist who was disgusted by the degeneracy of Rome, and who in about A.D. 100 extolled in his writings the hardihood and fierceness of the Teutonic barbarians and their leadership principle: "Their generals control them by example rather than by authority. If they are daring and adventurous and conspicuous in action, they procure obedience from the admiration that they inspire." Eighteenth- and nineteenth-century racist authors seized upon such writings as a cornerstone in their exaltation of the Aryans.

Another source contributing to the rise of European racism was the heritage of the ancient people of the North Sea Basin. Jonassen indicates that these people possessed a rather complete racist theory within their mythology, a racist theory which in most respects parallels the myths of modern times.[4] The *Rigsthula,* a poem of Viking society, describes the racial composition and the functions, relationships, and origins of the social classes on a mythological basis. According to the poem, the god Rig created the different classes of Viking society. Thrael, a member of the lowest class, is portrayed as black-haired with wrinkled skin, rough hands, knotted knuckles, thick fingers, an ugly face, a twisted back and big heels. Thrael's wife is depicted with crooked legs, stained feet, sunburned arms, and a flat nose. It was the duty of Thrael and his wife to carry burdens all day, dig turf, spread dung, and herd swine and goats.

Karl, the yeoman, on the other hand, is described as sturdy and strong with a ruddy face and flashing eyes. He managed the farm, built houses, and fashioned other artifacts. Mothir, a woman of a noble and still higher position, is depicted as having bright brows, a shining breast, and a neck "whiter than the new fallen snow." Her son, Jarl, by the god Rig, is portrayed in these words, "Blond he was, and bright his cheeks, grim as a snake's were his glowing eyes." Jarl's role as a warrior and ruler is described in detail. The poem represented a major ideological and mythological effort by the Vikings to explain nature, society, and themselves. It gave them answers to the complex questions of life.

The Thraels, the lowest class, were probably descendants of a short, brunet, round-headed race which the tall, blond, long-headed Norse had conquered when they moved into Scandinavia. It was the practice of the Vikings, in their raids and expeditions to England, Ireland,

---

[3] Christen T. Jonassen, "Some Historical and Theoretical Bases of Racism in Northwestern Europe," *Social Forces,* 30 (1951), 155–161.

[4] The following account is summarized from Jonassen, *Ibid.*

and continental Europe, to take captives whom they made into slaves. For the most part, these captives were shorter and darker than the Vikings. Accordingly, certain racial characteristics such as short stature, dark hair and skin, and a flat nose tended to become associated with inferior social status, and general inferiority. On the other hand, blondness, light skin, and certain facial features became associated with superiority. These beliefs were integrated within the mythology and tended to persist, although a certain amount of race mixture went on through the generations. Jonassen suggests that such notions formed a fertile mental atmosphere in which racism could grow and flourish.

Later European Roots of Racism

Apparently the most articulate early statement of racism was formulater by Count De Boulainvilliers about 1727 as an instrument for the advancement of the interests of the aristocrats. Count De Boulainvilliers was a Norman possessing an extravagant admiration for the feudal order that was already giving way to modern nationalism. He identified himself with the feudal lords whose position was on the decline. The taxes levied by the French Crown and the arrogant authority of Louis XIV roused in De Boulainvilliers the dream that the feudal nobility should assert themselves against the monolithic state and restore their old glory. In England a similar movement had given birth to the Magna Charta. De Boulainvilliers invoked racism as a weapon in the fight. He described the feudal lords as of the *Germani*, the Teutonic barbarians who had overrun the Roman Empire and of whom Tacitus had extollingly written. De Boulainvilliers believed that, by virtue of their racial heritage, the "Frankish" nobles were destined to be superior—a superiority he insisted they re-establish through ending the absolute monarchy. By the same token, he portrayed the masses as of inferior stock, as the old conquered Gallo-Romans (Celts and Mediterraneans).[5]

But despite De Boulainvilliers' racist argument, the nobility did not prove to be eternally destined to hold their advantaged position. By the time of the French Revolution, in 1791, the "two Frances" into which De Boulainvilliers had divided the people had shifted their relative positions. The populace now had the upper hand. The Abbé Sieyès accepted the claims of the nobles that they had racially inherited the fruits of the Frankish conquest. "Very well, we, the Gallo-Roman plebs, will now conquer the nobility by expelling and abolishing them. Our rights will supersede theirs on exactly the principle they invoke." Indeed the tables had been turned! As Benedict writes, "a less pre-

[5] Benedict, *op. cit.*, 174–176.

tentious statement of the fundamental racist dogmas is that nothing succeeds like success." [6]

It was, however, the work of Count Arthur de Gobineau that established and crystallized the Aryan myth. In many respects De Gobineau is to racism what Karl Marx is to communism and Adam Smith to capitalism. Prior to De Gobineau, the "Aryan controversy" chiefly concerned itself with the location of the homeland of the Aryan language and people by philology and anthropology. As such it had lacked any racist connotations. De Gobineau turned the issue into one with racial implications. His meditations were offered in the four volumes of *Essay on the Inequality of Human Races* (1853–1857). He viewed the Germans as racially inferior to the French because of the former's greater biological mixture—itself a highly questionable hypothesis. It was the English, he argued, who were the truly superior race.

Concerning himself with the issue of why nations decline, De Gobineau stated that neither religious fanaticism, religious decay, luxury, licentiousness, corruption, nor cruelty explains such decline, for many nations flourish despite one or more of these conditions. For him the critical element was that of racial composition. It was race which dominated all major problems of history. Dedicating his work to George V of Hanover, he wrote:

Gradually I have become convinced that race overshadows all other problems in history, that it holds the key to them all, and that the inequality of people from whose fusion a people is formed is enough to explain the whole course of its destiny. I convinced myself at last that everything great, noble, and fruitful in the works of man on this earth, in science, art and civilization, derives from a single starting point; it belongs to one family alone, the different branches of which have reigned in all the civilized countries of the universe.

It was the Aryans who were the superior peoples, the rulers.

De Gobineau explained the destiny of peoples in terms of racial inequality: The superior race is capable of considerable progress and civilization, while others such as the American Indians are limited by their racial inheritance. All of the principal civilizations were the achievement of the Aryans, who formed the highest branch of the white race. He sought to make this aristocratic "Aryan" race conscious of its "mission" in the high purposes of civilization and to convince the non-Aryans of their duty to respect this "mission." He viewed race mixture as resulting in racial decay and cultural decline. De Gobineau did not state explicitly what constituted a race. He confused race as a

[6] *Ibid.*, 177.

biological division with an ethnic group integrated by common cultural traits.

At the end of the nineteenth century De Gobineau's theories were introduced into Germany mainly through the work of Houston Stuart Chamberlain. In 1899, Chamberlain's bulky *Foundations of the Nineteenth Century* appeared in two volumes. It was widely heralded in Germany and exercised considerable influence upon the Kaiser and other German leaders. For Chamberlain the entire German people represented the superior racial group—not only the early Germanic tribes Tacitus had described, but Celts and Slavs as well. Chamberlain assumed that the blood mixture abhorred by De Gobineau had in this instance prevented sterility and made for German greatness. He defined his Great Race in such a manner so as to rule out no member of the German nation: "Whoever reveals himself German by his acts, whatever his genealogical tree, is a German." Thus race for him had a pragmatic, loose meaning that could be employed at will in the service of German nationalism. He likewise expounded many of the racist pronouncements against the Jews which became associated with Nazi Germany. His racism was taken over in substance by Hitler and the National Socialist Party.

THE IDEOLOGY OF WHITE SUPREMACY

The Southern Segregationist Credo

An integral component of the southern racial order is a body of ideas supporting and justifying the system. These can be summarized as follows:

I. *Segregation is part of a natural order and is instinctive in human nature.*

> Segregation is a natural order—created by God, in His wisdom, who made black men black and white men white. Each man should be proud of his race and should constantly strive to preserve its purity.
>
> Louisiana State Senator W. M. Rainach, a segregationist leader [7]

A. *Segregation is not a moral question.*

> It is useless for me to argue whether the racial instinct [for segregation] is right or wrong—it exists.
>
> Former Governor James F. Byrnes of South Carolina [8]

[7] *Southern School News*, 1 (November, 1954), 3.
[8] James F. Byrnes, "Race Relations Are Worsening," *U.S. News & World Report*, XLII (February 22, 1957), 113.

B. *Segregation is natural and best.*

. . . separateness of races is natural and best . . . members
of each race prefer to associate with other members of their
race and . . . they will do so naturally unless they are prodded
and inflamed and controlled by outside pressures.

> Report of the North Carolina Ad-
> visory Committee on Education
> (Pearsall Committee)[9]

C. *We are not bigots.*

. . . racial segregation is not the off-spring of racial bigotry or
racial prejudice. It results from the exercise of a fundamental
American freedom—the freedom to select one's associates. . . .

This freedom is bottomed on a basic law of nature—the law
that like seeks like . . . man finds his greatest happiness when
he is among people of similar cultural, historical and social
backgrounds.

> U.S. Senator Sam J. Ervin (D–
> N.C.)[10]

II. *The Negro is a different kind of human being.*

A. *There is a divergence of opinion among southern whites as
to whether the Negro is necessarily biologically inferior to
whites.*

1. *The Negro is inferior to whites.*

History is not so much the record of the events of nations
as a whole as it is the chronicle of the contributed civilizations of the superior races. . . . The negro race, though
one of the oldest, has never built a worthy civilization.

> President D. M. Nelson, of Missis-
> sippi College, Clinton, Miss.[11]

2. *It is not necessarily a question of Negro inferiority or
white superiority.*

I don't want to argue it [that Negroes are inherently in-
ferior] with anybody, but I don't go along with that. It
doesn't sound quite Christian to me. They're human beings
just like everybody else.

> Mayor Kenneth Cass of Greenville,
> S.C.[12]

[9] *Southern School News,* 2 (May, 1956), 7.
[10] Sam J. Ervin, "The Case of Segregation," *Look,* 20 (April 3, 1956), 32–33.
[11] Dr. D. M. Nelson, *Conflicting Views on Segregation,* pamphlet of the Association of Citizens' Councils, n.d.
[12] Robert Wallace, "The Voices of the White South," *Life,* 41 (September 17,
1956), 110.

B. *But Negroes are different from whites.*

The traditions of the races are greatly different. The environment and background of the races are greatly different. Actually there are great social and emotional differences that quickly come to the surface when aroused. Their mental processes are different. . . .

U.S. Senator John C. Stennis (D–Miss.)[13]

C. *Negroes are more prone to violence and crime.*

You don't know what they're [Negroes] going to do. You're leery. They carry razors, knives, rape women. You can't trust them. Don't know what they'll do. I'm scared of them.

Woman in Baltimore, Maryland [14]

D. *The moral standards of Negroes are lower than those of whites.*

One out of every 105 white births [in Mississippi] were illegitimate or less than 1%. 24.7% of the negro births were illegitimate, which means that 247 out of every 1000 negro births were born out of wedlock. . . . This is proof of the well-known fact that our negroes as a race make a mockery of the white man's holy institution of matrimony.

Mississippi Citizens Council leaflet [15]

E. *The Negro has a lower capacity to learn.*

Now, the Negroes are—I think as a general proposition—generally more retarded in school than the white children. And I think this is rather important—it's probably one of the things you can't say in your paper—but a Negro of 14 may be in the fourth grade with a white girl of 10 or 11, and this Negro is a fully developed man, sexually. I think that is one of the things, I mean, there's a little fear in there.

C. P. Liter, editor of the Baton Rouge (La.) *Advocate & State Times* [16]

[13] John C. Stennis, "The Race Issue," *U.S. News & World Report,* 39 (November, 18, 1955), 90.

[14] William Brink and Louis Harris, *The Negro Revolution in America* (New York: Simon and Schuster, 1964), 140.

[15] *Crime Report Reveals Menace of Integration,* leaflet, Association of Citizens' Councils, n.d.

[16] "Race Trouble To Grow in South: Mixed Schools Not in Sight," *U.S. News & World Report,* 40 (February 25, 1956), 135.

F. *The Negro is irresponsible.*

> The Negro is irresponsible in every degree. I think it is a basic trait, although other conditions—environment, economics and education—contribute to his so-called lethargy.
>
> > A Charleston, S.C., utility executive [17]

III. *Racial amalgamation or intermarriage is bad and dangerous.*

A. *Racial intermarriage will result in racial suicide.*

> We publish to the world that we protest the attempts being made to desegregate the races, because we believe such would inevitably lead into a hybrid monstrosity that would defy the word and will of God.
>
> > Resolution of the Missionary Baptist Association of Texas [18]

B. *The Negro male has designs on white women.*

> The average Negro who wants integration is not interested in equal educational and economic advantages with the White race, and when these things are dangled before him by the NAACP he is unmoved, but when they whisper in his ear that someday he will be able to live with a White woman he is very interested.
>
> > Rev. Leon C. Burns, Pastor of the West Seventh Street Church of Christ, Columbia, Tenn.[19]

IV. *Our race relations are harmonious.*

> . . . our colored citizens are happy and they are proud of Jackson [Mississippi]. . . . There is no racial tension here. We are all living in harmony together.
>
> > Mayor Allen Thompson, of Jackson, Miss.[20]

A. *Look how much we are doing for our colored people!*

> In the past 90 years—1865–1955—the Negro race has made the most amazing progress which has ever been made in the history of man in any comparative period of time.
>
> That progress has been helped, in fact has been made possible, by the cooperation and assistance of the white race.
>
> > Report of the North Carolina Advisory Committee on Education (Pearsall Committee) [21]

[17] *Southern School News,* 3 (January, 1957), 3.
[18] *Southern School News,* 1 (December, 1954), 15.
[19] *Augusta Courier,* 2 (June 17, 1957), 3.
[20] *Southern School News,* 3 (February, 1957), 12.
[21] *Southern School News,* 2 (May, 1956), 7.

B. *We don't hate Negroes—we're their friends.*

. . . I'm not anti-black or anti-nigger. I work niggers. I still have five who have worked for me 32 years. But they're still niggers.

> David Hawkins, leader in the Mississippi Citizens Councils [22]

We love our colored folk, just love 'em. Why, we have a maid, worked for us 18 years, and when she went to the hospital last year I paid all bills—glad to do it.

> A white Mississippian [23]

C. *The Negroes are contented.*

I have yet to meet one [Negro] who told me they wanted their children to go to school with white children.

> U.S. Congressman Charles E. Bennett (D–Fla.)[24]

D. *Trouble is caused by outsiders.*

If there are racial tensions in Mississippi, it is an indisputable fact that the responsibility rests squarely on the political and pressure agitators from outside the South rather than upon the shoulders of our people.

> Governor Hugh White, of Miss.[25]

E. *Northerners are hypocrites on the race issue.*

Schools in the North have to be pretty black before they'll hire a Negro teacher. There's a lot of hypocrisy about that. I resent too much admonition from the North.

> Superintendent of Wayne County Schools, Ky.[26]

F. *The South is being persecuted by the rest of the nation.*

Propagandists and politicians have blown up stories about segregation until the rest of the country believes it is a dirty word. The Southern white man has been ridiculed and pilloried before the nation, and indeed throughout the world, until he is one of the underprivileged minorities of the earth.

> Thomas R. Waring, editor of the Charleston (S.C.) *News & Courier* [27]

---

[22] *Southern School News,* 1 (April, 1955), 3.
[23] *New South,* 12 (February, 1957), 10.
[24] *Southern School News,* 1 (November, 1954), 3.
[25] *Southern School News,* 2 (February, 1956), 15.
[26] *Southern School News,* 2 (October, 1955), 7.
[27] *Southern School News,* 3 (November, 1956), 13.

The Evolution of White-Supremacist Ideology

The notion that segregation is part of a natural order is a lineal descendant of the pre-Civil War position that slavery was based upon the "laws of nature," an argument appearing early in the southern ideological arsenal. In 1700 the first positive statement of the anti-slavery school appeared in Boston, written by Samuel Sewell, then Judge of the superior court. His pamphlet *The Selling of Joseph, A Memorial* received wide distribution. The following year John Saffin replied to Sewell in another pamphlet, in which was probably the first written defense of slavery in America. He vigorously denied the general principle of natural equality, insisting instead that inequality was a rule of the universe.[28]

Sewell's argument was actually a carry-over from the pre-Enlightenment period. Social and economic inequalities were justified as part of the "natural order" and God's ordained plan for the world. Human servitude, economic classes, social estates, and even the differing status of men and women were explained on this ground. The position had been strongly influenced by Aristotle and other Greek thinkers who had justified slavery in logic as conforming to nature.

The eighteenth and early nineteenth centuries witnessed a major challenge to this thinking. John Locke, among others, argued that there could be no slavery under the law of nature; rather, slavery resulted from the withdrawal of the protection of natural law. Such spokesmen insisted that all men had certain natural and inalienable rights, rights that were rooted in the laws of nature. The pro-slavery advocates countered this argument by pointing to the state of inequality that existed in nature. Southerners such as John C. Calhoun asserted that, instead of being free and equal in a natural state, men were "born subject, not only to parental authority, but to the laws and institutions of the country where born, and under whose protection they draw their first breath." [29]

George Frederick Holmes, an ante-bellum teacher in several southern colleges, sought historical support for the natural-law position of inequality. He argued that as slavery existed "in a very considerable degree under all forms of civilized society, we may consider it a necessary consequence of social organization (or may even go further and

---

[28] This account is in large part summarized from James W. Vander Zanden, "The Ideology of White Supremacy," *Journal of the History of Ideas*, 20 (1959), 385–402.

[29] William Sumner Jenkins, *Pro-Slavery Thought in the Old South* (Chapel Hill: The University of North Carolina Press, 1935), 126.

with Aristotle regard it as a necessary constituent thereof) and as this is admitted to be natural, so we may consider its consequences to be consonant with the laws of nature." [30] As the slaveholders viewed nature, variety and inequality characterized every work of the Great Creator; in other words, nature was governed by unerring laws "which command the oak to be stronger than the willow; and the cypress to be taller than the shrub." [31]

The "natural-order" argument continued as a major support of the caste order in the post-bellum period, finding frequent expression in the defense of the southern racial structure. Thus, in 1907, Bishop William Montgomery Brown, prominent official in the Protestant Episcopal Church, could write that race prejudice was a "deep-rooted, God-implanted instinct," [32] and that the "Anglo-American citizen is prevented by a law of nature from allowing the Afro-American to be associated with him in the government of these United States . . ." [33] Accordingly, Bishop Brown reasoned, "From every point of view, the conclusion is unavoidable that it is not only right for Anglo-Americans to recognize the Color-Line in the social, political and religious realms, but more than that it would be a great sin not to do so." [34]

Closely associated in history with the natural-order position has been the elaborate Biblical argument initially formulated in defense of slavery. It was no wonder that in 1863 the Presbyterian church, South, met in General Synod and passed a resolution declaring slavery to be a divine institution, ordained by God. In the ante-bellum period perhaps no argument carried greater weight in southern thinking on the slave issue than the Biblical argument. Broadly stated, it held that the Negro was a descendant of Noah's son Ham, cursed by God and doomed to be a servant forever on account of an ancient sin. The contemporary South has inherited this ideological bulwark. An Arkansas minister states the position in these words: "My conception is that God started it. He separated the brothers Shem, Ham and Japheth and put a curse on the descendants of Ham. In the light of this, since God started it, I will not try to desegregate the races."

The second major ideological premise of the southern segregationist credo—the Negro is a different kind of human being—similarly has an extended lineage. As was seen in Chapter 4, slavery was initially explained primarily on religious grounds, namely, that the Negro was a

[30] *Ibid.,* 135.
[31] *Ibid.,* 138.
[32] William Montgomery Brown, *The Crucial Race Question* (Little Rock, 1907), 118.
[33] *Ibid.,* 125.
[34] *Ibid.,* 135.

heathen. With the passing of time and the conversion of Negroes to Christianity, the infidel buttress no longer constituted a satisfactory defense of slavery. Gradually, the biological argument emerged as a principal tenet of white supremacy. Jenkins observes, "The inferiority of the Negro was almost universally accepted in the South by all groups of pro-slavery theorists as a great primary truth." [35]

In the early 1840's, under the impetus of the work of Dr. Josiah Clark Nott, a physician of Mobile, Alabama, the theory of a separate origin of the white and Negro races began to gain currency in the South. According to this view, the two races were endowed with a different original nature. This nature was viewed as permanent, incapable of physical or intellectual alteration. Not only was the barrier between the races insurmountable, but nature was seen as setting limits beyond which the Negro was totally incapable of improvement. Thus, "no philanthropy, no legislation, no missionary labors can change this law: it is written in man's nature by the hand of his Creator." [36]

In the decades following the Civil War three major ideological positions can be distinguished on the issue of Negro inferiority. The first group held that the Negro was by nature inferior to the white, and that, while as a race Negroes might achieve a certain degree of progress, still they could do so only under the pressure and guidance of the whites. Nevertheless, Negroes could never reach the white intellectual, cultural, moral, or physical level. It was the doctrine of *permanent* Negro inferiority. This position viewed the Negro as essentially a completed product of evolution, incapable of being assimilated by the whites. Enoch Spencer Simmons, a member of the North Carolina bar, articulated this position in these words:

While we give the negro credit for much and believe him capable of more progressive advancement, in the way of learning and civilization, yet we know he is an inferior race, who, under the most favorable conditions, will not and cannot ever achieve what his white friend can, because it is not the purpose of God, the great wise Creator, that he should. . . .[37]

The belief in inborn Negro inferiority was widely held throughout the South and was frequently set forth by southern spokesmen and ideologists. Thomas Nelson Page, southern novelist who romanticized the ante-bellum plantation system, firmly believed in "the absolute and

[35] Jenkins, *op. cit.*, 252.

[36] Josiah Clark Nott and George R. Gliddon, *Types of Mankind* (Philadelphia, 1854), 79.

[37] Enoch Spencer Simmons, *A Solution of the Race Problem in the South* (Raleigh, N.C., 1898), 30.

unchangeable superiority of the white race—a superiority . . . not due to any mere adventitious circumstances, such as superior educational and other advantages during some centuries, but an inherent and essential superiority, based on superior intellect, virtue, and constancy." [38] Some southerners carried the position to the point of an unreasoning fear of the Negro which amounted to a phobia. Serious proposals were advanced for removing the Negro from the South and transporting him to Africa or to a state to be newly created. Rabid anti-Negro books and tracts made their appearance, such as Charles Carroll's *The Negro a Beast*.

Today the belief in Negro racial inferiority is still widespread throughout the South, but it appears to be on the decline. In 1942 the National Opinion Research Center polled white southerners on this question: "In general, do you think Negroes are as intelligent as white people—that is, can they learn things just as well if they are given the same education and training?" Only some 20 per cent of the respondents replied affirmatively. To the same question fourteen years later, in 1956, the affirmative responses had risen to slightly better than 50 per cent of the respondents.

The second post-bellum ideological position on the issue of Negro inferiority was characterized by its conviction of Negro inferiority, but it was less certain as to the "permanence" of the inferiority. In appreciating this position, it is important to realize that, even as late as the early decades of the twentieth century, it was widely believed in scientific circles that culture was a genetically inherited rather than an environmentally transmitted property, a belief now discredited but still prevalent in popular thinking. Accordingly, the Negro was viewed as retarded, as thousands of years behind the white race in development. However, this second group was not prepared to rule out the possibility of the Negro "catching up" with the "superior race." But if the Negro were to "catch up," it would be necessary that he be "elevated" under the guidance and supervision of an advanced, civilized race.

A third group rejected the point of view that the Negro was an inferior, or sought to skirt the issue as a major consideration. Instead it held that the Negro race was "different" from the white race. The "difference" was essentially one of social heritage, a heritage in which the white had been advantaged, the Negro disadvantaged. As a consequence the races could be distinguished on the basis of traits peculiar to them, e.g., the nature of the moral code and practices generally

[38] Thomas Nelson Page, *The Negro: The Southerner's Problem* (New York, 1904), 292–293.

prevalent among them. This position more or less characterized the thinking of a number of southern clergymen including Edgar Gardner Murphy and Methodist Bishop Atticus G. Haygood.

Another major tenet in the southern ideological system revolves about interracial marriage and racial amalgamation. In the ante-bellum South a number of prominent scholars, the most noted of whom was Dr. Josiah Clark Nott, advanced the theory that the races were not intended to mix. Nott argued that the offspring of whites and Negroes would speedily merge into one or the other of the original types, or become extinct from defective organization. According to Nott, "the superior races ought to be kept free from all adulterations, otherwise the world will retrograde, instead of advancing, in civilization." [39]

After the Civil War the belief was invested with new highly accentuated emotional qualities as it became linked with the cult of white womanhood—the "woman on the pedestal" pattern. The Negro male was depicted as ruled by an inordinate sexual craving for white women, making all Negro men potential rapists. By the turn of the twentieth century the miscegenation (interbreeding of races) doctrine had been elevated to a cardinal position in the southern ideological system. In 1904 Edgar Gardner Murphy could write, "The doctrine of race integrity, the rejection of racial fusion, is, perhaps the fundamental dogma of Southern life." It is this doctrine on interracial marriage that in the last analysis constitutes the South's main defense of the segregated system. As many white southerners perceive the segregation issue, *the* question remains, "Would you want your sister (daughter) to marry a Negro?"

Other Racist Themes

Although the ideology of white supremacy has tended through the years to occupy the center of the stage, other currents and forces were operative as well. Periodically, there emerged various campaigns against immigration groups, which were accompanied by virulent ideological pronouncements. Illustrative of such movements was that which culminated in 1921 in the enactment of the Quota Act, an act designed to halt mass European migration to America. Following 1890, the immigrants, who since the earliest colonization were drawn from northern and western Europe, began to come primarily from southern and eastern Europe. American racists were alarmed by the large number of immigrants coming from Poland, the Balkans, and Italy, as opposed to the "old" stock English, Germans, and Scandi-

[39] Nott and Gliddon, *op. cit.,* 405.

navians. Playing a central role in the exclusion movement were a number of racist books of which Madison Grant's *The Passing of the Great Race* was among the most prominent.

Grant argued that in Europe "the amount of Nordic blood in each nation is a very fair measure of its strength in war and standing in civilization." [40] But in Europe he found the Nordics receding, for him a desperate state of affairs, which is reflected in the title of his book *The Passing of the Great Race.* A similar prospect awaited America if the older immigrant groups did not keep their dominant position. Grant asserted that down to the time of the Civil War the United States was "purely Nordic . . . not only Nordic but also purely Teutonic, a very large majority being Anglo-Saxon in the most limited meaning of that term." [41]

It was a position greatly influenced by De Gobineau and Chamberlain. Lothrop Stoddard's *Rising Tide of Color* was another influential racist book during this period that included the thesis that racial intermixture was harmful and that this had been the source of the downfall of the great civilizations.[42]

The Negro as a Contrast Conception

Lewis C. Copeland suggests that the relations between the two races within the South has given rise to a distinctive conception of the Negro.[43] Whites sharply distinguish themselves from Negroes, conceiving of the latter in terms of a marked contrast. It is a dichotomy analogous to that between God and the Devil in religion. The Devil is a contrast conception set in opposition to God and represents the antithesis of Christian values. Through the evolution of this polar dichotomy, Christian values are exalted and made all the more impressive. This dichotomy is seen as running through the whole universe, dividing the natural and social world into either the kingdom of God or the kingdom of the Devil. Moral beliefs tend to be characterized by such a polarization of values. There are numerous such counter-conceptions as male and female, light and darkness, hot and cold, up and down, all of which carry certain moral connotations of good and bad, benevolent and malevolent.

[40] Madison Grant, *The Passing of the Great Race* (New York: Charles Scribner's Sons, 1916), 175.

[41] *Ibid.*, 72–74.

[42] Lothrop Stoddard, *The Rising Tide of Color* (New York: Charles Scribner's Sons, 1920).

[43] Lewis C. Copeland, "The Negro as a Contrast Conception," in Edgar T. Thompson, ed., *Race Relations and the Race Problem* (Durham, N.C.: Duke University Press, 1939), 152–179.

Within the South, there has emerged a similar polarization of social values and beliefs regarding whites and Negroes. From the white point of view, the Negro stands as the antithesis of the character and properties of the white man. The distinction makes of the Negro a counter-race—an image which is polar to that of the white race. Thus a sharp, distinct delineation has appeared. The Negro functions as a foil, a backdrop, for whites, through which the character of the latter is made all the more impressive.

For southern whites, Negroes, the "opposite race," are conspicuously contrasted to themselves in physical and social traits. The traits ascribed to the Negro are a reflection of the status given him in the social order. Accordingly, Negroes are often seen as subhuman and brutish, altogether unlike whites. The color of Negroes and whites takes on a moral connotation. God is portrayed as white, the Devil as black. Whites assign themselves the traits of virtue, purity, and worth, godlike characteristics, while they assign to Negroes the contrasting traits, the characteristics of the Devil. Whites possess emotional control and restraint; Negroes lack it. Whites are capable of continuous affection and mental concentration; Negroes are incapable. Whites are clean and moral; Negroes are dirty and immoral.

Thus Negroes are frequently depicted as "immoral and promiscuous just like animals." Unlike white people, they are thought to have little or no moral restaint. A southern white asserts, "The Negro has degraded Southern morality. We cannot have any moral standards with so many free and easy Negro women running loose. Most every Negro wench is a prostitute. I don't call it seduction by white men, for what really happens is the Negro women seduce the white men. Sex is at the basis of the whole problem." [44] A southern white woman observes, "We must deplore the low morals of the Negro, but we just have to recognize that they have a code of morals of their own—jungle morals. It's different from ours, and lower, and they can't be expected to be any better. Just go listen to their church service some time. It's just like the tom-toms of the jungle." [45]

In many respects southern ideology has made the Negro a devil, a boogeyman, the epitome of evil. The Negro becomes a foil, a backdrop, that sets off white social values and whites as a group, magnifying white self-esteem and status. By implication, anyone who behaves in a "bad," "offensive," or "degraded" manner is a Negro or "niggerish." When a white is very repulsive, he is said to be "just like a Negro" or "as mean as a Negro." Such connotations are likewise reflected in a

[44] *Ibid.*, 158.
[45] *Ibid.*, 158.

wide range of common expressions. To "nigger oneself" is to degrade oneself. Since the Negro is the personification of the dangerous and fearful, he is the demon in life, "the nigger in the woodpile." Coarse cloth is "Negro-cloth," and rank cheap grades of black tobacco are "niggerhead twist."

The contrast conception of the Negro appears in fables, anecdotes, jokes, and literature. In order to sound natural, whites attribute to Negroes in such stories a markedly dialect speech, while in striking contrast the white characters speak in the most polished and stilted phrases. The things whites laugh at in Negro life are significant as they represent traits considered distinctive. Similarly, the conception of the white woman is in sharp contrast to that of the Negro woman. The white woman stands for the home, purity, virtue, and the like. In conceptual polarity the Negro woman stands as a symbol of degradation. Negro women in common southern speech are never "ladies." Negroes are "colored women"; whites are "ladies." The net result of such contrast conceptions is to pose a counter-race to the whites, which functions ideologically to produce cohesion within white society and provides whites with a common element of belief and sentiment.

THE THOMAS THEOREM

The Self-fulfilling Prophecy

A number of decades ago, W. I. Thomas, probably the dean of American sociologists, noted, "If men define . . . situations as real, they are real in their consequences."[46] Thomas was pointing to the fact that men respond not only to the objective features of a situation, but also to the meaning the situation has for them.[47] Once the meaning has been assigned, it serves to determine not only men's behavior, but also some of the consequences of that behavior. Accordingly, the act of making the definition is also an act of making a prophecy. The fact that the definition is made creates conditions whereby the prophecy will be realized. Thus the definition is a "self-fulfilling prophecy," a self-fulfilling anticipation.

Daily life provides numerous illustrations of the workings of this theorem. A student with ability adequate to pass an examination is convinced that he is destined to fail. Anxious, the student devotes more

[46] W. I. Thomas, "The Relation of Research to the Social Process," in *Essays on Research in the Social Sciences* (Washington, D.C.: The Brookings Institution, 1931), 189.

[47] Robert K. Merton, *Social Theory and Social Structure* (New York: The Free Press of Glencoe, 1957), 421–422.

time to worry than to study, his mind preoccupied with thoughts of failing the examination. In turn he takes the examination and fails. What has happened? Initially the student was in a situation in which he was objectively capable of passing the examination. But he defined the examination as one which he could not pass. He defined the situation as real, and accordingly the situation was real in its consequences. By virtue of his definition, his behavior was influenced in such a manner that it brought about the very result anticipated; he failed. His prophecy was self-fulfilling.

In the beginning the self-fulfilling prophecy is a false *definition of the situation.* The resulting consequences never would have come into being in the absence of the false definition or prophecy. But, after acceptance of the false definition, new behavior is evoked that makes the originally false state of affairs come true. One of the most difficult points to grasp in this connection is that there is no conspiracy to make the definition come true. Rather the fulfillment occurs unintentionally by virtue of individuals acting as if it were true, that is, in accordance with their beliefs.

The operation of the self-fulfilling prophecy can be seen in the realm of race relations. Whites define the Negro as inferior. The definition is accepted as gospel, as actual reality. Such a definition is not intended by the whites to accomplish Negro inferiority; it is accepted as fact. But flowing from such a definition are a series of consequences. Whites allocate to Negroes a lesser share in the privileges and opportunities of the society, since they believe Negroes to be "inferior." Whites believe it would be senseless to provide Negroes with more in the way of privileges and opportunities, as it would be of no avail. But in so doing the whites do not give Negroes a chance to prove or disprove the point. Rather the consequences are built into the white behavior. It results in the very inferiority that was alleged in the initial definition. Whites then see Negroes in menial jobs, with limited education, in poor housing, and with various health problems, and find it easy to conclude that Negroes *are* inferior. Although there is no scientific support for the notion of Negro inferiority, whites, believing the notion, serve to bring about a disadvantaged state for the great mass of Negroes. Indeed it then appears to them that Negroes are "inferior." The prophecy is self-fulfilling. The fact of having made the definition creates the conditions whereby the prophecy is realized.

Such an interpretation is useful in understanding the southern segregationist credo. White southerners holding such beliefs are not necessarily dishonest or engaged in deliberate deceit. Their ideas conform in part to their personal experience and observation, selective as these may be. The Negro's living standards, though rising, are still low; rates of extramarital households and illegitimacy, of tuberculosis and venereal disease, and of crimes against persons and property are considerably higher among Negroes than among whites; and results of standardized, national I.Q., achievement, reading and related tests from Virginia to Texas show consistently lower scores for Negro than for white children when taken as a racial group. The average southern white is not aware of the multitude of social and cultural facts and forces that have fostered these situations. He does not understand the operation of the self-fulfilling prophecy or of his role in its operation. Rather he associates such traits with the visible physical characteristics of the Negro and concludes that the Negro is inherently inferior or at the very least "different."

Merton cites an illustration of the operation of the self-fulfilling prophecy in the initial white approach to Negro unionization:

. . . our fair-minded white citizen strongly supports a policy of excluding Negroes from his labor union. His views are, of course, based not upon prejudice, but upon the cold hard facts. And the facts seem clear enough. Negroes, "lately from the nonindustrial South," are undisciplined in traditions of trade unionism and the art of collective bargaining. The Negro is a strikebreaker. The Negro, with his "low standard of living," rushes in to take jobs at less than prevailing wages. The Negro is, in short, "a traitor to the working class," and should manifestly be excluded from union organization.[48]

But, as Merton indicates, the unionist and his kind have produced the very "facts" which are observed. By defining the situation as one in which Negroes were held to be at odds with unionism and in which they were excluded from unions, a series of consequences were invited that made it difficult for many Negroes to avoid the role of a strikebreaker.

Likewise with Jews. Jewish immigrants, like other immigrants, initially tended to associate with other Jews. Gentiles came to consider Jews as especially clannish, and placed barriers in the way of Jewish association with them. Accordingly, the Jews were forced to associate more exclusively within their own group. In turn the gentiles say, "See, the Jews are always sticking together."

The Vicious Circle

The self-fulfilling prophecy may or may not be circular in character. If a self-fulfilling prophecy is circular, *the end is again the beginning*, the reassertion of the beginning, perhaps in a strengthened form. The

[48] *Ibid.,* 424.

student failing an examination is a case in point. Having failed one examination, the student's self-confidence may be further undermined, his anxiety intensified, such that his studying for subsequent examinations may be further impaired. Accordingly, he fails those examinations as well. Once set in motion the vicious-circle process goes on and on of its own momentum. This is seen historically in the typical case of international armament: "armament in country A→fear in country B→armament in country B→fear in country A→armament in country A, and so on *ad infinitum*—or *ad bellum*." [49]

Myrdal, in his study of American race relations, speaks of the "self-perpetuating color bar" and concludes that "discrimination breeds discrimination." [50] White prejudice and discrimination keep the Negro low in standards of living, health, education, manners, and morals. This in turn gives support to white prejudice. White prejudice and Negro standards thus mutually "cause" each other.[51] In this sense, discrimination begets discrimination. This can be depicted as follows: "discrimination→lower income level→lower standard of living→lower education→lower earning capacity→discrimination." [52]

The discriminating group begins with an advantage. It possesses greater power and usually other means by which to assert its advantaged position, and which enable it to discriminate. Through discrimination it cuts the other group off from a wide range of economic and social privileges and opportunities. The state and process of discriminating give the advantaged group a new consciousness of its superiority, reinforcing the discriminatory pattern. Such discrimination is in turn ratified by the factual evidences of inferiority that accompany the lack of opportunity and by the disadvantaged state of those who live and breed in poverty, who suffer repeated frustration, who have little incentive to improve their lot, and who feel themselves to be the outcasts of society. Accordingly, discrimination evokes both attitudes and modes of life favorable to its perpetuation in both the group discriminating and the group discriminated against.[53]

Myrdal suggests that by this means a vicious circle can ensue. On the one hand, the Negroes' plane of living is kept down by discrimination from the side of the whites. On the other hand, the whites' reason for discrimination is partly dependent upon the Negroes' plane of living. "The Negroes' poverty, ignorance, superstition, slum dwellings,

---

[49] R. M. MacIver, *The More Perfect Union* (New York: The Macmillan Co., 1948), 63.

[50] Gunnar Myrdal, *An American Dilemma* (New York: Harper & Row, 1944).

[51] *Ibid.*, 75.

[52] MacIver, *op. cit.*, 64.

[53] *Ibid.*, 67–68.

health deficiencies, dirty appearance, disorderly conduct, bad odor and criminality stimulate and feed the antipathy of the whites for them." [54] Their antipathy intensified, the whites increase their discrimination. As a consequence, the Negroes' plane of living suffers, and white antipathy is fed even more. Thus, through time, there occurs a progressive, cumulative intensification of prejudice and discrimination.

Myrdal sees the Negroes' "plane of living," however, as a composite entity which includes levels of Negro employment, wages, housing, nutrition, clothing, health, education, stability in family relations, manners, cleanliness, orderliness, trustworthiness, law observance, loyalty to society-at-large, absence of criminality, and so on. The vicious-circle hypothesis can also work in the reverse direction. A movement in any of the Negro variables in the direction toward the corresponding white level will tend to decrease white prejudice and discrimination. Furthermore, a rise in any single one of the Negro variables, Myrdal asserts, will tend to raise all the other Negro variables. Thus, a rise in employment will tend to increase earnings, raise standards of living, and improve health, education, manners, and law observance; similarly, a better education is assumed to raise the chances of a higher-salaried job.[55]

Such formulations, however, must be carefully interpreted or they may mislead. Social systems are not indefinitely plastic. There are limits to the variation which occurs within them. The endless cumulation of effects is checked by such factors as the need for a certain amount of order, beyond which a system cannot proceed without disruption. Likewise, each variable in the situation is sustained by the others. If one is changed, there will be the pull and push of the others to bring it back into line. Furthermore, a given line of development may have one series of consequences at one stage and different or even opposite effects at later stages. Thus, whites may go along with Negro advancement in employment while such advancement is minimal or moderate, but, as the more crucial ingredients in the caste employment picture are approached, whites may respond with an intense reaction that may eventuate in a reversion to previous patterns.

It should also be noted that the vicious circle is not a creator of prejudice; it does not tell us how it comes into being. Rather it contributes to our understanding of how group prejudice is maintained— how it is sustained. There is still another limitation to the vicious-circle interpretation. The support of "the facts" is not essential to prejudice, as has been shown by the elaborate cultural equipment for

[54] Myrdal, op. cit., 1066.
[55] Ibid., 1066–1067.

prejudice that most Americans share even when they know no facts or when they have had no contact with the people toward whom the prejudice refers.

AN AMERICAN DILEMMA

The Myrdal Hypothesis

In 1944, after some three years of intensive study by a number of scholars and experts under the direction of Gunnar Myrdal, a major work in the field of American race relations appeared, *An American Dilemma*. The book immediately won wide recognition as a monumental work. The study was financed with funds secured under a grant from the Carnegie Corporation. Desiring to initiate a study with a fresh approach, uninfluenced by traditional attitudes and biases or earlier conclusions, the Carnegie Corporation "imported" as the general director of the study a Swedish social economist, Gunnar Myrdal.

The central thesis of the study is that, despite economic, social, and political factors, at bottom the race issue in America is an ideological question. The "American dilemma" is a moral dilemma:

. . . the ever-raging conflict between, on the one hand, the valuations preserved on the general plane which we shall call the "American Creed," where the American thinks, talks, and acts under the influence of high national and Christian precepts, and, on the other hand, the valuations on specific planes of individual and group living, where personal and local interests; economic, social, and sexual jealousies; considerations of community prestige and conformity; group prejudice against particular persons or types of people; and all sorts of miscellaneous wants, impulses, and habits dominate his outlook.[56]

The main norms of the American creed are centered in the belief in the common brotherhood of man as found in Christian teachings and the belief in equality and in the rights of liberty as found in the Declaration of Independence. It is the democratic creed—"all men are created equal"—a creed of equality and liberty. But contrasted with the creed is American racial and ethnic practice, an America of prejudice and discrimination. The creed and the practice are in conflict with one another. The result "is a problem in the heart of the American," a conflict that tears at his being.

According to Myrdal, a large amount of guilt is to be found among the dominant group regarding a segregated social system; the Negro problem "makes for moral uneasiness." [57] "The moral struggle goes on within people and not only between them." [58] A similar theme appears

[56] *Ibid.*, xlvii.
[57] *Ibid.*, xlv.
[58] *Ibid.*, xlviii.

in Rose's summary presentation of the Myrdal study. Rose indicates that our nation "labors persistently with its moral problems. It is taking its Creed very seriously indeed." [59] Or again: "Even a poor and uneducated white person in some isolated and backward rural region in the Deep South, who is violently prejudiced against the Negro and intent upon depriving him of civic rights and human independence, has also a compartment in his mind housing the entire American Creed of liberty, equality, justice, and fair opportunity for everybody." [60] This point of view has been a common assumption in American literature on race relations.

Thus central to Myrdal's thesis is the role of ideas: ". . . the Negro problem has its existence in the American's mind. There the decisive struggle goes on." [61] The "Negro problem," as Myrdal sees it, does not consist of, or have close relations with, various social trends in the economic, social, or political sense. If changes are to occur, they must occur in people's beliefs and valuations. Social trends are important only in so far as they influence what is in white people's minds. It is a point of view which enjoys considerable popular appeal.

A Critique of the Myrdal Hypothesis

Myrdal's position has not gone unchallenged. The major criticism directed at the conception of an "American dilemma" is that for Americans in general and southern whites in particular there actually is not any great moral dilemma, nor moral uneasiness on the matter. Cornell University sociologists, as part of a larger study in the early 1950's, asked a sample of southern whites in Savannah, Georgia, "Do you ever feel guilty about the way Negroes are treated—would you say never, sometimes, or fairly often?" Eight per cent replied "often," 33 per cent "sometimes," and 57 per cent "never." In fairness to Myrdal, however, it should be noted that the question rests upon the shaky assumption that people are aware of guilt, whereas guilt feelings are often unconscious.[62]

Golightly suggests that feelings of guilt result from the violation of group ideals that the individual accepts as a member of the group. The racial system and its accompanying practices are not defined for white southerners as a violation of their group ideals; rather the southern subculture defines the white-Negro race structure as desir-

[59] Arnold Rose, The Negro in America (New York: Harper & Row, 1944), 8.
[60] Ibid., 10.
[61] Myrdal, op. cit., 998.
[62] Robin M. Williams, Jr., Strangers Next Door (Englewood Cliffs, N.J.: 1964), 69–71.

able and appropriate. Whites need feel no guilt over personal discrimination against Negroes. In fact, the individual white is more apt to experience guilt or to suffer punishment if he violates the traditional patterns than if he practices discrimination.[63]

For a great many Americans the creed is not simply transmitted as a set of values pertinent to racial issues. The situation is analogous to Greek democracy, where democracy was accepted, but only for a segment of the population. Similarly in the South, although democracy is a deep and embedded value, it is democracy primarily for whites. Large numbers of southern whites do not see democracy as extending to Negroes anymore than Americans generally see democracy as extending to children (for instance, in the realm of voting rights). The doctrine of Negro inferiority or "differences" serves to place the Negro beyond the pale of the American democratic creed. This is illustrated by an experience of the author while walking near a Negro section in Augusta, Georgia. As he was passing a number of white children who were hurling stones and insults at a nearby group of Negro children, he inquired of the former, "Why are you throwing stones at those children?" They replied, "Mister, they ain't children, they're niggers!"

Campbell and Pettigrew, in a study of the performance of ministers during the Little Rock crisis in 1957 and 1958, conclude that neither the small-sect minister, typically segregationist and vocal, nor the denomination minister, typically integrationist and silent, gave significant evidence of guilt. They suggest that social isolation and hostile attitudes shelter the sect and segregationist ministers from communications that might force the moral issue, and that a southern segregationist credo further protects them. The integrationist, denomination ministers, on the other hand, defended themselves on the moral issue by values and beliefs centered around the obligations of their occupational role, e.g., the need to avoid alienating their congregations.[64] In still another study, of 279 students in a southern university, Campbell found that the Myrdal formulation was a drastic simplification of the normative dimensions of the issue.[65]

[63] Cornelius L. Golightly, "Race, Values and Guilt," *Social Forces*, 26 (1947), 132.

[64] Ernest Q. Campbell and Thomas F. Pettigrew, *Christians in Racial Crisis: A Study of the Little Rock Ministry* (Washington, D.C.: The Public Affairs Press, 1959).

[65] Ernest Q. Campbell, "Moral Discomfort and Racial Segregation: An Examination of the Myrdal Hypothesis," *Social Forces*, 93 (1961), 228–234. For a conceptual analysis of Myrdal's thesis, see Nahum Z. Medalia, "Myrdal's Assumptions on Race Relations: A Conceptual Commentary," *Social Forces*, 40 (1962), 223–227.

Discrimination and the American Creed

It would be a mistake to conclude that the American creed is a fixed and static cultural constant, unmodified in the course of time. Like any other aspect of culture, it is dynamic and subject to change. Nor does the creed exert the same measure of control over behavior in diverse times and places. To the extent to which the creed is a "sacred" and hallowed part of tradition, it is largely immune from direct attack. But, as is true of a great many other such traditions, it may be honored simply in the breach. Where the creed is at odds with other beliefs and practices it may be evaded, persisting as an empty cultural form partly because it is so flexible. There are many avenues available for conscientiously ignoring the creed in practice. Or, again, the creed may be reinterpreted in a manner consistent with practice. This, as we have seen, is what a large number of southern whites have done; by virtue of the segregationist credo, Negroes are placed beyond the pale of the creed. Accordingly, many Americans systematically deny through daily conduct what they affirm on periodic ceremonial or public occasions.[66]

It was this gap between creed and conduct, this disparity between ethos and behavior, which we have seen was central to Myrdal's study. Merton feels that such an analysis by itself is too simple. It is, Merton suggests, a relation between three values, not merely the two variables of official creed and private practice. The third variable Merton adds is that of the beliefs and attitudes of individuals regarding the principles of the creed. By the addition of this third variable a new distinction becomes apparent. Individuals may recognize the creed as an integral ingredient of their cultural tradition, without having any private conviction on its moral validity or its binding quality. So far as beliefs are concerned, two types can be identified: those individuals who genuinely believe in the creed and those who do not. Likewise, with respect to actual practice, two types can be identified: those individuals whose conduct does and those whose conduct does not conform to the creed.

Merton [67] formulates a logical syntax whereby the variables are diversely combined, forming the following typology of ethnic prejudice and discrimination.

[66] Robert K. Merton, "Discrimination and the American Creed," in R. M. MacIver, ed., *Discrimination and National Welfare* (New York: Harper & Row, 1949), 100–101.
[67] *Ibid.*, 103.

	Attitude Dimension: Prejudice and Non-prejudice [*]	*Behavior Dimension: Discrimination and Non-discrimination* [*]
I. Unprejudiced non-discriminator	+	+
II. Unprejudiced discriminator	+	−
III. Prejudiced non-discriminator	−	+
IV. Prejudiced discriminator	−	−

[*] Where (+) = conformity to the creed, and (−) = deviation from the creed.

Thus four major types can be identified in terms of their attitudes toward the creed and their behavior with respect to it. Each type can be found in every region of the nation and within every social class, though in varying numbers. Each of the types can now be examined more closely.[68]

Type I: The Unprejudiced Non-discriminator or All-Weather Liberal. This individual adheres to the creed in both belief and practice, and thus is neither prejudiced nor given to discrimination. The individuals of this group occupy a strategic position, Merton believes, in efforts to spearhead campaigns against prejudice and discrimination.

Type II: The Unprejudiced Discriminator or Fair-Weather Liberal. This individual is a man of expediency who, despite his own absence of prejudice, supports discriminatory practices when it is the easier or more profitable course. His expediency tends to take the form of silence, acquiescing in expressions of prejudice and discrimination. He is concerned lest he lose status or otherwise be penalized by his prejudiced associates. He may refuse to hire Negroes because "it may hurt business."

Type III: The Prejudiced Non-discriminator or Fair-Weather Illiberal. This individual is the reluctant conformist to the creed, the man of prejudice who does not believe in it but conforms for fear of being penalized. He is the prejudiced employer who discriminates against minorities until legal measures are brought to bear against him; the trade-union leader who although deeply prejudiced does away with Jim Crow in his union because of rank-and-file demands; and the businessman who foregoes his own prejudices when he finds a profitable market among minorities.

Type IV: The Prejudiced Discriminator or the All-Weather Illiberal. This individual is the bigot pure and unashamed, the man of prejudice who is consistent in his departures from the creed. He believes that differ-

[68] *Ibid.*, 103–110.

ential treatment of minority groups is not discrimination, but discriminating. Within wide areas of the South he is a social conformist; elsewhere in the nation he often tends to be a social deviant in terms of his attitudes and behavior toward minorities.

CONCLUSION

The study of ideology is useful in the consideration of ethnic and racial relations. The ideas that men hold have major consequences for their behavior. We have seen how men, by defining a situation as real—by accepting a false definition—can evoke new behavior that makes the originally false state of affairs come true. Such definitions and behavior can then get caught in the web of a vicious circle, in which the process goes on and on of its own momentum. Major sets of ideas may be in conflict with practice, confronting people, as Myrdal suggests, with a moral dilemma. Yet, although providing useful insights, ideological interpretations standing by themselves are inadequate for a comprehensive understanding of race and ethnic relations.

6

Personality Factors

The various factors of prejudice that we have thus far considered have dealt primarily with man's relation to man and to groups of men. Accordingly, the theories have frequently been referred to as "group-centered" approaches. In contrast to the "group-centered" approaches are those that are "personality-centered." Rather than focusing upon what occurs *between* people, "personality-centered" theories stress what occurs *within* people. These latter theories attempt to explain dominant-minority relations primarily in personality terms. Since prejudice is a state of mind, and as such is "carried" in specific individuals, some social scientists have looked for the sources of prejudice within the individual personality. These social scientists are often quite critical of "group-centered" social scientists who they feel view individuals as "interchangeable specimens of gutless creatures." [1]

The major insights that these theories contain are in many instances derived from psychoanalytic work. As has been true in our consideration of other factors of prejudice, we shall have to place strictures or limits upon the enthusiasm that has been evidenced by some theorists. This critical note will not in the least diminish our indebtedness to Sigmund Freud and the various psychoanalytic schools.

[1] Theodore M. Newcomb, "Sociology and Psychology," in John Gillin, ed., *For a Science of Social Man* (New York: The Macmillan Company, 1954), 237.

FRUSTRATION AND AGGRESSION

The Scapegoat Theory of Prejudice

One of the most, if not *the* most, popular of the various theories of prejudice is the scapegoat theory.[2] The major postulates of the theory are the following:

1. *Needs.* An individual experiences a variety of needs, be they induced biologically (hunger, thirst, sex, sleep, etc.) or socially (various rewards, rights, privileges, etc.).

2. *Frustration.* For one reason or another an individual often finds himself blocked from realizing his needs or desires. In a word, the individual is *frustrated.*

3. *Aggression.* A frustrated individual experiences anger which disposes him toward aggressive actions. Blocked in realizing his needs or desires (especially where the blockage is repeated and persistent), he becomes enraged; he wants to strike out, to destroy, to tear to pieces.

4. *Displacement.* An enraged person needs to vent his emotions and it makes little or no difference against whom he directs his aggressive feelings. If some specific person is guilty of contributing to his frustration, he will tend to direct his aggression against him. But at times this is not possible. It may be dangerous to attack another, especially if the person is a powerful figure. Thus a child frustrated by his parents or a student thwarted by a professor cannot generally strike back at the source; it would be too dangerous. Similarly frustration may stem not only from identifiable persons but from some impersonal event, "fate," pervasive source, or even one's own acts or thoughts of commission and omission. In such circumstances, there is no direct external source against whom one can retaliate. Nevertheless, the impulse to vent anger persists. Under such circumstances people unconsciously, at times consciously, tend to seek out a person, group, or object on which to "take out" their feelings, to find a "scapegoat." When hostilities are removed from the source or sources of frustration and discharged upon a scapegoat, the process is referred to as *displacement.* Displacement appears to be a common practice—for example,

---

[2] As examples of the scapegoat approach, see: John Dollard, *et al., Frustration and Aggression* (New Haven: Yale University Press, 1939); Talcott Parsons, "The Sociology of Modern Anti-Semitism," in Isacque Graeber and S. H. Britt, eds., *Jews in a Gentile World* (New York: The Macmillan Co., 1942), 101–122; Ellis Freeman, "The Motivation of Jew-Gentile Relationships," *Ibid.*, 149–178; Leonard Berkowitz, *Aggression: A Social Psychological Analysis* (New York: McGraw-Hill Book Company, Inc., 1962), chapter 6; and Aubrey J. Yates, *Frustration and Conflict* (London: Methuen & Co. Ltd., 1962), chapter 3.

more than one person has complained to a frustrated friend after receiving an unwarranted attack from him, "Don't take it out on me."

5. *Weak Victims.* Some sources for the displacement of hostile aggression are preferable to others, namely, those people who are too weak or defenseless to strike back, who are incapable of returning aggression with retaliatory aggression. They become the innocent victims of aggression. The student enraged by a poor grade, unable to retaliate against the professor, may respond to a trivial remark or act of a roommate with harsh, angry, and abusive words. The husband who encounters difficulties and irritations at work comes home in the evening ready, upon the slightest provocation, to snap at family members and vent his anger. Family members learn to watch for cues of such feelings, to "soft-pedal" requests, and to behave under such circumstances as unobtrusively as possible.

Aggression may also be deflected toward minorities, since they are generally portrayed as too weak or defenseless to strike back. A World War II veteran, commenting upon the possibility of unemployment during a depression, spontaneously asserts:

> We'd better not have it. Chicago'll blow wide open. On South Park the niggers are gettin' so smart. We'll have a race riot that'll make Detroit look like a Sunday School picnic. So many are bitter about the part the Negro played in the war. They got all the soft jobs—in the quartermasters, engineers. They're no good for anything else. The white got his ass shot off. They're pretty bitter. If both whites and niggers get laid off, that'll be bad. I'm gonna eat. I know how to use a gun.[3]

The southern reaction to Negroes following the Civil War can in part be understood as displaced hostility stemming from prevailing social disorganization and resentment toward the North. After the bloody Civil War the South turned its spent and fruitless hostility to the Negroes. Since southerners could not avenge themselves directly against the North, they turned their aggression against the Negroes, for whom the North had fought. To punish the Negroes represented a kind of deflected expression of hostility toward the victors, who had won the actual war but who could not win the fight for Negro freedom. Negroes and Yankees tend to be associated in the mind of the white southerner. Northern pressure upon the South often is followed by increased southern pressure on the Negro rather than by melioration of the Negro's lot.[4]

[3] Bruno Bettelheim and Morris Janowitz, *Dynamics of Prejudice* (New York: Harper & Row, 1950), 82.
[4] John Dollard, *Caste and Class in a Southern Town,* 3d ed. (New York: Doubleday & Co., Inc., 1957), 59.

6. *Rationalization.* Generally the expression of hostile impulses toward one's fellow men is discouraged, even prohibited by moral and ethical considerations, by norms. To "take out" one's feelings upon an innocent individual or group would conflict even more with such norms. Given the democratic creed of America, such behavior would bespeak rank injustice, hatred, and irrationality. It would tend to offend one's feelings of self-pride, morality, and intelligence. If one is to avoid feelings of self-condemnation, of guilt, it is essential that some excuse be available to sanction such behavior. The behavior, otherwise immoral, must be made to appear both rational and acceptable morally. What is rationally and morally inappropriate must be made appropriate. Humans are quite ingenious in coming up with excuses for their behavior. This process is referred to as *rationalization.* Individuals justify their behavior by finding some convincing reason why they can hate and discriminate against a minority group. Accordingly, a racist ideology tends to be evolved. People can then rationalize: "I hate Negroes because they are criminally inclined, dirty, immoral, lazy, and irresponsible." In this manner they can feel justified for their feelings.

Experimental Evidence of Scapegoating

Any number of studies have been conducted in an attempt to test the scapegoating hypothesis experimentally. One of the earliest of these was undertaken by Miller and Bugelski.[5] The subjects of the experiment were thirty-one young men between the ages of eighteen and twenty, working at a CCC camp. The researchers learned that the young men were about to experience a frustrating situation. As part of the educational program of the camp, they were going to be required to take a long, uninteresting test, a test promising to be so difficult that everyone was bound to fail miserably. Furthermore, the test would run far overtime so that the young men would miss what they had looked forward to as the most interesting event of the otherwise dull week: bank night at the local theater. This event was awaited with special eagerness, as the previous week one member of the group had won $200.

Accordingly, two frustrating experiences were awaiting the men. To the extent to which they were motivated to succeed on the tests, they were bound to experience frustration by virtue of failure. To the extent to which they were motivated to attend bank night, they were

[5] Neal E. Miller and Richard Bugelski, "Minor Studies of Aggression: II. The Influence of Frustrations Imposed by the In-Group on Attitudes Expressed Toward Out-Groups," *Journal of Psychology,* 25 (1948), 437–442.

bound to experience frustration by the interference of the testing program. The frustration and aggressive feelings that the experimenters anticipated under these circumstances were confirmed. Before and after the frustrating situation, the young men were tested as to their attitudes toward a number of minority groups. It was found that after the frustrating situations there was a definite decrease in the number of favorable items checked. The experimenters concluded that aggression aroused by the in-group authorities in blocking the desires of these young men were generalized and displaced to the out-group minorities. The production of generalized feelings of hostility appears to be particularly great when the frustration experienced is unreasonable, unjust, and unnecessary.[6]

Not all studies have confirmed the scapegoating hypothesis.[7] However, more recent investigations, especially those since 1958, have generally lent support to it.[8] Moreover, these recent studies have identified some of the limitations of the earlier experiments that failed to produce evidence of scapegoating. Experiments in scapegoating generally set up a situation in which the experimental subjects are made to fail in a task, are insulted by the experimenter, or are blocked from achieving some goal in which they are interested. Such frustration is presumed to create aggression that would reflect itself in an increase in prejudice as measured by attitude tests administered after the frustrating experience. The studies vary considerably, however, in the method by which subjects are frustrated, the measure of prejudice used, and the overall situation that defines the experimental context.

[6] N. Pastore, "A Neglected Factor in the Frustration-Aggression Hypothesis: A Comment," *Journal of Psychology*, 25 (1948), 271–279.

[7] See Bohdan Zawadzki, "Limitations of the Scapegoat Theory of Prejudice," *Journal of Abnormal and Social Psychology*, 43 (1948), 127–141; Gardner Lindzey, "Differences Between the High and Low in Prejudice and Their Implications for a Theory of Prejudice," *Journal of Personality*, 19 (1950), 16–40; Nancy C. Morse and Floyd H. Allport, "The Causation of Anti-Semitism: An Investigation of Seven Hypotheses," *Journal of Psychology*, 34 (1953), 197–233; and Ross Stagner and Clyde S. Congdon, "Another Failure to Demonstrate Displacement of Aggression," *Journal of Abnormal and Social Psychology*, 51 (1955), 659–696.

[8] See Emory Cowen, Judah Landes, and Donald E. Schaet, "The Effects of Mild Frustration on the Expression of Prejudiced Attitudes," *Journal of Abnormal and Social Psychology*, 58 (1959), 33–38; Leonard Berkowitz, *op. cit.*, chapter 6; Seymour Feshbach and Robert Singer, "The Effects of Personal and Shared Threats upon Social Prejudice," *Journal of Abnormal and Social Psychology*, 54 (1957), 411–416; Donald Weatherley, "Anti-Semitism and the Expression of Fantasy Aggression," *Journal of Abnormal and Social Psychology*, 62 (1961), 454–457; and George Stricker, "Scapegoating: An Experimental Investigation," *Journal of Abnormal and Social Psychology*, 67 (1963), 125–131.

Some Limitations of the Scapegoat Theory

The scapegoat theory undoubtedly provides some useful insights concerning sources of prejudice. Yet the explanation of prejudice is complex; it cannot be explained in terms of one mechanism. Standing by itself the theory suffers from a number of limitations:

1. Frustration does not always result in aggression. Reaction to frustration depends upon the set of circumstances and the individual's perception and evaluation of them. Frustration may not result in aggression at all. The individual may respond with some new or added effort by which to realize his goal. Or a substitute goal may be sought instead. Then, again, the individual may respond with regression, a lowering of his level of performance, an evasion of the situation by leaving it or "going out of the field," or by apathy and resignation. The reaction to frustration varies according to the circumstances and the individual's perception of them.[9]

2. Even should frustration foster aggressive impulses, aggression need not be displaced. Some individuals are intrapunitive—they direct their aggressive impulses inward against themselves rather than outward against the outside world. Such individuals tend to "bottle up" their rage—to take their rage out on themselves—a fact that symptomatically may express itself in headaches, ulcers, psychological depression, and so on. Ackerman and Jahoda indicate that among their anti-Semitic patients they failed to find any cases of deep depression, a fact that they attribute to the tendency of anti-Semites to handle rage through attacks upon others (extrapunitiveness) as opposed to intrapunitive reactions.[10]

3. The scapegoat theory fails to explain why a particular minority is selected for displacement where there are several to choose from.[11] Thus recourse has to be had to other theories to understand the choice of scapegoats—why some minorities are overlooked, others are hated, and still others are liked.

4. The scapegoat theory fails to explain why there is a striking difference in intensity of dislike toward different minorities.[12] As has been

[9] H. Himmelweit, "Frustration and Aggression: A Review of Recent Experimental Work," in T. H. Pear, ed., *Psychological Factors of Peace and War* (New York: Philosophical Library, Inc., 1950).

[10] Nathan W. Ackerman and Marie Jahoda, *Anti-Semitism and Emotional Disorder* (New York: Harper & Row, 1950), 243. Also see Gerald S. Lesser, "Extrapunitiveness and Ethnic Attitude," *Journal of Abnormal and Social Psychology,* 56 (1958), 281–282.

[11] Zawadzki, *op. cit.,* 127–141.

[12] *Ibid.*

noted in Chapter 3, the social-distance scales for the various minorities differ.

5. The scapegoat theory fails to explain why minorities at times displace their hostilities against dominant groups. For such minorities the dominant group is not a defenseless target; in fact, it may be quite powerful. The scapegoat may not always be a "safe goat" as the theory tends to imply.[13]

White and Lippitt, in a study of the impact of dictatorial adult leadership upon boys in a youth club, come to somewhat similar conclusions. Presumably the boys were frustrated by the autocratic behavior of the adult, but being afraid to aggress against him, "took out" their resentment upon other club members. But the scapegoats were never the weakest or most passive boys in the club. The boys singled out for aggression in one group "were both boys who could hold their own against any of the others taken singly," while in another club the scapegoat was the largest and heaviest boy. White and Lippitt argued that such scapegoats would not have been chosen if the sole aim of the aggression were to blow off steam safely; easier and safer targets supposedly would have been selected.[14]

6. The scapegoat theory tends to overlook the possibility of realistic social conflict. What may appear to be displacement in some instances may be aggression directed against the true source of the frustration.[15] This is especially likely where economic, power, or status competition occurs.

Some Modifications in the Scapegoat Theory

Our observations about the limitations of the scapegoat theory do not necessarily invalidate it. They do suggest, however, that a number of other factors or variables need to be taken into account. Let us examine a few of these:

1. *The Personality of the Displacer.* Berkowitz holds that highly prejudiced individuals will displace aggression more than non-prejudiced individuals when confronted with equally frustrating situations. In other words, whether or not displacement occurs depends not merely upon the objective fact of frustration or upon the availability of objects for displacement, but also upon the personality of the individual. Berkowitz's experiment involved female college students that had

[13] *Ibid.* and Gordon W. Allport, *The Nature of Prejudice* (Boston: Beacon Press, Inc., 1954), 351.

[14] R. K. White and R. Lippitt, *Autocracy and Democracy: An Experimental Inquiry* (New York: Harper & Row, 1960), 166.

[15] Allport, *op. cit.*, 351–352.

scored either very high or very low on an anti-Semitism attitude scale. These students were individually subjected either to an annoying, frustrating treatment by the experimenter or to a more neutral, non-frustrating experience with him. After this treatment, the girls were given a topic to discuss with another girl, but unknown to them this girl was actually the experimenter's confederate. A questionnaire rating by the confederate immediately after the conclusion of the discussion constituted the hostility index. In comparison with the nonfrustrated, highly anti-Semitic girls, the frustrated highly anti-Semitic girls gave evidence of increased unfriendliness toward their peer (in reality the confederate). On the other hand, tolerant coeds who received the harsh treatment displayed greater friendliness to the other girls. For the highly anti-Semitic girls, then, the hostility engendered by the frustrating experimenter presumably displaced to the neutral bystander; this displacement did not occur in the less prejudiced group. Similar results were obtained when the confederate was given a "Jewish" name. Hence, Berkowitz concludes that highly prejudiced individuals are more prone to scapegoating than less prejudiced individuals.[16]

2. *The Kind of Frustration Involved.* A number of social scientists have suggested that people are more likely to scapegoat in response to some kinds of frustration than others. Feshbach and Singer investigated this possibility in differing responses to personal and shared threats.[17] While a personal threat poses a danger primarily to the individual himself, a shared threat constitutes a danger to the larger society of which an individual is a part. Feshbach and Singer randomly assigned the members of introductory psychology classes to six groups: three personal threat groups (marital failure, mental illness, and severe personal injury), two shared threat groups (the danger of flood and hurricane and the possibility of atomic war), and a control group (a group that was exposed to none of the threats and to which the other five groups were later compared).

Tests measuring attitudes toward Negroes were administered to the students. Four weeks later five of the groups (but not the control group) were asked to discuss mimeographed statements about one of the five threats (each group receiving statements concerning a different threat). After the discussions, attitudes toward Negroes were again measured in each of the five groups and the control group. All three of the personal threat groups gained significantly in prejudice beyond the change in the control group. On the other hand, the flood and hurricane group experienced an appreciable decline in prejudice

16 Berkowitz, *op. cit.*, 143–144.
17 Feshbach and Singer, *op. cit.*, 411–416.

toward Negroes. Feshbach and Singer suggest that this was perhaps a result of a sense of shared fate. The group discussing the threat of an atomic war, however, displayed a gain in prejudice. It is conceivable that the frequent linkage of atomic war with the Soviet Union resulted in hostility to Russians, which the students in turn then displaced upon Negroes. In conclusion, this study by Feshbach and Singer suggests that some kinds of frustration are more likely to produce scapegoating than others.

3. *The Perceived Qualities of Potential Targets.* Critics of the scapegoat hypothesis have noted that aggression is not always displaced upon an innocent victim or upon the safest available target. This has led some social scientists to raise this question: Are some groups commonly perceived in such a fashion that they constitute particularly vulnerable or susceptible targets for the displacement of aggression? Berkowitz and his associates answer the question in the affirmative. Experimentally they have demonstrated that hostility will be displaced from the frustrater to another individual in direct ratio to the degree of dislike for this latter person.

In their experiments Berkowitz and his associates administered shocks to individuals who were working as partners on a common task. The subjects believed the shocks were applied by their partner and hence they acquired a dislike for him. Later the subjects were frustrated by one of the experimenters. The frustrated subjects were then presented with a task involving two potential targets for their hostility: the person they had been trained to dislike and a neutral individual. The study revealed that the frustrated subject directed considerably more aggression against the disliked person than against the neutral person. Berkowitz concludes that groups used as scapegoats are groups that individuals for one reason or another have *already* learned to dislike.

Berkowitz suggests still another point. A disliked group can be associated with an immediate frustrater, permitting the transfer of hostility aroused by the latter to the former. Hence, an industrial worker may become more hostile to the Jews in his community after receiving a cut in pay if he associates the disliked Jews with the non-Jewish factory owners. The worker may regard both the factory owners and Jews as rich and unscrupulous. Frustrated, he identifies Jews with the immediate frustrater (the factory owner), and displaces his rage from the factory owners to Jews.[18]

4. *The Role of Culture.* Whether or not an individual displays open aggression depends in part on the degree to which his culture or

[18] Berkowitz, *op. cit.,* 152–164.

subculture *permits* aggression. In some societies, aggressive behavior may be viewed as the mark of a "real man" and hence be encouraged and rewarded, for example, the Kwakiutl of the Pacific Northwest. In still other societies aggression may be regarded as an evil force that disrupts group harmony, for example, the Zuni of the American Southwest. Among some groups within the United States—sailors, marines, soldiers, lumberjacks, longshoremen, and oil field workers—a "he-man" subgroup actively fosters violent interpersonal aggression. The man who exclaims, "I don't believe in fighting" wins no popularity contests. Similarly, Cash describes the "one-hell-of-a-fellow" complex among Southern males.[19] Such males, more rare today than in former times, idealize violence and interpersonal aggression. In contrast, some groups define overt aggression and fighting as sinful or at least ungentlemanly and uncivilized. Many Christians define Christ's Sermon on the Mount as suggesting that aggression in any form is evil:

In brief, there are varieties of cultural settings in which aggression is expressed and even encouraged and others in which aggression is defined as improper or immoral. Whether or not one expresses his aggressions is not simply a consequence of the degree of psychological frustration. The definitions of appropriate behavior provided by the groups in which one acts are equally important in determining the outcome of frustration.[20]

We have noted that our earlier criticisms of the scapegoat theory do not necessarily invalidate it. They did suggest, however, that a number of other factors or variables need to be taken into account. Among these are the personality of the displacer, the kind of frustration involved, the perceived qualities of potential targets, and the role of culture.

PROJECTION

Projection involves the tendency of people to attribute to others motives or traits which they sense within themselves but which would be painful to acknowledge. It is a mechanism by which attitudes and behavior that cannot be accepted in the self are attributed to others. One sees others as he is himself. To the alcoholic it may be the other fellow who drinks too much; to the failing student it may be the teacher who is incompetent; to the football player making a stupid play it may be the quarterback who was in error; to the hostile and

[19] W. J. Cash, *The Mind of the South* (New York: Doubleday & Co., Inc., 1954).
[20] Frank R. Westie, "Race and Ethnic Relations," in R. E. L. Faris, ed., *Handbook of Modern Sociology* (Chicago: Rand McNally & Company, 1964), 610.

aggressive boy it may be the other lad who started the fight. For the businessman the thought that "I'm going to ruin this Jew and run him out of business" is one that generally evokes feelings of guilt and shame. In projection it becomes, "The Jews are trying to ruin me and run me out of business." Aggression against the Jew then becomes justified self-defense. The Jew is portrayed in such a manner that he "deserves" to be ruined for his "unethical" practices. Projection is a prevalent mechanism in dominant-minority relations.

The Cultural Heritage and Projection

Projection seems to play a central role in the frequent assignment to minorities of traits characterized by inordinate sexual desire. Within American life strong overtones of disapproval exist toward sex. Sexual desire is often viewed as "dirty," "filthy," "nasty," even as "sinful." The Fathers of the Christian Church contributed in no small way to the hostility of our modern culture toward sex. The ideal was developed that celibacy was superior to marriage. Paul declared, "But I say to the unmarried and to widows, it is good for them if they abide even as I. But if they have not continency, let them marry: for it is better to marry than to burn." [21] The mother of Christ, the Virgin Mary, was honored in part for her virginity, a cornerstone of her purity, since sex was seen as defiling and degrading. With time came the ascetic cults, the founding of monasteries, and the establishment of celibacy as a requirement for the clergy. Augustine in his *City of God* drew a distinction between the city of God and the city of the devil, implying a dichotomy and an antithesis between the flesh and the spirit. Christian leaders made frequent comments upon fleshy lust as being intrinsically evil.[22]

Given this cultural heritage that sexual desire is wrong, the feeling of such desire is often seen as a terrible thing, to be shunned at all costs. Yet it is an inevitable aspect of physical functioning; it cannot be entirely avoided—sexual desire makes itself felt. Many individuals are thus placed in a dilemma. On the one hand, they cannot deny the existence of the feeling; on the other hand, they cannot admit that they themselves harbor such feelings, feelings that by definition are "lustful" and "sinful." Unable to repress awareness of sexual desire, they instead repress the recognition of its origin within themselves, and the lustfulness is projected outside of themselves upon others. The mechanism can be stated in these terms: "I may feel sexual desire, but I am not

[21] Bible, I Cor. 7:8–9.
[22] Clifford Kirkpatrick, *The Family: As Process and Institution* (New York: The Ronald Press Co., 1955), 100–101.

responsible for it. You are. I am aware of lustful feelings. But it is *your* lust, *not mine*, that I am seeing."

Projection and Notions of Inordinate Negro Sexuality

Some authorities suggest that the projection of sexual desire is of considerable aid in helping us to understand the preoccupation of southern whites with Negro sexuality and the fear of Negro sexual attack. Discussions of the race issue with southern whites usually boil down to the question, "Would you want your sister (daughter) to marry a Negro?" But why such concern with this issue? As it takes two to make a legal marriage, supposedly the white sister or daughter could refuse a Negro suitor. On the conscious level the question does not make sense. It does, however, make sense if there is a repressed, that is, unconscious, feeling of sexual attraction among whites for Negroes.[23] A clear implication of the question is that white women would have no hesitation in marrying a Negro, and, in fact, would readily do so once there is genuine social equality between whites and Negroes.

There may be some foundation for the belief that there exists among whites an unconscious feeling of sexual attraction toward Negroes. It is probably no accident that prejudiced people call tolerant people "niggerlovers." The very choice of the word suggests that perhaps they are fighting the feeling of attraction themselves.[24] White stereotypes depict Negroes as uninhibited, rhythmic, and passionate. In a word, the Negro becomes an image—a symbol—for free and passionate sex. Experiencing sexual desire, white Americans, by virtue of their puritanical traditions (traditions which are particularly prevalent within the South), are often required to repress their feelings. But, in repressing them, it becomes easy to externalize them—to project these feelings upon the Negro. It is the Negro who is uninhibited, rhythmic, and passionate—the very qualities many whites would themselves like to express. Such projection is facilitated by the less stringent sex codes found among lower-socioeconomic-class Negroes. Accordingly, many whites do not find it difficult to embellish upon the theme of Negro sexuality.

By virtue of projection, the Negro becomes sexually tempting and attractive. "The Negro has sex appeal, *plus*—even the white man agrees to this!"[25] Negro women are commonly depicted in jokes, stories, and

---

[23] See: Dollard, *op. cit.*, 334; I. D. MacCrone, *Race Attitudes in South Africa* (London: Oxford University Press, 1937); and Calvin C. Hernton, *Sex and Racism in America* (New York: Doubleday & Company, Inc., 1965).

[24] See: Allport, *op. cit.*, 372–377.

[25] Hernton, *op. cit.*, 53.

folklore as especially voluptuous, sensual, and passionate, and, accordingly, implicitly desirable as sexual partners. Dollard indicates that the image of the Negro woman in southern white man's talk and fantasy was that of a seducing, accessible person dominated by sexual feeling and, so far as straight-out sexual gratification goes, desirable. In jokes the Negro woman was represented as a crude, direct person, with little suppression or veiling of her sexual interest.[26] The remark was current in Southerntown that a man did not know what sexual experience was until he had had a Negro woman.

Similarly, the Negro male is viewed as especially virile and capable. Dollard indicates that the idea seemed prevalent that Negro males were more like savages than humans and that their sexual appetites were more vigorous and ungoverned than those of white men. There was a belief in Southerntown that the genitals of Negro males were larger than those of whites: "One planter, for example, said he had had visual opportunity to confirm the fact; he had gone to one of his cabins, and on entering without warning, found a Negro man preparing for intercourse. Informant expressed surprise at the size of the penis and gave an indication by his arm and clenched fist of its great length and diameter."[27] Several authorities have noted, however, that there is no evidence to confirm the belief that the genitals of Negro males are larger than those of white males.[28] The interesting point here is that whites believe this to be true. Accordingly, it is not difficult to conclude on an unconscious level that one's daughter or sister may actually find Negro men attractive as husbands—for do not women generally find virile, capable men attractive? Simultaneously such projection permits vicarious gratification of forbidden desires. By focusing thoughts upon and telling stories of Negro immorality, the white can compensate in part for his inability or failure to implement his own desires.

The white image of the Negro, then, is such as to make the Negro sexually attractive. But such sentiments cannot be reckoned with openly—they are "disgraceful" and even "sinful." Although repressed—unconscious—they make their presence known in the preoccupation that many whites have with Negro sexuality, betraying sexual attraction. Thus, psychologists and psychiatrists note what many laymen have also observed, namely, those people who make vehement but unnecessary protestations of their innocence of, or of their horror at, cer-

[26] Dollard, op. cit., 137.

[27] Ibid., 160–161. Also see, 324–325.

[28] It appears that whites may be imputing to Negroes not only their own sexual desires, but a wish for exaggerated potency as well.

tain types of behavior reveal their own attraction to the behavior. It is not unusual to find in life the ex-prostitute who is a militant, fanatical crusader against vice or the ex-Communist who is a militant leader in the fight against Communism. A similar principle operates with the white who constantly argues, "Would you want your daughter (sister) to marry a Negro?"

Dr. Robert Seidenberg indicates an interesting case illustrating this general principle. One of his white patients inquired of him, "Is it true that Negroes have extra long penises and that they are erect all the time? Wouldn't it be disgusting to have intercourse with a Negro?" Later in therapy it was revealed that this woman could experience sexual pleasure with her husband only when she fantasied that a "large black" Negro was trying to rape her. In a word, her preoccupation with the issue and disavowal of it betrayed her own attraction to Negro males.[29]

The matter is frequently intensified by the fact that it is white males, not Negro males, who most frequently transgress the caste line and sexually engage women of the other racial group. If white men can find Negro girls so titillating why then may not white women find Negro men exciting? And if Negro men are especially accomplished copulators—indeed sexual athletes—white women may like them especially well. This final blow to the white man's pride in his masculinity has to be avoided at all costs. And it has been avoided at the cost of all Negroes who have ever been lynched under the faintest suspicion of intercourse with a white woman.

Projection and Fear of Negro Rape

The mechanism of projection is of value in understanding the agitating question of rape of white women by Negro men. The Negro man is held to possess an inordinate desire for white women, and southern communities have traditionally credited the slightest suspicion that such contacts have occurred. Although rapes do occur, the southern white's fear seem quite out of proportion to the actual danger. If the analysis thus far has some validity, the fear becomes comprehensible. Many whites unconsciously find the Negro sexually attractive. But such thoughts are too painful to acknowledge. They become permissible only when attributed to others, in this case the Negro male. The Negro male then appears as the aggressor.

[29] Robert Seidenberg, "The Sexual Basis of Social Prejudice," *Psychoanalytic Review*, 39 (1952), 90–95.

The situation is similar to that of the supermoral, sexually frustrated old maid who bars her door against fancied male aggressors. The old maid's sexual impulses, impulses she denies yet which are nevertheless real, are projected outside of herself upon fantasied male attackers. Indeed, "Methinks the lady doth protest too much." The projection to Negro men of large genitals makes the fear of rape seem all the more realistic and menacing. Furthermore, white men crossing the caste line for sexual liaison with Negro women tend to project to Negro men a similar desire on the part of the latter for white women. Within the South there is the constant possibility of aggressive sexual behavior by white men against Negro women; it is easy to believe—to project —that Negro men must constantly wish to retaliate against white women.[30]

The "Mammy" Complex

Lillian Smith, a proponent of this type of interpretation, adds another theme in her treatment of the theory. Not only is the Negro woman attractive to many white men, but, Smith argues, she also represents the Negro "mammy."

In the old days, a white child who had loved his colored nurse, his "mammy" with that passionate devotion which only small children feel, who had grown used to dark velvety skin, warm deep breast, rich soothing voice and the ease of a personality whose religion was centered in heaven not hell, who had felt when mind is tender the touch of a spirit almost free of sex anxiety, found it natural to seek in adolescence and adulthood a return of this profoundly pleasing experience.[31]

Contrasted with the permissive and relaxed relationship with his "mammy" was the white male's relationship with his white mother who authoritatively and repressively established the "do" and "don't" of behavior. Accordingly, the upper-class white male developed a dual sex interest, an interest in both Negro and white women. Yet his culture dictated that a monogamous—exclusive—relationship endure with a white woman. Simultaneously, "Deep down in him, he often reserves his play, his 'real' pleasure, his relaxed enjoyment of sex activities, and his fantasy, for women like his nurse [mammy] . . ."[32] A conflict ensues which in part is handled by expressing harshness and antagonism toward Negroes in an effort to dispel or deny the attraction to them.

[30] Dollard, op. cit., 162 ff. and 324–334.
[31] Lillian Smith, Killers of the Dream (New York: W. W. Norton & Co., Inc., 1949), 123.
[32] Ibid., 130.

Notions of Inordinate Sexuality Among Other Minorities

An inordinate sexual desire has also been attributed to various minority groups other than Negroes, probably stemming from somewhat similar mechanisms of projection. In the decades preceding the Civil War a rash of anti-Catholic books appeared as "convent disclosures." Later evidence exposed these "disclosures" as frauds, but not before intense anti-Catholic sentiment had been aroused by them. Nuns and priests were vividly depicted as engaging in licentious practices and infanticide.[33] Dark tales of sexual debauchery have long been a stand-by among Catholic-haters.

Among the more scurrilous of these attacks were those launched against the Catholic clergy after the turn of the twentieth century by the ex-Populist leader and United States senator from Georgia Tom Watson. In Watson's magazine, the confessional was depicted as a place "in which a lewd priest sows the minds of girls and married women with lascivious suggestions." It was "an open way to damnation along which untold thousands of our sisters have traveled to hell." The Catholic confessional was pictured as a snare where there were made "secret confessions to unmarried Lotharios, parading as priests and enjoying themselves carnally with the choicest women of the earth." Watson betrays his own probable subconscious projection of debauchery to priests in his assertion that in the confessional "the priest finds out what girls and married women he can seduce. Having discovered the trail, he wouldn't be human, if he did not take advantage of the opportunity." [34] Watson assumed—projected—that what was "human" for him held true for others as well.

Not dissimilar charges have been directed against Jews and rabbis. Watson, fanning the flames of hate against Leo Frank, a Jew framed in the rape-murder of a white fourteen-year-old Georgia girl, wrote, "Leo Frank was a typical young Jewish man of business who lives for pleasure *and runs after Gentile girls.* Every student of sociology knows that the black man's lust after the white woman *is not much fiercer than the lust of the licentious Jew for the Gentile.*" [35] Frank was subsequently hanged by an armed mob of twenty-five or thirty men grandiosely styling themselves "a vigilance committee." In Europe it has been a common practice to accuse Jews of gross sexual immorality. In Hitlerite Germany in particular, Jews were depicted as given to overindul-

---

[33] Gustavus Myers, *History of Bigotry in the United States,* revised by Henry M. Christman (New York: G. P. Putnam's Sons, Inc., 1960), 92–103.

[34] Watson's *Jeffersonian,* March, 1911. Quoted in *Ibid.,* 195–196.

[35] *Watson's Magazine,* January, 1915. Quoted in *Ibid.,* 203. Italics in the original.

gence, rape, and perversion. A special newspaper was formed for the purpose of warning the "chaste and innocent" Germans against alleged Jewish sexual perverts who ostensibly derived diabolical pleasure from raping "Aryan" women.[36] Yet it was precisely the Elite Guard of "Aryan" masculinity, the S.S., who were infamous for among other things raping Jewish women and harboring a high proportion of sexual perverts and homosexuals in their ranks.

The Jews as Living Inkblots

Historically the Jew has represented a particularly suitable projection screen for man's conflicts. It is easy to project one's own unacceptable feelings upon an outer object that lacks a clear, sharp structure of its own. Psychologists employ this principle in various "projective tests" of which the Rorschach test is the best known. In the formless inkblot, people are capable of "seeing" an extraordinary number of things. In the process of interpreting inkblots, individuals project their intimate fantasy life and general personality pattern. Thus, projective tests are useful tools in psychology. Ackerman and Jahoda note that for the anti-Semite "the Jew is a living Rorschach inkblot." [37] The Jew is portrayed culturally as many things: as "successful" and as "low class," as "capitalist" and as "Communist," as "clannish" and as "intruder into other people's society," as "oversexed" and as "impotent," as "strong" and as "weak." [38] Thus the image of the Jew is unstructured; he might be almost anything. As such, the Jew has constituted an especially suitable "inkblot" for the projection of traits and motives that one cannot acknowledge within oneself.

On the basis of an investigation of forty patients exhibiting anti-Semitism in psychoanalytic treatment, Ackerman and Jahoda concluded that not only do different people attribute different and mutually contradictory characterisics to Jews, but the same individual may make quite inconsistent accusations against them. One man asserts that Jews are degraded robbers and at still another time that they are too ethical. One woman contends that Jews are the incarnation of vulgarity but simultaneously they represent to her the symbol of a God figure.[39] Accordingly, Jews might represent almost anything and as such become a projection screen for inner conflict. One woman patient accused the Jews of being shams and fakers, capable of realizing high positions by unfair means. She herself was a highly successful business woman.

[36] Rudolph M. Loewenstein, *Christians and Jews* (New York: International Universities Press, Inc., 1951), 45.

[37] Ackerman and Jahoda, *op. cit.*, 58.

[38] *Ibid.*, 58.

[39] *Ibid.*, 57.

Psychiatric analysis indicated that the woman continuously accused herself of having secured success without merit, by being a "faker" who "bluffed" her way into positions of prestige.[40]

Bettelheim and Janowitz suggest that prejudiced individuals are prone to project onto Jews those tendencies represented by the demands of the person's own conscience or superego.[41] Within America, failure to realize success goals is generally attributed to the individual's own shortcomings. Such alleged traits of Jews as "ambitious," "hard working," "cooperative" (clannish), "resolute," "perseverant," "shrewd," and "intelligent" remind the individual of his own failure to live up to societal expectations, expectations that have become an integral part of his conscience. But, finding it too painful to admit his own shortcomings, the individual tends to excuse such shortcomings by blaming Jews for his failures.

Anti-Semitism and City-Hatred

Another essentially projection interpretation of anti-Semitism has been formulated by Arnold Rose.[42] Rose suggests that Jews are hated primarily because they serve as a symbol of city life. Residents of cities, as well as farm and village people, feel antagonistic to the city and what it stands for. Jews have been historically associated with economic success, political radicalism, and quick adaptiveness to a rapidly changing world, traits connected with life in the cities. The Jews constitute the urban people par excellence. In the United States, "New York" and "Jews" are almost interchangeable terms. Americans maintain a strong nostalgia for country life and the rural virtues. City dwellers picture rural life in idealistic terms where the virtues of honesty, clear thinking, and altruism are held to flourish.

Rose suggests that the host of contradictory antipathies directed against the Jews can be explained in terms of the association of these antipathies with city life. Jews are called both sharp businessmen (capitalists) and Communists, both urban products. They are believed to be superhumanly wise and yet weak and "unhandy," the stereotype of the "city slicker." They are depicted as cliquish and "pushy," both features of urban life. And so it goes. Yet, by the same token, city dwellers retain at least an unconscious recognition that the city is also necessary and good. Many of the desirable products of modern life presuppose cities; much we are proud of in "modern civilization" is the

---

[40] *Ibid.*, 59.
[41] Bettelheim and Janowitz, *op. cit.*, 43.
[42] Arnold M. Rose, "Anti-Semitism's Root in City-Hatred," *Commentary*, 6 (1944), 374–378.

result of cities. Thus cities are both admired and hated. By projecting the hatred of the city onto Jews, the prejudiced person is able to destroy and escape the city while simultaneously keeping it and living in it.

Limitations of Projection Theories

Projection theories suffer from many of the same shortcomings that characterize the frustration-aggression theories. Most particularly they fail to explain why a particular minority is selected for the projection of specific traits when there are several minorities to choose from. Even assuming for the moment the merit of projection theories, how is it that the stereotypes of various minorities differ? Yet there is an even more severe problem with regard to these theories. They are premised upon inferences from observable facts, not upon the facts themselves. In short, the evidence for them is at best circumstantial.

The theories need to be subjected to rigid experimental test, yet such testing would pose considerable methodological problems. This is of course a problem central to testing various psychiatric and psycho-analytic theories. Therapy apparently gives some confirmation to such notions. However, the rigid experimental testing so essential to science has, for the most part, been lacking. One theory could be substituted for another, and there could be any number of theories to explain the same phenomenon. Does this mean, then, that the projection theories outlined earlier are of no value? Of course not. As was noted, psychiatric work gives some confirmation of them. Similarly, for some time the virus theory of disease was generally accepted even though the evidence for it was at best circumstantial; later, more powerful microscopes lent support to the theory. Thus, merely because a theory lacks experimental support, in the absence of contrary evidence, it need not be rejected. Caution needs, however, to be reserved in relation to it.

THE PREJUDICED PERSONALITY

A number of researchers have advanced the hypothesis that prejudice constitutes an ingredient that is closely and intricately bound to an *entire* personality structure. It is a property or symptom of a basic personality organization. This point of view is to be contrasted with that which holds that prejudice represents a more or less *isolated* trait to be found in almost any kind of personality. This latter position suggests that prejudice is an independent personality tendency that manifests itself as a specific response to a specific stimulus. The prejudiced-personality theorists dispute this. They argue that individuals differ in their susceptibility to anti-democratic propaganda and in their readiness to exhibit anti-democratic tendencies. The crucial factor determining such susceptibility and readiness is the personality organization. The personality organization or structure may contain contradictions as well as consistencies, but these aspects are *organized* in that they represent constituent parts of a larger whole.

To understand prejudice, these researchers insist, one must examine the total personality. Personality is seen as a more or less enduring organization of forces operating within the individual. These persisting forces of personality are largely responsible for the responses of an individual in various situations; they give consistency to behavior. Although the personality arises from a social environment, it is not, once developed, a mere object of this environment. A structure has been developed within the individual that is capable of self-initiated action upon the social environment. A selection of the varying impinging stimuli is made on the basis of this relatively firmly established and unmodifiable structure.

Tolerant and Intolerant Personalities

Eugene Hartley undertook one of the earliest efforts to define a set of traits constituting the core of the intolerant personality.[43] He emphasized that the degree of tolerance expressed by individuals is a function of their personality complex and is not entirely determined by the specific group against which the attitude is directed. Individuals disposed to intolerance by their personalities tend to exhibit generalized antipathy to out-groups. Employing the Bogardus social-distance scale, Hartley measured the attitudes of several groups of college students toward a large number of racial, religious, national, and economic groupings. In order to test the hypothesis of generalized intolerance, he included in the list of thirty-two existing groups three non-existent groups—Danireans, Pireneans, and Wallonians. These three groups sound plausible but did not correspond to any existing ethnic designation.

The students were not informed of the fact that the three groups were fictional. Their responses to these three groups were correlated with the average tolerance expressed for the thirty-two existing groups. Using the Pearsonian product-moment coefficients of correlation, Hartley found correlations ranging from .78 to .85, computed separately for the students from the five schools who took the test. The high correlations confirmed the hypothesis as to the generality of tolerance and in-

[43] Eugene Hartley, *Problems of Prejudice* (New York: King's Crown Press, 1946).

tolerance. Intolerance toward one group tends to be accompanied by intolerance toward others, and relative tolerance toward one group tends to be accompanied by tolerance toward others. To understand attitudes toward a particular group, Hartley suggests, it is first necessary to have insight into the generalized tolerance attitudes of the individual. The individual's approach to one group can be seen as a particularization, a differentiation out from his generalized approach to peoples.

Based on his study, Hartley concluded that a relatively tolerant personality can be distinguished in terms of certain personality traits from the relatively intolerant personality. Although not necessarily definitive, his list of traits is of interest. The tolerant personality tended to exhibit little need for dominance, a strong need for friendliness, a fear of competition, a concern for societal betterment, and an appreciation of the contributions of others. The relatively intolerant personality, on the other hand, tended to be characterized by an unwillingness to accept responsibility; by a rejection of serious groups and political interests; by extreme egocentrism; by a dislike of agitators and radicals; by an interest in physical activity, the body, and health; and by emotionality rather than rationality.

The Authoritarian Personality

Perhaps the most ambitious and comprehensive effort to define a prejudiced-personality type was undertaken by a group of University of California psychologists at Berkeley. Considerable attention has since been focused upon their findings, which appeared in 1950 in a book entitled *The Authoritarian Personality.*[44] The work represents a milestone in research in the field of dominant-minority relations. Particularly impressive were their efforts to develop a series of tests for the measurement of anti-Semitism (the A-S Scale), ethnocentrism (the E Scale concerned with attitudes towards "Japs," "Okies," Negroes, Filipinos, zootsuiters, foreigners, criminals, and others), political and economic conservatism (the PEC Scale), and basic personality patterns (the F Scale). Together with these tests they employed detailed clinical interviews and projective tests on subjects who ranked among the highest 25 per cent and the lowest 25 per cent on the scale measuring anti-minority attitudes. The clinical interviews and projective tests were used to gain access to the conscious as well as unconscious aspects of the personalities of their subjects. The great majority of the subjects lived within the San Francisco Bay area and were drawn from the middle socioeconomic class. In addition, smaller groups of working-

[44] T. W. Adorno, Else Frenkel-Brunswik, Daniel J. Levinson, and R. Nevitt Sanford, *The Authoritarian Personality* (New York: Harper & Row, 1950).

class men and women, inmates at San Quentin State Prison, and patients at a psychiatric clinic were studied.

The Berkeley group state the major premise upon which they based their theory and research in these terms:

> . . . the political, economic, and social convictions of an individual often form a broad and coherent pattern, as if bound together by a "mentality" or "spirit," and . . . this pattern is an expression of deep-lying trends in his personality.[45]

By employing the questionnaire associated with the F Scale (referred to as the Implicit Antidemocratic Trends or Potentiality of Fascism Scale and by many subsequent researchers as the Authoritarian Scale), the Berkeley group believed they could measure an individual's basic personality patterns. They grouped the thirty-eight items composing the F Scale under nine general characteristics. These characteristics define the antidemocratic or potentially fascistic syndrome. *Syndrome* is a word commonly used medically to refer to a collection of concurrent symptoms associated with a disorder or disease. Let us examine these nine characteristics, defining each and then illustrating each with two statements found in the questionnaire:

1. Conventionalism. Conventionalism involves a rigid adherence to conventional, middle-class values.

> *Example:* "Obedience and respect for authority are the most important virtues children should learn."

> *Example:* "If people would talk less and work more, everybody would be better off."

2. Authoritarian Submission. Authoritarian submission entails a submissive, uncritical attitude toward idealized moral authorities of the in-group.

> *Example:* "Young people sometimes get rebellious ideas, but as they grow up they ought to get over them and settle down."

> *Example:* "Science has its place, but there are many important things that can never possibly be understood by the human mind."

3. Authoritarian Aggression. Authoritarian aggression involves a tendency to be on the lookout for, and to condemn, reject, and punish people who violate conventional values.

> *Example:* "An insult to our honor should always be punished."

> *Example:* "Homosexuals are hardly better than criminals and ought to be severely punished."

[45] *Ibid.*, 1.

4. Anti-Intraception. Anti-intraception entails an opposition to the subjective, the imaginative, and the tender-minded.

> *Example:* "The businessman and the manufacturer are much more important to society than the artist and the professor."

> *Example:* "Nowadays more and more people are prying into matters that should remain personal and private."

5. Superstition and Stereotypy. Superstition and stereotypy entail a belief that mystical determinants influence an individual's fate and a tendency to think in rigid categories.

> *Example:* "Some day it will probably be shown that astrology can explain a lot."

> *Example:* "Some people are born with an urge to jump from high places."

6. Power and "Toughness." Power and "toughness" are viewed as a preoccupation with the dominance-submission, strong-weak, leader-follower dimension, an identification with power figures, an overemphasis upon conventional morality, and an exaggerated assertion of strength and toughness.

> *Example:* "No weakness or difficulty can hold us back if we have enough will power."

> *Example:* "Most people don't realize how much our lives are controlled by plots hatched in secret places."

7. Destructiveness and Cynicism. Destructiveness and cynicism involve a generalized hostility toward and a vilification of humans.

> *Example:* "Human nature being what it is, there will always be war and conflict."

> *Example:* "Familiarity breeds contempt."

8. Projectivity. Projectivity entails a disposition to believe that wild and dangerous things go on in the world and more generally the projection outward of unconscious emotional impulses.

> *Example:* "Wars and social troubles may someday be ended by an earthquake or flood that will destroy the whole world."

> *Example:* "Nowadays when so many different kinds of people move around and mix together so much, a person has to protect himself especially carefully against catching an infection or disease from them."

9. **Sex.** Sex entails an exaggerated concern with sexual "goings-on."

Example: "The wild sex life of the old Greeks and Romans was tame compared to some of the goings-on in this country, even in places where people might least expect it."

Example: "Sex crimes, such as rape and attacks on children, deserve more than mere imprisonment; such criminals ought to be publicly whipped, or worse."

With the F Scale the Berkeley group hoped to identify a personality type that was potentially undemocratic and fascistic. Accordingly they expected F Scale scores to correlate with the scores realized from the Anti-Semitism, Ethnocentrism, and the Political and Economic Conservatism Scales. This indeed proved to be the case. For the first version of the F Scale the mean correlation with A-S (the Anti-Semitism Scale) was .53, with E (the Ethnocentrism Scale) it was .65, and with PEC (the Political and Economic Conservatism Scales), .54. The Berkeley researchers revised the F Scale several times by dropping items that did not correlate with total scores or that were not predictive of A-S and E scores. On the final version of the F Scale, the mean correlation with an E Scale that included anti-Semitic items was .75. Hence the Berkeley group felt that its work convincingly demonstrated that prejudice and authoritarianism (as defined by the F Scale) often constitute closely interrelated personality characteristics.

Genesis of the Authoritarian Personality in Childhood

The Berkeley researchers did not limit themselves to defining the predominant personality patterns of those ranking high in prejudice. They were also concerned with the early childhood interrelationships within the family that had fostered these patterns. In keeping with a predominantly Freudian approach, the Berkeley group viewed early relationships with parents and siblings as of paramount importance in determining the basic personality organization. The researchers undertook to identify a composite picture of the family patterns of the highly prejudiced. This picture emerged as an overview or abstraction taken from the total group. Accordingly, in specific cases individual exceptions and variations could be noted.

The home discipline of the prejudiced subjects was relatively harsh, arbitrary, and threatening.[46] One subject reported that his father "did not believe in sparing the rod for stealing candy or someone's peaches

[46] In this regard see: Donald Weatherley, "Maternal Responses to Childhood Aggression and Subsequent Anti-Semitism," *Journal of Abnormal and Social Psychology*, 66 (1963), 183–185.

off the tree." Another stated, "But mother had a way of punishing me—lock me in a closet—or threaten to give me to a neighborhood woman who she said was a witch." [47] Within these families, relationships tended to be rather clearly defined in terms of roles of dominance and submission rather than in equalitarian policies. As a result, the child developed an image of the parents as somewhat distant and forbidding. The child fearfully submitted to the demands of the parents and felt constrained to suppress impulses that were not acceptable to them. On the other hand, those low in prejudice tended to come from families placing less emphasis on obedience and greater emphasis on the unconditional giving of love and affection.

In a related study, children high in prejudice and children low in prejudice were asked to define the perfect boy. The highly prejudiced tended to define the perfect boy as being "polite," "having good manners," "being clean," whereas those low in prejudice tended to define the perfect boy in terms of "companionship" and "being fun." The tendency toward conformity in the prejudiced child found expression in frequent indorsement of such statements as "There is only one right way to do anything" and "Appearances are usually the best test." [48] The prejudiced children accepted the parental emphasis upon discipline to the extent that they described the perfect father in punitive and restrictive terms rather than in terms of love and understanding. Describing the perfect father, one child indicated, "He spanks you when you are bad and does not give you too much money. . . ." Another reported, "When you ask for something he ought not to give it to you right away. Not soft on you, strict." [49] The children low in prejudice, on the other hand, were more likely to be treated as an equal and given the opportunity to express feelings of rebellion or disagreement.

The goals which the parents of the highly prejudiced sought to instil were highly conventional in nature. The parents fostered the adoption of a rigid and externalized set of values: "That which is socially accepted and helpful in climbing the social ladder is 'good,' and that which deviates and is socially inferior is 'bad.'" The parents of the unprejudiced, on the other hand, were less status-ridden and showed less anxiety with respect to conformity and less intolerance toward socially unacceptable behavior. Rather than condemning, they tended to provide more guidance and support, helping the child to work out his

[47] Adorno, op. cit., 373.
[48] Else Frenkel-Brunswik, "A Study of Prejudice in Children," Human Relations, 1 (1948), 303.
[49] Ibid., 301.

problems and feelings rather than continuously demanding a suppression of them.[50]

The families of the highly prejudiced emphasized the faithful execution of prescribed roles and duties which often took preference over the exchange of free-flowing affection. Homelife induced a relative lack of mutuality in the area of emotion and shifted emphasis onto material benefits and goods. This tended to underlie the opportunistic character of the highly prejudiced person's interactions with others. Abundant cues were evident which suggested that beneath the self-negating submission to parents were considerable feelings of resentment toward them. Prejudiced subjects tended to feel themselves "forgotten," the victims of injustice who did not "get" enough of the things they deserved from parents.

Criticism of "The Authoritarian Personality"

Probably no other research in the field of race and ethnic relations has received greater attention than that of *The Authoritarian Personality*. Scores of studies have appeared criticizing, testing, refining, and qualifying the findings of the Berkeley group. By the end of 1956, six years after the publication of the volume, at least 230 publications appeared dealing with authoritarianism, an interest that continues unabated. Obviously, we are in no position here to review all the many criticisms of *The Authoritarian Personality*. We shall, however, note a number of the more vital ones.[51]

1. Many of the criticisms focus upon research methods. Critics point out, with some justification, that the sample of persons actually studied was not a representative or random sample of this population or of any other specifiable population. The subjects were primarily middle class and members of at least one formal organization (veterans' groups, labor unions, Kiwanis clubs, etc.). Yet middle class people and members of formal organizations differ in many respects from other segments of the population. Similarly some critics suggest that the study's scales are inadequate, in fact faulty, and that many items are ambiguous.

2. Some writers have suggested that a tendency toward "acquiescence" can account for part of the apparent relationship between an authoritarian personality type and prejudice.[52] The items in the F

---

[50] Adorno, *op. cit.*, 385–388.

[51] For an extended evaluation of *The Authoritarian Personality*, see: Richard Christie and Marie Jahoda, eds., *Studies in the Scope and Method of "The Authoritarian Personality"* (New York: The Free Press of Glencoe, 1954).

[52] There are many studies. See, for example, B. M. Bass, "Authoritarianism or Acquiescence," *Journal of Abnormal and Social Psychology*, 51 (1955), 616–

Scale are all "agree" items. A number of researchers have discovered that some people have a marked tendency to agree with almost any proposition, not only on the F Scale but on any and all scales, regardless of content. Conversely, other people disagree with practically every proposition, regardless of its nature. Couch and Keniston christen these types "Yeasayers" and "Naysayers" [53]:

> The difficulty lies in the fact that every time you agree with an item on the F-scale you chalk up a credit toward authoritarianism. If you agree that "obedience and respect for authority are the most important virtues children should learn," ping! you score one! If you agree that "to a greater extent than most people realize, our lives are governed by plots hatched in secret by politicians," ping! you score another point for authoritarianism. In other words, all the items are unidirectional, so worded that agreement always signifies authoritarianism. Only by disagreeing with every item can you obtain a completely "democratic" score.[54]

3. The Berkeley group held that the association between authoritarianism (as measured by the F Scale) and a variety of other attitudes (including prejudice) argues for the existence of a unified personality configuration. Not so, argue some critics. These writers note that authoritarian tendencies increase as intelligence, education, and socioeconomic class status go down.[55] Hence, some insist, the numerous components of authoritarianism are found together in a person simply because they are the norms of people with little education and low socioeconomic class status:

> . . . there is the real possibility that *both* authoritarian beliefs and prejudices may be learned in the same way that we learn that the world is round (or flat, or held up on the back of a giant turtle). The association of both prejudices and personality items with formal education forces us to take seriously the possibility that widespread indoctrination, relatively inde-

---

623; S. Messick and D. N. Jackson, "Authoritarianism or Acquiescence in Bass's Data," *Journal of Abnormal and Social Psychology*, 54 (1957), 424–426; "Reply" by Bass in the same volume, 426–427; N. L. Goge *et al.*, "The Psychological Meaning of Acquiescence Set for Authoritarianism," *Journal of Abnormal and Social Psychology*, 55 (1957), 98–103.

[53] A. Couch and K. Keniston, "Yeasayers and Naysayers: Agreeing Response Set as a Personality Variable," *Journal of Abnormal and Social Psychology*, 60 (1960), 151–175.

[54] Gordon W. Allport, "Prejudice: Is It Societal or Personal?" *Journal of Social Issues*, 18 (1962), 120–134.

[55] See, for example, H. H. Hyman and P. B. Sheatsley, " 'The Authoritarian Personality'—A Methodological Critique," in Christie and Jahoda, *op. cit.*, 50–122; W. J. MacKinnon and R. Centers, "Authoritarianism and Urban Stratification," *American Journal of Sociology*, 61 (1956), 610–620; and A. Kornhauser, H. L. Sheppard, and A. J. Mayer, *When Labor Votes* (New York: University Books, 1956).

pendent of individual psychological needs, may account for at least a considerable part of the correlation of authoritarianism and prejudice. Thus, *both* authoritarianism and prejudice may tend to be characteristic of persons in economically and socially deprived positions in the social structure.[56]

4. Some critics allege that authoritarianism may be spuriously related to prejudice through its association with status, anomie, or some other variable. Kaufman suggests, for example, on the basis of his study of 213 non-Jewish college undergraduates, that status is more closely related to anti-Semitism than is authoritarianism. By employing statistical measures, Kaufman undertook to determine the association between both authoritarianism and status and scores on the anti-Semitism scale. He attempted to discover through the use of partial correlations (statistical measures) the degree to which authoritarianism and status were each *independently* correlated with the anti-Semitism score. In other words, he measured the degree to which authoritarianism was correlated with anti-Semitism when the effect of status was allowed for, or to put it another way, was held constant. Similarly, he measured the degree to which status was correlated with prejudice when the effect of authoritarianism was allowed for. Since status and authoritarianism might go hand-in-hand, Kaufman wanted to look at the separate effect of each. The partial correlation of status and anti-Semitism was .48 (moderately high), while that of authoritarianism and anti-Semitism was .12 (quite low). Kaufman concluded that concern with status is the dominant dimension related to anti-Semitism and that the correlation he found of .53 between authoritarianism and anti-Semitism could be largely explained by their mutual relationship and concern with status. Thus, when the effect of status was held constant, the correlation between authoritarianism and anti-Semitism dropped to .12.[57]

Srole undertook to investigate the relationship of another variable, anomie, to prejudice. Anomie is a sociological concept derived from Durkheim which Srole used to designate a state of social malintegration within individuals, a state represented by disorganization, group alienation, and demoralization. In interviewing a sample of 401 white, native-born adults in Springfield, Massachusetts, Srole undertook to measure the association between both authoritarianism and anomie and scores on the prejudice scale. Using partial correlations, as did Kaufman, he was interested in discovering the degree to which authori-

[56] Robin M. Williams, Jr., *Strangers Next Door* (Englewood Cliffs, N.J.: Prentice-Hall, Inc., 1964), 90.

[57] Walter C. Kaufman, "Status, Authoritarianism, and Anti-Semitism," *American Journal of Sociology*, 62 (1957), 379–382.

tarianism and anomie each were *independently* correlated with the prejudice score. The partial correlation of anomie and prejudice was .35, while that of authoritarianism and prejudice was .12. On the basis of this sample, anomie appeared more closely associated with prejudice than authoritarianism.[58] Roberts and Rokeach, in a somewhat similar study of 86 adults, secured results differing from those of Srole. They found a correlation of .53 between authoritarianism and prejudice when anomie was held constant, and a correlation of .37 between anomie and prejudice when authoritarianism was held constant.[59] More definitive conclusions will have to await further research. Nevertheless, anomie appears to be a variable associated with prejudice.

5. A recurring criticism of *The Authoritarian Personality* deals with its tendency to equate authoritarian tendencies with a right-wing (fascistic) political orientation. May we not find, suggest some critics, intemperate and exaggerated love-prejudice just as we find intemperate and exaggerated hate-prejudice? They ask: what about Communistic authoritarianism of the left? Indeed, can one be authoritarian even if one's attitudes are "on the side of the angels?"

Rokeach takes this kind of position. He criticizes the F Scale as being a measure of right-wing authoritarianism rather than a measure of authoritarianism in general.[60] Authoritarianism as described by the Berkeley group, Rokeach argues, is a subspecies of a more general personality syndrome which he calls "dogmatism." Whereas Communists score relatively low on the Berkeley F and prejudice scales, they score higher on Rokeach's Dogmatism Scale than most other political groups. Rokeach stresses that authoritarianism should be viewed as a mode of thought (a structure characterized by a "closed mind," dependence upon some absolute authority, and patterns of intolerance toward certain groups) rather than as a set of beliefs (for instance, the favorableness or unfavorableness of attitudes toward certain minorities).

6. Finally, critics have often observed that the Berkeley group failed to give sufficient recognition to the role culture plays in prejudice. Where a society evolves elaborate definitions and norms governing interracial behavior, the mere presence of prejudice in a person tells us very little about his distinctive modes of personality. Under these circumstances prejudice and discrimination may constitute the characteristics of "normal" personalities. The matter is emphasized by com-

[58] Leo Srole, "Social Integration and Certain Corollaries: An Exploratory Study," *American Sociological Review*, 21 (1956), 709–716.

[59] Alan H. Roberts and Milton Rokeach, "Anomie, Authoritarianism, and Prejudice: Replication," *American Journal of Sociology*, 61 (1956), 355–358.

[60] Milton Rokeach, *The Open and Closed Mind* (New York: Basic Books, 1960).

parative studies of prejudice in the southern and northern United States. Evidence abounds to support the fact that white southerners are typically more intolerant of the Negro than white northerners. Available research tends to indicate that this is primarily the product of sociocultural factors and not the product of a higher incidence of authoritarian personalities within the South.

Public-opinion polls have shown the South to be one of the least anti-Semitic regions in the nation. Prothro found that two-fifths of his white-middle-class sample in Louisiana harbored intensely *unfavorable* attitudes toward Negroes together with *favorable* attitudes toward Jews.[61] If an authoritarian personality type constituted the crux of the problem, the South should display *both* a high incidence of anti-Semitism and a high incidence of prejudice against Negroes. Further, we should expect to find a higher incidence of authoritarian personalities in the South than in the North. Yet Pettigrew could not find any higher incidence of authoritarianism in four small southern towns in Georgia and North Carolina than in four roughly matched communities in New England. From his data, which included a study of various sociocultural variables, Pettigrew concluded that it was the sociocultural and social adjustment factors that accounted for the sharp differences between the North and the South, not differences in personality.[62] Nor does the authoritarian personality theory take into account inconsistency in prejudice and discrimination, for example, tolerance of Negroes in one's union but not in one's neighborhood.

After reviewing *The Authoritarian Personality* and various criticisms of it, what can we conclude? Perhaps Robin M. Williams, Jr., summarizes the situation best in this appraisal:

. . . there is every reason to accept the contention that authoritarianism, of the kind that is indexed by the F-scale, tends to enhance the likelihood of ethnic prejudice. But neither the authoritarian syndrome nor other related personality tendencies invariably constitute either a necessary or sufficient set of conditions for prejudice, much less discriminatory behavior.[63]

Hence, despite the lack of overall consensus on the study, the Berkeley research still commands considerable respect.

[61] E. Terry Prothro, "Ethnocentrism and Anti-Negro Attitudes in the Deep South," *Journal of Abnormal and Social Psychology*, 47 (1952), 105–108.

[62] Thomas F. Pettigrew, "Regional Differences in Anti-Negro Prejudice," *The Journal of Abnormal and Social Psychology*, 59 (1959), 28–36.

[63] Williams, *op. cit.*, 94.

III

INTERGROUP RELATIONS WITHIN AMERICA

7

Conflict

In the previous four chapters, attention has been focused upon the factors contributing to prejudice and discrimination. In this and the next three chapters, we will examine some of the chief processes and patterns of intergroup interaction within American life. We will devote one chapter each to the examination of conflict, segregation, stratification, and assimilation.

People are accustomed to associating interracial and interethnic relations, e.g., Negro-white, Jew-gentile, Italian-native American relations, with "social problems." The fact that conflict often represents an important ingredient in such relations probably furthers this point of view. It is not uncommon for conflict to be equated with violence. While it is true that riots, lynchings, and related forms of violence may periodically emerge when differing racial or ethnic groups are in contact, conflict need not be expressed exclusively in violent terms. Boycotts, strikes, wade-ins, sit-ins, passive resistance, legal litigation, at times even wit and humor, not to mention many other mechanisms, represent forms of conflict in which violence may be absent. Conflict may be thought of as a struggle over values and claims to wealth, power, and prestige in which the opponents aim to neutralize, injure, or eliminate their rivals. In its most extreme expression it may eventuate in the total annihilation of a group. This was the fate of a number of American Indian tribes.

CONFLICT AND THE SOCIAL ORDER

Conflict and Social Stability

It is not unusual for people to conclude that the absence of conflict in a relationship is an indication that the relationship is highly integrated, stable, and secure. Some married couples pride themselves on "never once having had a quarrel." It is assumed that this is a positive testimonial to the couples' love and happiness. Actually most marriage counselors and psychiatrists have come to a contrary conclusion. In any deep, intimate relationship such as marriage, some bickering is inevitable and its total absence is suggestive of the relationship's failure. The resolution of differences between people requires that some degree of quarreling and conflict ensue. Where all conflict is lacking, family stagnation is likely. The crucial issue in evaluating marital success is not the absence of conflict but how the couple quarrel, how often, over what they quarrel, and the intensity of the quarreling.[1]

Similarly, the absence of racial and ethnic conflict, in and of itself, is not necessarily suggestive of a stable, non-stressful relationship. It may merely be an indication that a dominant group has more or less successfully coerced and intimidated a minority. It is comparatively easy to confuse peace with satisfaction and silence with consent. Where a relationship is stable, where the participants feel that it will not be endangered by conflict, conflicts are quite likely to emerge. In fact, under some conditions, conflicts in intergroup relations may represent an index of a better integration of the minority within the community. A minority group which feels that the bonds uniting it to the dominant group are unstable tends to lack the security that is needed to act out hostility and engage in conflict. On the other hand, participation in overt conflict may be an indication that the minority feels sufficiently secure in its relationship with the dominant group to risk such expression, i.e., its members feel the consensual bond between the groups is strong enough to withstand antagonistic action. A study of the attitudes of Negroes in the army during the last war has suggested that those Negroes who were most positively motivated toward war and most ready to volunteer for combat were also the ones who tended to be most militant on race issues.[2]

---

[1] See: George Simpson, *People in Families* (New York: Thomas Y. Crowell Co., 1960), 202–206.

[2] Lewis A. Coser, *The Functions of Social Conflict* (New York: The Free Press of Glencoe, 1956), 83.

The Nature of Functions and Dysfunctions

The emphasis placed upon peace and harmony within the United States contributes in popular conception to the view that conflict is harmful. According to this view, any expression of conflict within a society or between groups is to be condemned. But this tends to overlook the fact that conflict often has a definite functional value for a social system. Within any society, various social patterns operate to maintain the social structure and the institutional systems. On a general level one may evaluate the consequences of any social trait or pattern as it relates to the survival, persistence, integration, or stability of the society as a whole. Those consequences that contribute positively to the system are referred to as *functions*. Those consequences that serve to diminish the integration or stability of a society or to lessen its possibility of survival and persistence are referred to as *dysfunctions*. Dysfunctions are the negative consequences of social patterns as they relate to the social structure.

It should not be assumed that functions are "good" and dysfunctions are "bad." These are ethical and moral judgments, value judgments. From a sociological viewpoint functions or dysfunctions do not have an ethical connotation; they are neither "good" nor "bad." Rather, sociologists assess the consequences of a social trait or pattern in relation to the social structure. The society is viewed as an ongoing system of interdependent parts in which the trait or pattern has a positive or negative role—is, respectively, functional or dysfunctional. A particular pattern may simultaneously be both functional and dysfunctional, i.e., in some respects it may play a positive role; in others, a negative role.

Functions and Dysfunctions of Ethnic and Racial Conflict

Ethnic and racial conflict may serve any number of functions within a society. First, conflict promotes group formation, and groups constitute the foundation stones of a society. Conflict facilitates the development of a consciousness of kind—it makes people aware of their shared or similar values. The distinction between "we," or the in-group, and "they," or the out-group, is established in and through conflict. Groups in turn bind people together within a set of social relationships; they are instrumentalities whereby people are interrelated through a set of roles and statuses. They define the positions people occupy in the social structure. Thus roles and statuses may be assigned to individuals on the basis of their membership in a particular ethnic

or racial group. By way of illustration, menial occupational roles are
rather consistently assigned to Negroes, tasks that are often indispensable for ongoing American life yet the performance of which is
usually seen as burdensome and undesirable.

Second, not only is a group defined and its boundaries established
through conflict, but conflict promotes group cohesion. Conflict serves
to make group members more conscious of their group bonds and is
likely to increase their participation.[3] Anti-Negro sentiment and anti-
Semitism may be functional in that they provide individuals who lack
a sense of cohesion within the society with an anchorage—with a sense
of group membership. They may provide them with a means of
identification in an estranged world.

Third, ethnic and racial conflict may function as a "safety valve" for
the society as a whole. Racial and religious prejudice provides for the
"safe" release of hostile and aggressive impulses that are culturally
tabooed without other social contexts. By channeling hostilities from
within family, occupational, and other crucial settings onto permissible
and less vital targets, the stability of existing social structures may be
promoted. This is the well-known scapegoating mechanism.[4]

Fourth, a multiplicity of conflicts between large numbers of differing groups within a society (conflicts among racial and ethnic groups,
labor vs. business, consumer groups vs. producer groups, business vs.
business, etc.) may be conducive to a democratic as opposed to a
totalitarian order. The multiple group affiliations of individuals contribute to a multiplicity of conflicts crisscrossing society. The various
groups operate as a check against one another. The individual's seg-
mental participation in numerous groups, rather than total absorption
by one group, results in a kind of balancing mechanism and prevents
deep cleavages along one axis, e.g., it prevents cleavage along rigid
class lines eventuating in class struggle. In totalitarian societies, on
the other hand, there is a maximum concentration of power in one
institution—the monolithic state.[5]

Finally, conflict may initiate other types of interaction between
groups, even between groups that previously were relatively isolated
from each other. The situation may be somewhat analogous to that of
children who meet for the first time. Conflict is often one way in which
the children enter into a relationship: Having first quarreled over the
use of a toy, they then may proceed to play with it cooperatively. In
this manner, each child serves to test the other. Within intergroup

[3] *Ibid.*, 87–95.
[4] *Ibid.*, 39–48.
[5] *Ibid.*, 76–81.

relations, conflict may perform a somewhat similar function. It becomes a means to "test" and "know" the previously unknown. The conflict acts as a stimulus for establishing new rules and norms, and may accordingly serve as a socializing agent for the contending groups.[6]

The dysfunctions of ethnic and racial conflict are often more readily apparent than are its functions. As the value system defines most forms of human conflict as harmful and morally wrong, greater attention tends to be focused upon its negative aspects. Conflict may reach a frequency and intensity whereby the social system is imperiled or undermined. Hostility is a potentially destructive and disruptive force within human interaction. Thus, societies usually take considerable care to regulate, suppress, and rechannel aggressive impulses. The dysfunctional impact of racial conflict has been reflected in some areas of the South where a number of school districts have undertaken to close public schools rather than permit their desegregation. To the extent to which education is a vital element in the American social structure, racial conflict serves to imperil major institutional functioning within these communities.

On the national level, racial or ethnic conflict may reach proportions that jeopardize national unity and undermine the national welfare. Energy and resources are drained and dissipated by friction that might otherwise find direction within more productive channels and cooperative activities. Similarly, fears and expectations of conflict may lead to an inefficient and ineffective employment of manpower and individual talents and capabilities. By the same token, since racial and ethnic conflict tends to be tabooed by the society-at-large as counter to the democratic creed, overt conflict may serve to promote moral guilt and concomitant psychological tension among segments of the population.

RACE RIOTS AND LYNCHINGS

Race riots are an especially violent form of racial conflict. Within the South, race riots have stemmed chiefly from Negro efforts to protest against their treatment or to improve their status. Guy B. Johnson observes:

Any organized effort of Negroes to improve their *status*, any disregard of the caste patterns by a group of Negroes, has been interpreted as concerted aggression. During Reconstruction, race riots centered around the political meetings of Negroes, the ballot box, and the presence of the Negro militia.

[6] *Ibid.*, 121–128.

The Atlanta riot of 1906 grew out of a "crime wave" of rape and murder of whites by Negroes which was played up in the newspapers until it appeared to be almost a concerted or planned aggression. The Houston riot of 1917 grew out of the presence of Negro soldiers who did not observe the rules of caste. In other words, they were "insolent" *en masse.* The Tulsa riot in 1921 occurred after a band of Negroes had gone to the county jail with the idea of preventing the lynching of a Negro prisoner. . . . In every riot which has occurred in the South, organized or concerted violation of caste principles has played the leading role.[7]

Grimshaw, on the basis of extensive studies of racial violence within the United States, comes to somewhat similar conclusions. He notes that racial violence has resulted not from conscious policy decisions of either the white or Negro group, but rather from reactions of whites to real or perceived assaults by Negroes upon the existing racial struc-ture. In brief, if the Negro "stays in his place," there is unlikely to be Negro-white violence. But Grimshaw observes that high social tension in and of itself does not necessarily explode in violence. Still a second ingredient is essential, namely that external controls be in-effective for preventing violence. Military and quasi-military organi-zations such as the police, state militia, and federal troops—agencies enjoying a monopoly of the legitimate use of force—can intervene to reduce the likelihood of violence in many instances.[8] Let us consider a number of concrete cases of intergroup violence.

The Detroit Race Riot of 1943

During World War II a number of serious race riots broke out in American cities including Los Angeles, Harlem, Beaumont, and Mobile. In the Harlem riot, 5 were killed, at least 307 were injured, some $5 million worth of property was destroyed (chiefly grocery stores and pawnshops), and at least 450 were arrested. The most critical of the wartime race riots, however, erupted in Detroit on June 30, 1943.

[7] Guy B. Johnson, "Patterns of Race Conflict," in Edgar T. Thompson, ed., *Race Relations and the Race Problem* (Durham, N.C.: Duke University Press, 1939), 146–147. Also see Stanley Lieberson and Arnold R. Silverman." Precipitants and Conditions of Race Riots," *American Sociological Review,* 30 (1965), 887–899.

[8] Allen D. Grimshaw, "Lawlessness and Violence in the United States and Their Special Manifestations in Changing Negro-White Relationships," *Journal of Negro History,* 44 (1959), 52–72; "Urban Racial Violence in the United States: Changing Ecological Considerations," *American Journal of Sociology,* 66 (1960), 109–119; "Relationships among Prejudice, Discrimination, Social Tension and Social Violence," *Journal of Intergroup Relations,* 2 (1961), 302–310; "Negro-White Relations in the Urban North: Two Areas of High Conflict Potential," *Journal of Intergroup Relations,* 3 (1962), 146–158; and "Actions of Police and Military in American Race Riots," *Phylon,* 24 (1963), 271–289.

Within Detroit, a climate of racial tension had been building up for some years. Two years earlier, in the spring of 1941, Negroes and whites were pitted against each other during a strike in Ford Motor's large River Rouge plant. In the same year a race riot had occurred at Northwestern High School, and earlier in 1942 riots had broken out at the Sojourner Truth Housing Project. Furthermore, Detroit abounded in hate groups. Through the years a climate of intolerance had been promoted by the utterances of Father Charles E. Coughlin, leader of the extreme-right-wing "Christian Front," and by two inflammatory demagogues, Gerald L. K. Smith and Frank J. Norris.[9]

During the early war years, a considerable influx of Negroes and whites from the South had supplied smoldering embers which contributed to racial tension. Whites from Kentucky, Tennessee, Oklahoma, and Arkansas, many of them former sharecroppers, brought with them Jim Crow notions of the Negro. From similar white groups within the South had come the lynch mobs of earlier periods. Within Detroit southern Negroes were able to secure jobs that gave them a wage and a sense of freedom which they had previously not known. Among southern white immigrants, for that matter many northerners as well, Detroit Negroes were seen as becoming too "uppity." The situation was compounded by Detroit's severe housing shortage that condemned thousands of both whites and Negroes to live in slums, tents, and trailers. Severe internal pressures had developed for housing in Paradise Valley, the Negro ghetto, that became the focus of the rioting. The area had been overcrowded prior to the war, and the crowded situation had been intensified by the new Negro immigration. Transportation and recreational facilities were also overburdened and overcrowded. Similarly, many Negroes smarted under discriminatory conditions at the very time when considerable appeal was being made to democratic slogans in the war against the totalitarian Axis powers. An increase of juvenile delinquency and crime during the war years provided large numbers of under-war-age youths who were ripe for mob behavior. In general, the frustrations and fears that inevitably accompany a major war fed aggressive impulses that searched for a scapegoat.

Such were the setting and the diverse currents that provided the backdrop for the Detroit riot. The initial outbreak flared Sunday evening, June 20, at Belle Isle, Detroit's 985-acre playground and beach. Four complaints of insult and injury had been lodged with the police

[9] This summary of the Detroit riot is based primarily upon Alfred McClung Lee and Norman Daymond Humphrey, *Race Riot* (New York: Holt, Rinehart & Winston, Inc.), 1943.

by both Negroes and whites several hours prior to the rioting. Versions differ regarding the chief incident that precipitated the riot. Whatever the triggering event, the riot began on the bridge leading to the island, and within a short time some 200 white sailors were fighting with Negroes. A number of Negroes were severely kicked and beaten. Rumors quickly spread through the Negro and white communities. Within two hours a Negro, Leo Tipton, grabbed a microphone in a Negro night club and urged the 500 patrons to "take care of a bunch of whites who killed a colored woman and her baby at Belle Isle Park." Another rumor circulated among whites who were leaving the defense plants about midnight that Negroes had raped and killed a white woman on the bridge. Both rumors were false.

Within Paradise Valley, the congested Negro ghetto, rioting broke out in the early morning hours of Monday, June 21. By 2:00 A.M. a white man had been stabbed in the chest, a policeman had suffered a possible skull fracture, and injured people were being taken into Detroit's Municipal Receiving Hospital at a rate of one a minute. Negroes stoned white workers inside a streetcar, and a Negro mob attacked whites coming off from work at the Chevrolet Gear and Axle Plant. Large groups of Negroes started looting stores and destroying white property in Negro districts. By 3:00 A.M. the situation appeared to be out of control, especially in Paradise Valley. An hour later, whites began ganging up on isolated Negroes along Woodward Avenue.

At 8:30 A.M. a Negro delegation met with Detroit Mayor Edward Jeffries asking him to call federal troops to quell the rioting. Shortly thereafter the police commissioner made a similar request, and the mayor phoned Michigan Governor Harry F. Kelly with a plea for troops. But complications were to delay the dispatch of troops for more than fifteen hours. During the day the rioting continued. Gangs of white hoodlums stopped and burned Negro cars on Woodward Avenue, the city's main north-south thoroughfare. Although police took action against Negro looters, there were numerous reports of their failure to protect Negroes from white attack. Humphrey gives this account of one such incident:

> There was an automobile burning on Woodward and up a side street a Negro was being horribly beaten. Eventually the mob let the Negro go, and he staggered down to the car tracks, and he tried to get on a streetcar. But the car wouldn't stop for him.
> The Negro was punch-drunk. There were policemen down the street, but they didn't pay any attention to him.
> I started shouting, "Hey, copper. Hey, copper." And I pointed to the Negro in the middle of the street. The policeman finally took notice of me, but instead of going in the direction in which I was pointing he walked over

to his parked scout car. Then two huge hoodlums began to slug the Negro, and he hung there on the side of the safety zone, taking the punches as if he were a bag of sand . . .[10]

In the Negro community crudely organized gangs of Negro hoodlums looted white-owned or -operated stores.

By early evening, 10,000 surging, angry whites had jammed the City Hall area. As the evening wore on, violence increased. White men stopped streetcars and removed and beat Negro passengers. Automobiles were overturned in the street, and some of them were set on fire. A large white mob attempted to invade the Negro slum, but it was momentarily stopped by police near the Frazer Hotel, a Negro hostelry. Negro snipers in the hotel opened fire on the police, and a pitched battle between the snipers and the police ensued. Police were peppered with bullets from hotel windows. They returned the fire, blazing away at windows and hurling tear-gas bombs.

Later that evening Governor Kelly made a formal, official request for federal troops. Shortly before midnight, President Franklin D. Roosevelt signed the proclamation requested by the governor, calling upon the "military forces of the United States" to put down the "domestic violence" in Michigan. The U.S. Army quickly restored order within Detroit and dispersed the mobs. Nevertheless, tension continued to prevail in Detroit for days thereafter.

In the rioting, 34 people had lost their lives (25 Negroes and 9 whites). Twelve Negroes were shot to death by police while looting stores and three others after they had fired shots at the police. The City Receiving Hospital treated 433 riot victims of whom 222 were whites and 211 Negroes. At least 101 riot victims were hospitalized.

The Los Angeles Zoot-Suit Riots

Beginning on June 3, 1943, some three weeks prior to the Detroit race riot, a series of sporadic acts of violence and rioting broke out in Los Angeles that were directed against Mexicans.[11] For some time prior to the Los Angeles outbreak, large numbers of Mexican adolescent males had been wearing a style of clothing featuring long suit-coats and trousers that were pegged at the cuff, draping fully around the knees and arranged in deep pleats at the waist—the term "zoot-suit" was applied to the clothing. In addition, "zooters," as they came to

---

[10] *Ibid.*, 32–33.
[11] This summary of the Los Angeles Zoot-Suit Riots is largely based upon Ralph H. Turner and Samuel J. Surace, "Zoot-suiters and Mexicans: Symbols in Crowd Behavior," *American Journal of Sociology*, 62 (1956), 14–20; and Carey McWilliams, *North from Mexico* (Philadelphia: J. B. Lippincott Co., 1948), 244–258.

be known, wore their hair long, full, and well greased. The underlying causes of the outbreak, as in the case of the Detroit riot, were
complex and multiple.

Early on the evening of June 3, a group of eleven sailors were walking along a street in one of the city's predominantly Mexican slum
areas. On one side of the street there was a large brewery, on the
other a series of small bars, boarded-up storefronts, and small shops.
The sailors, on leave from their station in Los Angeles, were set upon
by a gang of Mexicans youths. One of the sailors was seriously injured; the others suffered cuts and bruises. Underlying antagonism
toward Mexicans and indignation over the attack upon armed-service
personnel at a time of intense national patriotism led police officers at
the nearby sub-station to remain on duty after their regular hours for
the purpose of apprehending the attackers. The police were unsuccessful, but the incident served to whip up community anger against the
Mexican population.

In a vengeful mood, some 200 sailors decided on the following
evening to take the law into their own hands. They hired a fleet of
twenty taxicabs and with the assembled "task force" headed for the
east side of Los Angeles where most of the Mexicans resided. Soon a
Mexican youth in a zoot-suit was spotted walking along the street. The
sailors stopped the taxi fleet and administered a severe beating to the
youth. The sailors than re-embarked in their cabs until they sighted
another zooter. The same procedure was repeated. Four times in the
evening the same treatment was meted out to Mexican youths—2 seventeen years old, 1 nineteen, and 1 twenty-three. During the evening,
police took 9 of the sailors into custody and the Shore Patrol arrested
another 17. One of the leaders of the expedition indicated, "We're
out to do what the police have failed to do. We are going to clean up
this situation."

The following morning, June 5, the Los Angeles *Daily News* carried
the headline "Wild Night In L.A.—Sailor Zooter Clash." That evening, sailors were joined by scores of soldiers and marines. With arms
linked, they paraded through downtown Los Angeles four abreast.
Anyone wearing a zoot-suit was stopped and ordered to put away his
"drape" by the following night or suffer the consequences. Although
law-enforcement officials did not appreciably interfere with the demon-
stration, they did arrest and jail twenty-seven Mexican youths "on suspicion" of various offenses. The same evening, sailors entered an east-
side bar and ordered two zoot-suit customers to remove their clothes.
One complied, but the other refused and was beaten, and his clothes
were torn off his back. The next evening, attacks upon zoot-suiters
were intensified.

More serious rioting broke out on June 7. By then, civilian gangs of east-side Mexican adolescents organized retaliatory attacks against unwary naval personnel. This served to swell the cries of "outrage." On the evening of June 7, several thousand soldiers, sailors, and civilians marched through downtown Los Angeles beating up every zoot-suiter accessible. Movie houses were invaded, and Mexicans were dragged from their seats. Streetcars were halted, and Mexicans, along with occasional Filipinos and Negroes, were pulled out of the cars and beaten. Those who wore zoot-suits were stripped of their clothing amidst the jibes and molestations of the crowd. The mob then marched through the Mexican district.

By midnight, military authorities intervened and declared the entire downtown area of Los Angeles "out of bounds" for military personnel. The Military Police and the Shore Patrol swung into action, and the rioting quickly quieted down. Public outrage against zooters continued high. The Los Angeles City Council adopted a resolution making the wearing of zoot-suits a misdemeanor. On June 9 the Los Angeles *Daily News* carried an editorial declaring that "the time for temporizing is past. . . . The time has come to serve notice that the City of Los Angeles will no longer be terrorized by a relatively small handful of morons parading as zoot suit hoodlums. To delay action *now* means to court disaster later on."

The most prominently reported claim of both zooters and sailors as to the cause of the rioting was that the other group was molesting "our girls." Rumors circulated that zoot-suiters had been responsible for "assaults on female relatives of the servicemen." Similarly, the Mexican youths claimed the sailors were molesting and insulting Mexican girls. Although the forces contributing to the rioting were many, the precipitating factor appeared to be feelings by each group that the other was engaged in improper and acute sexual competition.

Turner and Surace suggest that a crucial underlying factor contributing to the riots was a displacement of favorable aspects of the symbol "Mexican" with the unfavorable symbol "zoot-suiter" in the period preceding the riots. They hypothesize that rioting against a group is usually preceded by a period in which the key symbol is stripped of its favorable connotations and instead comes to evoke feelings that are unambiguously unfavorable. In order to uncover trends in the popular image of Mexicans, Turner and Surace examined the portrayal of the Mexican community and population by the Los Angeles *Times* during the preceding decade.

Within southern California, there had developed a strong theme which depicted Mexicans favorably. The traditions and history of the old rancheros as the earliest settlers of California found a sympathetic and honored place within the heritage of the state. Similarly, there existed a series of positive stereotypes of the Mexican temperament as dashingly romantic, gay, and brave. Homage was paid to Mexican art, dance, crafts, music, and fifth of May festivities. On the other hand, there was the stereotype of the Mexican as a law violator, in which he was associated with marijuana, sex crimes, knife wielding, gang violence, and public relief burdens.

The image of the Mexican within California, then, was conflicting and ambiguous. But such an ambiguous symbol was incapable of arousing feelings that were uniformly and exclusively unfavorable. The force of the positive tradition was too strong to permit widespread approval of rioting against Mexicans. The symbol "zoot-suiter" functioned as a means by which ambiguous feelings toward Mexicans were circumvented. The symbol of the zoot-suiter provided the public sanction and the focused attention essential to the development of mob activity. It evoked none of the imagery of the romantic past. Rather the new symbol was one of a breed of people who were devoid of morals. The zooter costume became for the larger community "a badge of delinquency." Crime, sex violence, and gang attacks became the dominant ingredients in this theme. Thus the unfavorable symbol "zoot-suiter" came to displace the favorable aspects of the symbol "Mexican" and provided a context for the rioting.

Urban Racial Rioting

In the summer of 1964, rioting broke out among segments of the Negro population in Harlem, Brooklyn's Bedford-Stuyvesant, Philadelphia, Rochester, Chicago, and a number of communities in New Jersey, and in the summer of 1965 in Chicago and the Watts' district of Los Angeles. The 1965 Watts' riot was by far the most serious: 37 people were killed, 895 people were injured, 787 buildings were damaged and 209 buildings were demolished, and property damage was estimated at more than 175 million dollars.

As opposed to the well-disciplined, highly purposive behavior of organized civil rights protests, the 1964 and 1965 disturbances were characterized by diffuse terrorism, vandalism, looting, and rioting that was non-instrumental and chaotic and engaged in by atomistic individuals and small groups.[12] For the most part the rioters were the permanently dispossessed and the unemployed or underemployed—in

[12] Allen D. Grimshaw, "Changing Patterns of Racial Violence in the United States," *Notre Dame Lawyer*, in press, and Robin M. Williams, Jr., "Social Change and Conflict, 1944–1964," *Sociological Inquiry*, 35 (1965), 20.

brief, underprivileged Negroes in large city ghettos. The civil rights movement has offered these Negroes few tangible benefits and can realistically promise few benefits for the near future. Their disadvantaged state is largely the product of low education, lack of skills, family disorganization, illegitimacy, poor health, alcohol and narcotic addiction, and other conditions that cannot be much improved by concessions won through social protest.[13] As the Washington *Post* editorially observed:

. . . the protest now runs the whole wretchedness of slum life and there is no remedy that promises any immediate improvement. The rioting does not merely spring from Negroes' discontent, but from slum dwellers' inability to find any hope of relief.

The demonstrators' antagonist, in the South, is a specific registrar, or judge, or Governor, whose name and face is known to everyone. In the North the antagonist is anonymous, "the man," and the man is not only everyone who is white but some, including policemen, who are Negro.[14]

Moreover, Kenneth B. Clark has noted:

The inmates of the ghetto have no realistic stake in respecting property because in a basic sense they do not possess it. They are possessed by it. Property is, rather, an instrument for perpetuation of their own exploitation. Stores in the ghetto—which they rarely own—overcharge for inferior goods. They may obtain the symbols of America's vaunted high standard of living— radios, TV's, washing machines, refrigerators—but usually only through usurious carrying costs, one more symbol of the pattern of material exploitation. They do not respect property because property is almost invariably used to degrade them.[15]

The civil rights movement has led many underprivileged Negroes to define many of their problems in racial terms. Their deep despair and a sense of alienation has contributed to an unconcealed hatred of whites, a rejection of more moderate Negro leaders, and susceptibility to the appeals of demagogues. Often the policeman has become the focal point for the resentment of underprivileged adult Negroes and poorly supervised and unemployed Negro youth. The policeman in uniform is the striking, visible symbol of white power, prejudice, discrimination, and oppression (by white slum-owners and businessmen)

[13] Leonard Broom and Norval D. Glenn, *Transformation of the Negro American* (New York: Harper & Row, 1965), 184–185.

[14] "The Voice of Desperation," Washington *Post*, August 9, 1964.

[15] Kenneth B. Clark, "The Wonder Is There Have Been So Few Riots," *The New York Times Magazine*, September 5, 1965, p. 10.

that many Negroes feel have kept them down. Los Angeles Police
Chief William H. Parker asserts:

. . . the police officer, wherever he may be, is the visible symbol of *status
quo*—the "power structure," the "establishment," the authority of government, by whatever name you wish to brand it. In other words, the policeman is a physical object against which persons believing themselves to be
oppressed can vent their frustrations.[16]

In recent years urban racial outbreaks have often been triggered by
policemen arresting a Negro. A crowd assembles and attacks upon
the arresting policemen may ensue. But whatever the precipitating
incident, once the situation becomes one of open conflict, three things
occur: (1) those suppressive and repressive forces that normally operate to keep tensions partially controlled are weakened or removed;
(2) latent threats become actual and new threats emerge, both polar-
ized along the cleavage of racial and ethnic group membership; and
(3) acts formerly disapproved now become approved and virtuous,
giving legitimate sanction to expression of hostile and aggressive impulses.[17] A Negro woman drawn into Harlem rioting in 1964 explains:

I don't know what it was, but hearing the guns I felt like something was
crawling in me, like the whole damn world was no good, and the little kids
and the big ones and all of us was going to get killed because we don't
know what to do. And I see the cops are white and I was crying. Dear
God, I am crying! And I took this pop bottle and it was empty and I threw
it down on the cops, and I was crying and laughing.[18]

Lynchings

Lynching has been commonly defined as mob action that summarily
and illegally takes an individual's life. In lynchings the action is one-
sided and directed against particular persons. Thus lynchings are to
be contrasted with race riots where mob action is usually a two-way
encounter in which violence is more or less indiscriminately and, to
one degree or another, reciprocally directed by one racial group against
another. The term "lynching" is probably derived from the name of
Charles Lynch, a sympathizer with the colonists during the Revolutionary War. In the Bedford County area of Virginia where Lynch
made his home, Tories were actively harassing the Continentals and
plundering their property. In the absence of functioning courts or law-
enforcement officers, Lynch and several of his neighbors took matters

---

[16] "A Police Chief Talks of 'Police Brutality,'" *U.S. News & World Report*,
August 10, 1964, 33.
[17] Robin M. Williams, Jr., *Strangers Next Door* (Englewood Cliffs, N.J.: Prentice-
Hall, Inc., 1964), 384.
[18] *Time Magazine*, July 31, 1964, 11.

in their own hands. Suspected individuals were apprehended and brought to Lynch's house, where they were tried. If found guilty, the accused was usually given forty lashes across his bare back. "Lynch's Law" or "Lynch-Law" became the term used to designate the practice. However, Lynch and his associates did not have recourse to executions.

Following the Revolutionary War the practice spread. Corporal punishment—generally whipping, tarring and feathering, or banishment from the community—was summarily handed out to wrongdoers without recourse to legal action. In the frontier West, the death penalty was often substituted for corporal punishment. For cattle and horse stealing, highway robbery, and murder, death by hanging at the hands of a mob was not uncommon. Before the Civil War, lynching of Negroes was rare except in insurrection conspiracies. The financial investments in Negro slaves served to restrain mob action. But with the coming of Reconstruction and the disfranchisement of the white leadership together with "scalawag" and "carpetbagger" rule, lynching became a major instrument for "keeping the Negro in his place."

It is possible to gain an estimate of the number of lynchings since 1882 from an annual summary made by the Chicago *Tribune* between 1882 and 1917 and from the statistics kept by Tuskegee Institute since 1889. The largest number of lynchings occurred during the 1890's, when 420 whites and 1,111 Negroes met death at the hands of lynch mobs. Since the 1890's, lynchings have progressively declined. In the 1900's there were 885 lynchings (94 whites and 791 Negroes), in the 1910's 616 (53 whites and 563 Negroes), in the 1920's 315 (34 whites and 281 Negroes), and in the 1930's 131 (11 whites and 120 Negroes). By the 1940's the figure had fallen to 32, and during the 1950's the practice became virtually non-existent. Except for New England, lynchings have occurred in all sections of the nation but were most frequent in the South, including Texas.

Contrary to popular opinion, most Negro lynch victims have not been charged with rape. However, southern efforts to justify lynchings have traditionally revolved about the assertion that such fearsome tactics were essential to control and frighten Negroes lest they undertake wholesale sexual attacks upon white women. South Carolina Senator Cole L. Blease, defending lynching, told a political rally in 1930, "Whenever the Constitution comes between me and the virtue of the white women of the South, I say, to hell with the Constitution." Various studies have suggested that no more than 25 per cent of the Negroes lynched since 1882 were accused of rape or attempted rape. The Tuskegee statistics indicate that accusations of homicide were responsible for slightly better than 40 per cent of the lynchings. Robbery, theft, insulting white people, attempting to vote, not knowing a Negro's place, and related charges were of lesser significance in the total picture. In some instances the lynched victim was mistaken for another or was completely innocent of the alleged crime.

Lynchings have not infrequently involved considerable brutality and sadism. On occasion victims were tortured, mutilated, and burned alive. The Southern Commission on the Study of Lynching cites this case, occurring before 1930, which bears marked sadistic overtones:

> The sheriff along with the accused Negro was seized by the mob, and the two were carried to the scene of the crime. Here quickly assembled a thousand or more men, women, and children. The accused Negro was hung up in a sweet-gum tree by his arms, just high enough to keep his feet off the ground. Members of the mob tortured him for more than an hour. A pole was jabbed in his mouth. His toes were cut off joint by joint. His fingers were similarly removed, and members of the mob extracted his teeth with wire pliers. After further unmentionable mutilations, the Negro's still living body was saturated with gasoline and a lighted match was applied. As the flames leaped up, hundreds of shots were fired into the dying victim. During the day, thousands of people from miles around rode out to see the sight. Not till nightfall did the officers remove the body and bury it.[19]

Since lynchings have involved strong elements of popular excitement, they have offered otherwise disgruntled whites an opportunity to express pent-up emotions and feelings. The hard core of most lynch mobs was drawn predominantly from young, propertyless, unemployed whites, some of whom had court records.[20]

Efforts through the years to secure congressional approval for anti-lynching legislation have failed. On at least two occasions an anti-lynching measure passed the House of Representatives but was killed in the Senate by southern filibusters. With the virtual disappearance of lynchings, such legislation is today largely a dead issue. The South has traditionally opposed anti-lynching legislation on the grounds that it violated states' rights. Nevertheless, especially in more recent years, there has been widespread disapproval by white southerners of lynching practices. Although lynchings have now become an extremely rare occurrence, there are some who feel that the problem remains, but in substitute forms. Groups such as the Southern Regional Council point to bombings of homes, the needless shooting of Negroes by policemen "in the course of arrest," and related forms of violence as a continuing heritage of the lynch era.

19 Southern Commission on the Study of Lynching, *Lynchings and What They Mean* (Atlanta: 1931), 40.
20 See: Hadley Cantril, *The Psychology of Social Movements* (New York: John Wiley & Sons, Inc., 1941), 106–110.

CONFLICT ACCOMPANYING SCHOOL DESEGREGATION

Little Rock

Desegregation of southern schools has on a number of occasions erupted in mob action. Serious outbreaks occurred at Milford, Delaware; Henderson, Clay, and Sturgis, Kentucky; Clinton, Tennessee; Mansfield, Texas; and Little Rock, Arkansas. Of these outbreaks, that at Little Rock was one of the most serious and received considerable attention. Desegregation plans had been underway in Little Rock for nearly two and a half years prior to the serious trouble of September, 1957. Under court order to desegregate, Little Rock had prepared to admit 10 Negro students to previously all-white Central High School, a school accommodating 2,000 students.[21]

Developments in the city had followed a relatively uneventful course until August 22, 1957, twelve days before the scheduled opening of the schools. That evening Governor Marvin Griffin of Georgia addressed 350 persons attending a pro-segregation rally in Little Rock. Griffin was joined by Roy V. Harris, Georgia political leader and ardent segregationist, in calling for militant resistance to school desegregation. Strong pressure by segregationist groups was subsequently brought to bear upon Arkansas Governor Orval Faubus. Faubus related, "People are coming to me and saying if Georgia doesn't have integration, why does Arkansas have it?"

Five days before the opening of schools, segregationists secured from the county chancery court an injunction barring the school board from desegregating Central High School. Governor Faubus testified at the hearing that he had personal knowledge that revolvers had recently been taken from white and Negro students, and that violence threatened to ensue if desegregation were permitted. Little Rock Police Chief Marvin Potts, upon hearing of the Faubus testimony, denied knowing of any of the reports alleged by the governor. The next day, August 30, a federal district court issued a blanket injunction against any interference with integration of the Little Rock public schools. In so doing, it nullified the chancery court injunction.

On Monday night, September 2, before the start of classes Tuesday morning, Arkansas National Guard troops appeared at Central High School and surrounded it. An hour later, Governor Faubus announced that the guardsmen had been sent "to maintain or restore order and to protect the lives and property of citizens." He ordered the school to

[21] This summary of the developments at Little Rock is based upon reports in The *New York Times* and the *Southern School News*.

remain segregated. The action came as a surprise to both the school board and the city government, neither of which had been consulted or forewarned as to the action. After the posting of the guardsmen, the school board instructed the Negro students to remain away from school the next morning. In the interval, it asked the federal court what it should do. The court, in turn, ordered the school board to admit the Negro pupils to classes on Wednesday morning. On Wednesday, nine of the Negroes appeared, but the troops turned them away. A few hundred whites jeered at the Negroes, but no one was touched or injured.

On Thursday the school board returned to federal court, asking that the desegregation plan be delayed indefinitely. In the days that followed, Governor Faubus continued to insist that he had ordered the guardsmen to the school because of impending violence. However, newsmen on their own failed to verify his claims about weapon sales, the seizure of revolvers, and the existence of caravans from other communities. Later in court, city officials likewise were unable to produce evidence that violence was imminent. During the week of September 8, guardsmen remained on duty at Central High and the Negro students stayed away from classes. On Saturday, September 14, President Eisenhower met with Governor Faubus at Newport, Rhode Island, in hopes of ending the stalemate. But Faubus remained adamant.

Another week passed in which attention was focused upon courtroom action. On Friday, September 20, the federal district court granted a temporary injunction against interference with the court desegregation order by Faubus and the National Guard. Shortly thereafter Faubus ordered the guardsmen to leave the school. The following Monday, the Negro students were again to report to classes.

Monday, September 23, was a bright fall day in Little Rock. The spotlight had been on the city for better than three weeks. By 8:00 an angry crowd of some 500 whites milled before police barricades opposite the school. In the crowd whites murmured over and over, "The niggers won't get in!" Lynch talk circulated. At 8:45 the school buzzer sounded. Suddenly a yell went up: "There they are, they're coming." The crowd rushed four Negro newsmen mistaken for the students. Mob members jumped, pushed, kicked, and manhandled the Negroes. Then a cry sounded: "Look, they're going into our school." Nine Negro youths entered the school by a side door. Anger surged through the crowd. One woman cried, "Oh God, the niggers are in the school!"

Hysteria broke out among crowd members. Some of the women screamed and sobbed. Six white teen-agers wailed and shrieked, "The niggers are in our school!" A girl screamed to her white classmates inside, "Come on out, come on out, come on . . ." Tears flowed down her face; her body shook spasmodically. Suddenly a man hurled himself over the barricade, shouting, "Let's go over the top. Who's going over with me?" A number of men joined him, but police aided by state troopers pushed them back.

A little later a white student carrying his books came out of the school. The crowd cheered and clapped. In the next few minutes a number of other students came down the school steps. During the morning, crowd size and feelings continued to build up. By noon the crowd was so noisy and threatening that school and city authorities agreed to remove the Negro students. Shortly thereafter they were escorted from the school. That afternoon President Eisenhower denounced the "disgraceful occurrences" at Little Rock and issued a proclamation commanding all persons obstructing justice to cease and desist and disperse.

The next morning some 250 persons gathered before the school in defiance of the President's order. President Eisenhower then ordered 1,000 crack paratroopers of the 327th Airborne Battle Group into Little Rock and federalized the Arkansas National Guard in order to remove it from Governor Faubus' command. During the day, Little Rock police were confronted with scattered attacks and gang fights between Negroes and whites in various parts of the city.

That same evening, September 24, the paratroopers arrived at Central High School and proceeded to deploy their forces about the grounds. The next morning, nine Negro students arrived at the school in an olive-drab car with an escort of army jeeps. Under the tight guard of the paratroopers, the students entered the school without mishap. In the evening, the students were again escorted from the school by army vehicles. During the school day, paratroopers, brandishing fixed bayonets, dispersed incipient crowds about the area. One individual resisted, and a paratrooper struck him with his M-1 rifle. He incurred a gash just above his eye and was removed to a hospital.

In the days that followed, order was maintained both in and outside the school by troops. Efforts by a segregationist group to get students to boycott classes failed. Gradually the Arkansas National Guard took over more and more of the guard duty, the last of the paratroopers leaving on November 27. By that time, only a handful of soldiers were maintained at Central High. Within the classrooms and halls periodic "incidents" occurred: A white would spit in the face of a Negro, a Negro's gym shoes would be thrown out the window, hissing and remarks would be directed against the Negroes, books would be knocked from the Negroes' arms, etc. For a time a few white students attempted to be friendly to the Negroes, but these students were ostracized by other whites. Accordingly, the Negro students had to go it alone and were socially isolated. In February, one Negro girl was expelled and three white students were suspended for periodic involvement in conflicts.

Within the community, tensions continued. Guardsmen were eventually withdrawn from Little Rock when school recessed for summer on May 28, 1958. During the summer, Faubus was re-elected governor by an overwhelming majority of Arkansas voters. Charges and counter-charges were hurled with considerable frequency between segregationists, on the one hand, and integrationists and those who merely wished to see public education maintained, on the other. On the heels of his election victory, Faubus secured passage by the state legislature of legislation permitting the closing of desegregated schools. Subsequently he ordered Central High School closed, and it remained closed for a full year until the legislation was ruled unconstitutional.

Some Generalizations on Desegregation Disorders

The great majority of southern school districts have instituted desegregation without racial disorders. There were less than thirty outbreaks of any consequence in the first eight years following the initial Supreme Court school ruling. From the differing experiences of school districts—those with peaceful and those with turbulent transitions to desegregation—it is possible to come up with a series of tentative generalizations on some of the factors contributing to desegregation disorders.[22]

1. The incidence and severity of disturbances accompanying school desegregation, especially mob situations and student boycotts, have tended to vary inversely, within limits, with

   a. The degree of clarity and firmness with which authorities communicate the desegregation policy and procedure to the population
   b. The degree of firmness and resoluteness with which authorities institute and execute the program in the face of resistance
   c. The degree to which authorities make clear their readiness to use legal penalties against lawbreakers

It appears that sternness and steadfastness on the part of officials are of primary importance in realizing a peaceful transition to desegrega-

[22] This material is largely taken from James W. Vander Zanden, "Turmoil in the South," *Journal of Negro Education*, 29 (1960), 445–452.

tion. Indecision and wavering tend to be interpreted by the populace as signs of weakness and, as such, are frequently exploited by segregationists. Where desegregation proceeds by clear, resolute action, it tends to be more readily accepted and taken for granted. Firm administration promotes an atmosphere in which people tend to concede the legitimacy of the policy although they themselves may not abandon anti-Negro sentiments. Where people expect that authorities will invoke laws against violence, incitement to violence, and truancy, they are less disposed to participate in open conflict.

2. Where authorities take a firm, resolute position on desegregation, "law and order" forces within the community are more likely to come to the foreground and defend the action. In the absence of such a position, they have often been prone to remain silent. A "law and order" position has found particular strength among the urban middle class. This group tends to place a strong premium upon the "law of the land" and to fear that the alternative to compliance is violence and disorder.

3. When individuals come into an unfamiliar situation such as that posed by desegregation, they tend to be especially sensitive to cues as to what constitutes appropriate and acceptable behavior. Accordingly, clarity and decisiveness in early integration policy and practice, and firmness in handling "incidents" arising in classrooms, halls, and school grounds, tend to assume the utmost importance.

4. Where communities undertake to desegregate only one or a few schools, they often open the door to charges of "favoritism" and "unfairness," to an attitude that "we are being asked to do this, but the others aren't." As such they may intensify resentment and hostility, ingredients that can feed resistance.

5. The presence of widespread negative attitudes toward desegregation has not necessarily constituted an insuperable barrier to peaceful desegregation. In fact, within the South, desegregation has been accomplished in the face of mass white preference for the segregated system. Research has suggested that prejudiced people will accept, and participate in, a desegregated setting if such patterns are established and accepted as appropriate by the community-at-large. By the same token, many differing values and attitudes converge within desegregation situations. The values and attitudes of whites on racial issues are not the only relevant and important values and attitudes— respect for law and order, fear of violence and chaos, regard for public education, and respect for authority are other important variables.

6. There appears to be no greater likelihood of disturbances where large numbers of Negroes are admitted to an all-white institution than

where only a few Negroes are admitted. The relative and absolute numbers of Negro children involved in the desegregation situation do not seem to be of critical importance.

7. The Negro-white population ratio of a community does not provide a reliable index by which to gauge the intensity or incidence of overt resistance to school desegregation or the probability of disorders resulting from it. However, as an index of resistance activity, the ratio becomes increasingly reliable as the ecological unit of analysis is enlarged, i.e., sub-area–state–sub-region.

8. Community-wide education programs, designed to facilitate adult acceptance of desegregation and generally operating through parent-teacher associations and civic groups, have apparently tended to be of only minor consequence in minimizing disorders. Louisville, Kentucky, received considerable national acclaim for its educational program designed to prepare the public for desegregation. However, the decisive factor in that community's peaceful transition appears not to have been its educational activity. Rather, a determined, unequivocal program instituted and pursued by authorities and a stern, non-tolerant policy toward agitators apparently played the crucial roles. On the other hand in Clinton, Tennessee, where serious disorders occurred, school authorities also undertook to prepare the public but failed to take a resolute stand against "troublemakers." One shortcoming of the educational programs has been that they have operated primarily through various civic groups with predominantly middle-class membership and have failed to reach lower socio-economic groups, groups from among which demonstrators most notably have been drawn. Furthermore, the value of education in dealing with racial prejudice has come under increasing doubt as sociologists have raised serious questions as to its effectiveness.[23]

9. Publicity associated with desegregation appears to be a complex variable. Some school districts have successfully initiated desegregation by avoiding publicity; others have employed extensive programs of publicity. Publicity in and of itself need not contribute to the success of a program. It may be detrimental where outbreaks are likely to be contagious. In 1954 the Charleston, West Virginia, newspapers, *The Gazette* and *The Daily Mail,* played a major role in stemming a snow-balling movement throughout the state of student strikes and boycotts by ignoring and "playing down" the existing outbreaks. Publicity may also serve to generate debate and discussion, arousing segments of the population which are opposed to desegregation but which may otherwise remain inactive owing to a failure to grasp the meaning or immediacy of the program.

[23] See Chapter 16.

10. Communities with considerable economic and social insecurity appear to be especially susceptible to racial disorders. The disturbances at Cairo, Illinois, in 1952, and in Sturgis and Clay, Kentucky, in 1956, appear to have been closely related to the unsettled and unstable economic conditions within these communities.

A Portrait of the Hard-Core Segregationists

In the years intervening since the Supreme Court's 1954 school-desegregation ruling, it has become amply clear that some southern whites are less ready for desegregation than others. Although the myth is prevalent among some Americans that "Southerners are southerners and they're all alike," whites of the South are quite different in their attitudes on segregation and the strength with which they hold these attitudes. Which whites, then, are most ready for desegregation of the public schools and which are most resistant? It was to this question that Professor Melvin M. Tumin and his students at Princeton University addressed themselves in a field study of 287 white adult males in Guilford County, North Carolina (Greensboro is the county's major city).[24]

After investigating a series of variables, Tumin and his associates put together a collective portrait of the hard-core segregationists, those who would use force if necessary to maintain a segregated school system. The summary sketch reads as follows:

The hard core is slightly younger than its neighbors.
It attends church about as frequently.
It is as stable in its residence patterns, but is somewhat more concentrated in the rural areas.
There are many fewer white-collar workers in the group, and many fewer professionals, proportionately speaking.
All the other groups have significantly higher averages of numbers of years of school completed, though the actual differences are not very large.
Similarly, the hard core has a significantly smaller percentage of members who have achieved nine or more years of schooling. In this regard, it stands differentiated from all the other groups.
The hard core is not different from the other groups in the percentage of its members who have gone on in school beyond the grammar school level achieved by their fathers . . .
The mass society, through the agencies of the mass media, does not impinge upon the hard core to nearly the same extent as upon other groups.[25]

The group most ready for desegregation, on the other hand, contained significantly more individuals who had secured some college

24 Melvin M. Tumin, *Desegregation: Resistance and Readiness* (Princeton: Princeton University Press, 1958).
25 *Ibid.*, 180.

education, earned upward of $6,000 a year, were exposed to three or more mass media, and were occupationally located in professional and white-collar positions.[26]

The two groups likewise differed in the extent to which they revealed evidence of *anomie*—the extent to which the individual felt himself well or poorly integrated within his society. The group most ready for desegregation appeared to be most thoroughly integrated within the society; the most resistant group appeared to be the most alienated from society; while groups intermediate between the most and least ready groups fell between the latter two groups in their anomie scores.[27]

The majority of the residents of this North Carolina community were neither extreme segregationists nor extreme desegregationists. Tumin and his associates estimated that between 15 and 20 per cent of the population fell at each of the two poles. The remaining 60 to 70 per cent were estimated to have intermediary sets of attitudes and responses. It might be expected that, on any issue as sharply posed as that of segregation versus desegregation, a marked polarization of the two points of view would be found. However, only a portion of the community could be characterized as either ardent advocates or opponents of the proposed social change. Between the two ardent groups stood the majority of the population. The Princeton researchers suggest that the implications of this conclusion are crucial. The majority seemed susceptible to being moved to support either of the two opposing viewpoints. It appeared to be a fluid majority, one that was neither rigid in its convictions nor committed to an extent that would preclude its modifying its position with the trend of events. Accordingly, community leadership seemed likely to play a critical role in influencing the behavior of the majority in relation to desegregation.[28] The extent to which the Princeton findings hold for other areas of the South remains unknown. Greensboro enjoys a reputation as one of the most liberal and progressive cities in the South.

SOME OTHER FORMS OF CONFLICT

Litigation

Where there is recourse to courts of law, minority groups may seek to advance their status through this instrumentality. Conflict is then likely to find a legalized expression. The dominant and minority groups fight for their respective aspirations through legislation and litigation.

[26] *Ibid.*, 198.
[27] *Ibid.*, 185–187.
[28] *Ibid.*, 198–199.

The United States Constitution, especially since the adoption of the equality provisions of the Fourteenth Amendment, has provided an important weapon in the hands of racial and ethnic minorities.

An important part of the Negro attack upon the southern caste system has been waged within the legal arena. The vulnerability of Negroes, especially in the southern rural setting where various informal and economic controls have traditionally prevailed, served for decades to limit the means by which the Negro minority might advance its position. Accordingly, the National Association for the Advancement of Colored People focused its efforts primarily upon legal action. With the urbanization of large segments of the Negro population, new means such as the ballot, boycotts, and sit-ins have come increasingly to the forefront as weapons in the Negro arsenal.

The Supreme Court's school-desegregation ruling of May 17, 1954, was both a product of litigation and a source of subsequent litigation. By virtue of its unique position in the American governmental system, the nation's highest court was able to unleash forces capable of initiating tremendous social and cultural change within the South. The upsurge in conflict ensuing since the ruling suggests that the South is moving toward a new social equilibrium in Negro-white relations. The "separate but equal" doctrine formulated in 1896 in the famous case of Plessy v. Ferguson provided legal sanction to the southern normative system. In the 1896 decision the Supreme Court had held that laws requiring the separation of the races did not violate the Fourteenth Amendment so long as equal facilities were provided for Negroes. The court denied that the enforced separation of the races stamped Negroes with a badge of inferiority. "If this be so," the court said, "it is not by reason of anything found in the act [of separation], but solely because the colored race chooses to put that construction upon it." As Borinski observes, the Plessy v. Ferguson decision established an equilibrium in the southern social order by granting the Negro formal equality in principle and the whites separation in fact, in this manner preserving the caste order.[29] But, in a dynamic, ever changing society such as that in the United States, a social equilibrium established in 1896 could not be expected to prevail endlessly into the future. Within the 1896 adjustment there were elements of latent legal and social conflict. Southern whites did not really accept the equality of the Negro, and the Negroes did not really accept separation. As time progressed, circumstances altered. The May 17, 1954, ruling gave recognition to this fact and liquidated the old "separate but equal" doctrine.

29 Ernst Borinski, "The Litigation Curve and the Litigation Filibuster in Civil Rights Cases," *Social Forces,* 37 (1958), 142.

The new Supreme Court ruling did not, however, provide for a sudden or immediate liquidation of the old arrangement. In its decree of May 31, 1955, implementing the desegregation ruling, the court provided for the gradual realization of school desegregation. The 1955 decree in essence invited further litigation. Concrete plans for local desegregation were left in the hands of federal district judges. Furthermore, if desegregation were to be realized, unless southern communities would desegregate without judicial compulsion, separate legal action would have to be instituted in virtually every school district. Thus the Supreme Court allowed for the gradual institutionalization of social change without disrupting the social fabric through precipitous change.

Accordingly, the stage was set for acute legal conflict. Many southern states resorted to legal obstruction in hopes of frustrating desegregation. More than 200 new segregation laws were enacted. The strategy of the South was outlined in editorial candor in the influential and respected Richmond, Virginia, *News Leader* on June 1, 1955:

> To acknowledge the court's authority does not mean that the South is helpless. . . . Rather, it is to enter upon a long course of lawful resistance; it is to take advantage of every moment of the law's delays. . . . Litigate? Let us pledge ourselves to litigate this thing for 50 years. If one remedial law is ruled invalid, then let us try another; and if the second is ruled invalid, then let us enact a third.

On the other hand, the National Association for the Advancement of Colored People organized with considerable success to overturn through litigation these various legal devices. The courtroom thus became a major instrument of intergroup conflict. The Civil Rights Acts of 1957, 1960, 1964, and 1965 gave Negroes additional legal weapons with which to fight discrimination and segregation.

Sit-ins

As the Negro movement for full equality expanded in the early 1960's, new weapons were introduced with which to wage the struggle. "Sit-ins" at Jim Crow lunch counters (later expanded to libraries and other facilities), "wade-ins" at segregated beaches and pools, "kneel-ins" at all-white churches, "stand-ins" at voter registration offices, and "freedom rides" to bus terminals with Jim Crow seating and eating facilities became a new note on the American scene. The lunch-counter demonstrations emerged first and served as an inspiration for the later tactics, hence let us consider them at greater length. The movement was launched on February 1, 1960, when four Negro freshmen from North Carolina Agricultural and Technical College entered a Greensboro variety store and bought some merchandise.[30] About 4:30 in the afternoon, they sat down at a lunch counter reserved for whites, but they had not been served by closing time an hour later. The movement did not take formal, organized shape until the next day, when some seventy-five A & T students inaugurated a "sit-in" at the same lunch counter. The movement quickly snowballed throughout the South, involving Negro youth from at least thirty-nine colleges and white youth from another nine. "You sell us pencils, paper, toothpaste, and clothes," was the students' argument, "therefore you are inconsistent not to serve us meals." Negro students undertook to sit at lunch counters despite their failure to be served. In this manner facilities were tied up and the stores lost business. Success was not long in coming to the movement. Within a year and a half at least 126 southern cities had some eating facilities desegregated.

The sit-ins had a number of ingredients that provided a special appeal to the participants. For one thing they presented an opportunity for individual participation and direct action. There was no need to go through the intermediary of a team of lawyers and a court. The issue was clear-cut, not bogged down in legal jargon. Furthermore, the activity had a flare for the dramatic; it was spectacular and quickly gained the attention of the media of mass communication. The participants could acquire considerable satisfaction from their involvement in the movement. Feelings of rapport, solidarity, and mutuality flourished in the crowded atmosphere of the lunch counters and served to reinforce determination and to provide a euphoric sense of strength and achievement. And, with the opposition economically vulnerable, victory promised to be immediate.

The Citizens Councils and "Economic Pressure"

On the heels of the Supreme Court's 1954 decision outlawing mandatory school segregation, the battle cry "Racial integrity—states' rights" once again loomed over the southern horizon.[31] An advertisement of the Alabama Association of Citizens Councils, appearing in the Montgomery *Advertiser* on September 29, 1957, typified staunch segregationist sentiment:

The negro agitators are thick as fleas in Alabama. They are everywhere in our state. They have been touted and built up by Yankee and communist

[30] This material has largely been summarized from James W. Vander Zanden, "Sit-ins in Dixie," *The Midwest Quarterly*, 2 (1960), 11–19.

[31] This material has in large part been summarized from James W. Vander Zanden, "The Citizens Councils," *Alpha Kappa Deltan*, 29 (1959), 3–9.

newspapers. Now they think they can do anything and everything to destroy our Southern way of life.

There is no doubt that the timetable of integration calls for integration of Alabama schools by these agitators. Unless the white people prepare for this timetable of events, our Southern way of life will be washed away in a torrent of mongrelization. Our South will be destroyed.

The action of the Supreme Court confronted many southern whites with a situation that they viewed as a distinct threat. In quick order more than 100 resistance organizations mushroomed across the South. Of these the most notable and successful were the Citizens Councils of the Deep South states and their sister organizations in Virginia, North Carolina, Georgia, and Tennessee. Championing the two-pronged program of "racial integrity" and "states rights," the Councils had their origin in Sunflower County, Mississippi, where Negroes constituted 68 per cent of the population. Of Sunflower County, Robert Patterson, executive secretary of the Mississippi organization, noted to national columnist Homer Bigart, "Sir, this is not the United States. This is Sunflower County, Mississippi!"

The overwhelming bulk of the Citizens Council strength has resided in the heavily Negro-populated Black Belt counties of the Deep South. The region lies north of both the Gulf Coastal Plain and the long-leaf piney woods country, and south of the Piedmont. It is here where the heart of the "Old South" was located, where the old ways hang on with the greatest tenacity, where Negro subordination has been most intense, and where yet today a considerable stake remains in the preservation of the traditional racial patterns. Speaking of this fact, State Representative J. S. Williams of Mississippi has said:

> The citizens committee [Citizens Councils] of Mississippi is not a Ku Klux Klan, but our purpose is to give a direct answer to the National Association of [sic] Colored People. We have a heritage in the South for which we should ever be vigilant. . . . The NAACP's motto is "The Negro shall be free by 1962"—and shall we accept that?
>
> We can't have it, for if we do, it would ruin the economic system of the South. The men of the South are either for our council or against it. There can be no fence-straddling.

The Councils have sprung up in the Black Belt as resistance organizations. Accordingly their fate has been closely linked with the status of integrationist efforts. Mississippi Councils had shown success prior to the Supreme Court's 1955 school-desegregation-implementation decree. But they were not to "boom" until the decree was handed down and five NAACP petitions for immediate desegregation were filed in the state.   Then the movement surged in growth in terms of both chapters and membership.   The story was not too different in other Deep South states.   When the NAACP launched its offensive in the summer of 1955 to win school desegregation throughout the Deep South, the Citizens Councils mushroomed in chapters and membership.   But with the ebbing in the gravity and imminence of the desegregation threat in 1956, Council activity waned.   By then the Councils had successfully wiped out NAACP chapters and activity in the area.

The situation was well summarized by Charles N. Plowden, a banker, large landowner, and prominent figure in the Council of Summerton, South Carolina, a community from which one of the original cases before the Supreme Court had come.   Indicating that the Summerton Citizens Council was inactive, Plowden remarked, "There's no need to meet.   Everything's going along quiet."   The story was the same elsewhere.   With NAACP inactivity and with threats of imminent integration lessened, the scene was "quiet."   Robert Patterson, leader of the Mississippi Councils, had repeatedly asserted in organizing speeches, "Organized aggression must be met with organized resistance."   In short, movement begets counter-movement.   The corollary has also tended to be true, namely, if movement subsides, counter-movement tends to subside.

Although no reliable figure on the Councils' membership has been available, it is probable that it never exceeded 250,000.   The organization has engaged in a great variety of activities ranging from the backing of a Negro-college fund raising to the drafting and sponsoring of segregation legislation.   From time to time, various chapters and state associations have sponsored mass meetings and rallies, combed voter-registration lists to disqualify Negroes, sponsored regular television and radio programs, pressured for the dropping of the Negro Urban League from local Community Chests, combed textbooks for "subversiveness," and "exposed" the NAACP, the Southern Regional Council, and related integrationist groups as "Communist fronts."

Most controversial of Council activities and tactics has probably been its alleged use of economic boycotts and sanctions.   Some of its leaders publicly called for "economic pressure."   Fred Jones, a Council leader, declared, "We can accomplish our purposes largely with economic pressure in dealing with members of the Negro race who are not cooperating, and with members of the white race who fail to cooperate, we can apply social and political pressure."   United States Senator Herman Talmadge of Georgia, addressing an Alabama Council rally, recommended a social and economic boycott of "the scalawags and carpetbaggers who fail or refuse to join the fight to preserve segregation. Anyone who sells the South down the river—don't let him eat at your table, don't let him trade at your filling station and don't let him trade at your store."

AROUSAL AND RESOLUTION OF CONFLICT

Muzafer Sherif and his associates have conducted a number of experiments designed to show how conflict typically arises between two groups, and how, occasionally at least, hostility gives way to cordial relationships.[32] For experimental purposes they employed an isolated summer camp as the setting. For their subjects they chose boys 11 or 12 years old, all of whom were healthy, socially well adjusted, somewhat above average in intelligence, and from stable, white, Protestant, middle-class homes—in brief, boys with a homogeneous background. The several stages of one experiment were as follows:

1. During the first six days of the boys' stay in camp, Sherif and his associates aimed to develop two separate groups, each having high cohesiveness and each unaware of the other's existence. Although the two campsites were not far apart, they were out of sight and earshot of each other; each group had its own facilities for swimming, boating, making campfires, and the like. Group cohesiveness was fostered through the promotion of common and interdependent activities characterized by goals integral to actual situations—cookouts, preparing campfires, improving swimming facilities, treasure hunts, and so on. Before the end of the first stage each group had adopted a name ("Eagles" and "Rattlers"), had developed a recognized status hierarchy among its members, had formulated individual role assignments, and had evolved various norms (e.g., concerning "toughness" and cursing).

2. The second six days, stage 2, consisted of experimental efforts to create friction between the Rattlers and the Eagles. The experimenters brought the two groups into competitive contact with one another through games and tournaments in which cumulative scores were kept for each group (not for individuals). The experimenters also devised situations designed to be frustrating to one group and perceived by it as caused by the other group—for instance, a ball field considered by the Rattlers to belong to them was pre-empted by the Eagles (as arranged

[32] Muzafer Sherif, "Experiments in Group Conflict," *Scientific American,* 195 (1956), 54–58, and Muzafer Sherif, *et al., Intergroup Conflict and Cooperation: The Robbers Cave Experiment* (Norman, Oklahoma: University of Oklahoma Book Exchange, 1961).

by Sherif and his associates). Friction became commonplace. The Eagles, after a defeat in a tournament game, burned a banner left behind by the Rattlers; the next morning the Rattlers seized the Eagles' flag when they arrived on the athletic field. Other incidents of name-calling, scuffling, and raiding developed.

3. The third six-day period was designed as an integration phase. Sherif and his associates first undertook to test the hypothesis that pleasant social contacts between members of conflicting groups would reduce friction between them. The hostile Rattlers and Eagles were brought together for social events: going to the movies, eating in the same dining hall, and so on. But far from reducing conflict, these situations only provided new opportunities for the rival groups to berate and attack each other—for instance, in the dining hall, they would hurl paper, food, and vile names at each other.

Sherif and his associates then returned to a corollary of their initial assumption about the creation of conflict. Just as competition generates friction, they reasoned, working in common on a project should promote harmony. To test this hypothesis experimentally, they created a series of urgent, and natural, situations that challenged the boys. In this way superordinate-goal activities were introduced. One of these followed the shutting off of the common water supply by the experimenters, a development explained by the experimenters as the work of "vandals." A plan was formulated whereby the damage was repaired through a good deal of work on everyone's part. As the boys began to complain of thirst, Eagles and Rattlers found themselves working side by side. A similar opportunity offered itself when the boys requested a movie. The experimenters told them that the camp could not afford to rent one. The two groups then got together, chose the film by a vote, jointly financed the venture, and enjoyed the showing together. In due course, intergroup frictions were virtually eliminated, new friendships developed between individuals across group lines, and the groups actively sought opportunities to mingle, entertain, and "treat" each other.

The Sherif experiments demonstrate the role that competition plays in generating hostility and prejudice. It also shows that the possibilities for achieving harmony are greatly enhanced when groups are brought together to work toward common ends. Hostility gives way when groups pull together to achieve overriding goals that are real and compelling to all concerned. This often occurs, for instance, in real life situations during wartime when various racial and ethnic groups rally together to pursue the war effort against a common national enemy.

SUMMARY

Conflict often, but not inevitably, accompanies contact between differing racial, ethnic, and religious groups. It entails a struggle over values and claims to wealth, power, and prestige, in which the opponents aim to neutralize, injure, or eliminate their rivals. The absence of conflict between groups does not in and of itself indicate that the relationship is stable and non-stressful; peace is not to be equated with satisfaction nor silence with consent. Ethnic and racial conflict may be both functional and dysfunctional for a society. It may find both violent and non-violent forms of expression.

8

Segregation

Segregation may be thought of as a process or state whereby people are separated or set apart. As such, it serves to place limits upon social interaction. Segregation finds one form of expression in discrimination, where individuals are accorded differential treatment by virtue of their membership in a particular group. But discrimination should not be thought of as a practice exclusively limited to members of the dominant group; racial and ethnic minorities may discriminate against members of the dominant group, but their ability to do so is usually quite limited. Another form in which segregation finds expression is in physical or spatial separation. Through the operation of various ecological processes, contrasting types are sifted and sorted into different sub-parts of an area, as reflected in Chinatowns, Harlems, Little Italys, and ghettos in general.[1]

THE NEGRO

The Negro Within the South

One of the myths prevalent in wide areas of the nation is that the South represents a solid, monolithic entity. Nothing could be further from the truth. Perhaps no American region possesses greater internal diversity than the South in historical background, geography, cultural composition, economic structure, and political and social outlooks. Within the South at least four sub-regions can be recognized: (1) the lowlands and coastal plains—an area in which plantations and cotton

[1] James A. Quinn, *Human Ecology* (Englewood Cliffs, N.J.: Prentice-Hall, Inc., 1950), 352.

229

have traditionally flourished and in which Negroes constitute a sizable proportion of the population; (2) the piney woods—areas of poor soil scattered along the coasts and intermittently below the Piedmont, in which the plantation economy never took hold, where Negroes are dispersed in relatively small numbers, and where "poor whites" represent a large segment of the population; (3) the Piedmont—a country of rolling hills between the lowlands and the mountains, in which the plantation system was virtually absent, in which the southern textile industry became rooted following the 1880's, and in which urbanization has proceeded rapidly since the Civil War, as is represented by such cities as Birmingham, Atlanta, Charlotte, Greensboro, and Winston-Salem; (4) the highlands, or mountain region—an area made up of the southern extension of the Appalachian Mountains in which few Negroes reside.

The 1960 Census reports reveal that there were 18,871,381 Negroes in the United States, of which nearly 60 per cent lived in the South (compared with nearly 90 per cent in 1900). Of the South's 1960 Negro population, 58 per cent was urban and 42 per cent rural (compared with 17 per cent urban and 83 per cent rural in 1900).

The race patterns commonly identified with the South do not operate with the same uniformity or intensity within these sub-regions or within all the southern states. Generally the Deep South states with the highest Negro ratios have shown the greatest firmness and proliferation in the patterns. Similarly, the patterns have tended to operate most strongly in small communities, especially in rural areas.

Throughout the South, Negroes as a general rule are relegated to positions in the lower rungs of the job hierarchy. Discrimination plays a major role in influencing this pattern.[2] One study of 108 establishments in the Upper South, chiefly within the tobacco and textile industries, showed the existence of 105,000 jobs of which 17,000 were filled by Negroes. In these plants Negroes were totally excluded from white-collar employment in white-managed firms and had scarcely a toe hold in supervisory jobs.[3] A similar situation prevails in Birmingham, where nearly three-fourths of all employed Negro males worked as laborers and operatives, the latter in largely repetitive, semi-skilled

[2] See: Art Gallaher, Jr., *Houston: The Negro and Employment Opportunities in the South* (Atlanta: Southern Regional Council, 1961); Major J. Jones, *Chattanooga: The Negro and Employment Opportunities in the South* (Atlanta: Southern Regional Council, 1962); Carl Holman, *Atlanta: The Negro and Employment Opportunities in the South* (Atlanta: Southern Regional Council, 1962); and 1961 U.S. Commission on Civil Rights Report, *Book 3, Employment.*

[3] National Planning Association Committee of the South, *Selected Studies of Negro Employment in the South* (Washington, D.C.: National Planning Association, 1955), 205.

work. In contrast, only one-fourth of the white males were found in these categories.[4] In the 43 Birmingham firms studied, with few exceptions, Negroes were found in common, manual-labor jobs requiring only a few days training time and very little education.[5]

In addition to employment as laborers, Negro males find employment as handy men, janitors, and errand boys for local concerns (e.g., drug stores, auto agencies, grocery markets, etc.), attendants at service stations, as yardmen, and in the personal employment of wealthier whites. Most urban communities, even of relatively small size, have a number of independent Negro skilled artisans such as bricklayers, plasterers, and carpenters. There are also a scattering of Negro entrepreneurs and service workers, e.g., owners of grocery stores, barbershops, and gas stations, and insurance agents, cabdrivers, etc. A small segment finds employment in professional and quasi-professional pursuits such as preaching, funeral directing, and teaching. The overwhelming majority of Negro female employment is in domestic work—in Birmingham, for example, some 75 per cent of the gainfully employed Negro women are thus employed.[6]

As a general rule, firms do not pay Negroes less than whites for the *same* job classification or discriminate with regard to eligibility for insurance, pensions, medical care, and fringe benefits.[7] The differences that occur are attributable to differences in ability, seniority, or similar factors. However, Negroes are assigned to less skilled, often unattractive jobs—within the tobacco industry, for example, to the preparation of leaves, maintenance jobs, and warehouse operations. The tradition within particular industries usually determines what work is placed in the category of "Negro jobs." "Negro jobs" as a rule pay less than "white jobs" demanding comparable skills.[8]

In the rural communities of the lowlands and coastal plains, the Negroes are frequently found as tenant farmers on plantations. Farming is usually carried out on the basis of some sharecrop arrangement. Depending upon the items furnished the tenant (e.g., house, tools, mule, fertilizer, etc.), at the end of the season a given portion of the final crop goes to the landlord, in some cases as much as two-thirds. But with the increasing shift of southern agriculture from cotton to other crops, the large-scale introduction of cattle, and the mechanization of agriculture, factors that have been coupled with the growth in the attracting power of the cities and the North, Negroes have left the

---

[4] *Ibid.,* 232 ff.
[5] *Ibid.,* 241–242.
[6] *Ibid.,* 230.
[7] *Ibid.,* 173, 207, 290–291, 315, 345–346, 364–371, 376–382, and 416–418.
[8] *Ibid.,* 162–163 and 173.

rural South in large numbers. Census data show that Negro farm operators in the United States decreased from 925,710 in 1920 to 272,541 in 1959, and tenants from 698,839 to 138,048.

In the rural areas of the South a good deal of the relations between the races tends to rest primarily upon personal, face-to-face contact and interaction. The Negro is in a subordinate and dependent relationship with a dominant white, often the white planter. Lacking as he does access to the power structure, the Negro finds it necessary to rely upon personal influence with whites as a means of realizing protection, securing aid in time of difficulty, obtaining favors, and acquiring a sense of security. In large urban areas segregation and the complexity of urban life insulate many Negroes from contacts with whites. Life in the cities is characterized by a greater impersonality of contacts which serves to destroy the traditional rural basis of racial adjustment that rests upon intimate personal relations.

The relationships between Negroes and whites in the South are governed by what some have called the "etiquette of race relations." This pattern of racial etiquette involves rules pertaining to such forms of behavior as handshaking, the lifting of the hat, the use of front and rear entrances of homes, the employment of social forms and titles when meeting on the street and at work, etc.

The social worlds of the two races are separate and distinct. Many ordinary courtesies, dining together, fraternizing, and other semi-social acts of friendliness and informal social intercourse are not extended by whites to Negroes. Such behavior is interpreted by whites as "social equality" and is severely frowned upon. Visiting and entertaining do not take place across the color line. With but rare exceptions church membership, cliques, and voluntary associations do not cross racial lines. The exceptions are primarily found among professional groups such as ministerial and medical associations. Segregated schools have been traditional, but this pattern has been undercut by the Supreme Court's desegregation ruling of 1954 and recent civil rights legislation.

Except for the Reconstruction period, Negro election or appointment to public office has been a development limited almost exclusively to the post-World War II period. In the decade following the war, a relatively small number of Negroes within the South won election or appointment to city councils and boards of education. Since 1955, the election of Negroes to such posts has become more prevalent. Although still a limited development, Negroes in some cases have won election to state legislatures from predominantly Negro districts (as of 1965, Georgia, Tennessee, Texas, Oklahoma, Maryland, and Missouri had one or more Negro state legislators).

Negro voting has similarly been a development that for the most part has come about since World War II. With the turn of the twentieth century, Negro voting became a rare phenomenon in wide areas of the Deep and Mid-South, especially within rural communities. The situation was most acute in the heavily Negro-populated Black Belt counties, where Negroes outnumbered whites. In 1900, there were 286 such counties; by 1960, the number had been halved to only 144. Here either Negroes had traditionally been completely disfranchised or a handful of "good" Negroes had been permitted to vote. However, even "good" Negroes were allowed to vote only in the virtually meaningless general elections unil the 1940's. It was not until the Supreme Court ruled the Democratic white primary unconstitutional in 1944 that Negroes were allowed to vote in the crucial primary elections (with the weakness of the Republican party within the South, the winner of the Democratic primary normally was the victor in the general elections).

Poll taxes, literacy tests, and interpretation of the Constitution clauses, all of which were administered by local whites, traditionally served to minimize Negro voting. If these techniques were not successful, extralegal methods of intimidation were applied. Tactics of coercion were most prevalent in rural and small-town communities. Beginning with the passage of civil rights voting legislation in 1957, together with new voting legislation in 1960, 1964, and 1965, the United States government has initiated legal action within a number of "hard-core" areas (estimated to constitute less than 80 of the South's 1,107 counties) to compel county officials to register qualified Negro voters. Civil rights groups have also mobilized their resources toward a similar end, as in Selma, Alabama. In 1947 there were an estimated 595,000 registered Negro voters in the eleven states that once constituted the Confederacy, primarily in urban areas. By 1952 the number had risen to 1,008,614, by 1958 to 1,303,627, and by 1964 to 2,174,200. Indeed, Negro votes are assuming increasing importance within southern political life. Hence, in the 1964 Presidential election, of the six southern states carried by the Democratic Party, four (Arkansas, Florida, Tennessee, and Virginia) clearly would have gone Republican had it not been for the Negro vote. One other, North Carolina, might have. Only in Texas, President Johnson's home state, did the Democratic party clearly receive the majority of white votes.

In law enforcement and the courts, a double standard of justice has often tended to prevail for Negroes. This has been especially prevalent in the small towns and rural communities of the Deep South states. In cases where a Negro is tried for some crime against a white, it has traditionally been a relatively rare development for the court to decide in the Negro's favor, especially if the Negro is accused of an attack upon a white person. On the other hand, whites guilty of offenses against Negroes may not be prosecuted and when cases arise the police or judicial officials may discourage the action. Within some areas of the South a pattern of violence and intimidation emerged when legal action was considered uncertain or inadequate. Lynchings and whippings were notorious measures of extralegal punishment. It should not be concluded, however, that violence or intimidation against Negroes necessarily ran rampant. Checks operated within the white group to limit its use.

Segregation and dual facilities have characterized southern life for some sixty years. Dual school systems and dual churches had an even longer heritage. Negroes were segregated from whites in theaters, ball parks, waiting rooms, jails, and public conveyances. Separate parks, beaches, and swimming pools were operated for the two races although a comparable facility for the Negro group had not always existed. Signs labeled "WHITE" and "NEGRO" often appeared in buildings frequented by the two races, pointing to such separate facilities as rest rooms and drinking fountains. On the whole the two groups patronized different eating establishments, taverns, hotels, and recreational centers. Beginning in 1954, important inroads have been made through legal action, civil rights demonstrations, and economic boycotts in ending some of the more formal and legal manifestations of segregation in these areas (see Chapter 16).

The Negro in Large Northern Cities

Prior to 1915, there had been no significant migration of Negroes to the North or the West. In 1910 some 90 per cent of the nation's Negro population resided in the South. Beginning with World War I, Negroes began migrating in large numbers to northern cities. The migration continued unabated until 1930, when it dropped slightly during the Depression. It picked up again during World War II and has continued in large numbers since. In 1960, the Negro population of New York City alone stood at 1,087,931, or 14 per cent of that city's total. In the same year, Negroes within Chicago constituted 22 per cent of the population; Philadelphia, 26.4 per cent; Detroit, 28.9 per cent; Los Angeles, 13.5 per cent; Baltimore, 34.8 per cent; Cleveland, 28.6 per cent; and Washington, 53.9 per cent.

This northern migration brought with it the growth of segregated Negro communities within the larger cities. The initial settlement of Negroes was usually in the blighted areas near the center of the city.

As the Negro population grew, the "black ghetto" tended to expand block by block and neighborhood by neighborhood, sometimes by concentric circles, sometimes radially along the axes of major streets. The "better" residential sections kept being built farther and farther out, and, as the blighted sections were abandoned, the latter were opened to Negroes.[9] Since World War II, an additional process has emerged: Negroes are leapfrogging over white areas to establish Negro districts in deteriorating outlying areas. For the most part, the jumps are to the older, blighted areas of the city, but not exclusively. Thus in Milwaukee, there is an invasion occurring on the northwest boundary of the city in an area that is relatively new.[10] Within the Negro ghettos, housing is more expensive than comparable non-ghetto housing. A survey by the Massachusetts Advisory Committee to the United States Commission on Civil Rights found that Negro families in Boston pay $65 a month for housing for which the white population, for comparable space, pays $57 a month.

Along with the influx of Negroes into the nation's major urban centers, there has been a migration of middle- and upper-class white families into the suburbs. The trend has threatened to transform the cities into slums, with very large Negro populations, ringed by predominantly white suburbs.[11] The nation's capital is an example. Washington has the highest concentration of Negroes of any large American city, 53.9 per cent. Between 1950 and 1960, the number of Negroes inside the city of Washington increased by 130,934, while the number of white residents declined by 172,602. During the same period, the Negro population in the Washington suburbs increased by only 18,492, while the number of whites increased by 554,372.

A number of factors have contributed to the relative exclusion of Negroes from the suburbs. First, the sheer cost of suburban housing has placed it beyond the means of the great mass of Negroes, who, for the most part, are heavily concentrated in the lower income groups. Second, whites often have made it clear that Negroes would be unwelcome in the suburbs, and rather than experience social isolation many Negroes have chosen to avoid such communities. Third, restrictive zoning and various subdivision and building regulations have been employed to keep Negroes out. Some communities, for example, have set a minimum of two or more acres for a house site or have required

[9] Morton Grodzins, "Metropolitan Segregation," *Scientific American,* 197 (October, 1957), 33–41.

[10] William K. Brussat, "Incidental Findings on Urban Invasion," *American Sociological Review,* 16 (1951), 94–96.

[11] Leo F. Schnore and Harry Sharp, "Racial Changes in Metropolitan Areas, 1950–1960," *Social Forces,* 41 (1963), 247–252.

expensive street improvements but have waived these regulations for "desirable" developments while enforcing them for "undesirable" developments. Fourth, violence and coercion have occasionally been employed, such as the demonstrations that occurred before homes acquired by Negro families at Levittown, Pennsylvania.[12]

The shift in the ecological distribution of the nation's urban population, with the continuing influx of Negroes and the movement of higher-income whites to the suburbs, is having a number of consequences. Blighted areas appear to be spreading, in part the result of the fact that the Negro population has traditionally increased faster than the living space available to it. As Negroes move into new areas, one-family houses are converted to multiple dwellings and two or more Negro families may be squeezed into apartments previously occupied by a single white family. Likewise, business activities and associated property values within the central business districts have tended to decline. With non-white and low-income customers more and more predominant in the clientele of downtown stores, and with the appearance of suburban shopping centers, business establishments in the centers of the cities have tended to concentrate on cheaper merchandise. In large cities such as Chicago, Boston, and Los Angeles, the main streets are becoming infested with "sucker joints" for tourists— all-night jewelry auctions, stores with bargain linens and cheap neckties, hamburger stands, and bars with jazz bands.[13]

Patterns of residential segregation are pronounced within American cities. Demographers have developed an index of urban residential segregation that ranges in value from 0 to 100. If each city block contains only whites or only nonwhites, the index would assume a value of 100. On the other hand, if race plays no role at all in determining residential location, then any block chosen at random would have each racial group represented in the same proportion as in the city as a whole, and the index would assume a value of zero. Taeuber, computing indexes for 109 cities with Census data from 1940, 1950, and 1960, found that in each of these years between one-fourth and one-half of the 109 cities had index values above 90.0, and more than three-fourths had values above 80.0:

Substantively, the most interesting finding of this research is the universally high degree of residential segregation between whites and Negroes within the cities of the United States. Whether a city is in the North, South, or West; whether it is a large metropolitan center or a suburb; whether it is a coastal resort town, a rapidly growing industrial center, or a declining

[12] Grodzins, op. cit., 33–34.
[13] Ibid., 35 ff.

mining town; whether nonwhites constitute forty percent of the population or less than one percent; in every case white and Negro residences are highly segregated from each other. There is no need for cities to vie with each other for the title of "most segregated city"; there is room at the top for all of them! [14]

With the exception of two regions, the Northeast and the West (which showed declines in the index values for the period 1940–1960), residential segregation appears to be increasing within the United States.[15]

The residential segregation of Negroes contributes to segregation in other spheres of life. Schools are commonly districted on the basis of neighborhoods, with the result that segregated facilities emerge. Although there is no legal segregation of Negroes within northern schools, some city officials have attempted to exploit the spatial separation of the races by drawing school-district lines so as to minimize the number of mixed schools and the number of Negro children in predominantly white schools. Since elementary schools generally draw upon a smaller locality than high schools, segregation has been more prevalent in the former than the latter. Even where officials have the best of intentions, it is often difficult, if not impossible, to escape the consequences of segregated residential patterns in establishing school districts.

Chicago is a good illustration   The city's 530,000 public school pupils are essentially segregated as soon as they start school. Ninety per cent of the elementary students attend either all-white or all-Negro schools; only 18 per cent of the high school students go to integrated schools. De facto segregation results from a neighborhood school policy under which children attend schools close to home. Surveys conducted by Robert J. Havighurst and Philip M. Hauser, both of the University of Chicago, reveal that Negro schools are much more overcrowded than white schools, and served by the least experienced teachers. Even under ideal circumstances, it is more difficult to teach youngsters from slum environments. The Havighurst report observes:

These children come to school pitifully unready for the usual school experiences, even at the kindergarten level. Teachers remark that some don't even know their own names and have never held a pencil. Their speech is so different from that of the teachers and the primer that they almost

[14] Karl Taeuber, "Negro Residential Segregation: Trends and Measurement," *Social Problems*, 12 (1964), 48.

[15] Using a somewhat different index, Cowgill comes to somewhat similar conclusions. See Donald O. Cowgill, "Trends in Residential Segregation in American Cities, 1940–1950," *American Sociological Review*, 21 (1956), 43–47, and "Segregation Scores for Metropolitan Areas," *American Sociological Review*, 27 (1962), 400–402.

have a new language to learn. They have little practice in discriminating sounds, colors or shapes, part of the everyday experiences of the middle-class preschool child, whose family supplies educational toys and endless explanations.[16]

Patterns of spatial separation influence the development of separate Negro social institutions and associations. Many factors contribute to the perpetuation of separate Negro churches within northern cities, but the common role of the church as a neighborhood organization within American life cannot be overlooked as one such factor. The "black ghettos" have provided the foundation for separate Negro businesses, usually small establishments offering consumer goods or services. Social cliques and organizations often arise out of neighborhood patterns and accordingly take on a segregated character. The same situation holds true in the use of various recreational facilities including parks, beaches, swimming pools, theaters, and bowling alleys and in the use of eating places.

In northern cities Negroes experience no barriers to voting; in fact, various political factions may undertake strenuous efforts to get Negroes registered and, later, to the polls. Negroes may be elected to high positions of public office but as yet not to the very top positions. Negroes, however, have been elected to state legislatures and to the U.S. House of Representatives from predominantly Negro districts. The Negro vote in large northern cities has been gaining crucial importance in major elections. Since the New Deal period, Negro districts have voted overwhelmingly Democratic. Democrats within a number of northern states have been dependent upon the Negro vote to give them their margin of victory in close elections. When Republicans have been able to make inroads into this vote, or where a sizable number of Negroes stays away from the polls, Democrats have often lost elections. In presidential elections, New York, Pennsylvania, Illinois, Ohio, and Michigan command decisive electoral votes. In recent elections Negro voters in New York City, Philadelphia, Chicago, Cleveland, and Detroit have occupied a pivotal role in determining to which presidential candidate these states would swing. Accordingly, the Negro voice in government has been strengthened and, at times, Negroes have been able to exert influence beyond their numerical voting strength.

Within employment, Negroes are disproportionately represented in the lower rungs of the job hierarchy and underrepresented in skilled, clerical, business, and professional positions. The years have witnessed a slow erosion of the color line, yet a job ceiling is still prevalent in

[16] Jack Star, "Chicago's Troubled Schools," *Look*, May 4, 1965, 59.

Negro employment, relegating Negroes chiefly to the less skilled, menial, or unpleasant jobs. Government employment, however, is usually open to them on a non-discriminatory basis. One of the major problems confronting Negro workers is that they are usually the last to be hired, and accordingly, through the operation of seniority, the first to be fired. During economic recessions, their rate of unemployment generally runs more than double that of white workers. Similarly, their concentration within unskilled and semi-skilled jobs in industry, jobs particularly vulnerable to the vicissitudes of the business cycle, has rendered their position especially difficult. Long-term unemployment, the product of automation and other technological developments, has likewise had a lopsided effect upon Negroes. Anti-discrimination laws have been passed by a number of states, and anti-discriminatory clauses have been inserted in federal contracts offered to private industry, all of which have been designed to immunize Negroes against hiring bias. Still Siegel finds, employing Census data, that after making allowances for regional, educational, and occupational differences, it still costs Negroes roughly a thousand dollars a year just to be a Negro.[17]

Even if bias could be erased, Negroes as a group would still tend to be handicapped. The critical problem of Negro employment today has been created by large-scale economic and technological changes involving the elimination of many unskilled and semi-skilled jobs. In brief, a serious problem is posed for those who have to work with their hands in a society that appears to have less and less work for people with only hands. The 1960 Census reveals that in 68 selected American cities, 50 to 84 per cent of employed Negroes fell into unskilled and semi-skilled categories. And in these 68 cities, 15 to 62 per cent of all Negro families had an annual income of less than $3,000, the U.S. Government's "poverty line" figure. Negro employment problems are complicated by a high rate of school dropouts. For these 68 selected cities, the percentage of school dropouts among Negroes 25 years of age and over ranged from 54 per cent in Denver and Seattle to 88 per cent in Muskegon, Michigan.[18] Facts such as these lead Killian and Grigg, two prominent sociologists, to observe:

The level of living and the cultural standards of the masses of Negroes trapped in these densely populated, continuously deteriorating ghettos are not likely to keep pace with "the American way of life." Hence there is

17 Paul M. Siegel, "On the Cost of Being a Negro," *Sociological Inquiry,* 35 (1965), 41–57.

18 M. S. Handler, "U.S. Finds Negroes Trapped in Menial Jobs," *New York Times,* November 16, 1964.

great danger that, for countless Negroes, faith in America will be drowned in this black sea. Their isolation from white Americans will be magnified and, in their bitterness and isolation, they may be mobilized for violent conflict against people who need only to be recognized as white to be identified as enemies.[19]

Negroes experience no discrimination in the use of public conveyances or public facilities generally. In theaters there is no formal segregation, but there may be occasional informal efforts to discourage Negro attendance at a few of the exclusive ones. A similar situation holds true with regard to eating places. Lodges and secret societies for the most part exclude Negroes, and, except for social clubs characterized by relatively superficial contacts, a similar pattern prevails in the social sphere. Professional groups, however, are increasingly admitting Negroes to membership.[20]

The Negro Within a Small New England Town

A study by Frank F. Lee presents a picture of the race patterns of Branford, Connecticut—a small, industrial-vacation and suburban town of just over 10,000 people.[21] Negroes numbered about 170 persons, representing 1.5 or 2.0 per cent of the total. The community is located some ten miles east of New Haven. Until 1850, Branford's population was exclusively Protestant, but an influx of Catholics since that time has contributed to a sizable Catholic population. Ethnically the town is approximately 40 per cent Yankee, 14 per cent Scandinavian, 13 per cent Slav, 13 per cent Italian, and 10 per cent Irish.

Within the realm of employment, Negroes experienced a good deal of discrimination. Negro men were primarily limited to semi-skilled and unskilled labor in the foundries of the community. They appeared to be treated equally with whites up to and possibly including the supervisory ranks, but promotions above this level did not occur. Most of the workers belonged to an industrial union in which no discriminatory practices could be discovered. Negro women were chiefly employed in domestic work or in unskilled or semi-skilled jobs in a few of the smaller local factories.

[19] Lewis Killian and Charles Grigg, *Racial Crisis in America* (Englewood Cliffs, N.J.: Prentice-Hall, Inc., 1964), 116.

[20] See Irving Babow, "Discrimination in Places of Public Accommodation: Findings of the San Francisco Civil Rights Inventory," *The Journal of Intergroup Relations*, 2 (1961), 332–341.

[21] Frank F. Lee, "The Race Relations Pattern by Areas of Behavior in a Small New England Town," *American Sociological Review*, 10 (1954), 138–143, and *Negro and White in Connecticut Town* (New Haven: College and University Press, 1961).

Three-fifths of the Negro population were concentrated in a semi-segregated area near the railroad terminal and the town's major industries. A few white families were also found in this locale, but to Branford residents it was referred to as the "Negro section of town." A local foundry contributed to the residential pattern of segregation by developing a little Negro colony of its own within the area. Outside of this locality, it was practically impossible for Negroes to rent or buy a home. The citizens of Branford defeated a public-housing proposal, in part out of fear that Negroes would become tenants.

For the most part, the Negro and white worlds within Branford were separate. Although white churches appeared willing to welcome Negroes to their services, religiously inclined Negroes tended to go to the local African Methodist Episcopal Zion Church, the only major Negro institution in the community. The Roman Catholic church displayed few signs of discrimination, and Negroes apparently would have been welcomed. However, Branford's Negro Catholics generally did not participate in the church's services or activities. At times, Negroes attended the white-Protestant churches for special services, but within the more intimate social activities of the churches they appeared to find a cool reception.

Similarly, there was little joint Negro-white participation in adult social activities. Negroes were found in membership in two formal organizations, the chamber of commerce and the town band. It appeared unlikely that the more "social" groups and clubs would admit Negro members, although this did not apply as strongly to those with a younger membership. The Red Cross and the Visiting Nurse Association had no Negro members, and it was questionable if they would have been welcomed. Teen-age Negroes and whites jointly participated in three social activities: the American Legion baseball club, the Boy Scouts, and the Junior Musical Art Society, although Negro participation within the latter two groups was very limited.

Discrimination varied within public facilities. It was most apparent in the use of barbershops and bars, less so in the use of overnight accommodations, and virtually absent in the use of stores and professional services. By the same token, the pattern was not consistent, since one Negro might be turned away and still another admitted. Except for voting, Negroes were not engaged in political activity nor did they hold government positions. Negroes were accorded equal treatment within the courts and as applicants for public assistance. There was an absence of school segregation, and Negro children engaged with white children in almost all the school activities, although one school official exhibited antagonism toward Negroes. A number of Negro parents were members of the PTA, although they were not active members. There were no Negro teachers, and there seemed little prospect that any would be hired.

Legal discrimination was absent, Branford having no laws that would establish a specific status for the Negro. Lee notes that the northern race patterns differ from those in the South in that within the North the "place" definition of the Negro is less clear and detailed and there is less consensus regarding it. Accordingly there is more room for deviation within the North, with regard to both the overall pattern and the behavior of individual Negroes. By virtue of outstanding personality, ability, and personal acquaintanceship with strategically placed community leaders the individual Negro may be capable of considerably stretching the limits of his "place" definition; in some instances, he might even breach the barriers imposed upon him. This is not usually true within the South.

PUERTO RICANS

In 1898, Spain ceded Puerto Rico, a Caribbean island, 35 miles wide, 100 miles long, to the United States. Despite the rapid economic and political changes that followed, Puerto Rico retains in language, religion, and many other aspects its character as a Spanish colony. Since 1917, Puerto Ricans have been United States citizens, but until 1948 they did not elect their own governor. Although sending delegates to national party conventions, they do not vote for the president of the United States nor are they represented in Congress by voting members. Racial intermixture has been going on in Puerto Rico since the sixteenth century, and the variety of racial types ranges from blue-eyed, blond Caucasians to dark-skinned Negroes. While the Negroes were not discriminated against during Spanish occupancy, the Spanish Caucasians enjoyed a higher status, and whenever it was possible to do so Negro ancestry was denied. Since 1898, Puerto Ricans have adopted in some part American patterns of race consciousness, with distinctions on the basis of skin color and physical appearance. Nevertheless, discrimination is only subtly apparent in social affairs and is infrequent in other spheres of life, including economic employment.[22]

Puerto Ricans have been migrating to the mainland of the United States for over a hundred years, but it is only since the end of World War II that the migration has taken on mass proportions. Although there are scattered settlements of Puerto Ricans in other sections of

[22] C. Wright Mills, Clarence Senior, and Rose Kohn Goldsen, *The Puerto Rican Journey* (New York: Harper & Row, 1950), 3–6.

the nation, the greatest concentration has always been in New York City. The city's Puerto Ricans numbered 612,574 in the 1960 Census. The main focus of the Puerto Ricans within New York City has been east Harlem, but they are also found elsewhere in Manhattan, the south Bronx, and Brooklyn. A 1948 study of New York Puerto Ricans revealed that, over the years, women outnumbered men in the migration. In racial composition, 64 per cent of the migrants were white, reflecting the predominantly white character of the island's population; 16 per cent were intermediate, including the *indio,* those with copper cast to their skin and a tendency toward prominent cheekbones, and the *grifo,* those with light complexions, blue or gray eyes, but kinky hair, or some other combination of diverse racial features; and 20 per cent were Negro. The migrants were selected from the most productive age groups of the Puerto Rican population. Although less educated than the general population of New York, they were on the whole more educated than the average within Puerto Rico. Most of them had lived in the island's urban centers before coming to New York.[23]

One of the most striking aspects of the Puerto Rican communities of New York City is the dress of the women. Many of the women wear clothing of Spanish antecedents, with the dress or skirt gathered tightly at the waist and flaring out wide toward the hem. The women step along with a free hip movement, causing the hem to swish considerably, clockwise and back again. Scarves are commonly worn over their heads, the colors usually light in what might be called pastel tones except that they have a metallic or aniline dye look to them. The men often wear surplus army clothing that gives them an overall drab appearance. Duck-tailed haircuts and sideburns together with blue jeans and black-leather or colored jackets have been popular among the young men.[24]

A number of special institutions have grown up in Puerto Rican districts, most notably food shops, storefront churches, and travel agencies. The *bodegas,* the Spanish-American food shops, owe their existence to air transport and the great difference between the island's food habits and those prevailing within the United States. The storefront churches have a strong evangelical, puritanical, and even Holy Roller cast and are making inroads upon the traditional Roman Catholicism of the Puerto Ricans. The travel agencies can be spotted by the sign "PASAJES" (passages) on their fronts and deal mainly in "thrift"-class plane tickets to Puerto Rico.[25]

[23] *Ibid.,* 22–39.
[24] Christopher Rand, *The Puerto Ricans* (Fair Lawn, N.J.: Oxford University Press, 1958), 13–14.
[25] *Ibid,* 20–23.

The crucial motivating force in the migration appears to be the economic pull of New York; the island sources of information about the city are many and usually favorable. Population pressure on the island, as manifested in low living standards and lack of jobs, together with the city's reputation for economic opportunity serves to stimulate the migration. Many of the migrants also respond to the pull of relatives already settled in New York.[26] Language is one of the major problems confronting the immigrants. Spanish is the language of the island, and at least three-fifths of the migrants arrive in New York without a mastery of English adequate to make their way inconspicuously. Yet, to travel on subways or buses and to function in many other areas of life, some familiarity with English is necessary.[27]

The Puerto Rican migrants cluster primarily in the manufacturing and processing industries of New York, where some 50 to 60 per cent of those working find employment. Another 30 per cent are found in the service trades and domestic service. The jobs open to Puerto Ricans are restricted mainly to semi-skilled and unskilled jobs in the city's factories, hotels, restaurants, and other service trades. Although many migrants experience downward mobility in terms of their job level, their average earnings in New York are considerably higher than they enjoyed within Puerto Rico.[28] Only a small proportion of the women go into domestic work, while a considerable number find employment within the garment industry. Puerto Rico has an old tradition of fine needlework, and the Puerto Ricans are rated high within the garment industry in both "manual" and "finger" dexterity. The Spanish-speaking groups make up almost a fifth of the International Ladies Garment Workers Union's New York membership.[29] Several of the locals are predominantly Puerto Rican.

It takes no discerning eye to see the sea of misery confronting Puerto Rican newcomers. In 1960, Puerto Rican median family income in New York City was considerably lower than even nonwhite median income—$3,811 against $4,437. This was 63 per cent of the median income for *all* New York City families. Further, unemployment runs consistently higher than among nonwhites and whites.[30]

Puerto Rican problems are compounded by a high birth rate. In 1961, more than one-seventh of the births in New York City were of Puerto Rican parents (24,746 out of 168,383). The crude birth rate of

[26] Mills, Senior, and Goldsen, *op. cit.*, 43–59.
[27] *Ibid.*, 142.
[28] *Ibid.*, 68–75.
[29] Rand, *op. cit.*, 9–10.
[30] Nathan Glazer and Daniel P. Moynihan, *Beyond the Melting Pot* (Cambridge: The M.I.T. Press and Harvard University Press, 1963), 116–117.

the Puerto Rican population was 40 per thousand contrasted with roughly 30 for nonwhites, and 20 for all others. Although Puerto Ricans make no significant contribution to New York City's aged and disabled welfare load, they contribute one-half of the home-relief cases and one-third of the aid-to-dependent-children cases. More than half of the home-relief cases consists of homes with six persons or more, pointing to the problems that large families pose for Puerto Ricans.[31]

Puerto Ricans are concentrated in slum areas, finding housing in tenement buildings where apartments are at a premium. It is often necessary to "purchase" an apartment although ownership is not vested in the tenant, and monthly rent is collected. The "purchase" price may range as high as $1,500. In 1957, rentals ranged from $14 to $80 a month, exclusive of utilities. As a rule the apartments are self-contained, having from two to seven rooms, including a closet toilet. In some slum areas, however, a whole family may occupy only one room.[32] The slum buildings are often in a poor state of repair, but tenants are frequently afraid to report violations lest upon official inspection the whole building be condemned. If a building is condemned, new housing it difficult to come by. As a result a continuous deterioration of the buildings occurs. The dwellings are frequently infested with vermin: *ratas* (rats), *cucarachas* (cockroaches), and *chinches* (bedbugs). Leaking roofs, broken windows, and splintered steps are common.[33] Alleyways and streets are strewn with litter which remains to rot and decay. In winter, apartments that are equipped with central heating are often as cold as those without it. In summer, the sticky weather and the warmth exuded by hot-water pipes in the apartments combine with the smell of garbage and defective plumbing to push the residents into the streets, where the atmosphere is likely to be cooler and more fragrant.[34]

The schooling of Puerto Rican children has posed a number of problems for educators. A significant proportion (about 40 per cent) of the children are Spanish-speaking, possessing little or no facility in English. The number of teachers who are bilingual does not begin to approximate the needs of the school system. As a result children often learn little in school, although kept in school and promoted. In schools drawing Spanish-speaking Puerto Rican children and English-speaking non-Puerto Rican children, educational problems are compounded. The difficulties are often intensified by a sizable turnover of students

[31] *Ibid.*, 94 and 116–118.

[32] Elena Padilla, *Up From Puerto Rico* (New York: Columbia University Press, 1958), 7.

[33] Mills, Senior, and Goldsen, *op. cit.*, 92–93.

[34] Padilla, *op. cit.*, 8.

during the school year, through parental shifts in residence. Some have suggested that it might be desirable to set aside certain classes or even entire schools, for Spanish-speaking pupils. However, Puerto Rican leaders and spokesmen for civil-rights groups have generally opposed such proposals on grounds that segregation would inevitably ensue and that, within any such split, Spanish-speaking pupils would get the poorer facilities. The New York Board of Education, for its part, has decreed that all pupils shall be treated the same, regardless of race or language.[35]

In Puerto Rico, race is subordinate to social class; in New York it is made central to Puerto Rican life. As viewed by American culture, the Puerto Ricans are not a single racial type. A third of them clearly have Negroid characteristics. The world into which these Negroid Puerto Ricans move within New York is largely a Negro world, with all the restrictions commonly imposed upon it by the dominant white group.[36] It is particularly difficult for this group of Puerto Ricans, by virtue of racial barriers, to move out of the slums in Spanish Harlem, the south Bronx, and the lower east side.

The fair-skinned, Caucasian Puerto Ricans can find their way into the larger white world. But for those in the intermediate classification —the *indio* and *grifo*—the situation is more difficult. They occupy an ambiguous position within New York. The dark-skinned Puerto Ricans can move into the Negro group; the light-skinned, into the white group; yet the *indios* and *grifos* with light skin, hair, and eyes but a number of Negroid features do not find this course open to them. The *indios* and *grifos* distinguish between themselves and the dark Negroes, a distinction that is recognized on the island. Within Puerto Rico it was their personal aspirations and achievements which served to influence their position within the social order. But in New York this margin of privilege is no longer acknowledged. To continental Americans such individuals are Negroes. If they are to become assimilated, they must "become like" the Negro. Despite this fact, the *indios* and *grifos* continue to emphasize the desirability of whiteness in a society in which they are not considered white. They find they can hold only certain jobs, mix socially only with certain people, and for the most part be limited residentially to Puerto Rican or Negro neighborhoods.[37] Yet Fitzpatrick's study reveals that despite these problems, on the whole Puerto Ricans still maintain the pattern of a single ethnic community

---

[35] Rand, *op. cit.*, 111–116.
[36] Mills, Senior, and Goldsen, *op. cit.*, 87.
[37] *Ibid.*, 132–136, and Padilla, *op. cit.*, 72–78.

in which people mingle in social events of all kinds in disregard of the color marks that affect American behavior generally. Fitzpatrick found further confirming evidence for this conclusion in a survey of marriages in six Catholic parishes which revealed that 25 per cent of the Puerto Rican marriages involved people of noticeably different shades of color.[38]

The Puerto Rican migration has aroused some of the same distrust and fear that characterized previous migrations from Europe. The Puerto Rican influx is often viewed as a continuation of the "new immigration" from southern and eastern Europe, as contrasted with the "old immigration" from western and northern Europe. Various factors have contributed to this fact. A significant proportion of the Puerto Ricans are dark, even Negro; there is a rather high illiteracy rate among them; they come from a Catholic religious tradition; they lack training in full political participation; and the island from which they come is economically backward.

HISPANOS

Following the conclusion of the Mexican-American War in 1848, Mexico ceded to the United States a vast territory that encompassed California, Arizona, New Mexico, Nevada, Utah, and portions of a number of other states, and also approved the prior annexation of Texas. The area was greater in extent than Germany and France combined, and represented one-half of the territory that in 1821 constituted Mexico. Under the terms of the Treaty of Guadalupe Hidalgo, all Mexican citizens in the territory were to become United States citizens if they failed to leave the territory within one year. Very few returned to Mexico. At the time of the treaty, approximately 75,000 Spanish-speaking people lived in the Southwest: about 7,500 in California, roughly 1,000 in Arizona, perhaps 5,000 in Texas, and 60,000 in New Mexico. The overwhelming majority of these people were of mixed Spanish-Indian ancestry.[39] Many of them bear some of the proudest names of the Spanish explorers-soldiers-settlers who made this territory a part of New Spain in the 1500's and whose ancestors, mixing with the Indians, were third generation before the Pilgrims landed at Plymouth

[38] Joseph P. Fitzpatrick, "The Adjustment of Puerto Ricans in New York City," in Earl Raab, ed., *American Race Relations Today* (New York: Doubleday & Company, Inc., 1962), 176–177.

[39] Carey McWilliams, *North from Mexico* (Philadelphia: J. B. Lippincott Co., 1949), 51–52.

Rock. As the Hispanos sometimes say, "Some of our ancestors came over with Columbus; the others met him when he landed."

For those unacquainted with the Southwest and its history, it is important to recognize the distinction between the Hispanos (called also Spanish Colonials and Spanish Americans) and the Mexican Americans. The Hispanos are the descendants of those Mexicans who became citizens of the United States as a result of the Treaty of Guadalupe Hidalgo. The Mexican Americans, on the other hand, are relatively recent arrivals, migrating to the United States in large numbers since 1900. The Hispanos and Mexican Americans make up two very distinct groupings within the Spanish-speaking population of the Southwest.

The Hispanos constitute about a half of the population of New Mexico. They are predominantly a rural people who practice ways of agriculture prevalent in Mexico centuries ago. A "folk" people, they are still living culturally within the seventeenth century. Life is organized about an Old World and semi-communal village pattern with an economic foundation that rests upon stock raising and subsistence agriculture. Linguistically and culturally the Hispanos represent an extension of Latin America into the United States, and in large measure they have only limited contact with the outside world. Standards of living are low, and although their one-story adobe houses are extremely picturesque, their villages are none the less rural slums of the lowest order. Electricity, telephones, window screens, and an indoor water supply are rare or non-existent. Old medical practices and superstitions continue to prevail and contribute to poorer health conditions and considerably higher rates of infant mortality than the national average.

Within New Mexico both English and Spanish are official languages; voting instructions are in both languages; and a suspect may plead before the court in Spanish. The Hispanos enjoy full political rights; a number of them have been elected to major offices including those of governor and U.S. senator. On the whole the Hispanos may go to any school, be served at any cafe, stay at any hotel, and get a haircut at any barbershop. However, outside of their home villages, especially in the larger cities, they may encounter discrimination, but it is more of the type leveled at the Jew than at the Negro. On the social level they are not likely to be accepted; for the most part they live in a considerably segregated area, drink beer in predominantly Hispano-patronized bars, and attend their own social functions. Although segregation in the schools is banned, segregation tends to emerge on an informal basis largely through the operation of residential segregation. Hispanos tend to drop out of schools earlier than the "Anglos" and accordingly are found in considerably fewer numbers in high schools and colleges. Separate churches prevail for the most part, largely the products of language differences.[40]

MEXICAN AMERICANS

Probably as early as the 1890's, Mexican peasants from both sides of the Rio Grande would migrate for work from their homes, during the cotton harvest, to the old cotton-producing sections of East Texas and then, after the harvest, return to their homes. East Texas had long been a cotton-growing section in contrast with the cattle areas of South and West Texas. Although Negroes supplied the primary source of labor, Mexicans constituted a secondary source. About the turn of the twentieth century, cotton production started advancing into middle Texas and between 1910 and 1930 into West Texas, with the result that cattle were replaced in wide areas. Rather than having recourse to Negro and "poor white" sharecroppers and tenants for labor, as had been the practice in the old cotton-producing sections of the South, landlords and overseers relied primarily upon transient Mexican labor.[41]

By 1940 nearly 400,000 transient workers, two-thirds of whom were Mexicans, were engaged in following the "big swing" through the cotton-producing regions of Texas. Each year a vast army of migratory workers started harvesting cotton in the southern part of the state, moved northward into eastern Texas, and then proceeded into the central and western cotton-growing areas. The workers were organized by labor contractors and truckers. These latter individuals usually spoke English, knew the routes, dealt with the employers, and organized the expedition. They transported the workers in open or stake trucks, hired the crews out to employers, and oversaw the work.[42] At the present time probably more than a half of the Mexicans no longer use contractors. They may travel greater distances, stay a little longer at each farm, and stop at the smaller farms which a large labor contractor would skip. Where possible the workers prefer to drive their own cars, others may ride with friends or relatives or pay their own way on trucks.[43]

[40] This treatment of the Hispanos has in large part been summarized from materials in R. A. Schermerhorn, *These Our People* (Boston: D. C. Heath & Co., 1949), 180–183, and John H. Burma, *Spanish-speaking Groups in the United States* (Durham, N.C.: Duke University Press, 1954), 3–34.

[41] McWilliams, *op. cit.*, 169–170.

[42] *Ibid.*, 172.

[43] Burma, *op. cit.*, 54–55, and William Madsen, *The Mexican-Americans of South Texas* (New York: Holt, Rinehart & Winston, Inc., 1964), 29–31. Those readers who are interested in an anthropological treatment of the Mexican-American subculture will find Madsen a valuable source.

The conditions of life for transient workers have been difficult. Kibbe writes:

Generally speaking, the Latin American migratory worker going into West Texas is regarded as a necessary evil, nothing more nor less than an unavoidable adjunct to the harvest season. Judging by the treatment accorded him in that section of the State, one might assume that he is not a human being at all, but a species of farm implement that comes mysteriously and spontaneously into being coincident with the maturing of the cotton, that requires no upkeep or special consideration during the period of its usefulness, needs no protection from the elements, and when the crop has been harvested, vanishes into the limbo of forgotten things—until the next harvest season rolls around. He has no past, no future, only a brief and anonymous present.[44]

Sanitary facilities are especially inadequate and hygienic conditions are poor.

In addition to harvesting cotton, Mexican American transient workers usually find other seasonal agricultural work that rounds out the year's employment. During the winter and spring months, many of the workers find employment harvesting fruits and vegetables in the lower Rio Grande Valley and the Winter Gardens Area. Within the lush, irrigated lower Rio Grande Valley, a citrus fruit and vegetable industry sprang up in the 1920's. Although small in area, the "winter gardens" soon became a major source of citrus fruits and vegetables for the entire American market. The labor within this area has been primarily supplied by Mexican workers. During the summer months some of the labor migrates to the sugar-beet fields of Michigan, Minnesota, Iowa, Wisconsin, Ohio, Illinois, Nebraska, Montana, Colorado, Wyoming, and North Dakota.[45]

At the present time there are within the United States an estimated 3 million persons of Mexican descent, most of whom have either migrated to or been born in this nation since 1900. Their area of greatest concentration runs from the Gulf of Mexico across Texas, through New Mexico, up into Colorado, over through Arizona, and across California to the Pacific Ocean. Few immigrants have become naturalized American citizens, although their American-born children automatically acquire citizenship.

Beginning in 1942 the governments of the United States and Mexico reached yearly agreements on the number of Mexican nationals

[44] Pauline R. Kibbe, *Latin Americans in Texas* (Albuquerque: University of New Mexico Press, 1946), 176. Also see: Ozzie G. Simmons, "The Mutual Images and Expectations of Anglo-Americans and Mexican-Americans," *Daedalus,* 90 (1961), 286–299, and Madsen, *op. cit.,* 11–13.

[45] Kibbe, *op. cit.,* 191–206.

(*braceros*) to be admitted to this country for migrant farm work. These agreements specified minimum wages, minimum living and working conditions, and related benefits which were designed to protect Mexican nationals from exploitation while also protecting the standard of living of the American migrant labor force. Under these agreements as many as 450,000 *braceros* annually entered the United States for periods up to six months working as farm labor for growers of cotton, vegetables, fruits, and sugar beets in the Southwest and California. The program was terminated at the end of 1964, but a limited number of *braceros* nevertheless have been permitted entry from time to time as an emergency measure when crops are spoiling for lack of harvesters.

Much of the Mexican immigration to the United States is illegal, with the number of illegal immigrants probably exceeding the number entering legally. Mexican nationals swim or wade across the Rio Grande (hence the name given them, "wetbacks") to fill the considerable demand for workers to harvest the crops. The status of the wetbacks is quite uncertain. Whether they are deported or allowed to stay until the crops are harvested depends upon various economic, political, and social forces operating within the American scene. The wetbacks, by virtue of their illegal entry, are especially vulnerable to exploitation by labor contractors. The living conditions of wetbacks are often unbelievably poor and primitive.

Mexican Americans have also found employment in non-agricultural work. However, within the Southwest, their opportunities for industrial employment have been quite limited, their chances for promotion have been minimal and their wage rates have frequently been established on a discriminatory basis. Within industry, they have generally been restricted to jobs as common or unskilled laborers, the product of discrimination, limited education, and the lack of skills that can be utilized in urban American culture. Within the oil industry, for example, they have usually been employed as laborers, for the most part engaged in hard or menial work such as digging ditches and cleaning storage tanks and oil spills. In those oil refineries where they have been able to secure employment, their conditions of work closely parallel those of Negro workers. Mexican Americans are heavily represented among domestic servants; truckdrivers; highway, railroad, and irrigation workers; hotel porters, waiters, and bus boys; dishwashers and helpers in poolrooms and bars; and laborers in packing-shed or cannery jobs; etc.[46] Outside of the Southwest there are also sizable

46 *Ibid.*, 157–166.

Mexican populations in Chicago, Detroit, Gary, Kansas City, Omaha, and Denver. In Chicago, Mexicans first appeared as railroad laborers and later were employed in the steel mills, the packing plants, and the tanneries.

In southwestern towns and cities with any sizable Mexican-American population, separate "Mexican colonies" are prevalent. Dominant-group whites often refer to these colonies as "Mextown," "Spiktown," "Little Mexico," or some similar term. In smaller towns the Mexican section is usually set apart from the rest of the town by a railroad track, a highway, or a river. In larger communities, there is usually at least one section made up of Mexican Americans. Informal patterns of discrimination generally operate to maintain residential segregation and to bar Mexicans as renters or property owners from other neighborhoods. Nevertheless, the restrictions on Mexican-Americans have been rarely as strict as those upon Negroes in the United States, especially in higher income areas, where the assumption frequently has been that if one can afford to buy, he probably is "Spanish" and hence "white," and if he is poor he is "Mexican" and hence "non-white," and cannot buy anyhow.

A good many of the dwellings in the "Mexican colonies" are crudely built and in very bad repair. For the most part the homes are small wooden structures, often unpainted and of makeshift construction. Dwellings with one sleeping and living room are common, although there may also be a "kitchen house" that is either separated from or attached to the main structure. In rural communities, the structures may be very primitive, patched together from scraps of wood, tin, palm branches, tule, or a combination of materials. In unincorporated areas outside the city limits almost all forms of municipal service are lacking. Within the Mexican sections drainage systems are poor or absent, with the result that, after a rain, water frequently accumulates in the streets and roads. Many of the houses lack plumbing and indoor toilets.[47]

The level of formal education found among Mexicans tends to be low in terms of American standards. Thus they find themselves at a considerable disadvantage in the larger American society, where a premium is placed upon formal schooling and academic achievement. Their life is frequently geared by their cultural heritage to an agricultural tempo; conflicts between rural and urban values serve to complicate their adjustment to American life. Poor school attendance, limited average grade completion, and frequent school failures contribute to

[47] *Ibid.*, 123–125; McWilliams, *op. cit.*, 217–221; and Madsen, *op. cit.*, 10–11.

the situation. Some of the factors underlying these conditions are (1) high mobility necessitated by migratory work, (2) difficulties centering upon bilingualism, (3) the prevalence of low wage scales which force entire families, including children, into various jobs to augment total income, (4) illness and poor medical care which serve to depress school attendance, and (5) a sense of futility—"Why is José going to school? Isn't he going to pick fruit anyway?" [48]

Until relatively recently, Mexican children were often segregated for purposes of instruction, either in separate buildings or in segregated classes within the same building. Nevertheless, there was no overall pattern for the segregation.[49] Throughout most of the Southwest, segregation of Mexican-Americans was considered desirable but not absolutely essential, and in this way differed from the attitude of southern whites toward the segregation of Negroes. In some communities segregation was strict and complete, in others there was a "Mexican" school, but a few favored children with Spanish surnames who came from the top socioeconomic level of the Mexican-American subcommunity would attend the white school. Still others, lacking separate segregated schools, maintained segregated classrooms in the "white" school. Some communities even fluctuated between segregation and non-segregation depending upon the current number of Mexican-American students.[50] On the basis of pedagogical considerations some educators insisted that it was a sound practice to separate Mexican children who spoke little or no English during the first few grades until they had acquired an adequate mastery of English. But a strong factor influencing local decisions to maintain separate school systems was the prevalence of prejudice. As Mexican children advanced in age, the rate of dropouts from schools progressively increased. Within the separate Mexican schools, overcrowding, inferior equipment, less competent teachers, and short school terms tended to be the rule.

In the 1940's federal courts rendered two decisions that established the illegality of segregating Mexican Americans in public schools and forced the abandonment of the practice in Texas and California. In California, the courts ruled in the Mendez case (1947) that enforced segregation violated the Constitution of the United States by depriving the children of "liberty and property without the due process of law and by denying them the equal protection of the laws." The Delgado

---

[48] Edward C. McDonagh, "Status Levels of Mexicans," *Sociology and Social Research*, 33 (1949), 449–459; and Madsen, *op. cit.*, 106–108.

[49] Kibbe, *op. cit.*, 95 ff.

[50] John Burma, "The Civil Rights Situation of Mexican Americans and Spanish Americans," Jitsuichi Masuoka and Preston Valien, eds., *Race Relations* (Chapel Hill: The University of North Carolina Press, 1961), 157–158.

case (1948) in Texas accomplished the same end. However, Texas was permitted to maintain separate classes at the first-grade level for those who, on the basis of language-proficiency tests, did not have adequate command of English. Shortly after the decision, the Texas State Board of Education instructed local school districts to comply with the court rulings. These instructions were not implemented by all Texas school districts, as at least one suit was subsequently filed in federal courts to end segregation of Mexican children in the elementary school at Driscoll, Texas. By and large today the segregation of Mexican-American children closely resembles the segregation of Negro children in northern cities, i.e., it often occurs in fact, but it is far from absolute and usually is the product of neighborhood housing and prejudice, not of law. At the state university level, there never has been any real segregation, although informal and "social" segregation has certainly been prevalent.[51]

The legal status of Mexican Americans within the United States has tended to vary from state to state. One of the interesting aspects of the legal status of the Mexican immigrant has been his adverse reaction to becoming an American citizen. Most citizens of the United States of Mexican ancestry have acquired that status through birth in this country, not through the process of naturalization. McDonagh suggests that among the factors contributing to this situation were (1) the cost of securing the necessary documents, (2) language problems, (3) an inability to furnish adequate proof of legal entry, and the possibility of deportation once naturalization proceedings begin, (4) a deep loyalty to Mexico, and (5) a failure to ascertain the advantages of being an American citizen.[52]

Typically lacking citizenship, immigrants lack the right to vote. Native-born citizens, on the other hand, while in theory enjoying the right, often in point of fact were deprived of their voting rights through the operation of the Texas poll tax, petty annoyances at registration, and at times outright intimidation. Yet the single most important reason for low voter registration and participation has been widespread political apathy rather than really strong attempts of Anglos to abridge Mexican-American political rights. Since World War II, Mexican-American groups have displayed growing political interest, and as a result have elected their own people to political office, from Texas to California. Although not in large numbers, Mexican-Americans serve as members of school, health, park, and parole boards, as members of city councils, as judges, as state representatives, and as U.S. Congress-

---

[51] *Ibid.*, 159.
[52] McDonagh, *op. cit.*

men. Still the picture is not as yet rosy—in most sections of the South-west a Spanish name is a kiss-of-death at the polls.[53]

In the area of public accommodations, Mexican-Americans have at times experienced discrimination in restaurants, motels, theaters, parks, and swimming pools, especially in semi-rural communities and near the Mexican border. Similarly clerks may wait on Anglos in prefer-ence to Mexican-Americans, while service in barbershops and beauty parlors may be slow or nonexistent. Yet special toilet facilities, segre-gated waiting rooms, and refusal of service in libraries and other public facilities has been rare within the Southwest.[54] Overall, overt, formal discrimination in public accommodations has appreciably declined during the 1960's.[55]

CHINESE

It was during the gold-rush period in California that the first ex-tensive immigration of Chinese to the United States occurred. Initially, Chinese were welcomed as a source of cheap labor. The American fortune seekers who came expecting to find gold had no intention of performing menial or laborious tasks, or of earning their money as common laborers. Under these circumstances, "coolie" labor power was readily sought. Governor John MacDougall, in addressing the California legislature, in 1852, referred to the Chinese as the "most desirable of our adopted citizens" and recommended "a system of land grants to induce further immigration and settlement of that race." [56] Chinese were employed in building the Union Pacific, Northern Pacific, and Southern Pacific railroads; reclaiming swamplands; building levees and roads; mining; and a wide variety of manufacturing jobs.[57] By virtue of the shortage of women in the frontier West, Chinese were hired to do work usually done by women, such as cooking, washing, and gardening.

It was not long, however, before the speculative bubble of gold burst and whites were thrown into the employment market. Increas-ingly, American labor began feeling the competitive economic pinch of the cheap Chinese labor. From a total of 758 Chinese in the con-

[53] Burma, "The Civil Rights Situation of Mexican Americans and Spanish Amer-icans," 160–162.

[54] *Ibid.*, 165–166.

[55] Madsen, *op. cit.*, 13–14.

[56] R. D. McKenzie, *Oriental Exclusion* (Chicago: University of Chicago Press, 1928), 25–26.

[57] B. Schrieke, *Alien Americans* (New York: The Viking Press, Inc., 1936), 8–10.

tinental United States in 1850, the number rose to 105,465 in 1880, most of whom resided in California. The Chinese constituted a highly visible group. The newly arrived immigrant often shuffled along the street in a sort of dogtrot, displayed food habits different from those of the Americans, dressed in oriental clothes, wore his hair in a queue, spoke a languge that sounded queer to the American ear, and believed in omens, good-luck signs, and various superstitious practices. Out of this situation there arose the cry "The Chinese must go." Anti-Chinese feelings reached a feverish pitch following the business crash of 1876. Business houses failed; banks and mines were closed; and a drought hit agriculture. The Chinese were severely persecuted, subject to violence, riots, bloodshed, pillage, and incendiarism. Within San Francisco it was not uncommon to see Chinese pelted with stones or mud, beaten or kicked, harassed on the streets, and tormented by having their queues cut. Under the leadership of Denis Kearney, an Irish labor leader, the Workingmen's party was founded on a militant anti-Chinese program. It succeeded in electing candidates to major local and state offices.[58]

Some Chinese responded to this persecution by returning to China, but most responded by dispersing eastward throughout the United States. In 1880, some 22 per cent of the Chinese were in cities with a population of 25,000 and over, whereas 78 per cent were in less populated areas. But hand-in-hand with the dispersion of the Chinese went a trend toward greater urbanization. By 1890, 42.7 per cent were concentrated in urban centers having a population of 25,000 and over; by 1920, the figure had risen to 66 per cent.[59] Today at least 99 per cent of the Chinese are urbanites.

With the urbanization of the Chinese, Chinatowns made their appearance within various American cities. A Chinatown is a "ghetto" made up of Chinese, "a community within a non-Chinese community, having no independent economic structure but attached symbiotically to the larger economic, political, and social base."[60] Chinatowns arose both as voluntary and involuntary responses to common problems. The dominant group often erected barriers to Chinese entry into its lily-white neighborhoods. Further, meeting rebuffs in the larger society, many Chinese preferred to insulate themselves defensively from further

[58] *Ibid.*, 14.

[59] Rose Hum Lee, "The Decline of Chinatowns in the United States," *American Journal of Sociology*, 54 (1949), 422–432, reprinted in Arnold M. Rose, ed., *Race Prejudice and Discrimination* (New York: Alfred A. Knopf, Inc., 1951), 146–160, and *The Chinese in the United States of America* (Hong Kong: Hong Kong University Press, 1960), chapters 3 and 4.

[60] Lee, "The Decline of Chinatowns," 148.

rebuffs. Kinship and clan ties, a desire to preserve meaningful and cherished Chinese cultural traditions and practices, an inability to afford housing in other than low-rent areas, these and other factors operated to attract Chinese to common urban settlements.[61] Numerically San Francisco's Chinatown has been by far the largest, followed by that of New York and Los Angeles.

The smaller cities of the United States appear to be losing their Chinatowns, and, except in a few large cities, Chinatowns appear to be on the decline. Lee suggests that to survive, at least 360 Chinese must either be in the Chinatown itself or live within the same city or state where it is located. Although theoretically the ghetto is considered the "home" for the Chinese, many live outside of it for work or personal reasons. Once the Chinese population falls below the above figure, the Chinatown struggles vainly to survive—the population is not large enough to support separate economic and other institutions. Further, Chinatowns most often are located near central business districts. Urban expansion—with its attendant demolition of buildings, rezoning of land use, and widening of transportation arteries—together with the invasion of new immigrant groups have proved devastating to the continued maintenance of many American Chinatowns. In Pittsburgh, for instance, the Chinatown was totally obliterated by the building of a modern expressway. A population once dispersed seldom relocates, in toto, at a new site. Many Chinese utilize the opportunity to resettle elsewhere. The assimilation of second and third generation Chinese and the lowering of dominant group barriers have hastened the process.[62]

The Chinatown of Philadelphia is perhaps not untypical of Chinatowns generally within the United States. In 1940, it occupied one square block in a blighted area of Philadelphia. The stores abounded with all kinds of decorations: Signs were made of wooden boards with Chinese characters; neon-light signs lit up the fronts of most restaurants; and the store windows were full of big Chinese vases, porcelain statues of "Milo," and strips of red paper announcing the merchandise inside. Within Chinatown proper, there were eighteen stores, a curio shop, one needle manufacturing company, one barbership, and ten or twelve gambling houses.[63]

In 1940, some 922 Chinese resided in Philadelphia, of which about one-third lived in Chinatown proper. The occupational range of the

[61] D. Y. Yuan, "Voluntary Segregation: A Study of New Chinatown," *Phylon*, 24 (1963), 260–262.

[62] Lee, *The Chinese in the United States of America*, 65–68.

[63] David Te-Chao Cheng, *Acculturation of the Chinese in the United States* (Philadelphia: University of Pennsylvania, 1948), 72–73 and 80.

Chinese in Philadelphia was very limited. In 1945, it was estimated that 400 were employed as laundry operatives, 100 in restaurants, 18 in grocery stores, 2 in art-goods and curio shops, 12 in engineering, 4 as typists, and 11 in scattered occupations.[64] Outside of Chinatown, Chinese laundries were more or less evenly scattered throughout the city and were generally operated by unmarried men who made their residence within the laundry building. The laundryman functioned as an "intimate stranger" within the white community—intimate since he lived within the community and was known as "Charley Chinaman," yet a stranger since he tended to be culturally and socially isolated from the larger community. As such, he was often a lonely soul.[65] The Chinese restaurants were found in a number of sections of Philadelphia, the majority being concentrated in south Philadelphia where the Negro population predominated. The Chinese restaurants in the Negro section were small and dirty and served low-priced meals. A number of restaurants in west and north Philadelphia catered exclusively to white customers. In addition, there were a number of restaurants that catered to the customers in the Chinese gambling houses.[66]

The Chinese have experienced a long tradition of discrimination within the United States. In 1882 Congress passed the first Chinese Exclusion Act suspending for ten years all Chinese immigration, save for a small group of scholars, ministers, and merchants. In 1892 the Act was extended another ten years, and in 1902 the suspension of Chinese immigration was extended indefinitely. In 1943, under the impact of war conditions, President Roosevelt signed a law that provided for an annual Chinese quota of 105 and made Chinese aliens eligible for citizenship. Exclusion legislation contributed to the decline of the Chinese population in the United States from a high of 107,488 in 1890 to a low of 61,639 in 1920. Other factors contributing to the decline were the excess of departures from the United States over admissions, and the marked disproportion of the Chinese sex ratio within the United States (in 1910 there were 1,430.1 males to every 100 females; in 1940, 258.3 males to every 100 Chinese females). Between 1950 and 1960, the Chinese population within the continental United States increased to a new high of 198,958 (237,292 including Alaska and Hawaii).

California early enacted a series of anti-Chinese laws. Lawmakers successfully drove Chinese from mining activity within the state by a foreign miners' tax. An early legal decision prevented Chinese from testifying against a white man in court, a decision which placed them

[64] *Ibid.*, 80.
[65] *Ibid.*, 84–86.
[66] *Ibid.*, 90–94.

at the mercy of their persecutors. For a time, Chinese children were excluded from some public schools. San Francisco enacted various ordinances harassing Chinese laundries, including an act that made it a misdemeanor for any person on a sidewalk to carry baskets suspended on a pole across the shoulders, a typical Chinese practice. As late as 1952 the California constitution provided that corporations could neither directly nor indirectly employ Chinese; forbade the employment of Chinese in any state, county, municipal or public job; and empowered cities and towns to remove Chinese from within city limits. Most of this discriminatory legislation has either been repealed or declared unconstitutional.

JAPANESE

At the peak of the anti-Chinese agitation in the late 1870's and early 1880's, the Japanese population of the continental United States was virtually nil—the 1880 Census recorded only 148. By 1890 their number had risen to 2,039; by 1900, to 24,326; and by 1910, to 72,157. The immigrants moved through the port cities of Seattle and San Francisco into the surrounding areas and cities. As late as 1940 nearly 90 per cent of the Japanese population was concentrated in the Pacific Coast states—74 per cent in California and 39 per cent in Los Angeles County. As with the Chinese, the initial impetus in anti-Japanese feelings came from workingmen's groups: in Seattle, the Western Central Labor Union; and in San Francisco, the Labor Council. The anti-Japanese movement initially gained momentum in 1900, and, as a result of the previous decades of agitation against the Chinese, mounted quickly. Pressure came from labor and patriotic groups for legislation to exclude Japanese in much the manner as the Chinese had been excluded earlier.

The first formal step taken against the Japanese was the action taken by the San Francisco School Board in 1906 which attempted to segregate Oriental students in separate schools. By virtue of protests from the Japanese government, President Theodore Roosevelt prevailed upon San Francisco authorities to rescind the measure. As a sequel to this settlement, Roosevelt took steps to check Japanese immigration through the "Gentleman's Agreement" of 1907. Under the agreement Japan undertook to refuse laborers passports to the United States unless they were coming to join a husband, parent, or child; to resume a formerly acquired domicile; or to assume control of a previously owned farming enterprise. The agreement did not end immigration or check the agitation against the Japanese, but it did serve to change the type of immigrant admitted and to relieve tension between the United

States and Japan.[67] Prior to the agreement most Japanese immigrants were males, but, following 1907, a considerable number of women entered to become wives of the men who had preceded them. Many of these were arranged marriages. Some 38,000 brides entered the United States until the "Ladies Agreement" was reached in 1920, the product of stepped-up American agitation against the "yellow peril," in which Japan undertook to end this migration. By 1920 the Japanese population within the United States stood at 111,010. The Immigration Act of 1924 barred Japanese migration to the United States.

Prior to Pearl Harbor, 55 per cent of the Japanese within the United States were urban inhabitants. Within the cities they were largely concentrated in "little Tokyos," the result of various social and economic forces and restrictive covenants that prevented them from buying or renting housing outside their own areas. Similarly, informal restrictions served to bar them from occupations and professions for which their education had fitted them. Within Los Angeles, Japanese had established groceries, hotels, restaurants, fruit stands, barbershops, flower shops, nurseries, cleaning and dyeing shops, and similar establishments, most of which were small businesses run by a single family. Along the West Coast, Japanese were an important source of labor in lumber mills and fish canneries. They were also heavily concentrated in agriculture, often working on truck farms near urban centers. Immediately prior to American entry into World War II, Japanese raised about 42 per cent of the produce crops in California, including berries, onions, asparagus, celery, lettuce, peppers, tomatoes, cucumbers, spinach, and cauliflower. The bulk of the farmers operated as tenants, since state legislation forbade alien Japanese from owning land. In addition, there were about 1,600 Japanese-owned farms of which the titles were vested in American-born Japanese (American citizens).

While the Chinese generally reacted to native opposition with passivity, the Japanese responded with assertiveness. They demanded better employment and housing conditions, violated contracts, struck when the strike would be least opportune for the farmers, and were eager to become landowners. Strong, in a sample of 1,457 first-generation newcomers, found that during their first five years in the United States 80.7 per cent were common laborers. Twenty years later only 46.1 per cent were in this group, the rest becoming owners, managers, or tradesmen.[68] The Caucasian stereotype of the Japanese came to be

[67] Forrest E. La Violette, *Americans of Japanese Ancestry* (Toronto: Canadian Institute of International Affairs, 1946), 2–3.
[68] E. K. Strong, Jr., *Japanese in California* (Stanford, Calif.: Stanford University Press, 1933), 116.

that of an aggressive, cunning, and conniving individual, a stereotype in some respects similar to that of the Jew. It was a stereotype in sharp contrast with that of the Chinese, who were commonly depicted as humble and ignorant.

The Japanese success in establishing themselves in small-scale farming resulted in native demands for the restriction of Japanese land-ownership and tenure. In 1913, California enacted the first anti-alien landownership law barring aliens who were ineligible for citizenship from owning agricultural land, or from leasing land for periods longer than three years. In 1920, and again in 1923, the law was revised, each time being made more severe. The ingenious feature of the act was that the prohibition ran against "aliens ineligible to citizenship." Until 1870, American naturalization laws had defined aliens eligible to citizenship as "free white persons." In 1870 the word "white" was removed, but it was added again in 1875, largely through the impact of the anti-Chinese agitation in California.[69] On this basis the Japanese as alien "non-whites" were barred from citizenship. In 1922 the U.S. Supreme Court upheld this interpretation in the Ozawa case, declaring that a Japanese was not a "white" person and hence was ineligible to citizenship. It should be noted, however, that by birth American-born Japanese automatically became citizens.

Prior to World War II, West Coast Japanese were commonly denied free access to many places of public recreation, including swimming pools and dance halls, although in Los Angeles motion-picture houses did not discriminate against them. Intermarriage with Caucasians was forbidden in most western states. In restaurants they often received less courteous treatment than white patrons. On the other hand, although with some exceptions, store clerks usually treated them in a courteous manner, they were permitted to use the public libraries, and there was no discrimination against them at public schools. Since World War II, most of the discriminatory and repressive measures aimed at the Japanese have been either repealed or declared unconstitutional. In 1952 the Supreme Court declared that citizenship could not be denied anyone on the basis of race. Similarly, the alien land laws have been declared unconstitutional, and Japanese are now eligible for admission to the United States.

With the Japanese attack upon Pearl Harbor on December 7, 1941, there occurred an intense upsurge in anti-Japanese feelings on the West Coast. Rumors (later proved false) circulated of Japanese sabotage and "fifth-column" activities. Suspicions were aroused by the facts that Japanese sometimes lived near airfields and some of their number

[69] Carey McWilliams, *Prejudice* (Boston: Little, Brown & Co., 1944), 47–48.

engaged in coastwise fishing. Japanese known to have strong loyalties to their mother country were quickly rounded up by the FBI. Out of the war hysteria that followed the early months of the war, a decision was made by military leaders to evacuate the Japanese population from the Pacific Coast states and place them in internment centers. Ten centers were established in the West and Middle West, to which, beginning in the spring of 1942, some 100,000 Japanese were sent (see Chapter 11). Nearly two-thirds of these were American citizens.

The relocation worked a considerable hardship upon the Japanese. Businessmen and merchants, within the space of a few weeks, had to sell or liquidate their business interests and properties. Buyers, as a rule, were unwilling to pay reasonable prices when fully aware of the commercial disadvantage of the Japanese in having to make quick sales. Farmers were in the worst bargaining position possible, as evacuation came after planting and fertilizing but before harvesting. Unable to harvest their crops, they had to make the best bargain available.[70] Bloom and Riemer estimate that the evacuated Japanese suffered an economic loss of $367.5 million. A sample survey of 206 families showed the median loss per family to be $9,870 in terms of the 1941 value of the dollar.[71]

Soon after the evacuation, some of the interned Japanese were resettled in non-western parts of the United States. Students were often given permission to attend college; employment permits were given for some agricultural and industrial workers; and church groups, through the establishment of hostels, aided those unable to find employment. In December, 1944, the military ban on returning to the West Coast area was lifted. Although the wartime resettlement patterns entailed some dispersion of the Japanese through non-western portions of the United States, by 1950 some 80 per cent of the persons of Japanese descent within the country were living in western states. Initially, there was some opposition to the return of the Japanese to California and some serious incidents occurred. But the new storm raised a counter-reaction among the natives for fair play, and this became the dominant response. By virtue of the wartime evacuation, many formerly independent Japanese business establishments were disrupted and lost. Japanese farmers found it extremely difficult to re-establish themselves. The net result was the emergence of a new employment pattern, represented by a major shift from independent employment or employ-

---

[70] Dorothy Swaine Thomas and Richard S. Nichimoto, *The Spoilage* (Berkeley: University of California Press, 1946), 14–18.

[71] Leonard Bloom and Ruth Riemer, *Removal and Return* (Berkeley: University of California Press, 1949), 202–204.

ment by other Japanese to employment by non-Japanese employers. In 1960 the Japanese population of the continental United States stood at 260,059 (464,332 including Alaska and Hawaii).

JEWS

Within the United States there are an estimated 5.5 million Jews.[72] Of these, perhaps from 2 to 2.5 million reside in the five boroughs of New York City.[73] By virtue of their minority status, American Jews have experienced discrimination and residential segregation. In employment, Jews have frequently encountered barriers of one sort or another, the nature and extent of which are suggested by a number of surveys. In a study conducted by Jewish organizations in Chicago between 1952 and 1955, it was found that, of 40,000 job orders placed with Chicago's commercial employment agencies, 8,800, or 22 per cent, were restrictive against Jews. Of the 5,500 firms covered by the survey, 1,500, or 27 per cent, specified restrictions against Jews, including such statements as "Protestants only, no Jews or Orientals"; "We have no religious preference as long as they are of the Nordic race"; "We're desperate, but not desperate enough to hire Jews"; and "We only employ high type Anglo-Saxons." [74]

In 1956, the Institute of Industrial Relations of the University of California undertook a survey of job discrimination against Jews in the San Francisco Bay area. It reported that, of the 340 private employers in major industries interviewed, 75, or 22 per cent, acknowledged that they either barred Jews completely or limited their employment on a quota system.[75] Nationally the situation has vastly improved since the 1930's, when some employment agencies estimated that as high as 95 per cent of their job orders were closed to Jews. In the thirties, job ads stating "Gentiles Only" or "Christians Preferred" were common and accepted by newspapers, a practice that has virtually disappeared. Most newspapers will no longer accept job ads indicating religious requirements.[76]

Jews are conspicuously absent in the management teams of banks, public utilities, insurance companies, and certain large concerns in

[72] Ben B. Seligman, "Some Aspects of Jewish Demography," in Marshall Sklare, ed., *The Jews* (New York: The Free Press of Glencoe, Inc., 1958), 46.

[73] Ben B. Seligman, "The Jewish Population of New York City: 1952," in *Ibid.*, 95.

[74] Albert Weiss, "Jews Need Not Apply," in N. C. Belth, ed., *Barriers* (New York: Friendly House, 1958), 44.

[75] *Ibid.*, 45.

[76] *Ibid.*, 46–47.

heavy industry (including the automobile industry). It has been estimated that Jews constitute one-half of 1 per cent of the total executive
personnel in leading American industrial companies. Yet 8 per cent
of all college graduates and 25 per cent of Ivy League college graduates
are Jewish.[77]

Lewis B. Ward studied the hiring practices of 324 recruiters on
college campuses for some 250 major companies. Sorting out the recruiters in terms of the ethnic backgrounds of the students they hired,
80 hired only Protestant students, 42 hired only Catholic students, 14
hired only Jewish students, and 188 hired students from more than one
ethnic background. Those companies that hired only Protestants were
viewed by their recruiters as discouraging the taking of risks, as downgrading ability, and as placing a premium on "being a good Joe." This
contributed to a homogeneous environment that served to exclude
Jews.[78]

It was not uncommon prior to 1948 to find "restrictive covenant"
clauses in title deeds to property in fashionable sections of American
cities. Restrictive covenants served as instruments to bar particular
religious and racial groups, usually specifying that the property could
not be sold to any but "white gentiles." These agreements were enforceable within the courts and were a means by which Jews were
excluded from many neighborhoods. In 1948, the U.S. Supreme Court
ruled that such covenants were no longer enforceable in the courts, as
they violated the "equal protection" guaranty of the Fourteenth Amendment. Since then, new devices, of which "gentlemen's agreements"
have become the most prevalent, have been resorted to in order to
keep neighborhoods restricted. Some real-estate interests have also
attempted to circumvent the high court's ruling through new legal devices. Real-estate promoters may establish clubs or corporations to
which the landowner deeds his land, and, in turn, he is allowed the
use of it; the owner cannot, however, sell the property without the
consent of the club or corporation. Another scheme gives the community the option to purchase the land and to hold it for sale to an
approved buyer in the event the owner decides to dispose of the
property.[79]

[77] See: Benjamin R. Epstein and Arnold Forster, "*Some of My Best Friends . . .*"
(New York: Farrar, Straus, and Company, 1962); Lewis B. Ward, "The Ethnics
of Executive Selection," *Harvard Business Review*, 43 (1965), 6–40; and "Anti-
Jewish Bias Laid to Auto Men," *New York Times*, October 7, 1963, 32.

[78] Ward, *op. cit.*

[79] Arnold Forster, "The Hidden Barbed Wire in Housing," in Belth, *op. cit.*,
92–100.

Informal means may also be employed to exclude Jews from many communities. A case in Greenwich, Connecticut, is illustrative. A prominent real-estate broker in that community acknowledged to the Connecticut Commission on Civil Rights that she had written a memorandum to her sales staff warning against selling property to Jews. A part of the memorandum follows:

From this date on when anyone telephones us in answer to an ad in any newspaper and their name is, or appears to be, Jewish, do not meet them anywhere!

If it happens on Sunday, tell them we do not show on Sunday, take a phone number and throw it away!

If they walk into the office in answer to an ad we are running, screen them carefully . . .

We can do only one thing by cooperating with them [Jews] and that is to be liable to severe criticism by the board [Greenwich Real Estate Board] and our fellow brokers, as these people are everywhere and just roam from one broker to another hoping to get into Greenwich.[80]

Within colleges and universities there has been evidence through the years that discrimination operated among some schools in the admission of Jews. At times "quota systems" were maintained in which a specified number of Jewish students were accepted, despite the fact that other Jewish applicants may have been more qualified than many of the accepted gentile students. One nationwide survey in 1947 indicated that, of the applications from male students in the northeastern states who were ranked in the upper fifth of their high-school class, a Jewish application had a 53 per cent chance of acceptance, a Catholic 71 per cent, and a Protestant 74 per cent. In 1949 and in 1953, the Connecticut Commission on Civil Rights sponsored acceptance-and-rejection studies among the state's high-school graduates. The studies were designed to determine the extent of racial, religious, and ethnic discrimination in admission to institutions of higher learning. The commission concluded that the Jewish applicant had a comparatively limited range of choice and had to apply to a greater number of institutions.[81] Medical schools in particular have had a long tradition of imposing quotas on the number of Jewish admissions. However, in higher education generally and medical education in particular, there has been a marked decline since World War II in discrimination based upon religion.[82] Similarly there has been a decline in fraternity bias.[83]

[80] *New York Times*, September 15, 1961, 35.

[81] Benjamin R. Epstein and Arnold Forster, "Barriers in Higher Education," in Belth, *op. cit.*, 60–73.

[82] Harold Braverman, "Medical School Quotas," in *ibid.*, 74–77.

[83] Louis Krapin, "The Decline of Fraternity Bias," in *ibid.*, 78–88.

Country clubs, luncheon clubs, and related social clubs have represented an important area of discrimination directed against Jews. Exclusive clubs and informal gatherings of the "prestige classes" constitute strongholds of discrimination. In a 1961 study of 1,152 social clubs located in 46 states, the Anti-Defamation League found 67 per cent practicing religious discrimination (60 per cent were "Christian clubs," nearly 8 per cent "Jewish clubs," while roughly 33 per cent were non-discriminatory).[84]

This discrimination often has implications for the employment and promotion of Jews in the business world. One industrialist explained why he could not readily employ Jewish executives in his organization:

> It is important for our business that our plant managers maintain a certain status in their communities. They must join the country club and the leading city club. Today, that's where the big deals are discussed and made. They must be socially acceptable to the banking and business leaders of the town. They must be able to maintain a free and easy association with the people who count. If we promote Jewish personnel into key, sensitive positions, we run a risk of social non-acceptability. We avoid this by picking someone else.[85]

Discrimination is also found among hotels and resorts. A study by the Anti-Defamation League in 1956–1957 found that, of the 1,065 vacation hotels and motels from which they were able to secure information, 237, or 22.2 per cent, clearly discriminated against Jews.[86]

SUMMARY

We have seen that segregation often plays a major role within the United States in governing the relations between dominant- and minority-group members. The net effect of segregation is to place major limitations and restrictions upon social interaction between the members of these groups. It may find expression in discrimination, where an individual's membership in a particular racial, ethnic, or religious group becomes the foundation for differential and unequal treatment. Accordingly, minority-group members may find themselves disadvantaged in securing access to certain jobs, homes, health services, educational opportunities, and various public facilities and activities. Segregation similarly may find expression in spatial separation and the appearance of minority ghettos.

84 Epstein and Forster, *op. cit.*, Chapter 1.
85 N. C. Belth, "Discrimination and the Power Structure," in Belth, *op. cit.*, 11.
86 Albert Weiss, "Resorts: A National Survey," *ibid.*, 36.

9

Stratification

Within any society, people are ranked in a vertical arrangement—a hierarchy—that differentiates them as superior or inferior, higher or lower. This differential ranking of people is referred to as *social stratification*. Broadly considered, it is questionable whether any society, even the simplest, lacks some form of stratification. In this sense, social inequality is universal—in certain socially important respects, all societies differentiate between and rank people. This fact finds expression in the unequal distribution among the members of any society of scarce, divisible values, namely, wealth, power, and status. Accordingly, stratification represents institutionalized inequality in the allocation of rewards.

CLASS, ETHNIC, AND RACIAL STRATIFICATION

Social Stratification and Types of Social Organization

In considering social stratification, it is useful to distinguish between three types of social organization. First, there is role differentiation, i.e., a division of labor.[1] Early in human history it was discovered that a division of labor within society resulted in greater efficiency. The earliest and simplest expression of specialization was the division of labor between the sexes. With the growth in technology and societal complexity, the division of labor became increasingly specialized.

Second, there is the unequal distribution of rewards among the various roles making up the division of labor. Within any society there

[1] Dennis H. Wrong, "The Functional Theory of Stratification: Some Neglected Considerations," *American Sociological Review*, 24 (1959), 773.

are certain essential social functions or tasks that have to be performed. These functions are indispensable to the continuing and orderly existence of the society. But not all the functions are equally pleasant to the human organism, nor are they all equally in need of the same ability or talent. If all functions were equally rewarded, it is clear that some might never be performed. If doctors were given the same material rewards, status, and power that were given unskilled laborers, it is questionable whether enough young men would be willing to undergo the expensive and burdensome training necessary to become doctors. Accordingly, over an extended period of time, societies tend to evolve a system of differential rewards in order to instill in the proper individuals the desire to fill certain positions; once in these positions, the individuals need to be motivated to perform the duties attached to them. It is this system of unequal reward distribution that constitutes the foundation of stratification.[2]

Third, there is the tendency for the positions themselves, or at any rate the opportunities whereby the positions are secured, to be passed on from one generation to the next, giving rise to enduring classes or strata monopolizing certain positions. By virtue of family and kinship loyalties, one generation attempts to pass on to the next its advantaged position so that through time there exists a high correlation between the initial social positions of individuals at birth and their adult social positions. Accordingly, there emerges some degree of relative stability and permanence of the classes or strata. This contributes to the appearance of a common style of life and common values and sentiments that tend to be shared by the members of any given class and to set it off from other classes.[3] Thus, within the United States, the major social classes—the working, middle, and upper classes—can be distinguished in terms of their attitudes toward education; their systems of morality; their political, family, religious, and recreational behavior; and their patterns of life in general.

A Multi-dimensional Approach to Class

Consensus among sociologists as to the best or most appropriate definition of social class has as yet not been achieved. Although in agreement that the concept deals with the stratification of a population into higher and lower categories, scholars are in disagreement as to just

---

[2] Kingsley Davis and Wilbert E. Moore, "Some Principles of Stratification," *American Sociological Review*, 10 (1945), 242–249. For a more extended consideration of the functions performed by social stratification see James W. Vander Zanden, *Sociology: A Systematic Approach* (New York: The Ronald Press Company, 1965), Chapter 13.

[3] Wrong, *op. cit.*, 773.

what differences are to be emphasized. Whether class stratification is to be viewed as based upon income, power, occupation, education, group identification, level of consumption, family background, cultural differences, status, or a combination of these is a matter on which there is no substantial agreement.

In recent years, a multi-dimensional approach to class has gained increasing recognition and support. Three dimensions of class are frequently singled out: the economic, the status, and the power aspects. The *economic* dimension refers to the position that individuals occupy in the economic order as determined by income, property, access to credit, degree of dominance-subordination in employment relations, and degree of control over the determination of wages and prices of goods.[4] The *status* dimension refers to the relative standing or prestige enjoyed by individuals, based upon their position or role. The *power* dimension refers to the ability of individuals to influence or control the behavior of others. It can be seen that there are several analytically distinct dimensions of class, and that these are not necessarily identical; in fact, they may be disparate. Hangmen, prostitutes, and professional criminals are often paid exceedingly well, yet they may enjoy little status or power. University faculty members, while often ranking high in status, usually rank comparatively low in income and power. Some public officials may enjoy a good deal of power yet receive low wages and little status.

Stratification Based upon Racial and Ethnic Membership

Within American life there is, in addition to the stratification structure based upon social class, that based upon religious, ethnic, and racial membership. These two sets of stratification structures crisscross. A general formulation of this principle is found in Hollingshead's statement that a social structure may be "differentiated *vertically* along racial, ethnic and religious lines, and each of these vertical cleavages, in turn, is differentiated *horizontally* by a series of strata or classes that are encompassed within it. . . ."[5] Thus religious, ethnic, and racial groups are not arranged in a simple higher and lower ranking with respect to the class stratification system. Each of the religious, ethnic, and racial groups tends to span a range of higher and lower positions within the class structure, sometimes from the top to the bottom, sometimes within a narrower range. The most critical consequence of these

[4] Milton M. Gordon, *Social Class in American Sociology* (Durham, N.C.: Duke University Press, 1958), 240–243.
[5] August B. Hollingshead, "Trends in Social Stratification," *American Sociological Review*, 18 (1952), 679–686.

two stratification structures is that members of a minority group who achieve mobility into a higher class are not accorded many of the benefits bestowed upon members of the dominant group of the equivalent class.

The two systems need to be kept conceptually separate in order to discover the nature of their interrelationships. An illustration will help to clarify the matter. How does A, member of the old-American group and the "working class," articulate his status attitude toward B, a member of the Jewish (or Italian or Polish or Negro) group who has a high "middle class" status? In terms of the class hierarchy, the minority-group member would outrank the member of the old-American group. But, in terms of the ethnic or racial structure, the reverse situation would hold true. Reciprocally, the question becomes: How does B articulate his status attitude in relation to A? Do the attitudes of one stratification structure, either the ethnic and racial or class structure, tend to prevail? Do confusion and tension ensue from the crisscrossing of the two sets of patterns within specific behavior situations? [6]

The answers to these questions in part depend upon whether individual B is a member of the Jewish, Italian, Polish, or Negro group. The resolution of the matter would quite probably be reversed in some circumstances in the case of an Italian, on the one hand, and a Negro, on the other—the attitudes of the class structure tending to prevail in the former case, the attitudes of the racial and ethnic structure in the latter. Everett C. Hughes points to the dilemma of the Negro professional man: "The dilemma, for those whites who meet such a person, is that of having to choose whether to treat him as a Negro or as a member of his profession." [7] Similarly, within this situation the Negro professional faces a dilemma as to the choice of his proper role. In the realm of social organization, such matters are likely to be avoided by an "elaboration of social segregation," where the Negro professional man may serve only Negro clients. Where a white client makes use of a Negro's professional services, the contact is likely to remain purely professional and specific, rarely extended into a general social relationship.

The importance of keeping these two systems conceptually separate is seen in still another connection. It is known that family, clique, associational, and social relationships tend to be confined to members of one's own or closely adjoining classes. To what extent does the ethnic or racial factor divide the intimate group life of members of the same

[6] Gordon, op. cit., 252–253.
[7] Everett Cherrington Hughes, "Dilemmas and Contradictions of Status," American Journal of Sociology, L (1945), 357.

social class? By way of illustration, do middle-class Jews have more intimate social contacts with middle-class gentiles or with lower-class Jews? The same question can be asked of Italians, Poles, and Negroes in relation to the old-American group. The matter again depends to a considerable extent upon the ranking of the ethnic or racial minority on the social-distance scale.[8]

The distinction between the two systems is similarly of importance in considering social mobility, that is, the movement of people up and down the stratification hierarchy. In situations where the accent falls on democratic relations, status ideally is determined by what an individual can *do,* not by what he *is.* A distinction can be made between these two types of status, that is, between *achieved* status and *ascribed* status. Ascribed statuses are assigned to individuals, without reference to ability, on the basis of such characteristics as sex, age, and family membership. Achieved statuses are acquired by individuals through competition and individual effort.[9] Within the ethnic and racial structure of stratification, status is ascribed to the individual by the society; it is not rooted in his own competitive or individual effort. On the other hand, within the class structure, there is greater room for the achievement of status, although complete achievement often is limited by inheritance and unequal access to opportunities, both of which tend to be associated with family membership. To the extent to which status is ascribed (e.g., on the basis of religious, ethnic, and racial membership), social mobility within a social order is impaired; to the extent to which status is achieved, social mobility is facilitated.

PATTERNS OF STRATIFICATION

Stratification in "Yankee City"

The community provides an excellent setting from which to gain a view of the operation of the two sets of stratification structures, the ethnic and racial on the one hand, the class on the other. One of the earliest investigations into the structure and social life of a specific community was undertaken in the 1930's by W. Lloyd Warner and his associates. Warner, an American social anthropologist, selected a small New England town of about 17,000 as the setting for his research. The resultant series of volumes on "Yankee City" became a major landmark in the field of social stratification. "Yankee City" is a pseudonym of

[8] Gordon, *op. cit.,* 253.
[9] Ralph Linton, *The Study of Man* (New York: Appleton-Century-Crofts, Inc., 1936), 115 ff.

an actual community, the pseudonym being employed as a device to maintain the anonymity of the town's citizenry.

Yankee City is a small industrial New England community that gives the impression of a living tradition inherited from generations of Yankee forebears. Initially the city's economy rested upon shipping, shipbuilding, and fishing. Beginning in the 1840's, the economic base was extended to manufacturing, chiefly shoes, silverware, and textiles, which represent Yankee City's industrial foundation.

The Class Structure of Yankee City. By the 1930's, Warner found a well-developed social class system within Yankee City, which he described as falling within a sixfold division: upper-upper, lower-upper, upper-middle, lower-middle, upper-lower, and lower-lower. It should be noted that Warner's classificatory system rests primarily upon the status ingredient and tends to neglect the power and economic dimensions of class.

The *upper-upper* class represents "an aristocracy of birth and wealth." [10] It is an "old-family" class whose members can trace their lineage and wealth through many generations that likewise participated in an upper-class way of life. The members are old not only to the community but also to the class. Birth is crucial for membership. Although the men of this level are gainfully occupied, usually as large merchants, financiers, or in the higher professions, family wealth is inherited. Ideally the wealth should stem from the colonial and early-American sea trade when the city's merchants and sea captains amassed large fortunes. Upper-upper class people tend to be closely inter-married, either with members of the same class within Yankee City or with upper-uppers in Salem, Providence, Boston, or other New England cities. This group represented about 1.5 per cent of Yankee City's population.

The *lower-upper* class is in many respects similar to the upper-upper class in that the members of both live in large, expensive houses in exclusive residential sections and have somewhat similar patterns of participation in associations and informal social groups. In terms of wealth, the lower-uppers are able to meet the *means* test but they fail to meet the *lineage* test so essential for upper-upper class membership. Their wealth is as yet too new and too recently earned to have the sacred quality of wealth long present within a family line. Nevertheless, in term of wealth the lower-uppers have a slightly higher average

[10] The class characteristics are in part summarized from W. Lloyd Warner, Marchia Meeker, and Kenneth Eells, *Social Class in America* (Chicago: Science Research Associates, Inc., 1949).

income than upper-upper class members. Lower-upper class people tend to engage in conspicuous expenditure and fast living, behavior disdained by the upper-uppers. They aspire to upper-upper class membership, but they are barred by the absence of proper lineage. This group represents about 1.6 per cent of the population of Yankee City.

The *upper-middle* class comprises a group of substantial business-men and professionals—"solid, highly respectable" people but not "society." They often serve as leaders in civic affairs. They aspire to the classes above them and hope their good deeds and civic activities will win them acceptance by their social "superiors." About 10 per cent of the population of Yankee City is upper-middle class. The three higher classes, the two upper classes and the upper-middle, com-prise what Warner calls the "level above the common man." Together they represent approximately 13 per cent of the total population.

The *lower-middle* class, the top of the common-man level, is made up of small businessmen, clerical workers, other lower-level white-collar workers, and a few skilled workmen. Their homes are small and neat, located in the "side streets." They are proper and conservative, careful with their money, concerned about respectability, and labeled "good common people." They make up 28 per cent of the population.

The lower-middle class tends to shade imperceptibly into the *upper-lower* class; the dividing line between the two is often difficult to es-tablish with precision. Nevertheless, the two do not represent one class, the upper-lowers being distinguished as "poor but honest work-ers." The upper-lower class is made up of semi-skilled workers in factories, service workers, and a few small tradesmen. Its members live in the less desirable sections, have lower incomes, but are nevertheless viewed as "respectable." They represent 33 per cent of the population.

In contrast with the upper-lowers, the *lower-lower* class is not "respectable" and enjoys a "bad reputation" within the larger commu-nity. Its members are viewed as lazy, shiftless, and dependent, traits commonly viewed as opposite to "good middle-class virtues." They are thought to "live like animals," because it is believed that their sexual mores are not too exacting. They live in the least desirable sections of the community and comprise the largest proportion of in-dividuals on relief. They make up 25 per cent of Yankee City's popu-lation.

Yankee City's Patterns of Ethnic Stratification. The Irish were the earli-est of the ethnic groups coming to Yankee City, arriving in substantial numbers in the 1840's. However, factory positions were almost entirely filled by "natives" from within the city, since until the 1860's such jobs were commonly associated with middle-class status. Accordingly, Irish immigrants were able to find only unskilled employment as farm laborers, stevedores, carters, hod carriers, and domestics. In the 1860's the wage scales and working conditions within Yankee City were adversely affected, depressing the prestige value of factory work. This fact and the sharp decline in the city's maritime enterprises induced the movement of many middle-class "natives," especially young people, out of Yankee City in search of new opportunities elsewhere. Simultaneously the birth rate of the middle and upper classes began to decline. These two developments account for the fact that, in spite of only a slight expansion of the local economy since 1870, new immigrant arrivals have been able to find acceptance within the economic system. In the middle 1880's, French Canadians started arriving in Yankee City in some numbers. They were followed by Jews, Italians, Greeks, and Armenians, who in turn were followed by the Poles and Russians.[11]

At the time of Warner's study, there were 9,030 "natives" in Yankee City, 53.8 per cent of the total population. Of the ethnic groups, the

TABLE 10
Percentage, by Social Class, of Yankee City Ethnic Groups

Ethnic Group	Social Class *					
	UU	LU	UM	LM	UL	LL
Yankee	2.7	2.8	15.9	35.3	23.1	20.2
Total ethnic		0.2	3.5	20.4	44.3	31.6
Irish		0.3	5.9	27.5	53.7	12.5
French			1.0	13.1	40.3	45.6
Jewish			3.0	41.8	47.6	7.6
Italian			0.3	13.7	41.9	44.0
Armenian			1.2	17.9	50.8	30.1
Greek			2.2	5.4	35.8	56.6
Polish				0.7	9.8	89.5
Russian				4.3	25.5	70.2
Negro						100.0
Unknown			19.7	7.9	36.8	35.5
Total	1.4	1.6	10.3	28.4	32.9	25.4

* UU—Upper-Upper; LU—Lower-Upper; UM—Upper-Middle; LM—Lower-Middle; UL—Upper-Lower; LL—Lower-Lower.

SOURCE: W. Lloyd Warner and Paul S. Lunt, *The Social Life of a Modern Community* (New Haven: Yale University Press, 1941), Table 7, 225. By permission of the publishers.

11 W. Lloyd Warner and Leo Srole, *The Social Systems of American Ethnic Groups* (New Haven: Yale University Press, 1945), 31–32, and 46–47.

Irish were by far the largest. There were 3,943 Irish, 1,466 French Canadians, 677 Poles, 412 Greeks, 397 Jews, 284 Italians, 246 Armenians, 141 Russians, and 80 Negroes.[12] Table 10 gives the percentage breakdown by social class of the respective ethnic groups. Table 11 gives the percentage breakdown by ethnic groups of the six social classes. These tables demonstrate the disproportionate concentration of the nine ethnic groups, when compared with the native Yankee City group, in the level below the common man—in the lower-middle and the two lower classes. The entire upper-upper class and all but a small fraction of the lower-upper are "native." More than four-fifths of the upper-middle class are "native," but the proportion drops to two-thirds in the lower-middle. The ethnics, when compared with the "natives," are disproportionately concentrated in the two lower classes and, except for the Jews and the Irish, in the lower-lower class.

The tables also suggest that the average class status of an ethnic group tends to be associated with the length of time it has been in the city. The French Canadians and the Jews constitute the only important deviations from this pattern. There are, however, other considerations which suggest that the correlation between the position of a

TABLE 11

Percentage, by Ethnic Group, of Yankee City Social Classes

Ethnic Group	Social Class *					
	UU	LU	UM	LM	UL	LL
Yankee	100.0	95.4	83.4	67.1	38.0	42.8
Irish		4.6	13.4	22.7	38.3	11.5
French			0.8	4.1	10.7	15.6
Jewish			0.7	3.5	3.5	0.7
Italian			0.1	0.8	2.2	3.0
Armenian			0.2	0.9	2.3	1.8
Greek			0.5	0.5	2.7	5.5
Polish				0.1	0.1	14.3
Russian				0.1	0.7	2.3
Negro						1.9
Unknown			0.9	0.1	0.5	0.6
Total	100.0	100.0	100.0	100.0	100.0	100.0

* UU—Upper-Upper; LU—Lower-Upper; UM—Upper-Middle; LM—Lower-Middle; UL—Upper-Lower; LL—Lower-Lower.

SOURCE: W. Lloyd Warner and Paul S. Lunt, *The Social Life of a Modern Community* (New Haven: Yale University Press, 1941), Table 7, 225. By permission of the publishers.

12 *Ibid.*, 78.

group's status line and its length of settlement in Yankee City is less than perfect. The Armenians and the Greeks arrived in Yankee City during the same decade, yet the Armenians as a group have advanced their status position more than the Greeks. Furthermore, in terms of the time they have been in Yankee City and the status positions of more recently arrived groups, the Irish and the French Canadians do not enjoy the relatively high position that might be expected.[13]

In addition to the length of the group's establishment in Yankee City, certain secondary factors have contributed to the varying rates of mobility among the ethnic groups. One of the more important of these factors has been the type of motivation which induced migration to the United States. For the Jews, Armenians, and Russians, migration was undertaken with a view toward establishing themselves permanently within this country. Thus they were anxious to strike roots that would enable them to adapt themselves to the dictates of American life. On the other hand, a substantial portion of the Italians, Greeks, and Poles migrated with the expectation of returning to their homeland. They hoped to secure sufficient funds to increase their landholdings and their economic status in their native land. The number of those who actually repatriated themselves was comparatively small, but, until the decision was made to remain permanently in America, there was little impetus to meet any but the minimal demands of this society.

Proximity to the homeland, as in the case of the French Canadians, also has served to slow assimilation and, with it, the process of status advancement. Living only a few hundred miles from Quebec, the French Canadians were able to revisit their homeland easily. The French Canadians' strong identification with the family (in which initiative for mobility does not rest with the individual but with the family as personified by the father) has further served to retard the group's upward mobility. A large group population (by facilitating the institutional retention of ethnic patterns) similarly impedes a group's immersion within the larger society and thus serves to impair upward mobility, e.g., the Irish and French Canadians. And finally, as in the case of the Irish, status mobility may be retarded by virtue of the fact that a group is the first in order of appearance among the ethnic groups, arriving in a period of a fixed native population and of relatively limited opportunities for advancement within the social system. On the other hand, status mobility may be accelerated by similarities between the ethnic ancestral society and the general social-organization type of the "natives" (e.g., the Jews) or by similarities be-

13 *Ibid.*, 98–99.

tween the ethnic ancestral society and the religious complex of the "natives" (e.g., the Armenians).[14]

The occupational histories of the ethnic groups in Yankee City followed courses quite similar to one another. The workers of the newly arrived groups started at the very bottom of the occupational hierarchy and, through time, especially through generations, advanced upward to jobs with higher pay and increased prestige. To a considerable degree, each new group repeated the occupational history of the preceding one. Upon arrival, the Jews and Armenians were absorbed by the shoe factories, while the other ethnic groups were initially drawn into the textile mills. With the collapse of the local textile industry, the ethnics tended to widen their industrial representation, although for the most part they then moved into the shoe factories.

Warner divides the occupational classes into six groups and assigns numerical weights to each, as follows: (1) unskilled labor—1, (2) skilled factory—2, (3) skilled craft—2.5, (4) management-aid (e.g., foremen, secretaries, salesmen, clerks, etc.)—3, (5) management—4, and (6) professional—6. He was then able to secure an occupational index for each ethnic group—the absolute number in each of the classes in a given year is multiplied by the assigned numerical value of the class, and the sum of these products is then divided by the total employed population of the ethnic group. This quotient is a number between one and six and indicates the relative position of the ethnic group in terms of the occupational hierarchy. Table 12 reveals the occupa-

TABLE 12

Occupational-Status Indexes of Yankee City Ethnic Groups, by Decades

Group	1850	1864	1873	1883	1893	1903	1913	1923	1933
Irish	1.62	1.76	1.74	1.76	1.84	1.94	2.14	2.31	2.52
French					1.95	2.10	2.14	2.23	2.24
Jews							3.10	3.22	3.32
Italians							2.32	2.29	2.28
Armenians							2.46	2.51	2.56
Greeks								2.53	2.34
Poles								1.88	1.97
Russians									1.95
Total ethnics									2.42
Total natives									2.56

SOURCE: W. Lloyd Warner and Leo Srole, *The Social Systems of American Ethnic Groups* (New Haven: Yale University Press, 1945), Table 2, 60. Reproduced by permission.

[14] *Ibid.,* 99–102.

tional-status indexes of the ethnic groups by decades. The Jewish
occupational index in 1933 would probably have been above 3.75 if
account were taken of the fact that about one-third of the mature
members of the younger generation left Yankee City for the greater
occupational opportunities of other cities.[15]

The Irish, with the longest history in Yankee City, passed through
three phases: (1) 1850–1864—mobility moderate, (2) 1864–1903—
mobility slight, and (3) 1903–1933—mobility rapid. Social mobility
among the Irish has served to split the group along class lines. With
the scattering of the Irish through all but the topmost levels of the
class hierarchy, class differences and antagonisms have emerged that
have undermined the group's inner cohesion. The sharpest antagonisms exist between the lower classes (the lower-lower and upper-
lower) and the higher classes (the upper-middle and lower-upper).
The former refer to the latter as "lace-curtain Irish," a term not without
reproachful connotations, while the latter refer to the former as "shanty
Irish."[16] Warner observes that, by the 1930's, between the Irish and
the natives of the two lowest classes, and between the Irish and the
natives of the three highest classes, "there is a class solidarity greater
than the group solidarity between the Irish of the lowest and highest
classes or between the natives of the lowest and highest classes." [17]

The Norwegians of Jonesville

W. Lloyd Warner and his associates also undertook an investigation
of the social stratification of a midwestern town of about 6,000, to
which the pseudonym "Jonesville" (also called "Elmtown," "Prairie
City," and "Hometown" in the several publications reporting the research) was given.[18] Jonesville was established in the 1840's, receiving
its initial impetus from the completion of a canal that ran through the
town and connected the Mississippi River and Lake Michigan. Several
warehouses were built along the canal's banks, and barges could transport goods to and from the Jonesville vicinity. Surrounding agricultural areas used the canal as a means of shipping produce to market,
and in time Jonesville became a commercial center for farmers. Several
industries also located in Jonesville.

Jonesville is characterized by a five-class pyramid including an upper
class, two middle, and two lower classes. In contrast with Yankee City,

15 *Ibid.*, 59–61.
16 *Ibid.*, 93.
17 *Ibid.*, 94.
18 W. Lloyd Warner, *Democracy in Jonesville* (New York: Harper & Row,
1949).

there is an absence of an "old-family" (upper-upper) class. Two factors apparently have accounted for this situation. First, middle-western communities have been settled comparatively recently and thus for the most part have not had sufficient time to evolve an established old-family aristocracy based upon lineage. Secondly, the population of Jonesville has not been sufficient to make it possible for the older families to hold themselves aloof from the new rich and to organize their own exclusive group; there simply would not be enough people to make up a separate upper-upper class.[19]

The area surrounding Jonesville was settled in large numbers by Norwegians, who undertook farming as their main source of livelihood. After 1870, some of the Norse began to enter nearby towns including Jonesville, where they came into contact with people of other ethnic derivations. Within Jonesville the Norse were confronted with the fact that many of the local citizens viewed them as "foreigners" and looked down upon them as such. The Jonesville Norse found themselves at the bottom of the social and economic hierarchies as untrained and in-experienced laborers. Their subordinate position was the product of their relative lack of skill and the "foreigner" status assigned them by the "Americans." Also in the lower classes with the Norse at this time were the Irish and a mixed body of old Americans. In this early period the Irish and the Norse seem to have been in frequent conflict, numerous street fights and tavern brawls taking place between them. In marked contrast to their present strong opposition to the use of alcohol, the Norse were known as heavy drinkers. At the time of Warner's study, the Norse comprised about 15 to 20 per cent of the total population of Jonesville.

In the seventy years since the entrance of the Norse into Jonesville, two types of change have altered their class position. By virtue of better educational opportunities and the accumulation of wealth by the more successful members of the group, some Norse have secured entry into the commercial and professional activities of the town. Thus some of their number have been lifted into the lower-middle class, a few into the upper-middle class. The second change has been related to their religious life. Through the years there developed among the Norse an increasingly strict observance of the moral rules of Lutheran-ism, along with a more rigid enforcement of these rules through both formal and informal sanctions. This had the effect of setting the Norse even further apart from the "natives." But the strict observance of Lutheranism also had another effect. It contributed to a shift of behavior away from rough, wild, "disreputable" activities to "respecta-

[19] *Ibid.*, 25–26.

bility"—a shift from the lower-lower to the upper-lower class ("disreputability" and "respectability" being the distinction between the two groups).[20]

Their ethnic membership and the evolution of religious sectarianism have served to establish the Norse within Jonesville as a minority. Local Lutheranism has been extended and elaborated in a system of moral values that have placed the Norse beyond the mainstream of community life. Such relatively commonplace activities as dancing, card playing, smoking, and moviegoing are strenuously opposed. A Lutheran pastor cites this rationale for the disapproval of dancing: "It's not the dance itself that is sinful, it is what the dance leads to. You know that out of many a dance has come a fatherless child. I think that activities that are not sinful in themselves but will lead to sin should be stopped before the temptation of sin is placed before these boys and girls." [21]

The effect of these various taboos has been that the Norwegian Lutherans have been isolated from the usual patterns of community life. Their children are kept away from many school activities, and the ban on dancing serves to prevent their teen-agers from participating in much of the social life of their age group. Card playing, an avenue that is religiously barred to the Norse, constitutes a significant activity for bringing people into social contact and cliques. The taboo on drinking prevents the Norse from joining men's clubs or from participating in parties in which drinking is an accepted part of the ritual. These taboos interfere with Norse assimilation and close to them important avenues for upward mobility. In fact, social mobility appears to be the greatest threat to Lutheran sectarianism, in that mobility above the lower-middle class necessitates in large measure a rejection of some of the major elements in the sectarian ideology.[22]

Of those Norse who are organized in the church, only a few are members of the upper-middle class, about a third of the total are in the lower-middle class, and less than two-thirds in the upper-lower class. A few marginal individuals are in the lower-lower class. These class groups display significant differences in their religious behavior. Of the seven Norse who are in the upper-middle class, two are formally included in the chuch but are otherwise inactive. The others attend church occasionally but maintain most of their social life outside the Norse group. Since most of the members of Jonesville's upper-middle class are highly secular in attitude, it is necessary for upper-middle-

20 *Ibid.*, 171–173.
21 *Ibid.*, 185.
22 *Ibid.*, 173–176.

class Norse to participate at this level. The very fact of their middle-
class membership suggests that these individuals are relatively free
from sectarian attitudes and behavior. As such they may take an occasional drink, smoke in public, engage in card playing, and attend
movies. They retain their membership in the Lutheran group because
of recent mobility, kinship bonds, and economic advantage (the Norse
give preference to Norse businessmen because they seem to belong to
the sect).[23]

Teachers, some minor professional people, small businessmen, and
a large number of clerical workers are found among the lower-middle-
class members of the church. This group tends to fall into two categories: those who are marginal to the sect and those who are active
participants. The former represent a partly emancipated group which
tends to regard the church as the equivalent of other Jonesville
churches; they are essentially orthodox Lutherans who lack the local
sectarian orientation. These Norse participate freely in the community
life of their class level and as a result violate various of the sectarian
taboos. Within the church their participation is generally passive and
formal. On the whole they retain little evidence of ethnicity and
frequently marry outside the Lutheran group.

The second group of active, lower-middle-class Lutherans makes up
the controlling bloc in the formal church organization. Although they
do not themselves place emphasis upon personal conversion (emphasizing instead baptism and confirmation), they accept this form of religious experience out of deference to the upper-lower-class members.
This group stresses the Lutheran elements of church ideology but
seeks to minimize the Norwegian elements. They view themselves as
"Americans," not as "Norwegians," and seek to orient Lutheranism
away from an ethnic to a purely denominational basis. They favor
orthodoxy as opposed to a greater evangelical orientation.[24]

Approximately two-thirds of the total congregation are drawn from
the upper-lower class. This group constitutes the nucleus of both extreme sectarianism and Norwegian ethnicity. Since the spread among
them of upper-lower-class ("respectable") moral standards by 1900,
they have shown no improvement in their social and economic statuses.
The core of the upper-lower class is powerful within the church and
represents the pietistic tradition in its most extreme form. They stress
personal religious conversion rather than formal, ritualistic entry into
the church. This group comprises the backbone of the conservative element within the church which seeks to retain the Norwegian tradition,

23 *Ibid.*, 177–180.
24 *Ibid.*, 180–182.

especially the Norse-language service, in opposition to the "Americans" who desire to abolish this stigma of foreignness.[25]

Caste and Class in "Old City"

As part of their extended study of social stratification within American life, Warner and his colleagues initiated an investigation of a Deep South community of about 10,000, to which the pseudonym "Old City" was given.[26] Four social anthropologists, two white and two Negro, lived in Old City for two years in an effort to gain an understanding of the social structure and customs of the community's Negroes and whites. Old City is a trade center for the large plantations of the cotton counties that surround it. At the time of the study, Negroes represented more than half of Old City's population, and about 80 per cent of the population in the neighboring rural areas. Before the Civil War, the area comprised one of the most prosperous and flourishing cotton-growing areas of the South. Many of the planters amassed fortunes, built splendid, great homes, and lived in the manner of a white, feudal aristocracy. With the defeat of the South, the old social order of white master and Negro slave was destroyed, although cotton continued to be raised.[27]

The most important factor about the social structure of Old City— for that matter, of the South—is that it consists of a dual system of stratification, the class system on the one hand, the racial system on the other. The latter system, that of race, is often referred to as a *caste* system. Warner and his associates view stratification as any system of ranked statuses by which all the members of a society are placed in superior and inferior positions. As a result of this ranking, privileges, duties, obligations, and opportunities are unequally distributed among the various strata. In this sense both class and caste systems are stratification structures. But castes are to be distinguished from classes by two ingredients: castes are endogamous and prevent vertical mobility, while classes are not mandatorily endogamous and permit vertical mobility. In other words, a caste does not sanction marriage outside its own group and provides "no opportunity for members of the lower group to rise into the upper group or for the members of the upper to fall into the lower one." [28] On the other hand, a class permits its members to marry members of other classes and permits movement either up or down into higher or lower classes.

[25] *Ibid.,* 182–183.

[26] Allison Davis, Burleigh B. Gardner, and Mary R. Gardner, *Deep South* (Chicago: University of Chicago Press, 1941).

[27] *Ibid.,* 3–4.

[28] *Ibid.,* 9.

Warner and his associates suggest that, within Old City and the South generally, "there is a system of white and of Negro castes, and also a system of social classes *within each caste*, further stratifying groups and defining privileges." [29] The basis for determining membership in the respective castes is birth. Caste membership is an ascribed status, assigned to the individual on the basis of his parents' caste position. If both parents are defined by the community as whites, the child automatically becomes a member of the white caste. If one or both parents are defined by the community as Negroes, the child automatically becomes a member of the Negro caste. The important fact to be noted here is the role of the community definition of racial membership. *Biological* features in and of themselves do not determine such membership; it is rather a *social* definition. Thus a white-skinned man or woman may be *socially* defined as a Negro by the community, on the basis of some previous Negro ancestry. A relatively dark-skinned man or woman may be *socially* defined as a white by the community, on the basis of known white ancestry and the absence of known Negro ancestry.[30]

The caste system within the South is organized to an important extent about the control of sex. Not only have interracial marriages been traditionally prohibited by law, but the severest informal penalties have operated to enforce the code. Offspring of intercaste sexual relations are accordingly born out of sanctioned wedlock. Where children ensue from such relations, the community refuses the child and its parents a recognized family position in the upper white caste and forces the child into the lower Negro caste. Usually, the mother of a half-caste child is a Negro and by social definition the child becomes a Negro. But, if the mother is white, the community insists that all the child's family relationships be destroyed. The child may be placed with a Negro family, the father "run out of town" (or in the past lynched by community action), and the mother forced by social pressures to leave the community. In any event, the caste relationship is maintained by keeping all children who have a Negro parent in the lower group and by refusing to recognize the relation of the white parent to the child.[31]

The belief system centering about "the purity of southern white womanhood" functions as one device through which a half-caste child is barred from becoming a member of the upper caste. It rigorously serves to block sexual relations between white women and Negro men.

[29] Allison Davis and John Dollard, *Children of Bondage* (Washington, D.C.: American Council on Education, 1940), 12–13.
[30] Davis, Gardner, and Gardner, *op. cit.*, 7–8.
[31] *Ibid.*, 6.

But the ordinary double standard of American sexual mores continues to operate for white men within the caste situation. Sexual relations as "fun" are allowed to upper-caste men with the lower-caste women. But social condemnation would be the lot of a white man who would recognize the resulting offspring and accept the usual responsibility expected of an American father.[32]

The rank of the racial castes is determined by their privileges, duties, obligations, and opportunities in the society-at-large. This complex establishes the superordination of the white caste and the subordination of the Negro caste. *Within each caste* there is a system of social classes further stratifying the society and defining privileges, duties, obligations, and opportunities. Within Old City, six social classes are identified within the white caste—two upper classes, two middle classes, and two lower classes, a division similar to that found in Yankee City. However, within the Negro caste only a relatively slight differentiation by class has occurred, since segregation does not allow for the development of a sufficient occupational spread within the Negro group. For the most part, Negroes are concentrated in those jobs near the bottom of the occupational hierarchy. Nevertheless, an incipient, as yet roughly defined, five-class pyramid is present in the Negro community. The occupational status required to move into the Negro upper and middle classes is lower than would be the case in white society, so that an upper class Negro might be comparably ranked within the white class hierarchy as middle class.

Although there is no mobility *between* the two castes, there is internal class mobility *within* each caste. The development of class differentiation within the Negro caste has had major consequences for the pattern of American race relations. As Robert E. Park has noted, the castes were originally separated by a horizontal line, with all whites above all Negroes. With the development of Negro class differentiation, the situation has shifted.[33] The caste arrangement theoretically rests on the premise that *all* whites are considered superior to *all* Negroes. Yet the class differentiation among Negroes has served to contradict this assumption, for not *all* whites are superior to *all* Negroes in terms of various privileges, duties, obligations, and opportunities. Some Negroes rising to very high positions in the class hierarchy outrank in class status whites on the lower rungs of the class hierarchy. Though inferior in caste to any white person, the upper-class Negro is considered in social class to be superior to the lower-class white.

[32] *Ibid.*, 6–7.
[33] Robert E. Park, *Race and Culture* (New York: The Free Press of Glencoe, Inc., 1950), 243.

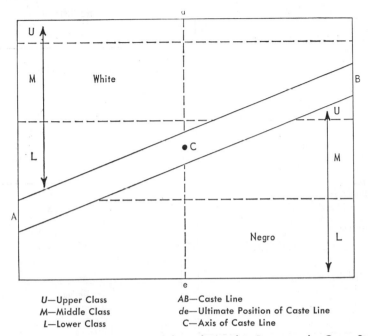

U—Upper Class   AB—Caste Line
M—Middle Class   de—Ultimate Position of Caste Line
L—Lower Class   C—Axis of Caste Line

Figure 2. Warner's Diagram of the Relationship Between the Caste System and the Class System in the Deep South. (Source: Reprinted from *Deep South* by Allison Davis, Burleigh B. Gardner, and Mary R. Gardner, by the University of Chicago Press, 1941. All rights reserved.)

Warner suggests that the caste line has shifted from its original horizontal position to one that is diagonal, so that higher class Negroes, although not equal to their white counterparts, are superior to lower-class whites. This situation is illustrated in Figure 2.

Warner considers it probable that, as educational, occupational, and related opportunities for Negroes improve, the caste line will move from its present diagonal position (*AB*) to a vertical position (*de*). Negroes and whites would have similar class positions but would continue to be separated by the vertical caste line. He speculates that even more drastic changes might follow from such a development:

It is possible that the ordinary social sanctions which apply to cross-caste "social" relations might finally be weakened with the increasing differentiation in the Negro community and the disappearance of caste differentials in power and prestige. Even the taboo on intermarriage might be relaxed. The children of such marriages would no longer necessarily be placed in the lower caste . . . the whole system of separate caste groups might disappear and new social forms develop to take its place.[34]

[34] Davis, Gardner, and Gardner, *op. cit.*, 11–12.

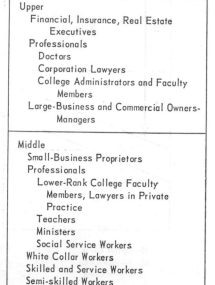

WHITE

| Upper |
| Financial, Industrial Executives |
| Large-Business Owners-Managers |
| Professionals |
| Doctors |
| Corporation Lawyers |
| Top University Administrators |

| Middle |
| Business Proprietors |
| Professionals |
| University Faculty Members |
| Teachers |
| Ministers |
| Social Service Workers |
| White Collar Workers |
| Skilled Workers |

| Lower |
| Semi-skilled Workers |
| Unskilled Laborers |
| Unemployed |
| Illegal |

NEGRO

| Upper |
| Financial, Insurance, Real Estate |
| Executives |
| Professionals |
| Doctors |
| Corporation Lawyers |
| College Administrators and Faculty |
| Members |
| Large-Business and Commercial Owners- |
| Managers |

| Middle |
| Small-Business Proprietors |
| Professionals |
| Lower-Rank College Faculty |
| Members, Lawyers in Private |
| Practice |
| Teachers |
| Ministers |
| Social Service Workers |
| White Collar Workers |
| Skilled and Service Workers |
| Semi-skilled Workers |

| Lower |
| Domestic and Other Servants |
| Unskilled Laborers |
| Unemployed |
| Illegal |

Figure 3. Stratification Structure of Crescent City. [Source: M. Elaine Burgess, *Negro Leadership in a Southern City* (Chapel Hill: University of North Carolina Press, 1960), 27. By permission.]

Time appears to be bearing out some of Warner's predictions, although it is still too early to determine whether the ban on intermarriage will be relaxed. In a recent study of "Crescent City" (a pseudonym for a North Carolina textile and tobacco center), Burgess notes:

It would be misleading to say that racial barriers have disappeared, or that Negroes are free to move within the community on the basis of equality with whites. But change is occurring, and with increasing rapidity. The caste-like structure, now in a state of transition, is giving way to a dual-class system, and there are increasing contacts between class equals across color lines.[35]

[35] M. Elaine Burgess, *Negro Leadership in a Southern City* (Chapel Hill: University of North Carolina Press, 1960), 28.

Rohrer and Edmonson report changes similar to those noted by Burgess in their consideration of the class structure of New Orleans.[36] Figure 3 portrays the stratification structure that Burgess discerned in Crescent City.

A number of writers, particularly Oliver C. Cox, have criticized the use of the concept "caste" to describe the race structure of the South.[37] Cox, on the basis of a comparison of the caste system of India with the race patterns of the South, concludes that a number of ingredients inherent in a "genuine" caste system are lacking in the United States, including rituals relating to eating and avoidance, hereditary occupation, etc. It seems, however, that Cox errs in equating caste with the East Indian caste system. He fails to recognize that some non-Hindu practices are in essence truly caste and similarly that some Hindu practices are essentially non-caste.[38] There may be some point in referring to southern race patterns as "caste-like" rather than as "caste," but the latter concept has by now become rather embedded within the terminology of the field of race relations. Furthermore, it has been for sociologists a useful concept by which to distinguish between the racial (i.e., the caste) and the class systems of stratification.

Stratification in "Georgia Town"

Employing the research tools evolved by Warner and his associates for the investigation of social class, Hill and McCall undertook a study of a community of about 5,000 in the "cracker" area of southeastern Georgia.[39] In contrast with Old City, "Georgia Town" (the pseudonym given the community) is not located in a plantation area. The inhabitants refer to themselves, and are referred to by others, as "crackers." The soils in southeastern Georgia and north-central Florida are composed of sand and sandy clay loams. By virtue of their relative infertility and the lure of better public lands in the West, the region tended to be bypassed in the stream of migration. The long-leaf pine grows in considerable profusion in the area and, thus, the early settlers

[36] John H. Rohrer and Munro S. Edmonson, *The Eighth Generation* (New York: Harper & Row, 1960), 26–27.

[37] Oliver Cromwell Cox, *Caste, Class, and Race* (New York: Doubleday & Co., Inc., 1948). Also see: Charles S. Johnson, *Growing Up in the Black Belt* (Washington, D.C.: American Council on Education, 1941), 325–327.

[38] Edward W. Pohlman, "Semantic Aspects of the Controversy over Negro-White Caste in the United States," *Social Forces*, 30 (1952), 416–419. For an excellent treatment of the controversy and a sound appraisal see Gerald D. Berreman, "Caste in India and the United States," *American Journal of Sociology*, 66 (1960), 120–127.

[39] Mozell C. Hill and Bevode C. McCall, "Social Stratification in 'Georgia Town,'" *American Sociological Review*, 15 (1950), 721–729.

termed the section the "Pine Barrens." [40]   In contrast to the agricultural patterns of ownership and management in plantation regions, the farms about Georgia Town are family farms that traditionally have practiced a good deal of subsistence production. The "cracker" culture represents a sub-type of culture within the larger regional culture of the South.

Georgia Town serves as a market center for surrounding rural areas. The area was first settled in 1740, and in 1790 it was organized as a county. In 1830, Georgia Town was designated the county seat, but by 1880 the community was still small, composed of a courthouse, a hotel, a general store, and six residences. Since 1880, the community has grown slowly and steadily. About 30 per cent of the population is Negro. As Georgia Town has grown, social differentiation and stratification have become more pronounced. More recently the importance of associations and church membership in influencing status and behavior has become more marked. Church missions have been established by Protestants and Roman Catholics, and associations such as the garden club, the country club, the Kiwanis club, the Lions, the Chamber of Commerce, the League of Women Voters, and others have been formed. [41]

Georgia Town is characterized by a five-class pyramid including an upper class, two middle, and two lower classes. In contrast with Yankee City and Old City, there is no "old-family" (upper-upper) class. The class status of each of the community's 4,933 citizens over twelve years of age was secured by means of the Warner "Index of Status Characteristics" (I.S.C.). These I.S.C. scores were computed from scales for occupation, source of income, house type, and dwelling area. Of the 3,429 whites, 142, or 4.1 per cent, were placed in the upper class, while only five Negroes (one family) possessed upper-class characteristics.

The class structure of Georgia Town can be contrasted with that of Yankee City and Jonesville in a number of significant respects. The percentages of individuals in the upper, upper-middle, and lower-middle classes are quite similar in all three communities. The percentage of the lower-lower class in Jonesville (12.5 per cent) is to be contrasted with that in Georgia Town (26.4 per cent) and that in Yankee City (25.2 per cent). However, the comparisons with Georgia Town obscure the important fact of caste, as the Negro and white groups are lumped together in the same categories. Actually, the

[40] Mozell C. Hill and Bevode C. McCall, " 'Cracker Culture': A Preliminary Definition," *Phylon*, 11 (1950), 223–231.
[41] "Social Stratification in 'Georgia Town,' " *op. cit.*, 722.

Negro population is largely concentrated within the lower positions of the class hierarchy, while the whites reflect a strong middle-class distribution.

The caste position of the Negroes within Georgia Town is reflected in the Warner I.S.C. scales. With regard to housing, 41.5 per cent of the houses occupied by Negroes were rated 7 (the lowest) on the scale and accordingly were in a very poor state of repair; only 1 per cent were rated excellent. In contrast, approximately 60 per cent of the houses occupied by whites were rated 4 and above, indicating that the condition varied from good to excellent. A similar picture emerged from the data on occupations. Sixty-four per cent of the occupations pursued by Negroes were rated 7 (heavy labor, public relief, domestic service, farm labor, etc.) and approximately 9 per cent were rated 4 and above (professional, proprietorial, clerical and kindred workers). On the other hand, approximately 70 per cent of the occupations engaged in by whites were rated 4 and above. In education, in terms of grades completed, the Negroes were concentrated at the bottom of the scale and the whites converged at the center and toward the top. In residential areas, the Negroes enjoyed the least desirable neighborhoods.[42]

MOBILITY

Upward Mobility Among Immigrant Stock in America

An integral element in "the American dream" has been the belief that any American who so wills can get ahead and make good. The saga of "from rags to riches" has contributed to an underlying faith in America and its capitalist democracy. The upward mobility of immigrant stock in the American status system has lent reinforcement to the belief. Since the Civil War, there has been a great excess in upward over downward mobility in American life. Immigrant groups have benefited from this fact and generally have been able to advance their position.

Insight as to the relative status and the upward mobility of ten nationality groups of European stock can be gained from Nam's analysis of data from the 1950 Census.[43] The census contained data on the foreign-born and second-generation populations of each of the nationalities. Nam was able to classify the two generations separately and thus obtain a basis for measuring their status change. For pur-

---

[42] *Ibid.*, 726–728.

[43] Charles B. Nam, "Nationality Groups and Social Stratification in America," *Social Forces,* 37 (1959), 328–333.

poses of measuring the status level of a group, Nam employed a version of the Alba Edwards socioeconomic scale of occupations. Although there are several dimensions to social stratification, an individual's occupation is generally regarded by sociologists as the most reliable single-item measure of his social status. The data in Table 13 portray the relative status positions of two generations of ten nationality groups and of the native population of native parentage.

The level of socioeconomic status was generally much higher for the second generation than for the first. The group average of the status indexes for the ten nationalities was 3.81 for the second generation, compared with 3.47 for the foreign-born. The relationship, however, varied for specific nationalities. Thus the index for the English and Welsh remained the same for the two generations, while the Germans experienced an almost negligible generational difference. The second-generation Irish, on the other hand, had a substantially higher status level than the foreign-born generation. The different rates of gen-

TABLE 13

Socioeconomic Status Indexes * of Selected European Nationality Groups, by Generation, and of the Native White Population of Native Parentage for the United States, 1950

Native		Foreign-born		Second Generation	
				Russians	4.87
		Russians	4.47		
				Swedes	3.97
		English & Welsh	3.92	English & Welsh	3.92
				Norwegians ⎱	
				Irish ⎰	3.91
				Germans	3.78
		Germans	3.75		
Total	3.72				
				Austrians	3.70
		Austrians	3.55		
		Swedes	3.50		
		Norwegians	3.43		
				Czechs	3.41
				Italians	3.39
				Poles	3.24
		Czechs	3.08		
		Italians	3.04		
		Irish	2.99		
		Poles	2.97		

* Standardized for age and urban-rural residence; the age-by-residence distribution of the native white population of native parentage used as a standard.

SOURCE: Charles B. Nam, "Nationality Groups and Social Stratification in America," *Social Forces,* 37 (1959), 330. By permission.

erational status mobility of the various groups contributed to a shifting of status ranks, although the Russians ranked first and the Poles ranked tenth among both generations. The explanation for the higher position of the Russians probably rests in the fact that a sizable proportion of the migrants from Russia were Jews fleeing persecution and prejudice in Czarist Russia. The Swedes improved their position, ranking fifth in status among the foreign-born and second among the second generation, while the Irish ranked ninth in status among the foreign-born and fourth among the second generation. Norwegians were likewise able to improve their rank on the status ladder.[44]

An analysis of census data by region indicates that the status *ranks* for each of the nationality groups, by generation, are relatively constant from region to region. But there are striking regional differences in the status *levels* of nationality groups. Thus, while the rank order of the nationality groups (i.e., the position of a group in relation to the other groups) tended to hold constant, their position within the occupational hierarchy (i.e., the figure representing a group's status index) varied from region to region. The status levels were considerably higher for all nationality groups in the South than for the other regions. Within the New England, Middle Atlantic, and East Central regions, the status indexes were similar but lower than those in the West North Central and Western regions and considerably lower than those in the South.[45] The higher status levels in the South probably reflected the southern caste patterning in occupations, with Negroes at the bottom of the socioeconomic hierarchy.

Group Characteristics Affecting Upward Mobility

Racial and ethnic groups have frequently exhibited markedly dissimilar rates of upward mobility. American Jews, for example, have climbed the social-status ladder more quickly and have achieved middle-class status more widely than any other ethnic group during the same period of American history.[46] Within the Northeast, Greeks have similarly tended to attain middle-class status more rapidly than most of the other groups. In general, ethnic groups with Roman Catholic

[44] *Ibid.*, 331.
[45] *Ibid.*, 332.
[46] Nathan Hurvitz, "Sources of Middle-Class Values of American Jews," *Social Forces*, 37 (1958), 117; Edward P. Hutchinson, *Immigrants and Their Children, 1850–1950* (New York: John Wiley, 1956), 180, 189–190, and 253–254; Fred L. Strodtbeck, Margaret R. McDonald, and Bernard C. Rosen, "Evaluation of Occupations: A Reflection of Jewish and Italian Mobility Differences," *American Sociological Review*, 22 (1957), 546–553; and Fred L. Strodtbeck, "Family Interaction, Values, and Achievement," in David C. McClelland, *et al.*, eds., *Talent and Society* (Princeton: Van Nostrand Co., Inc., 1958).

affiliation have witnessed less rapid upward mobility than non-Catholic groups. Likewise, Negro vertical mobility has been relatively slow.[47]

The factors responsible for these differential rates of upward mobility have varied with the group in question. Immigrant groups have differed in their possession of the various skills that are adaptive within an industrial setting. Many Jews came to America with occupational skills better suited to industrial living than those of their fellow immigrants. Similarly, ethnic and racial groups whose cultures were rooted within rural, peasant surroundings are less likely to possess the cultural values appropriate to achievement in America than are those with experiences in urban environments. While most of the Roman Catholic immigrants from eastern and southern Europe and Negroes from the South came from rural communities, many Jews and Levantine Greeks came from small towns or cities. Upward mobility has likewise been related to the ability of ethnic and racial groups to organize effectively in order to protect and further their interests. Where the ethnic group had previous Old World experience in facing the problem of minority-group adaptation, it was often prepared, as were the Jews and Greeks, to develop more quickly effective community organizations in America. The Jews had confronted a hostile gentile world for centuries in Europe, and the Greeks had faced Turkish persecution. The native Americans have also exhibited differing degrees of hostility to the various ethnic and racial groups, with the result that the nature and extent of the obstacles confronting them have differed. The latter factor can be seen in the case of Negroes, although it is less relevant in a comparison of the Jews with southern Italians or French Canadians.[48]

Rosen suggests that a crucial factor in social mobility is the individual's psychological and cultural orientation toward achievement. Individuals differ in their psychological need to excel, their desire to enter the competitive race for social status, and their levels of educational and vocational aspiration. Rosen examines the differences in (1) motivation, (2) values, and (3) aspirations of six racial and ethnic groups in order to determine the role of these three factors in the dissimilar rates of social mobility found among them. Employing ethnographic, attitudinal, and personality data, he discovered that the groups differed, and to some extent still do, in their orientation toward achievement.

1. *Motivation.* Motivation is generated by at least two kinds of socialization practices: achievement training that teaches the child to

[47] Bernard C. Rosen, "Race, Ethnicity and the Achievement Syndrome," *American Sociological Review*, 24 (1959), 47.
[48] *Ibid.*, 47–48.

do things well and independence training that teaches him to do things on his own. Achievement training fosters a strong valuation of high goals and the realization of such goals. Independence training promotes the development of self-reliant attitudes within the child and prepares him for relative autonomy in decision making. Rosen found that the various ethnic groups placed different emphases upon such training in the rearing of children. As a result, achievement motivation tended to be more characteristic of Greeks, Jews, and white Protestants than of Italians, French Canadians, and Negroes. The Italians, French Canadians, and Negroes came from agrarian societies or regions in which opportunities for achievement were severely curtailed by the social structure and where habits of resignation and fatalism prevailed. Under such conditions children were not typically encouraged to be achievers.[49]

2. *Values.* The achievement motive by itself is not a sufficient condition of upward mobility. It provides the internal impetus to excel, but it does not impel the individual to take the steps essential for achievement. In addition the individual must be prepared to plan, work hard, make sacrifices, and be physically mobile. Whether or not the individual will understand the importance of these ingredients depends in part upon the values transmitted to him by his group. The cultures of white Protestants, Jews, and Greeks stand out as orienting their members in terms of this value system considerably more than do the cultures of Italians and French Canadians. Rosen's hypothesis that Negroes would score low in value orientations proved to be wrong; the Negro score was not significantly different from those for white Protestants and Greeks although it was significantly lower than the Jewish score.[50]

3. *Aspirations.* Still a third element is necessary for social mobility: the individual's educational and vocational aspiration level. The elements of achievement motivation and values do not determine the areas in which the excellence and effort take place; they can be expressed in many kinds of behavior not conducive to social mobility, for example, deviant, recreational, or religious behavior. Thus, in addition, the individual needs to aim for high vocational goals and to prepare himself appropriately in order to move up the social ladder. Again the ethnic and racial groups differed in orienting their members toward vocational and educational preparation—the white Protestants, Jews,

[49] *Ibid.,* 50–53.
[50] *Ibid.,* 53–57.

and Greeks enjoyed considerable advantage over Italians and French Canadians. In terms of educational aspirations, the Negro score was comparable to those of Jews, white Protestants, and Greeks, although the vocational aspiration score of Negroes was the lowest of any of the six groups.[51]

The picture that emerges from Rosen's work and a number of other studies dealing with Negro mobility aspirations is somewhat confusing. Examining differences between "aspirations" and "plans" of children of different social classes and races, Stephensen found no significant differences between white and Negro ninth graders in occupational and educational aspirations. But despite the uniform level of occupational aspiration, the Negro students tended to *plan* lower than white students at each occupational level. By "plans" Stephensen meant the realistic expectations regarding future occupation as opposed to idealistic "aspirations."[52] On the other hand, Holloway and Berreman found white fifth and sixth graders at both middle and lower class levels aspiring higher than comparably graded Negroes. Nor did Holloway and Berreman find Negroes scaling down their occupational plans below their aspirational level any more than white students. Hence, in large measure they failed to replicate Stephensen's findings.[53] Perhaps the age differences between the students in the Stephensen and the Holloway-Berreman studies played a critical role. The results of a study by Gist and Bennett still further complicates the picture. They found that among ninth and twelfth grade students the occupational aspirations of Negroes and whites were roughly similar (a finding similar to that of Stephensen), but that Negro educational aspirations exceeded those of white students.[54] Obviously, more research is called for on these matters.

Factors Favoring an Excess in Upward over Downward Mobility

In a relatively unchanging society in which the occupational structure is more or less stable and stationary through time, individuals may realize upward mobility chiefly through one of two means: (1) displacement of individuals in higher positions, forcing the latter into downward mobility, or (2) replacement of individuals in higher posi-

[51] *Ibid.*, 57–60.

[52] Richard M. Stephensen, "Mobility Orientation and Stratification of 1,000 Ninth Graders," *American Sociological Review*, 22 (1957), 204–212.

[53] Robert G. Holloway and Joel V. Berreman, "The Educational and Occupational Aspirations and Plans of Negro and White Male Elementary School Students," *Pacific Sociological Review*, 2 (1959), 56–60.

[54] Noel P. Gist and William S. Bennett, Jr., "Aspirations of Negro and White Students," *Social Forces*, 42 (1963), 40–48.

tions as the latter for one reason or another retire or withdraw from the labor market. The United States, however, especially since the Civil War, has been characterized by a somewhat different situation. A number of factors have contributed to a great excess of upward over downward mobility. This fact has had a major impact upon the occupational status of the various ethnic and racial minorities. To the extent to which upward occupational mobility has been related to overall class status as well as to the relative status position of the various ethnic and racial groups in relation to the native Americans, the minorities have been able to experience on the whole a betterment in their position with American life.

Changes in the Occupational Structure. Changes in the occupational structure within the United States have been a major factor contributing to an excess of upward over downward circulation in the class hierarchy. Developments within technology have appreciably reduced the proportion of the population engaged in the physical labor of producing and handling material goods, while simultaneously increasing the proportion in professional, business, and clerical occupations.[55] The technical-scientific nature of industry has called for constantly greater numbers of technical employees while the increasingly complex nature of production and distribution has called for growing numbers of managerial employees. The increase in consumer goods has resulted in an increase in employment in distribution and trade; and an increase in leisure, in an increased demand for professional and personal services. Between 1870 and 1940, the proportion of the population employed in the production of physical goods fell from around 75 per cent to 50 per cent, and the trend has continued since. Clerical employees have multiplied, while the growth in the economic functions of government and of public services has further increased the number of white-collar workers.[56] It is estimated that in 1930 alone some 9 million persons who were white-collar workers would have been engaged in manual labor if the occupational distribution of 1870 had persisted.

Glenn suggests that since the 1940's there have been continuing changes in the occupational structure of the United States that have favored an excess of upward over downward mobility. In general, the proportion of workers in the more highly rewarded occupations increased and the proportion in the less highly rewarded ones declined, although there were many specific occupations that were exceptions to

[55] Elbridge Sibley, "Some Demographic Clues to Stratification," in Reinhard Bendix and Seymour Martin Lipset, eds., *Class, Status and Power* (New York: The Free Press of Glencoe, Inc., 1953), 381.
[56] Lewis Corey, "The Middle Class," in Bendix and Lipset, *op. cit.*, 373.

the pattern. During this same period Negro occupational differentiation increased, a fact reflected in their achieving relative gains in occupational position. The fact that within the nation as a whole there was more upward than downward occupational mobility probably facilitated these gains. In the absence of this favorable balance of upward over downward mobility, the upward occupational movement of Negroes would have resulted in about an equal amount of downward movement by whites. Had this been the case, Negro efforts at advancement would very likely have resulted in much greater white resistance. Thus a favorable balance of upward over downward mobility within a society is an important factor influencing the degree and nature of the resistance by a dominant group to a minority's advancement in status.[57]

Differential Birth Rates. Differential birth rates have also contributed to the excess of upward over downward mobility. The traditional pattern of an inverse relationship between fertility and social class (the higher the social class, the lower the fertility; the lower the social class, the higher the fertility) served to create a social vacuum within the upper strata. Recruits from the more prolific families of the level below the common man continuously flowed into the vacuum. The influence of this factor, however, has diminished since World War II with the increase in the fertility of the higher classes and a decrease in that of the lower classes.

Immigration and Mobility. The pattern of immigration similarly contributed to an excess of upward over downward mobility. Between 1900 and 1915, some 13 million to 14 million immigrants came to this nation. A disproportionate number of these were impecunious and unskilled when they arrived. Had these immigrants been distributed pro rata among the several social classes of the populaton, their arrival would have had no direct effect upon the rate or direction of vertical mobility. But this was not the case. Of the 642,724 immigrant workers admitted during the year ending June 30, 1914, 603,378 stated that they were engaged in manual occupations. Thus the immigrants included about 105,000 more blue-collar workers than would be found among an equal number of workers taken at random within the United States. If the same broad occupational distribution in the population were to be maintained, roughly an equal number of persons would have to have shifted from blue-collar to white-collar jobs during the same period.[58]

[57] Norval D. Glenn, "Changes in the American Occupational Structure and Occupational Gains of Negroes During the 1940's," *Social Forces*, 41 (1962), 188–195.

[58] Sibley, *op. cit.*, 382–383.

In some American cities the Irish were "helped" or "pushed" up the hierarchial ladder by the Italians who came after them and who displaced them in the lowest jobs. In turn, the Italians were "pushed" up the ladder by later arrivals from southeastern Europe and by Negro migrants from the South. Within New York City the process appears to be currently repeating itself with the Puerto Rican displacement of Negroes in some of the positions at the bottom of the job hierarchy.

SUMMARY

We have seen that, within the United States, people are differentiated vertically along racial, ethnic, and religious lines and horizontally along class lines. The racial, ethnic, and religious structure crisscrosses with the class structure. Thus members from these groups tend to span a range of higher and lower positions within the class structure. However, minority-group members are generally disproportionately represented in the lower strata while members of the dominant group are generally disproportionately represented in the upper strata. Although regional and community differences exist in the particular stratification patterns that have come to prevail, common elements are to be noted throughout the United States, including many of the criteria employed for evaluating any given individual's place in the stratification structure. Racial, ethnic, and religious membership also plays a role in influencing an individual's movement up or down within the stratification hierarchy.

10

Assimilation

The concept "assimilation" has been used by sociologists for at least sixty years, particularly with reference to immigrant groups in the United States. Nonetheless, it is one of the most elusive concepts employed in the study of race and ethnic relations. For the most part the concept has been applied to changes of a *cultural* and *social* sort, generally with implied direction toward greater *homogeneity*.[1] We may view assimilation as *a process whereby groups with diverse ways of thinking, feeling, and acting become fused together in a social unity and a common culture*. Assimilation, then, is an inclusive concept that may entail both *acculturation* and *integration*.

THE NATURE OF ASSIMILATION

Acculturation

For purposes of analysis we may distinguish between changes that are primarily cultural in nature and those that are primarily social. Let us consider cultural changes first—that is, alterations in the customs of a people, in those standardized ways of feeling, thinking, and acting that people acquire as members of society. We refer to this phenomenon as *acculturation*. Acculturation may take any number of forms[2]:

1. *Intercultural transmission.* Intercultural transmission involves the diffusion of elements or parts of culture from one group to another. It

[1] Stanley Lieberson, *Ethnic Patterns in American Cities* (New York: The Free Press of Glencoe, Inc., 1963), 7–8.

[2] See The Social Science Research Council Summer Seminar on Acculturation, "Acculturation: An Exploratory Formulation," *American Anthropologist*, 56 (1954).

is a matter of historical fact that each culture contains a minimum of traits and patterns unique to it or actually invented by it. It is easy, for example, to minimize America's debt to other cultures. As an illustration, consider the following account of the cultural content of a "one hundred per cent" American written as satire by a distinguished anthropologist:

If our patriot is old-fashioned enough to adhere to the so-called American breakfast, his coffee will be accompanied by an orange, domesticated in the Mediterranean region, a cantaloupe domesticated in Persia, or grapes, domesticated in Asia Minor. He will follow this with a bowl of cereal made from grain domesticated in the Near East and prepared by methods also invented there. From this he will go on to waffles, a Scandinavian invention, with plenty of butter, originally a Near-Eastern cosmetic. As a side dish he may have the egg of a bird domesticated in Southeastern Asia or strips of the flesh of an animal domesticated in the same region, which have been salted and smoked by a process invented in Northern Europe.[3]

2. *Cultural creativity.* Contact situations may not alone entail the borrowing or mixing of cultural traits. Acculturation is not merely a culture-receiving process; it is a culture-producing process as well. Acculturation may contribute to a creative synthesis between new and old elements and to the evolution of new cultural traits and configurations. Since culture is not a mere hodgepodge of traits but an organic whole, the process of taking over new cultural traits frequently involves the redefinition and remolding of a vast array of patterns in terms of the total cultural system. Cultural creativity may contribute to the emergence of a qualitatively new culture. This process can be seen in the fusion of the Indian and Spanish cultures to produce the Mestizo culture of Latin America and in the fusion of the Norman and Saxon cultures to produce the English culture.

3. *Cultural disintegration.* As a result of culture contact, rapid cultural change may be initiated that cannot be managed by the cultural system. The system may find itself overtaxed and disintegrate. This condition may be induced by the dominant culture forcing changes upon a people unprepared for them. Similarly, it may be the product of a people taking over great quantities of alien cultural material which their cultural system is unable to ingest and integrate into the whole. Vast disorganization may be the result, a condition reflected among many American Indian tribes.

[3] Ralph Linton, "One Hundred Per Cent American," *American Mercury,* 40 (1937), 427–429.

Acculturation may be accomplished through one group more or less completely taking over the culture of another, in the process relinquishing its own unique beliefs and behavior patterns. Such a group achieves fusion through a unilateral approximation of the other culture. This was essentially the case with a number of immigrant groups within some areas of the United States. Acculturation may also be accomplished through a bilateral, reciprocal fusion in which a genuine third culture appears through the merging of two or more cultures. Mestizo culture of Latin America reflects this process. Then again, if unilateral acculturation is viewed as one pole of a continuum and bilateral acculturation the other, various intermediary levels of acculturation may be recognized.

Integration

Integration entails alterations in the relationships between people, in those patterns of interaction that characterize people's daily lives. Whereas the focus of acculturation is upon the customs of a people, the focus of integration is upon the people who are practicing the customs. A racial or ethnic group commonly develops a network of organizations and informal social relationships that permit and encourage its members to remain within its confines for the meeting of a wide variety of needs. Social cliques, in-group dating and marriage, common residential patterns—even common occupations, schools, and religious affiliations—may characterize its members.[4]

Integration involves the fusion of groups in the sense that social interaction is no longer predicated upon one's racial or ethnic identity. The descendants of the former minority group and the former dominant group no longer make "dominant-minority" group distinctions. Individuals thus find their place within the community without reference to ethnic or racial origins. Hence, integration embraces the elimination of prejudice and discrimination. In this regard, Killian and Grigg observe:

At the present time, integration as a solution to the race problem demands that the Negro foreswear his identity as a Negro. But for a lasting solution, the meaning of "American" must lose its implicit racial modifier, "white." Even without biological amalgamation, integration requires a sincere acceptance by all Americans that it is just as good to be a black American as to be a white American.[5]

[4] Milton M. Gordon, *Assimilation in American Life* (New York: Oxford University Press, 1964), 31–51.

[5] Lewis Killian and Charles Grigg, *Racial Crisis in America* (Englewood Cliffs, N.J.: Prentice-Hall, Inc., 1964), 108.

Acculturation Without Integration

Acculturation appears to be a necessary precondition to integration.[6] But the reverse proposition does not hold. Acculturation can occur in the absence of integration. The Negro within the United States presents a good illustration of this. Although sharing with whites in the larger American culture, Negroes still experience much white prejudice and discrimination.

American Judaism presents still another illustration. For many American Jews traditional Judaism has been "dejudaized." In the realm of religion, there are congregations of the Orthodox, Conservative, and Reform varieties, named in order of their degree of adherence to the traditional rituals and practices. Synagogues and temples, particularly those of the Conservative and Reform persuasions, have made major acculturating adjustments to the standards of American life—for example, Conservative Judaism has introduced English into portions of the service and into the synagogue's business affairs, has altered the function of the rabbi, has abolished the segregation of the sexes in worship, has emphasized "decorum," and has cultivated the "multi-functional" synagogue with its age- and sex-graded recreational and educational programs.[7] Yet with the shift away from Orthodox Jewish cultural practices (acculturation), there has simultaneously occurred a strong desire for the preservation of a Jewish ethnic identity (opposition to total integration). Herbert Gans refers to this development as the emergence of "symbolic Judaism"—a kind of minimal adherence to specifically Jewish cultural patterns, in which emphasis is placed on a selection of nostalgic items of "Yiddish" background (for example, Yiddish culinary delicacies or Yiddish phrases), the possession in the home of tangible objects denoting Jewishness (for example, books or pictures with Jewish themes), a concern with "Jewish" problems, and a selection of festive religious traditions which help socialize the children into an awareness of and affection for a Jewish identity.[8]

Some Related Concepts

Assimilation is a social process that is to be distinguished from the biological process of *amalgamation*. Amalgamation involves the bio-

[6] Charles Wagley and Marvin Harris, *Minorities in the New World* (New York: Columbia University Press, 1958), 288.

[7] Marshall Sklare, *Conservative Judaism* (New York: The Free Press of Glencoe, Inc., 1955).

[8] Herbert J. Gans, "American Jewry: Present and Future," *Commentary*, 21 (1956), 422–430, and "The Future of American Jewry," *Commentary*, 21 (1956), 555–563. Also see: Erich Rosenthal, "Acculturation without Assimilation? The Jewish Community of Chicago, Illinois," *American Journal of Sociology*, 66 (1960), 275–288.

logical fusion of distinct racial and sub-racial groups. Assimilation does not necessarily imply the absence of physical visibility between groups; populations differing in the incidence of genetically transmitted racial characteristics may persist. It does imply, however, in terms of the end result, an absence of cultural and social distinctions based upon racial membership. Individuals, when assimilated, would no longer exhibit the cultural or social marks that identify them as members of an alien or out-group, nor would any racial characteristics that they possess function as the foundation for group prejudice or discrimination. Although for analytical purposes assimilation and amalgamation are two separate concepts, it should be noted that they usually go hand-in-hand. Assimilation promotes intermarriage and intermarriage promotes assimilation.

Assimilation also needs to be distinguished from naturalization and absorption. *Naturalization* refers to the acquisition of legal citizenship. *Absorption* is generally used to refer to the immigrant's ability to secure and sustain economic employment within the new country. The immigrant may adopt the occupational pattern of the new country or add to this pattern through the introduction of new economic acivities and occupations. On the whole, absorption proceeds more rapidly than acculturation or integration, because fewer changes in roles and institutions are required in the former than in the latter case.[9]

DIFFERING CONCEPTIONS OF ASSIMILATION

The "Melting Pot" Concept

Americans are by no means unanimous in their conception of how assimilation may "best" or "most desirably" proceed. Prior to World War I, the "melting pot" notion achieved considerable popularity, and it still enjoys currency in some quarters. According to this view, the multitude of whites from various European nations (Negroes and Orientals were not included) would fuse together within America, producing a new people and a new civilization—a people and a civilization that would achieve unparalleled glory in the annals of human history. Zangwill, a proponent of this thinking, declared with considerable enthusiasm:

America is God's Crucible, the great Melting Pot where all the races of Europe are melting and reforming!—Here you stand good folk, think I, when I see you at Ellis Island, here you stand, in your fifty groups, with your fifty languages and histories, and your fifty blood hatreds and rivalries. But you

[9] W. D. Borrie, *The Cultural Integration of Immigrants* (Paris: UNESCO, 1959), 101.

won't be long like that brothers, for these are the fires of God you come to—
these are the fires of God. . . . Germans and Frenchmen, Irishmen and
English, Jews and Russians, into the Crucible with you all! God is making
the American! . . . The real American has not yet arrived. . . . He will be
the fusion of all races, perhaps the coming superman. . . . Ah, Vera, what
is the glory of Rome and Jerusalem, where all races and nations come to
worship and look back, compared with the glory of America . . .[10]

Following World War I, the "melting pot" theory lost favor.[11] There
developed a growing awareness of the persistence of the cultural traits
that the immigrants brought with them. For many native Americans,
the great "crucible" of assimilation, the "melting pot," was not working
fast enough. Initially, northern Europeans had heavily predominated
among the immigrants to the United States, peoples whose cultures
were quite similar to that of the earlier settlers. But, by the turn of
the twentieth century, the tide had shifted—migrants from southern
and eastern Europe predominated. In 1882, some 87 per cent of the
migrants had come from northern and western Europe, whereas only
13 per cent had come from southern and eastern Europe. In 1907 the
situation had been reversed, the corresponding figures being 13 per
cent and 81 per cent, respectively. Native Americans were inclined to
view the new arrivals as "different," in some respects even as "unassimilable." This was coupled with a post-war intensification of the
fear of aliens and an abject terror after the Bolshevik Revolution of the
alien as a "radical" and "Red." A host of passions, prides, and prejudices surged to the foreground, and in 1921 Congress responded by
passing the emergency quota law of 1921 and later the Immigration
Act of 1924.

The "Americanization" Orientation

Within the context of the post-World War I situation, the "Americanization" movement gained momentum. Whereas the "melting pot"
theory had viewed the United States as evolving a new cultural way of
life through a fusion of European cultures, the "Americanization" viewpoint saw American culture as an essentially finished product on the
Anglo-Saxon pattern. It insisted that the immigrants promptly give up
their cultural traits and take over those of the dominant American
group. Differences were not to be long tolerated. Public schools,
patriotic societies, business organizations, among others, turned their
attention to "Americanizing" the immigrants. All evidences of foreign

[10] Israel Zangwill, *The Melting Pot: Drama in Four Acts* (New York: The Macmillan Co., 1921), 33 ff.
[11] For a more extensive consideration of melting pot theories see Gordon,
op. cit., Chapter 5.

heritage were to be quickly stamped out—aliens were to cease being "aliens" and to become "Americans." Other cultures were seen as "foreign"—as "peculiar," "inferior," and "a source of trouble." [12]

The "Americanization" notion found its reflection in academic circles and was popularized by Dr. Henry Pratt Fairchild. Fairchild viewed assimilation as closely analogous to the physiological process whereby an organism secures nourishment. Foodstuffs are consumed by the organism; ultimately the ingested food becomes an integral part of the physical organism and in this sense is assimilated.[13] Fairchild saw the process as a one-way street in which no reciprocal exchange is present; between human cultures, as between the body and food, no blending of consequence occurs: ". . . it appears that in social assimilation, as in physiological, . . . the receiving body sets the pattern. . . . And the process of assimilation does require that all foreigners . . . must be adapted to fit into an integrated whole without friction or disturbance." [14]

The Theory of "Cultural Pluralism"

Adherents of both the "melting pot" and "Americanization" concepts looked toward an essentially monocultural system. The former thought this could be achieved through "melting down" the immigrants and natives into a common whole; the latter, through divesting the immigrants of their "foreign ways" and remaking them into Anglicized Americans. Opposed to these notions, there has arisen another school of thought, that of "cultural pluralism," which has won considerable favor since World War II among sociologists, demographers, and social scientists generally. It aims at achieving uniformity within a society through immigrant conformity in those areas where this is felt to be necessary to the national well-being; yet simultaneously it permits immigrants to maintain their own cultural traits in other areas that are not felt to be as essential. It implies conformity within a framework of cultural pluralism—an imperfect fusion of a number of diverse cultural ingredients within the framework of a larger society.[15] Through time many of the foreign-born, as well as succeeding generations, would come to share increasingly in the common core of American life, while simultaneously retaining certain cultural characteristics of

[12] For a more extensive consideration of the "Americanization" orientation see *Ibid.*, Chapter 4.

[13] Henry Pratt Fairchild, *Immigration* (New York: The Macmillan Co., 1925), 396 ff.

[14] Henry Pratt Fairchild, *Race and Nationality* (New York: The Ronald Press Co., 1947), 109–112.

[15] Borrie, *op. cit.*, 93.

their own groups.[16]   The retention of various religious preferences constitutes the classic example of this type of phenomenon.   In brief, then,
pluralism involves a continuation of the minority as a distinct unit
within the larger society.

The proponents of this viewpoint suggest that cultural traits are
quite persistent.   This persistence, they argue, is a reality that cannot
be escaped; in fact, to attack group values—to undertake their suppression—is likely to strengthen them.   In addition, a number of advantages
may flow from a cultural pluralistic approach.   First, immigrants' retention of many of the traits of their original culture may constitute a
stabilizing link between their old way of life and the new.   Second, it
serves to avoid some of the dangers of social and personal disorganization that may follow from attempting to force the immigrants into a
world that they do not understand and that oversimplifies the com-
plexities of American social and cultural structures.[17]   Cultural pluralism, then, enables the immigrant to incorporate elements of the American culture at a pace that muffles and makes bearable the shock of
cultural collision.   Third, ethnic groups that cut across other social
groups—the most important of which are social classes—are an important factor in the maintenance of social solidarity and in the avoidance
of class consciousness and class conflict.   The pluralistic nature of
American society functions to provide various sources for the consolida-
tion of competing centers of power, a condition vital to the maintenance
of the democratic process.[18]   Where there is a maximum concentration of power in one institution, for example, the monolithic totalitarian state, there is a minimum degree of freedom.   Where there are
competing groups, institutions, and voluntary associations—competing
centers of power—democracy can flourish.   Thus America's diversity
in ethnic groups may contribute to the maintenance of the American
democratic order.

The cultural pluralistic school of thought puts less emphasis upon
the objective of assimilation in the sense of conformity in all social and
cultural areas.   It would accept cultural differences between immigrants and native Americans in certain areas and would insist upon the
right of groups and individuals to be different so long as the differences
do not lead to national disunity.   The adjustment between the groups
is viewed not as a one-way street but as a reciprocal process in which
the immigrant stock and the native Americans would each integrate

[16] *Ibid.*, 114. For a more extensive discussion of cultural pluralism see Gordon,
op. cit., Chapter 6.

[17] *Ibid.*, 92.

[18] Amitai Etzioni, "The Ghetto: A Re-evaluation," *Social Forces*, 37 (1959),
260.

with the other. This orientation is to be distinguished from that of the "melting pot," in its inclusion of non-European cultures in the process and in its willingness to tolerate—in fact, to welcome—differences over an extended period of time.

A NATURAL HISTORY OF RACE RELATIONS

The Cycle of Robert E. Park

One of America's outstanding students of race relations, the late Dr. Robert E. Park, of the University of Chicago, suggested that, whenever and wherever different racial and ethnic groups continuously meet, they inevitably pass through a series of irreversible stages. First, he indicates, the groups come into *contact;* invariably contact produces *competition;* from this competition some kind of adjustment or *accommodation* is realized; and, finally, there is *assimilation.*[19] Within the United States, Park saw the process unfolding in somewhat this fashion:

The newcomers typically came to America poor, the product of European peasant stock. They were largely uneducated, often ignorant of the English language, disillusioned by harsh treatment received at the hands of immigration officials, and bewildered by the strangeness, complexity, and tempo of city life. Accordingly, they found themselves largely isolated from the mainstream of American life. Condescendingly viewed as "greenhorns," they were exploited as cheap labor by natives, taken advantage of by loan sharks, and swindled by some of their own countrymen who already "knew the ropes." Within the labor market they were the victims of the business cycle—welcomed in the upturn, discharged and abused in the downturn. Their isolation was in part both a product of and a reflection of their ecological segregation within the city. Ghettos arose—Little Italys, Chinatowns, Little Bohemias, and Black Belts—the products of a number of forces: First, the immigrants were poor and hence were forced by rentals into the least desirable areas of the city—the slums. Second, they tended to huddle together in spatially compact areas, as their cultural likeness in language and traditions gave them a sense of comfort, belonging, and security. And third, the hostility and antagonism of the native population barred them from other areas while simultaneously reinforcing their disposition to reside with their "own kind."

Within the labor force the newcomers found themselves in competition for jobs with the natives and earlier arrivals. Conspicuous by virtue of their speech, traditions, customs, and manners, they became

[19] Robert E. Park, *Race and Culture* (New York: The Free Press of Glencoe, Inc., 1949), 150 ff.

a convenient foil for attacks by politicians searching for publicity and fame. Professional patriots, special interests, and anxious nationalists joined in the attacks. Sensational newspapers depicted a few crimes committed by immigrants as a "crime wave." In periods of economic depression their unpopularity was intensified by their disproportionate representation among the unemployed and those on relief. Their continuing influx within America and their tendency to have large families served to accentuate native fears of engulfment.

Although contact first contributed to competition and conflict, it eventually resulted in a division of labor and the establishment of a modus vivendi. Thus, in time, competition and conflict increasingly gave way to accommodation. English more and more replaced the mother tongue; some of the immigrants attended night school to learn English, the new customs, and new skills. Various "German-American," "Italian-American," "Polish-American," and other nationality newspapers grew up, bringing a wider knowledge of American affairs to those who could not read English. City political machines with their neighborhood ward bosses quickly gained an appreciation for the potential of the newcomers' votes. These party machines, often corrupt, contributed to the integration of the newcomers within American political and civic life. Party functionaries were quite adept at performing personal favors, providing relief in hard times, "fixing up" matters when immigrants got in trouble with the law, providing "Christmas baskets," and in general displaying personal interest in the immigrants. The children of the foreign-born functioned as carriers of the English language and American customs from the schools to the homes. And with time the birth rate of the ethnic groups began to decline. As they learned new skills, they started to climb up the occupational hierarchy; simultaneously, more recently arrived ethnic groups "pushed" them up the status ladder. Increasingly they gained acceptance and began the process of assimilation.

Critique of Park's Theory

Park's natural-history model has won considerable acceptance, and the theory has been applied in a number of well-known studies including Louis Wirth's *The Ghetto*.[20] The scheme, however, has come under criticism on several points. Etzioni suggests that, like many natural-history theories, Park's theory is not sufficiently specified to be tested.[21] He argues that Park formulated his theory in such a manner that different and even contradictory data can be interpreted to support

[20] Louis Wirth, *The Ghetto* (Chicago: University of Chicago Press, 1928).
[21] Etzioni, *op. cit.*, 255.

it. Etzioni in particular criticizes Park's frequent use of the term "eventually":

> When an ethnic group is assimilating, it is suggested that the hypothesis is supported; if an ethnic group is not assimilating, it is suggested that it has not yet reached the stage of assimilation. "Eventually," one can still hold, every ethnic group will be assimilated. As no time interval is mentioned and the sociological conditions under which the process of assimilation will take place are not spelled out, the whole scheme becomes unscientific.[22]

Park has also been criticized for his assumption that there is an inevitable and irreversible unilinear progression toward assimilation among differing groups. It appears that under some circumstances this does not occur. By way of illustration, some children of Jewish parents who have been converted to Christianity or who are of mixed Jewish-Christian marriages return to Judaism.[23] Similarly, the Nazi program in Germany served to reverse the long-run trend toward Jewish assimilation in that nation. Accordingly, Park's assumption seems to lack sound ground. The interaction between different racial and cultural groups takes many forms, and assimilation need not necessarily be the last stage. Indeed, the processes of competition, conflict, accommodation, and assimilation may more appropriately be viewed not as stages in a fixed sequence but as alternative situations. Furthermore, Park does not always make it clear as to exactly what forces are responsible for bringing about the transition from one stage to another.[24]

THE RATE OF ASSIMILATION

Warner's Propositions on Assimilation

W. Lloyd Warner and Leo Srole, on the basis of the Yankee City research, suggest three propositions as useful in predicting the relative rank and the rate of assimilation of various ethnic and racial groups within American life:

1. The greater the difference between the host and the immigrant *cultures*, the greater will be the subordination, the greater the strength of the ethnic social systems, and the longer the period necessary for the assimilation of the ethnic group.

2. The greater the *racial* difference between the populations of the immigrant and host societies, the greater the subordination of the immigrant group, the greater the strength of the social sub-system, and the longer the period necessary for assimilation.

[22] *Ibid.*, 255.
[23] *Ibid.*, 261.
[24] *Ibid.*, 255–256.

3. When the combined *cultural* and *biological* traits are highly divergent from those of the host society, the subordination of the group will be very great, their sub-system strong, the period of assimilation long, and the processes slow and usually painful.[25]

Warner and Srole employ the white "old-American" stock as the prototype of the host society. They then develop a scale by which to assess the position of any group in terms of its racial resemblance to the old American stock. Five categories are employed for analytical purposes:

1. Light Caucasoids
2. Dark Caucasoids
3. Mongoloid and Caucasoid mixture with Caucasoid appearance
4. Mongoloid and mixed peoples with a predominantly Mongoloid appearance
5. Negroes and all Negroid mixtures

A similar scale is constructed for assessing the position of groups in terms of cultural traits, of which religion and language are taken as being the most important for purposes of differentiation. This gives six parallel cultural types:

1. English-speaking Protestants
2. Non-English-speaking Protestants
3. English-speaking Catholics and non-Protestants
4. Catholics and other non-Protestants speaking an affiliated Indo-European tongue
5. English-speaking non-Christians
6. Non-Christians who do not speak English

Each of the five racial types has its six parallel cultural types. Thus the light Caucasoids can be divided into those who are English-speaking Protestants (English, Scotch, Northern Irish, Canadians, etc.), those who are non-English-speaking Protestants (Scandinavians, Germans, Dutch, etc.), and so on through the remaining six cultural types. As a group all six types of light Caucasoids rank above the dark Caucasoids. The dark Caucasoids, in turn, are divided into English-speaking Protestants (there is no actual group with these characteristics), non-English-speaking Protestants (Protestant Armenians), etc. The same process can be repeated down through and including racial type 5 (Negroes and all Negroid mixtures).

On the whole, Warner and Srole feel that their propositions (relating to the degree of ethnic and racial subordination, the strength of the

[25] W. Lloyd Warner and Leo Srole, *The Social Systems of American Ethnic Groups* (New Haven: Yale University Press, 1945), 285–286.

ethnic sub-system, and the timetable of assimilation) are confirmed when the various ethnic and racial groups are placed on this ethno-social scale. Most of the peoples from the British Isles have experienced slight subordination, developed weak sub-systems, and gone through a very short period of assimilation. Irish Catholics take many generations to assimilate, whereas the Protestant Irish are almost immediately assimilated. Jews from Germany and England, who tend to be light-skinned and not appreciably different in physical appearance from the old-American stock, on the whole assimilate more rapidly than do their co-religionists in the dark-skinned Caucasoid group. The rate of assimilation for Negroid Puerto Ricans, Cubans, and West Indians is very slow, and there is no predictable time when they will disappear into the total population. Lighter-skinned peoples from these same islands, although possessing cultural traits similar to the Negroid populations, have a more rapid rate of assimilation.[26]

While there is unquestionable merit in the Warner-Srole conceptual scheme, it does suffer from a certain degree of rigidity. Thus it is questionable whether a Portuguese or Sicilian Catholic (placed among the dark Caucasoids in cultural type 4) would be more subordinate within the United States than a light-skinned German-speaking Jew (placed among the light Caucasoids in cultural type 6). Likewise, there may exist significant regional variations such that the Japanese in New York City may enjoy a higher position than those in California. Variables other than cultural and racial differences may also prove of importance. To these we now turn our attention.

Some Additional Factors Influencing the Rate of Assimilation

The rate of a group's assimilation within American society is a function of many variables. While social scientists are generally in agreement that assimilation is a complex phenomenon, they are not necessarily in agreement as to just what factors tend to be most crucial in influencing the speed with which a group is assimilated. The evidence relating to the various variables is incomplete and controversial. Here we will outline a number of propositions in addition to those formulated by Warner and Srole. The propositions probably represent as good an "educated guess" as one can currently make.

1. *The larger the ratio of the incoming group to the resident population, the slower the rate of assimilation.*[27] Where the ratio of the immigrant group to the native population is small, the natives tend to

---

[26] *Ibid.*, 284 ff.
[27] Robin M. Williams, Jr., *The Reduction of Intergroup Tensions* (New York: Social Science Research Council, 1947), 58.

view the immigrants with both a disinterested aloofness and a patronizing air ("those quaint people"). But, as the ratio increases, the native population generally becomes more aware of their presence, often begins defining the immigrant group as a threat, and to one degree or another erects barriers to the new group's assimilation. One or two Chinese families within a community may for the most part be overlooked, yet simultaneously represent for the natives a passing focus for conversation ("those strange and interesting people"). The old-American stock may even derive considerable satisfaction and pride from their "open-minded," "tolerant," and "big-hearted" attitudes toward a few minority-groups members. It is not uncommon to hear the individual who feels guilty about his anti-Semitism declare, "Look! I don't hate Jews. Why one of my best friends is a Jew!" Similarly, a few Chinese or members of another minority may serve for the community much the same function as the "one Jewish friend": "Look! We don't hate Chinese or minorities. See what a tolerant community we are!" But as the number of Chinese increases, they are likely to be increasingly regarded as a threat and set off from the dominant group.

2. *The more rapid the influx of the incoming group, the slower the rate of assimilation.*[28] A rapid influx of immigrants is likely to arouse among the natives a fear of engulfment—a feeling that they are going to be overpowered, overwhelmed, and swallowed up. Accordingly, they are likely both to intensify their resistance to immigrant assimilation and to erect various segregating barriers. By the same token, the immigrants are likely to respond by taking refuge in an intensified ingroup coalescence.

3. *The greater the dispersion of the group especially in the same territorial pattern as the dominant group, the more rapid its assimilation.*[29] Where groups are concentrated in large numbers they tend to coalesce and perpetuate their native cultures. Where they are scattered, they are less capable of insulating themselves from the larger community and of preserving their native institutions, customs, and inmarriage patterns. Further, residential segregation has the effect of accenting the differences between groups by heightening their visibility.

4. *The higher the educational, income, and occupational levels of the incoming group, the more rapid its assimilation.*[30] To the extent to which a group's members are concentrated on the lowest rungs of the class hierarchy, they suffer the additional disadvantage of incurring

[28] *Ibid.*, 58.

[29] R. A. Schermerhorn, *These Our People* (Boston: D. C. Heath & Co., 1949), 460 and Lieberson, *op. cit.*

[30] S. Alexander Weinstock, "Some Factors that Retard or Accelerate the Rate of Acculturation," *Human Relations*, 17 (1964), 321–340.

various class prejudices and discrimination. Thus is is not uncommon to hear middle-class southern white parents declare, "I wouldn't mind if my kids would go to school with Ralph Bunche's kids, but I'd never let 'em go to school with our maid's or handy man's kids." In time an entire group may come to be stereotyped as menial workers and laborers, with a "job ceiling" emerging as that for Negroes. Similarly, groups at higher educational, income, and occupational levels tend to have greater access to the means for upward mobility, which, in turn, tends to be associated with a higher rate of assimilation.

5. *The greater the predisposition of the incoming group to change, the more rapid the rate of assimilation.*[31] Groups differ in the premium they assign to their traditional patterns as well as the premium they place upon admittance to the old-American group. Whereas the southern Irish on the whole retained a steadfast adherence to Catholicism, the Czechs, on their arrival, were more nominally Catholic and their defection from Catholicism was rapid. This fact probably accounts in part for the rapid assimilation of the Czechs, such that their position as a minority has dwindled to the vanishing point.[32]

6. *The greater the predisposition of the receiving community to recognize differences, the more rapid the rate of assimilation.*[33] Campaigns such as that of the "Americanization" movement following World War I often contribute to a "boomerang" effect in which assimilation, rather than being promoted, is actually delayed. Where group differences are accepted, people interact in a "matter-of-course" fashion and are less resistant to taking on new ways of behavior. But where differences are not accepted and where demands are raised that people divest themselves of particular traits, accentuated "consciousness of kind" and group cohesion tend to emerge, together with an intensified resistance to change. To attack group values is likely to strengthen them.

7. *The greater the degree of economic competition between the native and immigrant groups, the slower the rate of assimilation.* Economic competition is likely to contribute to hostile feelings, an intolerance of differences, an accentuated "consciousness of kind," and group cohesion.

8. *The greater the proximity and access to the homeland, the slower the rate of assimilation.*[34] French-Canadian assimilation in New Eng-

[31] Borrie, *op. cit.*, 94.
[32] Schermerhorn, *op. cit.*, 457.
[33] Borrie, *op. cit.*, 94–95.
[34] Warner and Srole, *op. cit.*, 100–101.

land and Mexican assimilation in the Southwest have been slowed by their respective geographical proximities to Quebec and Mexico. Proximity makes it relatively easy for immigrants to return to their original homes for periodic visits. Such visits may enable the immigrants to avoid deeply rooted ties and commitments within the new homeland. It also enables them to experience a reinforcement of previous cultural traditions and life patterns.

MARGINALITY

"The Marginal Man"

Individuals not infrequently find the process of assimilation turbulent, stressful, and emotionally disruptive. As early as 1928, Robert E. Park called attention to the individual who is torn between the conflicting demands of two cultural traditions, and referred to him as "the marginal man." [35] The marginal man as conceived by Park "is one whom fate has condemned to live in two societies and in two, not merely different but antagonistic, cultures." [36] He is an individual caught in the conflict of cultures, an individual who lives in two worlds, yet actually belongs to none. As an Amish student at a non-Amish college observed, "I feel like I am a man without a country. I don't fit in at home too well, and I don't fit in at school."

Although Park was probably the first to employ the concept of "the marginal man," the term has since become largely linked with the name of Everett V. Stonequist. Stonequist viewed the marginal man as an individual who, by virtue of migration, education, marriage, or some other influence, leaves one cultural group without making a satisfactory adjustment to another. Accordingly, he finds himself on the margin of each culture but a member of neither.[37] "He does not quite 'belong' or feel at home in either group." [38] Marginality may arise from (1) incomplete cultural assimilation in one or both societies, (2) failure to gain social acceptance within one or both societies, or (3) the persistence of inhibitions and loyalties derived from previous socialization.[39]

[35] Robert E. Park, "Human Migration and the Marginal Man," *American Journal of Sociology*, 33 (1928), 881–893.

[36] Everett V. Stonequist, *The Marginal Man* (New York: Charles Scribner's Sons, 1937), xv.

[37] *Ibid.*, 3.

[38] Everett V. Stonequist, "The Marginal Character of the Jews," in Isacque Graeber and S. H. Britt, eds., *Jews in a Gentile World* (New York: The Macmillan Co., 1942), 297.

[39] *Ibid.*, 297.

"Personality Traits" of the Marginal Man

Stonequist suggests that the marginal man, finding himself estranged from both cultures, typically develops a unique complex of personality traits. The marginal Jew, for example, sees himself from the Jewish standpoint and from the gentile standpoint; the marginal Negro, from that of the white as well as that of the Negro. As a consequence the marginal man develops a dual personality, a "double consciousness." As the product of two cultural traditions, there emerges a mental conflict, a clash between the dual identifications. According to Stonequist, the marginal man tends to react with violent emotion against the old identification; yet, though shaken, the old identification continues to exist and troubles his mind. The individual thus suffers from a divided loyalty, from an ambivalent state of mind. His entire life process is caught in a web of ambivalent attitudes and sentiments; he is torn between two courses of action that do not permit him to calmly take the one and leave the other.[40]

The marginal man, as the result of divided loyalty and ambivalent attitudes, is characterized by fluctuating and contradictory opinions and actions. His ambivalence frequently contributes to nervous strain and to irrational, moody, and "temperamental" conduct. He is an individual with excessive self- and race consciousness; he is hypersensitive, since he continuously views himself through the eyes of individuals from two conflicting cultural traditions. Often stigmatized by the dominant group as an inferior or made to feel unacceptable, he develops an inferiority complex. He attempts to compensate for his felt inferiority by assertive and excessive aggressiveness. In addition, he is characterized to a greater or lesser degree by egocentrism, withdrawing tendencies, a proclivity for rationalizing, and a hypercritical disposition.[41]

Critique of the Marginal-Man Concept

Kerckhoff and McCormack point out that the Park and Stonequist portrayal of the marginal man does not always make clear the nature of the relationship between the status and the personality characteristics.[42] It is not always certain whether a marginal man is one who is poised between two cultural worlds or one who exhibits the described personality characteristics, or both. This lack of clarity has led some

[40] *The Marginal Man*, 144–146.
[41] *Ibid.*, 146 ff.
[42] Alan C. Kerckhoff and Thomas C. McCormack, "Marginal Status and Marginal Personality," *Social Forces*, 34 (1955), 48–55.

social scientists to question, a number to reject, the concept of the marginal man. A number of writers have raised the issue with regard to the Jews, a group which Park and Stonequist had depicted as a virtual prototype of the marginal man.[43] Clearly that complex of personality traits which Stonequist described as characterizing the marginal man is at best characteristic of only a fraction of the American Jewish population. Others have raised similar questions about mulattoes. And the opposite objection can also be made, namely, that many individuals not occupying a classical marginal position display many of these same personality traits.

It seems essential, therefore, to make a clear distinction between the status of marginality and the individual's response to this status. A person occupying a marginal status is *an individual who has internalized to one degree or another the cultural patterns of a group that frequently functions as his reference group and to which he aspires to membership, but in which he does not find full or legitimate membership.*[44] These conditions are likely to foster marginality:

1. Where two groups with differing cultures or subcultures are in intensive and continuous contact
2. Where some of the members of one group for one reason or another come under the influence of another group or come to place a premium upon membership in the other group
3. Where the barriers between the two groups are sufficiently permeable for members of one group to internalize the patterns of the other
4. Where for one reason or another the patterns between the two groups cannot be easily harmonized or where cultural and/or racial barriers serve to block full and legitimate membership within another group [45]

A marginal individual is confronted with numerous situations in which his role is ill defined. But individuals differ in their definitions of situations and in their adjustments to them. In this sense, the phenomenon of marginality is more complex than Stonequist's list of personality traits would indicate. There are a number of diverse responses to marginal situations. Antonovsky, on the basis of a study of fifty-eight

[43] Milton M. Goldberg, "A Qualification of the Marginal Man Theory," *American Sociological Review,* 6 (1941), 52–58; and David I. Golovensky, "The Marginal Man Concept: An Analysis and Critique," *Social Forces,* 30 (1952), 333–339.

[44] See: Kerckhoff and McCormick, *op. cit.,* 50.

[45] See: Aaron Antonovsky, "Toward a Refinement of the 'Marginal Man' Concept," *Social Forces,* 35 (1956), 57.

Jewish men in New Haven, suggests a number of these differing responses as they relate to Jews.[46]

1. *Active Jewish orientation.* These Jews identified themselves with things Jewish, were opposed to assimilation, tended to reject non-Jewish patterns and identifications, and felt strong solidarity with Jewish groups. One remarked, "If you're not Jewish, then you can't understand anyway. And if you are, you don't have to ask questions; you already know what we feel. And all Jews feel alike, there's no need to go around studying them."[47] Another observed, "You say hello, goodbye, to the *goyim* [gentiles], but don't mix."[48]

2. *Passive Jewish orientation.* This group, although its reactions were in some ways similar to that of the first, was not quite as involved in, or as enthusiastic about, being Jewish. Nevertheless, its members were oriented toward the Jewish group and accepted their membership within it as fundamental. They were not, however, characterized by a clear, articulate desire to see Jews continue and survive as a distinct group. One remarked, "I see little point to being Jewish, but that's what I am. And there's little point in trying to be something else."[49]

3. *Ambivalent orientation.* This group appeared to approximate most closely Stonequist's complex of psychological attributes of marginality. Their relationship to both Jewish and non-Jewish groups was fundamentally unsatisfying and conflicting. It was reflected in this statement by a Jewish man, a statement which reflects his ambivalent identification in his references to Jews as "the Jewish people," "they," and "we": "*The Jewish people* can be their own worst enemy, by the so-called ghetto idea. I grant you that sometimes *they* have to band together in a so-called ghetto to have strength. But I feel that *we* must get along with our fellow beings; this means taking both the good and bad of the gentiles."[50]

4. *Dual orientation.* This group looked toward a slow but steady integration within the larger society and saw no insurmountable obstacles to it. They felt that the rewards to be gained from such integration were substantial.

[46] *Ibid.,* 57–62.
[47] *Ibid.,* 60.
[48] *Ibid.,* 60.
[49] *Ibid.,* 60.
[50] *Ibid.,* 60. Italics added.

5. *Passive general orientation.* This group of Jews were indifferent to, and in the process of drifting away from, Jewish culture; yet they did not actively seek to shut themselves off from Jewish life. Their solidarity with the Jewish group was nominal; they were completely indifferent to Jewish group survival; yet they were also indifferent to assimilation. One remarked, "Being Jewish is the least of my worries." [51]

6. *Active general orientation.* This group felt no solidarity with the Jewish group and came as close to assimilation as possible without hiding or denying their Jewishness.[52]

The Marginal Catholic

It should not be assumed that Jews represent the only religiously oriented group of which some of the members occupy a marginal status. Among Roman Catholics there appears to be a relatively high incidence of marginality. Father Joseph H. Fichter, a sociologist, studied 14,838 white urban Catholics living in three ecclesiastical parishes of a southern city.[53] He divided this group into four general categories: (1) *nuclear Catholics,* those who were the most active participants and the most faithful believers; (2) *modal Catholics,* those who were average "practicing" Catholics and regular parishioners; (3) *marginal Catholics,* those who conformed to a bare, arbitrary minimum of the patterns expected by the Catholic church; and (4) *dormant Catholics,* those who had "given up" Catholicism but had not joined another denomination. Some 5,786 individuals, or 38.9 per cent, were found to be dormant Catholics and accordingly "outside" the church. Of the remaining 9,052 individuals, approximately 21 per cent were marginal, 68 per cent modal, and 11 per cent nuclear.[54]

The marginal Catholic was an individual who was still under some degree of the church's control, yet who found himself very near its circumference. He was being pulled toward the center of one or more secular institutions; simultaneously, he felt himself pushed from Catholicism by the failure of the Catholic church to "change with the times." On the one hand, he accepted the values of the Catholic church; on the other hand, he rejected these values because of their disagreement with secular values. His religious role was ambiguous, since the Catholic church does not provide a clear-cut, formal position for the individual who is "neither hot nor cold." [55]

[51] *Ibid.,* 61.
[52] *Ibid.,* 61.
[53] Joseph H. Fichter, S.J., "The Marginal Catholic: An Institutional Approach," *Social Forces,* 32 (1953), 167–173.
[54] *Ibid.,* 169.
[55] *Ibid.,* 169.

Fichter used three criteria to determine the extent of marginality among Catholics in the three parishes:

1. *Mass attendance.* Unless the individual has a valid excuse, the Catholic church requires him to attend mass on Sundays and the designated feast days of the liturgical year. Some 1,792 individuals, or 19.8 per cent of the 9,052 Catholics, either attended mass only once during the preceding year or not at all.

2. *Sacraments of communion and penance.* Every Catholic is required to confess his sins and receive communion at least once a year during the paschal period (commonly referred to as "making one's Easter duty"). Some 1,946 Catholics, or 21.5 per cent, admitted their failure in this obligation during the preceding year.

3. *Catholic education of children.* Among the Catholics, there were 1,223 families with children of elementary-school age. Of these, 283, or 23.1 per cent, sent one or more of their children to the public school. Although there were exceptions, for the most part the *same* people were negligent in all three areas.

Fichter concludes that the mores and folkways of the larger society have gained ascendance over the mores and folkways of the church in the behavior and thinking of the marginal Catholic. Four factors apparently were most important in influencing the attitudes and behavior of the marginal Catholic.

First, the individual attempted to reconcile values and patterns of conduct which from his church's viewpoint were contradictory. This was particularly noted in two areas: that of race relations and that of business morality. In the former, the individual accepted the southern white norms of racial behavior in contrast to the Catholic church's teachings of brotherhood and love; in the latter, he accepted the "cutting of corners" in business in contrast to Catholic teachings that justice must operate at all times.[56]

A second factor which apparently contributed to marginal Catholicism was the individual's view that morality is relative and not, as the church believes, absolute. This was frequently seen in the individual's attitude toward Catholic doctrines on sex sins, birth control, and divorce. Although likely to praise and defend the "high morality" of his church's position, the marginal Catholic thought that circumstances made it impossible for him to act in accordance with these

[56] *Ibid.,* 171.

teachings. He tended to believe that "God truly understood his situation" although the priest in the confessional might not.

A third factor commonly influencing Catholics in the direction of marginality was anti-authoritarian sentiment. The principal figures of the Catholic church are arranged in a hierarchal system of ranks, based on appointment from above. The marginal Catholic frequently viewed this as an arbitrary and authoritarian arrangement that conflicted with American democratic ideals. Likewise, marginal Catholics often charged priests with being "dictatorial" and interfering in non-church matters. They insisted that priests confine themselves strictly to mass, sacraments, and rituals.

A fourth factor was associated with the changing nature of the parish. In the past, the parish ideally functioned as a community of persons carrying on a great many activities. Within America, however, traditional parish functions have increasingly been taken over by other institutions. This seems especially the case with regard to leisure-time activities. The marginal Catholic leans toward secularized activities and insists there is "nothing sinful to this." The net result is that he becomes more worldly in his thinking and thus marginal to the traditional center of the parish church.

INTERGROUP MARRIAGE

Intergroup marriage represents an important means through which both assimilation and racial amalgamation are realized. In the United States, intermarriage between peoples of differing nationality groups is a frequent occurrence; religious intermarriage is somewhat less common; while racial intermarriage is infrequent.

Interethnic Marriage

Although evidence suggests that nationality is not as binding a force as race or religion in mate selection, it nevertheless operates as a restrictive-selective factor. Although there are only a limited number of studies dealing with the incidence of interethnic marriage, available evidence suggests that out-group marriage is on the rise. Bugelski, for instance, studied the rate of in-group and out-group marriage for Poles and Italians in Buffalo, New York, a city with sizable Polish and Italian populations.[57] In 1930, in-group marriages were the common practice with more than two-thirds of the marriages involving partners of the same group. By 1960, Bugelski found the pattern virtually re-

[57] B. R. Bugelski, "Assimilation Through Intermarriage," *Social Forces*, 40 (1961), 148–153.

versed with more than two-thirds of the marriages involving partners from different ethnic groups. He concludes, "somewhere before 1975, the 'Polish Wedding' and the 'Italian Wedding' will be a thing of the past." [58] Studies of mate selection in New Haven show similar patterns,[59] while Wessel, in a study of ethnicity in Woonsocket, Rhode Island, found that the rate of outmarriage for the first generation was 9.6 per cent, for the second 20.9 per cent, and for the third 40.4 per cent.[60]

Interreligious Marriage

In the United States, intermarriage among the various Protestant denominations—Baptists, Methodists, Lutherans, Episcopalians, etc.— is quite common. When the matter of religious intermarriage is raised, reference is usually made to the pattern involving Protestants, Catholics, and Jews. All three of these major religious groups encourage their members to marry within the fold, but they exhibit considerable variation in their respective attitudes. Protestant churches tend to be the most flexible, Jews the most rigid, and the Catholic church falls somewhere in between. Provided certain stipulations are met, a Catholic priest will ordinarily marry a Catholic and a non-Catholic, but a Jewish rabbi generally will not marry a Jew and a non-Jew.[61]

Intermarriage between Catholics and Protestants represents the most significant interreligious marital pattern within the United States. Unfortunately there are insufficient data on the number of mixed marriages not sanctioned by the Catholic church. A study by John L. Thomas revealed that, during the decade from 1940 to 1950, mixed marriages sanctioned by Catholic nuptials represented 30 per cent of all Catholic marriages in the United States.[62] He further investigated mixed marriages in 132 parishes distributed throughout the East and Midwest. Of 29,581 mixed marriages, 11,710, or 39.6 per cent, were not sanctioned by Catholic nuptials.[63] A sample survey of the American population made by the Bureau of the Census in 1957 (based on

---

[58] *Ibid.*, 151.

[59] Ruby Jo Reeves Kennedy, "Single or Triple Melting-Pot? Intermarriage Trends in New Haven, 1870–1940," *American Journal of Sociology*, 49 (1944), 331–339, and August Hollingshead, "Cultural Factors in the Selection of Marriage Mates," *American Sociological Review*, 15 (1950), 624.

[60] B. B. Wessel, *An Ethnic Survey of Woonsocket, Rhode Island* (Chicago: University of Chicago Press, 1931), chapter 8.

[61] William M. Kephart, *The Family, Society, and the Individual* (Boston: Houghton Mifflin Co., 1961), 276.

[62] John L. Thomas, "The Factor of Religion in the Selection of Marriage Mates," *American Sociological Review*, 16 (1951), 488.

[63] *Ibid.*, 488–491.

35,000 households) found a rate of *existing* Catholic mixed marriages of 21.6 per cent. The comparable figure for Protestants was 8.6 per cent.[64] These figures, however, underestimate the rate of interreligious marriage as they fail to include the rate of conversion of one spouse to the faith of the other. In fact, some data of Lenski's for Detroit white Protestants and white Catholics indicate how frequent the conversion process may be and how it may be trending. Of the combined Protestant-Catholic white sample, 85 per cent reported that they and their spouses were of the same major faith, but only 68 per cent had been reared in the same religion. Furthermore, among the members of the third generation, who had been born in the North and who had contracted a marriage with a person of another major faith, there appeared to be a greater tendency toward conversion of one spouse to the faith of the other than among the comparable first- and second-generation members of the sample.[65]

Probably the most accurate figures available on religious intermarriage are to be found for the state of Iowa. Iowa marriage-application forms request each individual to cite his religious preference. In 1953, some 42 per cent of all Iowa marriages involving a Catholic party were mixed. For the same year, the Catholic Directory lists 30 per cent of all Iowa marriages that were sanctioned by the church as mixed. The state records reveal a much higher rate of Catholic-Protestant intermarriage, since the figures of the Catholic church do not include other-church and civil-ceremony marriages.[66]

Thomas suggests that three major factors influence the rate of Catholic intermarriage. First, where Catholics represent a relatively small proportion of the total population, rates of intermarriage tend to be high (provided that ethnic or other differences do not bar contacts between Catholics and non-Catholics). Thus, he found that mixed marriages sanctioned by the Catholic church constituted 70 per cent of the Catholic marriages in the dioceses of Raleigh, Charleston, and Savannah-Atlanta (dioceses with a small proportion of Catholics in the total population) but that they represented only 10 per cent of the marriages in the dioceses of El Paso, Corpus Christi, and Santa Fe (dioceses with a large proportion of Catholics in the total population). Second, the presence of cohesive ethnic groups within the community

[64] U.S. Bureau of the Census, *Current Population Reports: Population Characteristics,* Series P-20, 79 (1958), 2 and 8.

[65] Gerhard Lenski, *The Religious Factor,* rev. ed. (Garden City, N.Y.: Doubleday & Company, Inc., 1963).

[66] Loren Chancellor and Thomas Monahan, "Religious Preference and Interreligious Mixtures in Marriages and Divorces in Iowa," *American Journal of Sociology,* 60 (1955), 237.

serve to put a check on interreligious marriage. Third, the higher the socioeconomic class, the higher the proportion of mixed Catholic and non-Catholic marriages.[67]

In its 1957 sample of 35,000 American households, the Bureau of the Census found that 7.2 per cent of the Jews contracted a marriage with a gentile.[68] But here again the figure fails to note the rate of conversion. Further, it does not tell the *current* rate of interreligious marriage among Jews. Included in the figure were Jews who had taken their vows in Czarist Russian where intermarriage was forbidden as well as people who had married in the United States but who belonged to the virtually closed community of the immigrant generation. Hence, the current rate may well be double that of the Bureau's cumulative ratio. In this regard, Rosenthal, using a 1956 survey of Washington's Jewish population, found that 13.1 per cent of the households were characterized by a gentile spouse. He also provided tabulations on the rate of intermarriage for successive generations: 1.4 per cent for the first generation, 10.2 per cent for the second, and 17.9 per cent for the third. Since it can be assumed that the great majority of Washington's Jews who are marrying at the present time belong to the third generation, the 17.9 per cent figure is probably quite close to the current rate in that city.[69]

Although only some 63 per cent are actual church members, Americans generally think of themselves as being part of a religious community (Protestant, Catholic, or Jewish). Various data suggest that some 95 per cent of the American population readily identifies itself with one of the major religious groups (roughly two-thirds with Protestantism, one-fourth with Catholicism, and 3 per cent with Judaism).[70] Moreover, a transfer of membership is quite uncommon; probably no more than five per cent of adults have shifted from the religious group of their birth to another of the three major religious groups.[71] Evidence such as this has led some writers to suggest that America has developed not a single but a *triple* melting pot. They argue that the sharpest reduction of differences appears to have taken place *within* each of the three major groups rather than between them, that is, barriers to interaction, cooperation, and intermarriage have been lowered between Irish Catholics and Italian Catholics, between German Jews and Russian

[67] Thomas, *op. cit.*, 488–491.

[68] U.S. Bureau of the Census, *op. cit.*, 2 and 8.

[69] Marshall Sklare, "Intermarriage and the Jewish Future," *Commentary*, 37 (1964), 46–52.

[70] U.S. Bureau of the Census, *op. cit.*, 1.

[71] J. Milton Yinger, "Social Forces Involved in Group Identification or Withdrawal," *Daedalus*, 90 (1961), 249.

Jews, and between English Protestants and Swedish Protestants. Ruby Jo Kennedy, in a study of intermarriage in New Haven, found that while there is a decreasing emphasis on national origins in choosing a mate, there is still a considerable tendency to marry within one's own religious group: "Irish, Italians, and Poles intermarry mostly among themselves, and British-Americans, Germans, and Scandinavians do likewise, while Jews seldom marry Gentiles." [72] Apparently religious considerations play a major role, as the Irish, Italians, and Poles have traditionally been Catholic, and the British, Germans, and Scandinavians Protestant. Yet not all evidence supports the triple melting pot thesis. We have already noted the rather high incidence of Catholic marriage with non-Catholics. Further, Heiss, with reference to a midtown Manhattan population sample, discovered that 21 per cent of Catholic, 34 per cent of Protestant, and 18 per cent of Jewish marriages were mixed.[73]

Interracial Marriages

The incidence of Negro-white intermarriage within the United States is low. In 1965, 19 states still had laws that prohibited it, while the mores throughout the nation have generally functioned to limit its occurrence. In Boston in the period 1914–1938, 3.9 per cent of all marriages involving Negroes were Negro-white marriages and 0.13 per cent of all marriages involving whites were Negro-white marriages.[74] For the most part, interracial marriages are a phenomenon limited to northern urban centers. Studies of interracial marriages have revealed that most of the marriages take place between Negro men and white women. However, Golden's study of Negro-white marriages in Philadelphia from 1922 to 1947 reveals a smaller predominance in the percentage of Negro male–white female marriages, 58.5 per cent, than do most studies.[75] Wirth and Goldhamer, in their study of nativity in Boston and in New York State, found that foreign-born white males and native white females were over-represented in Negro-white marriages. Italian grooms were heavily represented. The authors conclude that "it is possible that color selection is in operation here and that among males the darker foreign nationalities are more likely to marry Negro

[72] Kennedy, *op. cit.*, 339.

[73] Jerold S. Heiss, "Premarital Characteristics of the Religiously Intermarried in an Urban Area," *American Sociological Review*, 25 (1960), 47–55.

[74] Louis Wirth and Herbert Goldhamer, "The Hybrid and the Problem of Miscegenation," in Otto Klineberg, ed., *Characteristics of the American Negro* (New York: Harper & Row, 1944), 277.

[75] Joseph Golden, "Characteristics of the Negro-White Intermarried in Philadelphia," *American Sociological Review*, 18 (1953), 177–183.

women." [76]   A similar pattern was found in Philadelphia.[77]   Contrary
to the popular stereotype, Bogue and Dizard, University of Chicago
sociologists, found that very few Negroes report they would encourage
their child to marry a white person.   In a sample of 721 Negro families
in Chicago, about one-half of the Negroes said they would tolerate it,
saying "It made no difference," while the other half indicated they
would oppose it.[78]

Probably the most satisfactory recent data for interracial marriage
is that supplied by John Burma for Los Angeles County.   Between
1948 and 1959 California recorded the race of applicants for marriage
licenses.   Of more than 375,000 total marriage licenses, some 3,200 were
found to be interracial.   Of these, Negro-white and Filipino-white marriages were the most common.   In the eleven-year period covered by
the study, the rate of interracial marriage tripled from 5.8 interracial
marriages out of every 1,000 marriages in 1949 to 16.1 in 1959.[79]

Golden's study of Negro-white marriages, based upon a Philadelphia
sample, provides any number of insights regarding the social characteristics of the spouses and the problems they encounter in a society that
for the most part disapproves of interracial marriage.   In terms of education, Golden found that the Negro-white couples had a median education that amounted to high-school completion.   The study did not
confirm the prevailing opinion that well-educated Negro men marry
ignorant white women.   Of forty-four Negro men, seventeen had married white women on the same educational level, twelve had married
educationally downward, while fifteen had married upward.   In terms
of the occupational matching of the spouses, a tendency was found
toward homogamy (like marrying like).[80]   On the other hand, less than
half of the marriages were religiously homogamous.[81]

Golden found that the social controls which operate to prevent interracial marriages affect the dating and courtship behavior of those who
attempt to undertake it.   Friends and relatives discourage the couple
from getting married, and various pressures may be applied to compel
them to discontinue the relationship.   Unless they frequent interracial
groupings, the couple find little opportunity to participate in larger

[76] Wirth and Goldhamer, op. cit., 288.
[77] Golden, op. cit., 179.
[78] "Negroes Are Cool to Mixed Marriage, 2 Sociologists Find," New York Times,
May 25, 1964.
[79] John H. Burma, "Interethnic Marriage in Los Angeles, 1948–1959," Social
Forces, 42 (1963), 156–165.
[80] Golden, op. cit., 182.
[81] Ibid., 182–183.

groups. Each is an outsider to the racial group of the other. The Negro partner is barred from places of entertainment that do not welcome Negroes, while the white partner is viewed suspiciously in most Negro circles. Since the community disapproves of interracial marriage and tends to view the couple during the courtship phase as maintaining an illicit relationship, most mixed couples carry on *sub rosa* courtship.[82]

The pattern of secrecy is frequently continued in the arrangements for the wedding. Some couples elope. Many from the Philadelphia area were married in Elkton, Maryland, or some other Gretna Green where "marrying parsons" perform the service with no embarrassing questions asked. In most cases the ceremony is civil rather than religious. In Philadelphia there were almost no formal church weddings attended by relatives and friends.[83]

The pattern of concealment is often continued after the wedding. Where the white spouse has carried on the courtship without the knowledge of his (or her) parents and siblings, the latter may not be notified of the marriage. In some instances the white spouse tells the parents of the *fait accompli* and hopes they will become reconciled to it. But it is not uncommon for the white spouse's family to refuse any contact with the Negro spouse. On the other hand, the family of the Negro spouse is usually willing to have contact with the white spouse. It appeared that, among the Philadelphia couples studied by Golden, the Negro spouse's family tended to respond to the white spouse in terms of the individual's merits and personal traits rather than as a violator of the mores. On the whole, the Negro community took a similar point of view. While disapproving of Negro-white marriage in general, the Negro community was generally prepared to view the white in terms of his (or her) personal qualities. Golden indicates that, although there was some reserve in the acceptance of the marriage, couples whose marriages had stood the test of time came to feel at home within the Negro community. The child-production record of the interracial couples was rather small. This may have been in part the product of their higher median age at marriage (28.3 years) and in part the product of an unwillingness to invite the additional hazard of children within the context of a relatively difficult setting.[84]

Although an interracial marriage did not appear to impair the prestige of the Negro spouse within the Negro community of Philadelphia,

---

[82] Joseph Golden, "Patterns of Negro-White Intermarriage," *American Sociological Review*, 19 (1954), 144.

[83] *Ibid.*, 144.

[84] *Ibid.*, 144–145.

the white spouse for one reason or another was often avoided by former white friends. A number of white wives joined Negro churches, while others attended white churches without their husbands. However, for the most part, they did not retain their previous organizational memberships. As with the children, the white spouses became Negroes socially. Their relations with the neighbors tended to be cordial but not intimate. Some of the whites lost their jobs when their interracial marriages were discovered, while a number of others were careful not to let the fact of their intermarriage become known to their occupational associates.

ASSIMILATION WITHIN HAWAII

Hawaii has often been referred to as a "polyracial paradise," "the showcase of American democracy," and "one of the most spectacular 'melting pots' in the world." [85] The 1960 Census revealed that, of a total population of 632,772, 32.2 per cent were Japanese, 31.9 per cent Caucasian, 10.9 per cent Filipino, 6.0 per cent Chinese, and 18.1 per cent Hawaiian and Korean. Geographically, Hawaii is an archipelago composed of eight inhabited islands and a chain of uninhabited islets that runs to Midway.

At the time of their discovery in 1778 by the English navigator Captain James Cook, the Hawaiian Islands had an estimated population of 300,000. Racially the Hawaiians are kindred to the Samoans and the Maoris, belonging to the Polynesian stock. Between 1782 and 1796, Kamehameha, a powerful chieftain on the largest island, Hawaii, established his rule over the other islands and founded the Kingdom of Hawaii. From the beginning, Kamehameha pursued a policy of fair play and goodwill in his dealings with "the peoples and ships of all nations." This policy was continued by his successors, and through the years circumstances in the Islands have favored the process of racial and cultural fusion.[86]

Although there were an estimated 300,000 Hawaiians in the Islands at the time of Cook's discovery, the native population has since steadily declined. Civil wars, new diseases, the intemperate use of alcohol, and low fertility were contributing factors. In 1823 the number of Hawaiians stood at 142,050; by 1860 the figure had dropped more than 53 per cent to 66,984; by 1900 there were only 29,799 Hawaiians and 9,857 part-Hawaiians. Since 1900, the number of part-Hawaiians has

[85] C. K. Cheng, "Assimilation in Hawaii and the Bid for Statehood," *Social Forces*, 30 (1951), 16.

[86] *Ibid.*, 16–17.

increased and they represent more than 80 per cent of that group classified as "Hawaiian" by the census.[87]

Large-scale sugar-cane production was introduced to the Islands in 1835, and, in the decades that followed, the export of sugar became of increasing importance to the Islands' economy. The rise in the sugar export became phenomenal following the conclusion of the U.S.– Hawaii Reciprocity Treaty in 1875. In 1877 the total Hawaiian sugar export to the United States amounted to 30,600,000 pounds; by 1898, the year of the American annexation of Hawaii, it reached 499,800,000 pounds. The expansion of the sugar industry gave a marked impetus to the Islands' productive and business enterprises and encouraged Caucasian immigration. In 1900 there were some 8,547 Caucasians in the Islands; by 1920, the number had risen two and a half times to 19,708. In response to the growing demands for labor on the large sugar plantations, more than 100,000 Chinese, Portuguese, and Japanese arrived between 1877 and 1896. By 1900 there were approximately 25,700 Chinese, 18,200 Portuguese, and 61,100 Japanese in the Islands. Until the 1920's, Japanese migration continued in considerable numbers; Japanese laborers were augmented at different times by Puerto Ricans, Koreans, Portuguese, and Filipinos.[88]

Hawaii still gives the appearance of a racial and cultural conglomeration characteristic of a growing polyethnic community. Many of the immigrant generation cling to their native languages, religions, traditions, and customs. A number of those who have achieved financial success have undertaken to perpetuate the native patterns; they have sponsored foreign language schools, newspapers, and radio programs and have organized national fraternal organizations.[89]

Although the Islands are often advertised as a "polyracial paradise," prejudices are by no means absent there. Among the descendants of old Caucasian families and newcomers from the continental United States, there are those who seek to erect and maintain social barriers based upon racial origin. This has been most prevalent in rural areas. Similarly, prejudices are found among the non-Caucasian groups—the Chinese, Filipinos, and Koreans, for example, harboring antipathy toward Japanese because of the aggressive policies pursued by Japan in the fifty-odd years before 1945. Likewise, there are intrarace prejudices, the Japanese from Japan looking down upon Okinawans, the *Punti* Chinese feeling antagonism for the *Hakka* Chinese, the old Caucasian families experiencing antipathy for the Caucasian newcomers,

[87] *Ibid.*, 18.
[88] *Ibid.*, 20.
[89] *Ibid.*, 22.

etc. Still, racial and ethnic membership plays a relatively insignificant role in the larger institutional setting of Hawaii. Japanese, Chinese, Hawaiians, and Caucasians have been elected to major public offices, and there is no evidence of bloc voting.[90]

Assimilation is taking place rapidly, especially among second- and third-generation non-Caucasians. Among the latter, disparaging attitudes prevail toward the languages, religions, traditions, and customs of their forebears. In matters of dress, speech, expression, mannerisms, and behavior patterns, their break with the immigrant generation has been unequivocal. Individuals who are more closely identified with ancestral patterns often become the objects of ridicule. On the whole there is an emergent integration of the non-Caucasions within the host American society and culture.

The Chinese are one of the oldest ethnic groups within the Islands. With the American annexation of Hawaii (1898), Chinese inflow was largely shut off through the application of American exclusion laws. Since the turn of the twentieth century, Chinese assimilation has proceeded at a rapid pace. Chinese are active in politics and enjoy a number of high political positions. They are well established in practically all the professions—11 per cent of the total licensed lawyers and 18 per cent of the total licensed doctors in the Islands are of Chinese ancestry. Within Honolulu they own property far out of proportion to their number: 25.4 per cent of the city's rental units have Chinese landlords, whereas 32.2 per cent and 29.2 per cent of the units have Caucasian and Japanese landlords, respectively. The Chinese Americans react with the same heedlessness and indifference to the turn of events within China as do native-born Americans in the continental United States toward the countries of their immigrant forebears. Although often celebrating Chinese festivals, staging Chinese plays, and decorating their homes with Chinese antiques, they are not particularly concerned about China or its destiny.[91]

The reputation of Hawaii as "the world's most successful experiment in mixed breeding" is not without foundation. Table 14 presents figures which suggest that, through the years, racial and ethnic intermarriages have increased. In the decade between 1945 and 1954, a total of 110,696 persons of all racial and ethnic extractions were married in

[90] Ibid., 22. Also see Andrew W. Lind, "Race Relations Frontiers in Hawaii," in Jitsuichi Masuoka and Preston Valien, eds., Race Relations (Chapel Hill: University of North Carolina Press, 1961), 58–77; and J. Milton Yinger, A Minority Group in American Society (New York: McGraw-Hill Book Company, 1965), 80–87.

[91] C. K. Cheng, "A Study of Chinese Assimilation in Hawaii," Social Forces, 32 (1953), 163–167.

TABLE 14

Percentages of Outmarriages in the Total Marriages of the Different
Racial and Ethnic Groups in Hawaii

	1913		1941		1949	
Group	Male	Female	Male	Female	Male	Female
Hawaiians	17.4	38.4	65.0	75.5	78.1	80.8
Puerto Ricans	19.6	22.9	25.0	48.5	40.7	57.0
Caucasians	13.8	8.7	21.9	10.2	36.9	16.3
Chinese	48.8	6.1	24.9	32.2	41.1	40.3
Japanese	0.7	0.3	4.5	10.1	6.4	16.8
Koreans	31.3	—	37.5	57.1	56.8	67.3
Filipinos	15.4	2.1	44.0	7.6	40.2	23.9

SOURCE: C. K. Cheng, "Assimilation in Hawaii and the Bid for Statehood," *Social Forces*, 30 (1951), 26. By permission.

Hawaii. Of this number, 31,432, or 28.4 per cent, married outside their own group. In absolute numbers, Caucasians and Hawaiians were the two groups most involved in intermarriages.[92]

A number of trends were noted by Cheng and Yamamura in their study of intergroup marriage in Hawaii. First, women from racial or ethnic groups with a more balanced sex ratio tend to marry outside their own groups in greater numbers than women from groups that have a less balanced sex ratio. Second, there is a greater tendency for the numerically smaller ethnic or racial groups to marry outside their own groups than is the case for the larger groups. Of the Koreans and Puerto Ricans, the smallest groups, 80.9 per cent of the former and 64.6 per cent of the latter are involved in outmarriages. On the other hand, of the Japanese and Caucasians, the largest groups, 22.4 per cent of the former and 41.3 per cent of the latter are involved in outmarriages. The comparatively higher outmarriage rate of the Caucasians is largely the product of a higher sex ratio than that of the Japanese. Third, there is a tendency for women in racial or ethnic intermarriages to marry upward on the social scale.[93]

MINIMUM ASSIMILATION: THE AMISH

Contact between groups does not inevitably result in assimilation. Groups may be in contact over a considerable period of time, yet assimilation may be held to a bare minimum. The "melting pot" does not

[92] C. K. Cheng and Douglas S. Yamamura, "Interracial Marriage and Divorce in Hawaii," *Social Forces*, 36 (1957), 81.
[93] *Ibid.*, 81.

always work. The Old Order Amish of Pennsylvania are a case in point. The Amish are a religious sect, an offshoot of the Mennonites. The group originated in Alsace and the upper Rhineland area of Germany and Switzerland during the Reformation conflicts of the sixteenth century. A schism occurred in the Mennonite movement in 1693, and Jacob Amman led his conservative followers, in time known as the Amish, from the larger group. The Amish were recruited from the peasantry and were both rural and lower class in background. The basic tenet of the group is that all practices and activities must be based upon a literal interpretation of the Bible, regardless of the laws or customs of the larger society. It appears that the movement originated as a revolt by a disadvantaged people against the culture of its day, a culture that had proved too punishing and too devoid of satisfactions to be followed longer. Because of religious persecution, the Amish migrated to Pennsylvania in the early 1700's. The group residing in Lancaster County is the oldest and most conservative of the Amish settlements in the United States.

The Amish are a kin-oriented, rural-dwelling, religion-centered people. Although frequently living adjacent to non-Amish farm neighbors, all Amish households in a geographic area form a "church district." The Amish are highly succesful as farmers, and their farms are acknowledged to be among the best in the world. Although very conservative generally, the Amish are not conservative in their farming techniques. They have adopted the new methods of rotating crops, applying fertilizer, and introducing new commercial agricultural products. While prohibiting the use of the tractor, they do employ some modern farm equipment including cultivators, sprayers, binders, and balers.

The Amish are oriented toward two major goals: (1) "the Christian way of life" as defined by the sect's interpretation of the Bible and (2) successful farming as defined by agricultural abundance rather than financial success. Their main objective in farming is to accumulate sufficient means to buy enough land to keep all the children on farms. To this end the Amish work hard, produce abundantly, and save extensively.

The Amish, far from being ashamed of their non-conformity, pride themselves on being a "peculiar people" who do not conform to the standards of the world. Non-conformity is held to be obligatory in those areas in which "worldly" standards are in conflict with those of the Bible. The sect members eschew the bearing of arms, going to war, public office, life insurance, and social security. Education beyond the eighth grade is opposed, since it is felt that higher education is both unnecessary and a danger in that it would draw the children away from the farm and the Amish way of life. They approve of elementary education in the "three R's," since literacy is required for reading the Bible. The fact that the Amish are trilingual contributes to their social isolation: Pennsylvania Dutch is the familiar tongue at home and in informal conversation; High German is used exclusively for services and ceremonials; and English (acquired in school) is employed with non-Amish Americans.[94]

Their attire is distinctive. Men wear their hair long, cut in bangs, with low-crown, wide-brim hats on their heads. Their coats lack collars, lapels, pockets, and buttons (they are fastened with hooks and eyes). Trousers are plain and worn with homemade suspenders. Shirts are plain and worn without neckties. Married men wear a beard, but a mustache (considered the mark of a military man) is forbidden; unmarried men shave. Amish women wear plain, solid-color dresses with near-ankle-length skirts. Their stockings are of black cotton; their shoes are of a high-laced, low-heeled type; and their head covering is a homemade bonnet ("store hats" are forbidden). Within Amish society styles of dress become very important symbols of group identity. The symbols indicate whether people are fulfilling the expectations of the group, for instance, a young man who wears a hat with a brim that is too narrow is liable for punishment.

Amish conservatism extends to wide areas of life. Telephones, radios, television sets, automobiles, washing machines, and electric lights are all forbidden. They eschew all forms of "worldly" amusement including attendance at sporting events, movies, dance halls, and bars. Ornaments and jewelry are prohibited.

Marriage to outsiders is not permitted. Their marriages are very stable; divorces are unknown; and their families are large. All religious services are held in the homes of the members—the custom being for the meetings to rotate among the homes in each district. They lack a paid clergy and a formal bureaucratic church organization. They select their bishops, ministers, and deacons by election from among the married men. After the Sunday service (which may last for four hours), a large dinner is served for all sect members in the home in which the service was held.

A number of factors have operated to keep Amish assimilation at a

[94] This summary of the Old Order Amish is based primarily upon John Gillin, *The Ways of Men* (New York: Appleton-Century-Crofts, Inc., 1948), 209–220; and John A. Hostetler, *Amish Society* (Baltimore: Johns Hopkins Press, 1963).

bare minimum. First, competing customs have had little opportunity
to be presented and tried out, by virtue of the group's non-conformity
and isolation. The Amish are kept from contact with most stimuli
or models by which they might learn other customs and practices.
Second, the group supplies plentiful rewards for following Amish practices. In time of difficulty or when he is starting a new farm, the
community comes to the individual's aid. The group also satisfies
various personal needs, for instance, ego-satisfaction, affection, companionship, and security. In a word, the Amish community provides
for all or most of the activities and needs of the people in it. Third,
the fear of punishment is considerable. The members are taught that
transgressions of God's will result, after death, in certain punishment
in the fires of Hell. The group also excommunicates and "shuns"
violators of its norms, withdrawing all social intercourse with the
wrongdoer. No member may knowingly eat at the table with an expelled member or have normal work or domestic relations with him.
If the case involves husband or wife, they are to suspend their usual
marital relations. Shunning constitutes a powerful instrument for keeping the church intact and for preventing members from involvement in
the wider society. Similarly it operates to keep the Old Order Amish
socially isolated from innovators within their own group.

Nevertheless, the Amish have not been able to shut the door entirely
upon social change. In recent decades both individual and group assimilation has increasingly occurred. Individual assimilation occurs
among those who for one reason or another voluntarily break with the
group or are involuntarily isolated from it. Group assimilation occurs
among entire congregations who come to consider themselves no longer
Old Order Amish. Among such groups, it is not unusual to find the
members adopting tractors, automobiles, and meeting houses, trimming
their hair and beards shorter and shorter, securing clothing more nearly
resembling that of other Americans, shifting to non-farm occupations,
and the like.

Among those who retain their Old Order allegiance, the individual
may still eschew electric lights, rubber-tired farm implements, and
telephones. Yet he may install propane gas on his farm, secure the
latest style gas-range, a kerosene-burning refrigerator, and an automatic, gas water-heater with a gasoline engine to keep up the water
pressure. His home may be lit with gasoline mantle lanterns. And although he does not have his own telephone, he may use that of a neighbor or a pay phone. Although still not buying a car, he may ride in
a cab or in the automobile of a non-Amish neighbor. In order to sell

Grade A milk, he may alter his barn, milk house, water supply, and his habits of working with farm animals. Hence, the Amish society is not static.

SUMMARY

We have seen that assimilation entails a process whereby groups with diverse ways of thinking, feeling, and acting become fused together in a social unity and a common culture. Americans have not been in agreement on how assimilation may "best" proceed, some adhering to the "melting pot" orientation, others to the "Americanization" approach, and still others to the position of cultural pluralism. Some scholars have suggested that contact between groups inevitably results in assimilation, a point of view that seems difficult to substantiate. Numerous variables influence the rate of assimilation, including the degree of racial and cultural differences that exist between the populations. As a result of assimilation, individuals may find themselves occupying a marginal status in which they have internalized to one degree or another the cultural patterns of a group functioning as their reference group and to which they aspire to membership, but in which they do not find full or legitimate membership.

IV

MINORITY REACTIONS TO DOMINANCE

11

Responding by Acceptance

How do minority group members think and feel about their subordinate status? How do they react to segregation, discrimination, disadvantaged conditions, and disparagement? What are their sentiments toward members of the dominant group? The answers to these questions are by no means simple. Any number of sociologists and anthropologists have attempted to classify minority reactions to dominance.[1] Yet none of these classificatory efforts has been entirely satisfactory. From these various approaches, however, we can identify four common patterns of reaction to dominance:

1. *Acceptance.* Minority-group members may come to acquiesce in—to accommodate themselves to—their disadvantaged and subordinate status.
2. *Aggression.* Minority-group members may respond to dominance by striking out against—engaging in hostile acts against—a status that is subordinate and disadvantaged.

[1] See, for example, Charles S. Johnson, *Patterns of Negro Segregation* (New York: Harper & Row, 1943), 244–315; M. R. Davie, *Negroes in American Society* (New York: McGraw-Hill, 1949), 434–457; George E. Simpson, "The Ras Tafari Movement in Jamaica: A Study of Race and Class Conflict," *Social Forces*, 34 (1955), 168–170; Robert B. Johnson, "Negro Reactions to Minority Group Status," in Milton L. Barron, ed., *American Minorities* (New York: Alfred A. Knopf, Inc., 1957), 210; Brewton Berry, *Race and Ethnic Relations*, 3d ed. (Boston: Houghton Mifflin Company, 1965), 380–403; and Donald M. Noel, Correlates of Anti-White Prejudice (unpublished doctoral dissertation, Cornell University, Ithaca, New York, 1961), chapter 6.

3. *Avoidance.* Minority-group members may attempt to shun—to escape from—situations in which they are likely to experience prejudice and discrimination.
4. *Assimilation.* Minority-group members may attempt to become socially and culturally fused with the dominant group.

We may view avoidance and assimilation as opposites, each constituting a pole on a continuum.[2] Each pole establishes an "outer limit" or standard between which transitional or intermediate reactions can be located. Confronted with a potential intergroup situation, the minority individual must tend either to avoid contact with the dominant group or merge himself socially and culturally with it. The continuum

avoidance   assimilation

reflects the fact that there are different degrees of avoidance and assimilation. A specific reaction is distributed somewhere along the continuum depending on the degree to which it constitutes avoiding or assimilating tendencies.

Similarly, we may view acceptance and aggression as opposites, each constituting a pole on a continuum.[3] Confronted with an intergroup situation—with contact with dominant group members—the minority

acceptance   aggression

individual must either tend to acquiesce in his disadvantaged and subordinate status or strike out against it.

These two continua pose choices that a minority individual must make when confronted with an intergroup situation. First, he must either allow intergroup contact to take place or he must avoid (or, at least, minimize) such contact. Second, once in the contact situation, he must either acquiesce in his subordinate status or strike out against it.

Minorities never follow one exclusive pattern of response. Intergroup relations are much too complex for any one pattern to be operative at all times. Rather, at times one pattern of reaction may come into play, at still other times another, and frequently some combination of responses may predominate. In this latter regard, based upon our two continua, we can identify four mixed response patterns: ac-

2 *Ibid.*
3 *Ibid.*

ceptance-avoidance, acceptance-assimilation, aggression-avoidance, and aggression-assimilation. In order to gain a clear picture of minority reactions to dominance, we shall devote one chapter each to acceptance,

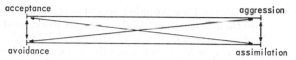

aggression, avoidance, and assimilation. In this chapter we shall be concerned with acceptance.

Some Expressions of Acceptance

Acceptance involves the renunciation of protest against the circumstances of minority status and the organization of responses so that instead accommodation appears. Daily life requires that humans accommodate themselves to various unpleasant situations. It is necessary to accept, and make the best of, disagreeable aspects of work, disagreeable traits in associates, disagreeable elements in the weather, and disagreeable facts of disease and death, in fact all the aspects of society that are limiting. Thus acceptance is not an adaptive mechanism found exclusively among minority peoples. They may, however, be required to employ it to an unusual degree. Here we shall examine some of the more typical manifestations of acceptance as it is reflected in minority-group adjustment to dominance. We shall draw chiefly upon studies of the American Negro, as the evidence here is more extensive than for perhaps any other minority.

Resignation

Some minority-group members feel that the wisest course is to accept what cannot be changed or avoided: "You don't like it, but what can you do?" Although minority-group status may be disliked, there is a conscious resignation to it or a sense of futility about changing one's lot. The minority member accepts his fate out of a feeling that there is nothing else to do. Such resignation reduces the wear and tear on one's personality. This was a common pattern of survival for Negroes during slavery times and continues to be followed by many. A Negro lower-class woman with six children said she instructed her children as her mother had instructed her: "When white folks don't treat you right, don't try to hit back. The Negro is weak—that what he is, and the white man is power. Vengeance is mine, says the Lord, and we gotta leave to Him to vengeance us. We are the underdogs." [4]

[4] E. Franklin Frazier, *Negro Youth at the Crossways* (Washington, D.C.: American Council on Education, 1940), 49. By permission.

A Negro policeman in Maryland describes his attitude of resignation, which he contrasts with his wife's militant responses to discrimination:

I have heard Negroes say they wouldn't accept certain jobs because white people call them by their first names. Take my own work, most of the men there call the Negroes arrested "darkey," "nigger," "shine," anything. I could get mad and put up a fight and make them resentful. It wouldn't do any good. I'd only be out of a good job, and they'd still go on calling Negroes whatever they please.

My wife has different ideas. She tells me to forget I'm colored and take seriously my authority to deal with whites. . . . She can't take a lot of things I put up with because her viewpoint is that she's as good as anyone else, and she'd cuss them out. I think I'm as good as some of those Irish cops, too, but I've got enough sense not to make an issue out of it. I got to eat, you know, and jobs are scarce.[5]

Outward Acceptance, Internal "Dignity"

Resignation may exist side-by-side with a feeling of pride in oneself and one's race or ethnic group. Although engaging in overt compliance and conformity with the dictates of the racial or ethnic structure, the individual may covertly or internally assert his feelings of individual worth and dignity. This type of formula is outlined by the late James Weldon Johnson, a Negro writer:

The pledge to myself which I have endeavored to keep through the greater part of my life is:

I will not allow one prejudiced person or one million or one hundred million to blight my life. I will not let prejudice or any of its attendant humiliations and injustices bear me down to spiritual defeat. My inner life is mine, and I shall defend and maintain its integrity against all the powers of hell.[6]

A Negro mother in the Deep South reports her experience in adjusting her daughter to minority status as follows:

I don't see how any Negro parent in the South can very well do otherwise than explain to the children the meaning of the differences which they observe. Race prejudice takes such queer forms that a child is very apt to run into it unexpectedly, and I think he or she should be prepared. I explain that the difference is really just in the minds of the whites. I tell my children that Negroes are every bit as good as whites. They [whites] make the difference they think is there apparent so that they can control Negroes. It just happens that the laws are made by whites and that Negroes perforce must in certain instances submit to humiliation because they can't do otherwise and live. This situation, however, should not fundamentally affect

---

[5] Johnson, *Patterns of Negro Segregation*, 238–239. By permission.
[6] James Weldon Johnson, *Negro Americans, What Now?* (New York: The Viking Press, Inc., 1934), 103.

the Negro's pride in himself. Negroes must realize that exterior features do not affect the inner being. I don't believe that we should let this prejudice discourage us and our faith in ourselves . . .[7]

Although teaching her children to comply with Jim Crow laws, this mother sought to instill in her children a sense of self-worth and dignity.

A twenty-two-year-old Chicago middle-class Negro male suggests that race prejudice does not particularly bother him. Although meeting with some unpleasant experiences with whites, he accepts his individual worth and shows satisfactions derived from his Negro membership without claiming racial superiority or showing excessive defensiveness:

I do not resent being born a Negro, although some friends have expressed the wish to be white or any other race except Negro. I am satisfied, although my color has retarded me, because each one is on this earth for a definite reason and the Lord, not man, is the final judge and if we behave in spite of color or creed we will come out winner.[8]

Internalization of Accepting Attitudes

It has been seen that some minority-group members *dislike* their disadvantaged status but become *resigned* to it. Others may go even further and *internalize* the attitudes associated with this status. They accept the existing order, neither questioning it nor doing anything about it. In essence they accept the dominant group's evaluation of themselves. They become indifferent to or even oblivious of their status. This is reflected in such statements as "I never think about it. I just take life as it comes, and go on from there." The attitude is typified by a Negro Birmingham millworker:

No telling what I would do if I had to set down to the table and eat a meal with a white man. I wouldn't enjoy it. I would be wondering what everybody that sees us would say. I tell you it would be hard. I would much rather wait until they finish if I had to eat at the same place with them. They would feel better, and I know I would.[9]

His attitude is made clearer in his philosophy toward voting:

I can't read and write, so I don't need to be voting just to be doing something. Ain't much need of these Negroes getting in that voting business, anyhow. The white folks running the country, and he [the Negro] can't do no good. That's the way it looks like it is to me.[10]

[7] Charles S. Johnson, *Growing Up in the Black Belt* (Washington, D.C.: American Council on Education, 1941), 251–252. By permission.

[8] W. Lloyd Warner, Buford H. Junker, and Walter A. Adams, *Color and Human Nature* (Washington, D.C.: American Council on Education, 1941), 62. By permission.

[9] Johnson, *Patterns of Negro Segregation*, 256. By permission of the publishers, Harper & Row.

[10] *Ibid.* By permission of the publishers, Harper & Row.

A Negro lower-class woman in Harlem tells about her life in the South:

To tell you the truth, I never had no trouble down there. I heard of people being treated bad but it never happened to me. The people I worked for, we got along fine. When you live there you know where you're supposed to go and what you're supposed to do and if you mind your own business you won't have any trouble. It's like that wherever you be. The world is like a bunch of bees. If you stir them up you get into trouble. If you let things be you won't have no trouble, but if you go looking for trouble, you'll get it.[11]

In some instances, such accommodating attitudes are taken over from those of parents and grandparents who had accepted the unequal status of the races as natural and inevitable. Frazier, in his study of Negroes in Washington, D.C., and in Louisville, Kentucky, found such patterns most prevalent among lower-class Negroes. A twenty-year-old Negro youth of fifth-grade education had accommodating attitudes impressed upon him by his parents. When he lived in North Carolina his parents had taught him "to do as we were told, be as courteous as possible to white people, don't talk back to them, and do your work as well as possible. They said 'niggers' that are liked by white people are those who don't give any trouble and don't ask for much." The youth indicated he thought this advice was good and he had tried to "follow it to the letter." He had not given "white people any trouble," but he had not "bitten his tongue in asking for things." He had discovered that "if you can act big enough monkey [clown], you can get almost what you want." [12]

THE CASE OF THE RURAL SOUTH

Within the rural areas of the South, traditional patterns of racial accommodation persist despite the changes that have occurred in agriculture through the years. On the whole a social system of white dominance and Negro subordination survives as a more or less fixed social and economic pattern. In the rural areas there is little room for Negroes as large landowners or professionals. For the most part, a Negro tenant population predominates, dependent upon white owners and planters. Farming is often carried on in large-scale units, plantations, that are subdivided into smaller units worked by tenants. The plantation system operates in such a manner as to control practically the

[11] Abram Kardiner and Lionel Ovesey, *The Mark of Oppression* (New York: W. W. Norton & Co., Inc., 1951), 146. By permission of A. Kardiner.
[12] Frazier, *op. cit.*, 42–43. By permission of the publishers, American Council on Education.

entire life of the families living within it. Work is seasonal and highly dependent upon such externally controlled factors as flood, drought, pests, and market prices. During the year, tenants are advanced credit by the landlords for living needs. By virtue of costly credit advances and low returns on labor, tenants realize little in the way of a cash surplus. With the increasing shift of southern agriculture from cotton to other crops, the large-scale introduction of cattle, and the mechanization of agriculture, factors that have been coupled with the growth in the attracting power of the cities and the North, Negroes have left the rural South in large numbers. Census data shows that Negro tenants decreased from 698,839 in 1920 to 138,048 in 1959. Within the next 10 to 25 years virtually all remaining Negro tenants will have migrated to cities and towns in both the South and the North.

The tenants have no stake in the land and no voice in determining such major decisions as to what or how much they will plant or when or where the crop will be sold. By virtue of their position, the tenants are dependent upon the white landlords. As a result of this dependence and the southern race structure of white dominance, the landlord exercises considerable influence and control over the lives of the Negro tenants. Such control represents a potent weapon in the hands of whites seeking to cope with any overt emergence of integrationist sentiment among tenants. A white Arkansas plantation manager, at the time of the Little Rock school disorders, pointed to the role of Negro dependence when asked if Negroes on his plantation might seek integration: "I can take care of things out here. It gets down to this—in winter time, when the groceries run out, they come to me." [13]

Poverty prevails among the Negro tenants to a degree equal to, if not greater than, among any other segment of the American population. It is reflected in indexes measuring living conditions, such as housing, income, education, and recreation. The houses are usually unpainted, small frame units of the "shotgun" type, typically resting on stones at each of the four corners. Underneath the home, a hound or two, a half-dozen chickens, and a few pigs may find a sheltered place. Many of the homes are not equipped with glass windows; instead, crude wooden shutters serve as window coverings. The privy is found as standard equipment.

The family, as in peasant societies generally, forms the principal and most important social group. The Negro family in the rural areas has grown out of customary practices originating during slavery or developing after slavery, in response to the conditions on the plantations.

[13] "Arkansas Man in the Street Has His Say About Little Rock," *U.S. News & World Report*, XLIII (October 11, 1957), 45.

Courtship usually begins at an early age through mutual attraction and often involves sexual relations. When pregnancy results, the couple may or may not marry. Many of the marriages are of the common-law type; the permanence of the relationship depends not only upon affection and sentiment but often upon the extent to which the couple can "work together" on the farm. Outside affairs are not uncommon. Couples may separate and "take up" with new mates. As a result of these sexual and marital practices, there is a high proportion of families with female heads. At times the pattern grows into a type of matriarchate family with the grandmother as the dominant figure. The mother acquires the status of a grandmother when her daughters become mothers and bring their children into the home.[14]

Where education is minimal and contact with the active currents of life is limited—where there is little communication with the larger world—traditional patterns of accommodation prevail. Within this context many Negroes go on from year to year without acute consciousness of race. Perplexed by their poverty when it becomes acute and taking such satisfactions as they may find from their group, they adjust to life and the racial system as they find it. More often than not, the racial situation is not generalized but conceived in terms of their personal relationships with "good" or "bad" landlords. The "white folks" see that they get "advances" for living, get out of trouble, and get attention when they are sick. Many Negroes do not consider the race issue important enough to discuss, or perhaps safe to discuss. A typical answer is "We git 'long fine with our white folks—course them po' [poor] whites make a lot of trouble." [15] Among them there is widespread ignorance of, or indifference to, current developments in the anti-segregation movement.

Within this setting, a Negro man explains how he instructs his son:

When I goes to a white man's house I stands in the yard and yells, and he comes to the door. If he tells me to come then I goes up to the door to talk to him, and I don't go in unless he tell me. If he tell me, then I goes in, but I don't set down lessen he tell me. And I don't talk to white folks direct like I does to colored. I lets him do the talking, let him take the lead. That's what he wants, and if he says something to me that I don't like, I says, "Now, Mr. _____, don't you think I oughta do such and such a thing," and then mos' likely he say "yes," but you better not go straight at the thing with a white man, he'll think you're smart. Yes, suh, I tells my chillen to do lak that. That's the way to get along.[16]

14 E. Franklin Frazier, *The Negro in the United States*, rev. ed. (New York: The Macmillan Co., 1957), 318–321.
15 Charles S. Johnson, *Patterns of Negro Segregation*, 245.
16 *Ibid.*, 247. By permission of the publishers, Harper & Row.

The movement among Negroes for civil rights has not typically stemmed from Negroes in the rural communities. Relatively isolated on the plantations through cultural and educational factors, and intimidated by the dominant whites, they have been generally removed from the mainstream of integrationist efforts. This is not an untypical situation. It is difficult to organize masses at the very lowest rungs of the society. It is among the urban and the more advantaged Negroes that the integrationist appeal has found its initial and greatest reception. College students in particular, propelled into the mainstream of American life and into currents of social mobility, have been in the forefront of such endeavors. On the other hand, rural Negroes have typically accommodated themselves to the prevalent racial and class structure or have migrated from the countryside.

THE CASE OF EVACUATED WEST COAST JAPANESE

Soon after the American entry into World War II, the United States undertook to remove all Japanese residents from the three West Coast states. Between March 2 and June 8, 1942, some 100,000 Japanese were moved into ten temporary relocation centers located in the West and Middle West. The mass evacuation was undertaken as a wartime measure in what was alleged to be the interest of national security. In the years intervening since this action, considerable controversy has stirred within America as to the wisdom, legitimacy, and fairness of the expulsion of the Japanese from their homes. The relocation centers were largely arranged in army-camp style; the inmates were housed in barracks, and the camps were surrounded by barbed wire. Involved were men, women, and children, both citizens and aliens.

An excellent study is available on the relocation center at Poston, Arizona, where nearly 10,000 of the evacuees were retained.[17] Leighton discusses the reactions of the Japanese to the difficult and stressful situation they found themselves in within the camp. He classifies these reactions as (1) cooperation, (2) withdrawal, and (3) aggressiveness. Here we are concerned with the cooperative and accommodative response, although there were also strong overtones of withdrawal and aggressiveness.

Reactions to life in the camp was not the same for all the evacuees. One factor playing a major role in influencing their responses was their membership in the Issei and Nisei groups. The Isseis were first-genera-

[17] Alexander H. Leighton, *The Governing of Men* (Princeton, N.J.: Princeton University Press, 1945).

tion immigrants who had come to the United States at about the turn of the century. They had not intended to make America their home but had hoped to acquire a little money and return to Japan. As a result they made no particular effort to learn English or to become part of the American community. Nevertheless, they did have contact with Americans through teachers of school-aged children, employers, and those ministers who took an interest in them. The Isseis were reluctant to give up their dream of returning to Japan, although they had gradually come to realize that its realization was unlikely. The war found them imbued with strong positive sentiments toward their native land of which they still were legally citizens. Yet, by the same token, they had lived a good portion of their lives in the United States and were tied to the fortunes of this nation. In this dilemma, the Isseis wanted Japan to win but simultaneously wanted no harm to come to America.

The Isseis came to Poston with a feeling that their lives' work had been wasted, and with bitterness, apathy, and fear. They felt that American declarations about equal rights and equal opportunity were pure fiction. They tended to mistrust and misinterpret much of what the officials of the relocation center did and said. They were not in the least interested in building a model community within the center. Nevertheless, for the most part, they obeyed the rules of the camp. They adjusted themselves to life in Poston, more or less resigned to their fate. They assisted their neighbors with odd jobs to promote mutual comfort, but they withheld themselves from more active participation in hard work.

The Niseis were the American-born, American-citizen, and American-raised children of the Isseis. Many of them spoke Japanese as their first language, but, from the age of six, when they entered school, they had become increasingly assimilated within American life. Many had become Christians, while others who remained Buddhists took on many characteristics of American religious behavior. In spite of social barriers, the Niseis had developed a fairly wide circle of American friends, and it was largely from these that they had acquired their goals and ideals, as well as their Americanized manners, language, and habits. In large measure they had grown away both from the customs of their parents and from their parents themselves.

Many of the Niseis came to the relocation center with burning feelings that "they can't do this to me!" They tended to be quite bewildered and at sea as to what they should do and what to expect. They were not particularly troubled or concerned with the future of Japan; rather their concerns revolved about a job, "three square meals," and what they would make of their lives. Although confused and suspicious, they still had faith in some American leaders. They came to the centers angry and discouraged, yet they were not without hope, "wanting to believe," "looking for a chance," and on the whole receptive to the ideas of community living entertained by the American officials. From among the Niseis came the active participants in community life.

On the whole, cooperation and accommodation were reflected among the evacuees in the development of self-government and liaison with the administration of the camp, in the maintenance of law and order, in obedience to regulations, in work on plans for community buildings, and, in short, in practically every aspect of daily living. Accommodation ranged from those who made outer and superficial adjustment to center life, making the best of a situation against which they internally rebelled, to those who, while preferring release from the camp, actively and willingly participated in the overall life of the camp. In addition, there were some instances of evacuees showing extreme dependence, and clinging to various American officials for support. Such evacuees were likely to agree to any proposal made by the American officials, even those that were ill advised, and would maintain that their food was satisfactory when by any normal standards it was inadequate.

APATHY AND REFORM MOVEMENTS

Acceptance and Negro Group Protest

A common lament heard among Negroes engaged in various reform activities is the considerable difficulty they experience in channeling and crystallizing Negro resentment into sustained, organized movements of protest and for integration. A Negro undergraduate student at the Ohio State University expresses this sentiment in a letter to the student newspaper:

For the record's sake, I AM Bitter . . . Why? I'll tell you why. Bitter because I recently returned from a rally for the Columbus Chapter of CORE (Committee on Racial Equality), and from a campus of many hundreds of Negro students there were, at the most, only eight OSU Negro students in attendance. However, the night before there were at least 100 Negro students in attendance for a talent show in the Ohio Union, all of who were informed of the rally the next day. . . .

Bitter because the picket lines at Rollerland [a roller-skating rink that operated with separate Negro and white nights] consists largely, if not completely, of caucasians.

Bitter because the Negro Greek letter organizations on this campus (Alpha Phi Alpha, Kappa Alpha Psi, Omega Psi Phi, Alpha Kappa Alpha and

Delta Sigma Theta) are nothing more than mere aggregations of individuals whose only apparent objectives are to see who can "sling" the most mud, or throw the biggest party.

Bitter because organizations such as the NAACP have been non-functional due mainly to the lack of memberships. YM-YWCA Human Relations Seminar that meets on Wednesday night is attended by as few as six persons. . . .[18]

The letter points up the fact that merely because a group finds itself in a minority or disadvantaged position does not necessarily mean that it will actively organize to improve its lot. Its position may be quite unfavorable, as in slavery, yet sustained social cohesion to alter its condition may be minimal. In the United States there were only three slave rebellions of any consequence, involving small numbers of slaves. In each instance they were discovered through betrayal by house slaves. This is not to suggest that there was an absence of powerful and resourceful leaders among the slaves. Nor does it mean that the Negroes accepted their state of slavery with docility. There were numerous *individual* protests. But organized rebellion on a *group* basis was infrequent and failed for a variety of reasons, the primary factor being that the fabric out of which social cohesion is made was eroded by slavery. Social cohesion was undermined by severe white repression, by individual slave efforts to gain advantage with the master, by dependence upon whites, by frequent identification with whites as well as latent self-hatred, by in-group distinctions between house slaves and field hands, and by general resignation.[19]

Upon emancipation, the slave, previously a piece of property with no rights at all, attained the status of a human being, although an underprivileged one. But the proclamation of freedom was not capable in and of itself of eradicating the heritage of slavery. In the period following the Civil War, the ex-slave's illiteracy, his lack of capital and property, his habituation to the past, and the continuing authority and power of the whites created new conditions for the continuance of dependence, techniques of self-ingratiation, self-hatred, and distinctions based on color, and for adjustments based upon acceptance of, and accommodation to, minority status. This is not to suggest that simultaneously other types of adjustments were not also made, but these will be discussed in subsequent chapters.

[18] "Complacency," *Ohio State Lantern,* April 24, 1961.
[19] Kardiner and Ovesey, *op. cit.,* 359–361; and Hortense Powdermaker, "The Channeling of Negro Aggression by the Cultural Process," in Clyde Kluckhohn and Henry A. Murray, eds., *Personality,* 2d ed. (New York: Alfred A. Knopf, Inc., 1956), 600–603.

Vested Interests in Minority Status

Behind the walls of segregation barring Negroes from full participation in American life, there have grown up various institutions similar to those of the white community. These institutions are largely the product of segregation, and many of them would be jeopardized if segregation were to come to an end. A sizable proportion of upper- and middle-class Negroes secure their positions by virtue of the existence of these separate institutions. Prior to the Supreme Court's desegregation ruling, the existence of a dual school system in the South gave Negro educators an exclusive monopoly in the education of Negro children and guaranteed them positions that since have often been endangered by desegregation. Many Negro entertainers benefit by the fact that large numbers of whites stereotype Negroes as being unusually rhythmic and accordingly there is a strong demand for their services. Some large companies find it expedient to keep one or two Negroes on their staffs so as to increase the company's appeal to Negro buyers, and thus sometimes an unqualified Negro may receive a large income. Owing to their vested interests, some Negroes are placed in an ambivalent position with regard to segregation. On the one hand, they may be anxious to do away with their disadvantaged minority status; on the other hand, they may realize that success in the battle against segregation would wipe out their advantaged position.

Some Negro institutions such as the separate church have grown up out of a long history. The segregated church has provided a field in which Negro leaders could realize social and economic security. Many Negro pastors feel a vested interest in ministering to the spiritual needs of Negroes. Because of the historic background and deep roots of the Negro church, religious integration will probably follow rather than precede the breakdown of the secular color line.[20] Some Negro religious leaders have been resistant to quite moderate proposals to undercut segregation. Frazier cites one such illustration:

. . . it was suggested in a midwestern city that as a means of breaking down segregation in churches, a white church might take on an assistant Negro minister. The suggestion was immediately opposed by the Negro ministers in the city. Seemingly, they feared that if the plan were carried out members of the segregated Negro churches would be drawn away, into the white church.[21]

[20] E. Franklin Frazier, "The Negro's Vested Interest in Segregation," in Arnold M. Rose, ed., Race Prejudice and Discrimination (New York: Alfred A. Knopf, Inc., 1951), 332–334.
[21] Ibid., 334.

Negro vested interests in separate Negro schools, libraries, hospitals, and welfare organizations offer in-group resistance to the breakdown of segregation. Separate schools traditionally freed Negro educators from competition with white teachers, since Negroes enjoyed exclusive rights to employment and leadership within the segregated Negro schools. Lamanna studied the reactions of teachers in 31 Negro schools in North Carolina to the prospect of school desegregation. While only a very small minority of the teachers preferred segregation, Lamanna found that a majority expected some Negro teachers to lose their jobs and that a significant minority expected to be adversely affected by desegregation.[22] Such fears and apprehensions take their toll of Negro teachers prepared to give battle against segregation. Some Negro physicians prefer to take advantage of a segregated practice and to have a primarily Negro clientele.[23] Indeed, some advocate separate hospitals on grounds that in them they would have more opportunities to develop their skills and to serve their "own people"—this despite the fact that Negro hospitals have generally been characterized by lower standards of medical care.

Negro business is especially vulnerable to a non-segregated world. The owners of a good many of these enterprises have attempted through the years to win mass Negro support for themselves through appeals to "race pride." Often the patrons of these enterprises have to pay higher prices for inferior goods and services. Negro restaurants in the black ghettos of large American cities illustrate this point. Frazier observes that "not only are Negro patrons forced to pay higher prices than are charged in comparable white restaurants but they must often tolerate poor service and outright incivility on the part of the employees." [24] Negro businesses, characterized as they are by the relatively modest nature of the enterprise, would find competition against large established white firms and chain stores difficult in a non-segregated society.

The class structure that has arisen in segregated Negro communities has been the product of discrimination in employment and of the social isolation of the Negro. As a result, occupations and incomes in the Negro community do not have the same relation to social status as they do in the white community. Negroes whose jobs and resources would place them in the middle class or even the lower middle class in the

[22] Richard A. Lamanna, "The Negro Teacher and Segregation: A Study of Strategic Decision-Makers and Their Vested Interests in Different Community Contexts," *Sociological Inquiry*, 35 (1965), 26–40.

[23] Kurt W. Back and Ida H. Simpson, "The Dilemma of the Negro Professional," *The Journal of Social Issues*, 20 (1964), 60–70.

[24] Frazier, "The Negro's Vested Interest in Segregation," 336.

white community may be upper class in the social pyramid of the Negro community. Within the Negro community these Negro professional and white-collar workers are able to assume an upper-class style of life. A non-segregated society would bring about a deflation of their status and prestige.[25]

The ambivalent position of many middle-and upper-class Negroes in relation to segregation is part of a more general problem of minority-group leadership. Lewin, in his observations about the Jews, speaks of the weaknesses of "leadership from the periphery," that is, leadership from minority-group members who are economically successful and who gain a degree of acceptance by the dominant group. These upper-class minority members can protect themselves to a certain extent from discrimination and prejudice. They can, for example, afford good housing and avoid slum living; their incomes are relatively high, enabling them to avoid discrimination in employment; they enjoy material comforts, prestige, and security; and they are sheltered from harsh day-to-day contact with members of the dominant group. Such individuals are frequently called upon for leadership by the minority group because of their status and power. But under such circumstances the minority tends to be led by leaders who are lukewarm toward the group, who may, under a thin cover of loyalty, be fundamentally eager to leave it. Minority upper-class leaders may thus be especially prone to soft-pedal any action that might arouse the antagonism of the dominant group.[26]

Displacement of Accommodating Leadership

The desegregation decisions of the Supreme Court since 1954 have contributed to the emergence of new patterns of Negro leadership in southern communities. These decisions withdrew legal support from the traditional framework of segregation and gave impetus to various integration movements. Prior to these decisions, Negro leadership within the South was predominantly of the "accommodating" or "compromise" type. These compromise leaders held their position primarily because they were acceptable to white leaders. Negroes accepted them because accommodation appeared to be the most practical and effective type of adjustment within a setting where segregation had legal sanction.[27]

---

[25] *Ibid.*, 337.

[26] Kurt Lewin, Resolving Social Conflicts (New York: Harper & Row, 1948), 195–197.

[27] Lewis M. Killian and Charles U. Smith, "Negro Protest Leaders in a Southern Community," *Social Forces*, 38 (1960), 253.

Following 1954, militant Negro leaders, reflecting the protest motive instead of the theme of patience and accommodation, have emerged with prominence on the southern horizon and have gained considerable recognition. The Rev. Martin Luther King, Jr., has symbolized this new type of leadership. Whereas the compromise leadership had typically operated in a non-controversial and often clandestine manner, the militant leadership has been characterized by its controversial, public, and activist techniques.

Thompson, in his study of Negro leadership in New Orleans, distinguishes between three types of Negro leaders [28]:

1. *The Uncle Tom.* The most characteristic feature of Uncle Tom leaders is their acceptance of the subordinate status assigned Negroes by white supremacists. They never make demands in terms of "Negro rights," but rather beg for favors. A New Orleans white lawyer describes one Uncle Tom leader whom he regards as a "great Negro leader": He came "hat in hand, stood at my desk, waiting for an invitation to be seated, as was his custom . . . as an humble, but great supplicant for the friendship of the white man for his race." [29] Uncle Tom leaders have tended to stress to other Negroes that they should "appreciate" what whites have done for "our people."

2. *The Racial Diplomat.* Unlike the Uncle Toms, the racial diplomat leaders do not accept segregation as right, but as effective diplomats, they display an astute understanding of the "ways of the South." They generally have a strong feeling of belonging in the local community and a keen sense of community pride. They identify with the problems of the total community and, as one racial diplomat put it, talk about the welfare of human beings, not just about "what is good for the Negro." They undertake to interpret the peculiar needs of Negroes in terms of general community well-being.

3. *Race Man.* The race man provides militant leadership. Such leaders see the world through race-colored glasses and they give a racial interpretation to a good many community events. They harbor a good deal of bitterness toward whites and accommodating Negro leaders—in short, any who are able and qualified to help the civil rights struggle but refuse to do so.[30]

Within New Orleans, the Negro community has increasingly come to reject Uncle Tom leaders, and since white men of power tend to refuse to do business with Negro diplomats and race men, an impasse has developed in that city's race relations.

The north-Florida city of Tallahassee is another southern community in which a new pattern of Negro leadership has emerged. A major

[28] Daniel C. Thompson, *The Negro Leadership Class* (Englewood Cliffs, N.J.: Prentice-Hall, Inc., 1963), Chapter 5.
[29] *Ibid.*, 62.
[30] Robert Johnson, *op. cit.*, 207.

challenge to the traditional race structure was posed when local Negroes initiated action against segregation on city buses. A boycott of the buses by Negroes followed. Out of this movement there emerged a new group of Negro leaders in Tallahassee. Killian and Smith undertook a study of this shift in Negro leadership.[31]

The new leaders of Tallahassee Negroes were closely identified with the bus boycott. As a result of the developments stemming from, and revolving around, the boycott, these protest leaders replaced the old accommodating leaders, the latter having remained aloof from or in opposition to the movement. Although the boycott had failed of its purpose to force desegregation of city buses, these new leaders were emerging as permanent leaders of the Negro community, not so much, Killian and Smith suggest, because of the attractiveness of their personalities or their skill at organizing but rather because they adhere to the form of militant leadership that is increasingly making its appearance among Negroes. The new leadership is not of the accommodating type. It aspires to gain its goals through formal demands and requests, boycotts, sit-ins, lawsuits, and voting. The protest leaders are not concerned, as were the old accommodating leaders, with whether or not the whites high within the power structure know, like, or want to deal with them. Burgess also notes the displacement of accommodating Negro leadership in "Crescent City," a North Carolina tobacco and textile center.[32]

Most of the Tallahassee white leaders are unwilling to deal with the Negro protest leadership, because of the latter's militancy and uncompromising opposition to segregation. By the same token, the accommodating leaders no longer could claim the support of the Negro population, no matter how acceptable they were to the whites. Killian and Smith conclude that, as long as this situation prevails, "the structure of the situation seems to permit only one kind of communication between the Negro community and the white power structure: formal, peremptory demands, backed by the threat of legal action, political reprisal, or economic boycott." [33]

VARIABLES AFFECTING THE RESPONSE OF MINORITY-GROUP MEMBERS

Being a member of a minority group does not mean the same thing to every person but, rather, operates within the context of many varia-

[31] Killian and Smith, *op. cit.*, 253–256.
[32] M. Elaine Burgess, *Negro Leadership in a Southern City* (Chapel Hill: University of North Carolina Press, 1960), Chapter 7.
[33] Killian and Smith, *op. cit.*, 256.

bles. Social scientists have repeatedly pointed to the fact that Negroes and other minority-group members react in different ways to their status. But social scientists are not always in agreement on the role and relative importance of the variables that influence the selection of the varying responses. One frequently cited variable is that of socio-economic class. It is generally agreed that attitudes of acceptance are most prevalent among lower-class Negroes. By virtue of such factors as their conditions of life, their minimal formal schooling, their greater isolation from divergent conceptions of the Negro's place in American society, and their frequent dependence upon whites, they are more in-clined toward acceptance patterns than are other socioeconomic groups.

Age is another variable of importance in influencing minority re-action. Powdermaker found in her study of a Mississippi community that the older generation of Negroes accepted the doctrine of white supremacy, believed that Negroes were inferior, and displayed the ex-pected respect and deference toward whites. Middle-aged Negroes were ambivalent; they did not necessarily believe that whites were superior to Negroes but in interacting with whites they acted as if they did. The younger generation was characterized by more or less open rebellion against the traditional race structure, expressing keen and outspoken resentment against whites.[34]

Kramer and Leventman similarly point to generational differences in the responses of Jews in a midwestern community to the problems posed by minority status. The first generation—immigrants from East-ern Europe—experienced the problem of economic and social survival in an alien society. They responded economically through employment in the garment and retail trades, socially through the establishment of a ritualistically correct community in a segregated ghetto, and re-ligiously through the acceptance of Orthodox Judaism and the acquisi-tion of a secular ethic of self-improvement. The second generation's life situation was characterized by marginality, which resulted in ten-sions pressing for improvement of its social position. It sought upward mobility into middle-class occupations and professions. Socially it sought to resolve its problems through the establishment of accul-turated but separate ethnic communities, while religiously it adapted Judaism to modern American life, reflected in Conservative and Reform Judaism. The third generation tended to accept the economic and religious resolutions of the second generation but rejected its social resolutions, namely, its isolation from the larger society. The third

[34] Hortense Powdermaker, *After Freedom* (New York: The Viking Press, Inc., 1939), 325 ff.

generation undertook to seek appropriate social status and acceptance in the community-at-large, e.g., movement to the suburbs.[35]

Variations in temperament and personality, sex, the nature of minority-dominant relations, the extent of the individual's experience in intergroup relations, and the distinctions made by a minority, e.g., in shades of color, are other relevant variables. The role of personality factors can be seen in this example of two Negro brothers:

> Two brothers, brought up in the same family and now in college, since their childhood days have shown marked differences in their modes of response to frustration by family authorities or the white world at large. The older one early began to conform to authoritative requirements and to resort to substitutive expression of his hostile impulses, while the younger one equally early developed the pattern of forcing his demands upon the environment by open and unrestrained expression of his feelings. Thus, the former invariably ran away from white boys when they came threateningly close to him; the latter, though younger, took almost every challenge without hesitation. At present one is literally engrossed in intergroup aggression, while the other seems to be relatively free from race feeling.[36]

Banks, in his study of Negroes in Columbus, Ohio, found that there were appreciable differences in Negro sensitivity to discrimination and segregation.[37] Age and sex proved to be of little significance. On the surface, occupation seemed to be a significant correlate of sensitivity —the higher the occupational level, the lower the sensitivity. Banks suggests that this correlation may well be a product of the fact that Negroes in the higher occupational levels enjoy a degree of economic security which makes it possible for them to avoid many discriminatory situations, or that they may attempt to dissociate themselves from the Negro community and identify themselves with the middle or upper classes of the white group. However, the variable most directly correlated with sensitivity to discrimination was the place of initial exposure to Negro-white relations. Negroes whose early conditioning was acquired in the South or who had spent several years there tended to be more sensitive than those whose conditioning had been acquired in the North.

[35] Judith R. Kramer and Seymour Leventman, *Children of the Gilded Ghetto* (New Haven: Yale University Press, 1961).

[36] Charles S. Johnson, *Patterns of Segregation*, 240–241. By permission of the publishers, Harper & Row.

[37] W. S. M. Banks II, "The Rank Order of Sensitivity to Discrimination of Negroes in Columbus, Ohio," *American Sociological Review*, 15 (1950), 529–534.

12

Responding by Aggression

Still another reaction to minority-group status is *aggression*. Some members of minority groups respond to dominance by striking out against—engaging in hostile acts against—a status that is subordinate and disadvantaged. Hostility represents an extremely common type of reaction to frustration. All individuals, not alone minorities, experience anger; they get "mad" from time to time. But the aggressive acting out of hostility is a potentially destructive and disruptive force within human interaction. Accordingly, societies undertake to regulate, suppress, and rechannel aggressive impulses. A major part of socialization is directed toward this end. Aggression takes a great variety of forms. Not infrequently it becomes so well camouflaged as to be virtually unrecognizable. This chapter will undertake to explore aggression as a response to minority-group status.

THE EXPRESSION OF HOSTILITY

Aggression Against the Dominant Group

Minority-group members generally find it the better part of wisdom to suppress and contain aggressive impulses toward members of the dominant group, by virtue of the greater retaliatory capabilities and resources commonly enjoyed by the latter. As a result, passive acceptance and resignation may ensue. Hostile protest is driven underground, bottled up within the individual. Yet it frequently remains a lurking and latent force. It is not unusual to hear minority-group members indicating to one another how infuriated—how "mad"—they may get from time to time over some discriminatory or insulting action on the part of dominant group members. Occasionally some may really "get mad" and strike back in the fury of frustration.

The bitterness and resentment that some Negroes feel regarding their subordinate and disadvantaged status is reflected in these statements by two Harlem Negroes:

The way the Man has us, he has us wanting to kill one another. Dog eat dog, amongst us! He has us, like we're so hungry up here, he has us up so tight! Like his rent is due, my rent is due. It's Friday. The Man wants sixty-five dollars. If you are three days over, or don't have the money; like that, he wants to give you a dispossess! Take you to court! The courts won't go along with you, they say get the money or get out! Yet they don't tell you how to get the money, you understand? They say get the money and pay the Man, but they don't say how to get it. Now, if you use illegal means to obey his ruling to try to get it—which he's not going to let you do— if you use illegal means to pay your bills according to his ruling—he will put you in jail.

—Man, age 31

The flag here in America is for the white man. The blue is for justice; the fifty white stars you see in the blue are for the fifty white states; and the white you see in it is the White House. It represents white folks. The red in it is the white man's blood—he doesn't even respect your blood, that's why he will lynch you, hang you, barbecue you and fry you.

—Man, age about 35 [1]

Outright aggression on the part of Negroes against white persons tends to represent a point of considerable sensitivity in the United States, especially within the South. In fact, in wide areas of the South, direct aggression by a Negro against a white traditionally posed a grave threat to the person of the Negro. The taboo against physical assault upon whites operated with its greatest severity in relation to adult Negro men. Much more open antagonism was tolerated from Negro women; they could often say and do things that would bring men a severe penalty. This probably was the product of the chivalry that our society expects of men toward women and of the lesser degree of fear commonly felt by whites of aggression by Negro women since it cannot take the form of sexual attack.[2]

[1] Kenneth B. Clark, *Dark Ghetto* (New York: Harper & Row, 1965), 2 and 6. By permission.
[2] John Dollard, *Caste and Class in a Southern Town*, 3d ed. (New York: Doubleday & Co., Inc., 1957), 289–290.

Outright aggression against whites may also be more the privilege of Negro children than of grownups. More severe sanctions have awaited mature Negroes who veered too far from their traditional roles. A Negro boy in the rural South relates an incident that might have resulted in serious repercussions if he had been an adult:

I guess the biggest fight I had was at a carnival they had here a few years ago. They had a greasy pig out there, and a white fellow was trying to catch it. When he got all greasy a group of colored boys I was with laughed at him. He came over where we were and said, "What you niggers laughing at?" Nobody said anything to him, and he wiped his greasy hands across my face. I hit him three times before he hit me once. People stopped the fight quickly—white and colored stopped it.[3]

The expression of direct aggression tends to be less characteristic of the Negro middle and upper classes, where respectability is a supreme norm and fighting and squabbling are severely censured. Lower-class Negroes are probably more prone to physical retaliation, as they are less hindered by norms of prudence and respectability. One lower-class Washington, D.C., Negro girl indicates this type of response:

I used to know one white girl and she was real nice. She's real big now, too, and she still plays with colored children. Most of 'em stop after they git big. She never did call me "nigger." If she did, I'd beat the devil out of her. . . . Yesterday a little white boy down near the school spit on me. I chased him, but I couldn't catch him. If I could a caught him, I'd a beat the hell out of him.[4]

Aggression may find many routes for expression. Negroes may "tell off" whites in harsh tongue-lashings. Hostility may find expression through secretive acts including the slashing of tires, setting fire to property, poisoning a valued dog, or "shooting from the bush," that is, murdering a white man under cover of night or from ambush. Gossipy tales may be spread that sooner or later reach the ears of whites and endanger the reputation of a hated white. Aggression may also take the form of gang attacks upon whites, a periodic problem in many large cities.

A far safer form for the expression of hostility is vicarious aggression. Clark suggests that Congressman Adam Clayton Powell's appeal to Harlem Negroes partly stems from the fact that a powerless people seek a concrete hero who will fight the battles they cannot fight for

[3] Charles S. Johnson, *Growing Up in the Black Belt* (Washington, D.C.: American Council on Education, 1941), 298. By permission.

[4] E. Franklin Frazier, *Negro Youth at the Crossways* (Washington, D.C.: American Council on Education, 1940), 78. By permission.

themselves. Added to the glamour of his flamboyant personal behavior, Powell provides the excitement and virtues of defiant racial protest; he is a hero that defies and taunts the white enemy. From Powell's behavior, Negroes can derive a gratifying joy of vicarious revenge without the attendant penalties of a real encounter.[5]

Hostility may find other channels for indirect expression. Automobiles may be used to this end. A Negro furnace worker in Texas said of his own experience: "I drive in a way that makes it look like I'll run over them [whites] if they walk in front of me when I have the right. I act like I don't see them. I have had some of them to curse at me for this, but I just laugh at them and keep on driving."[6] Politeness itself may be used as a weapon, as in the case of a Negro schoolteacher in Arkansas. Referring to white insurance men, she said:

Sometimes when they come here and act so smart—they always have some nasty joke to tell you—I make them stand out on the porch, and when it's cold it is not so comfortable. You know there is a way of being polite to white people that it is almost impolite. I say polite things, but I look at them hard and I don't smile, and while what I was saying is polite the way in which I say it isn't.[7]

Undercurrents of Hostility

In the previous chapter we observed that minority group members may come to acquiesce in—to accommodate themselves to—their disadvantaged and subordinate status. Yet despite overt, unaggressive accommodation to the racial structure, any number of writers note that Negroes harbor covert or latent aggressive impulses toward whites. Guy B. Johnson observes that "no system of human adjustment which is based upon the subordination of one group or race to another and the restriction of free competition between them can operate with perfect smoothness. There may be mutual adjustment, good will, and a high degree of cooperation, but always beneath the surface there will be the subtle play of friction . . ."[8]

[5] Clark, op. cit., 163.

[6] Charles S. Johnson, *Patterns of Negro Segregation* (New York: Harper & Row, 1943), 303.

[7] *Ibid.*, 304. By permission of the publishers, Harper & Row.

[8] Guy B. Johnson, "Patterns of Race Conflict," in Edgar T. Thompson, ed., *Race Relations and the Race Problem* (Durham, N.C.: Duke University Press, 1939), 126. Also see John Dollard, *Caste and Class in a Southern Town*, 3d ed. (New York: Doubleday & Co., Inc., 1957), 252; Hortense Powdermaker, "The Channeling of Negro Aggression by the Cultural Process," in Clyde Kluckhohn and Henry A. Murray, eds., *Personality*, 2d ed. (New York: Alfred A. Knopf, Inc., 1956), 602–603; and Robin M. Williams, Jr., *Strangers Next Door* (Englewood Cliffs, N.J.: Prentice-Hall, Inc., 1964), 300.

These feelings of latent hostility and aggression are not always conscious. McLean observes from her psychiatric treatment of Negroes that deep-seated sources of hostility and fear may be unconscious: "The intense fear of the white man with its consequent hostility and guilt may not be conscious in the Negro, but from my own psychoanalytic experience in treating Negro men and women, *I have yet to see a Negro who did not unconsciously have a deep fear of and hostility toward white people.*" [9]

To deal with and handle these undercurrents of fear and hostility, strong counter-mechanisms of one sort or another are mobilized. Kardiner and Ovesey note, on the basis of a study of twenty-five cases employing psychoanalytic techniques, that Negroes are trained by experience from earliest childhood in the suppression of aggression. Although possessing plenty of aggressive impulses, Negroes tend to fail on the side of implementing these feelings in overt behavior. "Watchfulness over this aggression is a constant preoccupation with every Negro. He does not discharge it because he is afraid to do so." [10] Although there is considerable resistance to discharging aggression toward whites, there is less resistance to discharge from Negro to Negro. Thus, most of the violence observed by Kardiner and Ovesey was of the beating-up variety, taking place largely between husbands and wives, and parents and children.

Karon, in a study of Negro personality characteristics in a northern and a southern city, concludes that Negroes in the South develop strong mechanisms of denial with respect to aggression. Such mechanisms are generalized not only to the race situation but to the whole of life. Compared with the Negroes in the northern city, southern Negroes are characterized by an increase in the number of people whose whole emotional life is deadened by the struggle not to be angry.[11]

Thus evidence points to the fact that there exist among Negroes deep undercurrents of hostility and aggression toward whites. Simultaneously, Negroes have been immersed in a cultural tradition calling for the suppression and repression of hostility and aggression toward whites. Thus many Negroes find themselves in a dilemma. They are placed in race situations in which hostility is an inevitable product; life confronts them with circumstances that constantly stimulate aggressive

[9] Helen V. McLean, "The Emotional Health of Negroes," *Journal of Negro Education,* 18 (1949), 286. Italics added.

[10] Abram Kardiner and Lionel Ovesey, *The Mark of Oppression* (New York: W. W. Norton & Co., Inc., 1951), 342.

[11] Bertram P. Karon, *The Negro Personality* (New York: Springer Publishing Co., 1958), 165–167.

thoughts and fantasies. Yet the expression of hostile and aggressive impulses is dangerous and defined as morally "sinful." [12]

Within this setting, the program of non-violent resistance to segregation offered a strong appeal to southern Negroes. The program, closely identified with the leadership of Rev. Martin Luther King, Jr., had particular appeal in the early 1960's during the early phases of the "Negro protest." King placed great stress upon non-violent means such as boycotts and sit-ins, and non-violent reactions in the face of attack. He gave articulate and forceful expression to the crosscurrents we have noted—the feelings of hostility toward whites on the one hand, and the dictates requiring suppression of these impulses on the other—and posed a solution to the dilemma.

King told Negroes that they had long been abused, insulted, and mistreated, that they had been "kicked about by the brutal feet of oppression." In essence, he repeatedly stressed to his Negro audiences, using such veiled euphemisms as "protest," that it was permissible and legitimate to feel hostility and to engage in aggressive activities against the existing racial order. Indeed, he emphasized the theme that Negroes have "a moral obligation" to fight segregation: "To accept passively an unjust system is to cooperate with that system; thereby the oppressed become as evil as the oppressor. Noncooperation with evil is as much a moral obligation as is cooperation with good." [13] He thus defined the traditional pattern of acceptance and resignation as immoral.

Simultaneously, King and his followers paid extensive homage to non-hatred and Christian love: "Love must be our regulating ideal. Once again we must hear the words of Jesus echoing across the centuries: 'Love your enemies, bless them that curse you, and pray for them that despitefully use you.'" In a sense, King's message to Negroes appeared to say that they could have their cake and eat it too; that they could protest but that really it was motivated not by animosity but by love. He aided Negroes to redefine as moral and acceptable what otherwise had been defined as immoral and unacceptable.

An incident at a Knoxville rally in support of the "Stay Away from Downtown" movement (part of a campaign to win the desegregation of that city's lunch counters) is illustrative. After a number of bitter

[12] James W. Vander Zanden, "The Non-Violent Resistance Movement Against Segregation," *American Journal of Sociology*, 68 (1963), 546. Also see: Jacob R. Fishman and Fredric Solomon, "Youth and Social Action: Perspectives on the Student Sit-In Movement," *American Journal of Orthopsychiatry*, 33 (1963), 872–882.

[13] Martin L. King, Jr., *Stride toward Freedom* (New York: Ballantine Books, 1958), 173.

and militant speeches, the chairman of the meeting came back to the microphone and reassuringly indicated, "We're making a lot of noise, but that doesn't mean we're angry at anybody. If you have no love in your heart, stay at home." [14] The assembled Negroes were permitted to vent their hostility but then, fittingly enough, were comforted, "We're really not angry." Indeed, anger constituted an appropriate reaction, yet it was felt necessary to deny it. As the "Negro protest" has gained momentum, many Negroes have become more comfortable in expressing protest sentiment. The King appeal, then, mediated between the conflicting traditions of the accommodating Negro and the militant Negro. In some respects it marked a transitional phase in the civil rights movement between accommodation and more militantly aggressive tactics.

The Hoodlum: Rebel Against Minority Status

For a lower-class boy who has internalized the glittering goals of "the American Dream" involving "the good life," his racial or ethnic background may be a formidable obstacle. Television and the movies have taught that American men should own convertibles and handsome clothes. A luxurious style of life is presented as within the grasp of every American. But as he gets into his teens he learns that his own prospects for "getting ahead" are poor. The role of the hoodlum offers one kind of response to this situation.

Many lower-class minority youths find themselves trapped at the bottom of the socioeconomic heap. Their racial or ethnic membership offers one obstacle, but there are also others. Sent to school because the law requires it and because their mothers may be anxious to get them out from underfoot, they regard the classroom as a kind of prison. Parents and friends, as contrasted with those in the middle and upper classes, usually do not hold education in awe, nor do they encourage strenuous efforts to learn. Accordingly, lower-class minority youth often lack the incentive for academic achievement, regardless of their intellectual potentialities. In time, many of them find themselves retarded in basic skills such as reading, and, whether promoted, "left back," or shunted into "slow" programs, others frequently define them as "dumb." School becomes still more unpleasant, and disinterest increases. By adolescence, the educational route no longer represents a realistic road to a higher standard of living.[15]

[14] Merrill Proudfoot, *Diary of a Sit-In* (Chapel Hill: University of North Carolina Press, 1962), 118.

[15] Jackson Toby, "Hoodlum or Business Man: An American Dilemma," in Marshall Sklare, ed., *The Jews* (New York: The Free Press of Glencoe, Inc., 1958), 544–545.

Similarly, lower-class minority youths generally come from neighborhoods where people are more prone to act upon their anti-social impulses. Predatory crime is not as universally frowned upon in deteriorated neighborhoods as it is in the more advantaged communities. Homelife may be complicated by chronic conflict; the death, desertion, or serious illness of the breadwinner; mental disorder or disease; alcoholism; gambling; promiscuity; or overburdened parents.[16]

With the educational route to a higher standard of living blocked by poor scholastic performance, the youth may quit school. But those who leave school find that unskilled work as a stock clerk, delivery boy, or soda jerk offers little chance for advancement. Difficulties with teachers may be carried over to supervisors, and employment is recurrently changed. Uncommitted to school or job, such a boy may start "hanging out" on street corners with other unsuccessful youths. The gang sets up a heroic rather than an economic basis for self-respect. The individual must demonstrate that he is not "chicken," and to do this he must display a reckless willingness to steal, to fight, and to indicate rebellion against conventional values. As Toby points out:

He must repudiate the bourgeois virtues associated with school and job: diligence, neatness, truthfulness, thrift. He becomes known as a "loafer" and a "troublemaker" in the community. When family and neighbors add their condemnations to those of teachers and employers, all bridges to respectability are burned, and he becomes progressively more concerned with winning "rep" inside the gang.[17]

The role of the hoodlum comes to represent rebellion against, and compensation for, permanent low status in the community-at-large. Since the larger society has clearly rejected him, he rejects—or appears to reject—the values and norms of that society.

Ethnic groups differ in their attitudes toward academic achievement, a factor apparently related to the incidence of delinquency among them. Both Jews and Italians came to the United States in large numbers at the turn of the century and settled in urban areas. But the two groups are to be distinguished in their attitudes toward intellectual accomplishment. Eastern European Jews regarded religious study as of immense importance for an adult male. Life in the United States gave a secular reinforcement to the Jewish reverence for learning. Immigrants from southern Italy, on the other hand, frequently viewed formal education as either a frill or the source of dangerous ideas. Children were encouraged in neglect of schoolwork and in truancy.[18]

[16] *Ibid.*, 542.
[17] *Ibid.*, 545–546.
[18] *Ibid.*, 548.

The Jews, through their emphasis upon academic achievement, tended to open a major route for the social ascent of their children. On the other hand, the Italian immigrants, with their conception of schools as of little worth, tended to deprive their children of the best opportunity for upward mobility. This factor may well be related to the disproportionately high incidence of delinquency among second-generation Italians and the low incidence of delinquency among second-generation Jews. Apparently, second-generation Jewish youths had less reason to become hoodlums. As Toby observes, "Their parents kept legitimate channels of social ascent open for them by inculcating the traditional attitude of respect for education and by transmitting the business know-how gleaned from hundreds of years of urban life in Europe." [19]

In-group Aggression

The dictates and requirements of the social order may be such that minority-group members must of necessity contain and suppress a good many of their hostile impulses toward the dominant group. Some of the aggression that otherwise might be directed at the dominant group may be redirected, or displaced, against one's fellows. Studies of lower-class Negro life have pointed to the relatively high incidence of internal aggression that tends to characterize the group. It is quite likely that this aggression represents in some part hostility that is deflected from the white group. Since whites occupy a powerful position by virtue of the racial structure, it is dangerous to vent aggressive impulses directly against them. It is safer to divert the hostility from the white group and focus it instead upon the Negro group. But it should not be assumed that all the aggression found within a minority is displaced from the dominant group. A good deal of it is the product of interaction within the minority group itself.

One of the most important sources of Negro aggression against Negroes derives from sexual jealousy. Among lower-class urban and southern rural Negroes, violence stemming from jealousy is relatively frequent. Johnson writes of the plantation area:

Jealousy and the violent expressions of this passion are manifested by both men and women during the courtship period, by legally married couples and by companions in a common-law relationship. Because Ben Mason began courting Alice Harris' daughter another woman shot him five times. But Ben Mason had not himself the best reputation. A few years earlier he had accidentally killed one girl while shooting at another who had spurned his attentions.[20]

[19] *Ibid.,* 549.
[20] Charles S. Johnson, *Shadow of the Plantation* (Chicago: University of Chicago Press, 1934), 51.

Dollard, in his study of Southerntown, similarly notes the prevalence of encounters deriving from sexual jealousy. Razor blades, ice picks, and knives were used as weapons by both men and women who felt themselves "wronged" by a lover.[21]

Similar patterns prevail among lower-class Negroes in large cities.[22] Drake and Cayton cite the case of a Negro night watchman who was employed at a junkyard. He would get home about seven o'clock in the morning and sleep during the day. One day, he woke earlier than usual and called his wife. Not finding her home, he dressed and went looking for her. He found her at her friend's house with two other men, consuming a bottle of whisky:

We began to argue and a rap came to the door. A young man said, "Is this the place that ordered the beer?" My wife said, "Yes, bring it in." She gave him a dollar bill and the boy was going to give her some change. She said, "It's on John"—meaning me. I got mad and I punched her. I chased the two men out and I grabbed her again. I told her to put her clothes on and get home. She was half drunk and she took a long time to get ready.

When we got down in front of the house she began to call me dirty names. I hit her on the face and she fell. She began to bleed, but I didn't care. I was so mad I could've killed her.[23]

Gambling is another frequent occasion for the expression of violence, as is a type of aggressive banter and boasting that occurs among groups of men gathered together. The banter takes the form of competition between men in which insulting remarks are exchanged about the other person's status, his performance, and even about the virtue of his wife, sweetheart, or mother. Although beginning in jest, the activity sometimes goes over into violent assault.[24] Dollard notes that there seems to be an actual idealization of personal violence among lower-class rural Negroes. It is not dissimilar from the admiration felt during the period of the frontier for the individual who was physically or morally capable of taking care of himself. Under circumstances where the formal machinery of law takes care of Negroes' grievances much less adequately than those of the whites, greater recourse is had to one's own competence in protecting and advancing one's interests.[25]

Violence may be a frequent accompaniment of family and marital conflict. An illustration is afforded from the case of a lower-class Negro subject in the Kardiner and Ovesey study. One morning the subject, a woman, phoned prior to one of the interview sessions and said, "My

---

21 Dollard, *op. cit.*, 269 ff.

22 St. Clair Drake and Horace R. Cayton, *Black Metropolis* (New York: Harcourt, Brace & World, Inc., 1945), 564 ff.

23 *Ibid.*, 588. By permission of the publishers, Harcourt, Brace & World, Inc.

24 Dollard, *op. cit.*, 272–274.

25 *Ibid.*, 274.

father got drunk yesterday and beat me up. My face is all swollen. Should I come anyway?" The interviewer was agreeable, and she appeared quite drunk on arrival. She told this story of what had occurred:

A friend of mine invited us over for drinks. When we got home my father hit my mother. He was kind of jealous she had gone. Well, naturally, I'm her daughter, so I hit him back and we started to fight. I wouldn't have gotten hurt if I hadn't been drinking myself. He bit me here. [She shows the teeth marks on her arm.] Then he kicked me here. [She displays a large bruise on her leg.] Then he tried to strangle me. . . . Then my husband came home. I told him he had to get me out of the house or I would kill my father. I'd kill him! Yet I love him in a way because he's my father; yet I hate him! I hate him!" [26]

Another day she phoned in tears, indicating her husband had beaten her up: "My face is still swollen, my arm is in a sling, and I can't hear out of one ear." [27]

Deflection of Hostility to Other Minorities

Not only may hostility be deflected from the dominant group and focused upon one's fellows, it may also be displaced upon other minorities. As was noted in Chapter 3, the social-distance rankings of minority-group members are quite similar to those of dominant-group members. However, while the minority tends to retain the standardized social-distance pattern, it moves its own ranking from one near the bottom of the scale to one at the top. Clearly the normative factor plays an important role in influencing the attitudes and behavior of one minority toward another. Simultaneously, hostility that cannot find direct expression against the dominant group may in some instances be rechanneled toward a permissive target, another minority. Other minorities are also weak, sometimes weaker than one's own group. Further, through aggression directed against another minority, the minority person borrows some measure of dominant group status.

Anti-Semitism among Negroes in the United States appears to be a development of relatively recent decades and in large measure is limited to urban settings. It has found fertile roots among Negro businessmen, who often find themselves competitors of Jewish merchants.[28]

[26] Abram Kardiner and Lionel Ovesey, *The Mark of Oppression* (New York: W. W. Norton & Co., Inc., 1951), 163. By permission of A. Kardiner.
[27] *Ibid.*, 165.
[28] Harold L. Sheppard, "The Negro Merchant: A Study of Negro Anti-Semitism," *American Journal of Sociology*, LIII (1947), 96–99, and Nathan Glazer and Daniel P. Moynihan, *Beyond the Melting Pot* (Cambridge, Mass.: M.I.T. Press and Harvard University Press, 1963), 71–77. For a consideration of Negro

Traditionally a large proportion of the white merchants who solicited Negro trade and established their businesses in Negro slums were Jews. Similarly, there were other areas of friction with Jews. Many of the housewives who hired Negro domestic workers in large cities were Jews, and many of the property owners who were willing to rent or sell homes to Negroes were Jews. A Negro owner of a small grocery store says:

When we first opened up, we had just as good a stock as any of them whites. But then the colored did not come in and buy and we went back. We had a struggle. A Jew across the street tried to move us out. But he's gone now. He tried to undersell us. Jews are dirty. He told the cake man and vegetable man that if they sold to me they could not sell to him.[29]

In several of the Delta towns in Mississippi, Chinese merchants have established businesses. Negroes frequently patronized them because they "feel freer." The situation provides an opportunity for some displaced hostility, since the non-whites offer a substitute target for Negro counter-aggression. A lower-class Negro reported this incident:

A bunch of us went in one of them Chinese stores. I asked for a match, and he got mad because I didn't say "Mr." . . . He called me a son-of-a-bitch, and told me to call him "Mr." I don't 'low no man to call me a son-of-a-bitch. I called him a Chinese son-of-a-bitch, and started to get him. One of them other Chinese said for him to let it drop.[30]

PROTEST

Humor

A very prevalent way of expressing hostile feelings is through humor. When friction and antagonism exist within important areas of interaction, joking and teasing function to discourage the development of serious overt aggression. Johnson relates an illustration of this phenomenon:

A factory hand in Cleveland, Mississippi, reported that at the place where he worked the white foreman and the Negro workers often exchanged jokes.

anti-Semitism also see: Richard L. Simpson, "Negro-Jewish Prejudice: Authoritarianism and Some Social Variables as Correlates," *Social Problems,* 7 (1959), 138–146; and J. S. Gray and A. J. Thompson, "Ethnic Prejudices of White and Negro College Students," *Journal of Abnormal and Social Psychology,* 48 (1953), 311–313.

[29] W. Lloyd Warner, Buford H. Junker, and Walter A. Adams, *Color and Human Nature* (Washington, D.C.: American Council on Education, 1941), 115. By permission.

[30] Charles S. Johnson, *Patterns of Negro Segregation,* 309. By permission of the publishers, Harper & Row.

One morning he told one of the boys, "Hurry up there, you son-of-a-bitch. Your mammy must not have given you any breakfast." The colored boy retorted, "You skinny bastard, look like your mammy never gives you anything to eat." Then they all laughed.[31]

Aggressive impulses that otherwise might not be tolerated find a permissive outlet behind the veil of joking. Hostility is often rendered harmless, or so it seems, through jest. But many a true word is said, and many genuine feelings are expressed, by means of the "joke." Thus, joking and teasing provide an important outlet for hostility.

Humor may also be a mechanism for expressing aggression toward the dominant group in the latter's absence. Through ridicule and sarcasm, hostile impulses are released. At times the jokes are so bitter as almost to lack humor:

It says in the white folks' newspaper that our women are trying to ruin the white folks' homes by quitting their jobs as maids.
Yeah. A lot of white women are mad because they have to bring up their own children.[32]

Some of the jokes have a strong protest character:

I went into the store at _____ to get some tobacco. I asked for "Prince Albert" and the clerk said "see the man on that can. He's white. Say 'Mister Prince Albert.'" I thought for a minute and then said "No thank you, sir; I believe I'll just take Bull Durham; I don't have to 'mister' him!" [33]

As Dollard points out, many jokes that Negroes tell have a delicate suppressed quality, in which the hostility is hard to locate but in which the individual has the baffled general feeling that the whites have been lampooned without knowing quite how. He relates this example in which the Negro exerts his stubborn self-respect and in which a fragile joke is had on the white man:

A Negro named George went into a white store to buy a hat. The clerk said, "Well, *Bill,* what will you have?" The Negro guessed he would have nothing. At the next store, "Well, *son,* what will you have?" He said nothing. And so on, through a list of names such as "uncle," "Mose," etc. Finally he came to a store where the clerk said, "Well, *George,* what will you have?" "A hat," he answered and bought it.[34]

Although such a joke may appear uproariously funny to a Negro, it would not appear at all humorous to most white persons.

[31] *Ibid.,* 308. By permission of the publishers, Harper & Row.
[32] Gunnar Myrdal, *An American Dilemma* (New York: Harper & Row, 1944), 961.
[33] John H. Burma, "Humor as a Technique in Race Conflict," *American Sociological Review,* 11 (1946), 713–714.
[34] Dollard, *op. cit.,* 309.

Humor may also provide Negroes with means whereby they can "laugh off" their misfortune and disadvantaged status and, perhaps simultaneously, take a dig at whites as in this joke:

A Negro drives through a red light in a Mississippi town. The sheriff yells, "Hey, boy, where you think you going?" The Negro thinks fast and answers: "Well, boss, when I see that green light on an' all them white folks' cars goin' through, I says to myself, 'That's the white folks light!' So I don' move. Then when that ol' red light comes on, I jus' steps on the gas. I says 'That mus' be us niggers' light!'" The sheriff replies, "You're a good boy, Sam, but next time you kin go on the white folks' light." [35]

Protest in Art

Through poetry, prose, and songs, racial and ethnic minorities may find vehicles by which to voice protest. Some of the Negro spirituals suggest underlying symbolism with important elements of protest hidden in them. A number such as "Go Down, Moses," "The Lord Delivered Daniel," and "Good News, Member" may well have been a subtle means by which to report the success of an escaped slave's flight via the Underground Railroad. "Heaven" and "Paradise" conceivably were symbolic representations of freedom and the North.

Opinions differ considerably as to how much the spirituals represented a vehicle for Negro hatred, revenge, and protest. A few authorities suggest that these elements were entirely lacking in the spirituals; others insist that they contained marked symbolic expressions of conscious protest; and still others are convinced that the spirituals represented a deep and profound sort of protest in which the meaning often was hidden from the singer himself in an unconscious form.[36] Whatever the case, the spirituals did represent a means of expressing the Negro's grim dissatisfaction with his worldly status. The emphasis upon other worldliness was reflected in such songs as "Dere's a Great Camp Meetin' in de Promised Land," "Look Away in de Heaven, Lord," "Fo' My Soul's Goin' to Heaven Jes' Sho's You Born," and "Heaven, Heaven, Everybody Talkin' 'Bout Heaven Ain't Goin' There." They typified the slaves' hope that life would be easier in the next world. In a sense they were "sorrow songs" molded by the hardships and suffering during slavery. "Nobody Knows" expressed such sentiment:

> Oh, nobody knows de trouble I've seen.
> Nobody knows but Jesus.
> Nobody knows de trouble I've seen.
> Glory hallelujah.

[35] Drake and Cayton, *op. cit.*, 723. By permission of the publishers, Harcourt, Brace & World, Inc.

[36] John Greenway, *American Folksongs of Protest* (New York: A. S. Barnes & Co., Inc., 1960), 79.

Sometimes I'm up, sometimes I'm down,
Oh, yes, Lord.
Sometimes I'm almost to de groun',
Oh, yes, Lord.

Although you see me goin' 'long so,
Oh, yes, Lord.
I have my trials here below,
Oh, yes, Lord.

Literature may also represent a vehicle for expressing protest. Among a group of Negroes, during the decades between the first and second world wars, a literary movement emerged that has been variously referred to as the "Harlem Renaissance," the "Black Renaissance," and the "New Negro Movement." For the most part, the work was the product of a race-conscious group. Poetry and prose became instruments for crying out against social and economic wrongs. The writers protested against segregation and lynching; demanded higher wages, shorter hours, and better working conditions; and insisted upon full social equality and first-class citizenship. Among them were Claude McKay, James Weldon Johnson, Jean Toomer, Countee Cullen, Langston Hughes, Walter White, W. E. B. Du Bois, and Richard Wright. Probably the best known of these was Richard Wright, whose *Uncle Tom's Children* (1938), *Native Son* (1940), and *Black Boy* (1945) depicted with stark, tragic realism the frustrations of many Negroes.[37] More recently, James Baldwin has emerged as a powerful protest writer.

Irresponsible and Awkward Work

Finding themselves in a disadvantaged and relatively powerless position, it is not unusual for minority-group members to work slowly or awkwardly, and at times even leave a job entirely without notice. Inefficient and sluggish activity represents a means of striking back at the dominant group, without necessarily provoking retaliation. It becomes a subtle instrument by which to mock the dominant group: "You say we are inferior, lazy, and no-good. Well, we'll just show you by being ignorant, awkward, slow, and inefficient. We'll take your money but we'll deliver little." A generalized lethargic disposition may become a rooted way of life and a response to difficult circumstances.

Franklin indicates that one type of reaction of Negroes to slavery was loafing on the job, feigning illness in the fields and on the auction

[37] See: John Hope Franklin, *From Slavery to Freedom* (New York: Alfred A. Knopf, 1952), 489–511.

block, and engaging in an elaborate program of sabotage. Since the slave was hard on farming tools and not disposed to exercise care with them, special tools were developed for him. He drove the animals with a cruelty that suggested revenge, and he was often so ruthless in his handling of the crops that the most careful supervision was necessary to ensure their survival until the harvest. Self-mutilation and suicide were likewise employed. In order to render themselves ineffective workers, some slaves mutilated themselves and cut off their toes and hands.[38]

Not only may minority-group members express resentment through inefficiency and low motivation, they may also show hostility through high labor turnover. Whites frequently complain that their "Negro help up and leave without so much as a word of notice." Quitting a job is a form of retaliation that exasperates whites and thus becomes an instrumentality by which Negroes can express hostility. This type of retaliation may not be in the interests of the Negro himself, but it evidently gives him some satisfaction. The constant shifting of tenant families from one plantation to another and the disappearance of a Negro cook or maid after a payday frequently involve some element of protest. It is as if the Negro were saying, "I may be inferior and you may have many advantages over me, but at least you do not own my body." [39]

Protest Organizations

As a response to their status as racial or ethnic minorities, some individuals have banded together in organized groups for the purpose of guarding and advancing the interests of their particular minority. Let us consider a number of these organizations:

National Association for the Advancement of Colored People. The NAACP, founded in 1909, works to achieve equal citizenship rights for Negroes through peaceful and lawful means. For the most part, it has sought its objectives through court and legislative action, although it has participated in some civil rights demonstrations. Probably its biggest legal victory was the historic 1954 Supreme Court order on school desegregation. Prior to the "Negro protest" of the 1960's, the NAACP was often looked upon by many Americans as a "radical" organization. However, in the spectrum of current civil rights organizations, the NAACP today seems quite conservative. Although an interracial organization, its membership, estimated at 500,000, is predominantly Negro.

[38] *Ibid.*, 206.
[39] Dollard, *op. cit.*, 302.

Southern Christian Leadership Conference. The Southern Christian Leadership Conference has been closely associated with the name of Rev. Martin Luther King, Jr., who spearheaded its organization in 1957. It has primarily concentrated upon mobilizing southern Negro communities for the realizing of "full citizenship rights, equality, and the integration of the Negro in all aspects of American life." The organization strongly reflects King's subscription to the Ghandian principle of non-violent struggle.

National Urban League. The National Urban League is one of the nation's older and more conservative civil rights organizations. It functions as a voluntary community service agency of civic, professional, business, labor, and religious leaders dedicated to the removal of "all forms of segregation and discrimination based on race or color." It uses research, conciliation, and negotiation to obtain equal job opportunities, better schools, housing, and improved family life and neighborhood conditions.

Congress of Racial Equality. Founded in 1942, the Congress of Racial Equality (CORE) has emerged as one of the most active of the large civil rights organizations. It has stressed the techniques of nonviolence, sit-ins, and peaceful demonstrations to end racial discrimination. It first employed the sit-in in 1942 in an effort to win desegregation of a Chicago restaurant. CORE did not gain prominence until the wave of 1960 sit-ins within the South. It has strong appeal for youth and it recruits many of its members from the nation's campuses.

Student Nonviolent Coordinating Committee. Although organized initially as an arm of the Southern Christian Leadership Conference, the Student Nonviolent Coordinating Committee (SNICK) soon broke away in a disagreement over leadership and tactics. A direct actionist organization, SNICK is among the more radical of the civil rights organizations. It has been particularly active in bringing the civil rights movement into rural Black Belt areas through voter-education work. The group has a youthful membership that is somewhat nebulous and shifting.

Southern Regional Council. The Southern Regional Council is a biracial organization formed in 1944 and dedicated to the improvement of social, civic, economic, and racial conditions in the South. It has cultivated a reputation for careful and objective research with a professionally trained staff in political science, law, economics, sociology, and journalism. It has also promoted the organization of state and local human relations councils.

Anti-Defamation League. Organized in 1913, the Anti-Defamation League specifically combats anti-Semitism, although it is also interested in fighting prejudice and discrimination against other minorities. It promotes anti-discriminatory legislation, investigates instances of intergroup tension, sponsors scores of workshops, and publishes a good deal of material against prejudice.

National Conference of Christians and Jews. The National Conference of Christians and Jews, founded in 1928, has been chiefly concerned with the promotion of harmonious relations among members of the different religious faiths. It has sponsored Brotherhood Week, seminars, and research on intergroup relations.

VARIABLES AFFECTING THE RESPONSE OF MINORITY-GROUP MEMBERS

Socioeconomic-class membership plays a crucial role in influencing patterns of reaction to dominance. Tendencies toward the direct expression of aggression among Negroes are probably most prevalent in the lower class. The large amount of social and family disorganization among lower-class Negroes encourages an explosive resolution of intense hostile impulses. Not only do children see considerable violence within their communities and families, but they are also the object of the violent behavior of their parents and immediate associates.[40] Furthermore, among the middle and upper classes respectability is a supreme norm and fighting and squabbling are severely scorned.

By virtue of their relatively greater isolation, the product of their disadvantaged position and lower levels of education, lower-class Negroes have been less influenced by movements and ideas of social protest than have the other classes. The strength of the NAACP and Urban League has traditionally resided in the middle and upper classes. Covert expressions of hostility in the form of petty sabotage, quitting of jobs, gossip, and pseudo-ignorant malingering tend to be more prevalent among the lower class than among the middle and upper classes.[41]

Robert Johnson, in his study of 150 Negroes in an upstate New York community, found that aggression, as a response to dominance, was more prevalent among the less educated, the southern-born, youths and adults under forty-five, females, and those whose interracial contact was minimal. Not infrequently, hostility was deflected toward other groups, especially the foreign born, who were resented for en-

[40] Frazier, *Negro Youth at the Crossways,* 52.
[41] Johnson, *Patterns of Negro Segregation,* 302.

joying privileges on their first day in America that were denied Negroes who were lifetime residents. Hostility was most closely related to place of birth. Lifetime residents of the northern community were generally less hostile than the southern-born. Buried racial antagonisms arising from southern experiences often came to the foreground in the more permissive setting of the North.[42]

[42] Robert Johnson, "Negro Reactions to Minority Group Status," in Milton L. Barron, ed., *American Minorities* (New York: Alfred A. Knopf, Inc., 1957), 201.

13

Responding by Avoidance

We noted earlier that assimilation may be viewed as the polar opposite of avoidance, and aggression as the polar opposite of acceptance. These two continua pose choices that a minority individual must make when confronted with an intergroup situation. First, he must either allow intergroup contact to take place or he must avoid (or, at least, minimize) such contact. Second, once in the contact situation, he must either acquiesce in his subordinate status or strike out against it. Thus far we have considered acceptance and aggression. In this chapter we shall consider avoidance as a reaction to dominance. Much of our treatment will entail a consideration of the American Negro, as the evidence is more extensive here than for perhaps any other minority.

INSULATION

Avoidance of Direct Contact

Experiencing a variety of rebuffs from the dominant group, minority-group members may respond with efforts directed at withdrawal and isolation from the stresses of intergroup contacts. Withdrawal and avoidance represent a relatively frequent type of response. Charles S. Johnson, in his study of southern Negro rural youth, found that 67.5 per cent of the youth stated that they stayed away from white youth as much as they could and 41.4 per cent said they would not play with white children if they could.[1] Goff, in a study of 150 Negro children in New York and St. Louis, found that 10 per cent of the responses of the children to difficulties in interracial settings were characterized by fighting, 7 per cent by arguing, and 82 per cent by withdrawing.[2] Consistent with these reports, TAT story-data (a personality test) reveal that a New York sample of lower class Negro boys of similar ages showed a greater need for passivity than a comparable sample of white boys.[3]

Robert Johnson in a study of Negro youth in Elmira, New York, found sentiment favoring insulation from whites quite prevalent as represented by indorsement of the following statements:

"Negroes should live around their own people." (27% agree.)
"If I had a choice between an all-Negro club and a mixed club, I would join the all-Negro club." (50% agree.)
"I would find it a little distasteful to:
Eat with a white person." (9% agree.)
Dance with a white person." (17% agree.)
Go to a party and find that most of the people there were white." (21% agree.)
Have a white person marry somebody in my family." (42% agree.) [4]

Negro adults in the same community (based on a sample of 150) showed similar patterns as reflected in their indorsement of the following statements:

"Negroes shouldn't go into business establishments where they think they're not wanted." (64% agree.)
"Suppose you were downtown with a group of your Negro friends, and they asked you to go with them into a restaurant that you were pretty sure didn't serve Negroes—would you go?" (71% would not go.) [5]

Williams suggests that the avoidance and isolation of Elmira Negroes is influenced not only by the objective existence of prejudice and dis-

[1] Charles S. Johnson, *Growing Up in the Black Belt* (Washington, D.C.: American Council on Education, 1941), 295.

[2] Regina Mary Goff, *Problems and Emotional Difficulties of Negro Children* (New York: Teachers College, Bureau of Publications, Columbia University, 1949), 46–47.

[3] P. H. Mussen, "Differences between the TAT Responses of Negro and White Boys," *Journal of Consulting Psychology*, 17 (1953), 373–376.

[4] Robert Johnson, "Negro Reactions to Minority Group Status," in Milton L. Barron, ed., *American Minorities* (New York: Alfred A. Knopf, Inc., 1957), 202.

[5] Robin M. Williams, Jr., *Strangers Next Door* (Englewood Cliffs, N.J.: Prentice-Hall, Inc., 1964), 249.

crimination, but also by a distorted conception of the prejudice and discrimination that still remains. Indeed, this distorted conception is partially the product of social isolation.[6]

The reluctance of Negroes to take advantage of desegregated facilities and the continuance of avoidance patterns often stems from an uneasiness and uncertainty about the new situation. Lingering fears from the past may lead some Negroes to expect that they will be humiliated and mistreated even at officially desegregated facilities. "Besides," goes an often heard remark, "how do I know how the white folks behave at such a place?" Yet the hard fact remains that the only way to learn "how the white folks behave" and "how to be ready" is to enter the new and threatening situation.

This vicious circle is quite similar to what psychologists describe as "avoidance learning." If we construct an experimental setting in which a subject's finger is repeatedly shocked electrically immediately after the flashing of a light, he quickly learns to avoid the painful shock by lifting his finger when the light comes on. But what happens when the electric shock is no longer applied? How can the subject acquire knowledge of the changed setting? As long as he lifts his finger at the light, he can never learn that the light is no longer associated with a shock. This is a critical element in avoidance learning. Negroes, too, have learned to withdraw from painful interracial settings. Even when these situations change and the discomfort is removed, many Negroes are reluctant to test them and discover the changes.[7]

Negroes cite a wide variety of factors as influencing their avoidance patterns. One of these is a dislike of whites. One Negro youth asserts, "I don't like white people. I wouldn't play with them. If they were kind I would, but they are mean and I don't have nothing to do with them. No'm, I don't know any white children at all. I ain't never played with them." [8]

In some cases there may be an absence of active antipathy toward whites, but whites may be avoided because of possible conflict. Such Negroes may be willing to have contact with whites but consider it inexpedient. An Arkansas Negro farmer explains this thinking in these terms:

I found that the best way to get along with white folks is to just be pretty careful and come in contact with them as little as possible. There are times

[6] *Ibid.*, 250.

[7] Thomas F. Pettigrew, *A Profile of the Negro American* (Princeton, N.J.: Van Nostrand Company, Inc., 1964), 162–163.

[8] Charles S. Johnson, *Growing Up in the Black Belt*, 296. By permission of the publishers, American Council on Education.

when you have to take a lot of things. Those things that you can avoid, you ought to. I am not a white folks' "nigger," and I try to keep out of trouble. I know, though, that I am in the South, and I know they can make it hard for me, so I just try to attend to my business and see if I can dodge a lot of trouble.[9]

Avoidance behavior may be found in the occupational sphere. Where competition exists with whites for jobs usually thought of as "white jobs," some Negroes will accept symbols of lower status as a method of expedience while performing work of a higher rank. A shipping clerk may wear overalls and accept the pay of a messenger; a nurse may permit herself to be called a domestic.[10]

Avoidance may be motivated by fear of discomfort or embarrassment and a desire to maintain self-respect. A Negro carpenter in a small North Carolina community reports such a situation:

The white dentist here makes a difference between white and colored. He's the only one here who does it, and I guess he wouldn't if there was a colored dentist here. You know he has special hours for colored, and he lets them all know they're colored. He insults the colored women so that none of them won't even pass his door. He's crazy about colored women. One of the colored teachers here didn't know about him, and she went to get some work done. He told her he would do the work and she wouldn't have to pay him a penny because she was just the girl he had been looking for. Of course she came away and told what he said. She was as mad as a hornet.[11]

Some middle-class Negroes, in an effort to maintain their self-esteem, may seek to avoid being addressed by their first name in this manner: "I always give my name to the clerks as M. F. Jameson, so they can't call me by my first name, Mary. One old girl was selling me some face powder, and I told her, 'Mrs. M. F. Jameson.' She said, 'What's your name?' I said, 'M. F. Jameson.' She said, 'What's your first name?' I said, 'M. F.' She said, 'That's a funny name.'"[12]

Avoidance may take the form of developing towns or communities composed principally or entirely of minority-group members. Even when residential segregation is not initiated and enforced by the dominant group, minority-group members may prefer to live in ghettos. In this manner they endeavor to avoid the continuous harassment incident to living in the larger community. Mozell C. Hill reports on some all-Negro communities in Oklahoma in which there is a positive feeling

[9] Charles S. Johnson, *Patterns of Negro Segregation* (New York: Harper & Row, 1943), 269. By permission.
[10] *Ibid.*, 273.
[11] *Ibid.*, 275–276. By permission of the publishers, Harper & Row.
[12] *Ibid.*, 279. By permission of the publishers, Harper & Row.

and consensus that the common welfare is best served by shunning social relations with whites.[13]

Mound Bayou, an all-Negro community in Mississippi, has fostered a tradition of race consciousness and avoidance of whites. A fourteen-year-old boy in Mound Bayou asserts:

I like it here. I like it because it's an all-colored town. You don't have to be around white people. You can laugh if you want to here. Down in Marigold or some place like that the white folks would be saying, "Nigger, do this and do that," but here you can play ball right out here in the street and nobody will run you away.[14]

Another Negro youth indicates:

I don't believe in white and colored mixing together. That's why I likes Mound Bayou, you don't have to mix with the white folks. Everything is run by colored people. If white folks lived here, you know we wouldn't have that big, three-story school house and all them teachers. Colored folks feel better when they don't have white folks around.[15]

Blinders Against Jim Crow

Upper- and middle-class Negro families often attempt on occasion to shield their children against racial discrimination and the contempt of whites. The parents may studiously avoid taking their children to places where they may be subjected to rebuffs because of minority-group membership. Sometimes the parents may go to fantastic extremes. Frazier relates the case of a Negro teacher who would not let anyone use the term "Negro" or "colored" in his home because he did not want his son to acquire the idea of his racial identity or of the inferior status involved with it. In another case the wife of a Negro professional man took great pains to keep her son from knowing that he was a Negro:

When he was a small child, she never alluded to race, color, or types in his presence. She brought him to Washington when he was three years old. When she took him with her on shopping trips to Fourteenth Street, and he would want to go to the movies, she would say, "No, dear, mother doesn't think this picture so interesting, we'll go another day or later." She never wanted him to feel he *could not* go. It was always a matter of choice. One day she took him with her to a fashionable bakery and confectionery to get some pecan buns. He was about six years old, and noticing people eating at small tables in the place, piped up, "Mummy, we don't have to go over to the Ten Cent Store to eat. We can have lunch here." Then she had to

13 Mozell C. Hill, "Basic Racial Attitudes Toward Whites in the Oklahoma All-Negro Community," *American Journal of Sociology*, 49 (1944), 519–523.

14 Charles S. Johnson, *Growing Up in the Black Belt*, 250. By permission of the publishers, American Council on Education.

15 *Ibid.*, 306. By permission of the publishers, American Council on Education.

explain that the hot dogs at the Ten Cent Store were much more appetizing than the lunches served at the confectioner's. The boy continued to believe he could have eaten at these places or gone to any movie until he was about eight years old . . .[16]

Middle- and upper-class Negroes, by virtue of their economic and social position, are often capable of escaping some of the consequences of minority status. As businessmen and professionals they can cater to Negro clientele and insulate themselves from contacts with whites. In transportation they can adopt, whenever possible, automobile travel in place of public facilities. They may do much of their shopping in neighborood stores where they are known and where the merchants may have financial reason to be courteous. Some may do much of their routine shopping by telephone since they feel their voice and diction may get better consideration than they would receive in face-to-face contact in the stores. Business contacts with whites can further be minimized by payments through the mails.

MIGRATION

Minority-group members may seek to deal with their disadvantaged position through migration. The stimulus to move may come from conditions at home that they desire to escape or from conditions elsewhere that attract them. More frequently forces of both "push" and "pull" are present. This has been reflected in the mass migration of Negroes from rural communities of the South to northern and southern urban centers. Except for the movement of some 40,000 southern Negroes to Kansas shortly after the Civil War, there was no significant migration to the North or the West until 1915. In view of the harsh and frequently severe circumstances of discrimination in the South, this is somewhat difficult to explain, especially since the North gave Negroes the vote, practical equality in justice, good schools, and public-welfare benefits. Rose suggests that among the factors accounting for the virtual absence of migration were the lack of a tradition of migration, the lack of sufficient job opportunities in the North, the lack of contacts in the North to ease the adjustment period, the lack of train fare, low morale, and a general accommodation to minority status.[17]

In 1910 some 90 per cent of the nation's Negro population was located in the South and 77 per cent in rural communities. Factors of

---

[16] E. Franklin Frazier, *Negro Youth at the Crossways* (Washington, D.C.: American Council on Education, 1940), 62. By permission.

[17] Arnold M. Rose, *The Negro's Morale* (Minneapolis: University of Minnesota Press, 1949), 37–38.

both "push" and "pull" operated to encourage the first major strivings of migration about 1915. Within the South "white infiltration" into types of work formerly monopolized by Negroes, the relative shift westward of cotton growing, the ravages of the boll weevil, and the drought of 1916 and 1917 served as special stimuli to Negro out-migration. World War I served as an added impetus. The draft moved a great number of Negro men from their home communities. The draft of white workers, the stopping of European immigration, and conditions of war prosperity forced northern industry to turn actively to Negroes for new workers.

The history of Negro migration during recent decades demonstrates clearly that the Negro population moves primarily in response to strong economic incentives. According to Census data, the growing inade-quacy of employment opportunities in southern agriculture induced a net migration from the South of over 700,000 Negroes between 1920 and 1930. During the 1930's, when few job openings were beckoning, net Negro migration out of the South fell below 350,000. During the decade of World War II large numbers of job openings for unskilled workers at rising rates of pay led an unprecedented 1,200,000 Negroes to leave the South. The migration rate during World War II was higher for Negro than for white men; it was particularly high among unskilled Negro workers. Since 1950, however, inter-county migration rates have been consistently lower for Negro than for white heads of families; the Negro migration rate has declined while the rate for the white population has remained fairly constant. It is likely that the recent decline in the Negro migration rate reflects the growing de-ficiency of employment opportunities for unskilled workers in the North.[18]

SEPARATISM

Diametrically opposed to the assimilationist response to minority-group status is the separatist approach. Whereas assimilation implies the absorption of the minority by the larger society, separatism has an opposite aim, secession by the minority. Separatism undertakes to maintain or realize a separate group identity that is usually linked with efforts to achieve territorial separation from the dominant group. In this respect it is a form of withdrawal or avoidance. Separatism, how-even, seldom involves simply avoidance. Indeed, separatist movements may most aptly be described as constituting an aggressive-avoidance

[18] U.S. Department of Commerce, *Negro-White Differences in Geographic Mobility* (Washington: Government Printing Office, 1964).

reaction. In this sense, it is a combined response, a fact that can be noted in a consideration of a number of separatist movements.

Zionism

The Zionist movement, arising in the nineteenth century among Jews and culminating in the establishment of the new nation Israel, represents one of the classic examples of a separatist movement. The movement constituted a reaction to the persecution that the Jews had experienced since their dispersion from their ancient homeland in Palestine. Theodor Herzl, great pioneer of Zionism, expressed the despair felt by many of the world's Jews in 1896 in a book that became an ideological cornerstone of the Zionist movement, *Der Judenstaat* (*The Jewish State*):

The Jewish question still exists. It would be foolish to deny it. It is a remnant of the Middle Ages, which civilized nations do not even yet seem able to shake off, try as they will. . . . The Jewish question exists wherever Jews live in perceptible numbers. Where it does not exist, it is carried by Jews in the course of their migrations. We naturally move to those places where we are not persecuted, and there our presence produces persecution. This is the case in every country, and will remain so, even in those highly civilized—for instance, France—until the Jewish question finds a solution on a political basis. The unfortunate Jews are now carrying the seeds of Anti-Semitism into England; they have already introduced it into America.[19]

For Zionists, assimilation was not the answer. In fact it was unwanted. Herzl wrote, "I referred previously to our 'assimilation.' I do not for a moment wish to imply that I desire such an end. Our national character is too historically famous, and, in spite of every degradation, too fine to make its annihilation desirable." [20] Herzl's answer to the Jewish question was "Let the sovereignty be granted us over a portion of the globe large enough to satisfy the rightful requirements of a nation; the rest we shall manage for ourselves." [21]

Many contemporary Jewish leaders are no less strong than Herzl in rejecting Jewish assimilation. Dr. Nahum Goldmann, president of the World Zionist Organization, has insisted that Jews intensify their efforts in all spheres of life to combat assimilation and to achieve a deepened identification with Israel as the center of Jewish life and activity:

We have become part and parcel of the life of the other peoples and with that we have lost the main basis of our separate existence. . . . The result is that we live in a period where a very large part of our people, especially

[19] Theodor Herzl, *The Jewish State* (New York: American Zionist Emergency Council, 1946), 75.
[20] *Ibid.*, 91.
[21] *Ibid.*, 92.

the young generation, is threatened by an anonymous process of erosion, of disintegration, not as a theory or as a conscientious ideology but by the fact of this day-to-day life. This process, if not halted and reversed, threatens Jewish survival more than persecution, inquisition, pogroms and mass murder of Jews did in the past.[22]

And Dr. John Slawson of the American Jewish Committee asserts that the "defense against assimilation" is even more urgent today than "defense against discrimination." [23]

The chief Zionist aim, as set forth by Herzl, was to secure "the survival of the Jewish people" and to solve "the Jewish problem" by establishing the Jews in Palestine with all the attributes of a modern nation: land, language (Hebrew), and sovereignty. The dispersion of the Jews throughout the world was seen as an intolerable condition that could be solved only by the establishment of a Jewish nation. Zionists saw the root of the Jewish problem as residing in the fact that the Jews lived as unwelcomed guests in lands occupied and ruled by others. If this were the case, then the solution seemed obvious. The Jews needed to establish themselves in a land not occupied and ruled by others, a land in which they themselves would be the hosts.

Zionists thought that the mere existence of the Jewish state would in large measure serve to solve the Jewish problem. Anti-Semitism was viewed as a kind of ghost fear aroused among the gentiles by the anomalous survival of the Jews despite their dispersion when, under similar circumstances, other peoples had become extinct or assimilated. In turn, anti-Semitism contributed to Jewish self-hatred and inferiority complexes. Zionists asserted that both types of problems could be solved by the creation of a Jewish nation to which world Jews could migrate. By the same token those Jews who continued to live in other nations would be benefited. Jewish rights could then be protected through international diplomatic channels. Since the Jews living in Palestine would enjoy status as a nation, the Jewish nation would occupy a position among the nations of the world and be in a position to advance the interests of world Jewry. In addition, Jews living outside of Palestine might derive a new sense of self-respect from the existence of a Jewish nation.[24]

Although the great majority of American Jews favored some sort of national homeland in Palestine, perhaps only one-third of them ever

22 "World Zionists Beset by Doubt," *New York Times,* January 12, 1965, and "Judaism in Peril Zionists Are Told," *New York Times,* December 31, 1964.

23 "Nation's Jews Found Retaining Identity as Group," *New York Times,* April 30, 1964.

24 Ben Halpern, *The Idea of the Jewish State* (Cambridge, Mass.: Harvard University Press, 1961).

actively engaged in programs with Zionist aims. The American Jewish Committee traditionally opposed many aspects of Zionism. With the establishment of Israel in 1948, the Committee assumed a policy of sympathy for the new nation. It was prepared to defend as legitimate a spontaneous, free sympathy of Jews with the Jewish state. But it denied that non-Palestine Jews were obligated to support Israel under any kind of attachment amounting to political allegiance. It forthrightly took the position that Jews outside of Palestine had only one political allegiance, their allegiance to the countries of their citizenship. The American Jewish Committee was anxious to make amply clear that the state of Israel neither "represented" nor "spoke on behalf of" Jews of any other country. The Committee sought and obtained formal assurances from Israel that, whatever Israel might do through channels open to it as a sovereign state in order to protect Jewish rights abroad, it did not act with any authority "on behalf of" non-Palestine Jews.[25] This stand of the Committee reflected the commitment of the great mass of American Jews to the United States and their primary loyalty to this nation. American Jewish migration to Israel since 1948 has been insignificant.

Since the establishment of Israel in 1948, the world Zionist movement has found itself divided. Israeli Zionist leaders insist that, to be qualitatively a full Jew, a Jew must settle in Israel. They strongly argue that it is obligatory for all Zionists to migrate to Israel now that the doors of the Jewish state are open to them. On the other hand, Zionists from the free West find it quite unreasonable that they should be expected to go to Israel as a duty.[26] As a result many American Zionists find themselves suspended in a kind of limbo somewhere between the Israeli stand and the various non-Zionist positions. Israeli Zionists, in essence, are saying, "Come or you excommunicate yourself"; non-Zionists are, in essence, urging, "Let us hoe our respective gardens." Many American Zionists find themselves trapped between the two positions.[27]

Garveyism

Immediately following World War I, a mass movement emerged among American Negroes with a strong separatist appeal. It was the most conspicuous and popular of the separatist movements that have grown up among American Negroes. It blossomed under the leadership of Marcus Garvey, a dark-skinned, stocky Negro from the West

[25] *Ibid.*, 216 ff.
[26] *Ibid.*, 232 ff.
[27] Judd L. Teller, "American Zionists Move Toward Clarity," *Commentary*, 12 (1951), 444–450.

Indies. Garvey possessed considerable gifts of leadership and ability as a master propagandist. His organization, The Universal Negro Improvement Association (UNIA), found a responsive setting for its appeal of black nationalism among large numbers of southern Negroes who had migrated to northern cities during and following the war. Among the migrants, there existed considerable disillusionment with the city as a promised land and with race riots and racial discrimination in the North. They had been uprooted from traditional patterns of life and found themselves confused and disoriented within their new surroundings. An old way of life had been displaced, but a new way of life had not as yet been realized. Migration had brought with it a destruction of old rural values, a disruption of social roots, and an isolation from traditional personal ties. Propelled into an urban industrial world, the migrants found themselves in an ambiguous position, role, and status.

This setting provided a fertile ground for a mass movement with a blatant racial and nationalistic appeal. A central ingredient in Garvey's appeal was the glorification of blackness. He exalted everything black and exhorted Negroes to be proud of their distinctive features and color. He told his listeners, "I am the equal of any white man. I want you to feel the same way." [28] One enthusiastic delegate to the first UNIA convention, in 1920, served notice that "it takes 1,000 white men to lick one Negro." [29] Garvey catered to the darker Negroes. He laughed at the light-skinned mulattoes, who, he asserted, were always seeking "excuses to get out of the Negro Race," and he scornfully accused his light-colored opponents, such as W. E. B. Du Bois, of the NAACP, of being "time-serving, bootlicking agencies of subserviency to the whites." [30]

Garvey angrily accused white scholars of distorting Negro history to make it appear unfavorable to Negroes. "Every student of history, of impartial mind," Garvey taught, "knows that the Negro once ruled the world, when white men were savages and barbarians living in caves; that thousands of Negro professors . . . taught in the Universities of Alexandria." [31] He glorified Negroes and told how whites were far below the darker race:

When Europe was inhabited by a race of cannibals, a race of savages, naked men, heathens and pagans, Africa was peopled with a race of cul-

[28] Edmund David Cronon, *Black Moses* (Madison: University of Wisconsin Press, 1955), 172.
[29] *Ibid.*, 172.
[30] *Ibid.*, 191.
[31] *Ibid.*, 176.

tured black men, who were masters in art, science and literature; men who were cultured and refined; men, who, it was said, were like the gods. Even the great poets of old sang in beautiful sonnets of the delight it afforded the gods to be in companionship with the Ethiopians. Why, then, should we lose hope? Black men, you were once great; you shall be great again. Lose not courage, lose not faith, go forward. The thing to do is to get organized.[32]

Along with his efforts to build Negro pride went a reorientation in religion as well. Garvey insisted that Negroes should end their subservience to the white man through the worship of a white God and worship instead a black God. For him Christ was a Negro.

Garvey advocated an aggressive philosophy of racial purity and social separation. He demanded that racial amalgamation end at once and warned that any member of the Universal Negro Improvement Association who married a white would be summarily expelled. Speaking to whites, he indicated, "We do not seek intermarriage, nor do we hanker after the impossible. We want the right to have a country of our own, and there foster and re-establish a culture and civilization exclusively ours."[33] It was a program of separation from whites. He denounced other Negro leaders as being bent on cultural assimilation, which he violently opposed. He viewed the National Association for the Advancement of Colored People as the worst offender because it "wants us all to become white by amalgamation, but they are not honest enough to come out with the truth."[34]

Garvey reassured whites that they need have no fears of the aims of the Universal Negro Improvement Association. He declared the organization was stoutly opposed to "miscegenation and race suicide" and believed strongly "in the purity of the Negro race and the purity of the white race."[35] He sought to warn the white world of the dangers lurking in social equality. "Some Negroes believe in social equality," he cautioned. "They want to intermarry with the white women of this country, and it is going to cause trouble later on. Some Negroes want the same jobs you have. They want to be Presidents of the nation."[36] Thus Garvey abandoned the fight for integration, a type of assimilationist appeal, and promoted racial compartmentalization, or separatism. His plans for the abdication of Negro rights in America brought him the open support of white supremacists and the Ku Klux Klan, which was reactivated following World War I.

[32] *Ibid.*, 176.
[33] *Ibid.*, 191–192.
[34] *Ibid.*, 192–193.
[35] *Ibid.*, 192–193.
[36] *Ibid.*, 193.

An integral aspect of Garvey's separatism was his program to lead
Negroes back to their African homeland. With his customary flare for
the dramatic he assured his followers that within a few years Africa
would be as completely dominated by Negroes as Europe was by
whites. He believed a great independent African nation was essential
for race redemption, and he was earnestly convinced that within Africa
Negroes would achieve their destiny as a great people. Garvey warned
whites, "We say to the white man who now dominates Africa that it is
to his interest to clear out of Africa now, because we are coming . . .
400,000,000 strong." [37] But it was never Garvey's intention that all New
World Negroes should return to Africa. Like many Zionists he felt
that, once a strong African nation was established, Negroes everywhere
would realize new prestige, strength, and protection.

In 1921 he created the "Empire of Africa" and made himself provi-
sional "President-General." To assist him he created the positions of
"Potentate" and "Supreme Deputy Potentate," and a nobility consisting
of "Knights of the Nile," "Knights of the Distinguished Service Order
of Ethiopia," and "Dukes of the Niger and of Uganda." Since the new
nation needed a military arm, Garvey founded the Universal African
Legion, the Universal Black Cross Nurses, the Universal African Motor
Corps, and the Black Eagle Flying Corps—all with uniforms and
officers. Great emphasis was placed upon ceremony, ritual, and pomp.
He staged parades and consecrated a black, red, and green flag for his
organization. Although he viewed Africa as the Negro homeland, he
himself had never set foot on African soil.

While the vision of a great Negro nation in Africa thrilled many
Negroes, probably few of them were really interested in returning to
Africa. The prospect of a great African nation served to give the newly
arrived migrants from the rural South a sense of identity in the face of
the disorientation of urban industrial life. It helped to answer the
question as to who they were, and it answered the question in terms
that served to build up self-respect and a feeling of being significant,
meaningful, and worthwhile. It identified Negroes as a people with a
heritage and a promising future. In the transition from a rural to an
urban way of life it provided a stopgap identity. And it simultaneously
provided emotional escape and a release for protest feelings.

Garvey set up his organization in New York City, with local branches
in Chicago, Philadelphia, Cincinnati, Detroit, Washington, and other
cities. In 1924 he claimed 6 million members. This figure is undoubtedly exaggerated, although the UNIA may have had as many as 100,000
dues-paying members. The number of Negroes who, though not actual

[37] *Ibid.*, 184.

members, identified themselves with the Garvey program probably was considerable and gave the movement a mass character. He published the *Negro World* as the official newspaper of the movement. He organized cooperative enterprises including grocery stores, laundries, restaurants, hotels, and printing plants.

The movement collapsed after 1923, not because Garvey's followers were disaffected, but because Garvey became entangled in a series of long-drawn-out legal suits. He was imprisoned in 1925, following conviction on a federal charge of using the mails to defraud in connection with the sale of stock for his Black Star Line, a steamship company. After two years he was released and deported as an undesirable alien. As a consequence of these reverses, the movement declined and lost membership rapidly.

In many respects Garvey resembled Theodor Herzl, pioneer of Jewish Zionism. Rose points out that, in their early years, neither Garvey nor Herzl had been exposed to very strong anti-minority feelings. When they later came into contact with prejudice, their predilection was to escape to a land free of discrimination, rather than to protest and to try to change the existing order. Both adopted a chauvinistic, even a religious, nationalism, and both condemned amalgamation and assimilation. Both sought support from those groups most hostile to their own minority. There is no evidence, however, that Garvey was familiar with Herzl's *Judenstaat*. The similarity between the two reflects the frequent similarity in reaction of minorities facing extremely difficult circumstances.[38]

The Black Muslims

Sometime in the midsummer of 1930, a peddler—variously known as Mr. Farrad Mohammad, Mr. F. Mohammad Ali, Professor Ford, Mr. Wali Farrad, and W. D. Fard—made his appearance in the Negro community of Detroit. Apparently he was an Arab, but his racial and national identity remains undocumented. In addition to peddling his silks and artifacts, he expounded a doctrine that was a hodge-podge of Christianity, Mohammedanism, and his own personal prejudices. As time passed, his teachings took the form of increasingly bitter attacks against the white race as well as the Bible. A number of people experienced sudden conversions and became his followers. Soon house-to-house meetings no longer could accommodate all those who wished to hear Fard. A hall was hired and named the Temple of Islam. With this, the Black Muslim movement was launched. Fard described himself to his followers as having been sent to awaken the "Black Nation"

[38] Rose, *op. cit.*, 43–44.

(American Negroes) to the full range of its possibilities in a world temporarily dominated by whites—"blue-eyed devils." [39]

One of Fard's earliest lieutenants was Elijah Muhammad, born Elijah Poole in Sandersville, Georgia, in 1897, the son of a sharecropping Baptist Negro minister. The family had moved to Detroit early in his life. Muhammad left school at the age of nine and took odd jobs around Detroit, later drifting around the country. When he returned to Detroit, he was attracted to Fard and his movement.[40] Sometime around June 1934, Fard mysteriously disappeared. Muhammad took over the leadership of "The Lost Nation of Islam," as the movement was known. In time Fard, no longer present, became identified with the god Allah. Muhammad assumed the title of Allah's "Prophet" and, more often, the "Messenger of Allah." [41] Factionalism developed within the movement, and Muhammad withdrew to Chicago, where the headquarters of the organization remains. Renewed factionalism in 1964 led Malcolm X, east coast leader of the Black Muslims, to break with Muhammad. Intense hostility and feuding developed between the followers of Muhammad and those of Malcolm X. On February 21, 1965, Malcolm X was shot to death while addressing a rally, apparently slain by followers of Muhammad.

The Black Muslims are not recognized as a legitimate Moslem group by any affiliate of the Federation of Islamic Associations in the United States and Canada nor by the world Islamic movement. The Black Muslims recognize Allah as the one true God. However, they view Him not as a unique deity but as the "Supreme Black Man" among "Black Men." For them, Allah is not a godhead complete in Himself, for all Black Men are defined as representing Allah, or at least participating in Him. Actually the group has elevated all Black Men (all non-whites) to a divine status. This is to be sharply contrasted with the Christian conception of God, since the Black Muslims define all members of Islam as God. Many of the teachings of the group are at variance with those of other Moslem groups.[42]

The Muslims do not consider themselves "Negroes." They resent and reject the word as no more than "a label the white man placed on us to make his discrimination more convenient." They prefer to call Negroes Black Men. They rarely use the word "Negro" without the qualifier "so-called." Muslims assert that Negroes have been kept in

[39] C. Eric Lincoln, *The Black Muslims in America* (Boston: Beacon Press, Inc., 1961), 10–14.
[40] William Worthy, "The Angriest Negroes," *Esquire*, LV (1961), 102.
[41] Lincoln, *op. cit.*, 15–16.
[42] *Ibid.*, 72–73, 218–219.

mental slavery by whites even while their bodies were free. Systematically and diabolically, whites have estranged them from their heritage and from themselves. "They have been educated in ignorance," and their origin, history, true names, and religion have been kept secret from them.[43] They have been "absolutely deaf, dumb and blind—brainwashed of all self-respect and knowledge of kind by the white Slavemaster." They are little more than "free slaves." [44]

In the Garvey spirit, the Negro past is extolled. In fact, Negroes are depicted as the original humans from whom all other races were made. In their mythology, the white race was created by Yakub, "a black scientist in rebellion against Allah." But this was an unfortunate development, as it peopled the world with whites, "blue-eyed devils," who are of comparatively low physical and moral stamina. Muhammad declares, "The human beast—the serpent, the dragon, the devil, and Satan—all mean one and the same; the people or race known as the white Caucasian race, sometimes called the European race." [45] The Muslims preach a virulent hatred of all whites. As one Muslim minister stated: "A white man's head is made to be busted." [46]

The Black Muslims stress the pursuit of a "righteous life." Their stringent code of morality prohibits the following: extra-marital sexual relations; the use of alcohol, tobacco, and narcotics; indulging in gambling, dancing, movie-going, dating, sports, long vacations from work, sleeping more than is necessary to health, quarreling between husband and wife, lying, stealing, discourtesy (especially to women), and insubordination to civil authority (except on the ground of religious obligation); and maintaining unclean personal habits and homes. Also prohibited are the eating of pork, cornbread, and kale (and generally any typical southern Negro food), hair straightening, or hair dyeing, excessive makeup for women, and loud laughter or singing.[47] A number of observers have noted that these puritanical ethical prescriptions place the Black Muslims in the mainstream of the dominant American middle class value system.[48] Hence, ironically, the movement functions in part to socialize lower class Negroes in the value system of the rejected white world.

[43] *Ibid.*, 68–69.
[44] *Ibid.*, 70.
[45] *Ibid.*, 77.
[46] Worthy, *op. cit.*, 104.
[47] E. U. Essien-Udom, *Black Nationalism* (New York: Dell Publishing Co., Inc., 1964), 28.
[48] *Ibid.*, and James H. Laue, "A Contemporary Revitalization Movement in American Race Relations: The 'Black Muslims,'" *Social Forces*, 42 (1964), 315–324.

The Black Muslims demand the absolute separation of the white and Negro races. In his booklet *The Supreme Wisdom*, Muhammad condemns integration as a kind of social opiate:

The Slavemaster's children are doing everything in their power to prevent the so-called Negroes from accepting their own God and salvation, by putting on a great show of false love and friendship.

This is being done through "integration," as it is called; that is, so-called Negroes and whites mixing together such as in schools, churches, and even intermarriage. . . . The poor slaves really think they are entering a condition of heaven with their former slaveholders, but it will prove to be their doom.[49]

The Black Muslims adamantly reject intermarriage. They remain convinced of their "superior racial heritage" and believe that admixture with whites would only serve to weaken the Black Nation physically and morally.[50]

The Black Muslims demand an entirely separate Negro economy. They argue that the Negro cannot achieve genuine freedom until he is economically independent. They point out that the total annual income of the American Negro is more than $20 billion, a sum greater than the total income of Canada. If this money were spent exclusively among Negro businessmen and invested in Negro enterprise, they argue that it would command the respect of every nation in the world. Their ideal would involve a complete economic withdrawal from the white community.[51] Members are urged to "buy black" even if they have to spend more for items in a Negro store. "The white man spends his money with his own kind, which is natural. You too, must do this. Help to make jobs for your own kind. Take a lesson from the Chinese and Japanese . . . and go all out to support your own kind."[52]

Muslim statements about their political goals are couched in mystical and vague terms. But they do periodically call for "a separate nation for ourselves, right here in America" or "some good earth, right here in America, where we can go off to ourselves." Muhammad told a Washington audience, "To integrate with evil is to be destroyed with evil. What we want—indeed, justice for us is to be set apart. We want, and must insist upon an area in this land that we can call our own, somewhere we can hold our heads with pride and dignity without the continued harassments and indignities of our oppressors."[53] Muhammad has called for "four or five states in America" to be turned over to him.

[49] Lincoln, *op. cit.*, 124.
[50] *Ibid.*, 89.
[51] *Ibid.*, 20 and 42.
[52] *Ibid.*, 93.
[53] *Ibid.*, 95.

Yet it is extraordinary that this demand for a national homeland has not been coupled with some sort of political program for its realization. Indeed, the Black Muslims have been an apolitical movement.

Black Muslims are uncompromising in their attitude toward whites. They insist they will continue to wage their fight until the white race disappears. There have been few physical conflicts with whites, and Muhammad urges his followers never to initiate a battle. But they are not pacifists. If attacked, Muslims are expected to fight back, and if necessary lay down their lives for the Black Nation. The organization has a secret army, the Fruit of Islam (FOI). It represents an elite group entrusted with top-security assignments. In an effort to maintain respectability, the Muslim leaders present the FOI as an ordinary physical-training program. But, in addition to body-building activities, its members receive training in judo, military drill, and the use of knives and blackjacks. Considerable suspicion has been aroused among law-enforcement agencies by Muslim attempts to shroud FOI activities in total secrecy. As a result of its power and secrecy, its high standards and strict discipline, the FOI enjoys considerable prestige among the Muslims.[54]

In 1960 the Black Muslims had between 5,000 and 15,000 registered followers, at least 50,000 believers, and a much larger number of sympathizers.[55] There were some sixty-nine temples in twenty-seven states from California to Massachusetts and Florida. The chief temple is on Chicago's South Side, where Muhammad has also established a Muslim restaurant, cleaning business, barbershop, grocery, butcher shop, and department store. In nearly every city with a temple, the organization has launched some business establishments. In addition, the Muslims own large farms in Michigan and near Atlanta and operate active parochial schools (known as "Universities of Islam") in a number of cities.

Through the years the Black Muslims have recruited their members primarily from among urban low-income groups with little schooling, many of them migrants from the rural South. Black nationalism has its roots in the frustrations, anxieties, and disillusionments of contemporary urban life that are complicated by segregation, discrimination, and poverty—by life within Negro ghettos at the periphery of white society. Its members are often strangers not only to the white society but also to the urbanized Negro community. The vast majority are the "unwanted from Dixie," who find themselves rejected by both the white society and by upward mobile and middle class Negroes who

[54] *Ibid.*, 199–203.
[55] Essien-Udom, *op. cit.*, 84.

resent, fear, and despise the migrants as a threat to an improved "Negro image." The result is a dual alienation giving rise to a sense of apathy, futility, and emptiness of purpose.[56] E. U. Essien-Udom, a Nigerian who studied the movement, asserts:

> In a psychological sense, many are lonesome within and outside their own group. They are rootless and restless. They are without an identity, i.e., a sense of belonging and membership in society. In this situation, there is neither hope nor optimism. In fact, most lower-class Negroes in these large cities see little or no "future" for themselves and posterity. This is partly because they have no faith in themselves or in their potential as black men in America and especially because important decisions which shape their lives appear entirely beyond their control.[57]

Black nationalism offers its members a way out. The convert to the movement is no longer a member of a despised minority. He belongs, at least spiritually, to a larger whole where people are "dark, proud, unapologetic." The movement combines the attractions of religion, nationalism, and political "pies in the sky" with a sense of belonging and self-esteem.[58]

Nativistic Movements

When societies with different cultures are in continuous contact, it is not unusual to find a situation of inequality existing between them. Under conditions of dominance whereby the one society holds the other in a subordinate and disadvantaged state, nativistic movements have been known to emerge. These movements represent a conscious, organized effort on the part of the members of the subordinate society to revive or perpetuate selected aspects of their culture. A notable ingredient of nativistic movements is the attempt to resist assimilation by the alien society that surrounds them. Strong undercurrents of withdrawal are present in which members of the subordinate society undertake to separate themselves from various elements and patterns of the dominant group's culture and to advance various current or remembered elements of their own culture. Simultaneously, strong overtones of aggressive behavior may be present.[59]

Among the North American Indians, nativistic movements represented one type of reaction to conditions of widespread deprivation. Under the impact of the white culture, Indian societies were undermined and their members thrown out of adjustment with significant features of

[56] *Ibid.*, 16–17, 23–24, 26–27, 95, 201–203, and 297–298.
[57] *Ibid.*, 354–355.
[58] *Ibid.*, 317 and 362.
[59] Ralph Linton, "Nativistic Movements," *American Anthropologist*, 45 (1943), 230–240.

their social environment. Old sets of norms were weakened by contact with the white culture, and as a consequence there arose a prevailing sense of confusion and a loss of orientation. No longer did there exist a foundation for security. The impact of the white culture not only deprived the Indians of their customary sense of direction and usual satisfactions, but it added to their sufferings by introducing the effects of new diseases and intoxicating liquor. Epidemics of measles, grippe, and whooping cough served to decimate their numbers.[60]

One of the fundamental myths of the Indian nativistic movements was the belief that a culture hero would one day appear and lead the tribal members to a terrestrial paradise. Through the intervention of the Great Spirit or his emissary, a "golden age" was to be ushered in within a short time. There was to be no sickness or death, only eternal happiness when the golden age arrived. Some twenty such movements were recorded in the United States prior to 1890. In anticipation of the establishment of the millennium, believers were instructed to return to the aboriginal mode of life. Traits and customs symbolic of foreign influence were to be put away.

Probably the best known of these movements was the "Ghost Dance" which spread among the Plains tribes in 1890. The movement had gone through an earlier phase in 1870 but by 1875 had exhausted itself. Wovoka, a Paiute, who was known to the whites as Jack Wilson, played a key role in the revived movement. During an illness Wovoka had experienced a trance that led him to believe he had been chosen by departed ancestors to initiate a movement among the Indians. His teachings were a composite of various beliefs and traditions long present in Indian life plus ingredients acquired from Christianity. Wovoka urged the Indians to live morally, to love one another, to live at peace with the world, and to prepare for a day when all Indians living and dead would be reunited in a state of everlasting happiness. A Messiah would appear in the future and would bring with him in bodily form their deceased ancestors. A great whirlwind would arise and all whites would perish. The buffalo and other game would be restored. It was essentially a doctrine of hope. The golden age would be a world without whites, in which once again Indians might attain stature. All this represented an effort to isolate the Indians from the disorganizing impact of white society.

Messengers went from tribe to tribe, bringing with them the new religion and teaching the dance. Some of the participants in the dance would wear a "ghost shirt," tailored in the Indian fashion and made of

[60] Bernard Barber, "Acculturation and Messianic Movements," *American Sociological Review*, 6 (1941), 663–669.

white cloth. The leader would carry red feathers, red cloth, and a "ghost stick" some six feet in length. Arrows with bone heads, bows, gaming wheels, and sticks found incorporation within the ritual. The dancers would shake with emotion and fall into hypnotic trances. During the trances, they would experience visions of departed Indians in the world beyond who were engaged in dancing, playing games, gathering for war dances, preparing for the hunt, and joining together in traditional fraternal organizations.

Somewhat similar nativistic movements occurred among groups of native Hawaiians in the wake of white contact. One such cult in the 1830's is described by an early historian:

> In Puna, a district at that time under my missionary superintendence, and about thirty miles from my place of residence, some young men took advantage of the state of things to bring themselves into notice. They devised a system of religion half Christian and half heathen. They promulgated that there were three gods—Jehovah, Jesus Christ, and Hapu (a young woman who had pretended to be a prophetess and had lately deceased). They dug up the bones of Hapu, adorned them with kapas [native cloth], flowers, and birds' feathers; deposited them in a prominent spot, and marked about this spot a definite enclosure. This they called *the place of refuge*. They went from house to house and from village to village, and exhorted the people with much earnestness and eloquence, to go to the place of refuge, saying, that the heavens and earth were about to meet and all who were not found in the place of refuge would be destroyed.[61]

VARIABLES AFFECTING THE RESPONSE OF MINORITY-GROUP MEMBERS

Robert Johnson, in his study of 150 Negroes in an upstate New York community of 60,000 persons, found the withdrawing or insulating response most prevalent among women, the southern-born, the less educated, and older Negroes. Among background characteristics, the most significant variables associated with insulating attitudes were education and regional origin. Educational level was divided between those with a grammar-school education or less and those with a high-school education or better. Regional origin was defined on the basis of birth in the North or the South. The results are shown in Table 15 (on page 396).

Charles S. Johnson, in his study of southern rural Negro youth, found that the desire to migrate to the North or West was related to the level of the father's education. Of youth whose fathers had completed only the second grade or less, 45.8 per cent wished to migrate from the

[61] Quoted by Edwin G. Burrows, *Hawaiian Americans* (New Haven: Yale University Press, 1947), 150.

TABLE 15

Relationship of Education and Regional Origin to Insulating Attitudes

	Better Educated Northern-born (33%)	Better Educated Southern-born (19%)	Less Educated Northern-born (15%)	Less Educated Southern-born (33%)
Per cent who agree that:				
Negroes should live around their own people	12%	21%	23%	47%
I would prefer an all-Negro club to a mixed club	31%	43%	59%	69%
I do not think it is all right for a Negro to marry a white person	29%	21%	50%	49%
I would find it distasteful to go to a party and find that most of the people are white	12%	11%	14%	37%

SOURCE: Robert Johnson, "Negro Reactions ' Minority Group Status," in Milton L. Barron, ed., *American Minorities* (New York: Alfred A. Knopf, Inc., 1957), 202–203.

South, compared with 70.5 per cent of those whose fathers had completed the tenth grade or more. The better-educated parents, although finding migration inconvenient for themselves, passed on their feelings that the race system of the South might be avoided through leaving the region.[62] Negro children between the ages of ten and fifteen showed the greatest tendency to avoid contact with whites. They had little contact with whites as employers, and playing with white children had become taboo for them at about the age of ten. As they reached later adolescence, they increasingly came into contact with whites in employer-employee relationships.[63]

As was noted earlier, middle- and upper-class Negroes, by virtue of their economic and social position, are often capable of insulating themselves from contacts with whites. At times, they may even undertake to shield their children from any realization of their membership in the Negro group and of its accompanying consequences. But it is an *individual* effort to escape from some of the harsher realities of minority-group status. *Collective* efforts to withdraw from association with the dominant group through separatist movements, e.g., Garveyism or the Black Muslims, have not won a sympathetic reception from members of the middle or upper classes. Although the appeal for a separate

[62] Charles S. Johnson, *Growing Up in the Black Belt*, 311–312.
[63] *Ibid.*, 319–320.

Negro economy or for Negro business may be considerable, indeed they may have a vested interest in it, the middle and upper classes are primarily oriented toward integration. Their aim is to participate in the total life of the community without necessarily merging with the dominant group. Lower socioeconomic groups, on the other hand, have generally shown themselves more receptive to separatist, nationalistic movements.

14

Responding by
Assimilation

In the previous chapter we considered avoidance as a minority group reaction to dominance. In this chapter we shall focus upon a response that is the polar opposite of avoidance—assimilation. As we noted in Chapter 10, assimilation is a process whereby groups with diverse ways of thinking, feeling, and acting become fused together in a social unity and a common culture. However, in contrast with Chapter 10, where we examined assimilation broadly as an *intergroup* process, in this chapter we shall consider assimilation more narrowly focusing not so much upon the interplay between dominant and minority individuals as upon the minority group itself. Hence, this chapter shall consider an approach or orientation found among some minority individuals that is characterized by a desire to lose their minority group identity and to become socially and culturally fused with the dominant group.

EUROPEAN IMMIGRANT GROUPS

Viewed over the long run, European immigrant groups within the United States have generally oriented themselves toward an assimilationist goal. Usually acculturation—alterations in a group's cultural practices—has proceeded more rapidly than integration—alterations in a group's network of formal and informal social relationships. Perhaps an actual case, that of the assimilation of southern Italians, may prove helpful. Certainly of the "new immigrants"—those arriving after 1880—

the Italians deserve special emphasis. They constitute the second-largest ethnic group within the United States, nearly 5 million Italians having migrated to this nation since 1820. Their recorded immigration is exceeded only by that of the Germans. Today there are within the United States some five million individuals who were born in Italy or had at least one Italian-born parent. The peak years of the Italian immigration were 1907 and 1913. The pre-World War I migration, which had reached 300,000 in a single year, was reduced to 5,807 by the quota system of 1924. Prior to 1900, Italians from northern provinces represented more than two-thirds of the total migrants from Italy. By the time of the quota law, four-fifths of all the Italians within the United States were from southern Italy, a fourth of these being from Sicily.[1]

Background of Southern Italian Immigrants

The Italians from southern Italy and Sicily came from an agrarian, small-village background. In their native land the lot of the peasants had been one of economic hardship. The soil was not especially fertile and rainfall was inadequate. Remnants of the feudal order persisted, and the peasant renter often received little to support his family. Onerous mortgage debts, usurious interest, exploitation by landlords, and unemployment were among the hardships that made America seem attractive by comparison. The people were largely illiterate and ridden by superstition. Christianity had become instituted by decree rather than conviction, and numerous ancient religious practices persisted, often taken over bodily into Catholic practice with little modification.[2]

The individual was closely and intimately linked with his family. The *famiglia*, the large family, included both blood relatives and in-laws up to the fourth degree. Family allegiance, solidarity, and affection were stressed. The *famiglia* represented a world within a world, in which obligation to family members was absolute. Outside of the family was a world of "strangers," and a benevolent act performed for a non-family member was often considered as a weak-headed deed. The individual's responsibility was to his family rather than to the community. Friendships outside of the family were not intimate. For the most part, the Italian family was patriarchal, the men exercising authority. Nevertheless, the mother enjoyed a powerful position.[3]

[1] R. A. Schermerhorn, *These Our People* (Boston: D. C. Heath & Co., 1949), 235.

[2] *Ibid.*, 242.

[3] *Ibid.*, 237–240. Also see: Nathan Glazer and Daniel P. Moynihan, *Beyond the Melting Pot* (Boston: The M.I.T. Press and Harvard University Press, 1963), 194–198.

Early Adjustments to American Life

By the turn of the twentieth century, the frontier and free lands had virtually vanished from the American scene. It was largely this fact that accounted for the settlement of the southern Italians within urban communities. New York City became the largest center of Italians in the United States, for that matter in the world, Rome not excluded. The introduction of the Italians to American life took place under difficult circumstances. In the cities they suffered from low wages, irregular and unskilled employment, child and woman labor, and poor housing in slum tenements. They were found in large numbers in the "sweatshops" of New York City; some earned their living as peddlers of vegetables and as pushcart vendors; and many others found work on the railroads, where they succeeded the Irish as laborers.

In the earlier years of the immigration, males highly predominated among the migrants. Lacking relatives or friends in the United States and unfamiliar with the language, money, and customs, the migrants frequently secured employment through an intermediary—the *padrone*. The *padrone* was usually an Italian who already "knew the ropes" and who found jobs for his fellow countrymen. Similarly he often made arrangements for room and board, banking, and other services. In some cases the *padrone* contracted for the labor of men in the old country and arranged for their passage to the United States. By virtue of the *padrone's* position and the ignorance of the immigrants, exploitation was not unusual.[4]

Many of the men had expectations of returning to Italy once they had amassed sufficient funds for realizing a "comfortable" existence in their homeland. An appreciable number managed to return, but, for the most part, circumstances did not permit the great majority to do so.[5] Accordingly, it became a common custom for those in America to send for other members of their families in order to have as many of them together as possible. With the passing of time, the Italian communities in American cities were characterized by polynucleated groups with one street made up of villagers from a hamlet in Avellino, still another from a community in Basilicata, and so on.

In large measure the immigrants were insulated from the larger American society. It was not unusual to find the dialect, cooking habits, and religious practices of the old country continuing without an appreciable break. "Little Italys" enabled the immigrants to cushion the shock of adjusting from a rural to an urban and from a foreign to

[4] *Ibid.*, 190–192.
[5] Schermerhorn, *op. cit.*, 246–247.

an American society. By the same token the "Little Italys" sheltered them from the hostility and antagonism of the native Americans who viewed them as "wops," "dagos," and "guinees." [6]

Mutual-aid societies, organized to reduce the ever-present risks of sickness, accident, and death, sprang up by the hundreds. In time their functions were broadened to include social activities; group mergers designed to overcome financial weakness contributed to an increase in their size and a decrease in their number. The Order of Sons of Italy of America, The Venetian Fraternal Order, and the Italo-American National Union were among the better-known fraternal insurance organizations. Similarly, a considerable number of Italian newspapers grew up within the United States. As late as World War II, there were some 130 Italian newspapers in this country, most of them weeklies. As assimilation proceeded, a newly coined Americanized Italian emerged: *"storo"* was a store; *"olzoppare"* was a holdup; *"mascina"* was a machine or an automobile; *"grosseria"* was a grocery, etc.[7] With the passage of time, Catholicism lapsed; it is estimated that some two-thirds of the Italian-American community is either outside of or only nominally in the Roman Catholic church.[8]

The Children of Southern Italian Immigrants

For a large part of each day, the children of the immigrant Italians were immersed within the mainstream of American life by the public-school system. From their teachers and school companions they learned to esteem American ways and to look down upon Italian ways as "foreign" and "undesirable." They often developed contempt for their parents as stupid, "greenhorns," and unknowing of American ways. A conflict ensued within the families between two ways of life, the one American, the other Italian. Considerable misunderstanding and frustration existed between the parents and the children and threatened to destroy family stability. The children frequently expressed American values and expectations and attempted to transmit them to the family situation. On the other hand, the parents sought to reinforce the pattern of the old-country peasant family.[9]

Child, in a study of the Italian colony in New Haven prior to World War II, distinguishes three types of reaction among American-born children of Italian parents to their situation: the *rebel*, the *in-group*,

[6] *Ibid.*, 248.
[7] *Ibid.*, 249–252.
[8] *Ibid.*, 255.
[9] Paul J. Campisi, "Ethnic Family Patterns: The Italian Family in the United States," *American Journal of Sociology*, LIII (1948), 443–449.

and the *apathetic*.[10] The *rebels* responded by revolting against their parents and the old traditions. They wished to be considered Americans and attempted to dissociate themselves from everything Italian. In contrast, the *in-groupers* strongly identified themselves with Italian symbols and traits and sought to shun American ways. They preferred membership in the Italian sub-community to full participation in the larger American society. The *apathetic* group attempted to retreat from the stresses and strains of conflict arising from the counter-pulls of the two ways of life. They undertook to avoid situations where nationality would be emphasized, and they minimized their membership within the Italian group. They attempted to get along both with the older generation and with their American associates, but their dual status often posed problems for them.

Acculturation of Southern Italian Immigrants

Today the families of the American-born children of southern-Italian immigrants tend to approximate the urban American family type. From the patriarchal, folk-peasant-type family of the Italian peasant, they have shifted toward the democratic and highly individualized pattern. Family solidarity has been increasingly undermined, and the small-family system—as opposed to the peasant large-family system— has come to prevail. Where previously the focus had been upon children living for their parents, among the American-born the situation has been reversed with the parents living for children. Families have become small in contrast to the relatively large families of the Italian immigrants. The age at marriage has risen; mates are no longer selected by parents; dowry rights are unrecognized; and a growing number of marriages are taking place outside of the Italian and Catholic groups. Few magical and superstitious notions persist in connection with pregnancy; during illness, increasing reliance is placed on physicians and specialists. Breast-feeding of infants is now rare, and birth control is the rule. The value of chastity has declined; chaperonage is no longer practiced; and divorce has become permissible.[11] Italian names are slowly being Anglicized, while second-generation children named Giuseppe by their parents introduce themselves as Joseph and give only the English name to their children. A number of Italian patterns, however, have survived, the most visible ones being food habits. Nonetheless, the food is milder and less spicy than that eaten by their parents. In summary, then, acculturation has almost com-

[10] Irvin L. Child, *Italian or American?* (New Haven: Yale University Press, 1943).

[11] Campisi, *op. cit.*

pletely eroded Italian cultural patterns among the second generation, and is likely to erase the rest in the third generation.[12]

Integration of Southern Italian Immigrants

Integration—the disappearance of the Italian social system—has proceeded much more slowly than acculturation. Gans, in a study of an Italian section in Boston, notes:

Indeed, the social structure of the West End . . . is still quite similar to that of the first generation. Social relationships are almost entirely limited to other Italians, because much sociability is based on kinship, and because most friendships are made in childhood, and are thus influenced by residential propinquity. Intermarriage with non-Italians is unusual among the second-generation, and is not favored by the third. As long as both parties are Catholic, however, disapproval is mild.[13]

Glazer and Moynihan, in their study of New York City ethnic groups, make a similar observation about that city's Italians:

Nor are these old Italian neighborhoods only shells of their former selves, inhabited exclusively by the older people. Many of the married sons and daughters have stayed close to their parents. Even the trek to the suburbs, when it does occur among Italians, is very often a trek of families of two generations, rather than simply of the young. And it is striking how the old neighborhoods have been artfully adapted to a higher standard of living rather than simply deserted, as they would have been by other groups, in more American style.[14]

This pattern—a lag of integration behind acculturation—has also been common among many other European immigrant groups.

PASSING

Undoubtedly one of the most complete forms of assimilation is leaving the minority group and "passing" as a member of the dominant group. This adjustment is a feasible alternative for those minority-group members who physically and culturally resemble the dominant group. The task is not particularly difficult for a German immigrant who decides to Anglicize his name and to become an Episcopalian rather than a Lutheran. Nevertheless, language accents, cultural differences, and community knowledge of his family background may in part frustrate his efforts. Still, his attempt to identify himself with the

[12] Herbert J. Gans, *The Urban Villagers* (New York: The Free Press of Glencoe, Inc., 1962), 32–34.
[13] *Ibid.*, 35.
[14] Glazer and Moynihan, *op. cit.*, 187.

dominant group may meet with little resistance, in fact it may be actually welcomed by the larger community as part of a process of Americanization.

As the position of the racial or ethnic minority declines in relation to the social-distance scale of the larger community, the possibility of successful passing becomes more difficult, especially when physical or cultural differences are discernible. Nevertheless, some minority-group members may succeed in the endeavor, as in the following case:

> I was a Jew, until a few years ago. Now, I am not!
> Many of you, the Jews whom I address, as well as many gentiles, may scoff at the notion of a Jew ever becoming a non-Jew. And my former people may blame me bitterly for changing.
> Fortunately, I cannot be reached. I have changed my name. I have changed my work. I have moved into a strange region and started afresh. My past is as finally sealed as though I had died and arisen with a new personality—for it is really necessary that a Jew change some important parts of his personality when he throws off his Jewishness.[15]

He changed his name and claimed to be descended from non-Jewish Adrianople Turks. He went west and "tried a variety of callings, but shunned the Jewish favorites." He later entered a western university and married. "I am now raising children who need never learn to endure snubs, who will never be tempted to retaliate against cruel discrimination. From this pleasant sunshine, I look back with horror at the somber world in which my race-proud kin persist on their ancient and unhappy course."

Broom, Beem, and Harris studied the characteristics of more than 1,000 persons in Los Angeles County who had petitioned to change their names. Although Jews constituted only 6 per cent of the population, 46 per cent of those petitioning to change their names were of Jewish origin. In comparison with non-Jewish petitioners, the Jewish group had a significantly higher percentage of foreign-born, married males, children included in the petition, older males, and residents in areas of high social rank and urbanization. The researchers concluded that the change in names probably represented a change in self-definition and group identification, especially by those who regarded their membership in the Jewish group as a barrier to further upward mobility.[16]

[15] Anonymous, "I Was a Jew," *Forum*, 103 (January, 1940), 8–9. Quoted by Brewton Berry, *Race and Ethnic Relations* (Boston: Houghton Mifflin Co., 1958), 489–490.

[16] Leonard Broom, Helen P. Beem, and Virginia Harris, "Characteristics of 1,108 Petitioners for Change of Name," *American Sociological Review*, 20 (1955), 33–39.

Where a sharp line is drawn on the basis of color, as in the case of Negroes, passing is open to only a small proportion. For those possessing light skin coloring and relatively Caucasian and non-Negroid hair texture and facial characteristics, it is a feasible alternative. How many Negroes pass permanently into the white group? Estimates range from a few thousand to tens of thousands annually within the United States. But, since present methods of making such estimates are quite inadequate, the actual number is not known. Negroes and passers themselves are reluctant to give information about those who pass, and census data and vital statistics are too inaccurate to catch discrepancies from one period to another.

There are various degrees of passing, accompanied by different degrees of estrangement from the Negro group and emotional identification with the white group. Thousands of light-skinned Negroes probably pass daily quite unintentionally. They are merely taken by others to be white. A second type of passing is for convenience in patronizing beauty parlors, buying theater tickets, eating in the better restaurants, etc. It is intentional but temporary. Still a third type occurs "for fun." Negroes may look upon passing as having fun at the expense of whites. Couples may attend white cabarets and exclusive dancing places just to see what they are like and to realize a thrill. A fourth type of passing is the product of economic necessity or advantage. Negroes may pass to obtain employment that otherwise would be barred to them. Usually such individuals continue to reside in the Negro community and find their social contacts there. Finally, passing may involve a complete crossing over to the other side of the color line.[17]

Seldom do people, regardless of the extent of their white features, grow up as Negroes and then suddenly make an intellectual decision to pass. Rather it is a step-by-step process in which emotional ties to the Negro group are severed and new relationships with whites achieved. Passing may initially be of the unintentional variety, but the realization that one can pass for white may lead to more adventurous passing for convenience or employment. As intimate relationships are established with white friends and fellow workers, the individual tends to be drawn gradually farther and farther away from his emotional attachments to the Negro community. The final break comes when the irritations of trying to remain colored and the attractiveness of the white world outweigh his inner agitation.[18]

[17] St. Clair Drake and Horace R. Cayton, *Black Metropolis* (New York: Harcourt, Brace & World, Inc., 1945), 160–163.
[18] *Ibid.*, 166.

Some writers also attempt to explain why many Negroes who can pass do not take advantage of the opportunity. Among the factors frequently cited are these: (1) fear and anxiety concerning possible later exposure of Negro identity; (2) race consciousness and pride; (3) loyalty to family and close friends; (4) a feeling of potential estrangement and loneliness as a white; (5) a perceived loss of status and esteem in the white world; (6) the considerable risks involved; and (7) a feeling that passing would entail too much well-thought-out and calculated planning.[19]

THE NEGRO PROTEST: AGGRESSION-ASSIMILATION

As European immigrants to the United States became acculturated, they lost many of the identifying "marks" or "signs" that set them apart from the dominant group. By the second and third generations, their English was usually indistinguishable from that of other Americans, while their distinct ethnic mannerisms, dress, gestures, food habits, religious practices, and the like became less pronounced. In brief, their "visibility"—those conspicuous features differentiating them from the dominant group and so essential for maintaining in-group and out-group boundaries—became less apparent. Although integration generally proceeded less rapidly than acculturation, the slower pace of integration was in part the product of the immigrant group's own doing; many of its members simply preferred to make their own group the primary focus for their informal and formal social relationships.

American Negroes, in contrast, have found themselves in quite different circumstances. Although for the most part culturally indistinguishable from dominant group whites, the fact of race has served to make them quite visible. Barriers premised upon race pose major obstacles to Negro integration. Yet despite experiencing persistent discrimination and segregation, evidence suggests that a substantial majority of Negro Americans share an integrationist outlook. A 1965 Newsweek poll, undertaken by public-opinion analyst Louis Harris, showed that by 6 to 1 Negroes wanted integrated schools and by 10 to 3 preferred racially mixed to all-Negro neighborhoods.[20]

Blocked in realizing their integrationist aspirations, some Negroes have responded with a social movement designed to break down the walls that bar them from full and equal participation within American

[19] James E. Conyers and T. H. Kennedy, "Negro Passing: To Pass or Not to Pass," *Phylon*, 24 (1963), 215–224.

[20] "The Negro in America—1965," *Newsweek*, February 15, 1965, 24–28.

life. Hence, a combined *aggression-assimilation* response has ensued. The current Negro protest represents aggression in that it constitutes a striking out against—a protest against—minority status; yet it also represents an assimilationist response reflecting a strong integrationist orientation.

The Aims of the Negro Protest

The Negro protest movement of the 1960's has not been directed against major deprivations inherent in the American social system as such, but, rather it has focused against "relative deprivations or inequalities" that Negroes experience as American citizens:

. . . its grand strategy is designed to achieve goals and effectuate values that are already acknowledged to be inherent in a political democracy and which are firmly established in our national culture. Consequently, Negro protest leaders do not advocate the overthrow of constitutional laws, changing the basic structure of our republican form of government, rearrangement of the American class structure, or the establishment of new political, economic, and ethical goals. Instead—except for a small extremist element—the Negro protest, itself, is a clear endorsement of the "American Creed" and a reaffirmation of the faith which the great majority of Negroes have in the essential goodness of the individual and in the democratic process.[21]

Yet in some respects, the Negro protest does resemble more typical revolutions. It stresses direct action (demonstrations, sit-ins, boycotts, etc.), possesses broad objectives (the elimination of the segregated order), and entails a genuine *mass* movement. And like revolutionary movements, it has achieved a heightened militancy and urgency, a sense that "even yesterday was too late." [22]

Nevertheless, in a technical sense, the Negro protest constitutes a reform and not a revolutionary movement. As Pettigrew observes:

It aims to modify, not to overturn, the society it confronts; it seeks to amend, not to ravage. Negro Americans are so firmly rooted in and shaped by their land that their . . . [movement] is attempting merely to guarantee full participation in the society as it otherwise exists. In short, they do not wish to deprecate or destroy that which they wish to join.[23]

The "Old" and "New" Protests

A good many Negroes have always resented the disadvantaged and subordinate status assigned them in American society. However, they

---

[21] Daniel C. Thompson, "The Rise of the Negro Protest," *The Annals of the American Academy of Political and Social Science*, 357 (1965), 20.

[22] Thomas F. Pettigrew, *A Profile of the Negro American* (Princeton, N.J.: Van Nostrand Co., Inc., 1964), 193.

[23] *Ibid.*

have been unable to do much about it, at least until recently, because
they have been virtually powerless. Hence, acceptance in large measure constituted the principal Negro reaction to dominance. Yet, even
so, the decades have witnessed at least periodic ripples of Negro protest. During slavery, over 200 slave plots and revolts were recorded.[24]
But two hundred slave plots is hardly a high number, considering that
chattel slavery lasted more than two centuries, that it flourished in an
area from Maryland to Texas, that it involved millions of slaves, and
that "plots" were often the products of the over-active fears and imagi-
nations of the whites.[25] The Civil War and Reconstruction brought
new strivings among segments of the Negro population for equality,
but these were crushed with the overthrow of the Reconstructionist
regimes and more particularly by the evolution of a Jim Crow system
in the 1890's.[26]

The twentieth century witnessed the formation of a number of civil
rights organizations, the most important of which was the National
Association for the Advancement of Colored People (the NAACP) in
1909. The NAACP established a legal redress committee soon after its
founding, and it won some important legal victories even in its early
days—beginning with the Supreme Court decision against the "grand-
father clauses" in 1915. It was this highly developed, selectively applied, legalistic approach on the part of the NAACP that led to the
Supreme Court's overthrow in 1954 of the legal foundation of segregation. Yet it was an approach that entailed "tokenism"—a small gain
here, and a small gain there involving usually a white university, park,
or other public facility, railroad pullman cars, and the like, gains frequently realized by middle class Negroes *for* middle class Negroes and
having little implications for the great mass of American Negroes. For
the most part, the great majority of Negroes were merely spectators
during the legal battle; extensive support in the local community was
not needed since one or a few plaintiffs were sufficient to enable the
NAACP lawyers to launch their legal attack and to pursue their
strategy until at least a token victory was won.[27]

The Negro protest of the 1960's is to be distinguished from these
earlier protest activities in a number of respects: (1) the shift from

[24] Herbert Aptheker, *American Negro Slave Revolts* (New York: Columbia University Press, 1943), 162.
[25] W. Haywood Burns, *The Voices of Negro Protest in America* (New York:
Oxford University Press, 1963), 2.
[26] C. Vann Woodward, *The Strange Career of Jim Crow*, rev. ed. (Fair Lawn,
N.J.: Oxford University Press, 1957). See Chapter 16 of this textbook for a
summary of Woodward's work dealing with the rise of Jim Crow.
[27] Lewis M. Killian, "Community Structure and the Role of the Negro Leader-
Agent," *Sociological Inquiry*, 35 (1965), 73.

primarily legal and educational means of protest to direct action (demonstrations, boycotts, sit-ins, wade-ins, and the like); (2) the shift in initiative from the hands of a relatively few professional desegregationists (e.g., NAACP lawyers and officials) to a large number of average citizens who are willing to confront the segregated system through direct action; (3) the broadening of objectives from a narrow attack upon a particular public facility (e.g., a particular school, recreational center, etc.) to a full-scale attack against the entire segregated order; and (4) the expansion of the movement to assume a *mass* character that cuts across divisions in the Negro community and reaches from coast-to-coast.[28]

The Montgomery Bus Boycott

The Montgomery bus boycott (1955–1956) marked a turning point in the Negro protest movement. Here the narrowly circumscribed boundaries of legalistic tactics were broken, and large numbers of Negroes in Montgomery became active participants in the civil rights struggle. The Montgomery movement constituted a spontaneous confrontation of the white community by an aggrieved and aroused Negro community. With Montgomery the Negro protest moved from selective attack to mass confrontation.[29]

The Montgomery movement developed many specific tactics—mass meetings, nonviolent techniques, mass boycotts, and legal-judiciary measures—that became "standard operating procedures" for the civil rights movement of the 1960's. The success of the Montgomery movement projected upon the national horizon a new group of militant Negro leaders represented by Rev. Martin Luther King, Jr.

The Montgomery movement was precipitated by an incident that occurred on December 1, 1955. Mrs. Rosa Parks, a forty-two-year-old Negro seamstress employed at a downtown department store, was returning home in the evening on a city bus. At one stop, several white passengers boarded the bus, whereupon the driver instructed four Negroes to stand so that the whites might sit. The bus driver was acting within his rights as prescribed by Alabama law. Three of the Negroes complied with the driver's instructions, but Mrs. Parks refused. The bus driver called a policeman, and Mrs. Parks was charged with violating the bus segregation law.

Word of Mrs. Parks's arrest spread throughout the Negro community. Talk was heard among some rowdy elements of initiating physi-

---

[28] See: James H. Laue, "The Changing Character of the Negro Protest," *The Annals of the American Academy of Political and Social Science*, 357 (1965), 119–126, and Pettigrew, *op. cit.*, 192–193.

[29] Killian, *op. cit.*, 73.

cal reprisals against Montgomery bus drivers. But a non-violent direction was given to resentment by a group of Negro ministers who called a one-day boycott of the buses for the day of the trial. The protest plans received wide dissemination through announcements at Negro church services and through news stories carried in the Montgomery press. On December 5, the day of the trial, a very high percentage of Negroes, perhaps as many as 75 per cent of the usual riders, stayed off the buses. Since Negroes represented about 70 per cent of the company's passengers, the protest was noticeable.

Mrs. Parks was fined $10 and $4 in costs. That evening a mass meeting was held in the local Holt Street Baptist Church. Some 5,000 Negroes, including 47 ministers, and 1 white minister of a Negro congregation were present. The crowd engaged in hymn singing and listened to militant attacks upon the Jim Crow system. A resolution was adopted continuing the bus boycott until such time as city and bus-company officials would agree to (1) more courteous treatment of Negroes, (2) seating on a first-come-first-serve basis, and (3) the employment of Negro bus drivers on predominantly Negro runs. The Montgomery Improvement Association was formed and Martin Luther King, Jr., was elected chairman. Twenty-seven years of age, King had secured his doctorate in religion from Boston University prior to becoming pastor of Montgomery's Dexter Avenue Baptist Church.

The Montgomery Improvement Association set up a car pool to get Negroes to work. Unsigned and unidentified schedules were posted on telephone poles and the sides of buildings. The city police responded to this challenge by becoming especially zealous in enforcing traffic laws, attempting in this manner to interfere with the operation through harassment.

Montgomery white leaders expected the movement to collapse. But the boycott continued into 1956 with considerable effectiveness—roughly 80 per cent of the usual Negro riders stayed off the buses. Exasperated, Montgomery Mayor W. A. Gayle issued a statement on January 23 announcing that he and members of the city commission had joined the Citizens Councils, the militant white segregationist group. He stated that Montgomery whites had "pussyfooted around on this boycott long enough."

Within a month of Mayor Gayle's announcement of his intention to take firm action, a grand jury returned indictments against some ninety Negroes including twenty-four ministers. The action was taken under an almost forgotten anti-labor law enacted in 1921. Negroes were angered by this development, but King cautioned, "Even if we are arrested every day, let no man drag you so low as to hate."

Despite police harassment, the boycott continued. The NAACP, at the request of Montgomery Negroes, undertook legal action challenging the legality of bus segregation in Alabama. During 1956 the case moved through the federal courts. On November 13, 1956, the United States Supreme Court upheld a lower federal court's ruling that invalidated the Alabama law and the city ordinance requiring bus segregation. The following evening some 2,000 Montgomery Negroes held another mass meeting and voted to end the eleven-month-old boycott as soon as the Supreme Court's decree was delivered to Montgomery. This occurred on December 21, 1956. Once again Negroes rode Montgomery buses, but no longer on a segregated basis.

After Montgomery

The sit-ins of 1960 (see Chapter 7) unleashed the Negro protest on a national scale. Cities across the nation—both North and South—became the scene for demonstrations, boycotts, sit-ins, and the like. In the course of these developments, Rev. Martin Luther King and his associates evolved a fourfold set of tactics which King explains in these terms:

1. Nonviolent demonstrators go into the streets to exercise their constitutional rights.
2. Racists resist by unleashing violence against them.
3. Americans of conscience in the name of decency demand federal intervention and legislation.
4. The Administration, under mass pressure, initiates measures of immediate intervention and remedial legislation.[30]

This fourfold strategy was effectively employed to secure passage of the Civil Rights Acts of 1964 and 1965. In the spring of 1963, Rev. King took the civil rights fight to Birmingham, Alabama, alleged to be the most segregated large city in the South, saying, "As Birmingham goes, so goes the whole South." He organized a siege of demonstrations against that city's segregation barriers (the first step). Over 3,000 Birmingham Negroes were arrested, while newspapers, magazines, and television stations beamed to the nation pictures of Negroes facing snarling police dogs and being bowled over by high-pressure fire hoses (the second step). Although little was accomplished in Birmingham itself, the civil rights issue quickly became the number-one topic not just in the South, but over the entire nation (the third step). Demonstrations quickly spread across the nation, some 1,122 being recorded within a four-month period. The demonstrations culminated on

[30] Martin Luther King, Jr., "Behind the Selma March," *Saturday Review of Literature*, April 3, 1965, 16.

August 28, 1963, in the "March on Washington" in which some 200,000 civil rights marchers demonstrated "for jobs and freedom." The wave of demonstrations spurred the Kennedy Administration to sponsor new civil rights legislation, legislation that was passed by Congress the following year (the fourth step).

The same strategy was employed in 1965 when many Negro leaders became convinced that a much more stringent law was needed to protect Negro voting rights. This time King took his campaign to Selma, Alabama. On Sunday, March 7th, some 520 Negroes prepared to march from Selma to Montgomery, the state capital, to dramatize their case to the nation (the first step). Television cameras recorded this scene: as the Negroes, marching two abreast, reached the Pettus Bridge crossing the Alabama River, Alabama state troopers unleashed a savage attack against the marchers with billy clubs and gas grenades (the second step). The nation was collectively outraged at this brutality. Soon thousands of sympathizers were bound for Selma, and the national spotlight was again focused upon the civil rights issue (the third step). The Johnson Administration responded with the Civil Rights Act of 1965 (the fourth step).

Factors Underlying the Negro Protest

We have noted that until relatively recently, the principal response of Negroes to their minority status was that of acceptance. Within the past decade, however, a number of forces have made Negroes susceptible to a protest or militant approach against racial segregation. Let us examine a few of these factors.

An Emergent, New Negro Self-Image. Heightened Negro self-respect has acted as a powerful stimulus to the protest movement. This improved Negro self-image has been partially fostered by an emergent redefinition of the Negro's status within American life. The supreme Court in particular has played an important role in this development. The net effect of the Supreme Court's recent desegregation decisions has been to advance in an authoritative, formal, and official fashion a new definition of the Negro as a first-class citizen. In its 1954 school ruling, the Supreme Court overturned the "separate but equal" doctrine formulated in 1896 in *Plessy* v. *Ferguson,* a decision that had relegated the Negro to second-class citizenship and gave legal sanction to a segregated racial order.[31] Presidential statements and Congressional enactment of new civil rights laws have reinforced the effect of the Supreme Court's decisions.

[31] James W. Vander Zanden, "The Non-Violent Resistance Movement Against Segregation," *American Journal of Sociology,* 68 (1963), 544–545.

These developments have been closely associated with another important stimulus to an improved Negro self-image, the emergence of the new nations of Africa. Rev. Martin Luther King, Jr. has observed:

> . . . today he [the Negro] looks beyond the borders of his own land and sees the decolonization and liberation of Africa and Asia; he sees colored peoples, yellow, black and brown, ruling over their own new nations. He sees colored statesmen voting on vital issues at the United Nations. . . .[32]

Such developments as these contributed to a new Negro self-image in which accommodation no longer constituted for many Negroes an acceptable response to segregation. And the civil rights movement itself, once it got under way, offered a further impetus to heightened Negro self-respect.

The Anticipation of Victory. Until the past decade, strong feelings of defeatism tended to characterize many Negroes. For those in the South in particular, the "road to a better life" appeared as an endless maze, with a mammoth white wall at every turn. Government officials, quasi-military personnel (e.g., the police), and business and educational leaders—in a word, the entire power structure—were usually lily-white. Concentrated largely in lower socioeconomic class positions many Negroes felt virtually powerless. The segregated order seemed impregnable. Indeed, segregation appeared to be—and in truth was—the "law of the land"; for example, the U.S. Army still had all-white and all-Negro units at the time of the Korean War, *Plessy* v. *Ferguson* still had the force of law, and since the defeat of Reconstruction the nation had been more or less willing to allow the South a measure of sovereignty on the race issue.

In the 1950's, however, especially with the Supreme Court's 1954 school ruling, this picture was altered. The machinery and resources of the federal government became decisively committed for the first time since Reconstruction to an anti-segregation program. Where previously widespread despair and hopelessness prevailed, now the situation was progressively defined as one that could be altered. This prospect of victory created a climate conducive to struggle.[33]

A Sense of Relative Deprivation. During World War II promotions were rapid and widespread in the Air Force and slow and piecemeal in the Military Police. Most of us probably would be inclined to predict that the men in the Air Force would be more satisfied with their

---

[32] Martin Luther King, Jr., "Civil Right No. 1—The Right to Vote," *New York Times Magazine*, March 14, 1965, 26.

[33] Vander Zanden, *op. cit.*, 545.

chances for promotion than the men in the Military Police since in absolute terms they were moving ahead faster in their careers. Yet research has demonstrated that the men in the Air Force were considerably more frustrated over promotions than those in the Military Police. Among the men in the Air Force it was not so much the *absolute* level of attainment that made for poor morale but a sense of *relative* deprivation—the dissatisfaction aroused by the discrepancy between what the Air Force men anticipated and what they attained. In contrast, the Military Police did not expect rapid promotions and they learned to live with relatively few advances in rank.[34]

We might also expect that Negroes should be more satisfied today than in any previous time in American history. Employment opportunities for Negroes have gradually expanded, their median annual family income increased 73 per cent between 1950 and 1960, and from 1940 to 1960 the number of Negroes who attended college more than doubled. Yet many Negroes find themselves in a position quite similar to the men in the Air Force. The prosperity of the war years and the 1950's gave Negroes a taste of "the good life," a taste of the affluent society. Negroes have gained enough to hope realistically for more. Hence barriers blocking their further advancement are felt as severely frustrating. Any number of observers have noted that revolutions are not made by persons who are utterly dispossessed and despairing, but by those who have already gained something, who hope for more, and who believe their aspirations to be legitimate and realistic.[35] Although the Negro protest constitutes more a reform than a revolutionary movement, these findings lend support to our appraisal that pressure for change occurs among people whose circumstances are improving.

The mass media—radio, television, magazines, and the press—penetrate, indeed invade, the Negro ghettos with the values and aspirations of the larger white-dominated society. Some nine out of ten Negro homes have a TV set, and a TV set that juts out an antenna that senses the white world and its ways as never before. Even a soap commercial can sow seeds of discontent if its setting is a modern suburban kitchen. Those who live in the congested Negro ghettos of our large cities are aware that others are not so disadvantaged. The Negro

[34] Robert K. Merton and Alice S. Kitt, "Contributions to the Theory of Reference Group Behavior," in Robert K. Merton and Paul F. Lazarsfeld, eds., *Continuities in Social Research: Studies in the Scope and Method of "The American Soldier"* (New York: The Free Press of Glencoe, Inc., 1950).

[35] See, for example, Crane Brinton, *The Anatomy of Revolution* (Englewood Cliffs, N.J.: Prentice-Hall, Inc., 1952), 53; Eric Hoffer, *The True Believer* (New York: Harper & Row, 1951), 7; James C. Davies, "Toward a Theory of Revolution," *American Sociological Review*, 27 (1962), 5–19; and James A. Geschwender, "Social Structure and the Negro Revolt," *Social Forces*, 43 (1964), 248–256.

protest is not so much a product of despair as a protest fed by rising expectations. Indeed, recent surveys testify to the fact that most Negroes feel they are doing better than five years ago and expect to do even better all around five years from now.[36]

Yet Negroes face formidable obstacles and frustrating barriers in realizing their aspirations. If Negroes are to satisfy their expectations there must be a marked *closing* of the gap between Negroes and whites as well as large *absolute* gains:

At the 1950 to 1960 rates of change in the relative standing of Negroes, they would attain equality with whites in education long before they would attain equality in occupation and income. But even the educational gap, as indicated by the ratio of the non-white to the white median years of school completed, would not close until the year 2022. And the income gap, as measured by the ratio of non-white to white median family income, would not close until 2410![37]

Further, at the 1950 to 1960 rate of change, non-whites in the United States would not attain equal proportional representation among clerical workers until 1992, among skilled workers until 2005, and among business managers and proprietors until 2730![38] Such a pace promises to be much too slow for a people whose expectations, as reflected in the slogan of the 1963 March on Washington, is "Jobs and Freedom Now!" A sharpening Negro awareness of these Negro-white differentials—of the considerable and continuing gap between Negroes and whites in education, jobs, and income—accentuates this sense of relative deprivation.

Additional Factors. We have examined a number of factors that during the past decade have made Negroes increasingly susceptible to the protest orientation. Still other factors are also at work. Among these we might note the "piling up" of Negroes in urban ghettos where communication and social movements can spread rapidly; the assumption by the movement of a strong religious flavor having a revivalistic impact; the exposure of many Negroes in the armed forces to a democratic and integrationist ideology; and the movement's early successes which begot pressures for still more change.

[36] William Brink and Louis Harris, *The Negro Revolution in America* (New York: Simon & Schuster, 1964), 234–242. Also see Geschwender, *op. cit.*, 248–256.

[37] Leonard Broom and Norval D. Glenn, "When Will America's Negroes Catch Up?," *New Society*, 25 (1965).

[38] Norval D. Glenn, "Some Changes in the Relative Status of American Non-whites, 1940 to 1960," *Phylon*, 24 (1963), 109–122; and Pettigrew, *op. cit.*, 188.

The Future

Barring a major war or economic depression it seems relatively safe to venture the prediction that the battle against formal and legalized segregation will probably be won in the foreseeable future. Recent civil rights legislation, judicial decisions, and presidential orders have indicated in a rather definitive manner that the United States as a whole will not tolerate direct, formal, and blatant segregation much longer. This is not to suggest that various individuals or sections of the nation will not attempt to "bootleg" segregation here and there, and perhaps with some measure of temporary success. Nor does it necessarily mean that there will be a *mass* entry of Negroes into formerly all-white schools, neighborhoods, or public accommodations. But the stigma of enforced legal segregation will be removed. The battle for desegregation is being won; in many respects it represents primarily a "mopping up" operation—the principle having been established.

Integration, however, the genuine, fundamental acceptance of individuals in their own right without reference to their group identity, is at best an extremely distant goal, perhaps even a goal of a century or so, not of decades. Without question, prejudice and discrimination (especially in informal social relationships) will persist, both North and South. But Negroes can expect that on the whole prejudice will no longer express itself in a direct, blatant, and frontal fashion. Rather prejudice will be of a more subtle, indirect variety, the kind experienced by Jews.

Further *de facto* segregation, separation that lacks explicit legal sanction, will persist, perhaps become even more prevalent in the immediate future. Residential-spatial patterning—the product of ecological processes through which contrasting types (e.g., different social classes, racial and ethnic groups, commercial and business activities, etc.) are sifted and sorted into different sub-parts of an area—will continue to contribute to *de facto* segregation in other spheres of life. Schools, churches, social cliques, recreational facilities, and the like, to the extent to which they arise out of neighborhood patterns, will bear the influence of this segregated patterning.

Obviously, a frontal civil rights attack based largely upon laws cannot do the job of eliminating the more subtle, indirect varieties of discrimination. Nor is an attack upon discrimination itself enough. The problems that confront the great mass of American Negroes will remain for a good many years even if all discrimination—formal as well as informal—were to end tomorrow. As James Q. Wilson, a political scientist, observes:

If every city and state adopts and enforces to the best of its ability laws preventing discrimination in employment, housing, public accommodations, and medical facilities; if every school district in the North and South were desegregated in fact as well as in name; if every level of government spent generously on welfare payments to indigent Negro families—if all these things occurred tomorrow, we would still be confronted with a social problem of considerable proportions.[39]

The heritage of Jim Crow lives on. For decades, indeed centuries, Negroes have been the victims of inequality and low status. The handicaps associated with poverty, high fertility, widespread family disorganization, a lack of skills, inadequate education, and low job seniority are not likely to be overcome in a few generations. Indeed, low status is self-perpetuating. President Johnson has cogently voiced his concern about these facts:

You do not take a person who for years has been hobbled by chains and liberate him, bring him up to the starting line of a race and . . . say, you're free to compete with all the others, and still justly believe that you have been completely fair.

Thus it is not enough just to open the gates of opportunity.

. . . the task is to give 20 million Negroes the same chance as every other American to learn and grow, to work and share in society, to develop their abilities—physical, mental and spiritual—and to pursue their individual happiness.
To this end equal opportunity is essential, but not enough, not enough. Men and women of all races are born with the same range of abilities. But ability is not just the product of birth; ability is stretched or stunted by the family that you live with and the neighborhood you live in, by the school you go to, and the poverty or the richness of your surroundings.[40]

Significantly President Johnson pledged that his Administration would work toward solving these problems.

One of the principal sources of President Johnson's information was a 78-page government study analyzing the plight of the Negro family entitled *The Negro Family: The Case for National Action* and commonly referred to as "The Moynihan Report" after its author, Daniel P. Moynihan. This study concludes:

The evidence—not final, but powerfully persuasive—is that the Negro family in the urban ghettos is crumbling. A middle-class group has managed to save itself, but for vast numbers of the unskilled, poorly educated

[39] James Q. Wilson, "The Changing Political Position of the Negro," in Arnold M. Rose, ed., *Assuring Freedom to the Free* (Detroit: Wayne State University Press, 1964), 182–183.
[40] Commencement address at Howard University, June 4, 1965.

city working class the fabric of conventional social relationships has all but disintegrated.

There are indications that the situation may have been arrested in the past few years, but the general postwar trend is unmistakable. So long as this situation persists, the cycle of poverty and disadvantage will continue to repeat itself. . . .[41]

The government study cites some of the following statistics to support its thesis:

Nearly a fourth of the Negro women living in cities who have ever married are divorced, separated, or living apart from their husbands in contrast to 7.9 percent among white women.

Between 1940 and 1963, the illegitimacy rate among Negroes rose from 16.8 to 23.6 percent; for whites, from 2 to 3 percent.

In 1950, 18 percent of all Negro families and 9 percent of all white families were headed by a female. In 1960, the percentage for white families was still 9 percent while that for Negro families had risen to 21 percent.

By the time they reach age 18, more than half of all Negro children have lived at least part of their lives in broken homes.

Currently, 14 percent of all Negro children are receiving aid to dependent children, compared to 2 percent of white children. Moreover, about 56 percent of Negro children receive such assistance at some time, compared to 8 percent of white children.

If present population trends continue, Negroes, who accounted for 1 in 10 in the population in 1950, will account for 1 in 8 by 1970. This population explosion, especially in the ghettos, has aggravated all the other problems and threatens to make them worse.[42]

Family disintegration and breakdown, the report suggests, is both a cause and a result of some of the gravest problems of the ghetto. The report cites studies that strongly suggest that children from broken homes have lower I.Q.'s, fall behind in school more often, drop out of school more readily, and commit more crimes than those who grow up with both parents.

Finally, the government report concludes that it is doubtful whether the establishment of equal rights and the kinds of general government programs thus far established—for example, manpower retraining and the antipoverty program—will do more than make opportunity available:

They cannot insure the outcome. The principal challenge of the next phase of the Negro revolution is to make certain that equality of results will now follow. If we do not, there will be no social peace in the United States for generations.[43]

[41] *The Negro Family* (Washington: U.S. Government Printing Office, 1965).
[42] *Ibid.*
[43] *Ibid.*

Hence, it would be misleading for white Americans to think that the Negro protest will subside in the face of civil rights gains. Indeed, the closer the Negro community gets to the attainment of its civil rights goals, the more impatient it is likely to become. Moreover, in terms of the increased publicity given to the struggle for equal rights, it will be easy for many lower class Negroes to define their vast problems— their discontent—primarily in racial terms. Certainly there is little ground for believing that the Negro protest will come to an end in the foreseeable future. If anything, it will grow in magnitude. Much depends on whether the bottle is seen as half full or half empty; whether one concentrates on what has been done or what remains to be done. While many whites see the bottle as half full, many Negroes see it as half empty.

As formal equality is attained in the field of civil rights, and as desegregation progresses, the focus of the protest will necessarily move ". . . away from an exclusive emphasis upon desegregation and equal opportunity toward a broader demand for a 'fair share' and advantages directly comparable to whites." [44] Many Negroes find themselves much in the position of the underprivileged urchin who has had his nose pressed against the window, longing for the goodies inside. In past years, segregation and discrimination barred him from entering the door. Now he can enter the store, but he lacks the economic resources for securing the goodies. Hence, Negroes will increasingly come to demand their "fair share" of "the good American life." In a word, equality of opportunity does not necessarily produce equality of results: on the contrary, to the extent that winners imply losers, equality of opportunity almost insures inequality of results. The Negro protest has become increasingly concerned not merely with removing the barriers to full *opportunity* but with achieving the fact of *equality of results*. By equality of results is meant a distribution of achievements among Negroes roughly comparable to that among whites.

VARIABLES AFFECTING THE RESPONSE OF MINORITY-GROUP MEMBERS

Generational differences appear to play an important part in the responses of minority individuals to their subordinate and disadvantaged status. Among European immigrants, the second and third generations generally have displayed stronger assimilationist strivings, particularly with an integrationist emphasis, than the first generation. Further, the Negro protest has found particular strength among Negro

[44] Pettigrew, *op. cit.*, 187.

youth. Solomon and Fishman, in their study of student participants in civil rights activities, note:

> Most of the young demonstrators whom we have been studying were at the threshold of their adolescence when the United States Supreme Court ruled unanimously that the segregated schools these youngsters had been attending were illegal. This public recognition of the desirability of desegregation and of its possible achievement in the near future was an experience in the adolescent development of these young people that was quite different from that of their parents and older siblings. Feeling that desegregation was now their right, the students experienced increasing frustration with the painful slowness of its implementation and with the seeming hypocrisy and helplessness of adults—white and Negro—who paid lip service to principles but took no risks for their realization.[45]

Similarly, assimilationist strivings have been particularly strong among middle class Negroes and European immigrants. Psychologically, such individuals have been quite prone to identify themselves with similarly situated dominant group members. Searles and Williams, in a study of Negro college student participation in sit-ins, conclude:

> Socialized to value respectability and achievement, educated to affirm their right of equal opportunity, legitimized in their expectations by civil rights legislation and an important body of opinion, living in a college environment where freedom from constraints and ease of communication facilitate the development of protest activity, these students have selected nonviolent protest as an acceptable means of demonstrating their anger at barriers to first-class citizenship. Far from being alienated, the students appear to be committed to the society and its middle class leaders.[46]

Indeed, for such youth, middle class white society has functioned as a key reference group.

Essien-Udom, in his study of the Black Muslims, suggests that the identification of middle class Negroes with the larger white society has contributed to a widening of the "social and psychological distance" between the Negro middle class and the Negro masses. Communication between the two classes is highly impersonal. Further, middle class Negroes often tend to look upon the Negro masses with shame and contempt. Essien-Udom notes that lower class Negroes do not share in any significant way in the opportunities which integration "victories" are supposed to win. Although they can vote, at least within the North, this has not brought them nearer to the "promised land."

---

[45] Fredric Solomon and Jacob R. Fishman, "The Psychosocial Meaning of Nonviolence in Student Civil Rights Activities," *Psychiatry*, 27 (1964), 91–99.

[46] Ruth Searles and J. Allen Williams, Jr., "Negro College Students' Participation in Sit-Ins," *Social Forces*, 40 (1962), 219.

And what do lower class Negroes gain when lunchcounters and other facilities are desegregated if they still cannot afford to buy the now-available goods and services? Essien-Udom suggests that facts such as these serve to estrange lower class from middle class Negroes and feed separatist movements among the former.[47]

[47] E. U. Essien-Udom, *Black Nationalism* (New York: Dell Publishing Co., Inc.. 1964), 328–329.

15

Additional Reactions to Dominance

In addition to acceptance, aggression, avoidance, and assimilation, we can distinguish a number of other responses that minority-group members may make to dominance. In turn, we shall consider obsessive sensitivity, efforts at ego enhancement, self-hatred, and flight from reality.

OBSESSIVE SENSITIVITY

Meeting rebuffs because of their racial or ethnic membership, some minority-group members react with hypersensitivity to contacts with members of the dominant group. They become so preoccupied with any manifestation of prejudice, that all dominant-group members are viewed with deep suspicion and relentlessly scrutinized for "telltale signs of bigotry." The customary slights, misunderstandings, and conflicts that are an integral aspect of any extended and intimate relationship are interpreted primarily in discriminatory and prejudicial terms. The dominant-group member is perceived as acting out of malice toward the member of the minority group. In short, the minority member develops a "chip on his shoulder."

Personal inadequacies, shortcomings, and failures are explained as the products of bigotry and prejudiced people. When white employers or supervisors criticize, demote, or discharge a minority-group member on the basis of an objective ascertainment and evaluation of the individual's skills and adjustment, it is easy for a minority person to shift the blame away from himself and to view it as solely a matter of racial or ethnic prejudice. The same holds true when a dominant-group member is promoted over him. Since prejudice is in reality often responsible for inequality in employment, his excuse appears plausible.

Since minority-group members may suffer insult and humiliation under a great variety of circumstances in interaction with the dominant group, a haunting anxiety may develop among the former of impending discomfort. Feelings of insecurity emerge as expressed in these statements made by three Jewish students:

> I wait in fear for an anti-Jewish remark; there is a physiological disturbance: a feeling of helplessness at all times, an anxiety, a dread.
>
> Anti-Semitism is a constant force in the Jew's life. . . .
>
> I have encountered at first hand very few overt expressions of anti-Semitism. Nevertheless, I am always aware of its presence offstage, as it were, ready to come into the act, and I never know what will be the cue for its entrance. I am never quite free of this foreboding of a dim sense of some vaguely impending doom.[1]

EFFORTS AT EGO ENHANCEMENT

Groups whose self-respect is constantly put on the defensive may react by seeking to inflate their feelings of self-worth through compensatory behavior. Just as a drowning man will grab almost anything in sight to give himself temporary support, so a group of people being constantly downtrodden may be expected to grab hold of almost any label or sign of status that will give them a sense of well-being. Exaggerated ethnic or social pride, enhanced status striving, or symbolic status striving may be the result.

Exaggerated Ethnic or Racial Pride

Not uncommon reactions to dominant-group discrimination and disparagement are exaggerated, inflated, and compensatory self-assertion and chauvinistic pride. These reactions represent an aggressive response to, and imitation of, the dominant-group attitudes, expressed in counter-symbols and reversed claims. These reactions have constituted an integral ingredient in the Zionist, Garvey, and Black Muslim movements discussed in the chapter on avoidance. Although predominantly separatist in character, strong aggressive overtones, reflected in assertive and demonstrative "nationalism" and a strong deprecation of the dominant group, have been important accompaniments of the movements.

[1] Gordon W. Allport, *The Nature of Prejudice* (Boston: Beacon Press, Inc., 1954), 144.

The effort to compensate for feelings of inferiority through exaggerated pride in blackness is reflected in this statement by a lower-class Negro woman:

Well, I don't care if I am the blackest one [in the family]—I'm glad I'm black. I wouldn't be yellah [light-skinned] for nothin'. If I was born again I'd want to be just as black, if anything, a little blacker. Hell, black is jest as good as any other color. I don't see why niggahs are always hollerin' about somebody bein' black, all niggahs are supposed to be black.[2]

Assertion of Negro superiority can be seen in this statement by another Negro:

Being a Negro means all the world to me because frankly I think [it] is the best race there is. It has been treated cruel and although the times are getting better for them, the white just tries to keep the Negro down because his intelligence would be much higher than white if he only had equalization in all aspects of present conditions.[3]

Drake and Cayton have noted the obsession of many Negro leaders in attempting to dispel notions that Negroes are the inferior creatures that their minority status implies. Since emancipation many of them have preached the necessity of fostering "race pride":

They have patiently attempted to popularize an expanding roster of Race Heroes—individuals who have attained success or prominence. "Catching up with the white folks" has been developed as the dominating theme of inspirational exhortations, and the Negro "firsts" and "onlies" are set up as Race Heroes. "Beating the white man at his own game" becomes a powerful motivation for achievement and explains the popularity of such personalities as Joe Louis or Jesse Owens, George Washington Carver or outstanding soldier-heroes. A myth of "special gifts" has also emerged, with Negroes (and whites also) believing that American Negroes have some inborn, unusual talent as dancers, musicians, artists and athletes.[4]

Donald Young has noted the "extravagant praise of ordinary accomplishments" in art produced by Negroes. The works of average but not distinguished authors are frequently spoken of in "prejudiced overpraise," and it constitutes "racial treason" to view them exclusively in terms of their merits.[5]

[2] E. Franklin Frazier, *Negro Youth at the Crossways* (Washington, D.C.: American Council on Education, 1940), 53. By permission.

[3] Martin M. Grossack, "Group Belongingness Among Negroes," *The Journal of Social Psychology*, 43 (1956), 172–173.

[4] St. Clair Drake and Horace R. Cayton, *Black Metropolis* (New York: Harcourt, Brace & World, Inc., 1945), 391. By permission.

[5] Donald Young, *American Minority Peoples* (New York: Harper & Row, 1932).

Enhanced Status Striving

Among European immigrants as well as members of many other minorities, tremendous importance has frequently been attached to matters of social status, especially status striving. Great stress was often placed upon upward mobility. Although working all day, some European immigrants attended night school to learn American ways of life, including English and history. Frequently, immigrant parents placed considerable pressure upon their children to acquire skills or education that would contribute to their advancement in the status hierarchy.

The pursuit of intellectual and professional goals seems to be especially rooted among many Jews. This stress upon educational attainment is undoubtedly the product of a long Jewish heritage and tradition emphasizing scholarship and intellectual endeavors. But one cannot overlook the fact that Jewish parents have frequently stimulated their children to excel intellectually in order to run an equal race with non-Jewish competitors. Jewish parents may stress that Jews have to be better prepared, have better academic records, and possess more experience than gentiles in order to be successful. Academic achievement thus may become a means to minimize or compensate for the burdens of rejected-minority status. On the other hand, the Irish tended to employ methods of political organization as a primary technique for enhancing their social and economic status.[6]

Enhanced striving has also been a reaction to minority status among some Negroes. A dark-skinned, very successful Negro businessman in Chicago is a case in point.[7] Married and about forty years old, he has responded to his racial position by getting ahead in the world, coming to "represent large buying power," and ultimately being "openly received by the whites." He indicates:

Where one has established himself the white people will recognize one. I know of several instances where the Negro, because of some success, has been openly received by the whites. It is then not a question of social equality, but the acceptance of someone who represents large buying power; that is the thing that means the continual turning of the wheels of industry.[8]

He attempts to minimize the personal effect of being ignored or subordinated by whites by evaluating his position in business or economic

[6] Kenneth B. Clark, "Jews in Contemporary America," *The Jewish Social Service Quarterly*, 31 (1954), 12–22.

[7] W. Lloyd Warner, Buford H. Junker, and Walter A. Adams, *Color and Human Nature* (Washington, D.C.: American Council on Education, 1941), 36–39.

[8] *Ibid.*, 36. By permission of the publishers, American Council on Education.

terms, as when he says, "I do not believe there is a white man in Chicago that can get more credit than I can. Of course, this was not obtained at first but had to be gradually built up." [9]

When he was a child, his parents enjoyed a comfortable living and instilled in him ambitions to get ahead in the world:

My father and mother had a lot to do with the forming of my life. My father never did any work for anyone else and often, through his determined attitude, managed to do things which seemed to be almost impossible. My mother was of the type that if you believed you could do a thing, she would continually tell you that the thing was possible, and do anything in her power to help you. So the first part of my life I was brought up under the force of my father and the help of my mother.[10]

He has no personal luxuries other than a car used in his work, and he avoids ostentatious display: "I continually put the profit back into my business." [11]

Among many middle- and upper-class Negroes considerable stress is placed upon appearing respectable and in this way countering white notions that all Negroes are lower class. Middle- and upper-class parents frequently admonish their children to "stop being common." Many parental warnings against fighting really "mean" that the children should avoid behaving in a manner which would identify them with the lower class. In this and other ways they may seek to differentiate themselves from lower-class Negroes, a concern related to their efforts to rise in the world.[12] In this way some middle class Negroes seek to minimize prejudice and discrimination—"We really are not like other Negroes." Indeed, there may be some foundation to this type of reaction. Evidence suggests that an inverse relationship exists between the class status of Negroes and the social distance which whites of all classes prefer to maintain between themselves and Negroes, that is, the higher the class status of Negroes, the less the social distance preferred by whites. Hence, people, even "prejudiced" people, do not react to Negroes simple as "a Negro," ignoring all other possible characteristics. Rather, other culturally provided orientations, including that of social class, enter into the picture and influence white responses.[13]

[9] Ibid., 38. By permission of the publishers, American Council on Education.
[10] Ibid., 36–37. By permission of the publishers, American Council on Education.
[11] Ibid., 37.
[12] Frazier, op. cit., 56–58.
[13] Frank R. Westie and Margaret L. Westie, "The Social-Distance Pyramid: Relationships between Caste and Class," American Journal of Sociology, 63 (1957), 190–196; and Melvin L. De Fleur and Frank R. Westie, "The Interpretation of Interracial Situations," Social Forces, 38 (1959), 17–23.

Yes, despite efforts to advance in social class, the frustrating role of the racial caste system may come to bear. Enhanced striving is not always capable of overcoming liabilities of minority-group status, a fact that may cause considerable anguish as in this case of an upper-class Negro youth:

> Sometimes I feel all right—I'd just as well though; I can't change it. At other times, I feel sorry because I am a Negro. There are many classes of us and many in these lower classes do not know how to conduct themselves; yet white people class us all alike. I can't understand that, particularly since there are different classes in their group and they don't fail to make the distinction. I have seen many Negro men who were famous but I realize they had and still have a task to rise above the ever present problem of color. It seems that you just can't get away from it—and you're still classed with the masses and we must be subjected to all racial indignities and are supposed to like it besides.[14]

Confronted with such a dilemma, some Negroes insist that their race "elevate" itself as a whole, thus placing the primary burden upon Negroes in an effort to "earn" white acceptance.

Education represents one of the primary vehicles for realizing upward mobility. Among many Negroes, education has become a fetish, revered in its own right. The symbolic value of "making good grades" or getting a certificate or a degree frequently becomes more important than the content of education. This formalism encourages the rote learning that characterizes a good deal of Negro education. Parents may relentlessly urge their children to become educated and may make great sacrifices to sent their children through college. It is not unusual to find students in Negro colleges whose way is being paid by a mother on her domestic worker's salary. The great premium assigned education is reflected in this statement of a deserted sharecropper mother of six children:

> I plan to let the children keep on in school as long as they want, until they want to leave. It sure is hard, but I'm willin' to struggle along to help them all I can. If a child ain't got a good education now days it be mighty hard on them. I went to the sixth and had to come out to work. I don't know nothin' but farmin' and it's hard makin' a livin' on the farm. My girl is the oldest and I'm goin' to help her stay in school. She's smart, too.[15]

Although such parents may themselves have only a few years schooling, they expect their children to become doctors, lawyers, and dentists. But the absence of an intellectual or scholarly tradition, the short-

[14] Frazier, op. cit., 65. By permission of the publishers, American Council on Education.

[15] Charles S. Johnson, Growing Up in the Black Belt (Washington, D.C.: American Council on Education, 1941), 116. By permission.

comings of segregated education, financial problems, and related factors more often than not interfere with the attainment of these goals.

Minority-group efforts to climb the economic ladder and advance their social status are often interpreted by the dominant group as aggressive actions. Lower-class whites in the South have tended to be especially sensitive to any suggestion of Negro "arrogance" and have at times been quick to suppress it with violence when it has been safe to do so. Dollard points out that, in some areas of the South, whites show considerable resentment when Negroes become skilled workers, seek the "frills" of education, acquire more than a small parcel of land, or even appear in good clothing on the streets during weekdays.[16] To the white is appears as an unwillingness of the Negro to accept his "place." Nor is the potentially aggressive content of striving necessarily lost upon many Negroes. In fact, they may take considerable delight in "showing up" whites through such behavior.

In effect, Negro efforts to gain symbols of status, including a high-priced automobile or home, may in part represent an endeavor to acquire attributes that are equated with equality. It is not difficult for whites to interpret such behavior as aggression. In essence it appears to many whites that Negroes with status symbols are saying, "Look, I'm your equal!"

Symbolic Status Striving

In the United States, as is true of any society, various symbols have emerged that have become associated with status and prestige. These symbols are part of the reward system employed by society in distributing personnel among the various positions and in securing essential services. Lacking genuine status in the society-at-large, some minority-group members undertake the cultivation of status symbols as a substitute for actual status. The situation is not too different from individuals with an inferiority complex who compensate for their feelings of low self-esteem through what appears to be a superiority complex. But the exaggerated and assertive character of the apparent superiority complex betrays its real nature. In much the same fashion, minority-group members may seek to inflate their egos and self-respect. Fraternal organizations with pomp, ritual, and status-exalting ranks and titles held especial appeal to many European immigrant groups. The processions of these groups, even their funerals, were often characterized by pride and polish. Similarly, Negro voluntary associations and churches often afford Negroes with an opportunity for self-expression

[16] John Dollard, *Caste and Class in a Southern Town* (New York: Doubleday & Co., Inc., 1957), 298–300.

and status recognition, and with an avenue to compete for prestige, to hold office, to exercise power, and to win applause and acclaim.[17]

Denied recognition and distinction, Negroes may attempt to compensate through the wildest extravagances in wearing exaggerated clothing, driving high-priced automobiles, or gaudily furnishing their homes. A twenty-eight-year-old Harlem Negro porter describes how he uses clothes for "flash": "In the colored race the people usually figure you on how you dress. Even if you ain't got a dime in the world, if you dress nice you can make with some of the biggest ones. I always like to wear something nice." [18] Likewise, since "nice-looking" women commonly represent status symbols for American men, he sought to date beautiful girls. Speaking of one of his dates, he confides:

I never did lay her. I take her out, number one, because she's a good mixer, and number two, because she's a good looker, a beautiful flash. Those kind of women you don't care much about laying, at least I don't. . . . You mostly use them as flash. You know what I mean as a flash? You're out cabareting and you want somebody with you that don't look beat-up, that looks sophisticated; someone who knows how to hold an interesting conversation with anybody, anytime, anywhere; someone who ain't going to make you ashamed.[19]

Frazier points to the role the Negro press plays in attempting to compensate for the collective inferiority of the Negro. Often the significance that the Negro press gives to Negro achievements bears little relation to the world of reality:

The appointments of Negroes to minor positions in the federal and state governments are reported as great achievements. In the Negro press mere police magistrates become judges. As the result of the exaggeration of the achievements of Negroes, myths grow up about the achievements of Negroes. Myths grow up concerning the importance of books written by Negroes. A Negro student who makes a good record in a northern university may be reported as a genius. The awarding of a doctorate to a Negro by a northern university is still reported as if it had great significance.[20]

Obscure and relatively unknown persons of Negro descent are frequently presented as individuals who played important roles in history. Thus, one Negro newspaper featured Samuel Johnson's Negro servant,

[17] Nicholas Babchuk and Ralph V. Thompson, "The Voluntary Associations of Negroes," *American Sociological Review,* 27 (1962), 647–655.

[18] Abram Kardiner and Lionel Ovesey, *The Mark of Oppression* (New York: W. W. Norton & Co., Inc., 1951), 109. By permission of A. Kardiner. Also see: Jack Schwartz, "Men's Clothing and the Negro," *Phylon,* 24 (1963), 224–231.

[19] Kardiner and Ovesey, *op. cit.,* 109. By permission of A. Kardiner.

[20] E. Franklin Frazier, *Black Bourgeoisie* (New York: The Free Press of Glencoe, Inc., 1957), 180–181.

who was painted by Sir Joshua Reynolds, as an example of the Negro in the art world.[21]

"Status" may be sought through "being seen" at exclusive places, having long fingernails (which takes one out of the manual-laboring class), joining clubs, and counting prominent people as friends. Advertisers in Negro newspapers are fond of introducing photographs of themselves, the picture not infrequently taking more space than the advertising matter. The society page reflects the love for positions of social prominence and for membership in clubs with high-sounding and mysterious titles. Some typical club and lodge names are: Original Sophisticated Eight; Les Jolies Jeune Filles; Twentieth Century Cavaliers; Sons and Daughters of Moses; The Grand Court of the Independent Order of Calanthe, Under the Jurisdiction of the Supreme Court Annexed to the Supreme Lodge Knights of Pythias, Colored, of North America, South America, Europe, Asia and Africa; and The Brotherly Love Continue Undertakers and Sons of America.[22]

Symbolic status striving may also be reflected in the pretentious use of language. A Negro drama critic writes, "Isabell Washington, irresistible in her charm, beauty and intrepidity, is rapturously intrinsic in every motive." At times unsophisticated Negroes may imitate the sounds of words but strip the words of their actual meaning, producing incongruous results. Such terms of salutation as the following may be used: "How does you sagashiate today?" and "How does yer wife appromulgate dis mawnin'?"[23] Effort at ego enhancement is likewise a factor in the fanciful and elaborate names adopted by many Negroes. Children may be named after such historical figures at George Washington or Abraham Lincoln or such movie stars as Loretta Young or Betty Grable.

SELF-HATRED

The late social psychologist Kurt Lewin suggests that within every minority group there exists a tendency toward self-hatred—an attitude toward one's own group characterized by aversion and dislike.[24] Such feelings of negative identification or rejection may have any number of sources:

[21] *Ibid.*, 180.

[22] Maurice R. Davie, *Negroes in American Society* (New York: McGraw-Hill Book Co., Inc., 1949), 442–443.

[23] *Ibid.*, 443.

[24] Kurt Lewin, *Resolving Social Conflicts* (New York: Harper & Row, 1948), 186–200.

1. Minority individuals may come to accept dominant group values by virtue of making the dominant group their reference group. Included within the accepted values are the dominant group's evaluations and conceptions of the minority group. Accordingly, the minority-group member may come to agree with the dominant group's appraisal, seeing himself and his group through its eyes. This process may underlie assimilationist strivings and under some circumstances lead to the individual's absorption into the dominant group.

2. Since belonging to the minority group may produce disadvantages in meeting various social and psychic needs, some individuals attempt to disaffiliate themselves from the minority and move outward into the dominant society. Yet they are often blocked by the dominant group in this, and as a result build up frustration and finally aggression. Since the dominant group is omnipotently powerful and statusful, this aggression is turned inward upon the self and upon the minority group.[25]

3. Learning that one is a minority individual, that one is a "Negro," a "Jew," or a "Mexican," is part of the process of acquiring one's self-identity. The child learns his racial or ethnic role in much the manner in which he learns his other roles. Yet his racial or ethnic role is defined for him by the larger society as demeaning and inferior. The self-image, then, that he comes to acquire has many negative and unfavorable properties promoting feelings of inferiority, a sense of humiliation, and a constriction of potentialities for self-development.

Self-hatred is seldom an open and uncomplicated reaction. Most of the time it takes the form of an indirect, unconscious self-hatred that may be accompanied by ambivalent feelings of superiority and chauvinism. Indeed, research suggests that Negroes who show the greatest prejudice towards whites also tend to manifest the strongest rejection of their own group and themselves.[26]

Jewish Anti-Semitism

Some Jews expend considerable energy in an effort to disassociate themselves from Jewish group membership, even to the point of engaging in severe anti-Semitic attacks upon Jews. Ackerman and Jahoda, in their study of anti-Semitism, found a number of anti-Semitic Jews among their case studies. One individual changed his Jewish-

[25] Ibid., 193.
[26] See: Donald L. Noel, "Group Identification among Negroes: An Empirical Analysis," Journal of Social Issues, 20 (1964), 71–84; and R. D. Trent, "The Relation between Expressed Self-Acceptance and Expressed Attitudes toward Negroes and Whites among Negro Children," Journal of Genetic Psychology, 91 (1957), 25–31.

sounding name and adopted Christianity, not because of religious conviction but in a desire to fortify himself against Jewish membership.
He considered Jews inferior, disliked Jewish girls, and sympathized
with Hitler's program against the Jews. Several individuals planned
conversion to Catholicism, and one woman underwent a nose operation
to alter her appearance so that she might pass as a Christian. To this
end she wore a cross. She hoped to get married but never to a Jew—
"Who wants to be a 'Mrs. Cohen'?" [27]

Other minorities may experience similar feelings. A Japanese-American student at a midwestern university observes:

> I feel whites are superior—up here [gesturing with her hand] and Japa-
> nese down here. They're [Japanese] just an inferior bunch of people—just
> passive. They aren't aggressive enough. They're in a rut. They're too
> complacent. I've assimilated white ways—I'm aggressive in getting what I
> want. The only way to get away from Japanese is to associate with whites.
> I don't date Japanese or associate with them. I'm going to marry an Amer-
> ican or else I will always be looked down upon.

Negro Self-Hatred

By virtue of his membership in the Negro group, the Negro suffers
considerably in terms of self-esteem and has every incentive for self-
hatred. In many respects even good performance is an irrelevant
factor in face of the fact that the Negro frequently gets a poor reflection
of himself in the behavior of whites, regardless of what he does or what
his merits are. He is identified by society as a Negro and of necessity
so identifies himself. But to compensate for his low self-esteem, he
may identify with whites. Kardiner and Ovesey observe that on the
basis of this process "self-hatred in varying degrees is a constant feature
in all minority groups." [28]

This identification with whites is reflected in this statement by one
Negro girl:

> I said I didn't want to be white but I don't know why I said so. . . . We
> are always trying to get white. That looks like we want to be white no
> matter what we say. . . . [Whites] have every advantage—the best of every-
> thing. After all, a colored person who says he doesn't want to be white
> must be kinda off. . . . If I had my life to live over again, I'm sure I would

[27] Nathan W. Ackerman and Marie Jahoda, *Anti-Semitism and Emotional Disorder* (New York: Harper & Row, 1950), 79–80, 101, 105, 107, and 117. Also see
Gerald Engel, Harriet E. O'Shea, Myron A. Fischl, and Geraldine M. Cummins, "An
Investigation of Anti-Semitic Feelings in Two Groups of College Students: Jewish
and Non-Jewish," *Journal of Social Psychology*, 48 (1958), 75–82.
[28] Kardiner and Ovesey, *op. cit.*, 297.

want to be born white—even looking like white is not the same thing. I would pass if I could; I don't blame people who can.[29]

A middle-class Washington, D.C., youth expresses similar sentiments:

But with all the disadvantages of being a Negro put in your way, if I could be born again, I'd want to be white. I think being white would make all the difference in the world in success and failure. With my ambition to be somebody and to do something worth while, having a white face would make a lot of difference. . . .[30]

The widespread wish among Negroes to be white (frequently unconscious) is reflected in the success of the flourishing Negro cosmetic industry specializing in skin bleaches and hair straighteners. A considerable portion of the advertising in Negro newspapers is taken up with the promotion of these products.

Charles S. Johnson in his interviews with southern Negro rural youths found among them such reactions to blackness as these: "Black is too black," "Black is ugly," "Black people are mean," "Black isn't like flesh," "Black is bad because people make fun, and I don't think it looks good either," "Black people are evil," "White looks better than black," "No black people hold good jobs," "Black people can't look nice in their clothes," "You can't get along with black people," "Black looks dirty," and "Black people have to go to the kitchen and scrub." Black youths are called by such derisive names as "Snow," "Gold Dust Boys," "Blue Gums," "Midnight," "Shadow," "Haint," "Dusty," "Polish," and "Shine." [31]

Self-hatred may find many subtle, indirect, and unconscious forms of expression. The case of a thirty-five-year-old former Negro schoolteacher living in Harlem is a case in point. The color black is anathema to her. With great distaste she remarks, "Ugh, black is dirty, bad, no-good, evil!" Feelings of actual nausea seize her when at a social gathering a dark man asks her to dance. She describes the bulk of the Negro population in the most prejudiced stereotypes:

I was waiting for a bus at 120th Street and 7th Avenue today. The people are all so loud and unclean. Two men tried to pick me up. They made a lot of loud wisecracks. It makes me mad and disgusted. Why do people have to be like this? All those people [whites] come by in cars and see them. You can imagine what they are saying. Then the bus came. It was full of Negroes going to the ball game. They had their whiskey bottles and their lunches. There was a lot of swearing and pushing. They don't bathe

29 Frazier, *Negro Youth at the Crossways*, 180. By permission of the publishers, American Council on Education.
30 *Ibid.*, 225. By permission of the publishers, American Council on Education.
31 Charles S. Johnson, *Growing Up in the Black Belt*, 259.

and they smell bad. I try to be calm about it but I get awfully discontented. I say to myself, "Why must I be a Negro?" [32]

The woman's children are both dark brown in color, and accordingly their births were a terrific shock to her. At the time of the first baby's birth she was certain she had been given the wrong baby and demanded an investigation. To make matters worse, the baby's hair grew out crinkly. She protests, "That was the final straw!" The child represented to her a piece of everything she hated in herself, particularly her Negro complexion. For a time she could not bring herself to take the baby out in public. When she started to do so, she covered the carriage. In desperation she tried giving the child daily baths in Clorox and hydrogen peroxide in an effort to whiten his skin, but to no avail. Her second child was also dark-skinned. In her children she constantly sees all the dreaded anti-Negro stereotypes. She unleashes a steady stream of criticism against the children: They don't read well, they can't eat properly, they are too loud, and they are ill-bred. As she cannot come out directly and accuse the children of having dark skins, of being Negroes, she displaces her anger on these minor items for which she never stops berating them. [33]

The Clarks, in a study of 253 Negro children aged three to seven, found that feelings of rejection for their own color appeared early. When asked to give their preferences for a white or colored doll, a majority of the Negro children preferred the white doll:

	Colored Doll, %	White Doll, %	Don't Know or No Answer, %
Give me the doll that you like to play with	32	67	1
Give me the doll that is a nice doll	38	59	3
Give me the doll that looks bad	59	17	24
Give me the doll that is a nice color	38	60	2

There are significant differences to be noted in the responses when analyzed by age groups. The strongest rejection of their own color occurred among the four- and five-year-olds. Among the six- and seven-year-olds there was a decrease in the prevalence of rejection, which suggests identification occurred to counter the self-devaluating beliefs they had acquired. [34]

[32] Kardiner and Ovesey, The Mark of Oppression, 252. By permission of A. Kardiner.

[33] Ibid., 253–254.

[34] Kenneth B. Clark and Mamie P. Clark, "Racial Identification and Preference in Negro Children," in Theodore M. Newcomb and E. L. Hartley, eds., Readings in Social Psychology (New York: Holt, Rinehart & Winston, Inc., 1947), 169–178.

Robert Johnson, in a study of 150 Negroes in an upstate New York community of 60,000, found a strong tendency among Negro youths to disparage their own group, as shown in responses to these propositions [35]:

	Per Cent Who Agree
If Negroes would prepare themselves, the white man would give them good jobs	59%
Negroes blame whites for their position, but it is really their own fault	50%
Negroes in this country need a lot more education before the white man gives them equal rights	47%
Negroes will never get ahead, because when one is succeeding, the others pull him down	41%
The white man is always trying to help the Negro but the Negroes won't try to help themselves	31%
Negroes are always shouting about their rights, and have nothing to offer	28%
Negroes would be better off if they acted more like white people	20%

Color Discriminations Within the Negro Group

As a result of the long history of racial interbreeding in America, the Negro population displays in its physical features a wide range and variety of traits and complexions. Conditions under which the mixed Negro-whites originated contributed to giving the mulatto a more favored position than the dark-skinned Negro in the American social hierarchy. Mulattoes were often the offspring of men who were both slaveowners and men of consequence. They lived in and near the homes of the slaveowners and thus were closer to the carriers of the dominant culture. They tended to share to some small extent in the prestige of their masters and progenitors and were the first to get the benefit of the schools. From time to time, some of their number inherited bits of property, were granted freedom, or were permitted to purchase land. As a result the mulattoes often enjoyed an advantaged position in relation to the darker-skinned field hands. Such distinctions tended to carry over into the post-emancipation era.

Whites often profess shock at the distinctions Negroes make among themselves. Probably most disconcerting to them are the color distinctions—the lines that Negroes draw between black and "light," "fair" and brown-skinned. Such color evaluations vividly reflect the standards of the dominant culture. Thus some whites are inclined to wonder how Negroes can expect whites to stop drawing the color line when they do it among themselves. However, the existence of color distinc-

[35] Robert Johnson, "Negro Reactions to Minority Group Status," in Milton L. Barron, ed., *American Minorities* (New York: Alfred A. Knopf, Inc., 1957), 205.

tions is not surprising in light of our preceding analysis of minority self-hatred.

Color distinctions may operate with considerable force within individual families, constituting an important source of friction. A lower-middle-class, dark-skinned Chicago woman indicates:

> The first time I was ever aware of prejudice and a color line within the race was when my mother left us. My father's mother, with whom we went to live, hated all but my oldest brother because we were dark. She disliked my mother because she was brownskin, and my mother is not a *dark* brownskin but a light brownskin. My brothers and I had hardly enough to eat. She was proud of her little grandchildren but not the dark ones. . . .[36]

Color distinctions play a prominent role in the lives of many Negroes. A twenty-six-year-old Harlem college student discusses the matter in these terms:

> All my cousins are almost white. My sister and I are darker. Grandma is very color-conscious. She speaks constantly of dark Negroes as "black bastards." She has a terrific prejudice against darker peoples. My father can pass. He has blue eyes and blond hair. He had high goals for his children. We could go only with certain crowds. There are only two crowds among Negroes—light and dark. He wanted us to go with the light. He always objected if he saw me with a dark Negro. All my girl friends were of one type, one color—light and fair.

The color theme is a recurrent concern with him:

> My wife's hair is straight and she doesn't look colored. . . . So many of my friends are fair and feel so superior and really are not. I was brought up in this clique. Shades to them are the most important thing.[37]

A common ideal held out by the Negro group to its members is to marry a mate lighter than oneself. Such mate-images are revealed when men are having "bull sessions" about women. One young man indicates to his fellows:

> I never go out with dark women because they just don't interest me. I prefer a light person for a sweetheart or a wife. They are more affectionate, lovable, and understanding. They are usually more attractive; they're prettier; they have good hair. They're more intelligent. I don't look for coal mines; I look for gold mines.[38]

[36] Warner, Junker, and Adams, *Color and Human Nature*, 14–15. By permission of the publishers, American Council on Education.

[37] Kardiner and Ovesey, *The Mark of Oppression*, 188. By permission of A. Kardiner.

[38] Drake and Cayton, *op. cit.*, 498. By permission of the publishers, Harcourt, Brace & World, Inc.

Such attitudes toward "marrying light" are often implanted at an early age. One mother confides, "I'm not prejudiced, but I don't want my children to marry dark people, because I feel they're hard to understand and I want my children to be happy. Of course, if they did marry someone dark-complexioned, I couldn't do anything about it. But I hope they don't." [39]

Martin investigated the beauty ratings of 50 male American Negroes and 50 male American whites. He asked his subjects to rank from most attractive to least attractive ten photographs of Negro women differing in the degree to which they displayed Negroid to Caucasoid features. His data supports the proposition that American males, Negro and white, share a common esthetic standard for judging beauty in which Caucasian features are considered to be more attractive than Negroid features. The Negro and white males were in almost complete agreement on the most attractive and least attractive females; both groups judged the more Negroid females to be less attractive. [40]

Clowning

Closely akin to self-hatred is behavior of self-debasement. In the presence of the dominant group, some minority-group members eradicate their own egos and attempt to ingratiate themselves and placate others through behavior which tends to degrade themselves. Clowning may represent behavior of this type. At times it may be undertaken quite consciously in order to win the favor and reward of dominant-group members. A fourteen-year-old daughter of a Washington, D.C., laborer depicts an activity of some lower-class Negro children that middle- and upper-class Negroes tend to resent as "being monkeys for whites": "We used to go down to the wharf an' sing an' dance for the white folks down there, an' they'd throw us money. They were real nice. Then, some time the ole police would come an' chase us away." [41] Similarly, it is not uncommon to find a Negro elevator man or attendant who wins his way by exaggerating his Negro accent and other stereotyped traits such as begging, laziness, and telling tall tales. His passengers give him coins and make him a pet.

Some minority-group members may organize their whole personality around deception and clowning. A twenty-one-year-old Washington, D.C., Negro male has evidently taken this path.

[39] *Ibid.,* 498. By permission of the publishers, Harcourt, Brace & World, Inc.
[40] James G. Martin, "Racial Ethnocentrism and Judgment of Beauty," *Journal of Social Psychology,* 63 (1964), 59–63.
[41] Frazier, *op. cit.,* 72. By permission of the publishers, American Council on Education.

I'm always being told I can't do something because I'm a "nigger." I don't feel badly about it all. I know being a "nigger" there are things I can't do, places I can't go, but I feel that where some tell me something I can't do, somebody will tell me I can do something I want to do. So I don't mind trying and if you know how to flatter and "jive" white people, you can get farther than they expect "niggers" to go. I usually make a big joke of it and act the part of the clown. I generally get just what I'm after. After all, I think that's all white people want anyway. They just want "niggers" to recognize them as superior, and I'm the man to play their game. I don't care what he says or does as long as he kicks in . . .[42]

Underneath, however, the youth harbors resentment and cynicism regarding such behavior: "I do hate to be called a 'nigger' by a white man, and if the odds aren't too great, he pays for each time he calls me 'nigger,' because I know he means something entirely different." [43]

Clowning may also be a conscious device designed to release tensions in interracial relations. In potentially dangerous situations with whites, Negroes may affect exaggerated physical response to tickling, wear their hats on their heads upside down, cut fantastic openings in their shoes for comfort, dance fancy jig steps, laugh loud and infectiously, roll their eyes, or sing ludicrous songs. Johnson tells of a lower-class Negro in the South who drove his old car, with defective brakes, into a new and expensive car carrying a white man and three white women. The new car was badly dented and scarred, and one of the women was slightly injured. The Negro avoided what might have been very painful consequences by the diversionary tactics of clowning:

Promptly the Negro began in a loud and terrorized voice to abuse his old car for having no better sense than to bump into "a white man's pretty automobile." He pointed to the damage it had done to the new car and to the passengers; stroked the crushed fenders and side with his hat; elaborated on the stubborn and sinful recklessness of his "no-count" vehicle; threatened to take an ax and beat it into scrap iron. An upper-class Negro chanced to be passing shortly after the crash; and when he saw the cars in difficulty, stopped his car a short distance away and walked back to see if he could be of any assistance. In the midst of the tirade against his "ole fool of a nothin'," the old Negro without shifting the tempo of his speech signaled frantically to the other one to go back. Misunderstanding the signal, the upper-class Negro came closer, and without looking directly at him the other whispered, "Man, go on out of the way befo' you git me in trouble." [44]

The incident was concluded with the white helping the Negro push his old car off the highway, and the matter was closed.

[42] *Ibid.*, 50–51. By permission of the publishers, American Council on Education.

[43] *Ibid.*, 50.

[44] Charles S. Johnson, *Patterns of Negro Segregation* (New York: Harper & Row, 1943), 283–284. By permission.

Clowning, or "acting the monkey," may also be a means to release tensions arising within the individual himself, especially in lower-class circles where the norms do not as strongly inhibit such expression. Similarly, the clowning reaction is sometimes employed as an attention-attracting device where the individual feels isolated.[45]

Servile Flattery

Servile flattery serves for some minority-group members a function similar to that of clowning. It may represent a studied device for getting what one wants. One Negro observes, "To get along with whites let them think at all times that they are better than you are, that the white man is boss, and act as humble as possible." In this manner the ego of the white is inflated. A Washington, D.C., skilled artisan advises his son, "You shouldn't act like you know too much. Treat white people courteous at all times and if necessary, do a little flattering and 'coat-tail' kissing." [46]

Dollard in his study of Southerntown indicates how Negroes may employ a servile, flattering type of response for manipulative purposes. For example, "A white man speaks to a Negro, 'How are you, Sam?' Sam: 'Oh, pretty good for an old nigger.'" [47] In this case the Negro assumes a derogatory attitude toward himself, calls himself by the name "nigger." By responding in this manner the Negro establishes himself as definitely knowing his place and puts himself in a good position to get whatever he wishes from the white. "Lower-class Negroes are quite expert at managing white people through their vanity. It is apparently a case of making the best of their status and exploiting the whites as best they can. . . . This is a sort of secondary compensation for the primary loss of self-esteem." [48] The "Sambo" or "Rastus" type of Negro takes off his hat, grins, strikes the white for a dollar, and frequently gets it in exchange for his servile, flattering type of submissiveness.

FLIGHT FROM REALITY

When people find themselves engulfed in strong counter-pulls, they are under pressure to find some way out. They may be in a conflict situation between what they have learned to need and simultaneously

[45] Robert L. Sutherland, *Color, Class, and Personality* (Washington, D.C.: American Council on Education, 1942), 57.

[46] Frazier, *Negro Youth at the Crossways*, 56. By permission of the publishers, American Council on Education.

[47] Dollard, *op. cit.*, 179.

[48] *Ibid.*, 179.

what they have learned they should not want or cannot have. Minority-group membership often poses such dilemmas for individuals. By virtue of their disadvantaged status they may be blocked from realizing many goals that the society-at-large seems to hold out for all its members. In American life, monetary success and upward mobility are two such goals that may be frustrated by the limitations of minority-group membership. In addition to facing direct barriers of discrimination, minority-group members are often disadvantaged in lacking equal access to the means by which success may be realized, such means as eduction, "contacts," and an initial "grubstake." Similarly, other needs may be directly frustrated by virtue of minority status or indirectly blocked by the social disorganization that may frequently accompany this status. Enmeshed within the severe counter-pulls of life, people may attempt to withdraw from stress, to flee from reality. Here we will briefly examine some such mechanisms, suggesting their role in minority-group adjustment.

Alcoholism

Dependence upon alcohol can be best understood if it is realized that alcohol is not a stimulant but rather an anesthesic, a sedative, or a narcotic in its action on the body and mind. It is probably this dulling of the more lively process of thought that appeals to persons who are in the process of becoming addicted. There are unpleasant or unbearable thoughts—intrusive worries, keen embarrassment, attacks of conscience, a sense of failure, frustrations—that cannot be thrown off. Generally speaking, alcohol may be used as an escape from the painful and burdensome feelings associated with such conditions. It becomes a means for fleeing from reality. Alcoholism is a complex phenomenon and certainly not the product of any one factor operating by itself. Involved are dynamics of personality and multiple social forces. There is no reason to believe that minority-group status in and of itself produces alcoholism, although it may contribute to the intensification of a number of underlying factors.

Thomas and Znaniecki have called attention to the unsettling effect of alcohol upon the life of the Polish peasant immigrants to America. Much of the disorganization due to the excessive use of alcohol in this country was the result of changed community attitudes toward such indulgence. In the peasant village, drunkenness on certain occasions and within socially prescribed limits was defined by custom and condoned by the group. Festivals and holidays traditionally had been occasions for prolonged drinking bouts, not only among the Poles but among many other European peasant groups as well. These immigrants composed a large portion of the unskilled American laboring population at the turn of the twentieth century.[49]

The character of drink-induced disorganization among the immigrants was in many cases directly related to the phenomenon of "culture shock": By virtue of their migration to America and immersion within a new cultural tradition, a changed outlook occurred among many concerning alcohol. In the United States the use of alcohol is frowned upon by large sections of the population. The European sanctions of convivial drunkenness are lacking. Frequently the peasant turned factory worker consumed alcohol as a compensation for his lack of economic success. For this group, a good deal of indulgence was "misery drinking." Alcohol served as a narcotic for their humiliations and frustrations. Economic instability reinforced their overindulgence. Often they harbored the conviction that sooner or later they would be fired, no matter how sober and conscientious they may have been. Thus, some reasoned, "Why not have some enjoyment while we can still pay for it?"

Drug Addiction

In addition to alcohol, there are other means of flight from reality. The narcotic drugs such as opium and its derivatives (morphine, heroin, codeine, etc.) enable the addict to control his "feeling tone" and to maintain "normal" feelings. By using the drug, the addict learns that he can regulate his moods more or less at will but that without the drug he tends to be a passive victim of his environment or of uncontrolled factors. A Negro addict observes:

I was just born black, poor and uneducated. And you only need three strikes all over the world to be out, and I have nothing to live for but this shot of dope.

I have nothing to shoot at. All I have to look forward to is a thrill and it's in a bag, and they run me up on the roof to get that. I don't have any place to turn, but I imagine you have. I'm poor and all I can look forward to is this bag [dope]. That's the only thrill in life for me, you know. I've never had anything, no opportunity, you know, to get any money, no nothing. All I can look forward to is what I can get out of this bag, and that's nothing really. . . . I figure if Whitey [whites] gives me half a chance, you know, when I came through school, I could have done something more than this, you know. I know it. But I didn't have the chance because, like I say, I had those three strikes against me.

I'm not really blaming him, you know, the younger ones, but all Whiteys

49 William I. Thomas and Florian Znaniecki, *The Polish Peasant in Europe and America* (New York: Alfred A. Knopf, Inc., 1927), 1691–1692.

are associated with their race, and I blame them all because there isn't anything else I can do, you know, but shoot dope.[50]

Negroes are even more disproportionately arrested for drug violations than they are for crime in general, representing roughly 60 per cent of all such arrests. However, it should be realized that the Negro has greater liability to arrest by law-enforcement agencies.[51] Promiscuous sex and heavy gambling may represent other avenues of escape from reality.

Fantasy

One of the most satisfying forms of substitute satisfaction available to the frustrated individual is that of fantasy, or daydreaming. Through fantasy the defeated person may find a retreat or escape from his feelings of inadequacy or insecurity. Thwarted in his efforts to secure ego satisfactions in the realm of reality, he may find release in fantasy. In his reveries, he may gain wishes denied him in the harsh world of obstacles. A lower-class Negro woman living in Harlem illustrates this type of adjustment and tells of her daydreams:

I've had them [daydreams] all my life. I've never wanted real expensive things because that I know I could never get, but I always wanted nice clothes and a nice apartment and nice furniture and a good husband, who don't drink. I don't care if he drinks as long as he don't get drunk and throw away all his money and forget about the food and rent and all that. I always wanted to be out in the country. I likes to be alone. I likes a nice country home in a small town. I likes a lot of flowers in my yard and chickens and lots of cats and dogs. That's my wish—those things.[52]

Aggressive impulses that cannot find overt expression may find an outlet in fantasy as in this case of a thirteen-year-old Negro boy:

I imagined I was working for a white man and he beat me and made me do everything for him, but he paid me my money every week. I imagined that I kept on working for him even though he beat me and treated me so mean . . . Then after I had worked for him a long time, I imagined that I got all his money. He had paid me all the money he had for working for him. I was rich and he was poor. I imagined that I bought his house and everything and then I hired him to work for me. . . . I made him work from "sun-up" till "sun-down." [53]

[50] Kenneth B. Clark, *Dark Ghetto* (New York: Harper & Row, 1965), 95. By permission. Also see, Harold Finestone, "Cats, Kicks, and Color," *Social Problems*, 5 (1957), 3–13.

[51] For a discussion of drug addiction among Puerto Ricans see: Dan Wakefield, *Island in the City: The World of Spanish Harlem* (Boston: Houghton Mifflin Co., 1959), 87–114.

[52] Kardiner and Ovesey, *op. cit.*, 144. By permission of A. Kardiner.

[53] Frazier, *op. cit.*, 81–82. By permission of the publishers, American Council on Education.

Fantasy may likewise find expression in folklore. The Brer Rabbit and Uncle Remus tales, gathered by the white journalist Joel Chandler Harris, are a case in point. The chief protagonist is an exceedingly clever animal, Brer Rabbit, who outwits all those who try to best him, particularly the Fox. Through his cleverness Brer Rabbit manages many hairbreadth escapes and eventually leads the Fox to his death. Bernard Wolfe suggests that the slaves identified themselves with the Rabbit while identifying whites with the Fox. The folklore represented in fantasy a camouflaged hatred of the whites.[54]

Neuroticism

As a result of the deprivations, frustrations, and conflicts associated with minority-group status, one might expect to find among such groups a higher incidence of disturbances in bodily function, thinking, feeling, and conduct. Actually the evidence on the matter is quite confusing and contradictory.[55] On the whole, however, mental health among minority groups does not appear greatly different from that found in society-at-large. Mental health is a product of a great multitude of factors. When pathological conditions appear among minority-group members, their subordinate status cannot be ignored as a factor, but it is certainly not the determining element.[56]

Nevertheless, emotional difficulties may be intensified by minority-group status. A twenty-seven-year-old Negro schoolteacher is a case in point. She had a low self-esteem, the product of childhood experiences in which her parents withheld emotional support from her and frankly favored her brother. She reacted to this situation with considerable resentment, which she consciously and unconsciously held within herself. Thus, in no position to give overt vent to her hostile impulses, she turned them against herself. This early pattern, characterized by the containment of resentment, became her chief means of

[54] Bernard Wolfe, "Uncle Remus and the Malevolent Rabbit," *Commentary*, 8 (1949), 31–41.

[55] For three contradictory points of view dealing with the comparative incidence of mental illness among whites and Negroes see David C. Wilson and Edna M. Lantaz, "Culture Change and Negro State Hospital Admissions," *American Journal of Psychiatry*, 114 (1957), 25–32; Benjamin Pasamanick, "A Survey of Mental Disease in an Urban Population," *American Journal of Psychiatry*, 119 (1962), 299–305; and Benjamin Malzberg, "Mental Disease among Negroes," *Mental Hygiene*, 43 (1959), 457–459. For a review of the literature dealing with mental illness among Negroes see Thomas F. Pettigrew, *A Profile of the Negro American* (Princeton, N.J.: Van Nostrand Co., 1964), 73–82.

[56] See: Kardiner and Ovesey, *op. cit.*; Warner, Junker, and Adams, *op. cit.*, 294–295; and Howard E. Mitchell, " 'Color Conflict' as a Defense," in Georgene Seward, ed., *Clinical Studies in Culture Conflict* (New York: The Ronald Press Co., 1958), 91–120.

dealing with aggressive feelings and was carried over into adulthood. The end products of such control became expressed in anxiety, headaches, nausea and vomiting, and high blood pressure. Her minority-group status complicated her efforts to acquire a sense of worthiness. Her encounters with the white world served to remind her that she was considered an inferior human being. By virtue of her early childhood experiences, she was especially sensitive to any situation confronting her with doubts concerning her self-worth and lovability. In response to overt discrimination, she often experienced a splitting headache, anxiety, nausea, and vomiting.[57]

"Gimme That Old-Time Religion"

Among any people, religion serves a variety of functions. Among some minority-group peoples, it takes on an additional function of providing a periodic escape from reality. Religious expression may permit individual immersion into a collectivity of ecstasy and exuberance in which daily cares and frustrations are temporarily forgotten. This is reflected in the widely prevalent form of religious expression found among rural and lower-class urban Negroes. In the countryside of the South the church is typically a small, conventional boxlike structure with a gabled roof and a small bell tower; in the slums of large northern cities there may be a scattering of regular church edifices, but, primarily, the churches are located in vacant stores, houses, abandoned theaters, and remodeled garages and halls.

Religious worship is typically characterized by expressiveness and lack of inhibition, in which the individual can give vent to his feelings whenever so moved. An integral element is excitement, which moves by concerted participation, at first slowly, but finally with rapid tempo, to a profound state of rapport and mutual responsiveness. The dramatic qualities of expressive action, suspense, and religious imagery intensify the mood. A feeling of expectancy develops, culminating in intense excitement whenever the preacher succeeds in reaching a dramatic climax in his sermon. At these points the responsiveness of the audience reaches its peak and individuals begin to exhibit ecstatic behavior.

The excitement is experienced as joyous and intermittently mirthful. During the prayers, sermon, and testimonials, rhythmic moans from the congregation and interjections of "Amen," "Praise the Lord," and "Hallelujah" encourage the speaker. Inner ecstasy gives way to shouts, musical responses, songs, rhythmic patting of hands and feet, and swaying of the body. Here and there in the audience the responses of

[57] Kardiner and Ovesey, *op. cit.*, 232–241.

individuals sometimes assume a lilting form almost birdlike in cadence. Even the preacher may fall into musical expression, intoning or chanting his phrases. Under the stress of emotion, worshipers may "get happy," flailing their arms about, crying, running up and down the aisles, yelling "Amen" and "Hallelujah!" Considerable release is experienced for pent up feelings and emotions. The individual can flee from reality into exuberant and euphoric feelings of joy and immense pleasure. Middle-class Negroes tend to disapprove of this type of service and to prefer a more restrained type of worship.[58]

VARIABLES AFFECTING THE RESPONSE OF MINORITY-GROUP MEMBERS

Personality factors apparently play an important role in influencing the adoption of the reactions to dominance which are considered in this chapter. Apparently not all personalities are equally susceptible to them. Socioeconomic factors also play an important role. Lower class Negroes appear to be more prone to escapist remedies than middle and upper class Negroes.[59] Further, fragmentary evidence suggests that lower class Negroes are less likely to identify with the Negro group and more likely to manifest group self-hatred than upper class Negroes.[60] On the other hand, the route toward upward mobility and a higher standard of living (status striving) tends to be severely restricted for lower-class Negroes, although feasible for many in the middle and upper classes. Lower-class Negroes in particular lack a heritage of, or reverence for, learning, and, accordingly, educational striving usually does not represent a realistic response for them. By the same token, they are almost completely lacking in the skills, training, and financial resources necessary for upward mobility. Nevertheless, despite these limitations, many lower-class Negroes seek advancement for themselves or their children within the class hierarchy.

[58] See: E. T. Kruefer, "Negro Religious Expression," *American Journal of Sociology*, 38 (1932–1933), 22–31; John Dollard, *Caste and Class in a Southern Town*, 3d ed. (New York: Doubleday & Co., Inc., 1957), 220–249; and Drake and Cayton, *op. cit.*, 611–657.

[59] Pettigrew, *op. cit.*, 53–54; and E. U. Essien-Udom, *Black Nationalism* (New York: Dell Publishing Co., Inc., 1964), 202–203.

[60] Noel, *op. cit.*, 80–81.

V

SOCIAL CHANGE

16

Minority-Dominant Patterns in Transition

In a world in which prejudice and discrimination seem to abound, it is sometimes difficult to grasp the fact that minority-dominant relations actually change. Yet change is an integral and inescapable feature of social existence. All social systems are constantly in a state of flux, although at times the shifts may be slow and virtually imperceptible. Patterns of American dominant-minority relations have been no exception, undergoing continuous change. The dynamic nature of intergroup relations and the magnitude of the forces that have been an ever present feature of American life can perhaps best be appreciated by examining a number of these patterns through time.

THE EARLY YEARS

In contemporary America, where racial conflicts and antipathies are periodically caught within the swirling currents of publicity, controversy, and emotion, it is sometimes difficult to picture an America where the race issue was of relatively little consequence and where instead religious bigotry and persecution provided the principal focus of turmoil. Yet this was the setting of America during its early years. During the 1620's and 1630's, when James I and his successor, Charles I, of England were pursuing High-Church policies, thousands of Puritans migrated to America, locating in New England. The Puritans stressed Low-Church practices and a Calvinist tradition. In Massachusetts, the

449

clergy dominated the government, and for this reason the colony has often been referred to as a theocracy. Only a minority of the settlers had the privilege of church membership, this being reserved for those who had expressed repentance and had been officially admitted to the local congregations. Nevertheless, all residents of the colony were required to conform to the faith. Separation of church and state was unknown in Massachusetts. For more than fifty years no one who did not belong to the Puritan church (in time known as the Congregational church) could vote or hold office. Thus only about one-fifth of the adult white males enjoyed the ballot.

Although they themselves had been the victims of religious intolerance in England, the Puritans had little sympathy for other religious dissenters. Dissent was equated with damnation. Members of the Society of Friends, derisively known as "Quakers" because of their quaking motions and trembling mode of delivery, were persecuted with fines, floggings, and banishment. Four Quakers who defied expulsion, one of them a woman, were hanged in Boston. Since the colonists were often at war with the Indians, Quaker opposition to war intensified Puritan irritation. As have many other peoples throughout history, the Puritans sought a scapegoat for their difficulties. Among the charges they leveled against the Quakers was that the latter incited Indians against them.

A sharp challenge to the authority of the Congregational clergy came from some of the residents of Massachusetts, among whom Roger Williams and Mrs. Anne Hutchinson were the chief spokesmen. The group was subsequently expelled from the colony, Williams for disseminating "newe & dangerous opinions" and Hutchinson as a "leper." Williams fled to the Rhode Island area, where he founded Providence and Newport in the late 1630's. There he established complete freedom of religion, even for Jews and Catholics—virtually unheard of at that time. No oaths regarding a person's religious beliefs were required, nor were taxes to support a state church or compulsory attendance at worship demanded. Simple manhood suffrage was practiced from the start, although it was later modified by property qualifications.

Stormy religious friction also characterized Maryland's early history. In 1632, Cecilius Calvert, the second Lord Baltimore, secured a charter from Charles I to establish the colony. As a Catholic, Calvert wanted to found a colony open to members of his faith. But Calvert did not exclude Protestants, since he was anxious to swell the number of settlers and thus make the venture profitable; in any case, the English government would have objected to an exclusively Catholic colony. It was not long before Protestants predominated in Maryland and, in keeping with the religious intolerance of the period, resented the presence of the Catholics. Bitterness was intensified by Jesuit activities and by the fact that the best offices in the colony were controlled by Catholics. By 1654, the Protestants had wrested control of Maryland from Calvert and had suppressed Catholicism. But, in 1657, with Oliver Cromwell's support, the supporters of Calvert regained control and restored religious tolerance. Religious friction persisted, and this together with economic difficulties contributed to a series of disorders and revolts. The result was that in 1691 England made Maryland a royal colony, and the Anglican church was established as the state church.

Whereas Maryland was founded by a Catholic, Pennsylvania was established by a Quaker, William Penn. The Quaker sect had arisen in England during the mid-1600's. Their "quaking" at religious services, their refusal to support the established Church of England with taxes, their use of "thees" and "thous" instead of more conventional titles, their refusal to take oaths and to participate in military service, among other behavior, often embroiled them with government officials. Penn joined the sect in 1660 and, by virtue of the persecution to which he and his co-religionists were subjected, sought asylum in the New World. In 1681, he managed to secure from the King an immense tract of land in America, in consideration of a monetary debt owed by the Crown to his deceased father. Penn established an unusually liberal regime in Pennsylvania, in which freedom of worship was guaranteed to all residents. However, under pressure from London, Penn was forced to deny Catholics and Jews the privilege of voting or of holding office. By virtue of the freedom and tolerance prevailing within Pennsylvania, many Quakers and other religious dissenters were attracted to the colony.

In New Jersey and Delaware, Quaker influence was also strong; these colonies, like Pennsylvania and Rhode Island, had no official religion. In other colonies the state-church system prevailed. In New England, except for Rhode Island, the Congregationalists were dominant; elsewhere the established church was the Anglican, as in England.

A number of forces, however, were at work, which as the years passed contributed to the separation of church and state, religious freedom, and greater religious tolerance. Opposition to the established Anglican and Congregational churches arose among many ordinary farmers and tradesmen who objected to their aristocratic control. The leading clergy- and laymen were commonly drawn from the upper classes, a fact that irritated and angered many of the communicants. The popularity of the dissenting sects grew as dissatisfaction with the

state churches intensified. Simultaneously, new immigrants contributed to the diversity of the religious beliefs within the colonies. The
Great Awakening, in the 1730's and 1740's, led by such outstanding
evangelists as Jonathan Edwards, George Whitefield, and John Wesley,
fostered revivalistic fervor and leveling tendencies that did much to
undermine the established churches and to further fractionize the
American population religiously. The great multiplicity of faiths made
intolerance impractical and disruptive of the social fabric.

SEGREGATION IN THE SOUTH

The Origins of "Jim Crow"

It is not uncommon for southerners and other Americans to assume
that the "Jim Crow" system in the South—legalized segregation—has
"always been that way." Or at any rate, if not always, then "since
slavery times" or "since the Civil War" or "since Reconstruction." A
good deal of national discussion over civil rights is premised on the
assumption that segregation practices are deeply rooted and, accordingly, ineradicable and not amenable to change. This thinking is part
of a prevalent myth that views southern race patterns as having been
immune to change, as having remained virtually untouched by the
passage of time.

The myth persists despite the fact that southerners have probably
been more familiar with the shifting fortunes of history than other
Americans have been. Their own history has amply demonstrated that
an old order and its institutions can perish quite quickly and rather
completely. Following the Civil War, a new order was instituted that
had behind it all the authority and confidence of a victorious North;
and then again, within a span of ten years, this new order was to give
way to still a third. Each successive regime in the South—slavery and
secession, emancipation and reconstruction, redemption and reunion
—had its characteristic economic organization, its system of politics,
and its social arrangements. And in each the race patterns were quite
distinct.[1]

C. Vann Woodward, a noted American historian, convincingly demonstrates the changing character of the southern racial structure in his
study of the rise of Jim Crow. He suggests that the assumption is often
incorrectly made that Reconstruction constituted an interruption of
normal relations between the races in the South. According to this

[1] C. Vann Woodward, *The Strange Career of Jim Crow,* rev. ed. (Fair Lawn,
N.J.: Oxford University Press, 1957). This account is summarized from the
source.

view, once the white southerners had overthrown the carpetbagger and scalawag regimes and established "home rule," while conceding that slavery was finished, they proceeded to restore to normality the disturbed relations between the two racial groups. This view overlooks the fact that segregation would have been impractical under slavery, as Negro domestic servants participated quite extensively in the life and households of the white upper classes. Furthermore, the institution of Jim Crowism did not follow automatically upon the overthrow of Reconstruction but was a development later in time.

Accounts written by both critics and friends of the South during the two decades following Reconstruction give ample testimony to the fact that Jim Crow was virtually absent from the region. Negroes generally received equality of treatment on common carriers, trains, and streetcars; were freely admitted to theaters, lectures, and exhibitions; and were served at the bars, restaurants, soda fountains, and ice-cream saloons patronized by whites. When, however, there was sufficient room, whites avoided sitting with Negroes, and within restaurants were usually served at separate tables. Similarly, Negroes were not disfranchised immediately after the overthrow of Reconstruction. Although Negroes were often coerced and defrauded, they continued to vote in large numbers in most parts of the South for more than two decades after Reconstruction.[2]

In South Carolina in 1898, when the movement for the institution of Jim Crow separation on railway cars was gathering momentum, the *Charleston News and Courier,* the oldest newspaper in the South, editorialized against the measure in these terms: "As we have got on fairly well for a third of a century, including a long period of reconstruction, without such a measure, we can probably get on as well hereafter without it, and certainly so extreme a measure should not be adopted and enforced without added and urgent cause." The editor then called attention to what he considered the *absurd* consequences to which such a law might lead:

If there must be Jim Crow cars on the railroads, there should be Jim Crow cars on the street railways. Also on all passenger boats. . . . If there are to be Jim Crow cars, moreover, there should be Jim Crow waiting saloons at all stations, and Jim Crow eating houses. . . . There should be Jim Crow sections of the jury box, and a separate Jim Crow dock and witness stand in every court—and a Jim Crow Bible for colored witnesses to kiss. It would be advisable also to have a Jim Crow section in county auditors' and treasurers' offices for the accommodation of colored taxpayers.[3]

[2] *Ibid.,* 15–25.
[3] *Ibid.,* 49–50.

What the editor of the Charleston paper obviously regarded as an absurdity became in a very short time a reality.

It should not be assumed that in the period between Reconstruction and the institution of the Jim Crow laws a golden age of race relations prevailed. It was precisely in the eighties and nineties that lynching attained its most staggering proportions. The absence of formalized segregation did not mean that Negroes were accepted as social equals by whites. Such acceptance was no more frequent before the introduction of the Jim Crow era than it was at the height of that era. Segregation probably entailed a further lowering of the Negro's status, but it did not imply a fall from full equality. Evidence indicates that Negroes were often denied their civil rights and discriminated against before the era of genuine segregation which was introduced in the 1890's. In education in particular, custom dictated the separate education of Negroes and whites. But after the 1890's the principle of segregation was consciously and deliberately applied to all possible areas of contact between the two groups and became a hard-and-fast dogma of southern life.

In the decades immediately following Reconstruction, southern leadership was predominantly characterized by a conservative philosophy on the race question. Negroes were viewed as belonging in a subordinate position, but the conservatives denied that this necessitated their being ostracized; similarly, they believed Negroes were inferior, but they denied that segregation must be the result. The conservatives looked with disapproval upon whites who championed the cause of the Negro, seeing such individuals as false friends who pretended friendship for the Negro to advance selfish ends of party advantage and private gain. At the same time, they disapproved of the Negrophobe fanatics who proposed an aggressive war against the Negro and a program of virulent racism.[4]

In contrast with the conservative philosophy, there arose in the 1890's another approach, worked out and expressed by the Populists. The Populists fancied themselves exponents of a new realism on the race issue, a realism that was neither the product of a liberal conscience on the one hand nor the product of a *noblesse oblige* paternalism on the other. It was the hope of an important segment of the Populist leadership that the great mass of southern white farmers and sharecroppers would join hands with their Negro counterparts in a fight against want, poverty, and the large business and landed interests of the period. A Texas Populist expressed the position in these terms: "They [Negroes] are in the ditch just like we are." Populist leaders

[4] *Ibid.*, 26–41.

such as Tom Watson, before he became a virulent racist, preached that the identity of interests of the farming groups of both races transcended differences in race. Eventually disillusioned, the Populists assumed a leading role in promoting a strong Jim Crow program.[5]

Prior to 1900, the only law of a Jim Crow type adopted by the majority of southern states was that applying to passengers aboard trains. South Carolina did not adopt such a measure until 1898, North Carolina not until 1899, and Virginia not until 1900. In the decade that followed, the application of mandatory segregation in new areas of life unfolded in fadlike fashion, each wave bringing additional laws. Across the South, law and custom dictated that "White Only" or "Colored" signs appear over entrances, exits, toilets, water fountains, waiting rooms, and ticket windows. Segregation became formally instituted in wide areas of life. Some southern communities even went to the extreme of enacting laws requiring the residential segregation of Negroes.[6] Similarly, various measures were adopted to disfranchise Negroes. Mississippi was the first state to move in this direction, with South Carolina following in 1895, Louisiana in 1898, North Carolina in 1900, Alabama in 1901, Virginia in 1902, Georgia in 1908, and Oklahoma in 1910.[7]

Woodward suggests that the South's adoption of extreme racism was due not so much to a conversion as it was to a relaxation of the opposition. By the 1890's and early 1900's, there developed a general weakening and discrediting of the numerous forces that had hitherto kept racism in check. As the years passed, opinion in the North shifted away from liberalism, in many respects keeping pace with opinion in the South, and conceded one point after another, so that at no time were the sections very far apart on race policy. Within the South itself the position of the conservatives was weakened and undermined, and their willingness and ability to hold the Negrophobe fanatics in check were diminished. Although the conservatives had reaped enormous prestige by their overthrow of the Reconstruction regimes, an accumulation of grievances, financial scandals, and alliances with northeastern capital and conservatives served to undercut their popularity in the South. The Populists for their part found their biracial partnership dissolving in frustration and bitterness, with their opponents raising the cry of white supremacy against them. For a good many of the Populists it became easy to blame the Negro for their defeat, to make him the scapegoat, and to vent their bitterness and hostility upon him.

[5] *Ibid.*, 41–47.
[6] *Ibid.*, 81–87.
[7] *Ibid.*, 66–68.

It was not long before former Populists were found in the forefront of many rabid anti-Negro movements. With the capitulation of northern liberalism, the diminution of the strength of the southern conservative position, and the flight of the Populists from biracialism, racism triumphed.[8]

The rise of the Jim Crow statutes in the South had the effect of tightening and freezing segregation and discrimination. In many instances these statutes actually served to instigate such practices. Prior to the enactment of these laws the Negro could and did do many things in the South which he was subsequently prevented from doing. It is clear, then, that formalized segregation is relatively new in the South and that the southern race patterns have not been immune to social change.

The Second Reconstruction

By the early years of the twentieth century, the Jim Crow order was well established in the South. The sanction of law was lent to racial ostracism that extended to churches and schools, to housing and jobs, to eating and drinking, not to mention public transportation, sports, hospitals, prisons, asylums, and even funeral homes and cemeteries. As Woodward observes:

> The new Southern system was regarded as the "final settlement," the "return to sanity," the "permanent system." Few stopped to reflect that previous systems had also been regarded as final, sane, and permanent by their supporters. The illusion of permanency was encouraged by the complacency of a long-critical North, the propaganda of reconciliation, and the resigned compliance of the Negro. The illusion was strengthened further by the passage of several decades during which change was averted or minimized.[9]

Since World War II, however, it has become increasingly apparent that another era of change is upon the South. Major assaults have been directed against segregation from a great many quarters, with demands that the South institute immediate reform. Perhaps most dramatic of these attacks have been the various decisions by the U.S. Supreme Court, especially since 1954. On May 17, 1954, the Supreme Court, consolidating cases arising in Delaware, Kansas, South Carolina, and Virginia, unanimously ruled that the "separate but equal" doctrine, which had been used to bar Negro children from white public schools, was unconstitutional. Mandatory school segregation was thus

[8] *Ibid.*, 51–64.
[9] *Ibid.*, 8.

struck down. In so doing, the Supreme Court again demonstrated that it could change its mind. Fifty-eight years earlier, in the case of *Plessy* v. *Ferguson,* it held the contrary. In the years that followed the 1954 ruling, the Supreme Court moved toward outlawing legalized segregation in all areas of American life. But in addition to that from the Supreme Court, there were many other pressures. Since World War II, demands mounted across America for civil-rights legislation. Similarly, executive orders of presidents, policy decisions of federal agencies and the military, and actions by labor unions, professional groups, churches and others contributed to the assault upon Jim Crow. This new era of change is sometimes referred to as the "Second Reconstruction."

Many white southerners responded to these changes and demands for change with resistance. Once again they unfurled the banner of states' rights and sought to retain for the South an independent sovereignty on the segregation issue—a South with its own government and laws dedicated to preserving its distinct racial order. A cursory examination would seem to suggest that the white supremacist forces within the South stand in a better position to wage the struggle than at the time of the first Reconstruction. Then, despite northern-imposed rule, mass white disfranchisement, Negro voting majorities in five states, federal troops, and exhaustion from the Civil War, the white South succeeded in overturning Reconstruction.

Yet, in point of fact, white supremacist forces find themselves in a weaker position today in their struggle to retain a free hand in the management of the South's racial affairs than at the time of the first Reconstruction. In the first place, as William G. Carleton has indicated, the national balance of power has shifted considerably since the 1870's.[10] The Radical Republicans had been compelled to back away from the first Reconstruction because in part they no longer could carry many sections of the North along with them. In the ninety or more years since this time, the situation has been drastically altered. The southern parts of Ohio, Indiana, and Illinois are nationally rather than southernly oriented. The industrial cities of these states, teeming with minorities, have been strong for civil rights. Kentucky and Missouri have increasingly arrayed themselves as "midwestern" states and Texas as a "western" state rather than as a "southern state. The true South is being progressively narrowed to a hard core of old planter states, while the traditional orientation of Virginia, Tennessee, North Carolina, and Florida within the southern orbit has been weakened.

[10] William G. Carleton, "The Second Reconstruction: An Analysis from the Deep South," *Antioch Review,* XVIII (Summer 1958), 180 ff.

Contrasted with the South of the first Reconstruction, the South today finds itself weakened in still a second respect. No major political party can concede to southern demands without seriously impairing its popularity outside the South. This was not the case during the nineteenth century, when the Democratic party emerged as the effective voice for the South in national politics. Today no northern Democrat of the stature of Samuel J. Tilden, Horatio Seymour, George H. Pendleton, Daniel Voorhees, or Thomas A. Hendricks has appeared to carry the southern torch. Rather, the northern leaders of the party have championed an anti-segregation program.[11]

The 1948 presidential election revealed the South's exposed and weakened position. Despite the fact that the anti-civil-rights Dixiecrat party carried four southern states with thirty-nine electoral votes, the Democrats won the presidential election. The election clearly demonstrated that southern failure to give bloc support to a Democratic presidential candidate need not inevitably result in his defeat. On the other hand, Negro votes in northern cities could prove pivotal in enabling a candidate to carry the states with the largest number of electoral votes. The net effect has been that the practical advantages of appealing to Negroes and other minority groups have tended to outweigh the practical advantages of attempting to retain southern allegiance.[12]

A third factor that has weakened the white supremacists' position as contrasted with their position in Reconstruction times has been the demands revolving about American world leadership and the fight against Communism. It was not until the past two or three decades that American racial practices became a critical issue in the world arena. Within the context of the present world situation, the racial issue is one from which the United States cannot retreat without severe international repercussions.

A fourth factor, a new ingredient on the southern scene—industrialization and urbanization—gives promise of further weakening the South's position in its fight to maintain segregation. As Professors J. Milton Yinger and George E. Simpson have pointed out, industrial growth is not simply a matter of building a few factories, power plants, or highways.[13] Production patterns are thoroughly entwined with habits of consumption, attitudes toward work, family patterns, religious values, and the distribution of political power. Alteration of one such

[11] *Ibid.*, 180 ff.
[12] James W. Vander Zanden, "Desegregation: The Future?" *South Atlantic Quarterly*, LX (1960), 206–208.
[13] J. Milton Yinger and George E. Simpson, "Can Segregation Survive in an Industrial Society?" *Antioch Review*, XVIII (Spring 1958), 15–24.

pattern has consequences for the whole and its parts. Thus, once a society takes the road of industrialization, a whole series of changes are inaugurated which undermine the segregated system. Strains in one part of the structure are felt throughout the whole system, as one part does not exist in a vacuum but is inextricably tied to the others.

Caste patterns arising in an agrarian-paternal society cannot be superimposed upon an industrial-urban foundation without severely changing their nature. A decline in agricultural jobs and an increase in industrial jobs with hourly pay rates, the beginnings of unionization, diversification of jobs for Negroes, greater social mobility, the growth in literacy and in awareness of democratic values, a maturing and developing urban middle class, a growing integration of the southern economy within the national economy—these and other forces are changing the South together with its race patterns. The impersonality of urban and industrial life leads one to ask "Can he do the job?" rather than "Does he belong?" Artificial restraints on the use of the labor force interfere with the rational organization of production.

Movement and Countermovement

When people feel dissatisfied with the institutions or norms existing within their society, they may undertake to initiate social change. Through more or less persistent and organized effort—a social movement—they attempt to change a situation they define as unsatisfactory. Although a good many forces have served to undermine and weaken the southern Jim Crow order, the fact cannot be overlooked that deliberate reform efforts have contributed in large measure to the overall process. Southern racial patterns have been challenged by a movement that in its organized aspect has included the National Association for the Advancement of Colored People (NAACP), the Congress of Racial Equality (CORE), the Southern Christian Leadership Conference, the united AFL-CIO labor movement, the nation's major church bodies (although a few southern denominations have been at most only lukewarm supporters), the major political parties through their platform statements and the declarations of their spokesmen, many civic organizations, and, probably most formidable of all, the federal government via presidential executive orders, new congressional enactments, and judicial rulings.

Yet social movements do not initiate social change simply because they arise. Cultural persistence poses one formidable impediment to social reform. Once a pattern of social relationships has been established, it tends to carry on unchanged, except as the dynamics of other social forces operate to undermine it. Generally people find comfort, security, and a sense of well-being in old, familiar, and established ways. New forms of behavior, adjustments, and situational definitions often confront people with ambiguities and contradictions. For many individuals, efforts to resolve such ambiguities and contradictions would set up disturbing tensions that would in turn involve serious difficulties. Accordingly, it is frequently easier to go along with the old way of doing things, especially when no incentive for inaugurating the new way is seen. The situation is compounded when people assign strong emotional qualities to the old way, such as many white southerners assign to their traditional race patterns. Thus the fact of cultural tenacity has proved a major obstacle to the integrationist movement.

Another impediment to social reform may be the emergence of a counter-movement—a resistance movement. Movement frequently begets counter-movement. Between the two movements a dynamic interaction may ensue, involving a more or less prolonged struggle. Thus integrationist efforts to topple the Jim Crow order have stimulated the rise of a large-scale resistance movement. This movement has attempted to minimize the consequences of the various assaults upon the region's racial system, and to save the existing system intact.[14] Let us turn to an examination of the southern resistance movement and the progressive accommodation of whites to desegregation.

Accommodation to Undesired Change

The Supreme Court's decision of May 17, 1954, holding segregated public schools unconstitutional, confronted the South with the demand that mandatory school segregation be ended. Three more or less distinct phases can be noted in the resistance that unfolded within the region to this new demand for change. Here we will focus our attention upon Virginia, South Carolina, Georgia, Alabama, Mississippi, Louisiana, and Arkansas, where the resistance was most intense.[15]

The first phase, from May 17, 1954, through May 31, 1955, was generally characterized by two co-existing themes. The first theme was a prevailing disbelief, "It won't happen!" For the great mass of southern whites the whole matter of desegregation appeared obtuse, one far off in Washington. It did not appear to them that desegregation could actually happen. Since the prospect of desegregation was a threatening, discomforting development, many southern whites responded by

14 James W. Vander Zanden, "Resistance and Social Movements," *Social Forces,* 37 (1959), 312–315.

15 Much of the account that follows is summarized from James W. Vander Zanden, "Accommodation to Undesired Change: The Case of the South," *The Journal of Negro Education,* 31 (1962), 30–35, and "Seven Years of Southern Resistance," *The Midwest Quarterly,* II (1961), 273–284.

magically denying the reality of the new situation. They reassured themselves that desegregation was unthinkable and thus would simply not take place. The second theme involved an attitude of "buying time." This orientation was most prevalent among state-government leaders. It was widely believed among them that some desegregation would be inescapable. But if it were inescapable, they nevertheless hoped to delay it, and delay became their major tactic. Overall, the southern scene was generally quiet and calm during the first year, with the region's leaders and newspapers reacting with restraint. Although new segregationist laws were added to the legal arsenal in hopes of delaying and circumventing the high court's ruling, their number was limited.

Then, on May 31, 1955, the Supreme Court handed down its decree *implementing* the ruling of the previous year. It declared that the federal district courts would have jurisdiction over lawsuits to enforce the ruling. It told the lower courts to be guided by "equitable principles" characterized by a "practical flexibility," but it warned that "constitutional principles cannot be allowed to yield simply because of disagreement with them." Defendant school districts were instructed that "a prompt and reasonable start toward full compliance" would be required and that admissions on a racially non-discriminatory basis must be made with "all deliberate speed."

The decree initiated the second phase of the resistance, characterized by a marked tightening of sentiment throughout the Deep and mid-South. The National Association for the Advancement of Colored People immediately followed the 1955 decree with a new offensive. Some 170 school boards in seventeen states were confronted with petitions signed by local Negroes demanding immediate school desegregation. The fiction "It can't happen" was exploded. Angered, whites inaugurated a policy of adamant resistance in which compromise was ruled out. Methods of resistance grew bolder. Within the heavily Negro-populated Black Belt areas, the white Citizens Councils mushroomed. Although these organizations had previously been limited to a handful of chapters, thousands now signed Council membership cards, and Council rallies were well attended. Newspapers published the names of Negroes who signed the petitions, and whites applied sanctions and social pressures against them. On the government level, state leaders rushed into law more than 200 new acts, in a desperate effort to find some legal mechanism through which to circumvent the Supreme Court's ruling.

By the fall of 1956 the school-desegregation battle appeared stalemated, with the segregationists in the saddle. For integrationists the situation was bleak. Negro Congressman Charles C. Diggs of Michigan lamented, "We cannot point to one instance of submission by Mississippi, Georgia, South Carolina, or Alabama to the Supreme Court's three-year-old decision outlawing school segregation. There is little question that the Deep South has won the first round in the battle for compliance with the decision of May 17, 1954." It was within this context that the Little Rock drama unfolded in late 1957, setting the basis for the third phase in the southern resistance.

It is conceivable that history will show that Little Rock represented the key battle between school integrationists and segregationists, the turning point of the struggle. Arkansas Governor Orval Faubus had called out the National Guard in an effort to block the desegregation of Little Rock Central High School (see Chapter 7). As a result, a historic precedent was inevitable. The issue posed by Faubus was whether a state could use the National Guard, the ultimate coercive instrumentality at its command, to enforce segregation. The issue could not be compromised, since a state either could or could not use armed forces to defy the federal courts. As developments unfolded, President Eisenhower decisively intervened, broke the stalemate, and turned the tide in favor of desegregation.

Confronted by the new situation posed by the developments at Little Rock, the white South could in essence take only one of two possible alternatives courses: Either it could intensify its resistance efforts and search for new weapons or it could begin the process of accommodation to school desegregation. The first course would have involved a continuation of the second stage, namely, adamant resistance and the rejection of compromise. Yet legal avenues for the total and more or less permanent blocking of desegregation had been effectively closed. Extralegal instrumentalities including violence and armed resistance would have offered still another means of blocking desegregation. But rioting, chaos, and violence would have jeopardized still other values. And Little Rock demonstrated that force would be met with force. If the South needed a reminder, memories of the Civil War still haunted the region, a war that demonstrated the folly of such an approach.

The South, accordingly, moved in the direction of the second alternative and began the process of accommodation to school desegregation. Virginia is a case in point. In Virginia, James Lindsay Almond, Jr., a fire-and-brimstone orator of the old school, became governor in January, 1958. Before his election as governor, Almond had served eight years as Virginia's Attorney General, and had been in the forefront of the fight to maintain the segregated order. It was a self-labeled program of "massive resistance" to desegregation. Campaigning for governor, Almond told Virginians, "There can be no surrender . . . I am willing to continue the fight to the last ditch, and then to dig another ditch. . . . If we yield one inch we are lost forever. . . . There can be no middle ground that will provide an avenue of escape. . . ."

Yet within thirteen months Almond stood before his 100-member House of Delegates and the 40-member Senate of Virginia, called into emergency session by him. "Massive resistance" had collapsed in the courts. Seven Virginia public schools had opened early in 1959 on a desegregated basis. Although his speech was elaborately embellished, paying homage to the cause of "massive resistance," Almond essentially declared that (1) the maintenance of completely segregated public schools was no longer possible in Virginia, (2) all legal avenues had been closed, and (3) the choice had become some integration if public schools were to be maintained or no public schools if total segregation was the goal. Significantly Almond cast his lot with the public schools and carried the state legislature with him. In subsequent speeches he explained, "I tell you now that we cannot overthrow the federal government, and we cannot reverse a final decree of a federal court." No mistake could be more costly than to "succumb to the blandishments of those who would have Virginia abandon public education and thereby consign a generation of children to the darkness of illiteracy, the pits of indolence and dependency and the dungeons of delinquency."

Defeated in their efforts to block school desegregation, southern leaders began to tell their constituents, "We have done everything possible to prevent desegregation. We can do no more. We are now in a situation where we will have to accept some Negroes in our white public schools. But we will do all in our power to see to it that the number of Negro children is held to a bare minimum. We will maintain our southern way of life!" Although school desegregation was often little more than "token," involving small numbers of Negroes, the walls of school segregation were breached.

Southern leaders such as Virginia's James Lindsay Almond, Jr., served to make school desegregation palatable to the white citizenry. Their loyalty to "southern institutions" could not generally be questioned. They functioned to redefine school desegregation in terms that made it no longer equivalent to social equality. They reassured whites that southern traditions would carry on, that they need not feel alarmed or threatened. And, simultaneously, social change continued.

Yet despite signs that white southerners were progressively accommodating themselves to school desegregation, "it was not until the introduction, debate, and enactment of the Civil Rights Act of 1964," as Attorney General Nicholas Katzenbach observes, "that America finally turned the corner in civil rights by outlawing all official, systematic discrimination in all parts of the country." The failure of southern whites to block school desegregation and the passage of new civil rights legislation led many southern leaders to take the course of still further accommodation to desegregation. Senator Richard B. Russell, longtime leader of Senate anti-civil rights forces, called upon his fellow Georgians to live with the new law:

> Violence and law violation will only compound our difficulties and increase our troubles. It is the understatement of the year to say that I do not like this statute [the 1964 Civil Rights Act]. However, it is now on the books. All good citizens will learn to live with the statute and abide by its final adjudication even though we reserve the right to advocate by legal means its repeal or modification. We put everything we had into the fight, but the odds against us mounted from day to day until we were finally gagged and overwhelmed.[16]

Within four months of the passage of the Civil Rights Act of 1964, a U.S. government survey of public accommodations in 53 cities in the 19 states which had no anti-Jim Crow public facilities' laws revealed that desegregation had been accomplished in two-thirds of the hotels in 51 cities and more than two-thirds of the motels in 46 cities; more than two-thirds of theaters in 49 cities; more than two-thirds of sports facilities in 48 cities; more than two-thirds of public parks in 50 cities; more than two-thirds of libraries in 52 cities; and more than two-thirds of chain restaurants in 50 cities (the largest downtown restaurants in major cities have generally desegregated although neighborhood lunch-eonettes and taverns often remain segregated). All this did not mean that all southern whites were bowing gracefully to desegregation, but that instances of accommodation more than offset instances of whites who chose the course of continuing resistance. However, it should be understood, the use of public facilities once restricted to whites has as yet *not* become a pattern among southern Negroes.

Economic pressures also played a major role in moving many southern white leaders along the road of accommodation to desegregation. In 1965, for instance, some $150 million in federal aid (more than $3 billion for the South as a whole) was scheduled to flow into Mississippi for a variety of programs (highways, school lunches, relief, farm programs, etc.), aid that could be cut off for non-compliance with the 1964 Civil Rights Act. Further, in 1964, only $37 million was spent on new plants in Mississippi, a drop of 28 per cent from the previous year. Industrialists were often reluctant to establish new plants in the state by virtue of its unsettled racial climate. It was little wonder that

[16] "Rights Obedience Urged by Russell," *New York Times,* July 16, 1964.

Governor Paul Johnson, although having campaigned vigorously on the race issue, told Mississippians in his inaugural address that in reality he was ready to "adjust":

National policies have a direct bearing on our economy, on our political freedom, on our daily living, whether we like it or not. . . . If I must fight, it will not be a rear guard defense of yesterday. It will be for our share of tomorrow.

Moreover, many white Mississippians had despaired of further resistance. In the words of a Hattiesburg merchant, "It's [resistance] brought us nothing but trouble since 1961—that's when the first freedom rides started. A lot of us are ready to try something else." Asked what else, he replied, "Well, adjustment—whatever you want to call it." [17]

Change, then, could not be shut out of the South. Initially many whites tended to deny the reality of the new situation, to magically dispense with the matter. When confronted with the actuality of impending change, they responded with die-hard resistance, bent upon blocking desegregation. Faced with a situation where they could no longer continue previous patterns without jeopardizing other cherished values, they undertook to accommodate themselves to the change while still hoping to minimize its impact. But in the process the race patterns of the South were being altered.

Strains in the Southern Social Structure

It would be a mistake to view the integrationist or segregationist movements as simply the product of forces revolving about the race issue. The matter is much more complex than this. In part these movements can be understood as symptomatic of the stresses and strains that have accompanied major changes in the entire structure of southern society. Before examining some of the consequences of these stresses and strains, it would be well to consider the profound transformations that have occurred in the social and economic structure of the South.[18]

The South is rapidly moving toward an industrial and commercial economy organized about cities and other metropolitan centers. New industries including light metals, synthetic textiles, plastics, and chemicals sprang up within the South to meet the World War II, then the

[17] Jules Loh, "Economics Fostering 'A New Mississippi,'" *Greensboro Daily News,* April 5, 1965.

[18] This discussion is in large measure summarized from James W. Vander Zanden, "Desegregation and Social Strains in the South," *Journal of Social Issues,* 15 (1959), 53–60.

postwar, demands. In the 1950's, factory employment in the South rose 31 per cent, more than four times as fast as in the non-southern states. Although as late as 1920 only one-fourth of the southern population lived in urban centers, by the 1950's urban dwellers comprised the majority of the region's population.

The vast and profound nature of these changes is perhaps most apparent in the states of the Deep South: South Carolina, Georgia, Alabama, Mississippi, and Louisiana. Since 1930, the long-term trend has been toward a marked decline in harvested cotton acreage. As Donald Bogue has observed, "cotton, like many monarchs these days, is king in name only and lives in exile in California." [19] Today Aberdeen, Angus and Hereford cattle graze on fields once white with long rows of cotton. In 1939, 46.5 per cent of the cash farm income of the Deep South states came from cotton, 25 per cent from livestock; in 1960 the figures had been reversed, 24 per cent of the cash farm income coming from cotton, 47 per cent from livestock. Between 1940 and 1960 the farm population declined by about one-half while the number of factory workers rose from 640,000 to 1,100,000. Income per person, in 1940 only half of the national average, had climbed to two-thirds of the national average by 1960.[20]

Changes of such magnitude have had vast ramifications in southern life and have had important consequences for the social positions and roles of its members, both Negro and white. It is through social positions and roles that societies integrate individuals within their component institutional structures, e.g., the positions of father, grandmother, and aunt place individuals within the institutional structure of the family; the positions of plumber, farmer, and educator place individuals within the economic institutional structure; and the positions of judge, mayor, and legislator place individuals in the governmental structure. By virtue of social change, new positions emerge and old positions are altered, at times even lost. As a result individuals occupying such positions and playing the associated roles may experience *role strain*.

Dissolution of Established Normative Expectations. One source of role strain develops when social change undermines the norms and expectations that provide the guideposts for people's daily lives. As we noted earlier in this chapter, a shift from an agrarian to an industrial-urban

[19] Donald J. Bogue, "Population Distribution and Composition in the New South," in *The New South and Higher Education* (The Department of Records and Research, Tuskegee Institute, Tuskegee, Ala., 1954), 3.

[20] Data from bulletins of the U.S. Department of Commerce, the U.S. Department of Agriculture, and the Federal Reserve Board.

society inevitably serves to undermine a racial-caste system erected upon an agricultural-paternal foundation. The southern system governing the relations between Negroes and whites had its birth in a rural-oriented, plantation society. When Negroes moved into the city, the elaborate requirements of the earlier system could hardly be maintained. Relationships in the city are too casual and too functional to require the constant manifestations of Negro subordination that prevailed in the countryside. Social change has likewise had an impact upon the economy, drawing people with obsolete skills into a developing commercial-industrial complex. Uprooted from rural communities, the workers have frequently experienced an undermining of old, traditional values and lifeways, a disruption of social ties, and an isolation from previously established primary ties and roots. They have had to learn new roles and concomitant statuses; yet the task of reconditioning behavior along new lines is one which many people find a difficult and uncomfortable process. Similarly the abandonment of the family as a work unit, as is traditional within a rural setting, requires new family adjustments by virtue of the changed roles of men, women, and children. At times social change may so undermine traditional normative guideposts that, at least in some settings, the individual literally "does not know what to expect."

Status Incongruities. A second source of role strain occurs when individuals, viewed in terms of the status hierarchy, come to occupy positions with incompatible status rankings. One of the most common expressions of status incongruity is the disparity between an individual's racial status and his class status. Within the semicaste arrangement of the rural South, *all* whites were considered superior to *all* Negroes. But in recent decades the class differentiation among Negroes has increasingly come to contradict this assumption, for in terms of social class and its associated privileges and opportunities, not *all* whites are superior to *all* Negroes. Indeed, this disparity between the racial and class statuses of many southern Negroes has contributed to the Negro protest—that is, many middle class, college-educated Negroes have the competence and motivation to seek not only the material rewards of success but also the assurance of a respected place within the community; in brief, their middle class status clashes with their status as a racially subordinate group.[21] Similarly, as we observed in Chapter 4, many Klansmen find themselves in a stressful situation by virtue of the contradiction posed by their internalization of the expectations of the

[21] Ruth Searles and J. Allen Williams, Jr., "Negro College Students' Participation in Sit-Ins," *Social Forces,* 40 (1962), 215–220.

American middle class and their inability to realize a stable, secure middle class status.

Status Redefinition. A third source of role strain develops when social change brings about a shift in the ranking of a given position in the status hierarchy, such that an individual comes to be ranked higher or lower than previously. This may entail a redefinition of the rights and duties associated with the position and of the amount of prestige accorded to it. Yet individuals occupying the position may be unwilling or incapable of altering their behavior in a manner consistent with the new definitions. Within an urban-industrial South, for instance, the old planter aristocracy finds its status deflated while the urban middle classes find their status inflated. Further, social change has brought about a new definition of the rights and status of Negroes in relation to those of whites.

Role strain often contributes to a state of tension within individuals. Profound transformations in a society's social and economic structure contribute to social maladjustment and malfunctioning, breeding a state of social unrest and dissatisfaction. People may experience anxiety, frustration, bewilderment, and tension—in a word, "discontent." The accumulated social and psychological effect may be a chronic, ubiquitous disturbance that seems to acquire an existence of its own and that the victim cannot trace to its source. Under such circumstances, people typically search for some level of stability. They become susceptible to social movements that give promise of providing them with a satisfactory life. For many Negroes the protest movement has fulfilled this function, whereas for many whites the segregationist movement has met a similar need. In the former case, the effort is directed toward realizing new, meaningful standards for behavior in keeping with an equalitarian order; in the latter case, the effort is directed toward realizing meaningful, satisfactory standards through reinstating the standards of an earlier period.[22]

PROGRESS IN DESEGREGATION

In essence we have noted that social change is an inescapable fact of social existence. Dominant-minority relations are continuously changing, never completely static. The rate of change, however, varies a good deal from one period to another. At times change proceeds slowly, hardly discernible from one generation to the next; at still other times change may be relatively rapid. It is this latter situation that

[22] For an extended discussion of these matters see James W. Vander Zanden, *Race Relations in Transition: The Segregation Crisis within the South* (New York: Random House, 1965).

has characterized American racial and ethnic patterns in recent years. Segregated institutions have been progressively undermined by a wide variety of forces.   Indeed, the pace of change has quickened in the face of recent judicial rulings and new civil rights' legislation. Table 16 summarizes our nation's major civil rights laws. Let us now turn to an examination of some recent desegregation trends.

TABLE 16

Major Civil Rights' Laws

Fourteenth Amendment. This amendment to the Constitution, adopted in 1868, declares that all persons born or naturalized in the United States are citizens, and provides that, if Congress chooses, a state's representation in Congress may be reduced if some citizens are denied the right to vote.

Fifteenth Amendment. This amendment, adopted in 1870, declares that "the right of the citizens of the United States to vote shall not be denied or abridged by the United States or by any state on account of race, color, or previous condition of servitude."

Legislation, 1865–1875. Of the many laws passed in this decade, six major laws survive, the others either struck down by Supreme Court decisions or repealed by Congress. These six laws restate the right of all citizens to vote regardless of race. Attempts to deprive anyone of any Constitutional right, interpreted as including voting, are made federal crimes, and guilty persons are also made liable for civil damage suits.

Hatch Act of 1939. Although not strictly a civil rights' law, this act makes it a crime to threaten, intimidate, or coerce voters in a federal election.

Civil Rights Act of 1957. This statute gives the Attorney General of the United States the power to enter court suits to protect the voting rights of any citizen in any election—federal, state, or local. A Civil Rights Commission was created and given subpoena powers to investigate violations of voting rights in any election.

Civil Rights Act of 1960. This statute makes defiance of court orders in voting cases a federal crime, requires preservation of all voting records for 22 months to prevent local officials from destroying registration forms and applications (these records are then available for court cases), and authorizes federal courts to appoint referees to see that qualified Negroes are allowed to register and vote should local registrars balk or resign to avoid complying with court orders.

Twenty-fourth Amendment. This amendment to the Constitution, adopted in 1964, abolishes the payment of poll taxes as a requirement for voting in federal elections.

Civil Rights Act of 1964. The voting rights section of this act applies to federal elections only. It provides that the same standards must be used in registering all voters; minor errors in applications cannot be used to disqualify registrants; a sixth-grade education is proof of literacy for voting purposes unless election officials can prove otherwise in court; literacy tests must be given in writing, with copies available to applicants; and a three-judge federal court must be impaneled to hear any case in which the Attorney General of the United States charges voting discrimination, with right of direct appeal to the U.S. Supreme Court.

The statute prohibits discrimination or refusal of service on account of race in hotels, motels, restaurants, gasoline stations, and places of amusement if their operations affect interstate commerce or if their discrimination "is supported by state action"; requires that Negroes have equal access to, and treatment in, publicly owned or operated facilities such as parks, stadiums, and swimming pools; empowers the Attorney General of the United States to bring school desegregation suits; and authorizes the use of federal technical and financial aid to assist school districts in desegregation.

The act further provides that no person shall be subjected to racial discrimination in any program receiving federal aid, and directs federal agencies to take steps against discrimination, including—as a last resort, and after hearings—withholding of federal funds from state or local agencies that discriminate. It bans discrimination by employers or unions with 100 or more employees or members the first year the act is effective, reducing over four years from 100 or more to 25 or more. And the statute permits the Attorney General of the United States to intervene in suits filed by private persons complaining that they have been denied rights guaranteed to them by the Fourteenth Amendment.

Civil Rights Act of 1965. This act extends some of the provisions of the 1964 statute to cover state and local as well as federal elections, and simplifies the intricate time-consuming judicial procedures required for enforcing present voting laws.

Education: The South

In public elementary and secondary schools within the South, compliance with the Supreme Court's 1954 desegregation decision has tended to follow geographical lines. The northern-tier, or border, states (Delaware, Kentucky, Maryland, Missouri, Oklahoma, and West Virginia) and the District of Columbia have most nearly complied. In the next ring of states, or the mid-South (Virginia, North Carolina, Tennessee, Florida, Texas, and Arkansas), compliance has often been "token." Desegregation has occurred, but the number of Negroes admitted to previously all-white schools has generally been quite limited. In the Deep South (South Carolina, Georgia, Alabama, Mississippi, and Louisiana), desegregation has encountered the greatest resistance and made the least progress.

The end of the school year in May 1965 found 380,054 Negroes attending schools with whites, or 10.9 per cent of the region's Negro students. The District of Columbia and the border states of Delaware, Kentucky, Maryland, Missouri, Oklahoma, and West Virginia accounted for 82.6 per cent (313,919) of the region's desegregated Negro students.[23] The situation is summarized in Table 17. Many school officials believe that the Civil Rights Act of 1964 will promote faster and more complete desegregation than that accomplished by the federal courts in the previous decade. Vice-President Hubert H. Humphrey, in charge of coordinating the Johnson Administration's civil rights activities, has bluntly told segregating school districts that if they do not comply with the act they not only face a loss of federal funds but legal action to bring about desegregation:

In reality the choice is simply this: to continue receiving federal aid and to desegregate anyway. A school district cannot escape the constitutional

[23] *Southern School News*, 11, June, 1965.

TABLE 17

School Segregation-Desegregation Status, May, 1965

	School Districts			Enrollment		In Desegregated Districts		Negroes in Schools with Whites	
	Total	With Negroes and Whites in Same District	Deseg.	White	Negro	White	Negro	No.	%
Alabama	118	118	9	549,593 **	293,426 **	131,241 **	87,457 **	101	.034
Arkansas	411	220	24	333,630 †	114,651 †	93,072	28,943	930	.811
Florida	67	67	22	1,014,920	247,475	817,842	175,969	6,612	2.67
Georgia	196	180	12	686,761	334,126	200,127	133,454	1,337	.400
Louisiana	67	67	3	472,923 *	313,314 *	63,591	88,677	3,581	1.14
Mississippi	163	163	4	299,748	279,106	34,620	21,929	57	.020
North Carolina	170	170	86	828,638	349,282	555,997	207,551	4,963	1.42
South Carolina	108	108	18	371,921	260,667	173,833	96,196	265	.102
Tennessee	152	141	65	724,327	173,673	475,877	136,936	9,289	5.35
Texas	1,379	862	450 *	2,086,752 *	344,312 *	1,600,000 *	245,000 *	27,000 *	7.84
Virginia	130	127	81	736,017	233,070	600,000 *	200,000 *	12,000 *	5.15
TOTAL	2,961	2,223	774	8,105,230	2,943,102	4,746,200	1,422,112	66,135	2.25
Delaware	79	45	45	83,164	19,367	78,942	14,064	12,051	62.2
District of Columbia	1	1	1	17,487	123,906	17,487	123,906	106,578	86.0
Kentucky	204	165	165	607,522	55,215	540,000 *	55,215	37,585	68.1
Maryland	24	23	23	566,375	169,207	561,300	169,207	86,205	50.9
Missouri	1,056	212 *	203 *	818,000 *	104,000 *	NA	95,000 *	44,000 *	42.3
Oklahoma	1,090	321	211	555,000 *	45,000 *	334,000 *	38,000 *	14,000 *	31.1
West Virginia	55	54	54	426,500	21,300	426,500 *	21,300	13,500 *	63.4
BORDER	2,509	821	702	3,074,048	537,995	1,958,229 ††	516,692	313,919	58.3
REGION	5,470	3,044	1,476	11,179,278	3,481,097	6,704,429 ††	1,938,804	380,054	10.9

* Estimated.   ** 1963–64.   † 1962–63.   †† Missouri not included.
SOURCE: Southern Education Reporting Service, June, 1965.

471

mandate to desegregate merely by rejecting all federal financial assistance. Those districts which do not meet the constitutional requirements will be subject to desegregation suits brought by the Department of Justice.[24]

By the end of the 1964–1965 school year, 133 of the previously all-white public colleges and universities in the South had desegregated, leaving 48 that had not declared a policy of non-discrimination. However, Negro enrollment in these institutions constituted only one per cent of the total. The American Council on Education observes:

Overall, the traditionally white institutions of higher education in the South play only a relatively minor role in the education of Negro undergraduates within their region. The gains that have been made over the past ten years in many cases represent important vindications of Constitutional rights, but they have had comparatively little practical effect in expanding opportunities for the great part of Negro youth. Even as the pace of integration in these institutions speeds up and as they approach a position of racial equity in their admissions policies, indications are that they will continue to provide only limited opportunities for Negroes. There are several factors that will make this so:

In the rising competition for college admission, Negro youth from segregated and frequently inferior public schools will tend to fare poorly against better prepared white applicants.

Economically, with average Negro family income in the South 48 percent of white family income, some predominantly white institutions, especially the private ones, may be financially beyond the reach of many talented, but disadvantaged Negro youth.

Many Negro students and parents will wish to avoid the tensions and social limitations of an overwhelmingly white milieu.

As a matter of simple equity it is vitally important that all institutions of higher education in the United States today open their doors to all qualified applicants on an equal basis. But the removal of procedural obstacles to equality of opportunity offers little expectation of that goal becoming a quick reality. Until such time as predominantly white colleges and universities in the South decide to offer "opportunity for equality," which would of necessity embrace the concept of "compensatory education," they will maintain their relatively minor role in the undergraduate education of southern Negroes.[25]

In point of fact, these observations also hold true in large measure for northern colleges and universities.

Education: The North

The situation with regard to school segregation in the North and West is characterized by the Federal Civil Rights Commission in these terms:

[24] A May 20, 1965, speech in New York.
[25] American Council on Education, "The Negro and Higher Education," *Expanding Opportunities*, 1 (1964), 3. By permission.

With rare exceptions such segregation as there has been in the North and West has been a matter of practice *without explicit legal sanction.* In some instances, nonetheless, official action has contributed to or caused segregation. Where this is true, a denial of equal protection may exist. . . .

Segregation in the public schools of the urban North and West results to a large extent from the familiar system of neighborhood schools in combination with residential concentrations of minority groups. These "ghettos" were not explicitly created by law. They arose largely because of the inability of minority-group members to find housing elsewhere. That is why the resulting segregation in schools is generally called *de facto,* to distinguish it from *de jure,* segregation.[26]

To combat patterns of de facto school segregation, a number of methods have been proposed including pairing systems, gerrymandering, and "busing." Let us examine each of these methods in turn. The *pairing* plan apparently was first adopted in Princeton, New Jersey, and soon after in a number of cities elsewhere in the country, including, on a limited basis, New York City. Where there are two nearby schools, one serving a white community and the other an adjacent Negro community, the two schools are placed in a common zone, one to serve children in grades one through three, and the other to serve children in the higher elementary grades. The plan has the advantage over other methods of keeping all the children in the new common zone together on the same basis, without the onus of some children being regarded as "belonging" to the school and others coming in from the "outside." The pairing method, however, is seldom feasible with senior high schools, since they are usually geographically far apart, have few grades that can be split, and offer courses that are taught across grade levels. Moreover, the plan offers little promise of success in sprawling, densely populated cities in which sections of immense ghetto areas are remote from white schools.[27]

Gerrymandering involves the changing of geographic boundary lines in such a manner that school zones have a maximum of heterogeneity of population. Just as schools were often previously gerrymandered to keep school populations homogeneous (all-white or all-Negro), gerrymandering now would be used for realizing desegregation. This method, however, also has a number of disadvantages. It exposes the school board and superintendent to constant political pressure for the purpose of revising the school zone lines or of granting permits for in-

---

[26] The U.S. Commission on Civil Rights Report, 1961, *Book 2, Education,* 99–100.

[27] Arnold Rose, *De Facto School Segregation* (New York: The National Conference of Christians and Jews, 1964), 38–39; and Kenneth B. Clark, *Dark Ghetto* (New York: Harper & Row, 1965), 114.

dividual exceptions in assigning students to a given school. And like the pairing plan, it is feasible only when Negro residential districts are geographically close to white residential districts; it can scarcely be used for those sections of Negro districts in large cities that are remote from white areas or are separated from the latter by political boundaries (e.g., separately incorporated suburbs).[28]

"*Busing*" entails the transportation of students by bus outside their neighborhood to schools where the other race predominates. A number of problems, however, are associated with bus transfer plans. First, it would add an additional expense to school budgets, already mounting rapidly because of the "baby bulge"—the increase in the birth rate during World War II and the post-war years. Second, it involves the complete abandonment of the principle of the neighborhood school. Third, it necessarily involves setting a racial quota for each school, or for the school system as a whole, a device that has questionable constitutional legality.[29] We have noted the limitations associated with plans for pairing, gerrymandering, and busing. Obviously, the "ultimate solution" to the "hard-core" problem of racial imbalance in schools is residential desegregation.

Urban Negro Population Growth and School Desegregation

The decades of the 1940's, 1950's, and 1960's have witnessed the most explosive growth of urban population in our nation's history. Even more striking has been the growth in the Negro population in urban centers. The Negro population of New York City rose from 9.2 per cent of the total in 1950 to 14 per cent in 1960; in Chicago, from 14 per cent to 22.9 per cent; in Philadelphia, from 18.3 per cent to 26.4 per cent; in Detroit, from 16.4 per cent to 28.9 per cent; in Los Angeles, from 10.7 per cent to 13.5 per cent; in Baltimore, from 23.8 per cent to 34.8 per cent; and in Washington, D.C., from 35.4 per cent to 53.9 per cent. The increase in the enrollment of Negro children in the public schools has been even more dramatic. In the decade 1950–1960, the trend has been for the enrollment of Negro children in the public schools in many cities to double, while the enrollment of whites either declined or increased only slightly. Many cities no longer keep statistics on the racial membership of schoolchildren, but figures are available for a number of large cities. The enrollment of Negro children in the public schools of Baltimore rose from 34.6 per cent of the total in 1950 to 51.4 per cent in 1960; in Washington, D.C., from 50.6 per cent to 79.5 per cent; and in Atlanta, from 31.8 per cent to 44.7 per cent.

[28] Rose, *op. cit.*, 39–41.
[29] *Ibid.*, 18–19, and 41–44.

This rather sudden and dramatic increase in the enrollment of Negro pupils has had a number of consequences for desegregation. Schools generally are located centrally to the residential population they serve. Desegregation tends to occur most rapidly in areas on the periphery of white neighborhoods into which Negro families are moving. Once the process has begun, generally within a period of a few years, the racial composition of the neighborhood changes, and so does that of the school. Schools frequently go through a process of segregation, desegregation, and then resegregation—from white to mixed to Negro.[30] Indeed, within our nation's large cities, the trend toward de facto segregation is accelerating.

Employment

A 1962 survey by the Department of Labor points to the general improvement in the occupational position of Negroes since 1940. The percentage gain of Negro males and females is higher than that of whites in all the non-farm occupations above the laborers' level except among Negro males in the professional, technical, and kindred workers category, where the overall increase of both groups is similar. Table 18 (page 476) reflects these gains. Nevertheless, the Federal Commission on Civil Rights noted in 1961 that, "despite a dramatic increase in types of employment available to Negroes during the past twenty years, the mass of Negro workers are still confined largely to the less skilled jobs." This pattern still prevails. The report also points to the fact that Negro concentration in the ranks of the unskilled and semi-skilled has made Negroes especially vulnerable to unemployment. The rate of unemployment for Negroes generally runs about twice that of the white population. Technical change and automation promise to intensify the problem of unemployment among Negro workers in the years ahead.

In early 1961, the late President Kennedy created by executive order the President's Committee on Equal Employment Opportunity. Under its terms the Committee was given the twin responsibilities of realizing equal employment opportunity in federal and federal-contract employment. The Committee has very substantial powers over contractors on government contracts, including the powers of public disclosure, injunctive and criminal proceedings, contract cancellation, and black-listing. The heart of the order is the provisions which require compliance reports. The burden is placed on the employer to demonstrate his compliance, rather than on the complaining employee or applicant.

[30] Clifton R. Jones, "Urban Negro Population Growth Influences Desegregation Rate," *Southern School News*, 9, June, 1962.

TABLE 18

Distribution of Employed Persons by Major Occupation Group, Color, and Sex, April, 1940, and April, 1962

Major occupation group and sex	Number (thousands)		Per Cent			
	White	Non-white	White		Nonwhite	
	1962		1940	1962	1940	1962
Males						
Total	40,104	4,079	100.0	100.0	100.0	100.0
Professional, technical, and kindred workers	4,924	181	5.9	12.3	1.9	4.4
Managers, officials, and proprietors, except farm	6,119	157	10.6	15.3	1.6	3.8
Clerical and kindred workers	2,891	255	7.1	7.2	1.2	6.2
Sales workers	2,576	65	6.7	6.4	.9	1.6
Craftsmen, foremen, and kindred workers	7,982	367	15.5	19.9	4.4	9.0
Operatives and kindred workers	7,497	968	18.8	18.7	12.2	23.7
Laborers, except farm and mine	2,352	895	7.5	5.9	20.5	21.9
Service workers, except private household	2,305	600	5.8	5.7	12.4	14.7
Private household workers	27	22	.2	.1	2.9	.5
Farmers and farm managers	2,379	221	14.0	5.9	21.3	5.4
Farm laborers and foremen	1,052	349	6.8	2.6	19.9	8.6
Occupation not reported			1.0		.7	
Females						
Total	19,914	2,727	100.0	100.0	100.0	100.0
Professional, technical, and kindred workers	2,740	201	14.3	13.8	4.3	7.4
Managers, officials, and proprietors, except farm	1,103	45	4.3	5.5	.8	1.7
Clerical and kindred workers	6,669	279	24.6	33.5	1.0	10.2
Sales workers	1,625	61	8.0	8.2	.6	2.2
Craftsmen, foremen, and kindred workers	220	18	1.2	1.1	.2	.7
Operatives and kindred workers	2,891	397	20.2	14.5	6.6	14.6
Laborers, except farm and mine	90	22	.9	.5	.9	.8
Service workers, except private household	2,752	613	11.3	13.8	10.5	22.5
Private household workers	1,259	1,016	10.8	6.3	58.0	37.3
Farmers and farm managers	130	7	1.2	.7	3.2	.3
Farm laborers and foremen	437	66	1.2	2.2	12.8	2.4
Occupation not reported			2.0		1.1	

NOTE. 1962 estimates are not completely comparable with 1940.

SOURCE: U.S. Department of Labor, *The Economic Situation of Negroes in the United States*, Bulletin S-3, Revised 1962 (Washington: U.S. Government Printing Office, 1962), 7.

The Kennedy and Johnson Administrations have actively undertaken to recruit and advance Negroes within the federal government. Although a survey in 1964 showed that 13.2 per cent of federal employees were Negro—slightly larger than the Negro proportion of the population—these were heavily concentrated in the lowest salary grades. In Grades GS-12 to GS-18, the highest salary grades, Negroes held only a little more than 1 per cent of the positions.

The Armed Services

With a few exceptions, the armed services of the United States practiced a policy of segregation until the post-World War II period. On July 26, 1948, President Truman issued an executive order calling upon the armed forces to put "into effect as rapidly as possible" a policy of desegregation. Two years earlier the Navy had initiated a policy of desegregation as a result of experiments with a number of desegregated ships during the war. On February 27, 1946, the Navy ordered that:

. . . all restrictions governing types of assignments for which Negro naval personnel are eligible are hereby lifted. Henceforth, they shall be eligible for all types of assignments in all ratings in all activities and all ships of the naval service. . . . In the utilization of housing, messing, and other facilities, no special or unusual provisions will be made for the accommodation of Negroes.

During World War II the racial policy of the Air Force was that of the parent Army—a 10 per cent restriction on Negro enlisted men, segregated units, and limited opportunities for advancement. On May 11, 1949, the Air Force initiated a new, non-discriminatory policy. Within six months' time, this new policy was in almost complete effect throughout the Air Force. In March 1950, the Army abolished the quota system limiting Negro enlistments to 10 per cent of total strength and in July 1951 eliminated segregation in its Far East Command in the Pacific, a product in part of an NAACP investigation of discriminatory practices against Negroes during the Korean War. It was not, however, until 1952 that desegregation was launched in a full-scale fashion among units in Europe and the United States. The Marine Corps was the last of the services to desegregate, the last of its two all-Negro units being integrated during 1952.

A 1963 report of the United States Commission on Civil Rights revealed that Negroes accounted for 11 per cent of the total personnel in the Army, 8 per cent in the Air Force, 7 per cent in the Marine Corps, and less than 5 per cent in the Navy. Negroes were found to constitute slightly more than 3 per cent of all Army officers in comparison with about 1 per cent in the Air Force, 0.3 per cent in the Navy, and 0.2 per cent in the Marines. The report noted that the Navy and Marines lag not only in number of Negro officers but also in the ranks they achieve.

Voting

In the period since World War II, Negro registration to vote in the South has climbed steadily, although gradually. In 1947 there were an estimated 595,000 registered Negro voters in the South; in 1952, 1,008,614; in 1958, 1,303,627; and in 1964, 2,174,200. The situation in the South at the time of the November 1964 election is reflected in Table 19. Federal action under recent civil rights legislation is pro-

TABLE 19

Southern Negro Voting Registration

State	Total Negro Voters as of 11/1/64	Increase Since 4/1/62	Per Cent of Eligible Negroes Registered	Per Cent of Eligible Whites Registered	Per Cent Negro of Total Registered Voters	Per Cent Negro of Total Voting Age Population
Alabama	111,000	42,700	23.0	70.7	10.4	26.2
Arkansas	105,000	36,000	54.4	71.7	14.6	18.4
Florida	300,000	117,500	63.7	84.0	12.0	15.2
Georgia	270,000	94,500	44.0	74.5	16.8	25.4
Louisiana	164,700	13,000	32.0	80.4	13.7	28.5
Mississippi	28,500	4,500	6.7	70.1	5.2	36.0
North Carolina	258,000	47,500	46.8	92.5	11.7	21.5
South Carolina	144,000	53,100	38.8	78.5	17.0	29.3
Tennessee	218,000	67,100	69.4	72.9	14.4	14.9
Texas	375,000	133,000	57.7	53.2	12.5	11.7
Virginia	200,000	89,900	45.7	55.9	16.0	18.8
Total	2,174,200	698,000	43.8	73.1	13.1	22.4

SOURCE: Testimony of Wiley A. Branton, director of the Southern Regional Council's Voter Education Project, before the United States Commission on Civil Rights.

gressively opening the door to Negro registration in the some 80 "hard-core" counties (of 1,107 counties in eleven southern states) where it has traditionally been impossible for Negroes to register and vote. Nonetheless, informal pressures still operate, especially in rural areas, to discourage Negro voter registration. In Tallahatchie County, Mississippi, for instance, where federal court injunctions have eliminated legal and procedural barriers to Negro registration, only about 200 of the 6,500 Negroes of voting age have registered. Observes one young Negro field hand in Tallahatchie County:

Maybe I could register and nothing would happen. Maybe my boss wouldn't fire me. Maybe no one would burn my house, throw me in the river or shoot through my door. Maybe. But I expect they would, so I haven't registered and don't intend to.[31]

In contrast, Negroes in large urban communities have in recent years generally encountered few if any obstacles to registration.

A continuing problem confronting civil rights forces in encouraging Negroes to register and vote has been political apathy stemming from such socioeconomic factors as low income, low educational attainment, and exclusion from many community services and activities. Matthews and Prothro, on the basis of their studies of Negro voting and registration, conclude:

. . . reformers should not expect miracles in their efforts, through political and legal means, to increase the size and effectiveness of the Negro vote in the South. The Negro registration rate is low, in rather large part, because of the social and economic characteristics of southerners—both Negro and white. These facts are not easily and quickly changed by law or political actions.[32]

Transportation

The segregation of Negroes in interstate travel has been under steady attack since the early 1940's. In a case decided in 1941, the Supreme Court held that Negroes could not be denied Pullman accommodations in railway travel. In June 1946, the Supreme Court ruled against segregation on interstate buses, and in the same year a federal court of appeals held unconstitutional the segregation of interstate Negro passengers by a railroad company. Several court actions, culminating in the Henderson decision of 1950, established the principle that a passenger, of whatever race, must be served without discrimination in dining cars of the railroads. Nevertheless, through manipulation, deception, and subterfuge, segregated practices often persisted even as late as 1954. On reserved-seat trains, the juggling of seat assignments according to the racial identity of the passenger was not uncommon.

The public-school decision of the Supreme Court in 1954 opened the way for further legal assaults upon segregated facilities. By the close of the 1950's, segregation still persisted on some carriers operating within intrastate lines and in the waiting rooms of many air, rail, and

[31] Kenneth G. Slocum, "Economic Threats Seen Persisting as a Barrier to Negro Vote in Dixie," *Wall Street Journal,* May 7, 1965.

[32] Donald R. Matthews and James W. Prothro, "Social and Economic Factors and Negro Voter Registration in the South," *American Political Science Review,* LVII (1963), 43.

bus terminals. However, court actions, boycotts, and at times voluntary policy have served to progressively end these practices. In 1956, segregation on Montgomery and Alabama public conveyances was held unconstitutional in a case growing out of the Montgomery bus boycott. Although bus desegregation remains a highly controversial issue in many southern communities, segregated seating on city buses is progressively coming to an end.

In a *Special Report* on waiting-room practices in twenty-one southern cities, issued in July, 1959, the Southern Regional Council concluded that "facilities in air line terminals are desegregated or rapidly being desegregated; that facilities in train stations are still largely segregated but are slowly becoming desegregated; that facilities in bus terminals are almost completely segregated." By January, 1962, the Department of Justice had secured written commitments from all rail lines serving the South to disallow segregation in all their terminals. After the "freedom rides" into the South in May, 1961, the Department of Justice petitioned the Interstate Commerce Commission for a regulation prohibiting any discrimination in interstate buses or bus terminals. The regulation was issued September 22 and became effective November 1, 1961. Compliance has been general, though not complete. The Department of Justice has moved quickly with legal suits against localities which prevent bus terminals from obeying. In many southern communities, "White" and "Negro" signs have come down over waiting rooms, but the waiting rooms remain partitioned, and Negroes and whites continue to segregate themselves in the traditional fashion.

Housing

Segregation in housing remains one of the most persistent areas of discrimination within American life. Racial discrimination in housing has taken many forms. Prior to 1948, the restrictive covenant constituted a widespread practice. Restrictive covenants are agreements between parties to the sale of real estate in which the purchaser agrees not to rent or sell his property to members of specified races, nationalities, or religions. In 1948 the Supreme Court held that restrictive covenants could not be enforced in courts of law; however, if the agreements are carried out by voluntary adherence to their terms, no violation of the Fourteenth Amendment is involved. Various practices have nevertheless operated to continue segregated housing: Mortgage lenders have commonly refused to make loans to Negroes in an area in which racial infiltration has occurred or is threatened; Negroes may be asked to pay more than the usual interest rates; building permits or the extension of utilities may be withheld from Negroes seeking to build in particular areas; real-estate brokers may refuse to show Negroes real estate in white neighborhoods; and club membership and various leasehold systems may be employed.

As of 1965, 18 states had adopted fair housing laws. These laws usually are directed at housing which is "publicly assisted" or "benefiting from public aid." In addition, laws in 12 states and in 35 cities cover some types of private housing as well. In some areas, fair housing laws have encountered strong opposition. Between 1963 and 1965, fair housing questions appeared on the ballot in local elections in Berkeley, California; Tacoma and Seattle, Washington; Detroit, Michigan; and Akron, Ohio; and in a statewide election in California. In every instance, civil rights forces lost. Probably the most stinging of these defeats for civil rights forces occurred in California where voters in 1964 adopted by a 2-to-1 margin a constitutional amendment voiding a fair housing law previously enacted by the state legislature. On the federal level, an executive order issued by the late President Kennedy in 1962 mainly affects *new* housing financed with federal aid through the Federal Housing Administration and the Veterans Administration. Critics contend, however, that this order has scarcely made a dent in housing discrimination and is applicable to less than 10 per cent of the nation's housing.

In Chapter 8, we noted that patterns of residential segregation are pronounced within American cities. Moreover, with the exception of two regions, the Northeast and West, residential segregation appears to be increasing within the United States. In our large central cities, Negro population continues to grow while white population declines. Meanwhile the suburbs, most of them segregated along racial lines, grow at a rapid rate. Within a generation, if present trends continue, several of our largest cities will have populations more than 50 per cent Negro. Hence, any strategic program for desegregation that fails to explore the full implications of facts such as these would be quite incomplete.

SUMMARY

In this chapter we have stressed that American patterns of dominant-minority relations have undergone continuous change. Although many Americans assume that race relations within the nation and the South have "always been that way," we have noted that this is simply not the case. Legalized segregation, for instance, is a relatively recent development of the late nineteenth and early twentieth centuries. Moreover, especially in recent years, formal segregation has been progressively challenged and undermined.

17

Toward Lessening Prejudice and Discrimination

We have seen that, through the years, American dominant-minority relations have undergone considerable change and alteration. Social institutions change not only through the operation of a vast number of impersonal and non-deliberative forces but because men may deliberately set out to change them. This has been the case as well with various patterns governing American ethnic, racial, and religious interaction. Prejudice and discrimination conflict with the assumptions underlying the American democratic creed, a creed stressing the dignity and worth of each individual and the right of each to enjoy equality and the privileges of liberty. Accordingly, a major social movement has arisen with the goal of bringing American minority practices into line with the democratic creed.

With the growing recognition that sociological findings can be applied in an effort to channel and change human behavior, sociologists have been increasingly called upon to contribute scientific knowledge that would be useful in realizing this goal. A value premise is of course implicit, namely, prejudice and discrimination are undesirable and should be combated. In response to these various demands, a body of sociological literature has emerged dealing with means by which democratic goals may be advanced. In this chapter our attention will be focused upon some of these findings.

SOME PRELIMINARY CONSIDERATIONS

Before proceeding with our consideration of techniques for combating prejudice and discrimination, it would be well to recognize the existence of a number of issues pertinent to a consideration of this sort. First, individuals and groups may display considerable diversity in the goals that they are pursuing. Some are oriented toward a "melting pot" approach in which the end desired is the fusion of the differing groups within one common American culture; others are directed toward an "Americanization" focus in which ethnic and racial minorities are asked to divest themselves of their distinctive traits and assume the ways of the dominant group; and still others favor an approach of cultural pluralism in which conformity would be realized in crucial areas but differences would be welcomed and tolerated in less essential areas. Sociology cannot answer the question as to which of these orientations is the most desirable—or, for that matter, if any of them are desirable. But it can shed light on the likely consequences of pursuing any one of them. This diversity in goals complicates the task of formulating an action approach for the lessening of discrimination and prejudice.

Second, as we have seen in our consideration of the sources of prejudice earlier in this book, social scientists are not necessarily in agreement on the causes of prejudice and discrimination. Some emphasize the economic or the power or the status factors; others, the cultural factor; still others, the ideological factor; while yet others stress various personality factors. By virtue of the great complexity of intergroup behavior and the multiplicity of factors involved, it is amply clear that an attack upon prejudice and discrimination must involve a many-sided approach. Accordingly, the matter is by no means simple. And, by virtue of their own predilections as well as the limited nature of our contemporary knowledge, social scientists are not necessarily in agreement as to how best to tackle the problem. Furthermore, our knowledge of the causes of prejudice furnishes us merely with cues for action. These cues or suggestions with regard to the methods best suited for lessening prejudice and discrimination need to be evaluated in their actual application by research.

Third, prejudice and discrimination are not the same phenomenon. It will be recalled that prejudice involves a state of mind whereas discrimination entails overt behavior. Attitudes and behavior are not to be equated.   A considerable gulf—even a conflict—may exist between the two.   Accordingly, one technique may be quite effective in combating prejudice but may be of little value in combating discrimination, and vice versa.   Education may be useful in altering attitudes, but the normative system dictating discrimination may continue to prevail.   Or discriminatory behavior may be punished via legal sanctions, and thus be minimized, yet prejudice may persist.

Fourth, prejudice and discrimination are not phenomena, as is sometimes implicitly assumed, that can be dealt with by focusing exclusively upon the dominant group.   While there is probably good foundation for placing emphasis upon changing the attitudes and behavior of dominant-group members, racial and ethnic patterns are in some measure reciprocal.   The antagonism between various racial and ethnic groups is not a one-way street in which the dominant group has a monopoly in adverse and negative feelings, ideas, and actions.   Accordingly, rounded action programs need to deal with both sides of the racial or ethnic equation.

This chapter will focus attention upon a number of strategies commonly suggested for combating prejudice and discrimination.   We will be particularly interested in considering evidence dealing with the effectiveness of these strategies.

PROPAGANDA

Propaganda in Combating Prejudice

For many people propaganda has gained a sinister connotation. They frequently equate propaganda with lies, deceit, and fraud. This view became especially prevalent during World War II, when propaganda was commonly identified with the hate and racist appeals of Nazi Germany.   More recently it has become associated with Communist and anti-American elements. However, as commonly used within the social sciences, the term has no necessary relation to truth or falsity.   It merely refers to a deliberate attempt to influence opinions or behavior to some predetermined end.[1]   Symbols are the vehicles by which propaganda is transmitted, be they written, printed, spoken, pictorial, or musical.

A major problem faced by those who would employ propaganda as a tool in fighting prejudice is the difficulty in reaching people who are not already in favor of the view it presents.   Communication research

---

[1] *Propaganda: How To Recognize It and Deal with It* (New York: Institute for Propaganda Analysis, Inc., 1938), 31.

has pointed up the fact that many people avoid points of view that are at odds with their own by simply not exposing themselves to such views. Those whom the propagandist would most like to influence by certain communications are often the least likely to be reached by them. People tend to listen only to ideas agreeing with their own opinions. It has been found, for example, that political propaganda within the United States which aims to win support from those who ordinarily give their allegiance to another party is usually unsuccessful. For one thing, Republicans, by and large, listen only to Republican speakers; Democrats expose themselves to Democratic speeches. A similar problem exists in the area of race relations. During World War II the government sponsored a weekly radio program, *Immigrants All, Americans All.* Each week the program dealt with the contribution of a specific nationality group within American life. Public-opinion research revealed that, when the program dealt with Italians, the great majority of listeners were Italians; when the Poles were presented, mostly people of Polish descent listened. Similarly, anti-prejudice propaganda is likely to reach a considerably smaller proportion of the prejudiced group than the non-prejudiced.

With the increasing role that motion pictures and television play in American recreational life, the potentialities for mass influence have been greatly enlarged. Accordingly, a number of studies have concerned themselves with the possible impact of these media upon racial and ethnic prejudice. The evidence suggests that motion pictures portraying an ethnic or racial group in adverse terms may function to increase prejudice. Peterson and Thurstone found, in their pioneer study of the phenomenon, that schoolchildren who saw *Birth of a Nation,* a film depicting Reconstruction from a white southern view, tended to exhibit a slight increase in prejudice toward Negroes.[2] On the other hand, a number of studies have revealed that movies with an anti-prejudice theme tend to reduce the expression of prejudice among those exposed to them.

Illustrative of these latter studies is Middleton's investigation of the impact of the movie *Gentleman's Agreement* upon the attitudes of a group of university students.[3] This film, which was first released to the public in 1947 and which received wide praise from critics, carries a strong message against anti-Semitic prejudice and sets forth an appeal for brotherhood, equality, and democracy. Middleton selected

[2] Ruth C. Peterson and L. L. Thurstone, *Motion Pictures and the Social Attitudes of Children* (New York: The Macmillan Co., 1933).

[3] Russell Middleton, "Ethnic Prejudice and Susceptibility to Persuasion," *American Sociological Review,* 25 (1960), 679–686.

an experimental group and a control group of students, the latter of which did not see the movie. Both groups completed an attitude questionnaire: the experimental group before and again after the movie; the control group before and again after the intervention of a comparable period of time. The control group was introduced into the study to check for any attitude changes that might result from the mere fact of taking the "test." It was conceivable that any changes noted in the attitudes of the experimental group after they had seen the film might be due not to the film but rather to the test itself. Thus the differences between the before and after scores of the experimental group might reflect not the influence of the movie but that of the intervening variable, the questionnaire administered the second time.

TABLE 20

Degree of Change in Expressed Anti-Semitism Following
the Showing of *Gentleman's Agreement*

Degree of Change in Anti-Semitism-Scale Scores	Experimental Group		Control Group	
	Number	Per Cent	Number	Per Cent
−11 or more	52	15.8	4	3.4
−4 through −10	112	34.0	27	23.3
No change or change of 3 points or less	112	34.0	49	42.3
+4 through +10	39	11.9	28	24.1
+11 or more	14	4.3	8	6.9
Total	329	100.0	116	100.0

Source: Russell Middleton, "Ethnic Prejudice and Susceptibility to Persuasion," *American Sociological Review*, 25 (1960), 682. By permission.

The results presented in Table 20 reflect the wisdom of having introduced the control group, as both the control and experimental groups displayed attitude changes. Nevertheless, the evidence strongly suggests that the film played a major role in reducing the expression of anti-Semitic prejudice. Subjects in the experimental group were five times more likely to display a reduction of eleven or more scale points than those in the control group. Reductions of four to ten scale points were also found to be more extensive among those in the experimental group. Yet the fact should not be overlooked that some 50 per cent of the individuals in the experimental group did not experience an appreciable diminution in expressed anti-Semitism; some even displayed an increase.

In connection with the use of anti-prejudice films, the question arises as to how well the effects of the film are retained over a period of time.

Our knowledge on this matter is still far from adequate. However, the evidence presently available suggests that there is usually a regression in attitudes—after the intervention of time, opinions tend to slip back toward the original view, but not all the way.[4] But such regression does not occur in all cases. Hovland, Lumsdaine, and Sheffield show that some opinion changes in the direction of the propagandist's position are larger after the lapse of time than immediately after the communication.[5] They refer to this as the "sleeper effect." They suggest that individuals may be suspicious of the motives of the propagandist and initially discount his position. Thus these individuals may give little or no evidence of an immediate change in their opinion. But with the passage of time they may remember and accept *what* was communicated although they may not remember *who* communicated it. Consequently they may be more inclined to agree with the position at a later date than immediately after it was presented.

The Evasion of Anti-prejudice Propaganda

The anti-prejudice propagandist faces a major task in confronting prejudiced individuals with his point of view. People are inclined to avoid communications that are contrary to their established beliefs. But what happens when prejudiced people are involuntarily confronted with anti-prejudice propaganda? It might be inferred that they would either fight the propaganda or give in to it. But often many people are unwilling to do either: They prefer to *evade* the implications of ideas opposed to their own. It is often much easier simply not to understand or to twist and to misinterpret a message than to defend oneself or to admit error. While educational level is related to the understanding of anti-prejudice communications, more people who are prejudiced are apt to misunderstand the message than comparably educated unprejudiced people.

Cooper and Jahoda [6] have assembled a convincing array of evidence which suggests techniques that prejudiced individuals may employ in order to avoid understanding anti-prejudice messages:

1. *Identification avoided—understanding "derailed"*: Individuals may undertake to extricate themselves from facing the implications of the message through misunderstanding the point of the communi-

[4] See, for example: Peterson and Thurstone, *op. cit.*

[5] Carl I. Hovland, Arthur A. Lumsdaine, and Fred D. Sheffield, *Experiments on Mass Communication* (Princeton, N.J.: Princeton University Press, 1949).

[6] Eunice Cooper and Marie Jahoda, "The Evasion of Propaganda: How Prejudiced People Respond to Anti-prejudice Propaganda," *The Journal of Psychology*, 23 (1947), 15–25.

cation. Although initially grasping the message, individuals may then disassociate themselves from it, and in the process lose the original understanding that they had. The process is reflected in a number of typical reactions to a series of cartoons lampooning a character dubbed Mr. Biggott. Mr. Biggott is depicted as a rather prudish figure with exaggerated anti-minority feelings. In one cartoon, Mr. Biggott, lying sick in bed, says to a somewhat startled doctor, "In case I should need a transfusion, doctor, I want to make certain I don't get anything but blue, sixth-generation American blood!" In another cartoon, Mr. Biggott says to a humble American Indian, "I'm sorry, Mr. Eaglefeather, but our company's policy is to employ 100 per cent Americans only!" The producers of the cartoons had hoped that the following process would occur: The prejudiced individual would see that Mr. Biggott's ideas about minorities were similar to his own, that Mr. Biggott was an absurd character, and that to have anti-minority ideas was to make one appear as ridiculous as Mr. Biggott. Presumably the individual would then reject his own prejudice in order to avoid identification with Mr. Biggott.

Yet a study of reactions to the cartoons showed quite a different result. Prejudiced individuals may first identify themselves with Mr. Biggott, as did one respondent who indicated, "I imagine he's a sour old bachelor. [laughing] I'm an old bachelor myself." He also appeared to be aware of Mr. Biggott's prejudices. But this did not end the matter. Criticism and disapproval of prejudice were implicit in the cartoons; Mr. Biggott had been made to appear ridiculous for holding such beliefs. Thus it was not uncommon for individuals to invent means by which to disassociate themselves from Mr. Biggott without necessarily surrendering their prejudice. Some people accomplished this task by making Mr. Biggott appear as an intellectual inferior, a Jew, a foreigner, a member of the lower class, etc. The net result was that they ended up losing the original understanding of the message. The "bachelor" in the above illustration finally concluded that the purpose of the cartoon was "to get the viewpoint of people to see if they coincide with the artist's idea of character and all." Clearly the issue of prejudice had become completely sidetracked.

2. *The message made invalid:* In other cases, individuals admitted understanding the message to a degree that did not permit their distortion of it. For them the process of disidentification often led to a more rationalized argument. They accepted the message on the surface but maintained the message was invalid for themselves. This was accomplished in one of two ways. Individuals might admit the general

principle but conclude that exceptions existed which entitled them to their prejudices. One cartoon concluded with a variant of the Golden Rule, "Live and let live." Prejudiced persons frequently expressed acceptance of the Golden Rule but would add, "But it's the Jews that don't let you live; they put themselves outside the rule." The second type of distortion involved an admission that the message was convincing in itself, but with the qualification that it did not contain a correct picture of usual life situations involving the minority group discussed. A case in point was a radio dramatization entitled *The Belgian Village*. In the story a Jewish couple in an occupied Belgian village were saved by the loyal support of the villagers who hid them from the Gestapo. The story was followed by an appeal for sympathy and tolerance toward the Jews. Many prejudiced individuals refused to admit the applicability of this dramatic story to other situations. They called it an "adventure story," "a war story," etc.

3. *Changing the frame of reference:* In some cases the perception of the prejudiced individuals was so colored by their prejudice that the message of the cartoon escaped them. They saw the issues that the cartoon presented in a frame of reference different from that which had been intended. One cartoon depicted a congressman who had native fascist, anti-minority views. He was shown in his office, interviewing an applicant who had with him a letter of recommendation saying that he had been in jail, had started race riots, and had smashed windows. The congressman was pleased and said, "Of course I can use you in my new party." Some prejudiced individuals imposed upon the cartoon their own ideology and made it appear that "bad politics" was the sole issue. One respondent observed, "It's about a strike . . . about trouble like strikes . . . He is starting a Communist Party." Still another, "It's a Jewish party that would help Jews get more power."

4. *The message is too difficult:* This type of evasion takes the same form as misunderstanding by unprejudiced people. Some individuals stated that "they didn't get the point." This was often due to the respondents' intellectual and educational limitations or to defects in the propaganda.

Boomerang Effects in Propaganda

It has been seen that individuals may consciously or unconsciously modify the stimuli they perceive from propaganda according to their own predispositions. Accordingly they may fail to understand the message contained in anti-prejudice propaganda. For somewhat similar reasons propaganda may "boomerang"—it may produce a result directly opposite to that intended by the propagandist. Instead of lessening prejudice, anti-prejudice propaganda may actually serve to promote it.[7]

Some psychologists, for instance, have suggested that there may be a boomerang effect in films showing cruelty against minority groups. Many prejudiced persons, far from being repelled, may actually be attracted by cruelty. Films depicting the persecution of minority-group victims may permit these prejudiced individuals to secure vicarious gratification for the very same sadistic impulses—in the process bringing hidden desires to the foreground.

Limits on the Effectiveness of Propaganda

It has been said that the impact of propaganda may be minimized through the tendency of individuals to avoid messages that are at odds with their own views; through a misunderstanding, twisting, and misinterpreting of the message; and through the operation of various boomerang effects. But there are still further limitations to the effectiveness of anti-prejudice propaganda. Evidence suggests that the impact of propaganda may be quite specific and that individuals often fail to carry the message over into other contexts. Allport tells of an insightful illustration of this principle. In the spring of 1951 the film *The Sound of Fury* was being shown in a Boston theater. The movie concluded with the clearly stated moral that conflicts can be solved only through patience and understanding, not through violence. The viewers, deeply moved by the dramatic story, applauded the moral. In the same program a newsreel was later shown in which the late Senator Robert Taft spoke on international relations. Taft made the identical point contained in the movie—conflict can be solved only through patience and understanding, not through violence. But the audience hissed him. Apparently the message had not carried over from one context to the next. People may alter their opinions within a very narrow area and fail to generalize these opinions to other areas.[8]

The impact of a single program may also be quite limited. Public-opinion experts stress that a single program may be relatively ineffective in reaching the public with a particular message. One program is not enough. A campaign is necessary. Several related programs often

[7] Eunice Cooper and Helen Dinerman, "Analysis of the Film 'Don't Be a Sucker': A Study in Communication," *Public Opinion Quarterly*, 15 (1951), 243–264.

[8] Gordon W. Allport, *The Nature of Prejudice* (Boston: Beacon Press, Inc., 1954), 493–494.

are capable of producing effects even greater than could be accounted for in terms of simple summation. Multiple exposure tends to produce a pyramiding stimulation.

Evidence likewise suggests that propaganda which serves to increase anxiety is ineffective propaganda. Janis and Feshbach found that, as the amount of fear-arousing material is increased, conformity to recommended actions tends to decrease.[9] Equivalent groups of high-school students were exposed to three different forms of communication on dental hygiene. The first group received a strong fear appeal, emphasizing the painful consequences of tooth decay and diseased gums; the second group received a more moderate appeal; and the third group received a minimal appeal that rarely alluded to the consequences of tooth neglect. The "strong" appeal aroused considerably greater fears and worry among the students concerning the condition of their teeth than did the "minimal" appeal. But the "strong" appeal failed to produce any significant change in dental-hygiene practices, whereas the "minimal" appeal produced an increase in such practices. Bettelheim and Janowitz came to somewhat similar conclusions in a study of anti-Semitic (pro-prejudice) propaganda. They found that anti-Semitic propaganda may reach its mark in the case of the insecure individual if it suggests actions that promise a decrease of insecurity, while simultaneously it does not arouse new anxiety.[10]

In conclusion, it appears that propaganda has a very limited direct effect in combating prejudice. This is not to suggest that there is no value in pro-democratic propaganda. Some authorities suggest that its effectiveness cannot be counted only in terms of winning the prejudiced over to a non-prejudiced view. Propaganda may strengthen the attitudes of those who are unprejudiced and make them less susceptible to pro-prejudice propaganda. Anti-prejudice propaganda may also give the impression to anti-Semites, segregationists, and others that public sentiment is against them. Accordingly, although continuing to hold their prejudiced attitudes, they may be less disposed to engage in discriminatory behavior.[11]

[9] Irving L. Janis and Seymour Feshbach, "Effects of Fear-arousing Communications," *Journal of Abnormal and Social Psychology*, 48 (1953), 78–92.

[10] Bruno Bettelheim and Morris Janowitz, "Reactions to Fascist Propaganda: A Pilot Study," *Public Opinion Quarterly*, 14 (1950), 53–60.

[11] For an overview review of the literature dealing with the impact of propaganda upon attitude change generally see Arthur R. Cohen, *Attitude Change and Social Influence* (New York: Basic Books, Inc., 1964); Bernard Berelson and Gary A. Steiner, *Human Behavior: An Inventory of Scientific Findings* (New York: Harcourt, Brace & World, Inc., 1964), Chapter 13; and Paul F. Secord and Carl W. Backman, *Social Psychology* (New York: McGraw-Hill Book Company, 1964), Chapters 3, 4, 5, and 6.

EDUCATION

"Give People the Facts!"

One of the prevalent assumptions underlying a good deal of the work in the area of intergroup relations is that prejudice will disappear if people are given the facts. The appeal to "education" as a cure-all for the most varied social problems is deeply rooted in the ideology of American life. Thus, within the setting of racial and ethnic relations, many intergroup workers believe that their primary task is to teach the facts about minority groups, and prejudice will be reduced. This view assumes that (1) people are predominantly rational beings and (2) prejudice is the product of ignorance. If people are rational and prejudice is due to "distorted stereotypes" and "warped social perception," then "correct" facts can be expected to change their hostile feelings. The naïveté of this view is apparent in terms of both the complexity of human behavior in general and prejudice in particular.

The assumption that education is a powerful cure-all for prejudice was one of the first premises within the field of minority relations to be subjected to the scrutiny of scientific investigation. Teachers in courses in race and minority relations were especially anxious to measure the impact of their courses upon their students' prejudices. The results were quite discouraging, especially as many of the teachers were highly motivated to curb prejudice. On the whole the studies coming out during the late 1920's and the 1930's generally revealed that education at best had negligible effects. By 1948, R. M. MacIver could conclude in his survey of strategies useful in combating prejudice, "All we can claim for instruction of a purely factual kind is that it tends to mitigate some of the more extreme expressions of prejudice." [12]

Today specialists in race relations tend to take a rather dim view of the effectiveness of anti-prejudice education. It suffers from many of the same problems as those of anti-prejudice propaganda. Individuals selectively perceive and interpret "facts" and protect themselves against facts they do not wish to believe.

Experimental evidence indicates that people most readily learn materials with which they agree. When given the experimental task of learning statements, individuals who favored segregation learned plausible prosegregation statements and implausible antisegregation statements much more readily than they did plausible antisegregation

[12] R. M. MacIver, *The More Perfect Union* (New York: The Macmillan Co., 1948), 222.

and implausible prosegregation statements. Individuals opposed to segregation showed the corresponding reverse tendencies.[13]

Still another limitation of education is its failure to penetrate beyond the level of verbal expression to overt conduct, i.e., to become translated into nondiscriminatory behavior. It is axiomatic that in learning situations rhetorical exhortations have little chance of success when they are in battle against actual behavior patterns. For example, a child will not tend to be honest because his father tells him to be (although he may mouth honest platitudes) if the same father is constantly engaged in dishonest practices himself.

Prejudice and Level of Education

Education is commonly looked upon in the United States as a source of liberation—as a means of freeing people from narrowness and provincialism. Since education stresses rational processes, it is often assumed that it causes people to control or reject the irrational and absurd. From this, many have concluded that education has value in and of itself as an instrument for eliminating prejudice. On the surface these surmises appear to be borne out by past research. Researchers have consistently reported finding a negative correlation between prejudice of all kinds and amount of formal education, i.e., the higher the level of education, the less the prejudice.[14]

More recently Charles H. Stember raised some serious questions regarding the accuracy of these findings.[15] He observed that past studies tended to understate the prevalence of prejudice among the educated. His research lends support to the critics of attitudinal studies on race issues who allege that educated groups, because of intellectual sophistication, are reluctant to state prejudiced sentiment since it runs contrary to the norms of the American democratic creed. Stember suggested that the educated tend to express their prejudices more subtly. When responding on attitude tests, they are capable of recognizing and avoiding the trap set with rather obviously biased clichés. Nevertheless, in substance they may agree with the prejudiced position.[16]

[13] E. E. Jones and R. Kohler, "The Effects of Plausibility on the Learning of Controversial Statements," *Journal of Abnormal and Social Psychology,* LVII (1958), 315–320.

[14] J. Harding, "Prejudice and Ethnic Relations," in G. Lindzey, ed., *Handbook of Social Psychology* (Reading, Mass.: Addison-Wesley Publishing Co., Inc., 1954), II, 1039.

[15] Charles H. Stember, *Education and Attitude Change* (New York: Institute of Human Relations Press, 1961).

[16] Also see: James W. Vander Zanden, "Voting on Segregationist Referenda," *The Public Opinion Quarterly,* 25 (1961), 92–105.

Stember assembled a number of studies of prejudice that had been conducted over the past several years and reanalyzed the data with appropriate controls. He found that the better educated differed from the less educated in (1) their beliefs and perceptions concerning minorities, (2) their attitudes toward discrimination, and (3) their acceptance of personal relationships with minority groups. In terms of beliefs and perceptions of minorities, the better educated were more likely than the less educated to give credence to certain anti-Jewish stereotypes: that Jews are a threat to the country, that many of them are Communists and racketeers, and that they are less willing than non-Jews to serve in the armed forces. On the other hand, the better educated were less likely to believe that Jews are unscrupulous in business, dishonest in public office, and too powerful or too demanding. Thus, although the less educated appear more likely to hold *traditional* stereotypes, the better educated may hold certain highly charged and derogatory stereotypes of minority groups.

Discrimination as a matter of policy or institutional practice appeared to be less acceptable to the educated than to the less educated, in terms of such issues as systematic job discrimination, school desegregation, desegregation of public transportation, admission of refugees to the United States, and acceptability of a Jewish candidate for the presidency. However, in terms of *informal* discrimination, it appears that the educated do not take as strong a position as they do on more formal discrimination. A similar, more definite picture appears with regard to issues of personal acceptance. The better educated are more inclined to accept casual relationships with minority-group members, but they appear less willing to accept contacts that verge on the more intimate aspects of life. Thus one study revealed that persons of the middle educational level are more likely than others to reject Negroes as guests in their homes.

Stember concluded that the impact of education is limited: "Its chief effect is to reduce traditional provincialism—to counteract the notion that members of minorities are strange creatures with exotic ways, and to diminish fear of casual personal contact. But the limits of acceptance are sharply drawn; while legal equality is supported, full social participation is not." [17]

Robin M. Williams, Jr., in his summary of the findings of Cornell sociologists, came to somewhat similar conclusions as Stember. He noted that the better educated tend to have more complex attitudes on issues since they have access to more facts, to divergent opinions, and to more subtle distinctions. Better educated people—in contrast

[17] Stember, *op. cit.*, 171.

with the less educated—are inclined to react to a more differentiated
social world. Their prejudice, when it exists, may in some ways be
harder, colder, more polite and more thoroughly buttressed by rationalizations, but it is less likely to be global, diffuse, and all-or-none in
character.[18] However, in terms of some types of behavior, education
appears to play no part, for example, it is not associated with willingness to have a member of one's family marry a Jew.[19] Hence, the
relationship between education and prejudice and between education
and discrimination is quite complex.

CONTACT

Interracial Contact and Prejudice

"Bring differing racial and ethnic groups into contact and their prejudices will wither away." This counsel is manifest in a good many
current activities to combat prejudice and discrimination. It assumes
that contact makes for intergroup friendliness. The simplified argument runs as follows: People in their daily lives are creatures of habit.
They more or less continually follow a beaten path—a path that leads
from home to work, then back home, then to a lodge meeting, back
home, on Sundays to church and back, and occasionally on a visit to
relatives and friends. Accordingly, people are exposed to few new
social environments and few contacts with people of other racial and
ethnic groups. Their lives are limited and they lack real experience
with members of minority groups. But this does not prevent them
from forming stereotypes and impressions about these groups. If
people with differing racial and ethnic origins are brought together,
their stereotypes and impressions will be challenged. They will see
that the minority groups are not in fact the people of the stereotypes.
They will then tend to give up their prejudices and engage in harmonious interaction.

In its more sophisticated expression this view suggests that segregation serves to promote distance and a lack of contact. Whites see
Negroes living under conditions in which the latter are assigned inferior positions. It is not too difficult for the whites to conclude that
Negroes are inferior and undesirable. Segregation thus operates to
reinforce prejudice. By the same token, segregation serves to limit
white opportunities for interacting with Negroes of similar status. The
net effect is that it shields whites from having to check their prejudiced

[18] Robin M. Williams, Jr., *Strangers Next Door* (Englewood Cliffs, N.J.:
Prentice-Hall, Inc., 1964), 374–375.
[19] *Ibid.*, 56.

beliefs against reality. Contact, on the other hand, if on a basis of equal status and under favorable circumstances, would function to re-move both these types of support for prejudice. The fact of sustained interracial contact itself challenges the assumption that segregation is right and inevitable, especially if such contact is sanctioned by an individual or organization that carries authority and prestige, e.g., an employer. Furthermore, provided the contact is sufficiently close, the white is faced with the necessity of somehow reconciling his own ob-servations and experiences with his previously held stereotypes.[20]

In and of itself, however, contact does not necessarily dispel preju-dice. In fact, superficial contact is often a means by which prejudice is increased. A white having casual contact with a Negro generally comes to the relationship possessing a well-formulated set of stereo-types. To a considerable extent the Negro he "sees" is the Negro of his stereotypes. Stereotypes sensitize individuals to signs that serve to confirm and reinforce the stereotyping process. The net result is that perception tends to be selective and distorted. What in other relation-ships may be taken to be a normal lack of knowledge on a matter is taken by many a white in interaction with a Negro to be evidence of Negro "ignorance" and "inferiority." Similarly, what may be other-wise taken to be appropriate aggressiveness is taken by many a gentile in interaction with a Jew to be evidence of Jewish "assertiveness" and "unbridled gall." When a Negro or Jew engages in behavior remotely resembling the Negro or Jewish stereotype, the incident "registers." [21]

When interacting with a member of a racial or ethnic minority, one has a tendency consciously or unconsciously to scrutinize the individual for behavior conforming to the stereotypes of his particular group—one is sensitized to the traits. In interaction with others, the trait would be overlooked or dismissed as a trait unique to the individual and not characteristic of a larger racial or ethnic group. Casual interaction does not usually lead to a challenging of stereotypes, as the contact is not sufficiently intimate to permit people to assess other individuals in a way other than the traditional manner based upon racial identity. Thus the character of the individual as a unique human does not necessarily penetrate the armor of the racial mythology.

Intergroup contact may fail to challenge stereotypes for still another reason—*exemption.* Occasionally an individual meets a member of

---

[20] In this connection see: Daniel M. Wilner, Rosabelle Price Walkley, and Stuart W. Cook, *Human Relations in Interracial Housing* (Minneapolis: University of Minnesota Press, 1955), 4–5.

[21] In this regard see Alice B. Riddleberger and Annabelle B. Motz, "Prejudice and Perception," *American Journal of Sociology,* 62 (1957), 498–503.

another racial or ethnic group who fails to fit that group's stereotype. But instead of altering or eliminating the stereotype, he makes the individual an exception—for example, a Negro who is remarkably energetic, hardworking, and self-disciplined may be excluded from the stereotype as an exception, as "not really" a Negro. Through exemption, an individual may retain his prejudice while circumventing discriminatory patterns for some particular purpose, for example, accepting a particular Negro in his social clique.[22]

There is also substantial agreement among social scientists that contact between members of groups holding very different social and economic status is likely to increase prejudice, whereas contact between groups having the same or a nearly equal status tends to reduce prejudice.[23] When white middle-class individuals have contact with only lower-class Negroes, the stereotype that Negroes are dirty, dumb, and shiftless is reinforced. Class prejudices are readily activated in unequal-status contacts. An individual's perception of an ethnic or racial group may be influenced by his class antagonisms. On the other hand, individuals possessing a common status tend to share common values and goals. Experiences along equal-status lines are more likely to run counter to the stereotypes of prejudiced individuals than are those that run along unequal status lines.

Evidence Relating to the Effects of Interracial Contact

A number of studies are suggestive of the effects of contact upon prejudice. One of the earliest studies employing a carefully planned experimental methodology was undertaken by F. Tredwell Smith.[24] Smith administered a battery of tests measuring attitudes toward Negroes to 345 students at Columbia University's Teachers College. Without reference to the test or experimental purpose, he obtained by invitation an experimental group of 46 students. A control group of 46 students closely paired with the experimental group by individual scores and approximately comparable in age, sex, and geographical origin was likewise secured. The experimental group was exposed to a four-day tour of Harlem, in which the members of the group visited with Negroes, saw a good deal of the community, and heard a number of lectures. Ten days later the original 345 students were retested, and Smith found that the control group (the group that had not been

---

[22] Williams, op. cit., 40–41 and 337–345.

[23] Gordon W. Allport and Bernard M. Kramer, "Some Roots of Prejudice," Journal of Psychology, 22 (1946), 9–39.

[24] F. Tredwell Smith, An Experiment in Modifying Attitudes Toward the Negro (New York: Teachers College, Bureau of Publications, Columbia University, 1943).

exposed to the tour) had not altered its attitudes. The experimental group, on the other hand, experienced a marked increase in favorable attitudes toward Negroes. Eleven months later, 40 members of the experimental group were retested, and most of them continued to display significantly more favorable attitudes than they had on the first test. Twenty-five members maintained all their original gains or increased them. The study lends support to the hypothesis that contact which provides for some depth in interaction will function to reduce prejudice.

A number of limitations must be noted, however, in appraising the Smith study. First, the Negroes involved in the contact situation tended to be of relatively high status—equal or superior to the social status of the participants. Second, the contact situation was "artificially" created—the participants did not *happen* to engage in contact with Negroes; rather the interaction was arranged. It is conceivable that group norms arose in this special setting in which prejudiced attitudes were defined as inappropriate and that it was this factor and not necessarily the contact which accounted for the attitude changes. In the "real" world such favoring circumstances might well be the exception. Third, the study measured changes in responses to verbal tests—attitude changes—and not behavior changes. To what extent such changes in attitudes were implemented in intergroup interaction is not known.

An interesting wartime illustration of the impact of interracial contact upon prejudice is afforded by the experiences of American troops in Europe in the closing months of World War II. Although it was the policy of the Army to have no mixed units of white and Negro soldiers, circumstances developed that militarily dictated that several Negro rifle platoons be attached to white companies. Although a certain amount of segregation remained in the arrangement, it did serve to bring the two races into close contact on a more or less equal footing. An agency of the U.S. War Department subsequently undertook a survey of 1,710 enlisted men for the purpose of determining white attitudes on the innovation. The men were asked, "Some Army divisions have companies which include Negro and white platoons. How would you feel about it if your outfit was set up something like that?" The responses to the question revealed that white troops who were more closely associated with Negro soldiers were more favorably disposed to the arrangement than those who had lacked such combat experience. The percentage of white enlisted men who indicated a strong dislike of the arrangement were distributed within the various types of contact situations as follows:

Field force units which did not have colored platoons in white companies
(1,450 cases)   62%
Men in the same division, but not in the same regiment, as colored troops
(112 cases)   24%
Men in the same regiment, but not in the same company, as colored troops
(68 cases)   20%
Men in a company with a Negro platoon (80 cases)   7% [25]

Evidence indicates, however, that these favorable attitudes in the more desegregated units were to some degree confined to Negro soldiers as *combat* companions. Many soldiers noted that relationships were better in combat than they were in the garrison situation. The investigators make this concluding observation:

. . . relationships in combat could be regarded as working relationships rather than social relationships. More precisely, they could be confined more narrowly to a functionally specific basis than could the contacts involved in community living. In particular, the combat situation was exclusively masculine, and issues of social relationships between men and women did not appear as they did in garrison. Far from being a "test case" in ordinary Negro-white relations, the combat setting may be regarded as a special case making for good relationships, for the sense of common danger and common obligation was high, the need for unity was at a maximum, and there was great consciousness of shared experience of an intensely emotional kind.[26]

Evidence from Interracial Housing

With the growth of public housing since World War II, a particularly fruitful laboratory has been provided social scientists for examining the impact of interracial apartment living upon racial attitudes and behavior. Interracial housing affords an unusual opportunity for intimate and prolonged contact between individuals of differing racial groups. Two studies have appeared, utilizing sophisticated methodological procedure, that have supplied valuable insights on interracial residential contact. The first study, by Deutsch and Collins, investigated four low-rent public-housing projects—two integrated interracial projects in New York City and two similar segregated biracial projects in Newark—for the purpose of determining the social and psychological effects of the two occupancy patterns upon race relations and attitudes.[27] In the two integrated housing projects, Negro and white

[25] Information and Education Division, U.S. War Department, "Opinions About Negro Infantry Platoons in White Companies of Seven Divisions," in Theodore M. Newcomb and E. L. Hartley, eds., *Readings in Social Psychology*, rev. ed. (New York: Holt, Rinehart & Winston, Inc., 1952), 502–506.

[26] Shirley A. Star, Robin M. Williams, Jr., and Samuel A. Stouffer, "Negro Infantry Platoons," in Harold Proshansky and Bernard Seidenberg, eds., *Basic Studies in Social Psychology* (New York: Holt, Rinehart & Winston, 1965), 683.

[27] Morton Deutsch and Mary Evans Collins, *Interracial Housing* (Minneapolis: University of Minnesota Press, 1951).

families were assigned to apartment buildings regardless of race; in the two segregated biracial projects, Negroes were assigned to buildings that were area-separated from those of the whites. Deutsch and Collins selected the projects in the two cities so as to match them in terms of Negro-white ratios and other relevant variables. Some 100 white housewives were intensively interviewed in each of the four projects.

Deutsch and Collins found marked differences between the two types of projects in racial relations and attitudes. Compared with the segregated biracial projects, the integrated interracial projects were characterized by

1. A higher incidence of friendly, neighborly contacts between the two racial groups
2. A social atmosphere more favorable to friendly interracial associations
3. An ascription of a higher incidence of favorable stereotypes and a lower incidence of unfavorable stereotypes to Negroes
4. A higher rate of acceptance of the interracial character of the project and of recommendations for an integrated occupancy pattern for future projects
5. A far greater proportion of those who reported they had undergone favorable attitude change toward Negroes as a consequence of living in the project

Similarly, as indicated in Table 21, the white residents in the integrated projects were more likely than those in the area-segregated projects to hold Negroes in the project in high "esteem." Considerably more of the housewives in the integrated projects made such statements as: "They're very nice; they have beautiful homes"; "A lot of them are nicer than the white people; when I was sick the lady across the hall came in and cooked soup"; "They're just the same as the white people here; except for color, there's no difference." On the other hand, many more women in the segregated projects made statements which implied Negroes were inferior.[28]

A second study confirmed the major findings of the Deutsch and Collins research. Employing a comparable research design, Wilner, Walkley, and Cook were able to verify the findings in a setting outside the metropolitan area of New York City.[29] The authors concluded that, the more intimate the contact between Negroes and whites, the more favorable the attitudes of the whites toward Negroes. Similarly, the more favorable the perceived social climate surrounding interracial

[28] *Ibid.*, 82–83.
[29] Wilner, Walkley, and Cook, *op. cit.*

TABLE 21

Percentages of Housewives Who Hold the Negroes in the Project
in Different Degrees of Esteem

Degree of Esteem	Integrated Interracial Projects, %		Segregated Bi-racial Projects, %	
	Koaltown	Sacktown	Bakerville	Frankville
Respect Negroes living in the project; view them as equal to white people in the project	72	79	43	39
Feel Negroes are inferior; characterize them as low-class, childish, primitive, etc.	11	13	37	35
Neutral or ambivalent	17	8	20	26

SOURCE: Morton Deutsch and Mary Evans Collins, *Interracial Housing* (Minneapolis: University of Minnesota Press, 1951), 82. By permission.

contact, the more favorable were the white attitudes. These studies suggest that contact, under the favorable conditions prevailing in the interracial public-housing projects, provides concrete experiences that test the white resident's pre-existing stereotypes and encourage the development of friendly relations and feelings. Works replicated these studies among Negro tenants in a single housing project that was partly desegregated and partly segregated and found that anti-white prejudice is also diminished through intimate and interracial contacts between status equals.[30]

Some Limits to the Effectiveness of Interracial Contact

Interracial contact has a number of limitations as a means of combating prejudice. One of the most frequently encountered of these limitations is the failure of many individuals to generalize their favorable attitudes toward particular minority-group members so as to include the whole minority group. In this way the experiences acquired within one specific context are not carried over into other interracial situations. Harding and Hogrefe investigated the attitudes of white department-store employees toward their Negro co-workers, for the purpose of determining whether or not the attitudes acquired within

[30] Ernest Works, "The Prejudice-Interaction Hypothesis from the Point of View of the Negro Minority Group," *American Journal of Sociology*, 67 (1961), 47–52.

the one context would carry over into others.[31] For purposes of the study, they secured the cooperation of two leading eastern department stores that had been employing Negroes in white-collar jobs. The study revealed that equal status job contact produced a large increase in the willingness of the white employees to work with Negroes on an equal basis. The white employees were also willing to continue this pattern in a new situation of the same type. But there was no significant change in their willingness to accept Negroes in *other* relationships—in sitting next to Negroes in buses or trains, sitting down with a Negro in a lunchroom or cafeteria, living in a new apartment building or housing project which contained both white and Negro families, and having a Negro for a personal friend. Thus the white employees tended to "compartmentalize" their experience of working with Negroes and did not generalize the experience to other situations involving Negroes.

A not too different kind of situation has prevailed in the coal fields of McDowell County, West Virginia. Within the coal mines the Negro and white miners work together as equals in a spirit of general goodwill. In a number of instances, Negroes work in superior status positions as motormen on mine lorries or as company physicians without any friction. The community outside the mine, however, constitutes an environment in which the spirit of integration dissolves and the white miners again become members of a superior caste. The boundary line between the two communities is the mouth of the mine. Here management assists the miners in recognizing their entrance into the outside world by providing separate baths and locker rooms. About one-fifth of the white miners behave in a consistently prejudiced fashion and another one-fifth in a consistently unprejudiced fashion both inside and outside the mine. The remaining three-fifths tend to shift their role and status upon passing from the mouth of the mine into the world-at-large. Thus, many miners handle their dual role and status through a certain degree of fractionation or segmentation of their personality. In this manner they escape the necessity of instituting a total reorientation in their attitudes and behavior toward Negroes.[32]

---

[31] John Harding and Russell Hogrefe, "Attitudes of White Department Store Employees Toward Negro Co-workers," *Journal of Social Issues,* 8 (1952), 18–28.

[32] Ralph D. Minard, "Race Relationships in the Pocahontas Coal Fields," *Journal of Social Issues,* 8 (1952), 29–44. For still other studies pointing to the fact of compartmentalizing and the failure to generalize to other situations see R. H. Gundlach, "Effects of On-the-Job Experiences with Negroes upon Racial Attitudes of White Workers in Union Shops," *Psychological Reports,* 2 (1956), 67–77; and E. B. Palmore, "The Introduction of Negroes into White Departments," *Human Organization,* 14 (1955), 27–28.

Deutsch and Collins and Wilner, Walkley, and Cook, in their respective studies of the effects of interracial housing upon interracial attitudes and behavior, found some evidence for the generalization of attitudes.[33] Nevertheless, there was a considerable gulf between the favorableness of attitudes toward the specific Negroes in the contact situation and the acceptance of the particular interracial experience, on the one hand, and the generalizing of favorable attitudes to Negroes as a group, on the other. Generalization to other non-white minorities was not significant.

When intergroup contacts do occur, the less prejudiced individuals, on the average, are most likely to develop those close associations and friendships that contribute to a further reduction of prejudice.[34] Nevertheless, even for those individuals who are highly prejudiced, intergroup contact on the whole tends to reduce prejudice.[35] Some of the conditions under which contacts between dominant- and minority-group members are most likely to result in a considerable change in the behavior and the attitudes of the prejudiced person seem to be:

1. The contact takes place between status equals.
2. The behavior of the objects of prejudice is at variance or does not conform with the beliefs of the prejudiced individual, e.g., the Negroes with whom the prejudiced has contact are not "lazy," "ignorant," "delinquent," etc.[36]
3. The contact is of sufficient duration and intimacy to sufficiently challenge the stereotypes of the prejudiced individual.[37]
4. The prevailing social norms dictate that prejudiced attitudes and behavior are inappropriate.
5. The members of the differing racial groups within the contact situation have a common interest, goal, or task that is the focus of the interaction.
6. The individuals involved are personally secure and have low aggressive needs.[38]
7. Positive support for change is forthcoming from reference groups outside the specific contact situation.[39]

[33] Deutsch and Collins, op. cit., 103; and Wilner, Walkley, and Cook, op. cit., 69.

[34] Williams, op. cit., 201.

[35] Ibid., Chapter 7.

[36] Deutsch and Collins, op. cit., 128.

[37] See I. N. Brophy, "The Luxury of Anti-Negro Prejudice," Public Opinion Quarterly, 9 (1946), 456–466.

[38] J. Allen Williams, Jr., "Reduction of Tension through Intergroup Contact: A Social Psychological Interpretation," Pacific Sociological Review, 7 (1964), 82.

[39] Ibid.

PSYCHOLOGICAL TECHNIQUES

Since prejudice is often deeply embedded in the functioning of the entire personality, some authorities insist that an effective program for combating prejudice must aim at reducing or rechanneling those elements within the personality that feed racial and ethnic antipathies. Focusing their attention upon the deep-seated anxieties, insecurities, and fears that frequently underlie and accompany prejudiced personalities, these specialists take a rather dim view of efforts that fail to come to grips with an individual's basic personality structure. The authors of *The Authoritarian Personality* are representative of this orientation. They suggest that educational approaches which employ rational arguments cannot be expected to have deep or lasting effects upon a phenomenon that is as intrinsically irrational in nature as is prejudice. Similarly, appeals to sympathy may backfire when they are directed toward people one of whose deepest fears is that they might be identified with weakness or suffering. Nor can closer contact with members of minority groups be expected to influence an individual when his basic personality organization impairs or even precludes him from establishing a deep or meaningful relationship with anybody, regardless of racial or ethnic membership.[40] What then can be done about prejudice? Adorno and his associates suggest that, ideally, psychological techniques need to be employed to change personality.[41]

Individual Therapy

Individual therapy is oriented toward the readjustment of individuals who are psychologically maladjusted. By means of therapy secured from a psychiatrist or trained counselor, an individual may undertake to cope with his emotional problems—his feelings of insecurity, inadequacy, and anxiety—and to find socially acceptable outlets for the expression of his needs. Clearly, individuals do not seek out a therapist for the express purpose of altering their attitudes toward minorities. However, in the process of gaining insight into the nature of their problems, their emotional need for racial prejudice and discriminatory behavior may be lessened. As they become increasingly capable of dealing with their problems and feelings on a mature, objective level, they will have less need to find immature, artificial outlets.

The man who, to compensate for his inner feelings of weakness and inadequacy, obsessively and relentlessly strives for a sense of power

---

[40] T. W. Adorno *et al.*, *The Authoritarian Personality* (New York: Harper & Row, 1950), 973.
[41] *Ibid.*, 974.

may desperately clutch at his membership in the dominant group (e.g., the white race) to provide himself with a sense of strength. To give himself the power he otherwise lacks, he may incessantly search out opportunities to vilify and humiliate Jews and Negroes. In the process he seeks to reassure himself, "I am powerful." The minority, being weak and helpless, gives him a sense of contrasting strength. But the power he realizes is not genuine, since it is external and not rooted in the personality itself. He has to constantly reassert and demonstrate his power in order to prove to himself and the world that he really is powerful. Accordingly, his involvement in racist behavior becomes a preoccupation. Through therapy he may come to realize an inner sense of strength and adequacy. As a result he will have less need to find some external, artificial bulwark for his sense of well-being.

As a means of combating prejudice, individual therapy has a number of obvious limitations. First, therapy usually takes a considerable period of time and arduous work, often encompassing more than two hundred hours distributed over a number of years. Second, the number of trained therapists is small and even inadequate for dealing with the number of individuals who might benefit from such services. Third, highly prejudiced individuals are frequently characterized by personality types that are relatively unresponsive to psychotherapeutic methods. And finally, available empirical evidence raises serious doubts whether short-term individual psychotherapy (averaging three times weekly for nine weeks) contributes much in the way of prejudice reduction,[42] while little is known on the impact of long-term individual psychotherapy.

Group Therapy

Group therapy has aims similar to those of individual therapy, but the former is organized about groups of maladjusted individuals. With the growing recognition of the role that groups play in the lives of human beings, increasing use has been made of therapy in a group situation. It offers a means by which individuals may overcome their feelings of isolation and rejection, and gain a sense of acceptance by other persons. Within the group, patients can find helpful new experiences and new insights that enable them to cope better with their problems and difficulties. Through the free, uninhibited atmosphere fostered within the group by the psychiatrist or counselor, individuals are led to break down barriers and to realize corrective emotional experiences.

[42] David Pearl, "Psychotherapy and Ethnocentrism," *Journal of Abnormal and Social Psychology*, 50 (1955), 227–229.

The indirect effects of group therapy upon prejudice are suggested in a study by Morris and Natalie Haimowitz.[43] As part of a training program in counseling, at the University of Chicago, twenty-four individuals participated over a six-week period in thirty-five hours of group therapy in which they discussed their personal problems. These individuals ranged in age from twenty-five to sixty, had a master's degree or its equivalent in psychology, and had at least three years of professional experience. Before and after the six-week training period, the members were administered the Bogardus social-distance test.

On the basis of the Bogardus test results, the individuals were classified as "friendly," "mildly hostile," or "strongly hostile" in their attitudes toward minority groups. The study revealed that, after the group-therapy experience, the number of individuals rated as "friendly" increased. The group designated "hostile" remained fairly constant. The changes that occurred took place among those who came to the therapy experience mildly hostile. There were no cases where a friendly individual became mildly or strongly hostile on the second test, and only one individual who had been strongly hostile on the first test displayed a shift on the second.

The authors suggest that the higher incidence of those classified as "friendly" after group therapy lends confirmation to the hypothesis that, with improved adjustment, hostility to minority groups declines. Through therapy, the individual becomes better able to cope directly and effectively with the source of his frustrations. He becomes less hostile in his reactions and has less need to displace whatever tensions do emerge. The authors conjecture that, for those individuals who are strongly hostile to minorities, prejudice assumes a more salient and basic part of their personalities. Since the therapeutic experience was relatively brief, it was not of sufficient duration to have an impact upon more deeply rooted patterns.

Two years later a follow-up study was made of seventeen of the twenty-four subjects in the study. The changes that had occurred between the pre- and post-therapy tests were maintained. Furthermore, there was a continued, though smaller, change during the succeeding two year period toward greater friendliness toward minorities. Yet evidence is also suggestive that individuals who were classified as "friendly" on the pre-test were not necessarily "tolerant" personalities. Although friendly toward racial and ethnic minorities, some of them indicated marked hostility toward Ku Klux Klansmen, Nazis, and Fascists. Thus one individual classified as "friendly" indicated that

---

[43] Morris L. Haimowitz and Natalie Reader Haimowitz, "Reducing Ethnic Hostility Through Psychotherapy," *Journal of Social Psychology*, 31 (1950), 231–241.

anyone associated with the Ku Klux Klan should be hung without trial. It appears that, in some cases of friendly disposition toward minorities, deep-lying hostility may be diverted into other channels.

Pearl, in still another study, comes to somewhat less optimistic conclusions regarding the value of group psychotherapy as an instrument for combating prejudice. He administered a series of attitude and personality scales (the same questionnaires utilized in *The Authoritarian Personality* studies) to 21 male, neurotic, hospitalized patients before and after psychotherapeutic treatment. A control group of seven randomly selected male tuberculous patients was given the same scales but not exposed to psychotherapeutic treatment. Pearl found no significant difference between the effectiveness of brief group therapy (12 hours of treatment) and intensive group therapy (60 hours of treatment) in reducing prejudice. But of even greater significance, the magnitude of the changes realized through group therapy was generally too small to be of great practical importance:

> Statistically significant shifts which yet leave highly ethnocentric individuals with strong ethnocentric ideology do not support the hope held by some that group psychotherapy may become a major technique for combating group prejudice. It would appear rather, that while psychotherapeutic treatment may play a role in any program designed to reduce ethnocentrism, it is not a panacea and must be utilized in conjunction with other approaches.[44]

Perhaps we shall want to reserve our judgment on the effectiveness of group psychotherapy, in light of the conflicting evidence, until such time as more research is available.

Prejudice Reduction Through Self-Insight

Katz and his associates have undertaken experiments dealing with the reduction of prejudice through the arousal of self-insight.[45] They suggest that an individual's attitudes (including prejudice) reflect deep motivational roots. Hence, to modify an individual's attitudes, Katz argues, it is necessary to produce self-insight into the associated underlying motivations. His experiments show that individuals holding negative stereotypes toward Negroes—and otherwise resistant to positive information about Negroes—have modified their attitudes

---

[44] Pearl, *op. cit.*, 229.

[45] D. Katz, C. McClintock, and I. Sarnoff, "The Measurement of Ego Defense as Related to Attitude Change," *Journal of Personality*, 25 (1957), 465–474; D. Katz, I. Sarnoff, and C. McClintock, "Ego-Defense and Attitude Change," *Human Relations*, 9 (1956), 27–45; I. Sarnoff and D. Katz, "The Motivational Basis of Attitude Change," *Journal of Abnormal and Social Psychology*, 49 (1954), 115–124; and E. Stotland, D. Katz, and M. Patchen, "The Reduction of Prejudice through the Arousal of Self-Insight," *Journal of Personality*, 27 (1959), 507–531.

through materials that give them insight into the dynamics of prejudice.

In the experiments, subjects read a case history designed to give self-insight into the psychodynamics of prejudice. This is followed by a threefold approach: (1) self-activity or self-involvement in which subjects are asked to order in logical sequence statements about the psychodynamics of prejudice; (2) the involvement of the subjects in making the materials that they read directly relevant to prejudice against Negroes; and (3) an appeal to the rationality and attitudinal self-consistency of the subjects. No significant changes occur immediately after the experiments but significant change does appear several weeks later. This fact is assumed to result from a "sleeper effect" associated with internal restructuring.

Catharsis

It is often of considerable value in therapy for individuals to express their true feelings freely and even explosively. Once having "blown their top" and expressed themselves vehemently and without inhibition, they may then be prepared to look at matters more objectively. Allport employed this procedure with effective results in an eight-hour course in race relations held for public officials.[46] As a result of a number of unpleasant instances of racial conflict, the police officers had been required to take the course. The fact that the course was compulsory was interpreted by the men as casting reflection upon their competence and fairness. Their feelings of injustice were compounded by their prejudices against various minority groups. By virtue of the tension that existed, instruction became impossible. The instruction provoked only a torrent of abuse, directed at the teacher and at minority groups. Members of the class complained, "Why does everyone pick on the police?" "We've never had any trouble. Why do we need this course?" "Why don't the Jews mind their business?"

The first six classes of the course were largely occupied with this kind of catharsis. Allport presented no counter-arguments and listened as sympathetically as possible to the hostile outbursts. The result was a "complacency shock":

In certain instances, to mix metaphors, the individual, given enough cathartic rope, proceeds to hang himself. He overdoes his stuff. He makes ridiculous statements. Then he subsides in confusion, his face red all over. He has convicted himself of gross exaggeration, one-sidedness, obvious injustice. Nor is it necessary for the leader to point out the limb where

[46] Gordon W. Allport, "Catharsis and the Reduction of Prejudice," *Journal of Social Issues*, 1 (1945), 1–8.

the luckless speaker dangles. It is more tactful not to do so. The speaker, having convicted himself of irrationality, finds himself both ashamed and deflated. Thus humbled, he is more ready to reconstruct his attitudes on a sounder line.

Catharsis does not cure prejudice, but it does serve to prepare the way for a less tense view of the situation.

THE LEGAL AND AUTHORITARIAN APPROACH

Can Laws Be Effective?

It is often said, "You cannot legislate against prejudice." This notion that laws are ineffective weapons against prejudice and discrimination is a frequently heard argument used against the enactment of various civil-rights measures. According to this assumption, laws must follow rather than precede social change and cannot by themselves change the norms of a society. The view was stated in classic fashion at the turn of the twentieth century by William Graham Sumner, a sociologist, who declared that "stateways [laws] cannot change folkways." Sumner believed that, when laws moved ahead of the customs or mores of the people, they were inevitably doomed to failure. The dismal failure of Prohibition in barring the manufacture, transportation, and sale of alcoholic beverages is commonly cited as proof of the position.

Although the argument against legislation sounds plausible, it is based upon a misunderstanding of the nature of laws and fails to distinguish between prejudice and discrimination. Laws can have little direct effect upon prejudice, since a state of mind—attitudes and feelings—is involved. But laws can prove effective weapons against overt acts of discrimination. Similarly, laws against murder and theft do not attempt to root out the desire to kill or steal; they seek to prevent these desires from becoming translated into overt acts. Laws are effective to the degree to which they act as deterrents to certain kinds of behavior, and therefore in part to the extent to which they are enforced. The fact that laws against murder and theft do not always succeed is no more evidence for the uselessness of such laws than is discrimination in employment evidence against fair-employment-practices acts. Many people feel that the fight against discrimination and segregation is more important than the fight against prejudiced attitudes and feelings. The former affect the right of an ethnic or racial minority to realize equality and freedom of opportunity. The latter may be considered a private matter.

Evidence on the Effectiveness of Laws

Probably one of the clearest instances of the effectiveness of authoritative methods in combating discrimination and segregation is the current undermining of southern Jim Crow institutions through legislative, executive, and judicial action. The federal government has undertaken a monumental project in the field of social engineering, and it is an unquestionable fact that it is succeeding. Although in some instances contributing to a higher incidence of interracial friction, federal action has compelled the South to alter its traditional patterns in the direction of desegregation. Similarly, desegregation in the nation's armed forces was realized through the authoritative intervention of a presidential executive order.

A study by Saenger and Gilbert provides insight into the impact that laws may have against discrimination.[47] The law in question was New York State's act against discrimination in job hiring. The study focused attention upon the reaction of customers to Negro sales personnel in establishments that had hired Negroes in response to the law. Since the law did not apply to customers, they could withdraw their trade from the integrated stores if they so desired. Saenger and Gilbert compared the attitudes of customers buying from Negro clerks with attitudes of customers buying from white clerks in a large New York department store. Trained interviewers were stationed near those sales counters where Negro and white clerks worked side-by-side. In this manner, customers who dealt with Negro clerks were distinguished from those dealing with neighboring white clerks. Both the customers of Negro clerks and those of white clerks were then followed out of the store and interviewed. Since the customers were not told that they had previously been observed, it was possible to compare their actual behavior with their attitudes.

In the interviews, the customers were asked to express their sentiments on the employment of Negro clerks. At least 20 per cent indicated that they would not buy in stores which hired them. Another 20 per cent gave limited approval provided Negro salesgirls were not used in departments handling food or clothing. The study revealed, however, that there was no relationship between what people said and what they did. No difference was found in prejudice between customers who had dealt with Negro clerks and customers who had dealt with white clerks. In both groups 38 per cent either disapproved of

<hr />

[47] Gerhart Saenger and E. Gilbert, "Customer Reactions to the Integration of Negro Sales Personnel," *International Journal of Opinion and Attitude Research,* 4 (1950), 57–76.

Negro clerks or wanted them excluded from some of the departments within the store. In fact, a number of women who had insisted a short time previously that they would not buy from Negroes were later observed buying from Negro clerks.

Saenger and Gilbert suggest a number of factors as contributing to the discrepancy between what people said and how they acted in relation to the Negro clerks. First, the prejudiced individual was caught in a conflict between two contradictory motivations: his prejudice on the one hand and his desire to shop where he found it most comfortable and convenient on the other. The individuals in the study tended to resolve the dilemma though acting contrary to their prejudice and completing their shopping as quickly and expediently as possible. Second, prejudiced individuals were caught in still another conflict: whether to follow the dictates of prejudice or whether to live up to America's democratic ideals. Either of these attitudes may be activated, depending upon the prejudiced individual's definition of the situation. Third, a desire to conform with prevailing public opinion may be uppermost in the individual's mind. He may prefer to translate his prejudice into overt action but, nevertheless, yield to local custom. The fact that Negroes were found in the stores as clerks tended to suggest to many individuals that the public approved of their presence. Individuals who are strongly prejudiced are often insecure and, accordingly, frequently have a deep need to conform. Thus, where they have the impression that others do not share their thinking, they are less likely to defend their prejudices and less likely to translate them into discriminatory behavior.

Killian, in his study of the adjustment of southern white migrants to life in Chicago, came to similar conclusions. Evidence gathered from employers and the migrants themselves revealed that southern whites were able to make a peaceful accommodation to the norms governing interracial situations within Chicago. Not only did they work in plants with Negroes, but they shared the same rest rooms and dressing rooms. The South continued as their principal reference group and they followed its practices of racial segregation when it was conveniently possible. When confronted with situations in which these ways could not be adhered to without personal sacrifice, they tended to make the necessary behavioral adjustments although attitude changes did not necessarily occur.[48]

Studies such as those we have cited show that what people do in intergroup situations seems to be almost independent of how they feel

[48] Lewis M. Killian, "The Effects of Southern White Workers on Race Relations in Northern Plants," *American Sociological Review*, 17 (1952), 327–331.

or what they think. The *social setting* appears to constitute the chief factor. As Allport notes, "Segregationists act like integrationists where social prescription requires; integrationists behave like segregationists when it is socially appropriate to do so." [49] Hence laws may play an important part in defining the social setting for individuals.

Two types of individuals appear to be particularly susceptible to the influence of anti-discriminatory laws: first, those who are themselves not prejudiced but who find it expedient or profitable to stand by silently or to give passive support to discrimination; second, those who are prejudiced but who are not prepared to pay a significant price for translating their attitudes into behavior, preferring instead the easier course of conformity. For these two groups, laws against discrimination frequently provide an impetus for overcoming previous patterns and for instituting non-discriminatory behavior; thus, the laws act as deterrents to discriminatory behavior. Taken together, these two groups probably make up a sizable majority of the population, the militant integrationists and militant segregationists representing smaller segments of the total population.

In evaluating the effectiveness of laws, we have stressed that they can play an important part in combating discrimination—overt behavior. But what about prejudice—a state of mind? The matter is by no means simple. As we have noted, at least in the short run, laws may have relatively little impact upon prejudice. Indeed, it is even conceivable that legally compelled desegregation may for a time intensify feelings of hostility and hence increase prejudice. Viewed from the long run, however, prejudice in some cases may be decreased. Evidence suggests that *specific* attitudes shape themselves to overt behavior. In considering intergroup contact, we observed that whites who actually work with Negroes, especially as equals, tend to develop favorable attitudes toward working with Negroes. Although this sentiment may not be generalized to other interracial situations, it nevertheless points to specific attitude change—to the lessening of prejudice in at least one sphere.

Some Limits to the Effectiveness of Law

In recent years, sociologists have increasingly come to recognize that laws can be effective instruments for reducing discrimination. But law, especially in a non-totalitarian society, is not all-powerful. Moreover, informal, indirect, subtle discrimination is much less susceptible to legal remedies than formal, direct, and blatant discrimination.

[49] Gordon W. Allport, "Prejudice: Is It Societal or Personal," *Journal of Social Issues,* 18 (1962), 123.

Frequently, civil rights legislation functions as a tool with an essentially negative character—it prescribes "thou shall nots." At still other times it may contribute to at best a "grudging acceptance" of minorities. Hence, although realizing desegregation, integration may remain a still distant goal. Accordingly, positive measures designed to promote intergroup goodwill are also called for.[50]

Laws are likely to be effective to the extent that they are enforced. But very often the victims of discrimination are ignorant of the laws or reluctant to make complaints under them, patterns most frequently encountered among those segments of minority groups most susceptible to discrimination, namely poorly educated, low-income groups.[51] The New York City "fair housing" ordinance is a case in point. New York City was the first community to enact a "fair housing" or "open occupancy" ordinance banning discrimination in the sale or rental of all housing except owner-occupied duplexes and rooms in private homes. Yet, the effect of the law appears to be limited. In the first three years of its operation, the New York City law adjusted slightly more than two hundred complaints to the satisfaction of the Negro complainant. While this indeed constitutes a gain, it is small when viewed in the perspective of New York's nearly one million Negroes. Most of the Negro complainants were middle-class Negroes in white-collar or professional occupations; lower-class Negroes, for whom the housing problem is perhaps most severe, hardly participated in the benefits of the open-occupancy law at all. And finally, nearly half of the complaints were from Negroes who already were living in areas that were predominantly white—Negroes who had already broken out of the ghetto.[52] It is perhaps somewhat unfair, however, to view a law's effectiveness in terms of the number of complainants benefiting from it. A good many landlords conceivably may have "fallen into line" with the law once it appeared on the books. These types of gains are difficult to measure.

SUMMARY

By virtue of the great complexity of intergroup behavior and the multiplicity of factors involved, it is clear that an attack upon prejudice and discrimination must involve a many-sided approach. Indeed,

[50] See Arthur Shostak, "Appeals from Discrimination in Federal Employment: A Case Study," *Social Forces*, 42 (1963), 174–178.

[51] Gerhart Saenger and Norma S. Gordon, "Influence of Discrimination on Minority Group Members in Its Relation to Attempts to Combat Discrimination," *Journal of Social Psychology*, 31 (1950), 95–120.

[52] Harold Goldblatt and Florence Cromien, "The Effective Reach of the Fair Housing Practices Law of the City of New York," *Social Problems*, 9 (1962), 365–370.

there appear to be no easy answers or quick solutions. If we consider our goal to be desegregation, the elimination of barriers, we are concerned mainly with social controls and institutional arrangements, in which case laws assume considerable importance. If we have integration as our goal, then the effectiveness of personal controls and the content of attitudes become central, in which case propaganda, education, contact, and psychological approaches (and under some circumstances laws) assume importance.

Bibliography

ACKERMAN, NATHAN W., and MARIE JAHODA. *Anti-Semitism and Emotional Disorder.* New York: Harper & Row, 1950.

ADAMS, R. *Intermarriage in Hawaii.* New York: The Macmillan Co., 1937.

ADORNO, T. W., ELSE FRENKEL-BRUNSWIK, DANIEL J. LEVINSON, and R. NEVITT SANFORD. *The Authoritarian Personality.* New York: Harper & Row, 1950.

ALLPORT, GORDON W. "Catharsis and the Reduction of Prejudice," *Journal of Social Issues,* 1 (1945), 1–8.

ALLPORT, GORDON W. *The Nature of Prejudice.* Boston: Beacon Press, Inc., 1954.

ALLPORT, GORDON W. "Prejudice: Is It Societal or Personal," *Journal of Social Issues,* 18 (1962), 120–134.

ALLPORT, GORDON W., and BERNARD M. KRAMER. "Some Roots of Prejudice," *Journal of Psychology,* 22 (1946), 9–39.

ALLPORT, GORDON W., and L. J. POSTMAN. "The Basic Psychology of Rumor," *Transactions of the New York Academy of Sciences,* Series II, 8 (1945), 61–81.

AMMONS, R. B. "Reactions in a Projective Doll-Play Interview of White Males Two to Six Years of Age to Differences in Skin Color and Facial Features," *The Journal of Genetic Psychology,* 76 (1950), 323–341.

ANTONOVSKY, AARON. "Toward a Refinement of the 'Marginal Man' Concept," *Social Forces,* 35 (1956), 57–62

ASHMORE, HARRY S. *The Negro and the Schools.* Chapel Hill: University of North Carolina Press, 1954.

BABCHUK, NICHOLAS, and RALPH V. THOMPSON. "The Voluntary Associations of Negroes," *American Sociological Review,* 27 (1962), 647–655.

BABOW, IRVING. "Discrimination in Places of Public Accommodation: Findings of the San Francisco Civil Rights Inventory," *Journal of Intergroup Relations,* 2 (1961), 332–341.

BACK, KURT W., and IDA HARPER SIMPSON. "The Dilemma of the Negro Professional," *Journal of Social Issues,* 20 (1964), 60–71.

515

BANKS, W. S. M., II. "The Rank Order of Sensitivity to Discriminations of Negroes in Columbus, Ohio," *American Sociological Review,* **15** (1950), 529–534.

BARBER, BERNARD. "Acculturation and Messianic Movements," *American Sociological Review,* **6** (1941), 663–669.

BARRON, MILTON L. "The Incidence of Jewish Intermarriage in Europe and America," *American Sociological Review,* **11** (1946), 6–13.

BARRON, MILTON L. *People Who Intermarry.* Syracuse, N.Y.: Syracuse University Press, 1948.

BARRON, MILTON L. "Research on Intermarriage: A Survey of Accomplishments and Prospects," *American Journal of Sociology,* **57** (1951), 249–255.

BARRON, MILTON L. *American Minorities.* New York: Alfred A. Knopf, Inc., 1957.

BARZUN, JACQUES. *The French Race: Theories of Its Origins and Their Social and Political Implications.* New York: Columbia University Press, 1932.

BARZUN, JACQUES. *Race: A Study in Modern Superstition.* New York: Harcourt, Brace & World, Inc., 1937.

BASS, BERNARD M. "Authoritarianism or Acquiescence," *Journal of Abnormal and Social Psychology,* **50** (1955), 616–623.

BEARD, CHARLES A. *An Economic Interpretation of the Constitution of the United States.* 2d ed. New York: The Macmillan Co., 1939.

BELL, DANIEL (ed.). *The New American Right.* New York: Criterion Books, 1955.

BELTH, N. C. (ed.). *Barriers.* New York: Friendly House Publishers, 1958.

BENDIX, REINHART, and SEYMOUR MARTIN LIPSET, eds., *Class, Status and Power.* New York: The Free Press of Glencoe, 1953.

BENEDICT, RUTH. *Race: Science and Politics.* New York: Modern Age Books, 1940.

BENOIT-SMULLYAN, S. "Status, Status Types, and Status Interrelations," *American Sociological Review,* **9** (1944), 151–161.

BERELSON, BERNARD, and PATRICIA J. SALTER. "Majority and Minority Americans: An Analysis of Magazine Fiction," *The Public Opinion Quarterly,* **X** (1946), 168–190.

BERELSON, BERNARD, and GARY A. STEINER. *Human Behavior: An Inventory of Scientific Findings.* New York: Harcourt, Brace & World, Inc., 1964.

BERKOWITZ, LEONARD. *Aggression: A Social Psychological Analysis.* New York: McGraw-Hill Book, Co., Inc., 1962.

BERREMAN, GERALD D. "Caste in India and the United States," *American Journal of Sociology,* **66** (1960), 120–127.

BERRY, BREWTON. *Race and Ethnic Relations.* 3d ed. Boston: Houghton Mifflin Co., 1965.

BERRY, BREWTON. *Almost White: A Study of Certain Racial Hybrids in the Eastern United States.* New York: The Macmillan Co., 1963.

BETTELHEIM, BRUNO, and MORRIS JANOWITZ. "Reactions to Fascist Propaganda: A Pilot Study," *The Public Opinion Quarterly,* **14** (1950), 53–60.

BETTELHEIM, BRUNO, and MORRIS JANOWITZ. *Social Change and Prejudice.* New York: The Free Press of Glencoe, Inc., 1964.

BETTELHEIM, BRUNO, MORRIS JANOWITZ, and E. A. SHILS. "A Study of the Social, Economic and Psychological Correlates of Intolerance Among Urban Veterans of

Enlisted Rank," *American Psychologist,* **2** (1947).

BIESANZ, JOHN, and LUKE M. SMITH. "Race Relations in Panama and the Canal Zone," *American Journal of Sociology,* **57** (1951), 7–14.

BLACK, PERCY, and RUTH DAVIDSON ATKINS. "Conformity Versus Prejudice as Exemplified in White-Negro Relations in the South: Some Methodological Considerations," *The Journal of Psychology,* **30** (1950), 109–121.

BLALOCK, H. M., JR. "Economic Discrimination and Negro Increase," *American Sociological Review,* **21** (1956), 584–588.

BLALOCK, H. M., JR. "A Power Analysis of Racial Discrimination," *Social Forces,* **39** (1960), 53–59.

BLAUSTEIN, ALBERT P., and CLARENCE C. FERGUSON, JR. *Desegregation and the Law.* New York: Random House, Inc., 1962.

BLOOD, ROBERT O., JR. "Discrimination without Prejudice," *Social Problems,* **3** (1955), 114–117.

BLOOM, LEONARD, and RUTH RIEMER. *Removal and Return.* Berkeley: University of California Press, 1949.

BLUMER, HERBERT. "Race Prejudice as a Sense of Group Position." In JITSUICHI MASUOKA and PRESTON VALIEN (eds.). *Race Relations.* Chapel Hill: University of North Carolina Press, 1961, 215–227.

BOGARDUS, EMORY S. *Immigration and Race Attitudes.* Boston: D. C. Heath & Co., 1928.

BOGARDUS, EMORY S. "Changes in Racial Distances," *International Journal of Opinion and Attitude Research,* **1** (1947).

BOGARDUS, EMORY S. "Stereotypes Versus Sociotypes," *Sociology and Social Research,* **34** (1950).

BOGARDUS, EMORY S. *Social Distance.* Yellow Springs, Ohio: Antioch Press, 1959.

BOGUE, DONALD J. "Population Distribution and Composition in the New South." In *The New South and Higher Education.* The Department of Records and Research, Tuskegee Institute, Tuskegee, Ala., 1954.

BOGUE, DONALD J. *The Population of the United States.* New York: The Free Press of Glencoe, 1959.

BONILLA, E. SEDA. "Social Structure and Race Relations," *Social Forces,* **40** (1961), 141–148.

BORINSKI, ERNST. "The Litigation Curve and The Litigation Filibuster in Civil Rights Cases," *Social Forces,* **37** (1958), 142–147.

BORRIE, W. D. *The Cultural Integration of Immigrants.* Paris: UNESCO, 1959.

BOSSARD, JAMES. "Nationality and Nativity as Factors in Marriage," *American Sociological Review,* **4** (1939), 792–798.

BOYD, WILLIAM C. *Genetics and the Races of Man.* Boston: Little Brown & Co., 1950.

BRAZZIEL, WILLIAM F. "Correlates of Southern Negro Personality," *Journal of Social Issues,* **20** (1964), 46–54.

BREED, WARREN. "Group Structure and Resistance to Desegregation in the Deep South," *Social Problems,* **10** (1962), 84–94.

BRINK, WILLIAM, and LOUIS HARRIS. *The Negro Revolution in America.* New York: Simon & Schuster, Inc., 1964.

BROOKOVER, WILBUR, and JOHN HOLLAND. "An Inquiry into the Meaning of Minority Group Attitude Expressions," *American Sociological Review,* **17** (1952), 196–202.

BROOM, LEONARD, HELEN P. BEEM, and VIRGINIA HARRIS. "Characteristics of 1,108 Petitioners for Change of Name," *American So-*

ciological Review **20** (1955), 33–39.

BROOM, LEONARD, and JOHN I. KITUSE. *The Managed Casualty: The Japanese-American Family in World War II.* Berkeley: University of California Press, 1956.

BROOM, LEONARD, and NORVAL D. GLENN. *Transformation of the Negro American.* New York: Harper & Row, Inc., 1965.

BROWN, ROGER W. "A Determinant of the Relationship Between Rigidity and Authoritarianism," *Journal of Abnormal and Social Psychology,* **48** (1953), 469–476.

BRUSSAT, WILLIAM K. "Incidental Findings on Urban Invasion," *American Sociological Review,* **16** (1951), 94–96.

BUGELSKI, B. R. "Assimilation Through Intermarriage," *Social Forces,* **40** (1961), 148–153.

BURGESS, M. ELAINE. *Negro Leadership in a Southern City.* Chapel Hill: University of North Carolina Press, 1962.

BURMA, JOHN H. "Humor as a Technique in Race Conflict," *American Sociological Review,* **11** (1946), 710–715.

BURMA, JOHN H. "Race Relations and Antidiscriminatory Legislation," *American Journal of Sociology,* **56** (1951), 416–423.

BURMA, JOHN H. "Research Note on the Measurement of Interracial Marriage," *American Journal of Sociology,* **57** (1952), 587–589.

BURMA, JOHN H. *Spanish-speaking Groups in the United States.* Durham, N.C.: Duke University Press, 1954.

BURMA, JOHN H. "Interethnic Marriage in Los Angeles, 1948–1959," *Social Forces,* **42** (1963), 156–165.

BURNS, W. HAYWOOD. *The Voices of Negro Protest in America.* New York: Oxford University Press, 1963.

BURROWS, EDWIN G. *Hawaiian Americans.* New Haven: Yale University Press, 1947.

CAHNMAN, WERNER J. "Socio-economic Causes of Antisemitism," *Social Problems,* **5** (1957), 21–29.

CAMPBELL, ERNEST Q., and THOMAS F. PETTIGREW. *Christians in Racial Crisis: A Study of the Little Rock Ministry.* Washington, D.C.: Public Affairs Press, 1959.

CAMPBELL, ERNEST Q. "Moral Discomfort and Racial Segregation: An Examination of the Myrdal Hypothesis," *Social Forces,* **39** (1961), 228–234.

CAMPISI, PAUL J. "Ethnic Family Patterns: The Italian Family in the United States," *American Journal of Sociology,* **LIII** (1948), 443–449.

CANTRIL, HADLEY. *The Psychology of Social Movements.* New York: John Wiley & Sons, Inc., 1941.

CARLETON, WILLIAM G. "The Second Reconstruction: An Analysis from the Deep South," *Antioch Review,* **XVIII** (1958).

CASH, W. J. *The Mind of the South.* New York: Doubleday & Co., Inc., 1954.

CASTLE, W. E. "Biological and Social Consequences of Race Crossing," *American Journal of Physical Anthropology,* **9** (1926), 145–156.

CASTLE, W. E. "Race Mixture and Physical Disharmonies," *Science,* **71** (1930), 603–606.

CHANCELLOR, LOREN, and THOMAS MONAHAN. "Religious Preference and Interreligious Mixtures in Marriages and Divorces in Iowa," *American Journal of Sociology,* **60** (1955), 233–239.

CHENG, C. K. "Assimilation in Hawaii and the Bid for Statehood," *Social Forces,* **30** (1951), 16–29.

CHENG, C. K. "A Study of Chinese Assimilation in Hawaii," *Social Forces*, **32** (1953), 163–167.

CHENG, C. K., and DOUGLAS, S. YAMAMURA. "Interracial Marriage and Divorce in Hawaii," *Social Forces*, **36** (1957).

CHENG, DAVID TE-CHAO. *Acculturation of the Chinese in the United States*. Philadephia: University of Pennsylvania, 1948.

CHILD, IRVIN L. *Italian or American?* New Haven: Yale University Press, 1943.

CHRISTIE, RICHARD, and MARIE JAHODA (eds.). *Studies in the Scope and Method of "The Authoritarian Personality."* New York: The Free Press of Glencoe, 1954.

CLARK, KENNETH B. "Jews in Contemporary America," *The Jewish Social Service Quarterly*, **31** (1954), 12–22.

CLARK, KENNETH B. "Desegregation: The Role of the Social Sciences," *Teachers College Record* **62** (1960), 16–17.

CLARK, KENNETH B. *Dark Ghetto*. New York: Harper & Row, 1965.

CLARK, KENNETH B., and MAMIE P. CLARK. "Racial Identification and Preference in Negro Children." In THEODORE M. NEWCOMB and E. L. HARTLEY (eds.), *Readings in Social Psychology*. New York: Holt, Rinehart & Winston, Inc., 1947.

COHEN, ARTHUR R. *Attitude Change and Social Influence*. New York: Basic Books, Inc., 1964.

COMAS, JUAN. *Racial Myths*. Paris: UNESCO, 1951.

CONANT, JAMES B. *Slums and Suburbs*. New York: McGraw-Hill Book Co., Inc., 1961.

CONYERS, JAMES E., and T. H. KENNEDY. "Negro Passing: To Pass or Not to Pass," *Phylon*, **24** (1963), 215–224.

COON, CARLETON S. *Races of Europe*. New York: The Macmillan Co., 1939.

COON, CARLETON S., STANLEY M. GARN, and JOSEPH B. BIRDSELL. *Races: A Study of the Problems of Race Formation in Man*. Springfield, Ill.: Charles C Thomas, Publishers, 1950.

COOPER, EUNICE, and HELEN DINERMAN. "Analysis of the Film 'Don't Be a Sucker': A Study in Communication," *The Public Opinion Quarterly*, **15** (1951), 243–264.

COOPER, EUNICE, and MARIE JAHODA. "The Evasion of Propaganda: How Prejudiced People Respond to Anti-prejudice Propaganda," *The Journal of Psychology*, **23** (1947), 15–25.

COPELAND, LEWIS C. "The Negro as a Contrast Concept." In EDGAR T. THOMPSON, ed., *Race Relations and the Race Problem*. Durham, N.C.: Duke University Press, 1939, 152–179.

COSER, LEWIS A. *The Functions of Social Conflict*. New York: The Free Press of Glencoe, 1956.

COTHRAN, TILMAN C. "The Negro Protest against Segregation in the South," *The Annals of the American Academy of Political and Social Science*, **357** (1965), 65–73.

COUCH, A., and KENISTON, K. "Yeasayers and Naysayers: Agreeing Response Set as a Personality Variable," *Journal of Abnormal and Social Psychology*, **60** (1960), 151–174.

COWEN, EMORY, JUDAH LANDES, and DONALD E. SCHAET. "The Effects of Mild Frustration on the Expression of Prejudiced Attitudes," *Journal of Abnormal and Social Psychology*, **58** (1959), 33–38.

COWGILL, DONALD O. "Trends in Residential Segregation in American Cities, 1940–1950," *American*

Sociological Review, **21** (1956), 43–47.

COWGILL, DONALD O. "Segregation Scores for Metropolitan Areas," *American Sociological Review,* **27** (1962), 400–402.

COX, OLIVER CROMWELL. *Caste, Class, and Race.* New York: Doubleday & Co, Inc., 1948.

CRAMER, M. RICHARD. "School Desegregation and New Industry: The Southern Community Leaders' Viewpoint," *Social Forces,* **41** (1963), 384–390.

CRONON, EDMUND DAVID. *Black Moses.* Madison: University of Wisconsin Press, 1955.

CUTRIGHT, PHILLIPS. "Negro Subordination and White Gains," *American Sociological Review,* **30** (1965), 110–112.

DAVENPORT, C. B. "The Effects of Race Intermingling," *Proceedings of the American Philosophical Society,* **56** (1929), 364–368.

DAVENPORT, C. B., and M. S. STEGGARDA. *Race Crossing in Jamaica.* Washington, D.C.: Carnegie Institute of Washington, 1929.

DAVIE, MAURICE R. *Negroes in American Society.* New York: McGraw-Hill Book Co., Inc., 1949.

DAVIES, JAMES C. "Toward a Theory of Revolution," *American Sociological Review,* **27** (1962), 5–19.

DAVIS, ALLISON, and JOHN DOLLARD. *Children of Bondage.* Washington, D.C.: American Council on Education, 1940.

DAVIS, ALLISON, BURLEIGH B. GARDNER, and MARY R. GARDNER. *Deep South.* Chicago: University of Chicago Press, 1941.

DAVIS, KINGSLEY, and WILBERT E. MOORE. "Some Principles of Stratification," *American Sociological Review,* **10** (1945), 242–249.

DEFLEUR, MELVIN L., and FRANK R. WESTIE. "Verbal Attitudes and Overt Acts," *American Sociological Review,* **23** (1958), 667–673.

DEFLEUR, MELVIN L., and FRANK R. WESTIE. "The Interpretation of Interracial Situations," *Social Forces,* **38** (1959), 17–23.

DEUTSCH, MARTIN, and BERT BROWN. "Social Influences in Negro-White Intelligence Difference," *Journal of Social Issues,* **20** (1964), 4–24.

DEUTSCH, MORTON, and MARY EVANS COLLINS. *Interracial Housing.* Minneapolis: University of Minnesota Press, 1951.

DOBZHANSKY, THEODOSIUS. "On Species and Races of Living and Fossil Man," *The American Journal of Physical Anthropology,* N.S., **2** (1944), 251–265.

DOBZHANSKY, THEODOSIUS. *Mankind Evolving.* New Haven: Yale University Press, 1962.

DOLLARD, JOHN. *Caste and Class in a Southern Town.* 3d ed. New York: Doubleday & Co., Inc., 1957.

DOLLARD, JOHN, *et al. Frustration and Aggression.* New Haven: Yale University Press, 1939.

DRAKE, ST. CLAIR, and HORACE R. CAYTON. *Black Metropolis.* New York: Harcourt, Brace & World, Inc., 1945.

DREGER, R. M., and K. S. MILLER. "Comparative Psychological Studies of Negroes and Whites in the United States," *Psychological Bulletin,* **57** (1960), 361–401.

DUNN, L. C., and T. DOBZHANSKY. *Heredity, Race and Society.* New York: The New American Library of World Literature, Inc., 1959.

EPPS, EDGAR G., IRWIN KATZ, and LELAND J. AXELSON. "Relation of Mother's Employment to Intellectual Performance of Negro College Students," *Social Problems,* **11** (1964), 414–419.

EPSTEIN, BENJAMIN R., and ARNOLD FORSTER. *"Some of My Best*

Friends . . ." New York: Farrar, Straus & Co., 1962.

ESSIEN-UDOM, E. U. *Black Nationalism.* New York: Dell Publishing Co., Inc., 1964.

ETZIONI, AMITAI. "The Ghetto: A Reevaluation," *Social Forces,* **37** (1959), 255–262.

FAIRCHILD, HENRY PRATT. *Immigration.* New York: The Macmillan Co., 1925.

FAIRCHILD, HENRY PRATT. *Race and Nationality.* New York: The Ronald Press Co., 1947.

FESHBACH, SEYMOUR, and ROBERT SINGER. "The Effects of Personal and Shared Threats upon Social Prejudice," *Journal of Abnormal and Social Psychology,* **54** (1957), 411–416.

FICHTER, JOSEPH H. "The Marginal Catholic: An Institutional Approach," *Social Forces,* **32** (1953), 167–173.

FINESTONE, HAROLD. "Cats, Kicks, and Color," *Social Problems,* **5** (1957), 3–13.

FISHMAN, JACOB R., and FREDRIC SOLOMON. "Youth and Social Action: 1. Perspectives on the Student Sit-in Movement," *American Journal of Orthopsychiatry,* **33** (1963), 872–882.

FLOWERMAN, S. H. "Mass Propaganda in the War Against Bigotry," *Journal of Abnormal and Social Psychology,* **42** (1947), 429–439.

FORSTER, NORA C., W. E. VINACKE, and J. M. DIGMAN. "Flexibility in a Variety of Problem Situations," *Journal of Abnormal and Social Psychology,* **50** (1955), 211–216.

FRANKLIN, JOHN HOPE. *From Slavery to Freedom.* New York: Alfred A. Knopf, Inc., 1952.

FRAZIER, E. FRANKLIN. *Negro Youth at the Crossways.* Washington, D.C.: American Council on Education, 1940.

FRAZIER, E. FRANKLIN. *The Negro Family in the United States.* Rev. ed. New York: Citadel Press, 1948.

FRAZIER, E. FRANKLIN. "The Negro's Vested Interest in Segregation." In ARNOLD M. ROSE, ed., *Race Prejudice and Discrimination.* New York: Alfred A. Knopf, Inc., 1951, 332–334.

FRAZIER, E. FRANKLIN. *Black Bourgeoisie.* New York: The Free Press of Glencoe, 1957.

FRAZIER, E. FRANKLIN. *The Negro in the United States.* Rev. ed. New York: The Macmillan Co., 1957.

FRAZIER, E. FRANKLIN. *Race and Culture Contacts in the Modern World.* New York: Alfred A. Knopf, Inc., 1957.

FREEMAN, ELLIS. "The Motivation of Jew-Gentile Relationships." In ISACQUE GRAEBER and S. H. BRITT, eds., *Jews in a Gentile World.* New York: The Macmillan Co., 1942, 149–178.

FRENKEL-BRUNSWIK, ELSE. "A Study of Prejudice in Children," *Human Relations,* **1** (1948), 295–306.

FRENKEL-BRUNSWIK, ELSE, and R. N. SANFORD. "Some Personality Factors in Anti-Semitism," *Journal of Psychology,* **20** (1945), 271–291.

FROMM, ERICH. *Escape from Freedom.* New York: Holt, Rinehart & Winston, Inc., 1941.

GALLAHER, ART, JR. *Houston: The Negro and Employment Opportunities in the South.* Atlanta: Southern Regional Council, 1961.

GANS, HERBERT J. *The Urban Villagers.* New York: The Free Press of Glencoe, 1962.

GARFINKEL, HERBERT. *When Negroes March.* New York: The Free Press of Glencoe, 1959.

GESCHWENDER, JAMES A. "Social Structure and The Negro Revolt," *Social Forces*, **43** (1964), 248–256.

GESCHWENDER, JAMES A. "Desegregation, the Educated Negro, and the Future of Social Protest in the South," *Sociological Inquiry*, **35** (1965), 58–69.

GILBERT, G. M. "Stereotype Persistence and Change Among College Students," *Journal of Abnormal and Social Psychology*, **46** (1951), 245–254.

GILLIN, JOHN. *The Ways of Men*. New York: Appleton-Century-Crofts, Inc., 1948.

GINZBERG, ELI. *The Negro Potential*. New York: Columbia University Press, 1956.

GINZBERG, ELI (ed.). *The Negro Challenge to the Business Community*. New York: McGraw-Hill Book Co., Inc., 1964.

GINZBERG, ELI, and ALFRED S. EICHNER. *The Troublesome Presence: American Democracy and the Negro*. New York: The Free Press of Glencoe, 1964.

GIST, NOEL P., and WILLIAM S. BENNETT, JR. "Aspirations of Negro and White Students," *Social Forces*, **42** (1963), 40–48.

GIST, NOEL P., and SYLVIA FLEIS FAVA. *Urban Sociology*. 5th ed. New York: Thomas Y. Crowell Co., 1964.

GLAZER, NATHAN, and DANIEL P. MOYNIHAN. *Beyond the Melting Pot*. Cambridge: M.I.T. Press and Harvard University Press, 1963.

GLENN, NORVAL D. "Changes in American Occupational Structure and Occupational Gains of Negroes During the 1940's," *Social Forces*, **41** (1962), 188–195.

GLENN, NORVAL D. "Occupational Benefits to Whites from the Subordination of Negroes," *American Sociological Review*, **28** (1963), 443–448.

GLENN, NORVAL D. "Negro Prestige Criteria: A Case Study in the Bases of Prestige," *American Journal of Sociology*, **68** (1963), 645-657.

GLENN, NORVAL D. "Some Changes in the Relative Status of American Nonwhites, 1940 to 1960," *Phylon*, **24** (1963), 109–122.

GLENN, NORVAL D. "The Relative Size of the Negro Population and Negro Occupational Status," *Social Forces*, **43** (1964), 42–49.

GOFF, REGINA MARY. *Problems and Emotional Difficulties of Negro Children*. New York: Teachers College, Bureau of Publications, Columbia University, 1949.

GOLDBERG, MILTON M. "A Qualification of the Marginal Man Theory," *American Sociological Review*, **6** (1941), 52–58.

GOLDBLATT, HAROLD, and FLORENCE CROMIEN. "The Effective Reach of the Fair Housing Practices Law of the City of New York," *Social Problems*, **9** (1962), 365–370.

GOLDEN, JOSEPH. "Characteristics of the Negro-White Intermarried in Philadelphia," *American Sociological Review*, **18** (1953), 177–183.

GOLDEN, JOSEPH. "Patterns of Negro-White Intermarriage," *American Sociological Review*, **19** (1954), 144–147.

GOLIGHTLY, CORNELIUS L. "Race, Values and Guilt," *Social Forces*, **26** (1947), 125–139.

GOLOVENSKY, DAVID I. "The Marginal Man Concept: An Analysis and Critique," *Social Forces*, **30** (1952), 333–339.

GOODMAN, M. E. *Race Awareness in Young Children*. Reading, Mass.: Addison-Wesley Publishing Co., Inc., 1952.

GORDON, MILTON M. *Social Class in American Sociology*. Durham,

N.C.: Duke University Press, 1958.

GORDON, MILTON M. *Assimilation in American Life.* New York: Oxford University Press, 1964.

GOSSETT, THOMAS F. *Race: The History of an Idea in America.* Dallas: Southern Methodist University Press, 1963.

GRAEBER, ISACQUE, and S. H. BRITT, eds. *Jews in a Gentile World.* New York: The Macmillan Co., 1942.

GRANT, MADISON. *The Passing of the Great Race.* New York: Charles Scribner's Sons, 1916.

GREENBLUM, JOSEPH, and LEONARD I. PEARLIN. "Vertical Mobility and Prejudice: A Socio-psychological Analysis." In REINHARD BENDIX and SEYMOUR MARTIN LIPSET, eds., *Class, Status and Power.* New York: The Free Press of Glencoe, 1953.

GREENWAY, JOHN. *American Folksongs of Protest.* New York: A. S. Barnes & Co., Inc., 1960.

GRIMES, ALAN P. *Equality in America.* New York: Oxford University Press, 1964.

GRIMSHAW, ALLEN D. "Lawlessness and Violence in the United States and Their Special Manifestations in Changing Negro-White Relationships," *Journal of Negro History,* 44 (1959), 52–72.

GRIMSHAW, ALLEN D. "Urban Racial Violence in the United States," *American Journal of Sociology,* 64 (1960), 109–120.

GRIMSHAW, ALLEN D. "Relationships among Prejudice, Discrimination, Social Tension and Social Violence," *Journal of Intergroup Relations,* 2 (1961), 302–310.

GRIMSHAW, ALLEN D. "Negro-White Relations in the Urban North: Two Areas of High Conflict Potential," *Journal of Intergroup Relations,* 3 (1962), 146–158.

GRIMSHAW, ALLEN D. "Actions of Police and Military in American Race Riots," *Phylon,* 24 (1963), 271–289.

GRODZINS, MORTON. "Metropolitan Segregation," *Scientific American,* 197 (October 1957), 33–41.

GROSSACK, MARTIN M. "Group Belongingness Among Negroes," *The Journal of Social Psychology,* 43 (1956), 167–180.

GROSSACK, MARTIN M. (ed.). *Mental Health and Segregation.* New York: Springer Publishing Co., Inc., 1963.

GROUP FOR THE ADVANCEMENT OF PSYCHIATRY. *Psychiatric Aspects of School Desegregation,* Report No. 37, 1957.

GUILFORD, J. P. "Racial Preferences of a Thousand American University Students," *Journal of Social Psychology,* 2 (1931), 179–204.

HAIMOWITZ, MORRIS L., and NATALIE READER HAIMOWITZ. "Reducing Ethnic Hostility Through Psychotherapy," *Journal of Social Psychology,* 31 (1950), 231–241.

HALLOWELL, A. IRVING. "Cultural Factors in the Structuralization of Perception." In J. H. ROHRER and M. SHERIF (eds.), *Social Psychology at the Crossroads.* New York: Harper & Row, 1951.

HALPERN, BEN. *The Idea of the Jewish State.* Cambridge, Mass.: Harvard University Press, 1961.

HALPERN, SAMUEL. *The Political World of American Zionism.* Detroit: Wayne State University Press, 1961.

HAMBLIN, ROBERT J. "The Dynamics of Racial Discrimination," *Social Problems,* 10 (1962), 103–120.

HANDLIN, OSCAR. *Boston's Immigrants, 1790–1865.* Cambridge, Mass.: Harvard University Press, 1941.

HANDLIN, OSCAR. *The Uprooted.* Boston: Little Brown & Co., 1951.

HANDLIN, OSCAR. *Race and Nationality in American Life.* New York: Doubleday & Co., Inc., 1957.

HANDLIN, OSCAR. *The Newcomers: Negroes and Puerto Ricans in a Changing Metropolis.* Cambridge, Mass.: Harvard University Press, 1959.

HARDING, J. "Prejudice and Ethnic Relations." In G. LINDZEY, ed., *Handbook of Social Psychology, II.* Reading, Mass.: Addison-Wesley Publishing Co., Inc., 1954.

HARDING, JOHN, and RUSSELL HOGREFE. "Attitudes of White Department Store Employees Toward Negro Co-workers," *Journal of Social Issues,* 8 (1952), 18–28.

HARTLEY, EUGENE. *Problems in Prejudice.* New York: King's Crown Press, 1946.

HEISS, JEROLD S. "Premarital Characteristics of the Religiously Intermarried in an Urban Area," *American Sociological Review,* 25 (1960), 47–55.

HERBERG, WILL. *Protestant, Catholic, Jew.* Garden City, N.Y.: Doubleday & Co., Inc., 1960.

HERNTON, CALVIN C. *Sex and Racism in America.* New York: Doubleday & Co., Inc., 1965.

HERZL, THEODOR. *The Jewish State.* New York: American Zionist Emergency Council, 1946.

HILL, MOZELL C. "Basic Racial Attitudes Toward Whites in the Oklahoma All-Negro Community," *American Journal of Sociology,* 49 (1944), 519–523.

HILL, MOZELL C., and BEVODE C. McCALL. "Cracker Culture: A Preliminary Definition," *Phylon,* 11 (1950), 223–231.

HILL, MOZELL C., and BEVODE C. McCALL. "Social Stratification in Georgia Town," *American Sociological Review,* 15 (1950), 721–729.

HIMMELWEIT, H. "Frustration and Aggression: A Review of Recent Experimental Work." In T. H. PEAR, ed., *Psychological Factors of Peace and War.* New York: Philosophical Library, Inc., 1950.

HOLLINGSHEAD, AUGUST. *Elmtown's Youth.* New York: John Wiley & Sons, Inc., 1949.

HOLLINGSHEAD, AUGUST. "Cultural Factors in the Selection of Marriage Mates," *American Sociological Review,* 15 (1950), 619–627.

HOLLINGSHEAD, AUGUST. "Trends in Social Stratification," *American Sociological Review,* 18 (1952), 679–686.

HOLLOWAY, ROBERT G., and JOEL V. BERREMAN. "The Educational and Occupational Aspirations and Plans of Negro and White Male Elementary School Students," *Pacific Sociological Review,* 2 (1959), 59–60.

HOLMAN, CARL. *Atlanta: The Negro and Employment Opportunities in the South.* Atlanta: Southern Regional Council, 1962.

HOOTON, E. A. *Up from the Ape.* New York: The Macmillan Co., 1949.

HORNEY, KAREN. *The Neurotic Personality of Our Time.* New York: W. W. Norton, Co., Inc., 1937.

HOROWITZ, EUGENE L., and RUTH E. HOROWITZ. "Development of Social Attitudes in Children," *Sociometry,* 1 (1938), 301–308.

HOSTETLER, JOHN A. *Amish Society.* Baltimore: John Hopkins Press, 1963.

HOVLAND, CARL I., ARTHUR A. LUMSDAINE, and FRED D. SHEFFIELD. *Experiments on Mass Communication.* Princeton, N.J.: Princeton University Press, 1949.

HUGHES, EVERETT C. "Dilemmas and Contradictions of Status," *American Journal of Sociology*, L (1945).

HUGHES, EVERETT C., and HELEN HUGHES. *Where People Meet: Ethnic and Racial Frontiers*. New York: The Free Press of Glencoe, 1952.

HUGHES, HELEN MacGILL, and LEWIS G. WATTS. "Portrait of the Self-Integrator," *Journal of Social Issues*, 20 (1964), 103–116.

HURVITZ, NATHAN. "Sources of Middle Class Values of American Jews," *Social Forces*, 37 (1958), 117–123.

HUTCHINSON, EDWARD P. *Immigrants and Their Children, 1850–1950*. New York: John Wiley & Sons, Inc., 1956.

HYMAN, H. H., and P. B. SHEATSLEY. "Attitudes Toward Desegregation," *Scientific American*, CXCV (1956), 35–39.

JANIS, IRVING L., and SEYMOUR FESHBACH. "Effects of Fear-arousing Communications," *Journal of Abnormal and Social Psychology*, 48 (1953), 78–92.

JANOWKY, OSCAR. Nationalities and National Minorities. New York: The Macmillan Co., 1945.

JENKINS, WILLIAM SUMNER. *Proslavery Thought in the Old South*. Chapel Hill: University of North Carolina Press, 1935.

JOHNSON, CHARLES S. *Shadow of the Plantation*. Chicago: University of Chicago Press, 1934.

JOHNSON, CHARLES S. *Growing Up in the Black Belt*. Washington, D.C.: American Council on Education, 1941.

JOHNSON, CHARLES S. *Patterns of Negro Segregation*. New York: Harper & Row, 1943.

JOHNSON, CHARLES S. *Into the Main-stream*. Chapel Hill: University of North Carolina Press, 1946.

JOHNSON, GUY B. "Patterns of Social Conflict." In EDGAR T. THOMPSON (ed.), *Race Relations and the Race Problem*. Durham, N.C.: Duke University Press, 1939.

JOHNSON, GUY B. "A Sociologist Looks at Racial Desegregation in the South," *Social Forces*, 32 (1954), 1–10.

JOHNSON, GUY B. "Racial Integration in Southern Higher Education," *Social Forces*, 34 (1956), 309–312.

JOHNSON, JAMES WELDON. *Negro Americans, What Now?* New York: The Viking Press, Inc., 1934.

JOHNSON, ROBERT. "Negro Reactions to Minority Group Status." In MILTON L. BARRON, ed., *American Minorities*. New York: Alfred A. Knopf, Inc., 1957, 192–214.

JONASSEN, CHRISTEN T. "Some Historical and Theoretical Bases of Racism in Northwestern Europe," *Social Forces*, 30 (1951), 155–161.

JONES, E. E., and R. KOHLER. "The Effects of Plausibility on the Learning of Controversial Statements," *Journal of Abnormal and Social Psychology*, LVII (1958), 315–320.

JONES, MAJOR J. *Chattanooga: The Negro and Employment Opportunities in the South*. Atlanta: Southern Regional Council, 1962.

KARDINER, ABRAM, and LIONEL OVESEY. *The Mark of Oppression*. New York. W. W. Norton & Co., Inc., 1951.

KARON, BERTRAM P. *The Negro Personality*. New York: Springer Publishing Co., 1958.

KATZ, D. "Psychological Barriers to Communication," *Annals American Academy of Political and Social Science*, 250 (1947).

KATZ, D., C. McCLINTOCK, and I. SARNOFF. "The Measurement of

Ego Defense as Related to Attitude Change," *Journal of Personality,* **25** (1957), 465–474.

KATZ, D., I. SARNOFF, and C. MC-CLINTOCK. "Ego-Defense and Attitude Change," *Human Relations,* **9** (1956), 27–45.

KATZ, IRWIN. *Conflict and Harmony in an Adolescent Interracial Group.* New York: New York University Press, 1955.

KATZ, IRWIN. "Review of Evidence Relating to Effects of Desegregation on the Intellectual Performance of Negroes," *American Psychologist,* **19** (1964), 381–399.

KATZ, IRWIN, JAMES M. ROBINSON, EDGAR G. EPPS, and PATRICIA WALY. "The Influence of Race of the Experimenter and Instructions Upon the Expression of Hostility by Negro Boys," *Journal of Social Issues,* **20** (1964), 54–60.

KAUFMAN, WALTER C. "Status, Authoritarianism and Anti-Semitism," *American Journal of Sociology,* **62** (1957), 379–382.

KENNEDY, RUBY JO REEVES. "Single or Triple Melting-Pot? Intermarriage Trends in New Haven, 1870–1940," *American Journal of Sociology,* **49** (1944), 331–339.

KENNEDY, RUBY JO REEVES. "Single or Triple Melting-Pot? Intermarriage Trends in New Haven, 1870–1950," *American Journal of Sociology,* **58** (1952), 56–59.

KEPHART, WILLIAM M. *The Family, Society, and the Individual.* Boston: Houghton Mifflin Co., 1961.

KERCKHOFF, ALAN C., and THOMAS C. MCCORMACK. "Marginal Status and Marginal Personality," *Social Forces,* **34** (1955), 48–55.

KEY, V. O., JR. *Southern Politics.* New York: Alfred A. Knopf, Inc., 1950.

KIBBE, PAULINE R. *Latin-Americans in Texas.* Albuquerque: University of New Mexico Press, 1946.

KILLIAN, LEWIS M. "The Effects of Southern White Workers on Race Relations in Northern Plants," *American Sociological Review,* **17** (1952), 327–331.

KILLIAN, LEWIS M. "The Adjustment of Southern White Migrants to Northern Urban Norms," *Social Forces,* **33** (1953), 66–69.

KILLIAN, LEWIS M. "Community Structure and the Role of the Negro Leader-Agent," *Sociological Inquiry,* **35** (1965), 69–80.

KILLIAN, LEWIS M., and CHARLES GRIGG. "Urbanism, Race, and Anomia," *American Journal of Sociology,* **67** (1962), 661–665.

KILLIAN, LEWIS M., and CHARLES M. GRIGG. *Racial Crisis in America.* Englewood Cliffs, N.J.: Prentice-Hall, Inc., 1964.

KILLIAN, LEWIS M., and CHARLES SMITH. "Negro Protest Leaders in a Southern Community," *Social Forces,* **38** (1960), 253–256.

KING, MARTIN LUTHER, JR. *Stride toward Freedom.* New York: Harper & Row, 1958.

KING, MARTIN LUTHER, JR. *Strength to Love.* New York: Harper & Row, 1963.

KING, MORTON B., JR. "The Minority Course," *American Sociological Review,* **21** (1956), 80–83.

KIRKPATRICK, CLIFFORD. *The Family: As Process and Institution.* 2d ed. New York: The Ronald Press Co., 1963.

KLINEBERG, OTTO. *Negro Intelligence and Selective Migration.* New York: Columbia University Press, 1935.

KLINEBERG, OTTO. *Race Differences.* New York: Harper & Row, 1935.

KLINEBERG, OTTO (ed.). *Characteristics of the American Negro.* New York: Harper & Row, 1944.

KLINEBERG, OTTO. *Race and Psychology.* Paris: UNESCO, 1951.

KLUCKHOHN, CLYDE. *Mirror for Man.* Greenwich, Conn.: Fawcett Publications, Inc., 1960.

KLUCKHOHN, CLYDE, and WILLIAM H. KELLY. "The Concept of Culture." In RALPH LINTON (ed.), *The Science of Man in the World Crisis.* New York: Columbia University Press, 1945.

KOENIG, FREDRICK W., and MORTON B. KING, JR. "Cognitive Simplicity and Prejudice," *Social Forces,* **40** (1962), 220–222.

KRAMER, BERNARD M. "Dimensions of Prejudice," *The Journal of Psychology,* **27** (1949), 389–451.

KRAMER, JUDITH R., and SEYMOUR LEVENTMAN. *Children of the Gilded Ghetto.* New Haven: Yale University Press, 1961.

KRUEFER, E. T. "Negro Religious Expression," *American Journal of Sociology,* 38 (1932–1933), 22–31.

KUTNER, BERNARD, CAROL WILKINS, and PENNY R. YARROW. "Verbal Attitudes and Overt Behavior Involving Racial Prejudice," *Journal of Abnormal and Social Psychology,* 47 (1952), 649–652.

KVARACEUS, WILLIAM C., et al. *Negro Self Concept.* New York: McGraw-Hill Book Co., Inc., 1965.

LAMANNA, RICHARD A. "The Negro Teacher and Desegregation: A Study of Strategic Decision-Makers and Their Vested Interests in Different Community Contexts," *Sociological Inquiry,* 35 (1965), 26–41.

LANG, KURT, and GLADYS ENGEL LANG, "Resistance to School Desegregation: a Case Study of Backlash among Jews," *Sociological Inquiry,* 35 (1965), 94–107.

LAPIERE, RICHARD T. "Attitudes vs. Actions," *Social Forces,* 13 (1934), 230–237.

LAUE, JAMES H. "A Contemporary Revitalization Movement in American Race Relations: The 'Black Muslims,'" *Social Forces,* **42** (1964), 315–324.

LAUE, JAMES H. "The Changing Character of the Negro Protest," *The Annals of the American Academy of Political and Social Science,* **357** (1965), 119–126.

LAUE, JAMES H., and LEON M. MC-CORKLE, JR. "The Association of Southern Women for the Prevention of Lynching: a Commentary on the Role of the 'Moderate,'" *Sociological Inquiry,* **35** (1965), 80-94.

LAURENTI, LUIGI. *Property Values and Race.* Berkeley: University of California Press, 1960.

LAVIOLETTE, FORREST E. *Americans of Japanese Ancestry.* Toronto: The Canadian Institute of International Affairs, 1946.

LAVIOLETTE, FORREST E., and K. H. SILVERT. "A Theory of Stereotypes," *Social Forces,* **29** (1951), 257–262.

LEE, ALFRED MCCLUNG, and NORMAN DAYMOND HUMPHREY. *Race Riot.* New York: Holt, Rinehart & Winston, Inc., 1943.

LEE, EVERETT S. "Negro Intelligence and Selective Migration: A Philadelphia Test of the Klineberg Hypothesis." *American Sociological Review,* 16 (1951), 227–233.

LEE, FRANK F. "The Race Relations Pattern by Areas of Behavior in a Small New England Town," *American Sociological Review,* 10 (1954), 138–143.

LEE, FRANK F. *Negro and White in Connecticut Town.* New Haven: College and University Press, 1961.

LEE, IRVING J. "How Do You Talk About People?" *Freedom Pamphlet.* New York: Anti-Defamation League of B'nai Brith, 1950.

LEE, ROSE HUM. "The Decline of Chinatowns in the United States," *American Journal of Sociology*, 54 (1949), 422–432.

LEE, ROSE HUM. *The Chinese in the United States of America*. Hong Kong: Hong Kong University Press, 1960.

LEIGHTON, ALEXANDER H. *The Governing of Men*. Princeton, N.J.: Princeton University Press, 1945.

LENSKI, GERHARD. *The Religious Factor*. Rev. ed. Garden City, New York: Doubleday & Co., Inc., 1963.

LESSER, GERALD S. "Extrapunitiveness and Ethnic Attitude," *Journal of Abnormal and Social Psychology*, 56 (1958), 281–282.

LEWIN, KURT. *Resolving Social Conflicts*. New York: Harper & Row, 1948.

LEWIS, HYLAN. *Blackways of Kent*. Chapel Hill: University of North Carolina Press, 1955.

LIEBERSON, STANLEY. "A Societal Theory of Race and Ethnic Relations," *American Sociological Review*, 26 (1961), 902–909.

LIEBERSON, STANLEY. *Ethnic Patterns in American Cities*. New York: The Free Press of Glencoe, 1963.

LINCOLN, C. ERIC. *The Black Muslims in America*. Boston: Beacon Press, Inc., 1961.

LINDZEY, GARDNER. "Differences Between the High and Low in Prejudice and Their Implications for a Theory of Prejudice," *Journal of Personality*, 19 (1950), 16–40.

LINDZEY, GARDNER. "An Experimental Examination of the Scapegoat Theory of Prejudice," *Journal of Abnormal and Social Psychology*, 45 (1950), 296–309.

LINN, LAWRENCE S. "Verbal Attitudes and Overt Behavior: A Study of Racial Discrimination," *Social Forces*, 43 (1965), 353–364.

LINTON, RALPH. *The Study of Man*. New York: Appleton-Century-Crofts, Inc., 1936.

LINTON, RALPH, ed. *Acculturation in Seven American Indian Tribes*. New York: Appleton-Century-Crofts, Inc., 1940.

LINTON, RALPH. "Nativistic Movements," *American Anthropologist*, 45 (1943), 230–240.

LINTON, RALPH. *The Cultural Background of Personality*. New York: Appleton-Century-Crofts, Inc., 1945.

LINTON, RALPH (ed.). *The Science of Man in the World Crisis*. New York: Columbia University Press, 1945.

LIPSET, SEYMOUR M. *Political Man*. New York: Doubleday & Co., Inc., 1960.

LITTLE, WILSON. *Spanish-speaking Children in Texas*. Austin: University of Texas Press, 1944.

LOEWENSTEIN, RUDOLPH M. *Christians and Jews*. New York: International Universities Press, Inc., 1951.

LOHMAN, JOSEPH D., and DIETRICH C. REITZES. "Note on Race Relations in a Mass Society," *American Journal of Sociology*, 58 (1952), 342–344.

LOHMAN, J. D., and D. C. REITZES. "Deliberately Organized Groups and Racial Behavior," *American Sociological Review*, 19 (1954), 342–344.

LOMAX, LOUIS E. *The Negro Revolt*. New York: Harper & Row, 1962.

LUSTIG, NORMAN I. "The Relationships Between Demographic Characteristics and Pro-integration Vote of White Precincts in a Metropolitan Southern County," *Social Forces*, 40 (1962), 205–208.

McDONAGH, EDWARD C. "Status Levels of Mexicans," *Sociology* and Social Research, 33 (1949), 449–459.

MacIver, R. M. The More Perfect Union. New York: The Macmillan Co., 1948.

MacIver, R. M. (ed.). Discrimination and National Welfare. New York: Institute for Religious and Social Studies, 1949.

McKenzie, R. D. Oriental Exclusion. Chicago: University of Chicago Press, 1928.

MacKinnon, William J., and Richard Centers. "Authoritarianism and Urban Stratification," American Journal of Sociology, 61 (1956), 610–620.

McLean, Helen V. "The Emotional Health of Negroes," Journal of Negro Education, 18 (1949).

McWilliams, Carey. Prejudice. Boston: Little Brown & Co., 1944.

McWilliams, Carey. A Mask for Privilege: Anti-Semitism in America. Boston: Little Brown & Co., 1948.

McWilliams, Carey. North from Mexico. Philadelphia: J. B. Lippincott Co., 1949.

Madsen, William. The Mexican-Americans of South Texas. New York: Holt, Rinehart & Winston, Inc., 1964.

Malzberg, Benjamin. "Mental Disease among Negroes," Mental Hygiene, 43 (1959), 457–459.

Mann, John H. "The Relationship between Cognitive, Affective, and Behavioral Aspects of Racial Prejudice," Journal of Social Psychology, 49 (1959), 223–228.

Martin, James G. "Racial Ethnocentrism and Judgment of Beauty, Journal of Social Psychology, 63 (1964), 59–63.

Mayer, John E. Jewish-Gentile Courtships. New York: The Free Press of Glencoe, 1961.

Medalia, Nahum Z. "Myrdal's Assumptions on Race Relations: A Conceptual Commentary," Social Forces, 40 (1962), 223–227.

Meltzer, H. "Group Differences in Nationality and Race Preference of Children," Sociometry, 2 (1939), 86–105.

Mendelson, Wallace. Discrimination. Englewood Cliffs, N.J.: Prentice-Hall, Inc., 1962.

Merton, Robert K. "Discrimination and the American Creed." In R. M. MacIver (ed.), Discrimination and National Welfare. New York: Harper & Row, 1949.

Merton, Robert K. Social Theory and Social Structure. Rev. ed. New York: The Free Press of Glencoe, 1957.

Merton, Robert K., and Alice S. Kitt. "Contributions to the Theory of Reference Group Behavior." In Robert K. Merton and Paul F. Lazarsfeld (eds.), Continuities in Social Research: Studies in the Scope and Method of "The Authoritarian Personality." New York: The Free Press of Glencoe, 1950.

Middleton, Russell. "Ethnic Prejudice and Susceptibility to Persuasion," American Sociological Review, 25 (1960), 679–686.

Middleton, Russell. "The Civil Rights Issue and Presidential Voting Among Southern Negroes and Whites," Social Forces, 40 (1962), 209–214.

Miller, Neal E., and Richard Bugelski, "Minor Studies of Aggression: II. The Influence of Frustrations Imposed by the In-group on Attitudes Expressed Toward Outgroups," Journal of Psychology, 25 (1948), 437–442.

Mills, C. Wright, Clarence Senior, and Rose Kohn Goldsen. The Puerto Rican Journey. New York: Harper & Row, 1950.

Minard, Ralph D. "Race Relationships in the Pocahontas Coal

Fields," *Journal of Social Issues,* 8 (1952), 29–44.

MITCHELL, HOWARD E. "'Color Conflict' as a Defense." In GEORGENE SEWARD (ed.), *Clinical Studies in Culture Conflict.* New York: The Ronald Press Co., 1958, 91–120.

MONTAGU, ASHLEY. *An Introduction to Physical Anthropology.* Springfield, Ill.: Charles C Thomas, Publishers, 1945.

MONTAGU, ASHLEY. *Man's Most Dangerous Myth: The Fallacy of Race.* 2d ed. New York: Columbia University Press, 1945.

MONTAGU, ASHLEY. *Statement on Race.* New York: Henry Schuman, Inc., 1951.

MONTAGU, ASHLEY. *Man: His First Million Years.* New York: A Mentor Book, 1958.

MONTAGU, ASHLEY. *Human Heredity.* Cleveland: The World Publishing Co., 1960.

MORLAND, J. KENNETH. "Racial Recognition by Nursery School Children in Lynchburg, Virginia," *Social Forces,* 37 (1958), 132–137.

MORSE, NANCY C., and FLOYD H. ALLPORT. "The Causation of Anti-Semitism: An Investigation of Seven Hypotheses," *The Journal of Psychology,* 34 (1953), 197–233.

MYERS, GUSTAVUS. *History of Bigotry in the United States.* Revised by HENRY M. CHRISTMAN. New York: G. P. Putnam's Sons, Inc., 1960.

MYRDAL, GUNNAR. *An American Dilemma.* New York: Harper & Row, 1944.

NAM, CHARLES B. "Nationality Groups and Social Stratification in America," *Social Forces,* 37 (1959), 328–333.

NATIONAL PLANNING ASSOCIATION COMMITTEE OF THE SOUTH. *Selected Studies of Negro Employ-ment in the South.* Washington, D.C.: National Planning Association, 1955.

NOEL, DONALD M. "Correlates of Anti-White Prejudice." Unpublished doctoral dissertation. Cornell University, Ithaca, New York, 1961.

NOEL, DONALD L. "Group Identification among Negroes: An Empirical Analysis," *Journal of Social Issues,* 20 (1964), 71–85.

NORTH, ROBERT D. "The Intelligence of Negroes," *Research Reports of the Anti-Defamation League,* 3 (November 1956).

ODUM, HOWARD W. *The Way of the South.* New York: The Macmillan Co., 1947.

PADILLA, ELENA. *Up from Puerto Rico.* New York: Columbia University Press, 1958.

PALMORE, ERDMAN P. "Ethnophaulisms and Ethnocentrism," *American Journal of Sociology,* 67 (1962), 442–445.

PALMORE, ERDMAN, and JOHN HOWE. "Residential Integration and Property Values," *Social Problems,* 10 (1962), 52–55.

PARK, ROBERT E. "Human Migration and the Marginal Man," *American Journal of Sociology,* 33 (1928), 881–893.

PARK, ROBERT E. *Race and Culture.* New York: The Free Press of Glencoe, 1949.

PARKER, SEYMOUR, and ROBERT KLEINER. "Status Position, Mobility, and Ethnic Identification of the Negro," *Journal of Social Issues,* 20 (1964), 85–103.

PARSONS, TALCOTT. "The Sociology of Modern Anti-Semitism." In ISACQUE GRAEBER and S. H. BRITT (eds.), *Jews in a Gentile World.* New York: The Macmillan Co., 1942, 101–122.

PARSONS, TALCOTT. "Certain Primary Sources and Patterns of Aggression in the Social Structure of the Western World," *Psychiatry,* **10** (1947), 167–181.

PASAMANICK, BENJAMIN. "A Survey of Mental Disease in an Urban Population," *Psychiatry,* **119** (1962), 299–305.

PASTORE, N. "A Neglected Factor in the Frustration-Aggression Hypothesis: A Comment," *Journal of Psychology,* **25** (1948), 271–279.

PEARL, DAVID. "Psychotherapy and Ethnocentrism," *Journal of Abnormal and Social Psychology,* **50** (1955), 227–229.

PEARLIN, LEONARD I. "Shifting Group Attachments and Attitudes Toward Negroes," *Social Forces,* **33** (1954), 47–50.

PECK, JAMES. *Freedom Ride.* New York: Simon & Schuster, Inc., 1962.

PETERSEN, WILLIAM. "A General Typology of Migration," *American Sociological Review,* **23** (1958), 256–266.

PETERSON, RUTH C., and L. L. THURSTONE. *Motion Pictures and the Social Attitudes of Children.* New York: The Macmillan Co., 1933.

PETTIGREW, THOMAS F. "Regional Differences in Anti-Negro Prejudice," *The Journal of Abnormal and Social Psychology,* **59** (1959), 28–36.

PETTIGREW, THOMAS F. "Social Psychology and Desegregation Research," *American Psychologist,* **16** (1961), 105-112.

PETTIGREW, THOMAS F. *A Profile of the Negro American.* Princeton, N.J.: Van Nostrand Company, Inc., 1964.

POHLMAN, EDWARD W. "Semantic Aspects of the Controversy over Negro-White Caste in the U.S.," *Social Forces,* **30** (1952), 416–419.

POLL, SOLOMON. *The Hasidic Community of Williamsburg.* New York: The Free Press of Glencoe, 1962.

POWDERMAKER, HORTENSE. *After Freedom.* New York: The Viking Press, Inc., 1939.

POWDERMAKER, HORTENSE. "The Channeling of Negro Aggression by the Cultural Process." In CLYDE KLUCKHOHN and HENRY A. MURRAY (eds.), *Personality.* 2d ed. New York: Alfred A. Knopf, Inc., 1956.

PRICE, MARGARET. *The Negro and the Ballot.* Atlanta: Southern Regional Council, 1959.

Propaganda: How To Recognize It and Deal with It. New York: Institute for Propaganda Analysis, Inc., 1938.

PROTHRO, E. TERRY. "Ethnocentrism and Anti-Negro Attitudes in the Deep South," *Journal of Abnormal and Social Psychology,* **47** (1952), 105–108.

PROTHRO, E. TERRY, and JOHN A. JENSEN. "Comparison of Some Ethnic and Religious Attitudes of Negro and White College Students in the Deep South," *Social Forces,* **30** (1952), 426–428.

PROUDFOOT, MERRILL. *Diary of a Sit-in.* Chapel Hill: University of North Carolina Press, 1962.

QUINN, JAMES A. *Human Ecology.* Englewood Cliffs, N.J.: Prentice-Hall, Inc., 1950.

QUINN, OLIVE WESTBROOKE. "The Transmission of Racial Attitudes Among White Southerners," *Social Forces,* **33** (1954), 41–47.

RAAB, EARL (ed.). *American Race Relations Today.* New York: Doubleday & Company, Inc., 1962.

RAAB, EARL (ed.). *Religious Conflict in America.* Garden City,

N.Y.: Doubleday & Company, Inc., 1964.

RAND, CHRISTOPHER. *The Puerto Ricans.* Fair Lawn, N.J.: Oxford University Press, 1958.

RAZRAR, GREGORY. "Ethnic Dislike and Stereotypes: A Laboratory Study," *Journal of Abnormal and Social Psychology,* 45 (1950), 7–27.

RECORD, WILSON. *The Negro and the Communist Party.* Chapel Hill: University of North Carolina Press, 1951.

RIDDLEBERGER, ALICE B., and ANNABELLE B. MOTZ. "Prejudice and Perception," *American Journal of Sociology,* 62 (1957), 498–503.

RINDER, IRWIN B. "Strangers in the Land: Social Relations in the Status Gap," *Social Problems,* 6 (1958), 253–260.

ROBERTS, ALAN H., and MILTON ROKEACH. "Anomie, Authoritarianism, and Prejudice: A Replication," *American Journal of Sociology,* 61 (1956), 355–358.

ROGERS, DAVID, and BERT SWANSON. "White Citizen Response to the Same Integration Plan: Comparisons of Local School Districts in a Northern City," *Sociological Inquiry,* 35 (1965), 123–131.

ROHRER, JOHN H. "The Intelligence of Osage Indians," *Journal of Social Psychology,* 16 (1942), 98–105.

ROHRER, JOHN H., and MUNRO S. EDMONSON. *The Eighth Generation.* New York: Harper & Row, 1960.

ROKEACH, MILTON. *The Open and Closed Mind.* New York: Basic Books, 1960.

ROSE, ARNOLD M. "Anti-Semitism's Root in City-Hatred," *Commentary,* 6 (1944), 374–378.

ROSE, ARNOLD M. *The Negro in America.* New York: Harper & Row, 1944.

ROSE, ARNOLD M. *The Negro's Morale.* Minneapolis: University of Minnesota Press, 1949.

ROSE, ARNOLD M. (ed.). *Race Prejudice and Discrimination.* New York: Alfred A. Knopf, Inc., 1951.

ROSE, ARNOLD M. "Inconsistencies in Attitudes toward Negro Housing," *Social Problems,* 8 (1961), 286–292.

ROSE, ARNOLD M. *Assuring Freedom to the Free.* Detroit: Wayne State University Press, 1964.

ROSE, ARNOLD M. *De Facto School Segregation.* New York: The National Conference of Christians and Jews, 1964.

ROSE, PETER I. *They and We.* New York: Random House, Inc., 1964.

ROSEN, BERNARD C. "Race, Ethnicity and Achievement Syndrome," *American Sociological Review,* 24 (1959), 47–60.

ROSENTHAL, ERICH. "Acculturation without Assimilation? The Jewish Community of Chicago, Illinois," *American Journal of Sociology,* 66 (1960), 275–288.

RUBIN, MORTON. *Plantation County.* Chapel Hill: University of North Carolina Press, 1951.

RUBIN, MORTON. "Social and Cultural Change in the Plantation Area," *The Journal of Social Issues,* 10 (1954), 28–35.

SAENGER, GERHART. *The Social Psychology of Prejudice.* New York: Harper & Row, 1953.

SAENGER, GERHART, and SAMUEL FLOWERMAN. "Stereotypes and Prejudicial Attitudes," *Human Relations,* 7 (1954), 217–238.

SAENGER, GERHART, and E. GILBERT. "Customer Reactions to the Integration of Negro Sales Personnel," *International Journal of Opinion and Attitude Research,* 4 (1950), 57–76.

SARNOFF, I., and D. KATZ. "The Motivational Basis of Attitude Change," *Journal of Abnormal and Social Psychology*, 49 (1954), 115–124.

SCHERMERHORN, R. A. *These Our People*. Boston: D. C. Heath & Co., 1949.

SCHERMERHORN, R. A. "Power as a Primary Concept in the Study of Minorities," *Social Forces*, 35 (1956), 53–56.

SCHERMERHORN, R. A. "Toward a General Theory of Minority Groups," *Phylon*, 25 (1964), 238–246.

SCHMITT, ROBERT C., and ROBERT A. SOUZA. "Social and Economic Characteristics of Interracial Households in Honolulu," *Social Problems*, 10 (1963), 264–268.

SCHNORE, LEO F., and HARRY SHARP. "Racial Changes in Metropolitan Areas, 1950–1960," *Social Forces*, 41 (1963), 247–252.

SCHRIEKE, B. *Alien Americans*. New York: The Viking Press, Inc., 1936.

SCHWARTZ, JACK. "Men's Clothing and the Negro," *Phylon*, 24 (1963), 224–231.

SEARLES, RUTH, and J. ALLEN WILLIAMS, JR. "Negro College Students' Participation in Sit-ins," *Social Forces*, 40 (1962), 215–219.

SECORD, PAUL F. "Stereotyping and Favorableness in the Perception of Negro Faces," *Journal of Abnormal and Social Psychology*, 59 (1959), 309–314.

SECORD, PAUL F., WILLIAM BEVAN, and BRENDA KATZ. "The Negro Stereotype and Perceptual Accentuation," *Journal of Abnormal and Social Psychology*, 53 (1956), 78–83.

SEIDENBERG, ROBERT. "The Sexual Basis of Social Prejudice," *Psychoanalytic Review*, 39 (1952), 90–95.

SHAPIRO, H. L. *Descendants of the Mutineers of the Bounty*. Honolulu: Memoirs of the Bernice P. Bishop Museum, 1929.

SHAW, CLIFFORD R., and HENRY D. McKAY. *Juvenile Delinquency and Urban Areas*. Chicago: University of Chicago Press, 1942.

SHEPPARD, HAROLD F. "The Negro Merchant: A Study of Negro Anti-Semitism," *American Sociological Review*, LIII (1947), 96–99.

SHERIF, MUZAFER. "The Problem of Inconsistency in Intergroup Relations," *Journal of Social Issues*, 5 (1949), 32–37.

SHERIF, MUZAFER. "Experiments in Group Conflict," *Scientific American*, 195 (1956), 54–58.

SHERIF, MUZAFER. "Superordinate Goals in the Reduction of Intergroup Conflict," *American Journal of Sociology*, 68 (1958), 349–356.

SHERIF, MUZAFER, and CAROLYN W. SHERIF. *Groups in Harmony and Tension*. New York: Harper & Row, 1953.

SHERIF, MUZAFER, and CAROLYN W. SHERIF. *Reference Groups*. New York: Harper & Row, 1964.

SHERIF, MUZAFER, et al. *Intergroup Conflict and Cooperation: The Robbers' Cave Experiment*. Norman, Oklahoma: University of Oklahoma Book Exchange, 1961.

SHEVAL, JUDITH T. *Immigrants on the Threshold*. New York: Atherton Press, 1963.

SHIBUTANI, TAMOTSU, and KIAN M. KWAN. *Ethnic Stratification*. New York: The Macmillan Co., 1965.

SHOSTAK, ARTHUR. "Appeals from Discrimination in Federal Employment: A Case Study," *Social Forces*, 42 (1963), 174–178.

SIBLEY, ELBRIDGE. "Some Demographic Clues to Stratification." In REINHARD BENDIX and SEYMOUR MARTIN LIPSET (eds.), *Class, Status and Power*. New York:

The Free Press of Glencoe, 1953, 381–388.

SIEGEL, PAUL M. "On the Cost of Being a Negro," *Sociological Inquiry*, **35** (1965), 41–58.

SILBERSTEIN, FRED B., and MELVIN SEEMAN. "Social Mobility and Prejudice," *American Journal of Sociology*, **65** (1959), 258–264.

SIMMONS, OZZIE G. "The Mutual Images and Expectations of Anglo-Americans and Mexican-Americans," *Daedalus*, **90** (1961), 286–299.

SIMON, WALTER B. "Race Relations and Class Structure," *Journal of Social Psychology*, **60** (1963), 187–193.

SIMPSON, GEORGE. *People in Families*. New York: Thomas Y. Crowell Co., 1960.

SIMPSON, GEORGE EATON, and J. MILTON YINGER. *Racial and Cultural Minorities*. 3d ed. New York: Harper & Row, 1965.

SIMPSON, RICHARD L. "Negro-Jewish Prejudice: Authoritarianism and Some Social Variables as Correlates," *Social Problems*, **7** (1959), 138–146.

SKLARE, MARSHALL. *Conservative Judaism*. New York: The Free Press of Glencoe, 1955.

SKLARE, MARSHALL (ed.). *The Jews*. New York: The Free Press of Glencoe, 1958.

SKLARE, MARSHALL. "Intermarriage and the Jewish Future," *Commentary*, **37** (1964), 46–52.

SMITH, F. TREDWELL. *An Experiment in Modifying Attitudes Toward the Negro*. New York: Teachers College, Bureau of Publications, Columbia University, 1943.

SMITH, LILLIAN. *Killers of a Dream*. New York: W. W. Norton & Co., Inc., 1949.

SOLOMON, FREDRIC, and JACOB R. FISHMAN. "The Psychosocial Meaning of Nonviolence in Student Civil Rights Activities," *Psychiatry*, **27** (1964), 91–99.

SOLOMON, FREDRIC, and JACOB R. FISHMAN. "Youth and Social Action: II. Action and Identity Formation in the First Student Sit-in Demonstrations," *Journal of Social Issues*, **20** (1964), 36–46.

SOLOMON, FREDRIC, et al. "Civil Rights Activity and Reduction of Crime among Negroes," *Archives of General Psychiatry*, **12** (1965), 227–236.

SOROKIN, PITIRIM A. *Contemporary Sociological Theories*. New York: Harper & Row, 1928.

SROLE, LEO. "Social Integration and Certain Corollaries: An Exploratory Study," *American Sociological Review*, **21** (1956), 709–716.

STAGNER, ROSS, and CLYDE S. CONGDON. "Another Failure To Demonstrate Displacement of Aggression," *Journal of Abnormal and Social Psychology*, **51** (1955), 695–696.

STAR, SHIRLEY A., ROBIN M. WILLIAMS, JR., and SAMUEL A. STOUFFER. "Negro Infantry Platoons." In HAROLD PROSHANSKY and BERNARD SEIDENBERG (eds.), *Basic Studies in Social Psychology*. New York: Holt, Rinehart & Winston, Inc., 1965, 680–685.

STEIN, HERMAN D., and JOHN W. MARTIN. "'Swastika Offenders': Variations in Etiology, Behavior, and Psycho-Social Characteristics," *Social Problems*, **10** (1962), 56–70.

STEMBER, CHARLES H. *Education and Attitude Change*. New York: Institute of Human Relations Press, 1961.

STEPHENSEN, RICHARD M. "Mobility Orientation and Stratification of 1,000 Ninth Graders," *American Sociological Review*, **22** (1957), 204–212.

STEVENSON, HAROLD W., and ED-
WARD C. STEWARD. "A Developmental Study of Racial Awareness
in Young Children," *Child Development*, 29 (1958), 399–409.

STODDARD, LOTHROP. *The Rising
Tide of Color*. New York: Charles
Scribner's Sons, 1920.

STONEQUIST, EVERETT V. *The Marginal Man*. New York: Charles
Scribner's Sons, 1937.

STONEQUIST, EVERETT V. "The Marginal Character of the Jews." In
ISACQUE GRAEBER and S. H. BRITT,
eds., *Jews in a Gentile World*.
New York: The Macmillan Co.,
1942.

STOTLAND, E., D. KATZ and M.
PATCHEN. "The Reduction of
Prejudice through the Arousal of
Self-Insight," *Journal of Person-
ality*, 27 (1959), 507–531.

STRICKER, GEORGE. "Scapegoating:
An Experimental Investigation,"
*Journal of Abnormal and Social
Psychology*, 67 (1963), 125–131.

STRONG, SAMUEL M. "Negro-White
Relations as Reflected in Social
Types," *American Sociological Re-
view*, 52 (1946), 23–30.

STRYKER, SHELDON. "Social Structure and Prejudice," *Social Problems*, 6 (1959), 340–354.

STUART, IRVING R. "Minorities vs.
Minorities; Cognitive, Affective,
and Conative Components of
Puerto Rican and Negro Acceptance and Rejection," *Journal of
Social Psychology*, 59 (1963), 93–
99.

SUTHERLAND, ROBERT L. *Color, Class
and Personality*. Washington,
D.C.: American Council on Education, 1942.

TAEUBER, CONRAD, and IRENE B.
TAEUBER. *The Changing Population of the United States*. New
York: John Wiley & Sons, Inc.,
1958.

TAEUBER, KARL. "Negro Residential
Segregation: Trends and Measurement," *Social Problems*, 12 (1964),
42–51.

TAFT, DONALD R. *Criminology*. 3d
ed. New York: The Macmillan
Co., 1956.

TAFT, DONALD R., and RICHARD ROB-
BINS. *International Migrations:
The Immigrant in the Modern
World*. New York: The Ronald
Press Co., 1955.

TALMADGE, HERMAN E. *You and
Segregation*. Birmingham: The
Vulcan Press, Inc., 1955.

TEAGUE, ROBERT L. "Negroes Say
Conditions in U.S. Explain Na-
tionalists' Militancy," *New York
Times*, March 2, 1961, 117.

TELLER, JUDD L. "American Zionists Move Toward Clarity," *Commentary*, 12 (1951), 444–450.

THOMAS, DOROTHY SWAINE, and
RICHARD S. NICHIMOTO. *The
Spoilage*. Berkeley: University of
California Press, 1946.

THOMAS, JOHN L. "The Factor of
Religion in the Selection of Marriage Mates," *American Sociological Review*, 16 (1951), 487–491.

THOMAS, W. I. "The Relation of Re-
search to the Social Process." In
*Essays on Research in the Social
Sciences*. Washington, D.C.: The
Brookings Institution, 1931.

THOMAS, WILLIAM I., and FLORIAN
ZNANIECKI. *The Polish Peasant in
Europe and America*. New York:
Alfred A. Knopf, Inc., 1927.

THOMPSON, DANIEL C. *The Negro
Leadership Class*. Englewood
Cliffs, N.J.: Prentice-Hall, Inc.,
1963.

THOMPSON, DANIEL C. "The Rise of
the Negro Protest," *The Annals of
the American Academy of Political and Social Science*, 357 (1965),
18–29.

THOMPSON, EDGAR T. (ed.). *Race
Relations and the Race Problem*.

Durham, N.C.: Duke University Press, 1939.

TOBY, JACKSON. "Hoodlum or Business Man: An American Dilemma." In MARSHALL SKLARE (ed.), *The Jews.* New York: The Free Press of Glencoe, 1958.

TRENT, R. D. "The Relation between Expressed Self-Acceptance and Expressed Attitudes toward Negroes and Whites among Negro Children," *Journal of Genetic Psychology,* **91** (1957), 25–31.

TRIANDIS, HARRY S., and LEIGH MINTURN TRIANDIS. "Race, Social Class, Religion, and Nationality as Determinants of Social Distance," *Journal of Abnormal and Social Psychology,* **61** (1960), 110–118.

TUMIN, MELVIN M. *Desegregation: Resistance and Readiness.* Princeton, N.J.: Princeton University Press, 1958.

TUMIN, MELVIN M. *An Inventory and Appraisal of Research on American Anti-Semitism.* New York: Freedom Books, 1961.

TUMIN, MELVIN M. *Race and Intelligence.* New York: Anti-Defamation League of B'nai B'rith, 1963.

TURNER, RALPH H., and SAMUEL J. SURACE. "Zoot Suiters and Mexicans: Symbols in Crowd Behavior," *American Journal of Sociology,* **62** (1956), 14–20.

VANDER ZANDEN, JAMES W. "The Citizens Councils," *Alpha Kappa Deltan,* **29** (1959), 3–9.

VANDER ZANDEN, JAMES W. "Desegregation and Social Strains in the South," *Journal of Social Issues,* **15** (1959), 53–60.

VANDER ZANDEN, JAMES W. "The Ideology of White Supremacy," *Journal of the History of Ideas,* **20** (1959), 385–402.

VANDER ZANDEN, JAMES W. "Resistance and Social Movements," *Social Forces,* **37** (1959), 312–315.

VANDER ZANDEN, JAMES W. "Desegregation: The Future? *"The South Atlantic Quarterly,* **LX** (1960), 205–216.

VANDER ZANDEN, JAMES W. "The Klan Revival," *American Journal of Sociology,* **LXV** (1960), 456–462.

VANDER ZANDEN, JAMES W. "Sit-ins in Dixie," *The Midwest Quarterly,* **2** (1960), 11–19.

VANDER ZANDEN, JAMES W. "Turmoil in the South," *Journal of Negro Education,* **29** (1960), 445–452.

VANDER ZANDEN, JAMES W. "Seven Years of Southern Resistance," *The Midwest Quarterly,* **2** (1961), 273–284.

VANDER ZANDEN, JAMES W. "Voting on Segregationist Referenda," *The Public Opinion Quarterly,* **25** (1961), 92–105.

VANDER ZANDEN, JAMES W. "Accommodation to Undesired Change: The Case of the South," *The Journal of Negro Education,* **31** (1962), 30–35.

VANDER ZANDEN, JAMES W. "The Non-Violent Resistance Movement Against Segregation," *American Journal of Sociology,* **68** (1963), 544–550.

VANDER ZANDEN, JAMES W. *Race Relations in Transition: The Segregation Crisis within the South.* New York: Random House, Inc., 1965.

VANDER ZANDEN, JAMES W. *Sociology: A Systematic Approach.* New York: The Ronald Press Co., 1965.

VINACKE, W. EDGAR. "Stereotyping Among National-Racial Groups in Hawaii: A Study of Ethnocentrism," *Journal of Social Psychology,* **30** (1949), 265–291.

VINACKE, W. EDGAR. "Stereotypes as Social Concepts," *Journal of Social Psychology,* **46** (1957).

WAGLEY, CHARLES, and MARVIN HARRIS. *Minorities in the New World.* New York: Columbia University Press, 1964.

WAKEFIELD, DAN. *Island in the City: The Problem of Spanish Harlem.* Boston: Houghton Mifflin Co., 1959.

WARD, LEWIS B. "The Ethnics of Executive Selection," *Harvard Business Review,* 43 (1965), 6–40.

WARNER, W. LLOYD. *Democracy in Jonesville.* New York: Harper & Row, 1949.

WARNER, W. LLOYD, and PAUL S. LUNT. *The Social Life of a Modern Community.* New Haven: Yale University Press, 1941.

WARNER, W. LLOYD, and LEO SROLE. *The Social Systems of American Ethnic Groups.* New Haven: Yale University Press, 1945.

WARNER, W. LLOYD, BUFORD H. JUNKER, and WALTER A. ADAMS. *Color and Human Nature.* Washington, D.C.: American Council on Education, 1941.

WARNER, W. LLOYD, MARCHIA MEEKER, and KENNETH EELLS. *Social Class in America.* Chicago: Science Research Associates, Inc., 1949.

WEATHERLEY, DONALD. "Anti-Semitism and the Expression of Fantasy Aggression," *Journal of Abnormal and Social Psychology,* 62 (1961), 454–457.

WEATHERLEY, DONALD. "Maternal Responses to Childhood Aggression and Subsequent Anti-Semitism," *Journal of Abnormal and Social Psychology,* 66 (1963), 183–185.

WEINSTOCK, S. ALEXANDER. "Some Factors that Retard or Accelerate the Rate of Acculturation," *Human Relations,* 17 (1964), 321–340.

WESSEL, B. B. *An Ethnic Survey of Woonsocket, Rhode Island.* Chicago: University of Chicago Press, 1931.

WESTIE, FRANK R., and MARGARET L. WESTIE. "The Social-Distance Pyramid: Relationships between Caste and Class," *American Journal of Sociology,* 63 (1957), 190–196.

WESTIE, FRANK R. "Race and Ethnic Relations." In R. E. L. FARIS (ed.), *Handbook of Modern Sociology.* Chicago: Rand McNally & Co., 1964, 576–618.

WHITE, R. K., and R. LIPPITT. *Autocracy and Democracy: An Experimental Inquiry.* New York: Harper & Row, 1960.

WILLIAMS, J. ALLEN, JR. "Reduction of Tension through Intergroup Contact: A Social Psychological Interpretation," *Pacific Sociological Review,* 7 (1964), 81–88.

WILLIAMS, ROBIN M., JR. *The Reduction of Intergroup Tension.* New York: Social Science Research Council, 1947.

WILLIAMS, ROBIN M., JR. *Strangers Next Door.* Englewood Cliffs, N.J.: Prentice-Hall, Inc., 1964.

WILLIAMS, ROBIN M., JR. "Social Change and Conflict, 1944–1964," *Sociological Inquiry,* 35 (1965), 8–26.

WILLIAMS, ROBIN M., JR., and MARGARET W. RYAN (eds.). *Schools in Transition.* Chapel Hill: University of North Carolina Press, 1954.

WILNER, DANIEL M., ROSABELLE PRICE WALKLEY, and STUART W. COOK. *Human Relations in Interracial Housing.* Minneapolis: University of Minnesota Press, 1955.

WILSON, DAVID C., and EDNA M. LANTAZ. "Culture Change and Negro State Hospital Admissions," *American Journal of Psychiatry,* 114 (1957), 25–32.

WIRTH, LOUIS. *The Ghetto.* Chicago: University of Chicago Press, 1928.

WIRTH, LOUIS. "The Problem of Minority Groups." In RALPH LINTON (ed.), *The Science of Man in the World Crisis*. New York: Columbia University Press, 1945, 347–372.

WIRTH, LOUIS, and HERBERT GOLDHAMER. "The Hybrid and the Problem of Miscegenation." In OTTO KLINEBERG (ed.), *Characteristics of the American Negro*. New York: Harper & Row, 1944.

WOLFE, BERNARD. "Uncle Remus and the Malevolent Rabbit," *Commentary*, 8 (1949), 31–41.

WOODWARD, C. VANN. *The Strange Career of Jim Crow*. Rev. ed. Fair Lawn, N.J.: Oxford University Press, 1957.

WORKS, ERNEST. "The Prejudice-Interaction Hypothesis from the Point of View of the Negro Minority Group," *American Journal of Sociology*, 67 (1961), 47–52.

WORTHY, WILLIAM. "The Angriest Negroes," *Esquire*, LV (1961), 102 ff.

WRONG, DENNIS H. "The Functional Theory of Stratification: Some Neglected Considerations," *American Sociological Review*, 24 (1959), 772–782.

YATES, AUBREY J. *Frustration and Conflict*. London: Methuen & Co. Ltd., 1962.

YINGER, J. MILTON, and GEORGE E. SIMPSON. "Can Segregation Survive in an Industrial Society?" *Antioch Review*, XVIII (1958), 15–24.

YINGER, J. MILTON. *Sociology Looks at Religion*. New York: The Macmillan Co., 1963.

YINGER, J. MILTON. *A Minority Group in American Society*. New York: McGraw-Hill Book Co., Inc., 1965.

YOUNG, DONALD. *American Minority Peoples*. New York: Harper & Row, 1932.

YOUNG, DONALD. *Research Memorandum on Minority Peoples in the Depression*. New York: Social Science Research Council, 1937.

YUAN, D. Y. "Voluntary Segregation: A Study of New Chinatown," *Phylon*, 24 (1963), 260–262.

ZANGWILL, ISRAEL. *The Melting Pot: Drama in Four Acts*. New York: The Macmillan Co., 1921.

ZAWADZKI, BOHDAN. "Limitations of the Scapegoat Theory of Prejudice," *Journal of Abnormal and Social Psychology*, 43 (1948), 127–141.

ZELIGS, R., and G. HENDRICKSON. "Racial Attitudes of 200 Sixth-Grade Children," *Sociology and Social Research*, 18 (1933), 26–36.

Author Index

539

Subject Index